THREADS OF LIFE

This publication has been supported
by La Trobe University.
Internet: http://www.latrobe.edu.au

RICHARD FREADMAN

THREADS *of* LIFE

AUTOBIOGRAPHY AND THE WILL

THE UNIVERSITY OF CHICAGO PRESS
Chicago and London

RICHARD FREADMAN is professor and head of the School of English at La Trobe University. He is the author of *Eliot, James, and the Fictional Self* (1986), coauthor of *Re-thinking Theory* (1992), and coeditor of *On Literary Theory and Philosophy* (1991) and *Renegotiating Ethics in Literature, Philosophy, and Theory.*

The University of Chicago Press, Chicago 60637
The University of Chicago Press, Ltd., London
© 2001 by The University of Chicago
All rights reserved. Published 2001
Printed in the United States of America

00 09 08 07 06 05 04 03 02 01 00   1 2 3 4 5
ISBN: 0-226-26142-5 (cloth)
ISBN: 0-226-26143-3 (paper)

Library of Congress Cataloging-in-Publication Data
Freadman, Richard, 1951–
   Threads of life : autobiography and the will / Richard Freadman.
     p. cm.
   Includes index.
     ISBN 0-226-26142-5 (cloth : alk. paper) — ISBN 0-226-26143-3 (paper : alk. paper)
     1. Autobiography. 2. Will. I. Title.
CT25 .F72 2000
920—dc21
                              00-039222

Chapter 4 of the present work appeared in a different version in *Renegotiating Ethics in Literature, Philosophy and Theory,* edited by Jane Adamson, Richard Freadman, and David Parker (1998). © 1998 Cambridge University Press.

Chapter 7 of the present work appeared in a different version in *The Ethics of Literature,* edited by Andrew Hadfield, Dominic Rainsford, and Tim Woods. Copyright © Hadfield/Rainsford/Woods. Reprinted with permission of Macmillan Press Ltd. and St. Martin's Press, LLC.

To the kids with love . . .

Ben, Madeleine and Elliot

CONTENTS

ACKNOWLEDGMENTS

As many an autobiography will show, innumerable people have a hand in what we become and what we do. This is certainly the case with this book. There are numerous people I want to thank. Some of these gave specialist advice on philosophical, theological, and theoretical matters. For their time and help I would like to thank Charles Altieri, Johann Arnason, Peter Beilharz, Rabbi Shimon Cowen, Rai Gaita, Kevin Hart, Graeme Marshall, Eric Osborn, John Passmore, Hayden Ramsay, Alex Segal, Patricia Harris Stablein, and Graham Storey.

Various friends, colleagues, and specialists read other sections of the book: Graham Burns, Trish Dutton, John Eakin, Ray Forsyth, John Gatt-Rutter, John Gillies, Terry Keefe, Derick Marsh, Michael Scammel, Alan Shapiro, Ron Shapiro, Patricia Harris Stablein, and John Wiltshire. My thanks to all of them.

Three friends took things well beyond the call of duty and read the manuscript right through as I was bringing it to a close. My thanks to Kevin Hart, Sally Morrison, and David Parker.

I'm also very grateful to the following friends and colleagues. My friend and colleague at La Trobe, John Gatt-Rutter, who provided constant encouragement, intellectual companionship, and expert scholarly counsel over a long period. ("Sling it my way," the ferociously busy but always obliging John used to say.) John Gillies, also a great La Trobe friend and intellectual companion, whose friendship, scholarly expertise, and encouragement have been unstinting and superb. Graeme Marshall, from the Philosophy Department at the University of Melbourne, has played a very special role. It was to Graeme, who has had a career-long interest in philosophical accounts of the will, that I went for guidance and discussion at key points in the project. He has been extraordinarily generous with his time and expertise, and has gone over many of the sections of philosophical exposition. I'm just glad that Graeme let me pay for the wine. I have benefited enormously from Patricia Harris Stablein's friendship, erudition, encouragement, and her expert counsel in matters concerning French language, culture, and literature, and seventeenth-century intellectual history. Other friends who have helped in important ways are Serge Lieberman, Renata Maimone, and Alex Segal.

I should add that though a seeker of comment, I don't always take the good advice I am given; so responsibility for errors and other inadequacies in the text remains squarely with me.

I am fortunate to work in a school where collegiality still reigns and where there is a culture that encourages research and discussion. I want to thank my colleagues for their cooperation, not least during the time when I have had to combine work on this book with the duties of Head of School. During this period Sue Thomas, Deputy Head of School, has been extremely helpful and supportive. I particularly want to thank one of my colleagues in the school, John Wiltshire, for expert comment on bits of the book and for his intellectual companionship over the years. Many thanks, too, to the administrative staff of the School of English for their expert and dependable work, often beyond the call of the job description: Renee Alford, Marie Mackenzie, Margaret Tarr, and Marilyn Richmond, and to the now retired Dorothy Johnson and Josephine Roberts. I've also learned plenty from thesis students working on autobiography whom I have supervised in recent years: Martin French, Hisako Fukisawa, Martin Redman, Anne Marie Sawyer, John Steyfburgen, and Graham Storey.

Again at La Trobe, special thanks to the staff at the Borchardt Library, especially Margot Hyslop, doyenne of the reference section; Sharon Karasmanis and the staff in the interlibrary loans section; and Jacki Saunders and the staff in the loans section. Sincere thanks to Cathy Coade, David Hird, Sue Jones, and Cathy Ward at the Information Technology Unit, and to Mai Lei and Mary Mulroney, the Faculty Computer Systems Officers. I wish to acknowledge the support of the La Trobe Faculty of Humanities and Social Sciences for several research grants that helped facilitate the research and writing of the book.

Some of the work on the book was done while I was a Visiting Fellow at the Centre for Philosophy and Public Issues, in the Philosophy Department at the University of Melbourne. My thanks to Tony Coady and Brian Scarlett, in particular, for an enjoyable and rewarding time there.

I have received help from various sources during research visits overseas. Thank you to Dr. Murray Simpson and the staff in the Koestler Archive at the University of Edinburgh; to Helen Sims, Secretary to the Koestler Chair in Parapsychology; and to Dr. John Beloff, a friend of Koestler's. Dr. Beloff was generous in speaking with me at length about Arthur Koestler. Mr. Bernard Crystal and the staff were most helpful when I conducted research in the Lionel Trilling Archive, at Columbia University Library, as were Megan Desnoyers and the staff at the Kennedy Library where I did research in the Ernest Hemingway archive. I am grateful to Quentin Anderson for a long conversation about Diana and Lionel Trilling; to James Trilling for conversations by phone and e-mail about his parents and my project; and to Stephen Koch, a friend and relative of Diana Trilling's, for an extended conversation about her.

On the editorial front, it has been my good fortune to work with Randolph Petilos at the University of Chicago Press. I could not have wished for a more committed and helpful editor. Thanks to Erin DeWitt for her expert work in copyediting the manuscript. At the Australian end, Richard McGregor's expertise has been of immense value in preparing the manuscript and compiling the index.

I owe special thanks, as always, to Diane. But this time the book is for the kids. Thanks to Ben (23) for keeping the computer happy and for all the help with the younger kids. Madeleine (12) practiced her typing on some passages from Augustine's *Confessions* and allowed me to cut and paste them into my manuscript. She also gave me generous access to her colossal collection of felt-tipped pens and drawing implements of various kinds—a huge help in getting my voluminous notes into some semblance of order. After some bracing initial negotiations, Elliot (4) agreed to wreak marginally less havoc in my study than in the rest of the house. This was a big help. His ascension into language and self-consciousness during the writing of this book on autobiography has been a constant source of enlightenment—and delight.

—*Richard B. Freadman,*
Melbourne,
August 1999

NOTE ON TEXTS AND TRANSLATIONS

For the works of philosophy and related disciplines that I cite in this book, I have generally used readily available editions, many of which are in any case standard texts. Unless otherwise indicated, references to Arthur Koestler's works are to the Danube Edition, published by Hutchinson of London; unless otherwise stated, references to Lionel Trilling's work are to the Uniform Edition, published by Harcourt Brace Jovanovich, New York. Where these editions are used, I cite the original dates of publication before giving details of place and publisher.

In the words of Eva Hoffman, a fine contemporary autobiographer, much gets "lost in translation."[1] Paul Ricoeur has demonstrated how profound some of the semantic and philosophical shifts are that can occur when terms like *self* undergo the process of translation.[2] Another case in point is the word *will*. In the chapters of this book that undertake detailed readings of autobiographical texts written in French, I attend to issues of translation. However, it has not been practicable to do so in the historical survey of concepts of the will that I give in chapters 2 and 3, and in the appendixes at the end of the book, "Some Earlier Conceptions of the Will: Maimonides to Mill" and "Some Other Late Modern Instances." A book-length study would be required to track shifting and cognate meanings of the word *will* as it occurs in English and various European languages. Such a study is beyond my competence—even if there had been time and room to do it here. But the reader should bear in mind that some of the quoted passages upon which I base my account of the philosophical history of the will may be open to challenge from the standpoint of translation.

INTRODUCTION

This book is first and foremost a study of autobiography. It focuses on a theme that, I argue, has been central to Western autobiography since its inception: the issue of the human will. Many readers of autobiography will be aware that some major autobiographers—Augustine and John Stuart Mill, for instance—write about the will in their autobiographies, and fine scholarly work has been done on the treatment of the will in Augustine's *Confessions,* Mill's *Autobiography,* and some other first-person narratives. But there is no sustained work of scholarship that takes account of just how central and pervasive explorations of the will are in Western autobiography. This book attempts to fill what is, I believe, a gap in our understanding of autobiography:[1] I argue that explorations of the will are a central and fundamental feature of the Western autobiographical "tradition"— an argument that I evidence through readings of various, though generally modern, autobiographical works.

Is it an accident that the gap to which I refer should exist? I suggest not. Late modern culture—by which I mean the cultural epoch that follows and is in part shaped by Nietzsche, Freud, and Marx—is deeply conflicted, confused, and even incurious about the will. The lacuna in scholarship about autobiography is just one example of a very general trend. We can ill afford such inadequate understandings of the will. Modern industrial society might seem to have extended the power of the human will as never before. And so in a sense it has. Yet we often hear how "disempowered" people feel in contemporary life—whether it be in massive, impersonal bureaucratic structures, or in particular ethnic and political regions of an increasingly global world, or in close human relationships, or just in the day-to-day business of having a life. In all of these areas, the will seems to be in trouble. And the same applies to some of the most powerful of our contemporary intellectual discourses. Free market economists claim that market forces will shape economic activity in ways that ensure the best possible outcomes. But what role does the will of particular individuals, particular economic actors, have in such pictures of our social world? In an important study of late modernity, the French social theorist Alain Touraine writes that we face "the real danger" of a "complete dissociation between system and actors, between the technical or economic world and the world of subjectivity."[2] Again, we like to think that our world more generally is a reasonably rational, predictable, rule-governed place; yet in fields like quantum mechanics and post-modern cultural theory, influential thinkers are saying that our cherished belief in a rule-governed and predictable world is a cultural fiction. If this is so, where does it leave us as people who think we can know about the world and can make rational choices about how to exercise our wills in light of that knowledge? We can ask similar questions about the will in secular culture: If there is no God-given design, no God-given moral code, what can guide our moral conduct? How do we know what would be a morally enlightened act of will, as opposed to one that is morally benighted or misguided?

These are tremendously pressing issues. They are also extremely complex, not least because the notion of the will is by no means clear. We use the noun *will* in daily conversation as if it were an unproblematic term, and even where we don't actually use the word itself, we often take it for granted in our attempts to make sense of the world. Take a typically unassuming comment from Nelson Mandela's autobiography. Of his decades in prison, he says:

> Part of being optimistic is keeping one's head pointed towards the sun, one's feet moving forward. There were many dark moments when my faith in humanity was sorely tested, but I would not and could not give myself up to despair. That way lay defeat and death.[3]

We understand this, and indeed Mandela's remarkable life more generally, as an example of his phenomenal strength of will. And one of the many reasons that we think this life remarkable is that it reveals deep links between strength of will and moral commitment. Mandela is one of those rare individuals who puts the power of the will to world-changing moral and political effect. There is much to be learned from such a man, not least from his autobiography; but in order to learn from it, we need a deep and respectful general interest in the will as a power in human life.

We also need to understand the will in order to deal with certain sorts of human frailty. People sometimes say, for instance, that a heavy drinker "lacks the willpower" to stay off the bottle. But what does this mean? Does it mean that the drinker "has" a will, but that his will is somehow "not strong enough" to eschew alcohol? Or is it a way of saying that maybe he doesn't have a will at all?[4] (The thought that someone might have "no will at all" can sound bizarre, but, as I show in this book, modern culture has produced some influential theories about human beings that actually assert that there is no such thing as the will.)

The relationship between the will and morality is one of the central themes of this book. This is thorny territory because it's all too easy to point the finger and say that someone is "doing the wrong thing" and could be doing "the right thing" if only he would "exercise his will." So—to take the case of the drinker again—someone might say: "Look, your drinking is wrecking your life and your family's life. It's morally appalling. You could do something about it if you really wanted to." But in certain views of the will, this is unfair to the drinker. The view that says that he has been "given" a weak will would suggest that he can't actually do anything about his drinking. His will isn't "strong enough" for him to change his behavior. Similarly, someone who says that there's "no such thing as the will" would presumably have to conclude that the drinker's habits are determined from "without" and that there's nothing he can do to change them. Either way, it doesn't seem that he can be held morally responsible for his heavy drinking or for his failure to scale down his drinking. The notion of moral responsibility only seems to enter the picture where someone can chose between options and act accordingly.

Consider another example (this isn't a book about problem drinking!) on the issue of responsibility. Someone might say of an inveterate gambler that she "won't take responsibility" for her own life. But what if she replies: "My gambling isn't a matter of moral weakness; it's a matter of bad luck: both of my parents were gamblers and I've inherited their addictive personality type. It's in the genes. There's nothing I can do about it"? This suggests an alternative reading of her situation that rejects the idea of the will as an enactment of moral responsibility, in favor of a notion of luck—in this instance "bad luck"; in particular bad *moral* luck. The gambler is really saying: "I've been unlucky in a moral way. I've had the misfortune to be born a person who can't do the right thing when it comes to gambling." In other words, in this morally significant area of her life, her will has been rendered powerless by misfortune.

Here's another take on this sort of situation, this time in terms of "excessive" eating. Someone of whom it is said that "he's eating himself into an early grave" replies: "I just look culpably out of control to you because you cling to the fiction that life is an orderly, controllable thing. If you were honest, you'd see that the disorder of my life reflects the craziness of life in general; that the will is itself a fiction—that we can't actually control things by exerting our wills. You might be able to resist fatty foods, but something else will get you—cocaine, maybe, or depression, or something random and out of the blue like a bus with brake failure." In saying this, he'd be appealing to some notion of "contingency"—to the idea that reality isn't law-governed and predictable, but is instead a random realm in which things happen in a purely accidental fashion. As I've said, this is a disturbing thought because in a purely contingent world, will—or at least will exercised on the basis of rational understanding and prediction—might seem to have no place.

At this stage we're starting to compile a set of perspectives on the will: I've talked about it in terms of "strength and weakness"; but we can also conceive of the will in less familiar terms such as its relation to "moral luck" and contingency. I've also been talking in a way that suggests that the notion of *free* will (we'll see later in the book that it's possible to believe in the existence of the will without believing in its freedom) often goes hand in hand with some idea of rational appraisal. Many people think that we are most free when we are most able to weigh our options and to act in the light of those appraisals.

The examples I've discussed all involve the idea of "having" a will. This in itself is an unexpectedly complex—and interesting—idea. Imagine that an intellectually adept woman who suffers from agoraphobia is responding to a plea from a friend who wants her to "buck up the courage" to leave the house for a few hours each day. She says: "You keep saying that I've 'got a will' and that I could use it to beat my fears, but it's not true. I've got a will, all right, but wills are things that are ultimately operated from outside us—by the genetic make-ups we're given; by the effects of our personal histories; by all sorts of circumstances that are beyond our control. 'Having' a will is like having some enzyme in my liver. It's 'my' enzyme, but I've got no control over it." The friend may be unimpressed, but, at least in some views of the will, the agoraphobic has a point.

This last vignette shows that an issue like the will can't adequately be addressed through a few reductive, logic-chopping examples. If there is such a thing as the will—and I argue in this book that there is—it's something that resides in that fantastically complex creature, the human being. It's not enough to talk about "the will." You have also to talk about "*his* will" or "*her* will"—to see will in the context of a life, with all of its dimensions, epochs, and forms of engagement with the world. And we have to understand that "social world" as a thing comprised of innumerable currents of ideology, convention, conflict, and possibility. One cannot properly discuss any allegedly "addictive" behavior pattern without looking at the social setting in which that behavior is designated as "addictive," at the motives and means whereby such designations are made, and at the history of the interactions between the behavior in question and the social world in which it has taken place.

Nor should we think about the will in merely problematical terms. We need to talk about "possibilities" and about the ways in which fine and effective acts of the will—moral, aesthetic, political, and other—occur in a complex and demanding world. This means looking closely at moral decisions in which things aren't just left or resigned to "luck"; at ways in which will seems to prevail in the face of life's awesome contingencies; at instances in which the will seems to be exercised as at least a relatively "free" power; at individuals who seem to evince strength of will; and at situations in which people behave as if ownership of the will involves a capacity to exert agency, at least to some degree. This is where an autobiography—and a life—like Nelson Mandela's comes in. The emblematic examples I'm giving in the introduction to this study of autobiography and its engagements with the will are, then, merely a way of setting the scene for much more detailed treatments of particular individual autobiographical instances later in the book—instances that, as it happens, sometimes concern such patterns as heavy drinking, gambling, moral weakness, and phobias, but that also involve various kinds of human achievement. The perspectives that I take on the will in the extended readings of autobiography in chapters 3 through 8 are basically the ones I have referred to above: will in terms of "moral luck," contingency, freedom, weakness, and ownership. I'll say more about this in a moment.

What happens if we change the quotation marks around what the people I've used as examples are reported to have said, so that they indicate not something spoken, but something *written*—written in an autobiography? Imagine that for some as-yet-unspecified reason the gambler has written an autobiography. On the face of it, this seems like a very good idea. Autobiography should suit her purposes well because it's a very good vehicle for someone who wants to try to understand the extent to which compulsion or freedom—determination or free will—can be invoked in order to explain and describe the life they have lived. I argue in this book that autobiography is indeed an excellent medium for such understandings; but I want to say more than this. I suggest that no person who is even minimally reflective can write his or her life *without* bumping up against such questions. Questions about compulsion and freedom may be particularly pressing for gamblers and others with allegedly "addictive" patterns, but *most of us ask such questions,* and necessarily so. This is one of the reasons that autobiography has become a central genre of human understanding. It's tailor-made for discussions of the will. If she uses the limitless resources of the genre well, the gambler might open out her "problem" in a tremendous range of dimensions: she might relate it not just to genetics, but to upbringing; she might see it in connection with factors she hadn't so far taken into account: feelings of depression or dread, for instance, which she escapes by making euphoric wagers; she might come to suspect that she gambles, in part at least, to escape deep conflicts within her sense of self; she might come to ponder the place that gambling plays in her culture—how it relates to forms of sociability, gender stereotypes, and other things. And these would be but a few of the connections that she might explore. The process of writing autobiography, like the writing in any genre, brings with it a whole world of possible connections. The process itself can facilitate forms of association, honesty, imagination that the person cannot attain in the more routine spaces that life provides for our search for understanding. (Some autobiographers find that they don't actually embark on the search until they start trying to write their life-story.) Perhaps the most precious thing of all is that, whatever its limitations might be, the gambler's narrative is *her* narrative. We may have all manner of theories, statistics, studies, and narrative representations of gambling, most of them framed in the third person. But this is the gambler's chance to tell us how it feels to *her.* For instance, to convey something about the "feeling of will-lessness" that she experiences when she "caves in to" compulsion, or about the unsuccessful battle her will "puts up" against these compulsions, or about the personal history in which this "addiction" has its genesis, and so on. In such matters, I suggest, there is no substitute for first-person accounts—not least because our more detached third-person accounts need to be able to consult them if we are to make any real headway with problems as complex as the ones I've been discussing. If I were to undertake a study of "compulsive" gambling—or alcoholism, or agoraphobia—the first thing I'd look for would be first-person accounts of these experiences by people who have experienced them. One such account is given in the autobiography of the self-flagellating Australian satirist Barry Humphries. Humphries's descriptions of his acute alcoholism are funny but also terrifying. He describes a disintegration of self that comes close to decimating everything—relationships, career, health, memory, any sense of orientation in the world. He recalls that during a major crack-up, "I felt I had forfeited all will of my own, and I was almost relieved to be a person to whom things just happened."[5]

It might of course be that what Humphries or others write about their personal patterns will be unreliable. They may indulge, as many autobiographers do, in self-justification, a degree of self-deception, and so on. Yet I contend that such is the revelatory power of autobiography that we ought not to reject these "fallacious" dimensions of first-person narrative out of hand: they will tell us something of these people's core fantasies about self and the world. We can't hope to have anything approaching deep understanding of a person unless we know a good deal about the texture, the trajectory, and the intensity of his or her fantasy life.

What might cause someone like the gambler to write her story? Perhaps late in a ruined life she thinks there might be some point in writing the story of that ruination. Why? Perhaps to explain herself to her now-estranged children? Or to warn other gamblers? Or maybe just to try to understand how this appalling mess came about? Maybe even to say that, shocking though the mess is, "I'm still human, I still have things to say and to offer, I'm not just defined by my gambling problem." Again, there seems to be much to commend her autobiographical impulse. It is indeed true that her life cannot just be reduced to her gambling problem; indeed she does have things to say, some of them stemming from other aspects of her life. Moreover, in deciding to write her life, and in executing that decision, she is actually exercising a degree of volition that has not been apparent elsewhere in her gambling-afflicted existence. The very writing of autobiography is itself perhaps an act of will, a way of imposing a certain shape and meaning on the life that one has had. We know that this activity can be therapeutic, "empowering"; in some instances it can even save lives. The writing of an autobiography can itself be a major life event. But we need to add a caveat here: Some autobiographies are so driven by their author's needs, obsessions, and fantasies that little freedom of will or reflection goes on in them. The narrative merely recapitulates compulsions that have dominated the writer's life. Hemingway's *A Moveable Feast,* the subject of chapter 4, is a case in point.

I now want to switch from compulsive behaviors to scholarship. We might expect that philosophers, theologians, and others who "work on the will" as an intellectual topic would be largely free of the confusions that dog the use of the term in daily conversation. But this is not the case. The philosophical, theological, psychological, and other literatures that deal with the will show remarkably little consistent understanding of what the will is. A good example here is the multivolumed *Encyclopedia of Philosophy,* the most extended reference work for the history of ideas we have. Turn to the entry for *will* and you'll find this: "*See* CHOOSING, DECIDING, AND DOING; DETERMINISM; VOLITION." In other words, the editors of this massive work seem to have concluded that the notion of will is historically too variable and unclear to admit of direct treatment. It has to be treated under other, albeit cognate, headings. Another indication of our intellectual unclearness about the will is the fact that we don't have a major scholarly work on the will in Western culture. The closest thing we have is an admirable but limited work by Vernon J. Bourke, *Will in Western Thought,*[6] which offers a taxonomy of different conceptions of the will. Others, like the formidable Hannah Arendt,[7] have written highly selective historical accounts. But that's about it. What are we to make of this?

As I have just said, some think that the uses to which the term *will* has been put are too variable to be susceptible of systematic presentation. I don't agree with this. Another explanation is that a good many scholars—philosophers, literary theorists, and others—believe that "there is no such thing as the will"; that is, there's no such "faculty" in the human person. All we can talk about are certain instances of "trying," "wanting," and the like, seen in particular descriptive and empirical contexts. Here again, I beg to differ, but it is important to note, right at the outset, that many major modernist thinkers have expressed doubts or downright disbelief when it comes to the will: Marx, Freud, Nietzsche—to name but a few of the most influential instances. This is another reason for saying that in the late modern period the will is in trouble. Thus Lionel Trilling writes of what he calls the "hypertrophy of the will" in modern life [8]—a condition in which the will is distended and disturbed in relation to other psychic faculties.

In this book I argue that the will is real, that it is susceptible of a fair degree of conceptual clarification, but that conceptual clarification alone will not enable us to explore the will as fully and richly as we need to do. For that, I suggest, we need to turn, among other things, to autobiography—the form that is so well suited, and historically attuned, to explorations of the will. This study, then, considers autobiography and the philosophy of the will as paired discourses, with the philosophy of the will as, so to speak, the subordinate partner of the pair. If I write in some detail about the history of conceptions of the will, it is in part because we cannot adequately grasp what autobiographers have to say about the will unless we have a reasonably clear understanding of various theories about, and terms that can be used to describe, the will. Some of this history appears in the first three chapters; most of the remainder occurs in appendix A, "Some Earlier Conceptions of the Will: Maimonides to Mill" and appendix B, "Some Other Late Modern Instances." The book also contains a glossary of terms, where the reader will find definitions of various conceptions of the will, along with definitions of other terms that crop up during the foregoing discussions. As between these sections and the chapters containing critical readings of particular autobiographies, I aim to provide a philosophically framed account of autobiography and its engagements with the will.

The structure of the book is as follows. Chapter 1, "Threads, Autobiography, Theory," explains and traces a figure that has traditionally been used to represent issues of human fate and volition. This is the figure, familiar from Greek culture onward, of the threads that the spinners work in shaping, or otherwise impinging upon, the formation of a human life. I argue that this figure expresses a great array of perspectives on matters of human "fate," "destiny," "will," and "free will," and that it is alive and in use in modern autobiography. Chapter 1 develops the claim for historical and empirical connections between autobiography and the will that I have just made. It also further elaborates on the structure and methodology of this book. Two principal points here: first, the methodology is interdisciplinary; second, though I discuss and sometimes use aspects of postmodern literary theory, my interdisciplinary method does not generally follow the patterns of interdisciplinarity that have become common in postmodern literary criticism and theory. The main methodological links in this book are between narrative theory, liberal social theory, moral philosophy, Freudian theory, ethics, and the history of ideas. Where I draw on philosophical accounts of the will and related topics, these accounts are intended to function as constituent parts of a theory of autobiography—a broadly humanistic theory that informs a particular critical approach to autobiographical texts. My section on methodology includes the question of the self (and its relation to the notion of the subject); it also introduces and defines the key analytic and descriptive terms that are used throughout the book. Here I give my definition of the will—a definition that sees it as an intrinsic power that is instantiated through engagement with various human faculties. I argue that the will is most "free" when instantiated through engagement with faculties of rationality (though I give an expanded account of rationality that includes modes of understanding that are more than merely cognitive), and least "free" when instantiated through engagement with nonrational (for instance, instinctual) faculties. I call this a *graduated conception of the will.*

Chapter 2, "Late Modernity and the Will," begins with a taxonomy of different conceptions of the will that are referred to throughout the book. After some preliminary discussion of the state of the will in late modernity, it gives evaluative expositions of several of the major accounts of the will that have been formulated in the modern period: those of Nietzsche, Marx, Freud, Sartre, Ryle, Derrida, and—on another note altogether—Mussolini and

Hitler. I locate these accounts in relation to the taxonomy that appears at the start of the chapter.

Chapter 3—"Theory and Practice: Will-less Autobiography?"—returns to one of the questions that emerged with respect to the problem gambler: What is the relationship between what she generally says about the will and what she finds herself saying about it when she writes her autobiography? She might say, with particular reference to her gambling: "I have no will," or, "My will is not free"; but can one write one's life-story based on premises such as these? In chapter 3 I consider what happens when a thinker who, qua thinker, denies the will or its freedom writes an autobiography. The thinkers in question are the influential French Marxist Louis Althusser; B. F. Skinner, the most famous of the behaviorist psychologists; and Roland Barthes, another highly influential avant-garde French intellectual. In each instance, I give an evaluative exposition of the thinker's account of the will (or its absence), and then follow up with a discussion of his autobiography. Hence "Theory and Practice": what these people say at the level of theory compared with what they do at the level of autobiographical practice.

The remaining chapters give detailed readings of particular autobiographies—readings that take into account the complete intellectual and literary oeuvre of the autobiographer under discussion and aspects of his or her cultural milieu. Each of these readings turns on what we might think of as a *thematics of the will*—a particular topic that comes up in thinking and writing about the will. These topics are the ones that I identified in the examples above. Chapter 4, "Moral Luck in Paris: Luck and Ethical Will in Hemingway's *A Moveable Feast,*" deals with Hemingway's autobiographical treatment of the notion of moral luck. I argue that Hemingway has a crude but insistent version of this doctrine and that his autobiographical (and other) engagements with the issue of will pay a heavy ethical price for this conception.

Chapter 5, "'Being and Making Oneself Be': Will and Contingency in Simone de Beauvoir's Autobiography," considers Beauvoir's treatment of the will's relation to contingency, principally in her four major volumes of autobiography. Here I trace her shifting conceptions of will: their status as a response to her horror of contingency and their ethical implications. The most significant shift considered is from the existential conviction that contingency enables—and in a sense requires—radical freedom of the will, to a view of the will as an ideologically and historically constrained power that must be put to proper political and ethical uses.

Chapter 6, "'Factor x': Arthur Koestler and the Ghost in the Machine," considers an autobiographer who was raised on the kind of deterministic metaphysic that is classically expressed in Newtonian mechanics, but who came to believe that the self could operate in various dimensions, including dimensions in which its will is free. Koestler thinks that human beings do indeed possess will as a free power. However, like some other prominent thinkers and autobiographers, he believes that we cannot ultimately explain the genesis or the nature of this power. The power is like a ghost in a machine (a phrase he takes over from the philosopher Gilbert Ryle and inflects for his own purposes). The chapter also presents Koestler as a practitioner of what I call *post-totalitarian autobiography*, that is, autobiography, written by intellectuals and writers, that seeks to explore and pronounce upon the phenomenon of totalitarianism.

Stephen Spender—the subject of chapter 7, "'Strange Identity': Stephen Spender and Weakness of Will"—is another post-totalitarian autobiographer. Of the figures I consider, he is the one who devotes most attention to the issue of weakness of will. After sketching in some of the philosophical history and particulars of this issue, I argue that Spender's autobiography, *World Within World*, narrates a passage from a condition in which the will is weak and the self that "possesses" it is decentered, to one in which the self exercises will in a more deliberate, rational, and existentially grounded way.

The final chapter, "'Custodians of Their Own Fates'?: Diana (and Lionel) Trilling in *The Beginning of the Journey*," turns on the issue of ostensible or possible ownership. In what sense—if at all—might we be said to "own" our own wills, or, to give the question a twist, to "own" the "fates" that we are "given"? This chapter reads Diana Trilling's autobiography, *The Beginning of the Journey*, for its account of this and other aspects of the will. Trilling writes extensively about the condition of her own will, but also about the condition of the will that she saw in her late and famous intellectual husband, the critic Lionel Trilling. I argue that both of the Trillings endorsed a view of the will as essentially deliberative, rational, and ethical, but that *The Beginning of the Journey* reveals a powerful and overriding attachment on the part of Diana Trilling to an alternative picture of the will as determined, ethically neutral, and rooted in the dark places of the self. This reading involves discussion of the Trillings' Jewishness, their cultural milieu, and, in particular, their engagements with Freudian theory.

These "thematics" constitute a structurally connected set of perspectives on the will; but, of course, there are many other perspectives that can be taken on this topic. The reader will encounter a good many of these in the course of the book, but the treatment I offer here does not pretend to be exhaustive. The philosophical, literary, and autobiographical culture of the will is a remarkably rich and complex thing.

CHAPTER ONE

Threads, Autobiography, Theory

The unexamined life is not worth living.
—Plato, *Socrates' Defense* (38b)

I. THREADS AND THE WILL

The following two passages were composed almost three thousand years apart:

> . . . There is not
> any advantage to be won from grim lamentation.
> Such is the way the gods spun life for unfortunate mortals,
> that we live in unhappiness, but the gods themselves have no sorrows.
> There are two urns that stand on the door-sill of Zeus. They are unlike
> for the gifts they bestow: an urn of evils, an urn of blessings.
> If Zeus who delights in thunder mingles these and bestows them
> on man, he shifts, and moves now in evil, again in good fortune.[1]

> I'd have liked to think I'd woven myself cunningly out of an assortment of
> odd threads and yarn, chosen with taste and freely, but from the moment I
> met Yvonne in that house in Longueville I've doubted that's really what I've
> done.[2]

The first is from the *Iliad,* the second from an Australian autobiography published in 1994. Inevitably they differ in all sorts of ways—generic, metaphysical, rhetorical, and other—and yet they have two related things in common: each tries to figure human life in threadlike terms, and each ponders the nature of human fate and the existence or otherwise of human freedom. In Homer's passage, Achilleus offers the distressed Priam the cold comfort of knowing that human fate is ineluctable. Robert Dessaix, by contrast, describes some of his feelings before and after he, an adopted person, meets his biological mother, Yvonne, in a house in Sydney. Hitherto he has seen himself as self-created—as both weaver and the figure woven. Now, however, when as an adult he finally meets his mother and sees himself in her eyes as she beholds him, he is not so sure. Perhaps other forces are at work in the world, weaving the selves that we experience as creations of our own consciousnesses, our own wills? Unlike Homer, Dessaix writes in a culture that often assumes the will to be at least partially free; but even in such a culture, reflection reveals this to be a fraught assumption.

The resemblances between these passages are apparently no mere coincidence. Throughout Western culture, threads and related figures constantly recur when writers and others, across a great range of ages, cultures, and genres, ponder the nature of human destiny and that term which, in one of its many guises, is often contrasted to destiny—the human will. The cultural evidence would suggest that there is something intuitively rich and apt about threads and related metaphors for such purposes. Certainly, most of the writers discussed in this study of autobiography and the will—twentieth-century writers from often contrastive cultural backgrounds—figure human life as a threadlike thing. Thus writes Stephen Spender, referring to certain incompatibilities that brought a love affair to an end:

> I did not satisfy her; and from my point of view, she was too clear, too decided, too much in possession of all the threads of her life, too confident in what she knew, too little mystified by what she did not know.[3]

Here Arthur Koestler grapples with the meaning, the "final truth," of the life of war hero and writer Richard Hillary:

> The final truth is probably a pattern composed of all the threads which we have picked up, and followed for a short while and dropped again. For the pattern is more than the sum total of the threads; it has its own symbolic design of which the threads know nothing. They are ordinary strings, woven of cause and effect; but in the completed design the effect seems to operate the cause. The threads are subject to causality; the pattern to finality.[4]

Simone de Beauvoir writes of a moment of profound change in personal and historical orientation; of August 1944, after the German occupation of France, she reports feeling:

> Not only was I not weaving my life, but its shape, the shape of the time I lived in, the shape of all I loved, depended on the future.[5]

And this is Diana Trilling writing about Mrs. Harris, the accused in a murder trial:

> Mrs. Harris's action spoke of depths of suffering and despair far beyond what most of us are pushed to though surely of the same basic stuff as the everyday pain that's woven into our experience.

And again, of Mrs. Harris and the toll the trial is taking upon her:

> Thread by thread she was being unwoven . . .[6]

Consideration of further classical sources suggests how various are the implications of thread-related figures for destiny and the will.[7] Even our word for the medium in which written representations are made—*text*—derives from the

Latin *texo,* "to weave." In Greek myth, Ariadne helps Theseus find his way out of the Minotaur's maze—the riddle that ensnares him—by laying what is in effect a hermeneutic thread that Theseus follows to freedom.[8] In classical literature, philosophy, and art, the Fates, or Moirai, are generally figured as spinners (and indeed, through a gendered etymological link, spinsters), their names deriving from the Greek *moira,* meaning "share" or "portion." In some sources, they are also weavers, singers, even writers. In the epics, fate or destiny are usually understood in deterministic terms: the course of an individual life is a matter of decree by Necessity. The individual's share is most fundamentally reflected in the timing and manner of his or her death. In this Necessity exercises its awesome life-fashioning prerogative in ways that are at once imperious, inscrutable, and, to human eyes at least, unsystematic. Yet in this complex, polytheistic system even the gods themselves are subject to Necessity. Thus Poseidon in the *Iliad* laments:

> "No, no. Great though he is, this that he has said is too much,
> if he will force me against my will, me, who am his equal
> in rank. Since we are three brothers born by Rheia to Kronos,
> Zeus, and I, and the third is Hades, lord of the dead men.
> All was divided among us three ways, each given his domain.
> I when the lots were shaken drew the grey sea to live in
> forever; Hades drew the lot of the mists and the darkness,
> and Zeus was allotted the wide sky, in the cloud and the bright air.
> But earth and high Olympos are common to all three."[9]

The gods, then, have their allotted fates and spheres of influence, but this is not a hierarchical world in the sense that one god or agency determines fate for all others. In this complex and ambiguous metaphysic, Necessity circulates through the system. Even the gods who are responsible for "earth" can at best defer or otherwise slightly amend human fates.[10] One's portion is generally allocated at the moment of birth. So in the *Iliad,* Hekabe grieves for her fallen son, Hektor, dead as Destiny had decreed:

> Let us sit apart in our palace
> now, and weep for Hektor, and the way at the first strong Destiny
> spun with his life line when he was born, when I gave birth to him,
> that the dogs with their shifting feet should feed on him, far from his
> parents,
> gone down before a stronger man . . .[11]

Hekabe grieves not just at Hektor's decease but at the violent and demeaning manner of his death. Some of the violent deaths of the epic heroes reflect an understanding of *moira* as a sort of malign and inscrutable force. In the *Theogony,* Hesiod speaks of

> the Destinies and ruthless Fates,
> Goddesses who track down the sins of men
> And gods, and never cease from awful rage
> Until they give the sinner punishment.

And he gives the Fates their most customary names:

> the Fates, to whom wise Zeus has paid
> The greatest honour: Clotho, Atropos,
> Lachesis, who give men all good and bad.[12]

Clotho again gives us the modern "cloth," "texture," "weave," "clothes"; *Atropos* means "irresistible"; *Lachesis* is literally "getting-by-lot." Yet some heroes are lucky, like Agamemnon, "blessed, child of fortune and favour";[13] and even in the apparently remorseless determinism of some of the epic passages, there lurks a contrastive idea: the idea of fate as a reward or punishment for the life choices the hero has made. Punishment, after all, presupposes the capacity to have acted otherwise.

The beginnings of the shift to this view are apparent in one of the most extended classical references to the Fates and spinning, in book 10 of Plato's *Republic*. Socrates tells Glaucon a story he has heard from the warrior Er, who recounts what he has seen of the "world beyond" after he has been slain in battle. I quote this extraordinarily powerful passage at some length:

> But when seven days had elapsed for each group [those who had been punished for their sins] in the meadow, they were required to rise up on the eighth and journey on, and they came in four days to a spot whence they discerned, extended from above throughout the heaven and the earth, a straight light like a pillar, most nearly resembling the rainbow, but brighter and purer. To this they came after going forward a day's journey, and they saw there at the middle of the light the extremities of its fastenings stretched from heaven, for this light was the girdle of the heavens like the undergirders of triremes, holding together in like manner the entire revolving vault. And from the extremities was stretched the spindle of Necessity, through which all the orbits turned. Its staff and its hook were made of adamant, and the whorl of these and other kinds was commingled. And the nature of the whorl was this.

Now follows an extended and at times obscure description of the whorl:[14]

> And the spindle turned on the knees of Necessity, and up above on each of the rims of the circles a Siren stood, borne around in its revolution and uttering one sound, one note, and from all the eight there was the concord of a single harmony. And there were three others who sat round about at equal intervals, each one on her throne, the Fates, daughters of Necessity, clad in white vestments with filleted heads, Lachesis, and Clotho, and Atropos, who sang in

unison with the music of the Sirens, Lachesis singing the things that were, Clotho the things that are, and Atropos the things that are to be.

Shortly after this comes the climactic moment in which lots for the next life are allocated:

> Now when they arrived they were straightway bidden to go before Lachesis, and then a certain prophet first marshaled them in orderly intervals, and thereupon took from the lap of Lachesis lots and patterns of lives and went up to a lofty platform and spoke, "This is the word of Lachesis, the maiden daughter of Necessity, 'Souls that live for a day, now is the beginning of another cycle of mortal generation where birth is the beacon of death. No divinity shall cast lots for you, but you shall choose your own deity. Let him to whom falls the first lot select a life to which he shall cleave of necessity. But virtue has no master over her, and each shall have more or less of her as he honors her or does her despite. The blame is his who chooses. God is blameless.'"

The prophet now flings the lots among them. And then:

> All the souls had chosen their lives in the order of their lots, they were marshaled and went before Lachesis. And she sent with each, as the guardian of his life and the fulfiller of his choice, the genius that he had chosen, and this divinity led the soul first to Clotho, under her hand and the turning of the spindle to ratify the destiny of his lot and choice, and after contact with her the genius again led the soul to the spinning of Atropos to make the web of its destiny irreversible, and then without a backward look it passed beneath the throne of Necessity.

Socrates comments:

> And there, dear Glaucon, it appears, is the supreme hazard for a man. And this is the chief reason why it should be our main concern that each of us, neglecting all other studies, should seek after and study this thing—if in any way he may be able to learn of and discover the man who will give him the ability and the knowledge to distinguish the life that is good from that which is bad, and always and everywhere to choose the best that the conditions allow . . .[15]

Here in capsule are some of the issues that have preoccupied writers—not least autobiographers—down the centuries. According to the passage, once woven (strictly speaking, in this instance, spun) the "web of destiny" is "irreversible"; indeed even "virtue" cannot "master" necessity once the weaving has been done. The Good Life, like all others, must bow before its fate. But there is a moment before the weaving in which the souls experience a kind of cessation of necessity; in which they can *choose* their own lots, their preferred and binding narrative configuration among the various "patterns of lives." With each lot comes the god to whom their life's necessity will thenceforth "cleave." Just one example of how later writers have negotiated notions such as these occurs in Simone de Beauvoir's autobiography, as in existentialism more generally, where there is a secular variant of the Platonic notion that one makes an inaugurating choice of life mode, and that particular, more incidental choices flow from that, as if by necessity. The existentialists thought that by an act of will one could make and remake that inaugurating choice over and over. But in her autobiographical writings, Beauvoir tells how she comes to see that all choices are situated and constrained, that one can only make the best choice that "conditions will allow." The will, like all human things, is conditioned.

Elsewhere, Beauvoir sees the myth of the spinners in a rather different light. In her survey of patriarchal mythology in *The Second Sex,* she argues that it is no mere coincidence that these mythological incarnations of the powers that constrain and crush human freedoms are women. The Moirai are an instance of the Western construction of woman as the occluded, threatening, and essentialized Other; the being who is responsible for the miseries of the race:

> The cult of germination has always been associated with the cult of the dead. The Earth Mother engulfs the bones of her children. They are women—the Parcae, the Moirai—who weave the destiny of mankind; but it is they, also, who cut the threads. In most popular representations Death is a woman, and it is for women to bewail the dead because death is their work.[16]

Interestingly, Beauvoir as autobiographer does not make this connection. In her life-writing, she uses the figure of threads and spinning, as so many male auto-biographers do, as a form of heuristic philosophical notation for issues of will and necessity. Though the gendered history of this figure is important and warrants detailed study in its own terms,[17] my primary concern in this book is with its use as a means of narrative-philosophical inquiry in life-writing.

So wherein lies the intuitive aptness of threads as a way of figuring human life and will? Whence the extraordinary cultural mobility of the metaphor? Threads can suggest many things.[18] In their familiar and ancient context of spinning and weaving, threads can metaphorically characterize both the "maker" and that which is made. The spinner or weaver is a kind of agent who brings things into being, albeit by drawing upon materials that, in some form or another, are already provided. In the case of weaving, the thing woven is thus the product of the kind of being that the weaver is: if a god, then the product of a god; if a human being, then the product of a human being. (But even this is to make a distinction that is not so absolute in some cultural frames where human beings are thought to reflect or include aspects of divinity.) The woven thing, the fabric, has features that can suggest an ontological similarity between it and the world in general: like woven fabric, aspects of that world are assumed to be comprised of multiple materials that are configured in complex but regular and resilient ways. In addition to this structural similarity, the cloth can have a more explicit representational dimension: there may be a figure woven into the fabric, a figure that reflects some aspect of the world. (Even an apparently nonrepresentational figure might reflect less manifestly visible aspects of reality.) A further level of complication and richness arises if the figure happens to be a representation of the weaver. This is what occurs in autobiography: the writer produces a text—*texo*—which is a medium whose intended function is to bear a representation of the writer him- or herself. To the extent that, day in, day out, in all manner of activities—career résumés, interviews, court testimonies, passing conversations over coffee, life reminiscences with friends and children, retrospective sessions in therapy—we all produce representations of ourselves, we constantly perform as weavers so conceived. Many would say that the perfect woven self-image—or autobiography—would be the one in which the image is absolutely identical with the person who weaves it; but it seems that, as Tristram Shandy discovers, this cannot be: in part because the very process of self-representation requires a reconstitutive translation of "self" into another medium; because, too, the woven image is subject to the laws of temporality according to which each new strand of the image would need to incorporate the image of the weaver incorporating the previous strand, and so on, and so on, ad infinitum; and also because we can never be fully "objective" about ourselves. And yet it might seem that the weaver is at least free to try to represent him- or herself; it might even be argued that if he or she believes or perhaps even *wills* the image in the fabric to be a true description of him- or herself, then there is an important sense in which it *is* indeed a true description. It might for instance be that such an image could be internalized in such a way that it becomes determinative of the fabric (threads again) of consciousness and so, in an important sense, just *is* who the weaver is—rather as in some sense we *are* the stuff of our fantasies about ourselves. So conceived, threads are a powerful metaphor for some conceptions of free will: we are the weavers, and through creative acts of consciousness, we essentially create ourselves. And this protean creative power can seem to extend beyond the self to that which surrounds it: the weaver's image can represent the world that he or she inhabits, even—so far as visual representation will allow—the nature of the relations between the "self" and the "world." Thus Henry James, in a passage that begins by commending his father's masterly prose style and then reflects upon his own practice as an autobiographical weaver, writes:

> But I hold my case for a rare command of manner thus proved, and need go no further; the more that I have dropped too many of those threads of my rather niggled tapestry that belong but to the experience of my own weaving hand and the interplay of which represents thereby a certain gained author-

ity. I disentangle these again, if the term be not portentous, though reflecting too, and again with complacency, that though I thus prize them as involved most in my own consciousness, this is just because of their attachment somewhere else to other matters and other lives.[19]

In a contemporary autobiography, Nicholas Mosley speaks of a person on whom a character in one of his novels is based:

> The other strand that was weaving in and out of both my life at this time and the story of *Meeting Place* was to do with Mary of the *Rainbearers*—who indeed in life was the person from whom, more than anyone else I had learned about the interweaving of threads to make a pattern: about how good can sometimes come out of apparent evil; how the recognition of a connection between inner choice and outer event can give life wonder and meaning.[20]

The written text, so well suited to causal and contextual explanation, is capable of detailed and nuanced accounts of the "self"-"world" relation, not least of the will's part ("inner choice") in the self's taking the forms it has. In another sense, it seems that there might be no limit to the weaver's freedom of self-representation: if she or he doesn't like the pattern, of self or world or both, the weaver can unpick the fabric and start again. Sometimes we say of people in periods of personal crisis that they have "unraveled." But the premise of the freedom-to-weave is often taken to suggest that given time and appropriate ministrations, that person will be able to "pull the strands back together again."

Conceived in other frames, however, weaving can have very different implications. What, for example, if our cultural metaphysic tells us that the weaver is not us but a god? Much will then depend on the kind of god that it is, whether, as the Judeo-Christian tradition often holds, God confers freedom of will on the human self, or whether, like Necessity, it is a remorselessly deterministic being. In general, if we are not the weaver, but merely the image woven by some extra-human agency, the weaving metaphor will tend to suggest a world structured by necessity, not by freedom. We might comfort ourselves by saying that the woven image resembles the weaver—that we are made in His image, that we have some special relationship with deity—or that in fashioning our image God-the-weaver seeks to close some gap that has opened up between deity and humanity, to restore our divinity, and so on. But still: destiny will seem ultimately to be out of our hands. This can even be the case in the model in which the human being is the weaver: the freedom-to-weave assumes that the threads are ours to dispose of as we wish. But what if, for example, they come with an image already impregnated in the fibers—an image of which we are unaware as we weave and that, as in Henry James's story about the figure in the carpet, we only perceive when the fabric is made? Again: the fibers themselves come with certain built-in capacities and limitations. We can't just do anything with them, any more than an autobiographer can do just anything with words. Moreover, what we do with the threads—or the words—will also depend on certain skills and genres that we have internalized: we will need the culturally provided skill of weaving (though this does not mean that we cannot modify and extend existing techniques); and we will need the genre of weaving, together with certain preexisting forms, styles, and objects of representation (here again, the weaver can modify and extend existing materials). All of these to some extent constrain, but also orchestrate, our recollections and even reconfigure the self that does the remembering, the weaving. Thus, in his major new study of autobiography, *Memory and Narrative,* James Olney writes of the autobiographer's search for self through "mutually reflexive acts of memory and narrative,"[21] a reflexivity he likens to a weave. Hence his subtitle: *The Weave of Life-Writing.* Much too will depend on the ends that we want the fabric to serve: a merely practical end might constrain or render superfluous certain aesthetic or representational strivings, just as the autobiography written as a warning to future generations may eschew psychological and stylistic subtlety. On the other hand, self-representation has its own aesthetics; thus some autobiographers and others see a human life itself as a form of art, replete with structures, meanings, and motifs that have their own aesthetic values and rationales. Like fibers, genres, and skills, the ends for which we fashion our self-representations will, in part at least, constrain or determine those representations.

A particularly complex and interesting variation on all of this might come about if the weaver were to incorporate into the image of self a representation of the kinds of powers that she or he is exercising in bringing the fabric and the image into being. Now the question as to whether or not the weaver is a free agent becomes one of the themes of the image itself. So the weaver's self-image might be that of a subject-being, monotonously producing standardized fabrics for the court that feature images of weaving itself. No suggestion of free will here. Conversely, the woven self-image could be about the might of the imagination and could picture self as a sovereign subject emerging from its own freely chosen, willed, activities of self-creation, as when Michel Leiris uses the French verb *filer* (to spin) in a typically layered rumination on his freedom or otherwise to narrate his own story. He speaks of wanting "to follow my bent in obeying only my inclinations and to leave the reader the job of deciding where my journey ends, if it leads to any definite place [*filer ma courbe en n'obéissant qu'à mes inclinations et laisser au lecteur le soin de déterminer à quoi menait mon trajet, si toutefois il menait à quelque lieu définissable*]."[22] One of the central contentions of this study of autobiography and the will is that the weaver-as-autobiographer often asks just this question: How free is my will, not only in the processes of self-representation, but in general? How free is the will in other aspects of life? What is the place of will in the world? Indeed there is an important sense in which autobiography in the West was *invented* to ask just such questions: Augustine, from whom autobiography as we now understand it principally derives, also largely invented the concept of the will as it is now understood.

Hence some of the reasons for the metaphor's mobility, its capacity to render the same issues in widely discrepant cultural frames. And there are further possible variations. For instance, it is one thing to think of human life as threadlike where threads are conceived in terms of fabric, another if by "threadlike" we mean one isolated thread. When we say that a gravely ill person's life is "hanging by a thread," we mean that he or she is frail, vulnerable, "fragile,"[23] close to extinction. This is quite contrary to what is implied by the much more robust sense of life—or a life—as fabric: a thing that derives strength and resilience from the structured multiplicity of the threads that make it up. Different again is the notion, as employed by Richard Wollheim in his *The Thread of Life*,[24] of the thread as the connecting element in the multidimensional process that is a person living his or her life; or James Olney's related figure of a "thread of consciousness" that links "various transformations of self."[25] Here the thread suggests continuity and, by implication at least, the robustness of an ongoing thing, its capacity for survival, reemergence, even under hostile and dramatically varying circumstances. Again in a more hermeneutic register, we talk of "losing the thread" of an argument, as if texts are indeed fabriclike things and our stories about the world are artifacts that require interpretive expertise, in both weaver and reader, if those stories are to be understood. Such stories, of course, include life-stories: biographies, autobiographies, and others. We also speak of the "cultural fabric." A famous variant of this is given by the narrator in George Eliot's *Middlemarch,* who tells the reader: "I at least have so much to do in unravelling certain human lots, and seeing how they were woven and interwoven." She promises to direct all her attention at the "particular web"[26] that is Middlemarch society, the web having become a prominent metaphor in nineteenth-century sociology. The web suggests a further dimension of this family of metaphors: a vibration emanating from one point on a web can be felt by the spider at any other point. Whatever happens in one place has effects everywhere. Just so, to loosen one thread in a fabric is to weaken and change the whole thing. So these are organicist metaphors. The web has another potential implication: like the net that often occurs in Greek tragedy, it is a place of entrapment.

I have suggested that the writers are doing what we all do much of the time. Lived lives, however reflective or unthinking, proceed from assumptions, beliefs, sometimes theories, about what sort of a thing the will is. Our very sense of our place in the world depends in large part on how far, and in what ways, we think we can shape our "destinies" and the world in which they are enacted through exertion of the will. Moreover, attitudes toward the will can be emotionally extremely complex. If some might find the sense of control that goes with a belief in the freedom and effectiveness of the will reassuring, the will can also occasion profound anxiety: anxiety about the uses to which malign and irrational people can put the will, and apprehensiveness occasioned by the fact that the will necessarily addresses itself to a frighteningly uncertain realm that has no present reality—the future. There are times, too, when as embodied beings we seem to be the bearers of forms of will over which we have little control, as in Arthur Frank's autobiographical account of illness and "the will of the body."[27] For some—like myself—the will is also just plain puzzling and fascinating: how many, while lying in bed on a very cold weekend morning with no immediate obligations, have wondered what is actually going on when that internal voice says, "You've been there long enough; now get up," and you do? The voice has already given this order several times, and you didn't get up. So why do you get up now? It seems that now your "will" has "stepped in"; or perhaps that it is taking a "stronger stand." But how? Why? At whose bidding? And how did "I" enlist the will's services in this matter in the first place? By a prior act of will, perhaps? But then, how did that prior act "get going"? Where did it come from? What is the relationship between "me" and "my" will? And so on. And note that similar questions arise in much more critical life situations: why and how does one person stay in what she or he knows to be a viciously destructive relationship, while another in an almost identical situation "summons the willpower" to leave?

There are various places I might turn to for an answer to such questions: psychology, philosophy, theology, for instance. But one's first recourse may well be to a source much closer to hand—my self. I seek to reconstruct and understand the processes involved through the activity of *introspection*. This, in a far more elaborate way, is what autobiographers have done over the centuries: they have "looked within" in order to try to understand the place and the powers that the self has in the world, to help provide what Richard Eldridge calls "a phenomenology of human agency in the world."[28] A classic example is Benjamin Franklin's autobiographical account of his "bold and arduous Project of arriving at moral Perfection"[29]—a project that entailed the exertion and recording of acts of will intended to neutralize his inclination to error and sin. And they have looked outward as well, to see what effects various kinds of actions, both volitional and constrained, have on that world. I'll refer to such foundational processes of self-location and self-description as *existential positing*,[30] and I want to suggest that one of the principal motivations for the writing (and indeed the reading) of autobiography has been to posit the self with reference to the will. As Paul Ricoeur says in a variation on Descartes's cogito, "I understand myself in the first place as he who says 'I will.'"[31] It is this profound link between autobiography and understandings of the will that I seek to explore in this book.

I think we need a term for the kind of autobiographer who indulges in extended philosophical contemplation of the world and her or his place in it—

contemplation that in some instance includes meditation upon the will. I shall call such autobiographers *reflective autobiographers* and will use the term *reflective autobiography* to designate first-person life-writing in which there is a significant and sophisticated component of reflection on the meaning and larger implications of the life being written, and of life in general; and in which there is a significant sense of reflective, critical distance between the attitudes and assumptions of the autobiographer and the attitudes and assumptions that were/are prevalent in his or her cultural-ideological milieu. (The notion that an autobiographer, or indeed anyone else, can attain "critical distance" from prevailing cultural ideology will prompt immediate resistance or skepticism among some readers: I take up this matter—indeed the whole question of the relationship between the self and its cultural situation—in the next section.)

Most reflective modern autobiographers seem to concede the constrained, conditioned status of the human will; they see the threads of a life as woven both for and by us. Some say we do more of the weaving than others, but always there is a tension between will and necessity; always we choose "the best that conditions allow." These autobiographers, and the history of debate about the will to which they contribute, make very clear that simple oppositions between "free will" and "determinism" are grossly inadequate; that the place of the will in human life is an immensely complex matter, both experientially and conceptually. Indeed one of the stories I have to tell in this book is about the perplexities that have beset late modernity in its attempts to figure, conceptualize, and appropriately exert the will. Late modernity does not generally think that the gods or their delegates do the weaving, and it might seem to follow from this that we are free and responsible authors of our own conduct; yet there have been many, especially in the last 130 years, who have wanted to deny the effectiveness—or even the existence—of the human will. Such thinkers have proposed alternative factors to account for what they perceive as our pervasive unfreedom: the unconscious or other aspects of our psychophysiological constitution, for instance, or various forms of ideological determination—patriarchal, racist, capitalistic, colonialist, and so on. Of course not all twentieth-century thinkers deny the existence or the effectiveness of the will; and, as we shall see, not all who deny the will when they have their theoretical hats on take the same view when they speak or write in a more "personal" vein. Among those who argue for the existence of the will are some prominent intellectual autobiographers who appear in this study: Spender, Koestler, Beauvoir, and Trilling. (Hemingway is another, and a complicated, matter.) Such writers impute the weaver's gift to the self: we spin the threads, we weave the pattern. Not entirely, of course: circumstance or some such agency has a big say; but modern voices such as these insist that the self has a substantial say as well. Such a position has its own long history.

Such exceptions notwithstanding, it is fair to say that in the intellectual culture of the century just passed in particular, the will has gone down in the world. I write, in part at least, to contest these developments; to make anew a case for the will as a real, if constrained, human power, and for the category of the will as an indispensable, if conceptually fraught, component in the description of human lives.

II. Reflective Autobiography and the Will: Augustine and Others

How the mind may seek and find itself is, therefore, a remarkable question: whither does it go in order to seek and whither does it come in order to find?
—Augustine, *The Trinity,* X (8)

In book 8 of the *Confessions,* Augustine recalls receiving a visit in Milan from Ponticianus, a baptized Christian and a high-ranking court official. Like Augustine himself, Ponticianus is something of an autobiographer. He narrates a crucial moment in his life to Augustine and Augustine's friend, Alypius. Ponticianus's account of this moment in turn becomes crucial—indeed transformative—in Augustine's life. Part of Ponticianus's autobiographical vignette concerns that other mode of life-writing with which autobiography is always deeply entwined: biography. Ponticianus tells how he and three friends had gone for a walk outside the Milan city walls. He and one colleague go their own way; the other two come to a house of Christians and here they find a copy of the *Life of Antony.* One of them is "set on fire" and "filled with love and sobering shame"[32] by what he reads; he undergoes an experience of conversion and decides to abandon his career in the court for a life of religious devotion. Ponticianus is moved when he hears this but does not follow his friend into the religious life. As Augustine listens to how Ponticianus's friend had emerged from "the turbulent hesitations of his heart,"[33] he is plunged anew into his own inner turbulence. He tries to shy away from the inevitable pain of self-confrontation, but realizes: "Lord, you turned my attention back to myself. You took me up from behind my own back where I had placed myself because I did not wish to observe myself."[34] Now follows a description of intense self-loathing and an experience of agonized equivocation during which self-accusation and inclination draw him toward God, yet for some reason his "soul hung back."[35] How can this be? How can his spirit "cry out" to enter "into my pact and covenant with you, my God," to make the journey that culminates in faith, and yet not make that journey? Augustine's approach to this question involves using autobiography to explore the nature and the intricacies of the human will. Passages such as these are among the *loci classici* of reflective autobiography:

> The one necessary condition, which meant not only going but at once arriving there, was to have the will to go—provided only that the will was strong

and unqualified, not the turning and twisting first this way, then that, of a will half-wounded, struggling with one part rising up and the other part falling down.[36]

As confessional autobiographer, he is engaging in an act of what we might term *retrospective introspection* that takes in not only the will in relation to God, but in relation to various other aspects of the soul, and even in relation to the body. He notes that when he wills certain physical movements they happen. Yet when it comes to the agonizingly crucial matter of willing God's grace:

> I was not doing what with an incomparably greater longing [than the longing that results in physical movements] I yearned to do, and could have done the moment I so resolved. For as soon as I had the will, I would have had a whole-hearted will. At this point the power to act is identical with the will. The willing itself was performative of the action. Nevertheless, it did not happen.[37]

This seems to him a "monstrous situation"[38] and he must know its cause. How is it possible that "the mind orders the mind to will. The recipient of the order is itself, yet it does not perform it"?[39] His explanation is momentous for Western understandings of the will, and for the tradition of Western autobiographical writing:

> The willing [of God's grace] is not wholehearted, so the command is not wholehearted. The strength of the command lies in the strength of the will, and the degree to which the command is not performed lies in the degree to which the will is not engaged. For it is the will that commands the will to exist, and it commands not another will but itself. So the will that commands is incomplete, and therefore what it commands does not happen. If it were complete, it would not need to command the will to exist, since it would exist already. Therefore there is no monstrous split between willing and not willing. We are dealing with a morbid condition of the mind which, when it is lifted up by the truth, does not unreservedly rise to it but is weighed down by habit. So there are two wills. Neither of them is complete, and what is present in the one is lacking to the other.[40]

Augustine here posits a specific faculty of the will; a faculty that is not ancillary to or merely the expression of rational understanding (he laments that "uneducated people"[41] can take the step he has so far been unable to take), and that is likewise not the mere servant of emotional or sensual urgings. Though part of the integrated organization of the soul, this will has the status of a logically and psychologically independent entity. In an effort to map the soul that is a crucial point of reference for later such attempts, Augustine divides the soul into three faculties, each an internal correlate of elements of the Trinity: *memoria* (memory: the Father), *intelligentia* (intellect: Logos), *voluntas* (will: Spirit).[42] The structure of the soul in some way resembles that of the Trinity. In *The Trinity*, which provides a more detailed and developed account of the soul thus conceived, he writes of "that God who is Trinity in our memory, understanding, and will."[43] As in the Trinity itself, none of the three constituents can act independently: memory, for instance, contains the objects needed for intellect to undertake cognitive activity, and the will, through a kind of "attention,"[44] brings those objects and the intellectual capacities into effective relation. In this sense, will enters into, is a constitutive part of, the process of cognition itself.[45] The quintessence and epitome of all activities of the soul is the state in which the individual turns away from the soul's life of "habit"—its entrenched condition of separation from God—and fully wills absolute accord with God's will. Augustine claims that if the will is fully "engaged," there will be no division within the soul: willing grace will be as spontaneous, effective, and immediate as willing the moving of a limb. If the will is undivided, "to act is identical with the will." Precisely how this state of engagement comes about is never made clear. Book 13 of the *Confessions* offers an explanation that is taken up in more detail in *The Trinity*. In this account the will is subsumed or gathered up into a greater power—the power of love. When Augustine says that "my weight is my love,"[46] he means that like all other things, the soul has a kind of center of gravity that, when found, sets it at rest, and that the love of God is that which brings the soul home and finally becalms it. When this happens, the will and the associated "turbulent hesitations of the heart" cease. That which remains is a transcendent, perdurable self, free of the contingent frailties of fallenness.

The narrative of book 8 continues: "From a hidden depth a profound self-examination had dredged up a heap of all my misery."[47] He takes leave of Alypius, sits under a fig tree in the garden, and weeps. All the while he is drawing closer to God. He hears a child's voice from a nearby house chanting: "'Pick up and read, pick up and read.'" Returning to Alypius, and recalling Ponticianus's story about the *Life of Antony,* he picks up the book of the apostle he had been reading and his eyes light on the passage:

> Not in riots and drunken parties, not in eroticism and indecencies, not in strife and rivalry, but put on the Lord Jesus Christ and make no provision for the flesh in its lusts. (Rom. 13:13–14)

The moment of conversion is upon him:

> I neither wished nor needed to read further. At once, with the last words of this sentence, it was as if a light of relief from all anxiety flooded into my heart. All the shadows of doubt were dispelled.[48]

The will is now said to be whole and wholly coincident with the will of God.[49] Will has become love. Augustine has taken life-writing into the domain of psychology and has sought to explain the orientation of a human being in the world on the basis of what his particular mix of recollection and introspection has revealed to him. The moment is extraordinarily dramatic, and on several levels: we witness the transformation of Augustine's soul, but from the perspective of readers who know that what we are witnessing, or at least the way it is being related, constitutes a watershed in the cultural history of the West. Augustine imputes a kind of inwardness to the self that proves to be foundational for modernity's sense of human individuality. And in rendering this sense of self, he revolutionizes self-life-writing.[50] In his hands, conventional religious confessional writing modulates into autobiography as we know it: a multifaceted account of self that is predicated on the assumptions of psychological depth and personal uniqueness, and on what is presumed to be the unprecedented particularity of any given life-story. At the same time, we know that in this remarkable text the modern philosophical conception of the will as an independent faculty is born. In the words of Albrecht Dihle: "From St. Augustine's reflections emerged the concept of a human will prior to and independent of the act of intellectual cognition, yet fundamentally different from sensual and irrational emotion." And again: "St. Augustine was, in fact, the inventor of our modern notion of the will."[51]

Though some have tried to find such a notion of will in, say, Aristotle,[52] the general consensus now is that the classical Greek philosophers were "intellectualists":[53] in other words, that they saw will as a function of logical thought, appetition (here meaning something like inclination) as logically inseparable from and consequent upon rationality. This meant that where the will is in operation it executes, and can only execute, a rational assessment as to what is the best or right course of action. If such a course is not "chosen," it is because other factors have interfered and have rendered the will-as-executor of rational assessment inoperative. Thus Plato's tripartite picture of the soul in *The Republic* comprises a "rational" part (*logos*), which "reckons and reasons the rational"; an "irrational and appetitive" part (*epithumia*) with which it "loves, hungers, thirsts, and feels the flutter and titillation of other desires"; and a third part, *thumos,* "the principle of high spirit . . . with which we feel anger."[54] It seems that acts of willing spring from reason, and that the virtuous man is the one in whom reason predominates. Where such acts do not occur it is because of "impulses which draw and drag" and "come through affections and diseases."[55] In book 3 of the *Nichomachean Ethics,* Aristotle likewise aligns "continent" (controlled) behavior with "choice" or will-as-executor of rational appraisal and "incontinent" (uncontrolled) conduct with nonrational "desire."[56] (Incontinence is the phenomenon of *akrasia,* which I discuss in chapter 5.) Later in the same work, however, Aristotle seems to shift ground and to entertain a somewhat different relationship between choice, reason, and appetition. He leaves open the possibility that choice springs from a form of reason that is impelled or perhaps conditioned by a prior inclination: "Choice is either desiderative thought or intellectual desire."[57] Aquinas (see appendix A, "Some Earlier Conceptions of the Will") was to endorse the "appetitive intellect" position, but Aristotle hedges his bets. Yet even if Aristotle had settled on choice conceived as inclination-driven intellection, he would not have been committed to a view of the will as a separate faculty, as it is envisaged by Augustine and in earlier Judeo-Christian scriptural accounts.

These historical considerations aside, the passages I have quoted from the *Confessions* have extraordinary iconic power in part because they depict something that is absolutely fundamental to human life: that process of existential positing in which the self forms a conception, however consciously or otherwise, of its place in the world—a conception that depends heavily on its understanding of the powers of the will. A belief that the will is marginal, ineffectual, or even nonexistent will be associated with a sense that the self is powerless, already given and shaped, the creature of greater and imperious powers. Conversely, to believe that the will is at least there and effective will entail some sense that the self has powers that are at its own disposal; that these powers might equip it, at least to some extent, to shape its own destiny; that if there are greater powers beyond the self, these may not be absolutely sovereign. I argue in this book that the sense of self and the sense of will are intricately entwined and that reflective autobiographers, who give the sense of self extended and probing narrative articulation, cannot help but factor the will into their narratives of self—however conscious or otherwise that factoring might be, and however sanguine or fearful they may feel about the will.

Augustine's autobiographical departure from the "intellectualist" view is a classic demonstration of what Olney calls "the dual, symbiotic activity of auto-biography-and-philosophy" that is so prominent in the history of autobiographical writing.[58] The *Confessions* is a particularly eminent example of reflective autobiography because Augustine is a giant among both philosophers and autobiographers. But it is worth noting that many other major philosophers have written autobiography as well, and that some of them have taken a particular interest, both in their philosophizing and their life-writing, in the will. In chapter 2 I discuss Nietzsche, Freud, Sartre, and Ryle in this context. But first some earlier examples, all of which are discussed in more detail in appendix A, "Some Earlier Conceptions of the Will: Maimonides to Mill."

Descartes is not a philosopher in a conventional sense; however, much of his philosophical prose is couched in a heuristic first-person mode, and his method of trying to resolve doubt through recourse to introspective analysis was to have a major influence on modern autobiographical writing. The second *Meditation* makes clear that the cogito incorporates more than just thought in its narrowly cognitive sense. The cogito includes a range of aspects and activities of consciousness. No less than Augustine, Descartes links introspection and (among other things) the will: "But what then am I? A thing which thinks. What is a thing which thinks? It is a thing which doubts, understands, [conceives], affirms, denies, wills . . ."[59] Hume's views about the will are complex: he wants to see the will as both determined and (to some extent at least) free. His is arguably a compatibilist account of the matter. The claim that the will can be both determined and free is reflected in the short autobiographical document that Hume wrote a few months before his death, *My Own Life*,[60] where his sanguinity of temperament is presented as the key determinant in his life.

Like Augustine's *Confessions,* the *Confessions* of Rousseau bring will and autobiography into close, albeit less systematic, relationship. Rousseau is yet another autobiographer who figures the complexities of the self in terms of threads or strands. Of an unjust childhood punishment and its psychological consequences, he writes: "I do not feel capable of unraveling the strands or even remotely following all that happened at that time within me."[61] Just prior to this he has made one of his most scandalous confessions: that he has a masochistic sexuality that stems, he believes, from his experience of corporal punishment at the hands of his foster mother, Mlle. Lambercier. He recalls the "admixture of sensuality"[62] he feels when she beats him; he continues in a tone of bemused lament:

> Who could have supposed that this childish punishment, received at the age of eight at the hands of a woman of thirty, would determine my tastes and desires, my passions, my very self for the rest of my life, and that in a sense diametrically opposed to the one in which they should normally have developed.[63]

This is Rousseau the "arch catastrophist"[64] in deterministic mode. Contrast this with John Stuart Mill's autobiographical treatment of the will in his *Autobiography,* a work that Olney likens to "a syllogism on private human experience":[65]

> During the later returns of my dejection, the doctrine of what is called Philosophical Necessity weighed on my existence like an incubus. I felt as if I was scientifically proved to be the helpless slave of antecedent circumstances; as if my character and that of all others had been formed for us by agencies beyond our control, and was wholly out of our own power. I often said to myself, what a relief it would be if I could disbelieve the doctrine of the formation of character by circumstances . . .[66]

He ponders the problem and eventually perceives that the term *Necessity* carries a misleading implication with respect to human action:

> I saw that though our character is formed by circumstances, our own desires can do much to shape those circumstances; and that what is really inspiriting and ennobling in the doctrine of freewill, is the conviction that we have real

power over the formation of our own character; that our will, by influencing some of our circumstances, can modify our future habits or capabilities of willing.[67]

The emphasis on "desires" is crucial: this is an autobiography that famously chronicles the discovery of an affective dimension in life, and it is this dimension that instigates the will's reflexive action upon character and its circumstances.

Of the autobiographers I discuss in detail in this book, all bar one are clearly what I have called reflective autobiographers. Althusser, Skinner, Barthes, Beauvoir, Koestler, Spender, and Diana Trilling all philosophize extensively, not least about the will. The exception is Hemingway, a writer whose work is apparently—I use the qualifier advisedly—suffused with a belief in the power of the will, but who does very little autobiographical philosophizing of note.

III. THEORY

Though not primarily a work of literary theory, this book does propose a theory of autobiography—a theory that draws upon philosophical accounts of the will and related topics, and that informs a literary critical approach to autobiographical texts.

I have proposed the term *reflective autobiography* and in so doing have referred to a significant sense of reflective, critical distance between the attitudes and assumptions of the autobiographer, and the attitudes and assumptions that were/are prevalent in his or her cultural-ideological milieu. I said that such a formulation would seem dubious to some readers. In saying this I had in mind—among others—certain postmodern "constructivist anti-humanist"[68] critics and theorists who claim that the self (to use that much-debated term for the moment) is wholly or largely constructed by ideological forces. In this view, there can be no "reflective, critical distance" between the self and the ideological world in which it is embedded—even though the emancipatory politics that often takes up the constructivist antihumanist premise in practice *requires* that such "distance" be possible: if it were not possible, there could be no way of transcending ideological determination, and so no possibility of emancipation from ideology.

The issue of "distance" from the ideological is one of several problems pertaining to the self that need to be considered in a study such as this that aims to give a philosophically framed account of autobiography and its engagements with the will. Bearing in mind that this is an interdisciplinary study, I now want to identify several theoretical problems pertaining to the self and to explain my position and methodological response to these problems. These are the notion of self, the possibility of knowledge of self through introspection, the problem of representation of self in autobiographical narrative, the issue of cultural specificity, the self's agential relation to culture, and the problem of explanation—the strategies and theories we employ to explain how self, whether in or beyond autobiographical narrative, comes to be the way it is. I shall take each point in turn and then offer some definitions of the will and related terms.

1. *The Self*

This is an admittedly vague and much-abused term, and it is sometimes said that it should now be replaced by the more "rigorously theorized" term *the subject.* I do not accept this. Despite the enormous effort and intellectual acumen that has been invested in what is termed "the critique of the subject" in contemporary literary theory and continental philosophy, the whole "question of the subject" remains, in my view, an intellectual minefield. A recent collection of essays purporting to give an authoritative and cutting-edge account of the critique of the subject is Eduardo Cadava et al., *Who Comes After the Subject?* Yet one comes away from the book with the impression that nothing even approaching consensus about the history and nature of conceptions of the subject has been reached. As Derrida says in an interview with Jean-Luc Nancy in the book, the subject "cannot be reduced to a homogeneity."[69] Derrida raises the question "by what right" we choose or refuse to identify particular philosophical constructs as "the subject."[70] The answer is not at all clear. What is clear is that a bemusing range of identifications are made in this volume, and elsewhere. For some, philosophical accounts of the subject start with Descartes and proceed through Kant and Husserl, thence to postmodern deconstructions (Derrida, Foucault, Levinas et al.). So conceived, the subject is associated with transcendental freedom, various forms of solipsistic disconnection from the social and ideological worlds, a disabling rationalism, and so on. For others, the essence of the subject lies in its *subjection* to certain structures of power and ideology; its lack of real or envisioned autonomy. Some of those who see solipsism as definitive of the subject agree with those who see subjection as its hallmark in the view that there are deep causal and conceptual links between the philosophy of the subject, on the one hand, and liberal humanism and capitalism, on the other.[71] However, such links are (to say the least) problematical for those who track philosophical accounts of the subject as far back as Aristotle.[72] But even among those who agree broadly on matters of chronology, the alleged connections between philosophies of the subject and these other historical tendencies are not in my view compellingly demonstrated. A fairly widely held view among the contributors to this volume is that the subject tends to be conceptualized as radically free in the sense that it "freely determines itself," that it possesses "pure will."[73] However, unless or until there is some consensus about what the subject *is,* this characterization, like a number of others, remains speculative. Another fairly common assumption is that there is an important distinction to be drawn between the "subject" and the "self," or "person" (see, for example, Vincent Descomes's essay "Apropos of the 'Critique of the Subject' and of the Critique of this Critique").[74] Here again, however, there are problems: How can the line be drawn if what is on one side of the divide (the subject) is so far from consensual characterization—as indeed is what is on the other side? And, as Derrida inquires, on what grounds do we separate, for instance, certain Cartesian assumptions about the inner life of the subject from selfhood in general?

Except when discussing poststructuralist authors, I have deliberately not made the distinction between self and subject in this study (indeed I seldom use the latter term). In part this is because of the conceptual and historical complexities to which I have just referred; it is also because, insofar as certain postmodern views adopt a deterministic standpoint—a standpoint that denies the will or its freedom—their determinism applies to human beings in general, regardless of whether these beings are conceptualized as subjects or selves. I suggest that familiar postmodern accounts of the nature and the history of the subject should not be allowed to eclipse some histories of the issue that depart from standard postmodern accounts; for instance, competing intellectual histories of the self such as Charles Taylor's monumental *Sources of the Self: The Making of the Modern Identity*[75] or a (post)modernist account like Anthony Cascardi's *The Subject of Modernity*.[76]

When I speak of the "self," therefore, I am not speaking of an alleged philosophical construct such as the "subject"; I am speaking of real, empirical human beings who possess an extraordinary range of attributes (psychological, physiological, cultural), whose lives in cultural situations evince a vast array of forms of participation in and connection with those situations, and whose characteristics admit of various forms of theoretical description (though I contend that no form of theoretical description can ever exhaust the complexity of the self). "Self" is a global and inclusive term, and this in my view is one of its strengths. In this book, it is also a heuristic term: we need empirical and conceptual presuppositions about self in order, for instance, to read autobiography, but we read autobiography, in part at least, to extend these empirical and conceptual awarenesses—to find out more than we could otherwise know about particular selves, and about the self in general. "Self" might be thought of as a heuristic sign: it designates something, a something to which we attribute certain properties—for instance, the possession of a will—but on the understanding that its referent is open to empirical and conceptual elaboration and specification. We might therefore read reflective autobiography on the assumption that there is a will, but also in the hope that we may learn from such reading more than we had known hitherto about the will. We even have to leave open the possibility that reading autobiography might in fact undermine our belief in the will—a matter I take up in chapter 3.

ii. Introspection

Another reason for eschewing the term "subject" is that it tends for many to be associated with Cartesianism, not least with a Cartesian understanding of introspection. Postmodern literary theory is generally very hostile to Cartesian assumptions, and it will generally follow from this that advocates of postmodern assumptions will repudiate the notion of introspection. On the other hand, it's also no doubt true that postmodern theory's dislike of Cartesianism is partly rooted in an already-embedded hostility to the notion of introspection and its assumed complicity in various "liberal humanist" and capitalist understandings of self/subject. Indeed, one of the hallmarks of postmodern theory's accounts of the self/subject is its resistance to the notion that we might actually learn something that is (a) reliable and (b) valuable through introspective activity. This resistance, which can take on an almost obsessive intensity,[77] sits oddly with postmodern theory's often deep commitment to depth psychology.

Of course, introspection is a much-debated topic, and many philosophers, philosophical psychologists, behaviorists, and others now deny that there is any such thing as introspection. There is a substantial literature on this subject. William Lyons's *The Disappearance of Introspection*[78] contains a valuable historical summary of various views. As Lyons shows, introspection is too complex a matter to admit of easy, categorical pronouncements (as in the genre of pronouncements about "the death of the subject"). Even the meaning of the term is not self-evident. Does it refer to some kind of passive registration of what's going on in the mind, registration that is simultaneous with the occurrence being registered; or to a deliberate and active act of attention to what's going on in the mind, an act performed by some part of the mind "other" than the part in which the thing observed is occurring? Is it in fact possible to conceive of attentive monitoring that goes on in consciousness simultaneously with that which is being monitored, or does it make more sense to talk of "retrospection"[79]—a looking back on the contents of consciousness—rather than "introspection," a (simultaneous) looking in upon them? Again, if we know what sort of a thing introspection is, it might seem to follow that we know what sort of mental phenomena it deals with. But what are these phenomena? Here are some candidates: thought processes, sensations, and motivational states. The last of these might well include willing.

There have been various objections to the notion of introspection. For instance, if it does indeed involve one "part" of the mind monitoring another, doesn't this entail a splitting of consciousness that might render the very notion of consciousness conceptually incoherent? Even if we accept the monitoring idea, it arguably can't mean simultaneous monitoring, in which case what we do when we "retrieve" the contents of consciousness is more like an act of memory, or retrospection, than an act of monitoring. But is the notion of retrieval apposite? How do we know that our understanding of what has gone on in our minds is accurate? Since they can't generally be checked, it may well be that in fact they are reconstructions of a notably unreliable kind—a thought that will ring bells with many who have, say, checked recollections of inner events against diary jottings made about them at the time. If these reconstructions are indeed unreliable, then perhaps they are more like "constructions," or acts of imagination than of "retrieval"? If there were such a thing as introspection, it ought perhaps to follow that we would be able recover an experience that could be so designated; yet if we try to recover such experiences, it seems that we actually only retrieve and recount the contents of introspective acts: we can perhaps retrieve a feeling of anger, but can we retrieve any sensation that corresponds to the act of retrieval itself? Lyons thinks not; he argues that "phenomenologically it seems impossible to detect our introspections."[80] Another very important possible objection is that we cannot experience what might be thought of as unmediated experience of our own inner states. Such experience, like all others, must be filtered through our learned patterns of understanding, and these patterns must come, in large part at least, from the cultural grammar in which we have developed as perceiving, meaning-making beings. Lyons, who in fact only endorses a modified conception of introspection, argues that "our 'introspection' of our motives, desires, deliberations, plans, decisions or intentions will be colored by and adapted from our own particular culture's 'rough-and-ready' view of the mind and its operations."[81] A further, though more circumscribed, objection might be raised by a Freudian: If it is true that most of our decisive inner events are unconscious, then introspection, even if it is said to exist, can be of only limited value, because, unassisted, it cannot give us access to the most important dimension of the psyche's functioning.

I want to affirm the actuality and the power of introspection; and to say that it can give us substantial insight into ourselves as will-bearing agents. In this respect I am in sympathy with Descartes, some of the seventeenth-century philosophical psychologists (see appendix A, "Some Earlier Conceptions of the Will: Maimonides to Mill"), and, indeed, Augustine, who in a foreshadowing of Descartes says this in *The Trinity*:

> But since we are investigating the nature of the mind, let us not take into consideration any knowledge that is obtained from without through the senses of the body, and consider more attentively the principle which we have laid down: that every mind knows and is certain concerning itself. For men have doubted whether the power to live, to remember, to understand, to will, to think, to know, and to judge is due to air, to fire, or to the brain, or to the blood, or to atoms, or to a fifth body . . . On the other hand who would doubt

that he lives, remembers, understands, wills, thinks, knows, and judges? For even if he doubts, he lives . . .[82]

However, I only want—and I think need—to make certain claims in support of the "insight" to which I refer. The notion of introspection I employ in this book does not require that looking inward be simultaneous with that which is looked upon. Autobiographers always look back upon whatever it is that they recount in their narratives. Autobiography just is retrospective in nature. If we concede—as I do—that "introspection" is really a species of retrospection, then the autobiographer gives us introspection at a double remove: she or he gives us a narrated recollection of a recollection of an inner event. The concern about a "split" in consciousness becomes less pressing on the retrospection view, since that which is being attended to is now removed in temporal terms from that which is attending. It might, however, be argued that retrospection entails unreliability since there is a lag between event and its monitoring, and that the lag will be longer, and the unreliability therefore greater, in the case of the autobiographer who narrates what is already a recollection. This is quite likely, and it seems pointless to argue for the absolute reliability of introspection. On the other hand, it seems equally pointless to insist that introspection is constitutively wholly unreliable. In the first place, no one is generally in a position to make such a judgment. For the most part, others don't know what "goes on in our heads." If the findings of introspection cannot generally be objectively confirmed, neither can they generally objectively be denied. Further, the whole question of what an introspectively generated finding "means" is complicated by the fact that in something so subjective as introspection, things are being filtered through a particular individual's sense of what is true, of what things mean. If an autobiographer says that "a certain feeling was the starting point for my nervous breakdown," this, her understanding of the feeling and its consequences, could not be rejected out of hand. It is very much a part of *her truth,* of how she experiences her life—and perhaps of *her* sense of self more generally.

Yet I do not want to present introspection as a radically private event. In terms of the objects of introspection, it may be that when we look in and back upon certain sense experiences, we encounter them in a fairly "direct" way; but when it comes to something like the will, it is surely clear that, as Lyons argues, our looking in and back is heavily mediated by cultural—and, crucially, *ideological*—understandings. In the case of the will, the very notion of personhood that I internalize from my culture must enter deeply into my understanding of my volitional states and actions. For this reason, among others, we can never wholly achieve what Derrida calls "presence":[83] in one of his accounts, an unattainable state in which consciousness is entirely transparent to, and coincident with, itself. Even the greatest conceptual innovators like Augustine are subject to the claims of cultural mediation. Thus Augustine's philosophical account of the will, not least its puzzling over the failures of volition that he sees in himself, owes much to the general tenor of Saint Paul's conception of will—the Paul who laments: "The good which I want to do, I fail to do; but what I do is the wrong which is against my will; and if what I do is against my will, clearly it is no longer I who am the agent, but sin that has its lodging in me" (Rom. 7:19–21). And Paul in his turn is reflecting a long-standing biblical discourse of fall, salvation, and moral conduct.[84] Again, Augustine's customary word for the will—*voluntas*—is derived from Roman jurisprudence. As Dihle says, in formulating his philosophical conception of the will Augustine was "greatly helped and tacitly guided by the Latin vocabulary of his time";[85] I would add that his introspective experience of what he later designated as the will was also mediated by cultural categories. A Freudian would say that there was much that Augustine could not penetrate through introspection because it was unconscious. This is no doubt true. But it is also true that in a Freudian account the unconscious can be penetrated through that form of assisted retrospection we call psychoanalysis. In principle, the same is true for the autobiographer, who can also look back and in with the assistance of psychoanalytic understandings.

When I use the term "introspection" in this book, I refer to retrospective accounts of internal events that generally possess a higher degree of probable authenticity than could be provided from any other vantage point and that must be taken seriously—not least because they constitute some particular person's truth about themselves. For my purposes, it is not necessary to give a detailed account of the precise mechanisms whereby introspectively derived phenomena come into being.[86] Nor does it matter that an autobiographer probably doesn't (even this isn't entirely clear) tell us what it feels like to introspect. For my purposes, it is quite sufficient to be able to say—as I think we can—that introspection can give relatively authoritative access to some of the cognitive and perceptual states that are associated with willing.

III. *Self-Representation and Representation of the Self*

If the representations of my inward phenomena that I effect through introspection are to a significant degree mediated by various forms of cultural understanding, then it will follow that the representations I give of those inward phenomena in an autobiographical narrative will also be (to a significant degree) culturally mediated. The same will apply to representations of aspects of my self that are not inward—to actions and other manifest forms of behavior—because here, too, I cannot make sense of what I "do" without the assistance of a cultural grammar that groups certain kinds and sources of action into intelligible categories and sees them in terms of certain general understandings of self and world. At both of these levels—"internal" and "external"—self-representation is mediated by what we might loosely call *cultural categories.* But these categories are in turn implicated in another source of mediation: language. Postmodern theory, not least postmodern theory of autobiography,[87] has made a great deal of language's role in self-representation and has concluded from its belief that language is an inherently fictitious medium that self-representation too must be inherently fictitious. I've argued elsewhere that in recent decades literary studies in general has suffered because such postmodern assumptions have been accepted with too little thought and qualification.[88]

How might some of these matters be reconceptualized? We use language to report on a vast spectrum of aspects of the world, some (the date of my birth) quite straightforward, others (what I mean when I say I love someone) less so. Poststructuralist views of language tend to see it as a kind of meaning-imposition where no meaning actually resides. (I say "tend" because there are so many varieties of poststructuralism.) We impose signs on phenomena and because no meaning "inheres" in these phenomena, there is no real meaning—not even relatively stable meaning—to be had. But we might equally see signs as heuristic devices through which we learn to agree on what certain aspects of our world "mean"; that is, "mean" to those who participate in various kinds of cultural conversation.[89] Agreement on external phenomena (the date of my birth) is not difficult, but agreement on internal phenomena is more so. Yet cultural conversation does necessarily, and very definitely, reach down to internal and less readily formulable registers of experience.[90] We *do* in fact want and need to know what we mean when we say we feel love for someone, and what the significance of such a feeling is. Indeed we constantly discuss just this point in a whole range of communicative media. One such medium is autobiography, and I want to suggest that autobiography—along with lyric poetry, psychoanalytic narratives, conversations over coffee, and other forms—is one of the principal genres in which cultural conversation reaches down to the inner life and gives it articulation in ways that are powerful, sometimes alarming, sometimes edifying, but generally educative. In writing autobiography, as elsewhere, the very struggle to articulate and evaluate experience can change the way we understand such experience, and indeed the values we assign to it. It is unbalanced, then, to see language as something that can only impede self-representation of this kind. Because language is constitutively social, there will be certain regions of subjectivity that it cannot represent, or cannot represent without distortion; but there are other such regions for which it is a powerfully—indeed *the* most powerfully— *enabling* medium for self-representation.

Another (and related) rationale for postmodern denials of authentic self-representation has been the notion that representation is necessarily metaphoric in nature. There is ample historical support for this view, not least in respect to the will. For instance, Augustine's tripartite division of the soul into *memoria, intelligentia,* and *voluntas* is one of innumerable attempts over the centuries to map the divisions and components of the soul. It is a striking fact that neither of the two attempts that are best known in our own time—Plato's and Freud's—have a faculty that corresponds in any direct way to the will. But Augustine's does. In appendix A, "Some Earlier Conceptions of the Will: Maimonides to Mill," I survey some of the other influential attempts to map the soul (or psyche) and the place of the will therein. Here we need to say something about the nature of such enterprises in general.

Many—though by no means all—such attempts try to understand the soul/psyche as if it were a map comprised of particular "regions" that can in turn be thought of as distinct psychological "faculties." But as we know from our encounters with Freudian thought, the map metaphor doesn't quite do. Like others, Freud's attempt to chart the psyche involves not only "regions" that might be thought of as inert, but also *forces* that link or transcend or even transform or energize such "regions" to the point where it seems that we are talking not about a map but about a set of processes involving protean psychophysiological constituents. What, for instance, is the "censor mechanism" that "represses" painful materials "down" into the unconscious? Is this mechanism a thing, a process, a combination of both? Where does it reside? And what is the unconscious—a place, a combination of places, a place containing forces, a set of forces that constitute and play a part in certain larger processes? And so on. Similarly, in the case of Augustine's "map," it is clear that "will" is more than just a region-*cum*-faculty. It is also a force, a kind of tailored psychic energy, which is there to bring certain other psychic elements—the power to perceive and the perceptions that the mind remembers—into particular modes of relatedness.

One does not need to accept poststructuralist accounts of the self in order to sound a cautionary note about the metaphoricity and conceptual slipperiness of conceptions of the self and of the will's place in such conceptions. We are dealing here with matters that are indeed hard to represent and hard to grasp. But let us not be too fatalistic about this. Metaphor, too, can be an enabling medium: if we are agreed on *x*—agreement that arises from cultural conversation—and by metaphoric association or substitution we liken *x* to *y*, we may be able to agree on the nature of *y*. Our broad cultural endorsement of Freud's sedimentation metaphor of the psyche comes about, in part at least, because we are already familiar with and agreed-upon some of the implications of sedimentation elsewhere (in the discourse of geology, for instance).

I want to suggest that autobiography is valuable precisely (though not exclusively) *because it offers such a deep, complex, and potentially authoritative report* on the nature of the psyche and on such phenomena as the will. This does not entail saying that autobiographers necessarily tell or capture *all* of the "truth" about themselves; it does not entail that metaphoric association or substitution provides a definitive means of representation. Moreover, though I believe substantial truth-telling about the self in narrative to be possible, it is not a necessary part of the case I make here that *entire* "truthfulness" in this sense be ascribed to particular autobiographical texts. What *is* essential to the case is that such texts be seen as possessing significant representational power in respect to the self; that texts of this kind have the ability to *envisage the psyche* in certain ways; and that these ways represent actual or possible modes of being in the world. Such narratives make culturally available for our consideration complex conceptions of what it means to have a mind and a self and a will. I call these conceptions *metaphors of self-constitution,* by which I mean a pivotal or controlling metaphor in an autobiography that expresses an understanding both of what the—or a—self is like; and of the forces that bring it into being, that constitute it as the thing it is.[91] And note that how we characterize the will depends in large part on how we characterize the self, and that (in some cases) the reverse also applies. Some such conceptions will "ring true"; others may become true because we embrace and enact them in our own lives. Autobiographers don't just report a self; they *envision* one. But we needn't on this account imagine that in some loose and unspecified sense the entire enterprise of autobiography is fictitious—a thing no "truer" to "actual selves" or "real life" than a novel.

IV. *Cultural Specificity*

All autobiographers, no matter how they might feel or wish to be, write from a position of cultural embeddedness in the sense that they participate in and cannot help but reproduce elements of their cultural environment in their narratives; and this applies to various dimensions of their narratives: to central concepts, motifs, understandings of the self, conceptions of life, the Good Life, and so on. We need, then, to acknowledge the *cultural specificity* of, say, Augustine's conception of the will. In addition, it's important to see that cultural specificity (to the extent that it is present) does not necessarily foreclose the possibility that a particular account of the will might have some very broad—even universal—cultural legitimacy. This is to say that on the matter of the will, Augustine (or someone else) might just be right about some aspect that is so central to the human constitution that he makes a discovery that holds for very different and chronologically distant cultural situations. Such a claim would need of course to be argued in great detail; but let us note here, at the outset, that theories about the will often aspire to transcultural, transhistorical validity, and that we cannot dismiss such aspirations out of hand.

Cultural specificity goes beyond the theological and philosophical content to the very structure of Augustine's narrative. By this I mean not only to the sequencing of events and meditative passages, but also to the very rhetorical configuration of the text. Modern autobiographers generally address their ruminations to the reader (or to some combination of the self and the reader); but Augustine, of course, addresses his to God—a God, indeed, who already knows the content of the narrative; who in a sense overhears what He himself has brought into being. This culturally remote mode of doing autobiography has all sorts of interesting implications. One of these registers in what I shall term *protocols of self-disclosure*: that is, culturally appointed and accepted norms for the revelation of self in narrative.[92] Such protocols are conditioned (not necessarily determined) by broader cultural assumptions: in this case, the belief in the existence of an omnipotent God who already knows what is in one's heart gives rise to a narrative structure in which one is telling a divine auditor what He already knows. Among the things God already knows is the structure of the soul of the confessor—a structure that, according to Augustine, resembles God's own nature. Another of the purposes of Augustine's narrative is to find out what the soul's structure is, or should be, and then to recount the process by which it attains a proper disposition such that the will accomplishes its appointed part in the life of the individual. When it does so, God's grace is upon it.

v. *Self's Agential Relation to Culture*

Augustine's capacity to take over the term *voluntas* from jurisprudence and invest it with a new array of psychological and anthropological meanings and to establish these meanings for later tradition through a revolutionary reconfiguration of religious confessional writing—these are achievements that entail not only reflecting existing cultural norms and materials, but *transforming* them, even bringing new ones into being. We need, then, to acknowledge the cultural specificity of Augustine's conception of the will without seeing "specificity" as a synonym for *conventionality.* I shall adapt a sociological term here and speak of the *reflexive monitoring*[93] that takes place in such autobiographies: the sense in which thought draws upon and then modifies existing social understandings, and in which the same process works in reverse. In this context it is interesting to note that Augustine's conversion is described two-thirds of the way into the narrative, and that the remainder of the text is largely taken up with philosophical reflection. The reflective autobiographer is able both to absorb and to transform culturally given understandings because he or she possesses something more than merely passive receptivity to social messages. He or she possesses a power that is best designated as agency.

In broad terms I understand agency to involve the capacity to act (or not act) on the strength of complex kinds and combinations of reflective, deliberative, and appraisive activity. In putting it this way, I am following the account given by Charles Taylor in his essay "What Is Human Agency?". Taylor follows Harry G. Frankfurt in distinguishing between "first-order" and "second-order" desires.[94] The former are the kinds that animals have (these may involve making simple choices); the latter are the kinds of which human beings are capable. However, it is clear that not all human beings reflect or deliberate to the same extent or in the same manner. Taylor makes a further distinction between "weak" and "strong" "evaluators"—that is, between those who weigh alternative inclinations in terms of simple self-interest and pleasure, on the one hand, and those who weigh inclinations in a more "qualitative" manner, on the other.[95] Thus (my example) the "weak evaluator" might weigh the options he confronts in his marriage (to stay or leave, what to do about the children) in terms simply of his own gratification, while the "strong evaluator" will try to make an assessment of the moral quality and status of the various inclinations he experiences. Taylor says that this latter distinction is so fundamental that it amounts to a distinction between "different kinds of self" and that we rightly impute to the "strong evaluator" a "depth" that is lacking in the "weak" one.[96] I want to highlight five aspects of this account. First, it has a strong *moral* dimension: highly developed forms of agency are characterized by moral awareness and discernment, and this in turn means that agents bear moral responsibility for their moral choices (and indeed for their moral evaluations). Second, it opposes behaviorist-style accounts[97] in that it says that people can and are to be understood and assessed not simply by what they do, but by the kind and quality of the evaluations they make.[98] Third, this view also opposes the Sartrean "radical choice"[99] account of freedom in that it sees moral deliberation as requiring a weighing of, and a sense of "pull"[100] between, alternative courses of action that is not envisaged in the way the Sartrean chooser seizes an alternative and seizes his or her freedom by doing so. Fourth, Taylor, who sees "man" as a "self-interpreting animal,"[101] insists on a strong connection between agency and language. One dimension of this connection is that the "strong evaluator" will seek, and will be good at finding, ways to articulate evaluations—their grounds, their implications, their sources—but this in turn implies an awareness that evaluations are necessarily clouded and subject to revision.[102] Finally, it is obvious that Taylor's view ascribes certain kinds of freedom of will to the agent; and the more "depth" a particular agent has, the more rich and developed that freedom will be, because the great value of insight lies in our opportunity to review and change the way we behave. Self-interpretation entails the chance for self-transformation.

Anthony Giddens's account of agency acknowledges, as we surely must, that the sense of self-as-agent has to be constituted through a social system. The system enables the abstract potentiality of agency to be instantiated in particular individual selves. This system will of course include language—at the most elementary levels the acquisition of first- and third-person pronouns; it will also include various cultural stories about the world and about what a person is or should be. Here ideology (conceived as false stories about the world and our place in it) assumes a rightfully prominent place. However, Giddens postulates a "reflexive" relationship between a self and a social system. We aren't just "structural dopes"; we at once reflect, reflect upon, and react back upon the structures in which we take shape, transforming those structures in the light of acts of "discursive penetration."[103] So structure must be thought as a "duality" in that it is "both medium and outcome of the reproduction of practices."[104] Agency must entail a developed form of reflective consciousness in order for what Giddens calls "reflexive monitoring of conduct"[105]—our evaluative awareness of our conduct and its place within the social system—to occur. Giddens rejects the structuralist "demystification of the claims of consciousness" and argues that social theory "must promote *a recovery of the subject* without lapsing into subjectivism."[106] Though their purposes and emphases are different, both Taylor and Giddens see complex forms of evaluative and inwardly directed consciousness as a necessary condition of agency, and a main claim of this book is that autobiography constitutes one of the most elaborated and valuable sources of knowledge about consciousness so conceived. Importantly, both Giddens and Taylor are at pains to say that the individual so construed is not incompatible with something like a Freudian depth psychological account (provided that Freud is not understood to be a wholesale determinist): processes like articulation, evaluation, and cultural competence draw upon and across conscious, preconscious, and unconscious levels of mental activity.[107] So—contrary to a familiar postmodern claim—(post)-Freudian conceptions of the self do *not* rule out the concept of a human agent possessed of significant kinds and margins of freedom.

Agents, then, are not "structural dopes"; they are complexly enmeshed in and responsive to social environments; they think, feel, and act out of various "levels" of self; they are susceptible to description under a variety of terms including *cause, motive, reasons, intentions*—all such terms apply because the human agent is a multidimensional creature. Above all, it would seem that the agent is inconceivable without something that corresponds to what we customarily think of as the will.

VI. *Explanatory Postulates*

If, as I have been arguing, there is an invaluable and inescapable *heuristic* dimension to autobiography, we might want to say that in reflective forms of the genre, certain notions can function, as they do in other discourses, as what might be termed *explanatory postulates*. The will is a case in point. There are those—autobiographers among them—who lay great claim to having some kind of palpable "experience" of the will: of "getting it going," of feeling it as one exerts it, of seeing its effects, and so on. Such experiences are common to all people, including—and this point deserves emphasis—those who deny the existence of the will. But this kind of subjective sense is at some remove from the theoretical accounts we might want to give of, say, the will. Theory presses a notion such as "will" into a range of explanatory and speculative functions. But what of the sort of autobiography, like Augustine's *Confessions,* which is itself, in many places and among other things, a work of theory in a quite familiar sense? Here too will functions not only as a thing experienced and reconstructed through introspection, but as an explanatory postulate: something that is called on to account for other observed aspects of life and self. Augustine's notion of the will is essential to his explanation of the soul's spiritual journey, of the self's relationship to God; and his manner of embedding explanation in narrative was to be highly influential for later reflective autobiographers. One of the many respects in which the *Confessions* is a central text is that it sets up a particular kind of *rhythm of recollection and reflection* such that experience is tested against theory and theory against the proceeds of experience. Similar patterns occur not only in later spiritual autobiography, but in modern secular variants as well.

VII. *Will and Related Terms*

I shall term my conception of the will a *graduated conception.* According to this, the will is a power to precipitate, where "precipitate" leaves open the question whether the power causes certain things to happen or assists/augments processes that are already in motion. In this undifferentiated form, all higher organisms possess this power. In this sense, will is an inherent power in the human being. This power can be thought of as a "faculty," but this is merely a way of saying that it—the power—has some degree of phenomenological and conceptual autonomy. It does not entail ascribing a particular "location," either figural or neurological, to the power in question. (I see little philosophical necessity to do either of these things.) I say "some degree of phenomenological and conceptual autonomy" because the will is a particular kind of power: a kind that is instantiated through engagement with other faculties. Here we need something like a Freudian account of the psyche. Here, too, the notion of graduation enters the picture. I suggest that the will can take a whole range of forms, and that the form(s) it takes will depend upon the other faculty or faculties with which it engages on particular occasions. "Graduation" is meant to suggest a spectrum. If in Freudian terms the will is instantiated through engagement with unconscious forces—say, the forces of the id—it (the will) will take forms that resemble the instinctual "blind striving" that Schopenhauer imputes to it. If, on the other hand, the will is instantiated through engagement with faculties whose mode is that of deliberative reasoning, then the effect will be to instantiate the will as a power that acts in the light of rational deliberation—the Greek or Spinozan position. If the Schopenhauerian view can be located at one end of the graduated spectrum, the Greek or Spinozan ones would be at the other; and between these will lie an almost infinite series of intermediate possibilities, made up of differing mixes of rational, instinctual, and so on. Note at this point, however, that I have not essentialized the will as either rational or instinctual—or indeed as anything else. In its undifferentiated form it is a kind of potentiality that awaits instantiation that is specified by its mode of engagement with other faculties. Note also that I am picturing the process (unlike, say, Derrida) in temporal terms: as a process of transition from potentiality to instantiation. This particular transition also comes under the general rubric of "graduation."

We now need to ask where—if anywhere—*freedom* of the will comes in. I want to suggest that freedom resides on the band of the continuum in which will is instantiated through substantial engagement with deliberative appraisal, and it would follow from this that the further toward the Greeks and Spinoza one goes the freer the will is. Conversely, the further in the other direction one goes—in the direction of the will's determination by unconscious, instinctual, irrational factors—the less free it is. I want to add some qualifications here. First, even at the furthest reach of the instinctual part of the spectrum, there can, in my view, be no question as to whether the will exists: the will (in its mode of potentiality) is inherent in everyone; the point is that the more it takes its orders from instinctual, unconscious, and irrational pressures, the less free it is. Second, the spectrum analogy should not be taken as suggesting that, at its furthest experiential reaches, there can ever be a "pure" form of rational or instinctual instantiation of the will. I take it to be an empirical fact of human psychology that traces of irrational and unconscious elements will always be present in the processes of rational deliberation, and that the contrary is also true. Third, we need to consider ethical implications. Can one, for example, say that a particular individual is morally at fault for performing a destructive act of will that is almost wholly determined by unconscious and instinctual forces? I believe that the answer is no, because acts so determined are not free, which is to say that they are not within the power of the actor to resist. However, there is the following prescriptive ethical point: that with respect to social life and the responsibilities we have to others, the modalities of will that involve a profound engagement with rational and deliberative faculties are preferable, because it is only in such modalities that the will can partake effectively of a cultural system that builds in socially requisite forms of accommodation, consideration, regulation, regularity, and cognizance of communal rules and expectations. Importantly, such modalities are characteristic features of *agency* in its developed forms—the forms described by Charles Taylor, for example. Developed forms of agency cannot occur at the other end of the spectrum. Harry G. Frankfurt's notion of "second-order volitions" helps further to elaborate the sense of agency in question here. Frankfurt points out that it is entirely possible for an amoral hedonist to employ rational calculation in pursuit of his or her pleasures. The hallmark of the moral agent (or "person"[108]—confrontingly enough, Frankfurt regards the two terms as virtually synonymous) is not therefore the capacity for mere calculative rationality; rather, the moral agent is a person who wills that his or her will shall be in, and that it shall enact, a preferred moral disposition. To will the will in this way is to perform a "second-order volition";[109] and only a rational agent who is richly cognizant of moral possibilities and implications, and who is capable of reflecting rationally upon and choosing between complex moral alternatives, can formulate preferences of this kind.

We now need to ask what sorts of conditions might cause the will to be (relatively) free or unfree respectively. A detailed taxonomy would require a book unto itself, but here are some general pointers. First, regarding unfreeness. The sorts of factors that might impede the instantiation of the will through engagement with the deliberative faculties include motivations being unconscious, whether because they are instinctual or because repressed (for whatever reason); ideological conditioning, which precludes deliberation except insofar as it conforms to particular, falsifying preconceptions; and contingent factors such as the sheer complexity of that which has to be contemplated, lack of information about it, and so on. By contrast, (relatively) free exercise of the will might occur when these impediments are minimal or limited in their impact. Crucially, they can be limited by the ways in which we learn from experience. The more we learn, the less apt we are to be determined by pressures that we cannot reflect upon (depending of course on what it is we learn). Such learning is possible for various reasons. One is that certain kinds of conditioning—say, ideological conditioning—are internally vulnerable because, as Marxists sometimes point out, ideology itself is internally conflicted and will often yield knowledge of its own chinks and frailties. Another is that in a discourse like psychoanalysis, we have a tool for reducing the determinative power of the unconscious and increasing the role of the ego's powers of rational deliberation. What might prompt someone to submit to—to direct the will toward—psychoanalysis? It might be something as basic as pain, or some combination of pain and perceived conflict or dysfunctionality in the self. Situations permitting (relatively) free exercise of the will can also occur when causal pressures have been diluted to such a degree that their impact upon the will is slight. Here I want to suggest a further application for the notion of graduation. I use the term *receding causal efficacy* to refer to the fact that even if (as some conceptions of system entail) there is a sense in which all causal factors bear, however indirectly, on all occurrences within a system, causal influences come in greater and less degrees: they are "graduated" in the sense that the more proximate the cause, for example, the greater its causal impact; and the contrary also applies. The advent of the Second World War might have some oblique causal role in the fact that a twelve-year-old boy, besotted by the mythology of military might, buys an imitation gun in a toy shop in Melbourne, Australia, in 1998. However, the causal efficacy of the Second World War will be so attenuated in this case that its actual impact on the boy's choice of toy will be minimal. We would be better served to explain the purchase with reference to more proximate influences in his life and culture. But the reverse would be true for someone in his seventies who buys tranquilizers in a Melbourne pharmacy in 1998, if the need for this medication were directly caused by trauma experienced during the Second World War. My point is that causal factors can "thin out," and that some choices, for example, are made by agents who are embedded in "thin" or "attenuated" causal settings. Where this happens, the will is more free than where causal antecedents are more proximate, and (so?) more powerful. Hypothetically at least, an agent in a setting that is entirely free of strong causal antecedents, at least in respect to the choice or act in question, would be capable of spontaneous acts of will in the Kantian sense: acts that are entirely caused, inaugurated, by an act of free choosing. But it is doubtful that such choices can in fact occur in so pure a form. Someone acting in a highly attenuated causal setting would in a fairly unproblematic way possess a power that Mill and others talk about: the power to intervene in causal sequences. But I want to make the stronger claim (as indeed does Mill) that by virtue of the will's inherent presence, agents possess this power even where causal antecedents are proximate and strong. The threads of life don't just construct us; we have an inherent ability to weave the threads that converge through patterns of antecedence on the point that is the "I."

Reference to ideology reminds us that acts of will, whatever their character, take place in social settings; and clearly "my" capacity to behave as a (relatively) free exerter of the will—as someone who acts in the light of deliberation, for instance—depends upon prior forms of acculturation. There can be no "I" that could formulate intentions without the social Other, and no sense of identity without complex forms of identity allocation that go on in social groups. Nor can I formulate projects that find expression in particular acts of will unless I have culturally given concepts, repertoires of aims, and the like. Similarly, I would not—could not—embark upon the sort of act of will that is involved in writing an autobiography unless I had access to already-embedded cultural understandings of recognizable life-structures, character types, and so on. Here I use Hayden White's term *modes of emplotment*.[110] There has been much work on how we internalize such materials. There is no need or scope for me to venture upon these issues. But, with respect to the (relative) freedom of the will, the point I want to emphasize is that however we internalize these materials, and whatever the cultural grammar[111] that provides them, the agent is distinguished by a capacity to *draw upon* such materials *without being wholly determined by them*. To use Anthony Giddens's term again, the relationship between an agent and existing narrative modes is, like the relation between an agent and a social system, *reflexive:* the narrative mode or system acts upon us, but we also react back upon it.

Claims such as these can be made from a third-person point of view as we observe social actions. But what of that much-debated inner "space" where some claim that willings take place? Allowing as we must for the ambiguities attendant upon the figure of the "space," I believe that human beings do possess inwardness of this kind, and that we know this both from introspection and from the first-person reports of others—not least autobiographers. However, it is also the case that conceptions, and even experiences, of "inner" and "outer" spaces have a high degree of cultural specificity—a point to which I will return in chapter 4. Many of the writers so far discussed inquire whether we can gaze into this "space" and, as it were, witness willings as they happen. Here I think we need to acknowledge a feature of human descriptions that is noted with due reverence by some thinkers (Hobbes and Hume, for instance), but hopelessly mishandled by others like Skinner: namely, the irreducible element of *mystery*. We simply cannot be sure about many of the activities of consciousness. Clinical attempts to isolate an inner phenomenon that is willing are of passing interest;[112] but so complex are the processes under scrutiny, and so massive the methodological impediments to such research, that these experiments ultimately resolve nothing. Here again, first-person experience, including that reported by autobiographers, must count for a lot. We all know the feeling of willing that comes when we resolve to do something; and as Hume notes, we learn from experience that there are certain patterns of linkage between the feeling of willing and the advent of certain resultant happenings. To claim that the "willing" feeling is illusory seems gratuitous: why distrust our subjective experience to this degree, and how could such feelings be invalidated from a third-person point of view? Ryle and others have claimed that what we experience at such times is not what we think it is: that the alleged link between willings and doings is never actually experienced. This may be, but does it matter? As I've noted, it can be objected that what we see when we gaze within is never contemporaneous with the gaze itself: like anything that consciousness registers, willings have in a sense already happened when consciousness gets round to registering them in some form of synthetic understanding. Again, this may be (the questions arising here don't warrant elaboration for my purposes); but even if it is, the difficulty can be accommodated by my distinction between *introspection* and *retrospection*. There is a sense in which introspection is inevitably a retrospective mode. But having made this fine distinction, I propose to disregard it and, in what follows, to use the more familiar term *introspection* for the general activity of looking within one's consciousness.

In chapters 2, 3 and in the two appendixes, "Some Earlier Conceptions of the Will" and "Some Other Late Modern Instances," I survey various conceptions of the will in roughly chronological terms. The best way to organize such an inquiry is to combine chronology, context, and a set of descriptive categories that help us to pick out various conceptualizations. Vernon J. Bourke provides some such categories in his valuable study *Will in Western Thought*. This book, to which I have already referred, is one of the very few attempts at a comprehensive treatment.[113] It is organized conceptually and leaves a lot of work still to be done on historical lines of development (as well as on post-1960s developments). Bourke classifies various thinkers' accounts of the will under eight nonchronological headings:.

- *Will as Intellectual Preference:* Here the exercise of will is thought to be indistinguishable from cognition, both logically and in practical terms. Will can only enact what is rationally deemed to be the best course of action. Where such courses of action are not pursued, it is because the will has been rendered inoperative and some other influence (passion, for instance) has taken over.
- *Will as Rational Appetite:* In this view willing is an entirely different kind of activity from cognition. Will is seen as a psychic power enabling its possessor to incline toward objects intellectually apprehended as good (and the reverse for "bad" objects). Understanding is not the initial cause of volitions; rather, understanding, or the objects it makes known, provides the sense of purpose, and the understanding of the mode in which a purpose might be achieved, which attracts the appetitive (inclining) thing that is the will to operate in certain ways.
- *Freedom as the Genus of Volition:* In this view the will is by definition free. To speak of the will as constrained or blocked, whether by internal or external factors, is a contradiction in terms. Many people actually take this view for granted: they assume (erroneously) that will and free will are synonymous.
- *Will as Dynamic Power:* This conception sees the will as a kind of raw power or energy that the individual possesses and can exert.
- *Heart, Affection, and Will:* This view sees love as the central and definitive aspect of volition.
- *The Will of the People:* The notion that a collection of individuals can possess a single will, either by virtue of some binding force that makes each will identical, or because the various things they will coalesce to form one supra-will.
- *Will as the Source of Law:* This view sees laws as being promulgated by some fiat of a legislator and as binding upon those for whom the laws were brought down.
- *Will as Reality:* In this view will is the very stuff of life—a kind of life force that is in, and is constitutive of, everything.

To these, I add two categories of my own:

- *Determinism:* Here the existence of the will is conceded, but its freedom is denied; that is, it is said to be fully determined by forces external to itself.
- *Conceptual Denial:* Here the very existence of the will is denied.[114]

We now need to ask how the concept of a *cause* relates to this notion of will. Aristotle's fourfold typology of causes is foundational. He distinguishes between *efficient cause* (that by which a change is wrought), *final cause* (the end or purpose for which a change is pursued), *material cause* (that in which a change is wrought), and *formal cause* (that into which something is changed).[115] Alisdair MacIntyre identifies three often used senses for the word *cause*: One, the Humean view (taken up by Mill) that one event is the cause of another if and only if the first kind of event can universally be seen to result in the second kind, and vice versa. Here the occurrence of the first event is both a necessary and sufficient condition for the occurrence of the second. Two, the view that a cause is a necessary but not a necessarily sufficient condition for bringing something about. Three, the idea of "cause" as a "lever," a means of setting in train something that brings something else about.[116] The authors of the autobiographical texts in this study use the term *cause* in each of these ways (and often without much consistency). For my purposes it is sufficient to note the distinctions between one, two, and three. But there is a cardinal feature of "causes" that holds for each of these versions, and that is, as MacIntyre puts it, that a cause will "stand in an external, contingent relation to an action."[117] In other words, in this view a cause is clearly prior to and independent of the outcome it brings about. This sounds clear enough, but when we start to complicate the picture—as we must, even for purposes such as mine—complexities appear.

One complication is to make a distinction between *event causation* and *agent causation,* where the first refers to events that cause other events and the latter to intentional human activities that bring certain things about. This is a crucial distinction for autobiography because, as I have argued, one of autobiography's main aims is often to explore the distinction between "circumstantial" things that happen to or shape me and things that come about because I or other persons have knowingly or willingly brought them about. There is a large philosophical literature that shows how hard it is to draw this distinction, but it will do for our purposes. However, we need to note one complication that results: when we speak of an agent as a cause, we are assumed to be speaking about a being who has the ability to formulate intentions for doing this or that. But intentions would normally be understood to be deeply entwined with actions, certainly with some kinds of action; so the supposed externality of cause to effect starts to break down. There is no need for detailed assessment of this problem here. Once again, it is sufficient to note it with a view to the way autobiographers talk about causes, intentions, and the like, and to note that the dividing lines between, for instance, cause, intention, and reasons are very hard to draw with any precision.

Rational exercise of will involves, among other things, certain kinds of intentional behavior. Our habitual sense of the term *intention* is a good guide: to have an intention is to mean to bring something about. Here again, it is useful to complicate matters somewhat. For a start, there are intendings that can be associated (a question-begging term) with various kinds of mental states or processes. Some of these will involve what we might call *rational deliberation*: "thinking things through," consciously formulating particular plans with a clearly identified purpose or end in view. Here we tend to operate through modes like *reasons* and *justifications*. Others may be less deliberative, less conscious, more a matter of inclining to act "unthinkingly," out of particular emotional and psychological "states." Such cases are less likely to involve having a clearly pinpointed end in view, and they tend to fall into two (perhaps more) classes: those where the inclination to act does not take the form of conscious awareness, but where there is, in principle, no reason that we cannot be aware of it (I'll term these *preconscious intentions*), and those where the inclination is unconscious in the Freudian sense: it is buried and we can have no (unassisted) access to it (*unconscious intentions*). I want to add a further qualification that is critical for the reading of complex literature, including complex autobiographical literature, and this is the counterbehaviorist claim that there are internal, mentalistic phenomena that (a) can precede and result in actions, (b) may not result in any observable action but are nevertheless "real" and consequential. Trying to help someone without them—or anyone—knowing that you are doing it, and without any help in fact being rendered, is an example here. Some intentions have outcomes; others don't—but it is just as important to attend to the second kind as the first, not least because so much of a person's moral being will be reflected in such internal states and inclinations. Autobiography is an invaluable source of information about just such states and inclinations, whether they be the kind that have observable outcomes or the kind that do not.

A motive might seem to be closely akin to an intention, and so in some cases it is. There are various possible overlaps between motive, cause, reason, intention, and so on. Again, though, I want to rely on customary usage for a sense of the term *motive* that is (a) reasonably distinct from the others and (b) useful for reading autobiography. We use the term in connection with situations in which there is a suggestion of foul play, deception, or disingenuousness. The term is often used in connection with the idea of the *ulterior*, of things not being what they are presented as being. So the motive for a murder is a thing associated with an illegal act; it is also often a hidden thing or one that the culprit will seek to disguise or disclaim. Motives are often termed *ulterior* when the reason given or implied for behavior is a front: the man who is delightful with an unsuspecting woman's children because he wants to seduce her. A theory like Freud's needs and employs such a notion of motive.

Having given this theoretical account of will and its engagements with autobiography, I now want to consider will in a more historical context. The autobiographers discussed in this study all write in an epoch I term *late modernity*. I argue that their preoccupation with the will and related phenomena comes about, in part at least, because late modernity has inherited deeply conflicted accounts of the will. Before turning to the autobiographical texts themselves, I want to explore some of these accounts—their sources, claims, implications, and internal contradictions.

CHAPTER TWO

Late Modernity and the Will

I. BACKGROUND

I have argued that we need to think more carefully about the will than we generally do, but also that such thinking is not easy. One of the principal sources of difficulty is conceptual: attempts to generate theories of the will run into a variety of logical complexities. They can also produce eye-opening surprises. For instance, it ought now to be clear that issues pertaining to the will are far too complex to be encapsulated in simple binaries like "free will versus determinism." As we've seen, it's entirely possible to be both a determinist and a believer in the existence of the will. The question "Is there such a thing as the will?" is not the same question as "Is the will free?" What's more, some philosophers argue a "compatibility" thesis according to which it is possible to be both a determinist and a believer in free will, the idea being that the agent qua entity may be fully determined and yet, for reasons that remain a metaphysical mystery, be capable of exercising free will.[1] Lest the reader feel adrift on a sea of will-related issues, I list in an endnote many of the questions that have come up, or will come up, in the course of this philosophically framed account of autobiography and its engagements with the will.[2]

But serious thinking never goes on in a cultural vacuum, and this includes thinking about the will. Another source of complication in theorizing the will is that various cultures and historical epochs have conceptualized it in so many different ways. Cultural context will inevitably shape the questions one asks, and the answers one proposes, about the will. It might not occur to someone in an intensely secular cultural situation to ask whether some deity directs the actions of her will, let alone to answer in the affirmative. But someone in a deeply theistic environment might ask just such a question and might conclude that deity operates on the individual will in just this way. Secularization—which tends to displace will-thinking from the relation between deity and the individual, or between the individual and a divinely ordained metaphysical context, to the individual as primary or sole locus of the will—has been but one of several major cultural shifts in the West that have impinged upon thinking about the will in recent centuries. Little wonder that the Nietzsche who famously announced that "God is dead" also appealed to the individual will's powers of overcoming and mastery.

The cultural shifts in question are extraordinarily complex; so much so indeed that the most authoritative histories of modernity and the self tell their stories in several dimensions, and in terms of crisscrossing and even chronologically convoluted developments. Touraine's *Critique of Modernity* is a case in point, as is Charles Taylor's majestic *Sources of the Self*.[3] Yet notwithstanding the complexities, and the various historical accounts that have been offered, it seems undeniable that the modern world has what might be called a distinctive and emphatic sentiment of freedom; or, to put it another way, a distinctive sense of the will and its powers. In very rough terms we might say that late modernity[4] imagines for the self a deeper, more radical form of freedom than had been imputed to the self in earlier periods. This is what Taylor calls the idea of "the free, self-determining subject"[5] in modern culture. A suitably dramatic way to think of this is to compare the self as imagined in earlier theistic European culture with the self of, say, Sartrean existentialism. The point is not that earlier understandings denied that human beings possess free will. On the contrary, such freedom is a fundamental postulate of many strains of the Judeo-Christian tradition.[6] Rather, the issue is one of the kind and degree of freedom that is envisaged. Freedom of the will in theistic Europe is itself seen as God-given; and it unfolds against—is constrained by—a complex metaphysical background. When we get to Sartre (thanks in large part to Nietzsche), that background has vanished. Freedom of will is now the freedom to structure the world as its possessor chooses. To the extent that the issue of origins even arises, the origin of the will's freedom lies in some primordial, naturalistic structure of things. So radically free is this will that it can give birth to the "self" that "possesses it."[7]

Why did this more radical sentiment of freedom come about? There are many possible explanations, and many of these overlap both chronologically and causally. If we put things in terms of broad cultural developments, some of the following come to mind: industrialization, which has transformed and extended our sense of the powers we possess; capitalism, with its insistent focus on the individual as a maker and possessor of wealth; secularization, for reasons given above; democratization, which, by weakening the hold of traditional hierarchical social formations, has expanded the possibilities of liberty; the scientific revolution and its redefinition of our place in a law-governed naturalistic universe; the rise of the middle class; and so on. Other and related factors might better be seen in terms of particular intellectual movements: Renaissance Humanism's imputation of greater centrality to the individual human being; the empiricism of the seventeenth century and beyond, which gradually removes the belief in a transcendental guarantee for human understanding; the Reformation's emphasis on individual conscience; eighteenth-century political thought, which imputes to Society a moral authority that had hitherto been reserved for deity, and which ascribes to the individual an unprecedented freedom to participate in consensual societal arrangements; Enlightenment rationality, so deeply imbued with the culture of individual deliberation—an aspect of a deepening sense of human interiority that flows on into Romanticism and beyond. We can also construe these developments in terms of major thinkers: Kant, who lifts the discourse of freedom out of its earlier theological framework and empowers the rational will of the individual; Hegel, whose theodicy of the Spirit at once echoes and transcends redemptive Christian understandings of freedom; Schopenhauer, who, though indebted to Kant in some respects, seems to drive a wedge between will and rationality, but who holds out renewed hope of mystical transcendence; Nietzsche, who takes over Schopenhauer's dynamic sense of will but rejects his transcendental dimension. Freud, on the other hand, pictures an individual who is deeply shaped and scarred by a past that the will cannot finally overcome. Postmodernism is inclined to see the self as fragmented and the will as chimerical, an aspect of a mythology that wants to perceive the self as unified and self-determining.

Many of the cultural factors just mentioned have in common a tendency to undermine ethical understandings of the will: capitalism, in the sense that it gives such high priority to worldly success and acquisitiveness; Freudianism, insofar as it is interested in the psychological rather than the moral viability of the self; postmodernism, because it often repudiates the cultural "master-narratives" from which ethical norms can be derived, and because its conception of the fragmented self cannot readily sustain the burdens of moral agency. In appendix A, "Some Earlier Conceptions of the Will: Maimonides to Mill," I take up the history of earlier conceptions of the will in more detail, by way of an account of some influential and representative theories.

I believe that the twentieth century's legacy with respect to the will is vexed and problematical. Its cultural prophets in Nietzsche, Marx, and Freud all give the appearance of endorsing the will, yet none actually does so, except in the most qualified and internally contradictory ways. Will in the twentieth century was also massively complicated by the rhetoric and the realities of totalitarianism, and in the latter part of the century by the onward march of global capitalism, with its crude culture of the imperial and bionic will. Psychologist Leslie Farber, writing in 1965 with a particular clinical and historical focus on anxiety, calls this "the Age of the Disordered Will";[8] another clinician, Rollo May, calls for "conjunctive processes of being"[9] that will reunite what he sees as the now-sundered forces of love and will. Lionel Trilling, critic and cultural commentator, expresses concern in a book about the liberal imagination at what he calls the "hypertrophy of the will"—a condition in which the will is distended and dangerously distorted by a disturbance in the economy of the faculties that share its psychic domain.[10] Alain Touraine argues that we have replaced the deliberative rationality of the Enlightenment with "a purely instrumental conception of rationality,"[11] which drastically contracts the will's access to rational counsel and subordinates self to massive, impersonal social forces. We've all seen the shelves upon shelves in the self-help section of bookstores, bulging with exhortations to will harder and assurances that if you will hard enough you will overcome anything and everything—even the reality of your own death. Thus Michael Domeyko Rowland, prophet of "absolute happiness," reminds his readers that "it is also well known amongst religious people that God has granted free will to humans" and insists that "the first step to absolute happiness is to take full, total and complete responsibility as the creator of every single aspect of your life."[12] G. Gordon Liddy, too, is in no doubt about the colossal potency of the will. His autobiography is called just that—*Will.* The higher climes of culture sometimes reflect this ethos of individualism and its fixation on the imperial will; but, as I have argued, modern and postmodern literature, for instance, has often tended to evacuate the self to such a degree that will falls out of the picture. And the same has been true for much of the work that has gone on under the banner of literary theory and for a good deal of analytic philosophy.[13] To generalize, one might say that the way things are now is somewhat schizoid: contemporary Western culture often seems split between a "mass" cultural addiction to the unconditioned[14] and a "high" cultural renunciation of the will and its attendant powers of agency. I would like to see the will become the subject of more inquiring intellectual and cultural curiosity, and to see less of the premise of necessary extremity in the way we discuss matters such as these. Some writers and intellectuals are setting an example here: the social novelists, for example, and the social, political, and philosophical theorists whose descriptions of human society and the self are premised on the existence of human agency: Jürgen Habermas, Charles Taylor, Alisdair MacIntyre, Anthony Giddens, C. B. Macpherson, John Rawls, and Charles Altieri, to name but a few.[15] As liberalism in many of the Western democracies veers increasingly to the right, work of this kind takes on special urgency and importance.

But of course there is often an immense gap between the specialization of such work and the public discourses it seeks to understand and to influence. This applies equally to academic work that is skeptical about the will. The analytic philosophy of action has generated its own calculus for representing phenomena like causation and will. Here is an example chosen at random from Donald Davidson's *Essays on Actions and Events:*

where x and y are events,
$(x = y$ if and only if $((z)$ (z caused $x \longleftrightarrow z$ caused $y)$ and (z) (x caused $z \longleftrightarrow y$ caused $z))$.[16]

I don't wish to disparage such work. It can have real intellectual power and has an important part to play. But clearly this is a highly technical and greatly specialized way of going about things: events and consequences are reduced to and assigned symbolic values, and relations between these factored as symbolic representations of conceivable states of affairs. The nonspecialist reader cannot profit directly from this. Nor can such work easily accommodate the experiential complexity of real human situations. I believe that literature can help here, and, in particular, that autobiography can offer a great deal as an accessible mode of inquiry into the will—a mode of inquiry that retains a good deal of the human nuance, the buzz of situational complexity, that we need in order to understand the nature and powers of the will.

II. Ambivalent Prophets of Late Modernity: Nietzsche, Marx, Freud

The great cultural prophets of late modernity can seem at first glance to be visionary proponents of the will: the legend of Nietzsche is of a prophet who espouses the human need and power to overcome. Marx foreshadows and urges what seems to be a great historical act of will that promises liberation for the oppressed. Even Freud, a gloomier figure in the popular imagination, proposes a therapy for releasing the wretched from subjection to the most crippling forms of neurosis. Each seems a fit spokesperson for late modernity's confident expectation of progress, its orientation toward a future that humankind will increasingly be able to shape. Each seems a prophet of liberty: Nietzsche, postmetaphysical liberty; Marx, political liberty; Freud, psychological liberty. Yet these impressions cannot survive a closer reading of Nietzsche, Marx, or Freud. Their accounts of the will are in fact profoundly conflicted, and even seriously deficient. For this among other reasons, their legacy has been deeply problematical.

1. *Nietzsche: Assertion and Denial*

Of all the major thinkers who write extensively about the will, Nietzsche's contribution is perhaps the most puzzling. In part this is because of the wanton excess of his style (or rather styles, since there are many); in part, also, because his views about the will have often to be reconstructed from aphorisms, most notably from his later work and his notes. But the chief source of puzzlement is conceptual and, in my view, it is this: Nietzsche's work seems divided between a titanic Romantic assertion of the power of the will, on the one hand, and, on the other, a denial that will, at least as it is commonly understood, even exists. In terms of the categories I set out in the last chapter, Nietzsche's account of will comprises elements of at least four views: Will as Dynamic Power, Will as Reality, Will as the Source of Law, and Conceptual Denial.

Nietzsche's "Overman" is widely seen as a kind of superbeing, forging his journey into the future through irresistible acts of will. Thus Zarathustra, prophet and prototype of the Overman, proclaims himself "a seer of that which must come. A seer, a willer, a creator, a future himself and a bridge to the future."[17] The Overman occupies—or will occupy—a place that is "above the steam and filth of human lowlands [where] there is a *higher, brighter* humanity

. . . one belongs to it, not because one is more talented or more virtuous or more heroic or more loving than the men below, but—because one is colder, brighter, more far-seeing, more solitary" than they. The Overman "lives among clouds and lightning as among one's own kind."[18] Hence his many resounding invocations: "Let your will say: the overman *shall be* the meaning of the earth! I beseech you, my brothers, *remain faithful to the earth*."[19] Amidst the mediocrity and the "paralysis of will"[20] that he finds in German culture, Nietzsche proposes to "teach man the future of man as his *will*, as dependent on a human will, and to prepare for great enterprises."[21]

The "fully emancipated man" can be "master of his will," "truly free and possessor of a long-range, pertinacious will."[22] In his own tragically (but how ironically?) boastful autobiography, *Ecce Homo*, written months before his decline into insanity, Nietzsche tells the reader: "My humanity is a continual self-overcoming."[23] In this he seems to offer himself as an exemplar of the anti-Christian "struggle against the morality of unselfing."[24] This impassioned, even messianic, sense of the will can be understood in various ways: as a reaction against the passivity of Schopenhauer's vision of ultimate exemption from the will;[25] as a refusal of what he perceived as centuries of Christian self-abasement (Hannah Arendt draws a telling contrast between Paul's "I-will-and-I-can*not*" and the fact that there is an "I-can inherent in every I-will" for Nietzsche);[26] as an attempt to rescue humankind from Rousseau's atavistic sentimentalizing of the species; perhaps more than anything, as a proto-existential enjoining of humankind to fashion its own world after the demise of God—the "event" famously proclaimed by Nietzsche himself: "*God is dead!*"[27]

By contrast to the above, there is the Nietzsche who says quite categorically that "The will of psychology hitherto . . . *does not exist at all*," and that "there is no such thing as 'will.'"[28] And there are more extended statements such as this:

> A quantum of strength is equivalent to a quantum of urge, will, activity, and it is only the snare of language (of the arch-fallacies of reason petrified in language), presenting all activity as conditioned by an agent—the "subject"— that blinds us to this fact. For, just as popular superstition divorces the lightning from its brilliance, viewing the latter as an activity whose subject is the lightning, so does popular morality divorce strength from its manifestations, as though there were behind the strong a neutral agent, free to manifest its strength or contain it. But no such agent exists; there is no "being" behind the doing, acting, becoming; the "doer" has simply been added to the deed by the imagination—the doing is everything.[29]

It is clear from this that Nietzsche rejects the sort of dualistic picture we find in Descartes, where intentions are said to be formulated in a kind of inner sanctum of the individual mind and then enacted through physical or other exertions. Nietzsche, by contrast, often writes as if "intentions" and "actions" are all of a piece—aspects of a continuum—and that the "self," far from being the initiator of such events, is in fact nothing more than the sum of these events, or perhaps the product of them. Alexander Nehamas glosses this position, which I identify as a version of Conceptual Denial accounts of the will, as an aspect of a "sweeping monism": "the view that not only opposites but all things in general are essentially interrelated and derive their character from their interrelations."[30] "All things" would here include "motives," "acts," and "agents," such that all are part of a seamless fabric that cannot be segmented into discrete items or events. This organicist conception typifies Nietzsche's rejection of the Kantian[31] (and Schopenhauerian) thing-in-itself. And just as the reference to "the snare of language" foreshadows poststructuralist views about representation, so the organicist conception of a world of differential relations without substances foreshadows (post-)Saussurean accounts of the world in general.[32] But the metaphor of fabric doesn't fully capture Nietzsche's sense here, because, as his allusion to a "quantum of strength" shows, he conceives of the world in terms of dynamic circulations of energy: "motive," "will," and "action" are fictions we use to segment something that is more like a flow than a fabric. As Nehamas says, in this flow "parts actually determine what each other is through their interconnections."[33] Insofar as anything can be said to follow from such a highly abstracted ontological figure as this, it would seem logical for Nietzsche to conclude, as he does, that traditional antitheses between free will and determinism have no place in this scheme of things. Such antitheses are mere "mythology."[34] There can be no question of "two successive states, the one 'cause,' the other 'effect'"; rather, there is "a struggle between two elements of unequal power: a new arrangement of forces is achieved according to the measure of power of each of them."[35]

But what is this agent-less power? The answer is by no means clear, but it seems that in part at least Nietzsche follows Schopenhauer in assuming that there is a kind of life force in everything. This, at least in one of its usages, is what Nietzsche means by the "will to power": "Life *is* will to power."[36] Like Schopenhauer's will, it is in everything, not least—indeed most notably and in its highest manifestation—in human beings: "*The world is the will to power—and nothing besides!* And you yourselves are also this will to power—and nothing besides!"[37] This is a version of the Will as Reality view, combined with the Will as Dynamic Power one (and inflected with Will as the Source of Law, the Overman being a kind of legislator). Coming from a writer who so often enjoins humankind to aspire to a higher pitch of civilization and who saw himself as a revolutionary psychologist,[38] such a reduction of human interiority to a preeminent and atavistic drive is surely surprising. But surprising though it may be, it is consistent with Nietzsche's tendency to deny the actuality of what we believe to be "inner experiences"[39] and his habit of figuring the will in naturalistic terms. A famous naturalistic figure is the simile of the wave in *The Gay Science:*

> *Will and wave.*—How greedily this wave approaches, as if it were after something! How it crawls with terrifying haste into the inmost nooks of this labyrinthine cliff! It seems that it is trying to anticipate someone; it seems that something of value, high value, must be hidden there.—And now it comes back, a little more slowly but still quite white with excitement; is it disappointed? Has it found what it looked for? Does it pretend to be disappointed?—But already another wave is approaching, still more greedily and savagely than the first, and its soul, too, seems to be full of secrets and the lust to dig up treasures. Thus live waves—thus live we who will—more I shall not say.[40]

John Stuart Mill also employs a tidal figure when envisaging the will.[41] He uses it to inquire whether we are carried by the tide (antecedent conditions) or whether we possess the freedom to swim against it. Nietzsche's simile dispossesses the self of its will: will is an impersonal force that surges wavelike through "consciousness," promising forms of knowledge and engagement that it never yields, the surge, the promise and the failure to fulfill, endlessly repeated in a world that disallows any kind of finality. And since will is not "of" consciousness, it is mere "superstition"[42] to imagine that consciousness can know will through introspection.

Schopenhauer locates the road to knowledge—access to the Ideas—in a state of transcendent but passive recognition of the nature of the world. Hegel's theodicy[43] brings the Spirit back to its lost state of total comprehension of reality. Nietzsche rejects both of these visions. For him, knowledge is linked to striving, overcoming, activity (though, as Arendt points out, his doctrine of "eternal recurrence" actually denies the future that is the will's necessary habitat);[44] yet there is no end point, no Archimedean position, no Absolute Idea, at which this striving can finally arrive. In short, his perspectivist epistemology[45] says that no such position exists: each individual will have a view of reality, but there is no ascertainable "truth" about the world according to which the truth of that or any other view can be assessed. It follows that no "true" perception of the world can be gained by assembling a range, or even all, of the views of individuals: "The concept 'truth' is nonsensical. The entire domain of 'true-false' applies only to relations, not to an 'in-itself.'"[46] Human knowledge is irreducibly positional, subjective. Hence the assertion, recently revived for postmodern literary theory by Derrida, that all acts of knowing are acts of interpreting: the "value of the world lies in interpretation . . . previous interpretations have been perspective valuations by virtue of which we can survive in life, i.e., in the will to power, for the growth of power."[47] In these terms it is possible to speak not only of a will to power, but also of a will to truth and a will to knowledge. Nehamas defines the will to power as "an activity that affects and in fact constitutes the character of everything in the world and that is itself the result of such effects." He continues: "The will to power is an activity that consists in expanding a particular sphere of influence, physical or mental, as far as it can possibly go. As such, it ranges from the crudest to the most sophisticated, from mere physical resistance to brute subjugation to rational persuasion."[48] In this view, "rational" activity is never merely a disinterested quest for the "truth"—it always has a self-serving agenda: "to establish a world in which one's best impulses and strongest needs can find expression."[49] It is not clear to me what "best" can mean, or how it can be ascertained, in this context; nor is the status of the "self" that seeks to procure its own interests entirely clear. But an apologist for Nietzsche might respond that such queries presuppose the very metaphysical views that Nietzsche wishes to reject, and that his "self" must be thought of as—and as the product of—process. We have seen that he does not picture the "I" of identity as a given substance from which choices, actions, and the like issue. Rather, the "I" is a provisional consequence of a process of self-fashioning. Of Goethe he says that "what he aspired to was *totality;* he strove against the separation of reason, sensuality, feeling, will . . . he disciplined himself to a whole, he *created* himself."[50] The will to power, then, works upon the self, bringing it into being and making of its being the highest manifestation it can: "Becoming as invention, willing, self-denial, overcoming of oneself: no subject but an action, a positing, creative, no 'causes and effects.'"[51] Goethe's alleged quest for "totality" indicates that this process of self-fashioning is also one of reconciling conflicting tendencies, tendencies that are both "within" the self and in the culture that surrounds it: the "strongest" human being (Shakespeare is another example) is one in which "instincts that conflict powerfully . . . are controlled."[52] The "great man" is like "*the bow with the great tension.*"[53] Nietzsche's famous injunction that we must "give style" to ourselves needs to be seen in the context of this emphasis upon control in the culture of the self. Passages like the ones just quoted suggest that the Overman is not a creature of mere Dionysian assertion and excess: as Nehamas argues, he creates and integrates himself much as a writer creates and integrates a character out of multiple and miscellaneous materials. "Style," then, suggests the achieved coherence of art: "*One thing is needful.*—To 'give style' to one's character—a great and rare art!"[54] Hence Nehamas's subtitle: *Life as Literature.* Nietzsche can even speak of this power of self-fashioning as if it were a kind of ultimate freedom of the will: "One could conceive of such a pleasure and power of self-determination, such a *freedom* of the will that the spirit would take leave of all faith and every wish for certainty . . ."[55]

But in what sense can the Overman be said to possess such freedom of the will? Nietzsche's answer seems to be that there is a sort of formal "self," an anonymous potentiality, which harbors and is indeed characterized by the will. But the entity in which this will resides is brought into being as *identity*, and is continually transformed, by that will. Each transformative act changes the self, changes its identity, because the self is nothing other than the sum and process of its acts. There is "no 'being' behind the doing, acting, becoming." A variant of this account is that the "synthetic concept 'I'" is actually split between that which commands and that which obeys, and that what we experience as the sensation of willing is in fact the feeling caused by the will overcoming that in the "self" which resists the commands that determine the will.[56]

Nietzsche, then, rejects what one of his admirers among the novelists, D. H. Lawrence, called "the old stable *ego* of the character."[57] He argues that our mistaken metaphysics and ontologies spring in large part from our tendency to read a kind of ego-substance into things. And the concept of the will is deeply implicated in such misapprehensions: "The logical-metaphysical postulates, the belief in substance, accident, attribute etc., derive their convincing force from our habit of regarding all our deeds as consequences of our will—so that the ego, as substance, does not vanish in the multiplicity of change.—But there is no such thing as will."[58] We are purveyors of power in a differential universe. The role of will in all of this is by now I hope roughly (if not unambiguously) apparent. But what—to return to my other key term—of autobiography? What form, or forms of justification, might it assume in such a universe?

Nietzsche often wrote in the first person; he authored an autobiography; he also believed that "every great philosophy" is a kind of "involuntary and unconscious memoir."[59] Yet his reconceptualization of human psychology and identity leaves little room for the kind of effective introspection that we habitually associate with autobiography. The Cartesian ego-substance has gone; self does not find validation in some internal theater of consciousness:

> The whole of life would be possible without, as it were, seeing itself in a mirror. Even now, for that matter, by far the greatest portion of our life actually takes place without this mirror effect; and this is true even of our thinking, feeling, and willing life, however offensive this may sound to older philosophers.[60]

Again, in *The Will to Power* he dismisses the idea that there is a will and that we can know it through introspection as mere "superstition."[61] Here his debt to Schopenhauer, who locates the better part of willing in the unconscious, is clear, though it is less clear how an unconscious in, say, a Freudian sense can exist in the self-as-process that Nietzsche envisages. But the implication for autobiography would seem to be twofold: there is no ego-substance for autobiography to "mirror," and introspection cannot penetrate the processes of the will. What, then, *can* autobiography do? In Nietzschean terms, it can express the will to power by attempting to persuade the reader to a certain view of the author, thereby "expanding" "its sphere of influence." And no doubt all autobiography does express some will to power in just this sense. It can also exemplify the process of self-fashioning, and Nietzsche does this by refracting his first-person narratives through an array of histrionic, constructed, and highly rhetorical selves, each bidding for its own centrality in the world, its own self-serving vision of the world. It can fashion the self as a novelist fashions a character, bringing "multiplicity" under the control of some higher purpose. And so on. But what it cannot do—and what Nietzsche does not do, whether in *Ecce Homo* or elsewhere—is to capture the richness of lived, reflexive human interiority. The story the Overman has to tell is of creating something—a "self"—out of nothing, and of doing so through the action of a force—the will—which, though "in" every self, is not determined by or reflective of any self in particular. How we get from nothing to a something that is nevertheless not a thing at all is, as Nietzsche seems sometimes to realize, a story that can't be told. Yet, as I shall argue in my readings of Barthes, Hemingway, and Beauvoir, Nietzsche's perplexing legacy with respect to the will was to haunt some of the most important autobiographical writing of the twentieth century.

II. *Marx: Self-Generation and the Will*

In a passage in volume 1 of *Capital,* Marx undertakes to reveal to the reader "the secret of profit making." In order to do so, he tells us, we must "take leave" of a "noisy sphere, where everything takes place on the surface and in view of all men." He goes on:

> This sphere that we are deserting, within whose boundaries the sale and purchase of labour-power goes on, is in fact a very Eden of the innate rights of man. There alone rule Freedom, Equality, Property and Bentham. Freedom, because both buyer and seller of a commodity, say of labour-power, are constrained only by their own free will. They contract as free agents, and the agreement they come to, is but the form in which they give legal expression to their common will. Equality, because each enters into relation with the other, as with a simple owner of commodities, and they exchange equivalent for equivalent. Property, because each disposes only of what is his own. And Bentham, because each looks only to himself. The only force that brings them together and puts them in relation with each other, is the selfishness, the gain and the private interests of each. Each looks to himself only, and no one troubles himself about the rest, and just because they do so, do they all, in accordance with the pre-established harmony of things, or under the auspices of an all-shrewd providence, work together to their mutual advantage, for the common weal and in the interest of all.[62]

This sphere is Edenic in two senses: first, because in a more perfect world, things would indeed function in roughly this way; and second, because it is, in Marx's view, utopian, ideological cant to imagine that things can so function under the reign of capitalism. The world has to be changed in order to bring such a possibility about—even after the revolutions of 1848. As one of Marx's most famous formulations says, philosophy must now play a part in effecting such change: "The philosophers have only *interpreted* the world, in various ways; the point is to *change* it."[63] He speaks, of course, as both a beneficiary and a strong critic of Hegel, who, he thinks, uses philosophy "not to discover the truth of empirical existence but to discover the empirical existence of the truth."[64] There is no Spirit whose high intellectual destiny will mystically put the world to rights. That outcome has to be sought and fought for. If Marx's attitude to the precapitalist era is not always consistent (in the *Manifesto of the Communist Party*, he and Engels blame capitalism for decimating "all feudal, patriarchal, idyllic relations"),[65] he on the whole offers no Hegelian theodicy, but rather a process of assisted teleological development through which humankind helps to create social forms that are at once Edenic and unprecedented.

Central to his Edenic vision is the will. Buyer and seller "are constrained only by their free will," and contractual arrangements "give legal expression to their common will." Rousseau's[66] presence is obvious: some conception of the Will of the People lurks behind such statements. To be "constrained" only by one's free will is, in Marx's terms, to be free. Humankind, he believes, "is in the most literal sense of the word a ςωουπολιτιχόν [social animal], not merely a gregarious animal, but an animal which can individuate itself only in the midst of society."[67] For this social animal to be able to enter freely into contractual arrangements is one of the highest imaginable manifestations of what Marx (after Feuerbach) calls its "species-being." Under such circumstance the will in a sense belongs to, is an expression of, the individual being: "Each one of your relations to man—and to nature—must be a *particular expression,* corresponding to the object of your will, of your *real intellectual* life";[68] it is (again in a sense) a part of that person, a faculty that she or he can exercise in the light of rational and collective self-interest. This is a version of the doctrine of Will as Rational Appetite.

But why only "in a sense"? Because the will is both a faculty of the self and *the* faculty that brings the self into being: "Man makes his life activity itself an object of his will and consciousness. He has conscious life activity."[69] But capitalism, through the estrangement of labor, sunders this unity of self and will, the circuit of willing and self-construction. The will now becomes external to the self: "Through this *alien mediator* [money] man gazes at his will, his activity, his relation to others as at a power independent of them and of himself."[70] What Hegel calls "civil society"—the actual, as opposed to statutory, relations between members of a society—finds expression in a form of will that is both externalized and hierarchized. Productive relations cause effective political "will" to be vested with those who control and profit from the productive processes in question: "The individuals who rule in these conditions—leaving aside the fact that their power must assume the form of the *state*—have to give their will, which is determined by these definite conditions, a universal expression as the will of the State, as law."[71] The laborer is plunged into a kind of abyss of disorientation— a circumstantially engendered version of Hegel's alienated Spirit and a fore- shadowing of the more metaphysical condition posited by existential and post- modern accounts—in which "all things are *other* than themselves . . . my activity is *other* than itself."[72] *Capital* gives several devastating descriptions of the laborer in this radically disenfranchised condition. Here is one:

> Within the capitalist system all methods for raising the social productiveness of labour are brought about at the cost of the individual labourer; all means for the development of production transform themselves into means of dom- ination over, and exploitation of, the producers; they mutilate the labourer into a fragment of a man, degrade him to the level of an appendage of a ma- chine, destroy every remnant of charm in his work and turn it into a hated toil; they estrange from him the intellectual potentialities of the labour- process in the same proportion as science is incorporated in it as an inde- pendent power; they distort the conditions under which he works, subject him during the labour-process to a despotism the more hateful for its mean- ness; they transform his life-time into working-time, and drag his wife and child beneath the wheels of the Juggernaut of capital . . .[73]

Thus subjected, he is stripped of "power"—of will—and of the "intellectual" agency of self-creation. Marx is another writer who is apt to see human life in threadlike terms, but here threads have a particularly ominous and literal mean- ing. Many of the laborers described in *Capital* and elsewhere are in fact weavers: "the poor spinner"[74] of *Capital* is a real, empirically apprehended human being; a victim of the social-economic world Marx seeks to anatomize. When Marx uses threads as a metaphor, its force is sinisterly deterministic: "In its beginnings, the credit system sneaks in as a modest helper of accumulation and draws by in- visible threads the money resources scattered all over the surface of society into the hands of individual or associated capitalists."[75] Marx's rewriting of Hegel is matched by his reconceptualization of Kant's categorical imperative as a mode of political intervention: "the *categorical imperative to overthrow all conditions* in which man is a debased, enslaved, neglected and contemptible being."[76] The will is thus turned from a task of universal moral prescription to one of particu- lar social-political transformation.

This particular will may belong to an enlightened individual—a Marxist in- tellectual, for instance—but its great historical location is within a class: it be- comes the collective—or general—will of the proletariat. And this class comes about not by accident or choice, but by a kind of historical necessity—the pro- letariat is the necessary corollary of capitalism: "When the proletariat proclaims the *dissolution of the existing world order,* it is only declaring the secret of its own existence, for it *is* the *actual* dissolution of that order."[77] In other words, it has become a class in the sense that it is aware of itself and its historical destiny as such, and it is this awareness that will guide its will in doing what "it will be compelled to do."[78] But like all classes, its ultimate destiny is to do away with itself—to release the free will of the self-creating agent from the thralls of capitalism.

The reduction of this man to a mere "fragment" of the person he has been, or can be, would seem to imply that there is a mode of full being that is travestied by his current predicament. And this in turn might suggest that Marx has a developed theory—or at least a detailed picture—of what such a mode of being might be like, and of how will actually functions in the emancipated condition of self-creation. But I side with those who can find no such theory, nor indeed any such picture, in Marx's writings, and this applies to both his early and late works.[79] At best there are impressionistic hints, like the following from the *Economic and Philosophical Manuscripts*: "*Communism* is the *positive* supersession of *private property* as *human self-estrangement,* and hence the true *appropriation* of the *human* essence through and for man."[80] But what—and this has become a notorious question—is the nature of this "essence" that is so "appropriated"? In Marx's case—as in Nietzsche's and, as we shall see, in Sartre's—no substantive answer can be given to this question: Marx does not offer a detailed human ontology or psychology. This does not mean that he has no theory of human nature whatsoever; it means, rather, that his theory is of a kind that posits the capacity for change and transformation as the essence of the person. The human being is a kind of open-ended potentiality whose forms, when they are not determined—that is, constrained—by history, will be determined by creative consciousness itself. And this latter form of determination is the product of freedom of will—at least as it finds expression in given social contexts. For it is of the "essence" of humankind that it is a social being. Of "social man" Marx writes:

> Only through the objectively unfolded wealth of human nature can the wealth of subjective *human* sensitivity—a musical ear, an eye for the beauty of form, in short, *senses* capable of human gratification—be either cultivated or created. For not only the five senses, but also the so-called spiritual senses, the practical senses (will, love etc.), in a word, the *human* sense, the humanity of the senses—all these come into being only through the existence of *their* objects, through *humanized* nature.[81]

So the circuit of the will takes in another dimension: it resides in but also creates the self; it is also created through the social forms that it brings about. If the figure of unfolding suggests a preordained shape for the self and its world, Marx's preeminent figure is of a kind of spontaneous birth of the will out of the will, the self out of the self: humankind's "self-mediated *birth.*"[82]

Marx's reluctance to be more precise, to specify other and more fixed aspects of the human "essence," has several sources. One, of course, is tactical: for him the purpose of theory, such as it is, is to precipitate and guide action, not to fix particular accounts of the world. Another is his identification of fixed ontologies of the self with the culture and ideology of the bourgeoisie. "The ideas of the ruling class are in every epoch the ruling ideas";[83] and this applies crucially to ideas about human nature, the self. Hence Marx and Engels's stated desire to crush atomistic "bourgeois individuality"[84]—the corollary at the level of "mental production" of the processes of capitalistic "material production."[85] In another famous formulation, Marx writes:

> The mode of production of material life conditions the general process of social, political and intellectual life. It is not the consciousness of men that determines their existence, but their social existence that determines their consciousness.[86]

The shift from "conditions" to "determines" is, as many have noted, problematical here since to be conditioned is to possess some degree of freedom of the will, while to be determined is to be utterly shaped by the will of some external force or set of conditions. But whether Marx means "conditions" or "determines," it is clear enough that the nature of human beings is in this view consequent upon particular economic-cultural formations, and that as these formations are transformed so too will be the forms of "human nature." Since such transformations cannot be predicted with any certainty, the point is to have theories that set them in motion, rather than ontologies that try to anticipate or circumscribe the outcomes of historical struggle—so the argument seems to run. Yet it is clear that a powerfully deterministic account of the will is present here; at least of the will in its known—as opposed to its envisioned—modalities.

The conditions-determines issue provides a suitable context for asking what implications Marx's account of the will might have for autobiography. Clearly, if the emphasis falls on "determines," autobiography can have only a heavily contingent mode of being: at best it can reflect the economic-ideological formation that its author inhabits, though the autobiography of a free being under pure communism might be expected to enjoy all the freedoms of the blessed state of the unconditioned. There again, such a narrative, lacking the tensions and resistances of life-writing as we know it, might be of limited interest. If, on the other hand, the emphasis falls on "conditions," then the outlook for autobiography would seem to be more promising, albeit more familiar. Marx's awareness that aspects of the "superstructure"—cultural forms of which autobiography must surely be one—can have a substantial degree of autonomy from the economic "base"[87] would suggest that the autobiographer can to some extent transcend the forces that shape him or her, and that the story of how this transcendence comes about might include an account of the will that is so central to bringing it about. It might even be that autobiography can be seen as an instance of the self-creation that for Marx is definitive of the species. Certainly, his conception of language and consciousness as inherently dialogical is richly suggestive here: "Language, like consciousness, only arises from the need, the necessity of intercourse with other men."[88] Autobiography might well be seen as an example par excellence of such "intercourse"—provided that it is not autobiography of the atomistic, Cartesian kind, but rather life-writing that partakes of Marx's grand narrative of greater freedom and integration in social contexts. But then even the atomistic, disconnected autobiographer might be of evidential interest for Marxist analyses that seek to chart bourgeois ideology.

What Marx's writings about the self in general, and will in particular, do not offer is a developed sense of human interiority. These writings comprise elements of three conceptions of will: the Will of the People, Will as Rational Appetite, and Determinism. Some Marxists will say that his theories do not preclude an interior dimension—that the autobiographer as self-creator is free to bring interiority into being and to the notice of the reader. Critics might say that Marx's account of humankind leaves no margin for the highly individualized forms of selfhood we most value in autobiography. We will see presently how Althusser, one of the major modern apologists for Marx, in fact writes his own life, and how two recanted Marxists—Koestler and Spender—write theirs. In Koestler's and Spender's autobiographies, there is an added dimension of interest in that both include in their narratives an account of how and why they repudiated Marxist accounts of self and will.

Late in *Capital,* Marx seems to concede that the wholly unconditioned is a chimera, that human activity always goes on in the context of constraining circumstance: he speaks of "the true realm of freedom, which, however, can blossom forth only with this realm of necessity as its basis."[89] If taken as representing his final position, this would suggest that even under pure communism, the will inhabits a world of constraining forces and circumstances. This is in part a logical point: the concept of will makes no sense without a contrastive concept of constraint. But it is also a metaphysical point (though Marxists will dispute this): it involves the claim that humankind inhabits a reality in which the freedoms of the will are always and inevitably challenged, always and inevitably qualified.

III. *Freud: Pseudo-Agency in a Deterministic World*

In "A Difficulty in the Path of Psycho-Analysis," Freud acknowledges Schopenhauer's status as one of the "forerunners" of psychoanalysis. Of this "great thinker" he says that his

> unconscious "Will" is equivalent to the mental instincts of psycho-analysis. It was this same thinker, moreover, who in words of unforgettable impressiveness admonished mankind of the importance, still so greatly under-estimated by it, of its sexual craving.[90]

The comment ignores the mystical dimension of Schopenhauer's thought, though even here there are similarities between the two thinkers: Freud's notion of the "oceanic experience" is itself quasi-mystical. And the affinities go deeper still. Like Schopenhauer, Freud believes that our common sensation of unconstrained volition is nothing more than "the illusion of Free Will."[91] But perhaps the most complex and important similarity between the thought of the two men lies in the question they raise about the provenance of "character" in individual conduct: is character, as Schopenhauer thought, a given that imposes determinatively upon the will; or can character be changed in ways that—and that are intended to—at least change the messages to which the will responds?

Such questions in turn raise some of the most difficult issues in the interpretation of Freud's thought. I am largely persuaded by Frank Sulloway's contention that "Freud's entire life's work in science was characterized by an abiding faith in the notion that all vital phenomena, including psychical ones, are rigidly and lawfully determined by the principle of cause and effect."[92] If this is indeed true of his "entire life's work," the famous remappings of regions of the psyche make no difference here. While they may revise particular aspects of the earlier accounts of psychic dynamics, they leave untouched the conception of causation that shaped those accounts. That conception, and with it Freud's conception of the will, is deterministic. Yet, Freud's conception of the therapeutic process of psychoanalysis seems to require some qualification of the deterministic premise. He repeatedly characterizes psychoanalysis in terms like the following in *The Ego and the Id*: it is "an instrument to enable the ego to achieve a progressive conquest of the id."[93] And in this same study he clearly equates the ego with reason and the id with passion: "The ego represents what may be called reason and common sense, in contrast to the id, which contains the passions." Then follows the famous equestrian analogy according to which the ego is like a man on horseback: the id is the horse, and ego uses the borrowed force of the horse to guide it. Freud continues: "In the same way the ego is in the habit of transforming the id's will into action as if it were its own."[94] The analogy is roughly consistent with Freud's later belief that the ego forms out of the abandoned cathexes of the id: that it makes of passional and instinctual id energies the stuff of the quasi-rational social being.

Several issues arise here. First, it is prima facie hard to reconcile Freud's version of determinism with his conception of psychoanalysis: if we are determined by our characters and our pasts, how can any "instrument" help to give us the rationally informed will to act in ways that are other than a repetition of these determining factors? Second, it is noticeable—and perhaps inevitable—that the passage about the ego's transformation of id materials is framed in terms that essentially delegate agent-status to various aspects of the psyche. So in the first instance the id is an agentlike thing that has "will," but this will is then commandeered by the ego, which then redirects it in the light of rational appraisal and common sense. A kind of allegorizing of the psyche into agent-substitutes and subsections is constantly at work in Freud. In the present case, it would seem that the will is determined in each of its manifestations—first by the id, then by the ego—and is therefore not free. However, even this is not entirely clear, because Freud's thought is very much in the mainstream of European rationalism, which says, in effect, that the more rational our reasons for acting the more free we are.

Freud's views on the free will–determinism issue are most clearly and concertedly set out in the chapter "Determinism, Belief in Chance and Superstition—Some Points of View" in *The Psychopathology of Everyday Life*. Having argued that apparently random activities like naming the first number that comes into your head are in fact not random, but pre- or unconsciously determined, he suggests that this insight might help with another problem:

> Many people, as is well known, contest the assumption of complete psychical determinism by appealing to a special feeling of conviction that there is a free will. This feeling of conviction exists; and it does not give way before a belief in determinism. Like every normal feeling it must have something to warrant it. But so far as I can observe, it does not manifest itself in the great and important decisions of the will: on these occasions the feeling that we have is rather one of psychical compulsion, and we are glad to invoke it on our behalf. ("Here I stand: I can do no other." [Martin Luther's declaration at the Diet of Worms.]) On the other hand, it is precisely with regard to the unimportant, indifferent decisions that we would like to claim that we could just as well have acted otherwise: that we have acted of our free—and unmotivated—will. According to our analyses it is not necessary to dispute the right to the feeling of conviction of having a free will. If the distinction between conscious and unconscious motivation is taken into account, our feeling of conviction informs us that conscious motivation does not extend to all our motor decisions. *De minimis non curat lex.* But what is thus left free by the one side receives its motivation from the other side, from the unconscious; and in this way determination in the psychical sphere is still carried out without any gap.[95]

The figure of the seamless—gapless—will is reminiscent of Augustine's conceptual imagery of the will in its full and "incomplete" states. Freud's use of such imagery makes his position clear: we sometimes feel that we possess free will, but when this happens it is because our true motives for acting as we do are unconscious. Again: "The deeply rooted belief in psychic freedom and choice . . . is quite unscientific and must give ground before the claims of a determinism which governs mental life."[96] No action is "unmotivated," that is, the will always acts in obedience to some determination from some part of the psyche, or from stored psychic residues of the individual's personal history. For Freud, indeed, a motive can take several forms:[97] it can work either consciously or unconsciously; if it is unconscious, it is so because the ego has a motive for repressing it. A motive in this sense operates like a cause—something that determines particular (conscious and unconscious) motivational states from without. Frank Sulloway notes that according to Freud, such intricate systematicity even holds for "free association" in psychoanalysis. He notes that Freud's term—*Einfall*—means something like "intrusion," suggesting the intrusion of preconscious materials into consciousness.[98] Such an intrusion is not in Freud's view random. Quite the contrary, that which rises "up" from the preconscious does so in a systematically determined way. If this were not so, psychoanalysis would not be able to uncover the systematic mechanisms of neurosis, nor indeed of "normal" psychological functioning. Indeed one of Freud's great contributions is to have demonstrated that neurotic behavior is not a matter of chance, of meaningless scramblings of normal functions, but that it is, on the contrary, a directed and systematic activity that possesses not only an etiology of its own, but a kind of will of its own. Freud also posits the existence of a "counter-will"[99] which, in *its* own systematic way, works against repressive psychic mechanisms that are present both in normal and neurotic individuals.

In chapter 3, I inquire how three representative modern thinkers who deny the existence of free will in their intellectual work go about writing their life-stories. In his own, and rather impersonal, autobiography, *An Autobiographical Study*, Freud does not dwell in any detail on this issue in his own life.[100] He does however say this of his decision to become a doctor:

> Although we lived in very limited circumstances, my father insisted that, in my choice of profession, I should follow my own inclinations. Neither at that time, nor indeed in my later life, did I feel any particular predilection for the career of a physician. I was moved, rather, by a sort of curiosity, which was, however, directed more towards human concerns than towards natural objects; nor had I grasped the importance of observation as one of the best means of gratifying it.[101]

The phrasing is interesting: the individual is "moved," the will is determined, by something that seems to come from without—"curiosity"; yet curiosity is a deeply subjective sensation, one we might be more inclined to picture as coming from "within" than "without." Moreover, curiosity is suffused with its own will-like impulse to project the self into the world. There is a blur here between cause and effect, such that curiosity seems to be its own cause, or its own effect. But in Freud's terms curiosity is the cause; the "choice" of medicine, the effect. The odd passivity of this passage contrasts interestingly, and perhaps tactically, with what we know to have been Freud's fierce, almost messianic levels of ambition. It is almost as if he takes little responsibility for the "choice" he makes. And this might seem to be a logical extension of his overall position.

But in his mind it is not. Like Schopenhauer and others, Freud does not believe that the determination, the unfreedom, of the will, is incompatible with moral responsibility. On the contrary, the whole drift of psychoanalysis is toward greater self-understanding, greater rationality, and common sense in exerting the will, greater self-control through the activity of a properly disposed superego: "Analysis does not set out to make pathological reactions impossible, but to give the patient's ego *freedom* to decide one way or the other."[102] Freud's reconceptualization of Kant's categorical imperative locates it in the superego[103]—a psychic dimension that has both parental and archaic roots, and that is somewhat ambiguously located between ego and id. The superego carries and contains ethical awarenesses; it also assists the ego in resisting and mastering the instinctual drives of the id. The ambiguity of the superego's position—it is described as both a "grade" of the ego and as "a representative of the internal world, of the id"[104]—may complicate our sense of whether it functions as a motive or a cause in conduct, but however it functions it works as a determinant of the will. In this sense, Freud's general causal picture is maintained. However, because it assists in the colonization of the id by the rational powers of the ego, the superego helps us to more aware of how we are constituted and to switch the determinative power over the will from id to ego. She or he who is most self-aware and rational is not thereby more free, but is thereby more responsible for his or her actions.

Since I shall be considering some autobiographies that are heavily influenced by Freudian theory, I want to make a few remarks here about Freud and autobiography. Quite apart from ways in which we may use Freud to interpret autobiography, it is clear that there are deep connections between psychoanalysis and autobiographical texts. Both are forms of "talking cure"—as Freud called psychoanalysis. Each depends heavily upon a mixture of recollection and fantasy; each is to some extent driven by and draws upon internal conflict. And there is a further point that has to do with Freud's enormous cultural influence on modernity: his picture of the psyche has been so powerful that for many autobiographers it conditions the sense of what is involved in the act of introspection, of life-narration: not only the sort of effort, courage, and pain involved, but, quite specifically, what one can expect to find when one introspects. Freud's topography has to a remarkable degree become late modernity's landscape of the mind. Among intellectual autobiographers there tends to be this interesting twist: many have in fact undergone analysis, and their autobiographies record what they think they have learned about their unconscious lives through the analytic experience. Stephen Spender and Arthur Koestler are both cases in point. But, as I argue in chapter 8, a still more emphatic example of such autobiographical mediations of Freud is Diana Trilling's *The Beginning of the Journey*—

a book that powerfully, if often unwittingly, captures that paradoxical sense in which Freud sees us as at once wholly determined and partially free—as pseudo-agents in a deterministic world.

III. EMPHATIC DECLARATIONS: LATER TWENTIETH-CENTURY VIEWS

With the exception of certain views to which I shall refer in the last section of this chapter, the later twentieth century's accounts of the will have been marked by a tendency to emphatic declaration: the will is either affirmed in a manner of high and even messianic drama; or it is denied with equal trenchancy—as for example in the many modernist aesthetic manifestos espousing impersonalist doctrines that eviscerate the inner realm of intentionality, or sever the links between it and action.[105] There are many reasons for this polarization of views, including: the ambivalent legacy of the prophets of late modernity; the devastation of confidence in culture and in the human individual that was wrought by the two world wars; secular society's hardening of skeptical attitudes to alleged interior psycho-spiritual phenomena; the advent of modern totalitarian doctrine and practice; and the increasing influence of science, including sciences of human and social behavior, as the dominant paradigm of human understanding.

1. *Sartrean Existentialism: The Drama of Affirmation*

In Sartre's *Nausea* Antoine Roquentin comes to Bouville to conclude his biographical research on the Marquis de Rollebon. In trying to write this life, to get all the relevant detail in and interpreted, Roquentin finds himself overcome with feelings of paralysis, suffocation, and nausea. After abandoning this enterprise, he has a vision of what he calls contingency:

> The essential thing is contingency. I mean that one cannot define existence as necessity. To exist is simply *to be there;* those who exist let themselves be encountered, but you can never deduce anything from them. I believe there are people who have understood this. Only they tried to overcome this contingency by inventing a necessary, causal being. But no necessary being can explain existence: contingency is not a delusion, a probability which can be dissipated; it is the absolute, consequently, the perfect free gift.[106]

The passage brings out much that is central to Sartre's, and to other post-Heideggerian, understandings of the will.[107] The world is not structured or causally determined. It is a realm of chance, not necessity. One can respond to this absurd reality by denying the absurdity and constructing causal explanations and constraining life protocols, by making oneself thinglike, an entity stripped of the burdens and freedom of consciousness. This is the solution of those who aspire simply to "be." Or one can face the absurdity, which means facing the fact that one is free, that one is not necessarily captive to, the consequence of, any causal sequence. So conceived, contingency is the "free gift" of freedom. As Sartre says in *Being and Nothingness*: "Freedom is precisely the nothingness which *is made-to-be* at the heart of man and which forces human-reality to *make itself* instead of *to be*."[108] Clearly such a view has profound implications for autobiography: Sartre's contention that "between past and present there is an absolute hetero-geneity"[109] would, if taken literally, require a radically new mode of life-writing in which "the self" (this entity must now dwell in quotes) is, as it were, recreated, or seen to have been reinvented, ex nihilo from moment to moment. If such a mode of selfhood were indeed possible, autobiography might have a central, or at least an exemplary, role to play in the ongoing processes of self-creation. Sartre's own autobiography of childhood, *The Words*, is open in proclaiming: "I loathe my childhood";[110] yet it also claims that one cannot recapture the sub-jective truth of one's own life in narrative because narrative will always take its bearings from retrospective insights that falsify moment-to-moment experience. And this holds for things like one's "passions," "blunders," "prejudices," and also various kinds of willings, such as "bygone acts of resistance."[111] Not surprisingly, *The Words* evinces a strong sense of causal shaping of the young bourgeois self. But it ends at age nine. In chapter 5 of this book, I examine Simone de Beau-voir's more extended, indeed massive, autobiographical oeuvre as a response to contingency and as an inquiry into the limits and possibilities of existential self-writing.

Roquentin's revelation suggests that life is deeply paradoxical: it is, strictly speaking, meaningless, yet the individual confronts the possibility, even the obligation, to create meaning out of freedom. The will is central to this process: rather than being paralyzed by absurdity, "it" should be precipitated into action (which includes the making of meaning). To this extent, Sartre's view of the will is a version of the Freedom as the Genus of Volition concep-tion. I've put "it" in quotes, however, because Sartre, while depending heavily on a notion of the will, does not want to essentialize it—or indeed any other psychological phenomena. The key here is the term *nothingness*, which appears in the quote above and gives his greatest existential work its title: *Being and Nothingness*. Sartre is profoundly anti-Cartesian in (among other ways) refus-ing to think of the self as a substance—hence the repeated references to terms such as "the ontological mirage of the Self."[112] Like Hegel (prior to his account of the Spirit's ascension to Absolute knowledge), Nietzsche, and Marx, Sartre envisages the self not as essence but as possibility. It possesses Hegelian nega-tivity—the capacity to imagine itself as other than it "is"—though it has no prospect of arriving at some state of ultimate or universal self-realization. Its condition is one of "condemnation to freedom,"[113] both in the sense that it is the recipient of the unsolicited "gift" of freedom and that it must bear the an-guish of never coming to rest, of never being wholly coincident with itself.

Hegel's "unhappy consciousness" is not then a passing stage on the way to universal self-realization—it is the very condition of all human life at all times: "Human reality therefore is by nature an unhappy consciousness with no possibility of surpassing its unhappy state";[114] self-transcendence, self-surpassing, is the one imperative in this world. Sartre rejects Kant's categorical imperative on the ground that the individual is merely "dissembling" the "anguish" that freedom brings if he or she tries to legislate for others.[115]

We cannot, then, claim that freedom—say, the freedom of the will—is a part of humankind's essence. Rather: "Human freedom precedes essence in man and makes it possible; the essence of the human being is suspended in his freedom . . . Man does not exist *first* in order to be free *subsequently;* there is no difference between the being of man and his *being-free*."[116] Freedom is a given in the constitution of the world; nevertheless, we must will it in order to seize it, and we must have the courage to endure the anguish that this involves. But what is the nature of this (in)essential will? The question is by no means easy to answer, and I side with those who think that the most Sartre offers is a kind of paradoxical gesturing at something that by his own admission cannot ultimately be formulated.

Sartre tells us in *Being and Nothingness*: "This brief study does not attempt to exhaust the question of the will; on the contrary, it would be desirable to attempt a phenomenological description of the will for itself. But this is not our goal."[117] What he does is to argue roughly as follows. The self is engaged in choices of both a global and a local nature. The local ones involve particular decisions (do I marry this person?); the global ones have to do with longer-term choices of the modes in which we will live, our fundamental existential orientation toward the world. The choice of global orientation is freely chosen, though "freely" does not entail that the will acts in the face of no constraints. On the contrary, "freedom can exist only as *restricted*,"[118] by which he means that there is always a set of circumstantial givens—a situation, what he terms *facticity*—within which, and against which, our choices are made. So "freedom can be truly free only by constituting facticity as its own restriction."[119] There is a further sense in which the global choice—the choice of a "project"—is not free, albeit a paradoxical one: it is "conditioned," but what conditions it is, precisely, the "self's" impulsion to its own transcendence: "The will is determined within the compass of motives and ends already posited by the for-itself in a transcendent projection of itself toward its possibles."[120] The will, then, is conditioned by an inaugurating choice of freedom, and this choice in turn conditions all subsequent self-transcending choices. But the will is not a "privileged" part or faculty of the psyche; it has no executive function. It is rather an "event" that exists on account of a primordial freedom that is in the world, that comes into the world through humankind: "The will is not a privileged manifestation of freedom but . . . is a psychic event of a peculiar structure which is constituted on the same plane as other psychic events and which is supported, neither more nor less than the others, by an original, ontological freedom."[121]

It seems fair to say that in this view will can (at least in a sense) be exerted but not located. It isn't "in" consciousness because there is no Cartesian consciousness that could contain the will and then direct it at the world. Consciousness is, on the contrary, intentional in the Husserlian sense; it only exists in and through particular engagements with the world: "Consciousness *of* something is self-consciousness."[122] We only "have" consciousness, including a consciousness of self, when we are conscious *of.* Herein lies one of the main terms of Sartre's repudiation of the Freudian unconscious. For Sartre, there can be no dimension of consciousness of which we are constitutively unaware, because to have consciousness is, precisely, to *be* aware, or at least to have, in principle, no barriers to awareness. This in turn means that Sartre rejects the Freudian doctrine of unconscious causation—there is no unconscious, and because of this there can be no distinction between a cause and a motive: only that of which we are conscious can act upon the will; all causes must therefore be motives (where "motives" are construed as intentional): "The cause, the motive, and the end are three indissoluble terms of the thrust of a free and living consciousness which projects itself towards its possibilities and makes itself defined by these possibilities."[123] The reference to "end" here further elaborates Sartre's position: we don't merely choose with particular ends in view; it is also the case that our "ends," which are never really "ends" but transitional forms of consciousness, come to us as a *consequence* of our choices. I return to this partially inverted notion of choice in chapter 7, where I discuss Stephen Spender's autobiography.

If we combine this notion of "choice" with Sartre's contention that the past has—or need have—no determining power over the will, we have a radical notion of freedom, albeit one that is in a sense "decentered" in that the possessor of this will and this freedom is never a settled entity, always a thing in process, in motion. Like others in this study, Sartre uses the figure of threads, and, as in other cases, it reveals a lot about the outlook of the writer in question. He describes the for-itself—the being that self-surpasses—as diasporic, an entity that is never at home, at one with itself. Always spinning new forms of itself out of itself, it sustains the provisional entity that is the infinite array of other things it can be (its "nihilations") by a "thread" of continuity: "It is the being which holds to itself by a single thread, or more precisely it is the being which by being causes all possible dimensions of its nihilation to exist."[124] Seen in one way, this diasporic self is a titanic thing, paving the abyss it strides upon; but from another vantage point, it is an exceedingly thin thing, a substanceless, empty always-becoming that never becomes anything, anyone, in particular. Threads here betoken a relation between the "self" and "its" intentions and acts so tenuous that one might just as easily say that self and destiny have been sundered, as claim that destiny is scripted by the self. Here Sartre's existential vision can only be described as deeply paradoxical. Like Nietzsche's, it seems to hypostasize the will while at the same time denying the will any psychic location, any status as possession of a self, and certainly any "privileged" status. It is an affirmation of the will that seems dramatic; but the drama comes, at least in part, from the high-wire habit of Sartre's imagination—an imagination that has in this instance affirmed will in a way that renders it so ontologically insubstantial as to be almost, and vertiginously, indistinguishable from will-lessness.

Nevertheless, Sartre can say that "it is not enough to will; it is necessary to will to will,"[125] the implication being that the "self" does in fact have to exert a certain inborn power in order to kick the process of self-transcendence into action—if this were not so, there would be no point in existential injunctions to free choosing—and in so exerting the will, one is doing something of value. Sartre's position seems to combine elements of Will as Dynamic Power with Freedom as the Genus of Volition. Here the vexed problem of existential ethics rears its head. I want to forestall most discussion of this until I consider Beauvoir's supplement to existentialist ethics, *The Ethics of Ambiguity*, in chapter 5. For the moment, a typical passage from Sartre's notoriously slim conclusion to *Being and Nothingness*, "Ethical Implications," will suffice: the moral agent's "freedom" will "become conscious of itself and will reveal itself in anguish as the unique source of value and the nothingness by which the *world* exists."[126] The agent so pictured is radically separate; not a would-be Kantian legislator for all people, but a being through whose authentic self-transcendence value comes into the world. The problem as to how interpersonal moral values come into being under these conditions has often been noted and was never solved by Sartre. Existentialism was doomed to be a mode of atomistic Romanticism, rebellious, individualistic, but incapable of detailed social or ethical elaboration.

Still, it is a vision that holds out, and was to achieve, the possibility of high drama for writers of autobiography. The great existential autobiographers like Beauvoir were able to read the existential predilection for anguish, sudden transformation, liberation, and rebellion into an almost solipsistic realm of psychological depth and complexity—a realm that, as Beauvoir was to acknowledge in her autobiography, was an unadmitted residue of bourgeois individualism in a doctrine that purported to renounce psychological depth. But there is one further dimension of Sartrean existentialism I have not so far noted, and that explains its importance for autobiography. Sartre insists that the self is by definition an intersubjective thing: it depends for its existence on the existence of the Other. Here again Hegel's influence is powerful. But the Other is not just a person other than my (ostensible) self. When I self-transcend, when I seek or attain self-consciousness, I am in fact *othering myself*, creating another self: "To know is to *make oneself other*."[127] The autobiographer, of course, sunders the self in the effort to know it, creates a second self that becomes the subject of the writing self's narrative. As Wordsworth writes in *The Prelude*:

That, sometimes, when I think of it, I seem
Two consciousnesses, conscious of myself
And of some other Being.[128]

Thus appears a gap that most autobiographers want to fill: they want (to change
the metaphor) to close the circle between the writing and the written self. It cannot be done, and one of Sartre's great contributions to the understanding of autobiography is to have given us a powerful and intricate explanation of why this
is the case.

II. *Anglo-American Analytic Philosophy: Gilbert Ryle*

At the end of his most influential work, *The Concept of Mind*, the British analytic philosopher[129] Gilbert Ryle anticipates charges that the book will be seen
as a work of behaviorism. While he denies that he has any interest in defending
behaviorism as such, he pays it the compliment of saying that it has helped to rid
philosophy and philosophical psychology of the concept of mind that is his target throughout: namely, the Cartesian model that sees mind and bodily actions
as ontologically distinct and that (among other things) sees human actions as
being caused in all cases by prior mental acts of will, or "volitions." His famous
figure for this model is the "ghost in the machine," where the machine is the
"body" and the "ghost" is the mysterious theater of the mind. Ryle doesn't mince
words. This doctrine "should be treated as one of the curios of theory"; we
should dismiss as a mere philosophical myth the picture of experiences as
"episodes which constitute the shadow-drama on the ghostly boards of the mental stage."[130] These are memorable and influential formulations, and they entail
the Conceptual Denial of the will; but the stakes are high. Chapter 6 of this
study deals with Arthur Koestler, who titled one of his books *The Ghost in the
Machine* and did so in express opposition to what he saw as the limitations of
Ryle's account of human action, motivation, and self-consciousness.

Whatever his hesitations about behaviorism, there is indeed a case for seeing
The Concept of Mind as an immensely sophisticated philosophical analogue of
some aspects of behaviorist theory. Ryle shares with B. F. Skinner[131] not only an
aggressively dismissive attitude to Cartesianism, but also the view that in the tradition he is writing against the "occult inner thrusts" that are postulated as the
willed causes of actions "were screened from scientific observation."[132] Their existence could not be verified or corroborated. Further, we construct descriptions
of allegedly mental activity according to the same principles, and using the same
sorts of terms, that we use in characterizing observable behavior. Of perceived
qualities like strength of will, effort of will, and resoluteness, Ryle says:

> Note that it is no part of the definition of resoluteness or of irresoluteness that
> a resolution should actually have been formed. A resolute man may firmly re-

sist temptations to abandon or postpone his task, though he never went through a prefatory ritual-process of making up his mind to complete it. But naturally such a man will also be disposed to perform any vows which he has made to others or to himself.[133]

In other words, we can see, characterize, and commend the man's resolution without recourse to some (as Ryle sees it) vocabulary of phantom inner states. What's more, the resolute man will reflect his disposition in whatever he does, so that "it is not a single-track disposition or, for that and other reasons, a disposition to execute occult operations of one special kind."[134] I understand this to mean that, as many philosophers now hold, there are various tryings, willings, and so on, but that no faculty of the will lies behind or beyond these particular activities. Importantly, Ryle does not want to deny that inner states and activities of varying complexity exist ("when a person does something voluntarily . . . his action certainly reflects some quality or qualities of mind");[135] his point is that, first, we cannot get reliable information about such states, and, second, it is both customary and sufficient to characterize behaviors in terms of whether they are appropriate, intelligent, expert, and so on.

Ryle marshals an array of arguments against the doctrine of "ghostly inner thrusts": he asserts that nobody, save those who endorse the theory that there are "hidden operations of willing," ever talks about their experience of such "operations";[136] he suggests that though the doctrine claims that all human actions are caused by such antecedent mental states, there are in fact many actions that are not so caused.[137] Noting that the doctrine sees the alleged connection between volition and movement as mysterious, he contends that there's no way of knowing what causal chains were in operation;[138] and he submits that the doctrine's view that some mental process are themselves caused by volitions can only lead in two absurd directions: either volitions themselves are caused, in which case action is not voluntary, or the old process of infinite regress sets in as we seek an illusory inaugurating volition in the prehistory of the action.[139] The first of these claims—that nobody ever describes their volitions—has particular relevance for this study of autobiography and the will. Here is part of what Ryle says about this matter:

> Despite the fact that theorists have, since the Stoics and Saint Augustine, recommended us to describe our conduct [our acts of choice] in this way, no one, save to endorse the theory, ever describes his own conduct, or that of his acquaintances, in the recommended idioms. No one ever says such things as that at 10 A.M. he was occupied in willing this or that, or that he performed five quick and easy volitions and two slow and difficult volitions between midday and lunch-time.[140]

In fact, writers of autobiography, both in earlier traditions of religious autobiography and in post-Freudian forms, *do* often speak in very much this way about their inner lives. (And in any case, even if nobody did, it wouldn't prove that there are no such things as volitions.) Even if the technical term *volition* is seldom used by modern nonphilosophical writers, the autobiographers discussed in this study try repeatedly to characterize and anatomize the inner states in which they will certain actions, and the nature of the connections (or the interventions) between willing and acting. I discuss this issue in detail in chapter 7 with reference to Stephen Spender's autobiography, *World Within World.* In one of the examples I refer to, Spender describes a particular moment in which he makes a decision to get to know a young man who becomes his lover: "At that moment I made a decision to get to know him, when I quite well might not have done so. There was a moment of pure arbitrariness when I thought: 'I need not do this, but I will do it.'"[141] Such reports are entirely characteristic of reflective autobiography; indeed they constitute a compelling reason for reading autobiography as a mode of inquiry into the will. Even Ryle himself, in an autobiographical essay written for a collection of papers about his work, employs this kind of self-description. Explaining how his friend Wittgenstein and those who reverenced his work led Ryle to broaden his philosophical affiliations, Ryle says: "It made me resolve, not indeed to be a philosophical polyglot; but to avoid being a monoglot."[142] Of course it might be objected that the accounts of willing and acting that these people give cannot be verified; but neither, as I have noted in chapter 1, can they be disconfirmed. A further point here: Accounts of the human individual cannot be limited to modes of inquiry that fall under the rubric of scientific verification. As Charles Taylor argues, the attempt to render human behavior in this way reflects a naturalist premise that "the terms of everyday life, those in which we go about living our lives, are to be relegated to the realm of mere appearance."[143] Those "terms" include the "experience" of "volition" and the ways in which we talk about it. Ryle wants to acknowledge the existence of this dimension but to leave it out of explanatory descriptions of human behavior. In this he shares a dire limitation with Skinner. Ryle is eloquent in his reassurances about the human implications of a causally structured world: "Not only is there plenty of room for purpose where everything is governed by mechanical laws, but there would be no place for purpose if things were not so governed. Predictability is a necessary condition of planning."[144] But his proposed way of understanding people leaves little room for the experience of agency—an experience that is deeply implicated both in the way we plan (and perform other complex cognitive and imaginative processes) and in the forms that our plannings, imaginings, and willings take.

III. *Postmodern Literary Theory's World Without Will: Derrida*

We have seen that many writers who deny the existence of the will, or who take issue with traditional accounts of it, nevertheless spend a good deal of time on the topic. This is not however the case in much postmodern literary (and cultural) theory. Here references to the will are scarce, both in major primary texts and in the dozens of introductions to and handbooks about theory that have appeared since the 1960s. Where a will-like word is used, it is often *desire;* but the term is seldom specified in any conceptually detailed way. With some important exceptions like Harold Bloom, whose early work on poetic influence turns on the notion of a "*wilful revisionism"* that is practiced by the oedipal poet against precursor writers,[145] postmodern theory exhibits a deep hostility to the whole notion of a complex agential self and to the culture that has given it philosophical and literary expression. One aim of this study of autobiography and the will is to show that these matters are more complex than antihumanist literary theory allows, and that it is no mere coincidence that work in other areas—humanistic literary and social theory, some regions of philosophy, among others—continues to strive for complex and adequate agential accounts of the self.[146]

Since postmodern literary theory has so little to say about—even against—the will, there is no need to say a great deal about such theory here, even though its influence in literary studies has been massive. The two main sources of such theory tend to be Nietzsche, whom I have already discussed, and Saussure. The main tenets of the Saussurean position are by now so familiar that the barest outline will suffice: All cultural phenomena are "signifying systems." Such systems are self-sufficient, self-determining, and have the integrity of an already-complete organism at any given moment. They are hierarchically organized into levels of increasing complexity, and meaning is generated within the system not through direct correspondence or reference between a symbol and aspects of an "objective reality" but through differential relations between the terms that comprise the system. A distinction is drawn between the shared system of communicative possibilities (*langue*) and particular communicative acts (*parole*). Communicators are largely unaware that they possess the competence that comes to them through the *langue,* and later elaborations of structuralism insist that they themselves are constituted in and through the system. They enact systemic possibilities but they are not agents. Jonathan Culler, one of the early Anglo-American exponents of structuralism, writes that "structural analysis . . . refuses to make the thinking subject an explanatory cause" and that the "individual subject" is only retained in such analysis in the sense that "meaning must move through him."[147]

Having briefly sketched these immensely influential ideas, I will now move to two very powerful later developments, each of which has profoundly shaped an intellectual environment in which the will is simply assumed to be a dead issue: Althusserian structuralist Marxism and the linguistic poststructuralism of Derrida and Roland Barthes.

Poststructuralism comes in various forms and has permeated various intellectual movements. One form descends from Nietzsche through Foucault and is predominantly concerned with power and its relation to knowledge. Another, which also owes much to Nietzsche and has been taken up by Derrida and others, focuses more specifically on language and its relation to metaphysical traditions. This more linguistic wing of poststructuralism also includes some of the later work of Roland Barthes. Here again, a brief exposition will suffice: In the context of a wide-ranging intellectual reassessment that focuses particularly on Husserl, Derrida reconsiders and recasts Saussure's differential account of meaning; however, he associates this with a concept of structure that, like Althusser's, is decentered.[148] Since there is no controlling perspective from "outside" the system and no controlling center "within" it, the differential activity of signification is endlessly deferred. What Derrida calls "the myth of consciousness"[149] falsely imputes to language users a capacity (a) to translate intentions into linguistic meanings that accurately embody them, and (b) to have those meanings accurately received by hearers/readers. Language users are both participants in and products of the "play" of differential meaning: participants to the extent that they are language users, and products because consciousness itself is in some way linguistically produced. Since consciousness and self derive from decentered, differential, open "systematicity," the self too is decentered. Here again, it seems problematical to talk of agency. Derrida does not often write about the will as such, but one of his early essays offers a characterization of the will that seems to have undergone relatively little change in his later work. Having drawn a distinction between "pure speech" (the realm of pure transcendence) and "inscription" (the modes of human—linguistic—expression), he speaks of the "attempt-to-write," by which he seems to mean the impulse and the aspiration to engage in inscriptive practices like writing. He continues:

> The attempt-to-write cannot be understood on the basis of voluntarism. The will to write [*vouloir-écrire*] is not an ulterior determination of a primal will [*vouloir primitif*]. On the contrary, the will to write reawakens the willful sense of the will [*le sens de volonté de la volonté*]: freedom, break with the domain of empirical history, a break whose aim is reconciliation with the hidden essence of the empirical, with pure historicity. The will and the attempt to write are not the desire to write, for it is a question here not of affectivity but of freedom and duty. In its relationship to Being, the attempt-to-write poses itself as the only way out of affectivity. A way out that can only be aimed at, and without certainty that deliverance is possible or that it is outside affectivity. To be affected is to be finite: to write could still be to deceive finitude, and to reach Being—a kind of Being which could neither be, nor affect me by *itself*—from without existence. To write would be to attempt to forget difference: to forget writing in the presence of so-called living and pure speech.[150]

The passage, and indeed the entire essay, is extraordinarily complex; so much so that the attempt to arrive at a confident paraphrastic reading is probably futile.[151] It does seem clear, however, that the possessor of the "will-to-write" is not a subject in any substantive agential sense; there is no preexisting self, armed with preexisting powers, intentions, and meanings, that commits these meanings to language through some act of free choosing: "The attempt-to-write cannot be understood on the basis of voluntarism." Rather, it is the act of inscription itself that brings meaning—or rather, perhaps, in the first instance, the possibility of meaning-making—into being. And among the meanings that thus come into being is first-person consciousness itself. Language (in the broad sense) is constitutive of subjectivity. It is tempting now to say that "once subjectivity is so constituted" certain things follow; and I will indeed put it this way, at least for the moment. So—once subjectivity is so constituted, certain things follow: there now exists an entity that assumes what might be termed the sentiments of agency; the feeling, for instance, of possessing a will—the reawakening of the "willful sense of the will"—takes root, and it supports certain agential aspirations, including the desire for transcendence ("pure historicity"). But transcendence (here associated with "affectivity") is neither a preferred nor a possible objective: one cannot "forget difference." What is possible, and what is preferred, is the ethical engagement that the being-possessed-of-the-sentiment-of-agency can now enact. This is a matter not of "affectivity but of freedom and duty": to feel like a moral agent, and to self-posit oneself as such, is to make possible ethical conduct ("duty") and to exercise some kind of volition ("freedom") in one's moral life.

In this reading, will seems to enter the picture as an event consequent upon the construction of consciousness through language. Will is not, then, a given constituent of the human being. Nor is it more than a kind of illusion—something we ascribe to ourselves under the general and fictional rubric of personhood. But to read the passage as a temporal sequence, as I have just done, is too simple, because Derrida does not conceive of things in terms of origins, linear developments, and outcomes. Difference entails ceaseless patterns of reciprocal constitution and differentiation, proliferation, play, and so on. Consciousness and language, which partake of these patterns, are not amenable to ontological description. Thus the passage, and the essay more generally, offers no real specification of consciousness, subjectivity, or the subject. Whether we see the process described as linear, circular, dialectical, or whatever, it is impossible to say where the subject is, what its powers are, how subjectivity relates to, say, identity, and so on. The subject is what Derrida elsewhere calls a "trace structure": it's a kind of echo of something that has long since moved on, that indeed never possessed substantive being or location, something whose essence is to be always elsewhere, always other than it is.[152] Little wonder that the "will" in this passage seems such a spectral thing. The "attempt-to-write" is not willed by anyone; the sense of the will, such as it "is," is "reawakened" (but when and how was it awake in the first place?), but this reawakening is itself illusory in the sense that the condition-of-being-able-to-will arises from an endless process of fictionalizing. Derrida's deconstructive discourse, while always "willful" in its own Nietzschean way, cannot and does not seek to give any substantive account of the will, nor of the subject that (at some levels of his descriptions) might be said to possess one. Such a conception does not correspond to any of the categorizations of will we have thus far considered. Indeed it is intended to deconstruct such categorizations. It contains elements of Determinism, Conceptual Denial, and even, perhaps, the Freedom as the Genus of Volition view. It is something like this heady and radically paradoxical mix that infuses Roland Barthes's "autobiography," *Roland Barthes by Roland Barthes.*

IV. TOTALITARIANISM

Any survey of autobiography and its relation to the will that includes the twentieth century must take account of passages such as these, from two of the century's most notorious "autobiographical" works:

> Infinite then were the problems and the worries [after his assumption of power]. I had to decide everything, and I had a will firm enough to summon up all the political postulates that I had enunciated and sustained with pen and paper, in meetings and in my parliamentary speeches. This was not only a problem of strength to last, to endure, to stand erect in any wind, but also, above all, a problem of the will.

And:

> A new sense of justice, of serious purpose, of harmony and concord guides now the destinies of all the peoples and classes of Italy. There are neither vexations nor violence, but there is exaltation of what is good and exaltation of the virtue of heroism. In every class, among all citizens, nothing is done against the state, nothing is done outside the state.[153]

And from another source:

> In the Jewish people the will to self-sacrifice does not go beyond the individual's naked instinct of self-preservation. Their apparently great sense of solidarity is based on the very primitive herd instinct that is seen in many other living creatures in this world.

And finally:

> The more unified the application of a people's will to fight, the greater will be the magnetic attraction of a movement and the mightier will be the impetus of the thrust. It belongs to the genius of a great leader to make even adver-

saries far removed from one another seem to belong to a single category, because in weak and uncertain characters the knowledge of having different en-
emies can only too readily lead to the beginning of doubt in their own
right.[154]

It is in response to sentiments such as these, by Mussolini and Hitler, respectively, and the deeds done in their name, that many intellectuals after the Second World War turned to the writing of reflective autobiography. The autobiographies of Simone de Beauvoir, Arthur Koestler, Stephen Spender, and Diana
Trilling are cases in point.

CHAPTER THREE

Theory and Practice
Will-less Autobiography? Althusser, Skinner, and Barthes

In the previous chapter I argued that much thinking about the will in the modern period has been ambivalent and indeed deeply conflicted. Though we like to think of the great prophetic figures of cultural late modernity—Nietzsche, Marx, and Freud—as champions of human emancipation, their intellectual positions are in many respects profoundly deterministic. Where they are not deterministic, they are often contradictory, since any commitment they may have to various forms and degrees of human freedom must conflict with their deterministic presuppositions. Nor does the situation improve in the decades that follow. Sartrean existentialism appears to affirm the will, yet in conceptual terms, at least, that which is affirmed is puzzling and lacking in substance. The analytic philosopher Gilbert Ryle, whose thinking bears clear similarities to behaviorist psychological theory, repudiates the concept of the will. Postmodernism as expounded by Derrida appears to deconstruct the concept of will, or perhaps to eviscerate it in the play of deconstructive deferral.

It is one thing to deny the will (or its freedom) in theory, but can such denials be sustained when one narrates one's life-story? That is the question posed in this chapter. I shall consider three enormously influential figures, each of whom reflects aspects of the views outlined in the last chapter: the French structuralist Marxist Louis Althusser, one of the central figures in postmodern literary theory; B. F. Skinner, the most famous and influential of behaviorist psychologists; and Roland Barthes, the French intellectual whose intellectual phases included a commitment to poststructuralism. Qua theorist, each of these denies the will or its freedom; but each also wrote extended autobiographical works. Taking these figures in turn, I shall first discuss what they have to say about the will in theoretical terms, and then see what happens when they pick up the autobiographical pen. Here again, I aim to give a philosophically framed account of autobiography and its engagements with the will.

I. Althusserian Theory: Structuralist Marxism

Althusser's relationship with structuralism, and with post-Saussurean theory in general, is a complex matter. While at times he denied his affiliation with the movement,[1] it is clear that he has close affinities with it in at least four respects:

his rejection of humanistic conceptions of the individual self; his preoccupation with scientific analysis and discourse; his strong methodological focus on structures; and a particular synchronic conception of social formations. To the extent that Althusser talks about the will, the following passage is characteristic:

> In ideology men do indeed express, not the relation between them and their conditions of existence, but *the way* they live the relation between them and their conditions of existence: this presupposes both a real relation and an "*imaginary,*" "*lived*" relation. Ideology, then, is the expression of the relation between men and their "world," that is, the (overdetermined) unity of the real relation and the imaginary relation between them and their real conditions of existence. In ideology the real relation is inevitably invested in the imaginary relation, a relation that *expresses* a *will* (conservative, conformist, reformist or revolutionary), a hope or a nostalgia, rather than describing a reality.[2]

Ideology is, then, a "second degree relation":[3] it is a story that depicts and rationalizes; but what it depicts and rationalizes are not the real relations that people have with their world (say, the actualities of economic exploitation), but rather the relations they have as a consequence of the false beliefs they hold about their relations with their world. Ideology mediates and saturates our sense of our place in the world—so much so, in fact, that there is no place "outside" ideology from which we can view our situation. In part, this is because "man is an ideological animal by nature" whose very subjectivity is constituted in and by ideology: "*The category of the subject is only constitutive of all ideology insofar as all ideology has the function (which defines it) of 'constituting' concrete individuals as subjects.*"[4] So, if I myself am an ideological product, my consciousness cannot (wholly?) transcend ideology. And this applies not only to class-bound societies, but to all societies whatsoever, since "man is an ideological animal." There are, however, two partial exceptions to this rule: "authentic" (in other words, truly distinguished) art that puts us in a particular relation to knowledge and helps us to "*see*" something that "*alludes* to reality";[5] the other is science. Science "may well arise from an ideology, detach itself from its field in order to constitute itself as a science,"[6] thereby creating a capacity to impact upon ideology in some significant way. According to Althusser, Marxism is one such science—indeed, along with Freudianism, it is *the* science par excellence. One of Althusser's most influential contributions to Marxist scholarship is to claim that there is an "epistemological break" between early and later Marx[7] and to claim the later, and allegedly definitive Marx, as the greatest antihumanist prophet of late modernity. So conceived, he claims scientific Marxism can help map certain features of social formations; it can even help map some of the contours of ideology itself.

That ideology is said to be "overdetermined" is further evidence of Althusser's other great debt—to Freud. Althusser uses the term, as Freud sometimes does, to mean a configuration that results from various kinds of causes, where none of these is sufficient to explain the configuration on its own.[8] Among other things, this means that a social formation cannot be said in any simple sense to arise from determination by the economic "base," though Althusser does say that the base determines "*in the last instance.*"[9] (One of the impressive features of Althusser's position is that like the later Marx and Engels, and like Trotsky, he posits a relation of "relative autonomy"[10] between base and superstructural phenomena such as art.) In place of the simple dualistic model of base and superstructure, he proposes a model comprising various mutually impacting and impinging levels. This is his notion of "metonymic" or "structural" "causality," where "structures" and their "effects" react upon one another in such complex ways that there is a sense in which the structure (or "cause") is actually immanent in its "effects." In *Reading Capital,* he puts it thus:

> This implies therefore that the effects are not outside the structure, are not a pre-existing object, element or space in which the structure arrives to *imprint its mark:* on the contrary, it implies that the structure is immanent in its effects, a cause immanent in its effects in the Spinozist sense of the term, that *the whole existence of the structure consists of its effects,* in short that the structure, which is merely a specific combination of its peculiar elements, is nothing outside its effects.[11]

Althusser refers to the notion of structure described here as "decentered structure."[12] Unlike Hegel's notion of totality, in which the essence of the whole is expressed in each of its parts, this one has no transcendent controlling dimension. There will be temporary and uneven patterns of "dominance" and "contradiction," and certain permutations will produce the possibility of radical social transformation, but there can be no stable dominant perspective. Importantly, "*contradiction is the motor of all development*"[13]—"contradiction" and not agents, then, make history. Hence Althusser's famous notion of history as a process "*without any locatable subject.*"[14] So what is the status of the "subject" in all of this?

Several points here. One is that the decentered notion of structure is accompanied in Althusser's writings (as it is in much poststructuralism) by a decentered notion of the subject: since the subject is constituted in and through ideology, and since ideology is necessarily and inescapably false, the subject does not have access to authentic modes of knowing, being, or even striving. Thus the will, for instance, is "expressive of" an "imaginary relation"—a misleading sense of one's real relation to the "real." The will, then, is trapped inside ideology; it is congenitally inauthentic. People are also trapped in the sense that they occupy positions and "functions" within a system that determines and fixes them: "The structure of the relations of production determines the *places* and *functions* occupied and adopted by the agents of production, who are never anything more than the occupants of these places, insofar as they are the 'supports' of these functions."[15] This support role for the subject shows—if such a demonstration were needed—that Althusser's account is a strange and intractable version of event causation. As Anthony Giddens has argued, Althusser offers no real account of agency. In Giddens's words: "Althusser's agents are structural dopes of . . . stunning mediocrity."[16] Giddens also argues that the Althusserian model repeats one of the cardinal limitations of structuralism in failing to distinguish adequately between the "structures" (in Giddens's terms, virtual structural properties of a social system) and "system" (the lived practices of the social entity),[17] and he points out that the absence of an agent in the theory is both a symptom and a cause of this deficiency: it is agents who translate virtual properties into practices and who react back upon and change those properties.[18] More of this in the next section. Such criticisms are not restricted to non-Marxist commentators. Writing of Althusser, Ted Benton enters the following complaint from the standpoint of a phenomenological, humanist Marxism: "The abandonment of humanist Marxism means the breaking of the bond through which that tradition linked Marxist theory, the subjective experience of historical actors, and their transformative action."[19] Another way of putting (part of) this would be to say that Althusser has severed the connections between experience, subjectivity, will, and action.

II. "THE TORN UNITY OF DESIRE": ALTHUSSER AS AUTOBIOGRAPHER

1. *After Such Silence*

Louis Althusser wrote two autobiographical works. The first, *The Facts*,[20] written in 1976, concludes with the protests in Paris of 1968. It is a pained but lucid narrative that sets out, among other things, some of the "facts" of his unhappy childhood and his later battle with manic-depressive illness. But the most sensational of the unhappy "facts" of his life is necessarily missing from this volume: it was in November 1980 that Althusser, apparently in a delusional state, strangled his wife, Hélène. John Sturrock has aptly characterized this incident as "an opaque act of will."[21] On account of his mental condition at the time, Althusser was exempted from entering a plea. He spent the next two years in institutional care. In 1985, after some further periods of institutionalization, he wrote his extended autobiographical narrative, *The Future Lasts a Long Time*. "Alas," he tells us here, "I am no Rousseau" (p. 29). Indeed he is not; but in terms of tortured exhibitionism, the sheer anguish and the scale of internal conflict reported (he writes of "the endless pain of being alive" [p. 157]), Althusser's autobiography loses nothing by comparison with Rousseau's. Even Althusser's horrific centerpiece—the murder of Hélène—is reminiscent of the most macabre of Rousseau's "confessions": his abandonment of his five children. *The Facts* and

The Future Lasts a Long Time were published posthumously in 1992, Althusser having died of a heart attack in October 1990.

The Future Lasts a Long Time covers much of the "factual" ground up to 1968 with which the first volume deals, but its mode and its motivation are very different. The mode is far more agonized and the style correspondingly more uneven. As Althusser tells it, the motivation for writing is principally to redress the silence that occurred as a result of his not having his day in court. Unlike the convicted criminal who says his piece, serves his time, and is then free to resume some semblance of his former life,[22] Althusser has not told his side of the story and has had to suffer misrepresentation by some sections of the press. He wants to "intervene *personally* and *publicly* to offer my own testimony" (p. 18) and to achieve, rather as Rousseau seeks to do in *The Reveries of a Solitary Walker,* what he calls "*a definitive state of anonymity*" (p. 210)—the state in which there is nothing more to discover because the autobiography has told it all. This is his way of resuming his former life:

> I again seek, in a somewhat paradoxical manner, *a definitive state of anonymity*; not the anonymity afforded by the fact I was declared unfit to plead, which was like a tombstone over me, but by publishing all there is to know about me, thus putting an end to further requests for me to be indiscreet. This time journalists and other media people will have had their fill, though you will see that they will not necessarily be satisfied. First, because they will not have done any of it for themselves, and secondly because they will have nothing to add to what I have written; not even commentary, because I have provided my own!! (pp. 210–11)

II. *Paradoxes and Contradictions*

Paradoxical is an apt adjective for this narrative: notwithstanding Althusser's theoretical commitment to the view that "truth" is entombed in impenetrable layers of ideology, this autobiography, like the earlier one, appeals constantly to an empirically verifiable notion of the "facts." Paradox is also apparent in what is perhaps the narrative's organizing binary: that between agency and passive submission to fate. To "intervene *personally* and *publicly*" is to take a decisive role in shaping opinions and events that might flow from them. Yet such agential activity sits uneasily with Althusser's theoretical understanding of the subject as a "support"[23] for ideological structures, just as his determination to tell his own factual story seems to conflict with his theoretical claim that the subject is necessarily inauthentic because it is trapped in an "imaginary relation" to the real— "a relation that *expresses a will*" that is not and cannot be his or her own.[24]

The passive, will-less part of the binary assails the reader at the outset as the narrative begins with Althusser's recollection of the murder. The scene is like something out of Poe, Hoffman, or, better still, Camus or Robbe-Grillet. Althusser wakes up in his dressing gown at the foot of the bed in his and Hélène's flat:

> The grey light of a November morning—it was almost nine o'clock on Sunday the sixteenth—filtered through the tall window to the left, on to the end of the bed. The window was framed by a pair of very old Empire red curtains which had hung there a long time, tattered with age and burnt by the sun.
>
> Hélène, also in a dressing gown, lay before me on her back.
>
> Her pelvis was resting on the edge of the bed, her legs dangled on the carpet.
>
> Kneeling beside her, leaning across her body, I was massaging her neck. I would often silently massage the nape of her neck and her back. I had learnt the technique as a prisoner-of-war from little Clerc, a professional footballer who was an expert at all sorts of things.
>
> But on this occasion I was massaging the front of her neck. I pressed my thumbs into the hollow at the top of the breastbone and then, still pressing, slowly moved them both, one to the left, the other to the right, up towards her ears where the flesh was hard. I continued massaging her in a V-shape. The muscles in my forearms began to feel very tired; I was aware that they always did when I was massaging.
>
> Hélène's face was calm and motionless; her eyes were open and staring at the ceiling.
>
> Suddenly, I was terror-struck. Her eyes stared interminably, and I noticed the tip of her tongue was showing between her teeth and lips, strange and still.
>
> I had seen dead bodies before, of course, but never in my life looked into the face of someone who had been strangled. Yet I knew she had been strangled. But how? I stood up and screamed: "I've strangled Hélène!" (pp. 15–16)

Immediately we see that the whole issue of agency and fated passivity in this autobiography is massively complicated by the specter of insanity. The murder description has Althusser's hands commit the strangulation, but against his will. He is moved by an irresistible force that, though psychologically internal to his being, has the impact of sheer, brute externality. Madness here functions as a cause—a form of event causation. It is madness that "makes" him kill her.

However, this picture is fascinatingly complicated by the narrative's account of the status and etiology of the "madness" in question. This account is, like everything in the book, somewhat equivocal: it veers between a medicalist account of his illness (he suffered perhaps fifteen severe depressions and attempted suicide on at least one occasion), which sees his manic-depression as a biochemical violation of his organic integrity, and a psychoanalytic explanation, which traces his illness to psychological causes in his familial history. Of the two, the psychoanalytic dimension is the most prominent. Indeed, when Althusser announces the nature of his intended project in the narrative, he gives the reader to expect a psychohistory of the self: "I give notice that what follows is not a diary, not my memoirs, not an autobiography. In discarding everything else, I simply wanted to remember those emotional experiences which had an impact on me and helped shape my life; my life as I see it and as others may, I think, see it too" (p. 29). (If Veasey's translated "shape" may be a little strong, Althusser does nevertheless use the *passé composé* of the verb *marquer*—*ont marqué* [*p. 25*]—to suggest a substantial causal relationship between past and present.) Again, he tells us that he is writing "the 'genealogy' of the emotional traumas of my psyche" (p. 192). In this view, the murder of Hélène might be read as the product of unconscious causation.

The phrasing is interesting: "helped shape" (or *mark*) and "genealogy" both suggest something less than a full determination of the psyche by its emotional history. Still, that history is presented as extraordinarily powerful. Indeed, echoing the title of his most famous—and a thoroughly deterministic—essay, "Ideology and Ideological State Apparatuses," Althusser declares that the "Family" is "the most powerful ideological State apparatus" (p. 105). But what exactly does this mean? Clearly the family as a social institution bears affinities with some other social institutions, like, for instance, the legal system. To this extent, the family can be said to be shaped by and subject to various ideological forces. However, *The Future Lasts a Long Time* is a deeply Freudian (and Lacanian) book, and, as one might expect of such a work, it sees the family as far more than merely a social construction. In this account—a version that is not sustained by biographical research[25]—the Althusser family is the very stuff of primordial Freudian family romance, replete with a castrating mother, an intimidating father (who bears some resemblance to two other fathers who will appear in this study: those of Stephen Spender and Arthur Koestler), and a feminized son who as an adult manifests all manner of resultant angers, conflicts, and neuroses and who projects mother-hatred onto other women. If it is always hard to draw the line between social-ideological and primordial causation in the case of family dynamics, it has to be said that Althusser's autobiography is especially unclear about any such distinction. And to the extent that it is unclear about this, it is necessarily unclear about Louis-as-subject, since he is held to be a causal casualty of the family itself.

The majority of autobiographies discussed in detail in this book exhibit some Freudian influence, but *The Future Lasts a Long Time* shares with Diana Trilling's volume *The Beginning of the Journey* the distinction of being what might be termed a constitutively Freudian life-narrative. By this I mean that an essentially Freudian understanding of the psyche not only infuses the book's general understanding of what the self—and this self in particular—is like, but that both the self that is fashioned in the narrative and the self that has allegedly been fashioned in "life" are to a great extent the products of the experience of psychoanalysis. This is hardly surprising given that both authors sought psychoanalysis in part to overcome phobias. So Althusser's and Trilling's autobiographies are mediated at several levels by Freudianism[26] and, among other things, this mediation shapes the depiction of significant others in their lives—that de facto biographical activity that goes on in all autobiography. Take the depiction of Althusser's mother, for instance.

Mme. Althusser is like a Grimms' tale stepmother writ large (he even spent some of his childhood in forested regions of Algeria). She may love him in her way (p. 53), but what she offers is less a love than a kind of semi-intentional deprivation. The mother had been engaged to Louis's uncle—also called Louis—but had accepted his father's hand in marriage when the uncle was killed during the First World War. The young Louis is convinced that the mother never really loved *him;* that her love was for her fallen fiancé and that he, the son, was a mere and even a resented intermediary between mother and the true beloved: "When she looked at me, it was not me she saw, but *another person,* the *other* Louis" (p. 53). And in a passage that echoes throughout the book:

> In my case, death represented a man my mother loved more than anyone else, more than me. In her "love" for me, something chilled and marked me from earliest childhood and determined my fate for a very long time. It was not a phantasy but the very *reality* of my life. That is how phantasy becomes real for every individual. (pp. 53–54/*p. 48*)

The verbs *marked* [*m'a marqué*] and *determined* [*fixant*] again suggest that the self is the helpless victim of circumstance; yet here again, there is a kind of escape clause: "for a very long time" implies that the determinative history of the self is not for *all* time; that the processes of receding causal efficacy set in, either because the history in question loses determinative power over time, or because the self-as-agent finds ways of breaking its history's hold, or both. If the past lasts a long time, so too—as the book's title insists—does the future. And the future, it would seem, holds out the promise of freedoms that the past would not allow.

This indeed proves to be Althusser's claim. But before freedom is allowed a look in, the mother gets one of the great autobiographical goings-over from the oedipally impaired son. He does not doubt that as a breast-fed baby he had an erotic bond with his mother (p. 55), and his early stature in the oedipal triangle was assisted by the fact that his mother never really loved, and was indeed (according to Louis) sexually traumatized by, his father. The son, then, should have won an easy victory—except that all such victories are hard because they block individuation; and except that in this case the son was the recipient of love actually intended for another—the other Louis. Louis experiences—or at least recollects—this maternal emotional misidentification in appalled and appalling terms. Like her, he is the victim of a debilitating and annihilating sexual ravishment: "I had been raped and castrated by my mother, who felt she had been raped by my father" (p. 51). This particular comment refers to one of a series of emasculating episodes: the mother pulls back the boy's sheets and pointing to semen stains says, "'Now you are a man, my son!'" (p. 51). However reliable or otherwise these memories may be, the humiliation of it all still rankles with Althusser at age seventy-three, as do other such occurrences. The resultant rage at the mother (see for instance pages 138–39) is quite ferocious, and these incidents are allocated a fearsome causative power in the narrative, at least until it reaches the late stages of his life. When as a result of his relationship with Hélène he finally feels that he achieves adult individuality, there is a ghoulish note of triumph over the mother: "At last I had my revenge on my mother! I was a man" (p. 130). (Incidentally, the mother was alive and apparently reasonably alert in a nursing home at the time, though Louis insists that she showed virtually no interest in him.)

The most grievous consequence that he imputes to such episodes, and to his mother's flawed love in general, is that it compelled in him a sadomasochistic patterning with women in which he overcompensated for sadistic rage at emotional deprivation (real or imagined) by needing to "seduce" and serve the woman in question. Here the Althusser of the autobiography takes his place in a French tradition of sadomasochistic love that includes the troubadour poets, Baudelaire, Mallarmé, Robbe-Grillet, Ricardou, Roussel, and others—a tradition that is not without its own cultural kudos and that has its own protocols of self-disclosure. Of the "contradiction" involved in being loved in lieu of another, Althusser says: "Clearly, the only means I had of escaping this 'contradiction' or ambivalence was to *seduce* my mother (as one might seduce a stranger one met) so that she would look at me and love me for myself"(p. 55). I want to come back to the all-important phrase "for myself" presently. But let's note here some of the life consequences that Althusser adduces from this need to seduce: these include an almost compulsive philandering (a trait he shares with Arthur Koestler); a refusal of sexual experience that might compromise the oedipal bond until the age of twenty-one; an experience of sexual nausea so powerful that after he first sleeps with Hélène, he suffers the first of his major and devastating depressions: he recalls that "a far more violent and deep-seated feeling of repulsion gripped me, which was much more powerful than my own will [*plus forte que toutes mes résolutions*]" (p. 124/*p. 116*); a repetition of the sadomasochistic pattern in his long relationship with Hélène (he says of first meeting her: "I was filled with a powerful desire to serve her . . . right to the very end, I never abandoned this supreme mission" [p. 116]); a body of intellectual work that owes much both in orientation and structure to the configuration of the oedipal bond; and—very importantly—a sense of something amounting almost to a spiritual challenge; a sense that he must overcome the past that constrains him, that he must learn to love in a way that his mother did not love him.

III. *Learning to Love*

The man who is "chilled and marked" by inauthentic love faces the most awful of human fates: that he himself will be inauthentic in love—a creature of "artifice" and "seduction" (p. 58) whose deepest connections with others are manipulative bids for existential validation through acknowledgment by the Other: "Inside, I was no more than someone consciously adept at orchestrating his muscles, and unconsciously and diabolically adept at seducing and manipulating other people, at least those whose love I sought" (p. 89).

In chapter 7 I argue that Stephen Spender's autobiography, *World Within World*, explores similar fears and that, like Althusser, he sees the problem as deeply implicated in a certain flawed condition of the will. Althusser is quite explicit in his belief that the coldness, castration, and feminization he suffered in his relationship with his mother consigned him for many years to an inauthentic mode of loving that was also an inauthentic modality of the will. In his adolescent diary he cites "the will to power [*volonté de puissance*]" above secret declarations of love for a girl called Simone:

> Each day [I] started a new page by summoning the "will to power," an expression I had picked up somewhere and which gave me the resolve to escape from the void I was in and to assert myself by means of a hollow will [*d'une volonté vide*] which could not take the place of what nature had given me. (p. 91/*p. 83*)

The boy who is not loved "for myself" has no self, and thus no affective will, with which to love others—so the claim goes: "It seems that my mother's impersonal love, directed not towards me but through me to someone who was dead, made it impossible for me to exist in my own right or in relation to another person, especially if that other person was a woman. I felt powerless or impotent in the full sense of the word" (pp. 136–37). He recalls feeling "deprived of my physical and psychological being" and asserts that if "a part of you is removed, thus permanently denying your wholeness as a person, you can legitimately refer to it as a form of amputation, of castration therefore" (p. 137). In this condition he is capable not of love, but only of "*l'unité déchirée du désir.*" Veasey renders this as the "fractured unity of desire" (p. 285/*p. 278*); however, *déchirer* pertains particularly to the tearing or shredding of fabric, the implication in Althusser's context being that the self is a kind of threadlike weave compromised by trauma. I have underscored this implication in my title for this section.

"Your wholeness as a person"—what is this beacon of bourgeois humanism doing in the autobiography of the most famous antihumanist Marxist theorist of the era? Well, it is no aberration. On the contrary, *The Future Lasts a Long Time* is dominated by such "bourgeois humanist" discourses of the self and its intersubjective modes. Thus does Althusser ask the cardinal question: "How does one de-fine the ability to love?" (p. 137). And here, at some length, is his reply:

> An individual must have a sense of wholeness as a being and of his "potency" [*puissance*], though not merely for the sake of pleasure or from an excess of narcissism. On the contrary, he must be capable of giving fully, positively, and without weakness. In the same way, to be loved is to be capable of being seen and accepted as a free agent in one's giving [*reconnu comme libre en ses dons mêmes*], so that the gift is "transmitted," or finds its way, to the other and elic-its in response another act of giving from deep within. Being loved is precisely the free exchange of the gift of love. But if one is to be the free "subject" and "object" of this exchange, one must, as it were, be able to initiate it. One has to begin by giving wholeheartedly, if one wishes to receive a similar or even greater love in return (this exchange is quite the opposite of a utilitarian cal-culation). Obviously, one needs to be an entirely free agent if one is to do this, with one's physical and spiritual integrity undamaged. (pp. 137–38/*p. 129*)

This is an astonishing passage in all sorts of ways. The traces of a Marxist (and indeed Rousseauian) view are there in the notion of a "free exchange," and no doubt Althusser would argue that such exchanges are most likely to occur in "a human community purged of all market relationships" (p. 240)—his definition of communism. However, the emphasis here on the free human agent, the sub-stantial self who gives and receives from some sort of core of authentic being, the enormous qualitative and ethical emphasis on profound intersubjective ex-change—all of these things reflect a view that is a far cry indeed from the im-personal, agent-less theory of Althusser the Marxist philosopher. Unlike Warren Montag, I cannot read in such passages the "voice" of "materialist inspiration."[27] And there is this further qualification: *The Future Lasts a Long Time* does not claim that learning to love depends on the decimation of ideological state appa-ratuses or of possessive-capitalistic ideology in general. What it reports is a painful, gradual, but ultimately (we gather) availing process of learning to love in a social world that, qua theorist, Althusser sees as inimical to such spiritual-psychological developments. He reports that around 1975 he was "finally be-ginning to understand what loving meant" (p. 245). The "fractured unity of de-sire" is becoming whole again.

iv. *Psyche and Theory*

Of the ideological state apparatuses, including the all-powerful family, that have shaped his life, Althusser writes: "I am surprised I have been unable to do with-out them in understanding what happened to me" (p. 30). Why he should be surprised is not clear: after all, it is entirely consistent with his theoretical posi-tion, according to which such "apparatuses" determine the subjectivity of indi-viduals, that such "violent organisations" (p. 30) should play a dominant role in the narrative. This apparent inconsistency underscores the complexity of the relationship between Althusser's Marxist theory and his practice as an autobiographer. In fact—and this is one of the fascinations of the book—he himself is much exercised by this issue. He describes himself as "the author of a body of philosophical work which was abstract and impersonal, but passionately concerned with the self" (p. 170). He notes that even some of the dominant structural motifs in his theorizing derive from structures in his psychological history. Hence the suggestion that the epistemological "break" that he detected between Marx's early and later writings derives from his (Althusser's) tortured separation from his mother (p. 174). He even announces:

> What I really want to discuss . . . is how I came to invest and inscribe my objective, public activities with my subjective phantasies (this is not a matter of lucid reflection but something obscure and largely unconscious). (p. 160)

This skeptical intellectual honesty is arguably one of the great virtues of *The Future Lasts a Long Time*—unless like Sturrock one sees this dimension of the book as a devilishly disingenuous appeal for sympathy.[28] Not even Althusser's own most cherished theoretical presuppositions are immune from the suspicion of occluded and covert motivation. And the same applies to his political activities; he sees his maverick role within the Communist Party as a reflection of his three dominant fantasies: "solitude, responsibility, mastery" (p. 197).

So where, in his eyes, does this leave his theoretical writing? The answer is by no means clear. Some passages in *The Future Lasts a Long Time* reaffirm foundational theoretical claims. Thus, for instance, the doctrine of history as a "process without a subject"[29] is reiterated: "The course of history is determined not by the attitudes of individuals but by class conflict and class positions" (p. 195). In his theoretical writings this idea entails that, like history itself, the individual subject is "decentered." Yet, as I have suggested, the authorial subject in the autobiography does not seem to reflect this view. On the contrary, what we find there is a multidimensional subjectivity, tortured, certainly; but also intent upon understanding and transcending its own suffering. Its highest aspiration is to be an emotional-spiritual agent, a free and loving giver and receiver of gifts. Althusser's Catholicism is very much in evidence in this dimension of the book—much more so than his Marxism.

Understand and transcend: these imperatives throw out a dual challenge to his theoretical position. In order to understand, one must do what his theory sees as impossible: First, one must achieve discursive penetration of the layers of ideological obfuscation that characterize one's imaginary relation with the world and get to the "stark reality" (p. 224) that lies beyond ideology. This he seeks to do in the autobiography. Second, one must assert a highly personalized form of the will—a modality that has no place in the theory. In Althusser's case this involves various processes, including a redirection of the will away from "the will to *self-destruction*" (p. 277) and toward a more integrated, untorn state of the self. Such redirection may go on in and be more suited to certain particular political contexts, but in *The Future Lasts a Long Time* it is not seen as being itself a political matter. Nor is the book's discourse of personal salvation through love presented as being reducible to political processes. There is a manifest gap throughout between what we might as well term the *political* and the *personal dimensions*.

Yet both dimensions play a part in the causal account that is offered. This account is another version of Althusserian overdetermination according to which phenomena have multiple causes, none of which is sufficient on its own to bring about the outcome in question. There are three principal modes of causation in *The Future Lasts a Long Time.* Two of these are instances of event causation: Althusser's organic predisposition to mental illness, and the ideological state apparatuses that so damage him. But the third has to do with agent causation: Althusser here credits the human individual with a will that can transform even the most tragic and unpromising personal materials. And in the overall configuration of the book, it is this cause that prevails, notwithstanding the "endless pain of being alive." So causation here is not "metonymic"; the will is a mover not an effect. He tells us that this position derives (at least in part) from Spinoza's account of *conatus* (p. 242)—a modality of willing that fuses body and soul.

The preeminence of will is arguably the most striking aspect of Althusser's legacy as an autobiographer. Could it be accounted for in terms of the theoretical writings? We recall that he made two exceptions to the dictum that human beings could not cut through ideology to the real: one was science; the other was great art. Clearly autobiography is not a science. But is it art in the sense he meant when he granted it the status of an exception to the rule? No doubt it can be. It is in the case of his beloved Rousseau. Yet he is the first to acknowledge that he is no Rousseau. This is not great autobiographical art. *The Future Lasts a Long Time* is the self-disclosing narrative of a man who wishes to make an archetypal journey—from a torn to a unified state of being; from a life in which the threads seem to be woven from without to one in which the self does much of the weaving. He tells us that at "sixty-seven . . . I feel younger now than I have ever done" (p. 279). The wish is itself predicated on an understanding of selfhood that Althusserian antihumanist theory cannot accommodate; and the narrative draws upon understandings of human inwardness without which Western autobiography can scarcely be written.

III. SKINNERIAN BEHAVIORISM:
A "SCIENCE OF HUMAN BEHAVIOR"

B. F. Skinner's views about the will are given pithy expression in one of his later works, *About Behaviorism:*

The conditions which determine the form of probability of an operant are in a person's history. Since they are not conspicuously represented in the current setting, they are easily overlooked. It is then easy to believe that the will is free and that the person is free to choose. The issue is determinism. The spontaneous generation of behavior has reached the same stage as the spontaneous generation of maggots and micro-organisms in Pasteur's day.[30]

Though not the father of behaviorism—that honor rests with John B. Watson—Skinner is its doyen, and several of his principal ideas are captured in the passage just quoted. What he is after is a "science" of behavior that will see behavior as a "lawful scientific datum";[31] in other words, as something that, like all other natural phenomena, is law-governed and susceptible of prediction, once—and to the extent that—the laws in question are known. This scientist vision renders the human individual as an "operant" (an organism whose behavior is to be studied); hence its common designation as "operant behaviorism." The study of the human organism's behavior is conducted according to two foundational beliefs: that behavior is, and must be seen as, a reaction to, and an engagement with, some environmental setting,[32] and that the organism in question does not have the properties of an agent in any developed sense. The existence of an agent as "strong evaluator" is inconceivable in Skinner's view of the world. This fierce opponent of Descartes rejects all "mentalistic"[33] explanations of behavior, and indeed the entire dualistic premise that there are separate realms of mind and matter. Mentalistic explanation is predicated on the spurious belief in an "inner man" from whom behavior "emanates": "The function of the inner man is to provide an explanation which will not be explained in turn. Explanation stops with him. He is not a mediator between past history and current behavior, he is a *center* from which behavior emanates."[34] Such a view, he thinks, belongs back with Pasteur and the maggots, and it is from the blight of mentalistic explanation that behaviorism promises to rescue us. It can show, for instance, that behavior is not freely chosen, but rather the upshot of the individual's history, a history comprised of "aversive," "neutral," and "reinforcing" experiences, otherwise known as environmental "contingencies."[35] To cut a long and category-spawning story short: the organism will repeat behaviors that its history has found to be positive (reinforcing) and avoid ones that its history says are negative (aversive). Though it is easy to miss the historical antecedents in "the current setting," a science of behavior knows that they are there and can reconstruct their lawful operation under laboratory conditions. Since humans are not generally available for such research, other organisms—principally white rats—are used; but this is not a problem because the "lawfulness" of nature will emerge in the study of any natural organism.[36]

As some of his titles show, Skinner is among the most confronting of modern writers on—or rather against—the will. *Walden Two,* the title of his utopian novel of social engineering, is a calculated affront to a cultural imagination suffused with reverence for personal freedom; but the most confronting title of all is *Beyond Freedom and Dignity,* a book that implores us to shed our attachment to the inner and "autonomous"[37] man and, with it, our commitments to the associated notions of "freedom" and "dignity." Since the issue of dignity is not central to Skinner's writing, I will leave it aside and consider the more pivotal matter of freedom. In one of the wide-eyed conversations that make up the majority of *Walden Two,* Frazier, the mastermind behind the utopian Walden Two community, explains:

> "That's the source of the tremendous power of positive reinforcement—there's no restraint and no revolt. By a careful cultural design, we control not the final behavior, but the *inclination* to behave—the motives, the desires, the wishes.
>
> "The curious thing is that in that case *the question of freedom never arises.*"[38]

In other words, if the organism's environment is engineered in the right way, it (or he or she) will only want to do what is best for it (or him or her) and for the group as a whole. (Little is said about how conflicts between personal and collective interests might be resolved.) Freedom can only be an issue if something you want to do is blocked by a constraint. For Skinner, then, freedom means absence of constraint. This is why he rejects the charge that behaviorism sees a human being as an "automaton."[39] For him, the fulfillment of an engineered wish is freedom. Skinner also refutes the claim that he denies the complexity of human behavior. Our activities are complex all right, but this doesn't mean that we're free: "Since human behavior is enormously complex and the human organism is of limited dimensions, many acts may involve processes to which the Principle of Indeterminacy applies. It does not follow that human behavior is free, but only that it may be beyond the range of a predictive or controlling science."[40] In a similar vein on the will: "Self-determination does not follow from complexity."[41] Statements such as these seem to suggest that Skinner does not want to deny that we have inner "mentalistic" states; he simply wants to suggest that such states are not susceptible of observation (and of corroboration by other observers), and that they can therefore have no part in the "science" of behavior. Nevertheless, the stridency of his antimentalistic rhetoric often reveals a hostility to "mentalistic" notions per se, and whatever his final view on the matter, the rhetoric has had a major impoverishing impact on modern conceptions of the human agent and of a whole range of inner phenomena that are identified under descriptors such as the "will." Not least of the problems here is that Skinner sees the very *will to freedom* so precious to proponents of the open society as itself causally determined: "Man's struggle for freedom is not due to a will to be free but to certain behavioral processes characteristic of the human organism, the chief effect of which is the avoidance of or escape from so-called 'aversive' features of the environment."[42] So it is not just freedom, but the very sentiment of freedom, that is under attack; and it may be that such repudiations of "will" reflect a Conceptual Denial position with respect to the will. At the very least, Skinner's account of "behavioral process" amounts to a radical and unqualified determinism.

For those of us who find the entire mind-set of Skinner's work utterly bemusing, a useful clue might lie in a remark in *Contingencies of Reinforcement*, where he argues that to resist cultural engineering is "to leave further changes in our culture to accident, and accident is the tyrant really to be feared."[43] Leaving aside the question as to how "accident" can happen in a law-governed world, it is clear that Skinner's entire project is motivated by a kind of horror of the accidental, and that the chaos that can be wrought by a fully endowed, capricious human agent is not just methodologically, but psychologically, antipathetic to him. Interestingly, he shares with modern thinkers who in other respects would loathe his entire scientist outlook a belief that there is no such thing as a unified human "self": "The concept of a self may have an early advantage in representing a relatively coherent response system, but it may lead us to expect consistencies and functional integrities which do not exist." And a little further on: "If the environment of which behavior is a function is not consistent from moment to moment, there is no reason to expect consistency in behavior."[44] So "we" are whatever we are at a point in the history of "our" environmental stimuli; as the stimuli change so do "we." Skinner, then, espouses a radical causal determinism. Agency does not function as a cause. Nevertheless, he thinks that there is one sense in which "the individual does appear to shape his own destiny." Skinner explains: "He is often able to do something about the variables affecting him."[45] Like the cultural engineer, the individual organism can act on his or her environment in ways that will change the contingencies that act on him or her. To this extent some measure of self-control, self-scripting even, is available to us. After all, the moment-to-moment "self" is the ideal candidate for change.

Skinner's belief in the organism's capacity to act effectively upon its environment is by no means consistent. In *Beyond Freedom and Dignity*, he writes that "it is the environment which acts upon the perceiving person, not the perceiving person who acts upon the environment."[46] Here some of the many massive philosophical—and, importantly, commonsense—objections to Skinner's project come into view. Another quotation will help sharpen the point:

> When a man controls himself, chooses a course of action, thinks out the solution to a problem, or strives toward an increase in self-knowledge, he is *behaving*. He controls himself precisely as he would control the behavior of anyone else—through the manipulation of variables of which behavior is a function.[47]

This passage construes activities such as thinking, striving (a form of willing) as cases of "*behaving*." Most of us would agree with Skinner on this point. The catch is that Skinner does not agree with himself: his assault on mentalistic accounts says

that we must bracket out activities like thought and willing that are not susceptible of observational description under the rubric of behavior. But what is "behavior"? For Skinner's enterprise to have any real validity, it must be possible to draw
a firm line between allegedly nebulous "inner" happenings and discernible external acts. But any such line is notoriously hard to draw, not least, as the above passage shows, for Skinner himself. Further, most of what we want to know about
human beings (as distinct from rats) as social and individual "organisms" arises
from and requires attention to those features that make us distinctively human:
our "inner" lives and selves, our complex consciousnesses. A Skinnerian social science, which aspires to leave this dimension out, is a contradiction in terms.

On the will again, we need to ask a question of a more pragmatic kind. Who
does the social engineering, and how? Two points here: One, those who do it
would need to have all the attributes of developed, discriminating, deliberative
agency. They would need to be strong evaluators. Yet in Skinner's account nobody
is like this. Two, aspirants to the big engineering jobs would embody a will to
power whose political dangers are all too familiar. Skinner associates the threat of
nuclear war, the Holocaust, and other such catastrophes with the realm of the "accidental" that he so fears.[48] For him, control is the answer. Those of us who dis-
agree see in his denial of will, agency, complexity of selfhood, combined with a
naive faith in control, a recipe for the repetition of the great tragedies of the twentieth century.

Can anyone actually experience the world, be a self, in the manner that Skinner's project would suggest? How does this denier of freedom of the will write his
own life? Where does introspection, for example, fit in this antimentalistic view
of the world? It is rather typical of Skinner that he does not in fact repudiate introspection with anything like the antimentalist fervor that his rhetoric and theory would require. In *About Behaviorism* he warns that we cannot be guaranteed
that self-knowledge that comes through introspection will be "accurate" because
"we are not always watching what happens when we behave"; nevertheless, it is
"important to examine the reasons for one's own behavior as carefully as possible
because they are essential, as I have said, to good self-management."[49] So there
definitely *are* "reasons" and other such inner phenomena; what's more, we must
penetrate and take account of such things if we are to manage ourselves through
managing the variables that shape us. But this is just what, inter alia, Skinner's
"science" won't allow. If not the "science," then perhaps the autobiography?

IV. "The Autobiography of a Nonperson": B. F. Skinner and Behaviorist Autobiography

1. A "Behavioristic Proust"

On the penultimate page of his massive three-volume autobiography, B. F. Skinner writes: "If I am right about behavior, I have written the autobiography of a

nonperson."[50] Skinner, of course, is supremely confident about his account of behavior; so we can conclude that in his view he has indeed written an autobiography of a "nonperson." We can further conclude that this is what he set out to do.

Such an autobiographical aspiration might sound postmodern and, as we have seen, Skinner's account of the self as decentered and lacking the characteristics of a persisting entity is reminiscent of certain postmodern views. However, this is about where the resemblance ends: Skinner's manner of self-narration is fundamentally conventional—much more so, indeed, than either his scientific or his "literary" rhetoric would suggest. The rhetoric is boldly encapsulated in his three autobiographical titles, each of which suggests that his narrative is, as it were, governed by the scientific laws whose discovery the narrative seeks to document. *Particulars of My Life* suggests a specific set of determinative "contingencies" that have rendered this life unique (at least in some ways). *The Shaping of a Behaviorist* appears to shift the focus from the particulars to the processes whereby life's contingencies do their determinative work. *A Matter of Consequences* refers to life outcomes, but, as per the theory, these consequences are said to flow from effects of environmental shaping of the self, not from developments that have their origin in subjectivity or individual agency. To write as and of a "nonperson" would suggest that Skinner the autobiographer, like Skinner the scientist, wants to delete the mentalistic from human descriptions, to construe the autobiographical subject as operant:

> I am sometimes asked, "Do you think of yourself as you think of the organisms you study?" The answer is yes. So far as I know, my behavior at any given moment has been nothing more than the product of my genetic endowment, my personal history and the current setting. That does not mean that I can explain everything that I do or have done. I know more about myself than about anyone else, but it is still far from enough. Nevertheless, I have tried to *interpret* my life in the light of what I have learned from my research. (*MC*, p. 400)

Skinner knows himself not by introspection but by observational induction and law-seeking, law-governed analysis. His relationship to himself is, purportedly at least, one of pure externality. Carlyle's characterization of Mill's *Autobiography* as the "autobiography of a logical Steam-engine"[51] might seem apt for Skinner, who spends large tracts of his narrative on the minutiae of professional life, who proclaims that "I . . . do not think feelings are important" (*MC*, p. 399), and who aspires to be "a sort of behavioristic Proust" (*SB*, p. 16).

However, the first title of the series alerts us to another, and in some respects competing, facet of the Skinner persona. The lines on which the title is based are Prince Hal's, speaking to Falstaff: "Do thou stand for my father and examine me upon the particulars of my life."[52] The use of a Shakespearean reference reflects one of the volume's central preoccupations: its account of Skinner's intense early literary ambitions and of how they set the scene for his eventual re-pudiation of the literary life in favor of science. These particular lines are care-fully chosen, because, like Shakespeare's play, Skinner's first volume focuses heavily on a father-son relationship: the father, a demanding but emotionally needy small-town lawyer; the son Frederic (1904–1990), a would-be prodigal who dreams of literary fame but later achieves professional renown as a Harvard academic, cultural prognosticator, and self-appointed social engineer. It is a suc-cess that threatens and undermines the father's already fragile self-esteem, even as it completes the task that the success-hungry father had taken on.

But to speak in this way is surely to trespass on territory that would be strictly off-limits in an autobiography that really was about a "nonperson," if by this we understand a human entity that can be understood without reference to the kind of reflective consciousness that enables it to possess an identity. Skinner may want the behaviorist resonance of "particulars" to predominate in his use of the Shakespeare quotation, but inevitably its psychological implications come powerfully to the fore. Inevitably because, even in a work like this, which is often leached of the subjective, one cannot write autobiography without engaging, however reluctantly, with a world of psychological nuance, notation, allusion, explanation—in other words, with that "mentalistic" world that, qua theorist, Skinner rejects. Proustian behaviorist autobiography is a contradiction in terms, a psychological and generic impossibility. Hard though he tries, Skinner cannot wholly rid his text of introspection. However, the attempt yields some interest-ing ruses: "Can I tell you what I really think of myself? I can at least offer some objective evidence. In many of my notes I record my failures and mistakes, and the explanations are never excuses. In 1966:

> I do not admire myself as a person. My successes do not override my short-comings. Last night at dinner Babs Spiegal said that I was the one person she knew who had not been changed by success. This morning I thought of a quip: 'Yes, I was impossible *before* I was successful.' (*MC*, p. 410)

That he does not "admire himself as a person" is an understanding that, in the first instance, can only come from introspection. The fact that introspection yields a personal jotting that in time assumes the status of "evidence" for some kind of pseudo-objective research into the self is irrelevant. The jotting too is a form of autobiography; it becomes incorporated into the more elaborated auto-biography Skinner later writes; but no mysterious process intervenes to convert the interiority of introspectively garnered insight into the "objectivity" of evi-dence. This technique of making inwardness appear to metamorphose into be-havioral data figures prominently in Skinner's autobiography, especially in the final volume. It is quite simply a form of narrative sleight of hand.

Skinner thinks that he has probably committed "intellectual suicide" by writ-ing his autobiography: "By tracing what I have done to my environmental history rather than assigning it to a mysterious creative process, I have relinquished all chance of being called a Great Thinker" (*MC,* p. 411). But this, I suggest, is not where the real risk lies. What really threatens his status as a Great Thinker here is the inevitable revelation that the narrative rendering of human lives, be they other lives or one's own, cannot proceed without a powerful "mentalistic" dimension. And this fact says a great deal not just about narrative, which after all reflects the structures of human experience, but about the very nature of the human "organism."

ii. *Feeling and Dispassion*

In an interview Skinner says of tragic incidents like his brother's death at the age of sixteen in 1922: "I tend to take major things of that kind without any emotion, yet I think I am an emotional person. When something happens I accept it."[53] Even allowing for the fact that the comment was made in the last year of his life when he was dying of leukemia, it is typically unsatisfactory and puzzling. Skinner's entire account of feeling suffers from a conceptual fuzziness that fails adequately to distinguish between four (and perhaps more) questions: Do we in fact have feelings? If we do, can we know anything about them? If so, can we report upon them? Again, if yes to the above, are feelings to be understood as the causes of what we do, or merely as responses to external causal contingencies? I have quoted one of Skinner's characteristic repudiations of mentalistic explanation of behavior. He attacks the view that "the function of the inner man is to provide an explanation which will not be explained in turn. Explanation stops with him. He is not a mediator between past history and current behavior, he is a *center* from which behavior emanates."[54] His rejection of this position would suggest that though we may have feelings (a fact that he does not of course deny), they cannot be said ultimately to be determinative of what we do. They themselves are environmentally determined. Explanation can only stop with the environment, and we learn about this through observation of it and through observing the ways in which human beings behave in response to it. It would also follow that, insofar as it seeks to know and report on such feelings, autobiography is at best a grand humanistic illusion.[55] At worst a con. The underlying question here is ontological: Does the human being possess spontaneous causal power? If she or he does, then prima facie, there is reason to suppose feelings cannot be implicated in the operations of such power. And this could apply even if feelings are in some sense externally caused. In all his writings, Skinner mistakenly assumes that questions about how feelings function can be settled by explaining how they are caused.

Unlike Althusser and Barthes, Skinner does not seriously inquire into the psychological roots of the existential orientation that finds expression in his theories. This indeed is one of the great—albeit predictable and in some ways apposite—limitations of his autobiography. He is in some respects a reflective autobiographer, but where it matters most, reflection is often suppressed—indeed, one suspects, repressed. This is not to say, however, that feelings don't find their way into his pages. At times of course they do, and indeed *Particulars of My Life* is a quite deeply felt book in which the world he grew up in and the people with whom he shared his early life are often lovingly evoked. And Skinner, once the would-be man of letters, *can* write. This of himself at age six: "And so the years passed, and I became aware of their passing" (*PML*, p. 32); and of his father: "Life was to abrade him, to wear him down. He struggled to satisfy that craving for a sense of worth with which his mother had damned him, but forty years later he would throw himself on his bed, weeping, and cry 'I am no good, I am no good'" (*PML*, p. 38). The phrasing of this is typically deterministic, indeed fatalistic: the father has been "damned" by certain maternal attitudes, and from these contingencies certain consequences are said inevitably to flow. The father could not have been other than he was.

The relationship between feeling and fatalism is a key to Skinner's autobiography. This is how he describes his reaction to his brother's childhood death from what appears to have been a massive cerebral hemorrhage:

> I submitted to that tragic loss with little or no struggle. At one moment on a fair Sunday morning [his parents had gone to church] I was telling my brother about my college experiences . . . and fifteen minutes later he was dead. There was nothing I could do. It was Alex Clark who called the doctor, and when he came, I could only stand by and watch. The doctors who performed the autopsy asked me about the symptoms, and I described among other things the rather strange way in which my brother vomited—with no coughing or retching. They told my father that my objectivity was helpful. With the same objectivity I had watched my parents as they reacted to the discovery that my brother was dead. (*PML*, pp. 209–10)

The dispassion here may in part be a shock reaction to the sheer enormity of the event, or perhaps a defensive reaction against the event's power to hurt. Skinner's explanation—that he submits because there is nothing to be done—links dispassion, fatalism, and passivity. And he records similar feelings about the death of his maternal grandfather (he writes with more, though by no means abundant, feeling about the death of his parents). But the numbness he records—and indeed almost flaunts—on these occasions is not reflective of the autobiography as a whole. In fact, he recalls many pleasures—in music, success, sex, intellectual inquiry, parenting. There is also a good deal of pain, some of it, like the anguish he feels at his father's crushing sentiment of inadequacy, diffused throughout many hundreds of pages. He writes of his paternal grandmother's enormous "ambition" (*PML*, p. 9) and of how she passed this on to his father, yet he scarcely states what is surely obvious: that the damning legacy is passed on to him as a kind of oedipal patrimony that in turn fuels his own massive ambitions—ambitions so imperious that his career is marked by the maverick's acceptance of ridicule as a price worth paying for notoriety. So the issue is not whether he feels, or even whether feelings matter—he *does* feel ("Yet— yet—I am unhappy," he laments in one of those jottings that are supposed to function as mere objective research data in the autobiography, *MC*, p. 219); and the feelings are clearly important to him. The issue is what sort of feelings he has, what sort he acknowledges, and the kinds of determinative power that he imputes to these feelings.

An undercurrent in these volumes of which he seems unaware is the fear that one might not be able to feel, or to feel enough, or that the presumed objects of one's feelings might not be real. Skinner would appear to have been highly narcissistic, and it may be that like many narcissists he was privately— perhaps unconsciously—haunted by the tenuousness of his emotional ties to the world. One of the most striking things about *Particulars of My Life* is the frequency and openness with which he refers to his youthful autoerotic activities. A reading of the complete autobiography certainly suggests that he had reason to be haunted. One example: he devotes many pages of *The Shaping of a Behaviorist* to the years of the Second World War, yet there is remarkably little about the war itself or the atrocities that were taking place. Most of his retrospective attention is focused on a project he designed, which was to train pigeons to guide bombs to enemy targets. There is much about the project; even more about the cool reception he received from the military bureaucracy. But not a lot else. Now and again, the fear of failing adequately to feel rears its head. Here too he tends to defer to quoted notes, like this one about Julie, the elder of his two daughters. Having not seen much of her in recent years (he was a devoted father), he reflects: "It is almost as an abstraction that I love Julie so dearly" (*MC*, p. 222). This is not of course to say that the narcissist does not feel—he or she does; rather that his or her relationship to feeling, and its patterns of connection to others and to the world, may be highly complicated. This, I suspect, is the case with Skinner; but, though trained as a psychologist (he taught some subjects in clinical psychology), he cannot bring himself to look squarely at such matters. Instead as both scientist and autobiographer, he pursues a vast fiction of impersonality, and a part of this fiction is his ostensible denial of the power of the will.

III. *The Spinners Know Better*

Skinner's autobiography echoes his scientific denial of the will in various ways. Sometimes he quotes earlier formulations of his own, as in notes he made for an attack on C. I. Lewis's *Mind and the World Order* (notes that again confuse questions of genesis and function): "'Instinct' and 'will' are describable simply as changes in the response to a given stimulus. They are not things which cause changes" (*SB*, p. 117). Then there is his constant use of behaviorist terminology when narrating all aspects of his and others' behavior, even the most apparently "private" kind. On his relationship with Julie again: "How much has her behavior reinforced mine? How much has reinforcing mine meant to her?" (*MC,* p. 222). He also spends a good deal of time on his disputes with Chomsky, Joseph Wood Krutch, Carl Rogers, and others who rejected his deterministic account of behavior. With obvious pleasure he quotes (*MC,* p. 122) from a poem that John Hollander wrote after a widely publicized debate between Skinner and Rogers. Hollander's playful poem construes the debate about the will in terms of Atropos, her sisters, and the threads of life:

> I once saw Dr. Johnson in a vision;
> His hat was in his hand, and a decision
> Of import on his lips. "There is," he said,
> "Free Will, and there's an end on't." All the same,
> Atropos and her sisters, overhead,
> Grinned at this invocation of their name.[56]

In Skinner's view, someone who holds a belief in the freedom of the will is merely doing so in response to some stimulus. (Logically the same must apply to a view like his own, but he does not seem to think that this impugns the authority of his position.) Though the literary encouragement he so cherished from Robert Frost was based on his short stories (*PML,* p. 248), Skinner also wrote poetry into his early adult years. One of his poems is entitled "Hymn to Labor, or Action as the Solution of Doubt." The poem, which is quoted in *Particulars of My Life* (p. 284), is undistinguished, but it is of interest in that it appears in the section where he narrates a period of indecision about his future, and in which he recalls being blighted by some of the inertia that so often characterizes adolescence and early adulthood. The essentially conventional nature of Skinner's autobiography is again apparent here: he writes in the mode of a *Künstlerroman* about the phase in which he moves back home after college and tries to become a writer. Here again, he draws upon jottings done at the time. The tone of some of these is deeply, indeed self-indulgently, introspective: "But why should I despise the things I attain? Is it because I am secretly conscious of my inferiority and feel that if I achieve a 'great' thing I must have been mistaken as to its greatness?" (*PML,* p. 282). The dominant theme of these musings—as in some of Althusser's self-characterizations and in Stephen Spender's youthful diary entries—is the fear that one has no effective will, that one is trapped in a kind of will-less state: "I see clearly now that the only thing left for me to do in life is to justify myself for doing nothing" (*PML,* p. 283). Yet, in the same notebook passage he says this: "We must make use of our knowledge and intellect to choose those desires which will give us (in the sum total) the greatest pleasure" (*PML,* p. 282). So there is the idea of fatalistic resignation and passivity, on the one hand, and of choice, on the other.

This portrait of the artist as a young man ends with a repudiation of art. Looking back, he realizes: "The truth was, I had no reason to write anything. I had nothing to say" (*PML,* p. 264). Such moments of candor do occur in these volumes, though like this one they tend to be associated with Skinner's need for notoriety and self-dramatization. When it comes to the really important question of why and how he made the decision to abandon writing for science, the narrative is much less informative. Not least of the problems is that under the pressure of issues that might really threaten his deterministic premise, his prose plunges into utter conventionality: "I was floundering in a stormy sea and perilously close to drowning, but help was on the way" (*PML,* p. 298). That help in question is a discussion by Bertrand Russell of John Watson's work. Skinner reads Russell (and then Watson) because he feels conflicted about his life direction. We might see his reading of such material as a choice he makes, but, looking back, Skinner sees it as a response to stimuli and as a fortuitous visitation from the realm of accident in which life takes place: "help was on the way." There are begrudging glimpses of his inner processes at the time: he thinks that he has been pursuing his interest in behavior in the wrong place (literature), and that science was the new "art form" of the twentieth century (*PML,* p. 291); he writes of his having "turned rather bitterly" against literature (*SB,* p. 90). But neither the nature of that turning nor the reasons for its bitterness are properly explored. Skinner would say that this is because the causes of these changes were environmental and because he received aversive conditioning when he tried to write and reinforcing conditioning when he read Watson. But that is too simple. The deafening silence at the center of these volumes concerns the decision he makes to become a scientist; the way that, following his period of will-lessness, the scientific vocation engaged, fired, and then sustained his will.

In fact, as his notebook notion of choosing certain "desires" shows, the will is actually always present as a covert power in Skinner's work. It is there in the very notion of social engineering in which we choose to change the world in certain ways so that it will condition us in the most desirable fashion. Such a choice is consistent not only with the existence of the will, but with a will that is at least partially free. Choices so conceived are contrary to Skinner's intermittent conceptual denials of the will and to his avowed determinism. The will is there, too—though he tries to deny it—in the autobiography when he says that "we control the world around us, but only because that world has taught us to do so and induces us to do so" (*MC,* p. 407). He claims that "the main course of my life was set by a series of accidents" (*MC,* p. 400). And in a sense this is true for everyone. But Skinner's horror of the accidental results in a rage for objective observation, prediction, and control; a rage that cannot bear to speak its own emotional origins, and that cannot acknowledge the most frightening and potentially capricious power of all—the power that attends the partial freedom of the human will.

V. Barthesian Poststructuralism and the Subject

Roland Barthes's career as a theorist-critic moved through various phases, including structuralist and poststructuralist ones. Like Derrida, Barthes often characterizes human behavior in terms of language use and reception; indeed in the highly rarefied world of Barthes, reading becomes the quintessential human activity. His celebrated short essay "The Death of the Author" pictures the reader, as structuralism generally pictures the subject, not as an agent but as a conduit for externally imposed and constituting processes: "The reader is the space on which all the quotations that make up a writing are inscribed without any of them being lost . . . the reader is without history, biography, psychology; he is simply that *someone* who holds together in a single field all the traces by which the written text is constituted."[57] In *S/Z*, a work that marks his transition from structuralist to poststructuralist modes, Barthes says this of subjectivity: "Subjectivity is a plenary image, with which I may be thought to encumber the text, but whose deceptive plenitude is merely the wake of all the codes which constitute me, so that my subjectivity has ultimately the generality of stereo- types."[58] The self, then, is both empty and inauthentic: empty because constructed and directed from without; inauthentic because, textlike, it is made up of quotations, stereotypical bits of cultural material. It is not so much a divided as a fragmented self.

The following passage from the "autobiography" I discuss in the next section is as good an introduction to Barthes on the self as any:

> For classical metaphysics, there was no disadvantage in "dividing" the person . . . quite the contrary, decked out in two opposing terms, the person advanced like a good paradigm (*high/low, flesh/spirit, heaven/earth*); the parties to the conflict were reconciled in the establishment of a meaning: the meaning of Man. This is why, when we speak today of a divided subject, it is never to acknowledge his simple contradictions, his double postulations, etc.; it is a *diffraction* which is intended, a dispersion of energy in which there remains neither a central core nor a structure of meaning: I am not contradictory, I am dispersed.[59]

He goes on to liken the—his—self to a "disintegrating statue" and to see it as an unclassifiable thing, drained of substance, split between incommensurable tendencies and selves: "You are at one and the same time (or alternately) obsessive, hysterical, paranoiac, and perverse to the last degree (not to mention certain erotic psychoses)."[60] It is not surprising that *Roland Barthes by Roland Barthes* is an autobiography whose protagonist often seems passive, vulnerable, a subtle sensibility in a murderously insistent world. The dispersed self is bereft of will. But can autobiography be so bereft?

VI. Dispersing the Enticements of the Imaginary: "Roland Barthes" on "Roland Barthes"

The line between autobiographical and other modes of writing is notoriously hard to draw, but in the case of Roland Barthes it is even harder than usual. While some of his early semiological writings read like detached cultural analysis, other semiological pieces such as those collected in *Mythologies*[61] give quite personalized expression to Barthes's spectacularly ambivalent attitude to the ideological systems of his day. *A Lover's Discourse,*[62] a later work, does not explicitly offer itself as autobiography, yet it operates in a generic zone that includes elements of autobiography, fictional autobiography, the diaristic register of Gide's and Stendhal's journals, and much else. It is fitting that in this instance the line should be so hard to draw because Barthes repeatedly denied that any such line could be more than a fictional demarcation. Yet here some qualification is necessary. His last book, *Camera Lucida,* seems to endorse the possibility of representational "truth"[63] with respect to the subject and to impute to the self a developed, humanistic sense of interiority[64]—features that are consistent with some sort of substantial demarcation between autobiography and other forms of writing. However, *Roland Barthes by Roland Barthes,*[65] published in 1975, reflects the contrary view: the "self" under discussion here is very much the "plenary" self of the post-Nietzschean Barthes.[66] It is, ostensibly at least, a self without a stable "core" of interiority and without any stable relation to the "real." Here too the narrative mode combines elements of autobiography, fictional autobiography, journal, but also the aphoristic modes of Montaigne, Pascal, Nietzsche, and Kierkegaard, and the estranging theatricality of Brecht.

1. *Doxa and Paradox*

Barthes defines *Doxa* as "a popular opinion" (p. 71). It is his version of the natural attitude, the taken-for-granted construction of the world (or some part thereof) that as an avant-garde intellectual he subjects to "a transgressive avant-garde action" (p. 131); in this instance, to a particular kind of defiant but dazzling cultural critique. His aim is nothing less than "the *decomposition* of bourgeois consciousness" (p. 63), the very bastion of the natural attitude. For him *Doxa* is linear, the heir to Enlightenment rationalism: it is hedged about with institutional protocols; policed by generic, stylistic, and epistemological prescriptions and proscriptions; driven by social agendas to which it will not, cannot, admit. *Doxa* is the ethos of the "stereotype" (p. 90). Barthes's style (a mode composed of many styles) is scandalously antithetical to all of this: freewheeling, lateral, transgressive, veering between and conflating "private" and "public" discourses, fired by an elaborately cultured anger that suspects and seeks out agendas at all levels of cultural discourse. It reproaches those subjects of the natural attitude who are "*unwilling to let go of a stereotype* [*faute de lâcher un stéréo-type*]" (p. 90/*p. 93*).

The converse of *Doxa*, and perhaps the dominant trope of *Roland Barthes by Roland Barthes*, is "paradox": "a *Doxa* . . . is posited, intolerable; to free myself of it, I postulate a paradox" (p. 71). And when paradox hardens into *Doxa*, as it is wont to do, it too must be subjected to the deconstructive energies of paradox. This process—posit-negate-posit-negate—amounts to a kind of open-ended dialectic. Because the process is unending, no postulation can ever be "*the last word*," and this applies no less to the self in autobiography than to anything else. *Roland Barthes by Roland Barthes* "is not a book of 'confessions'" (p. 120), because to confess is to come to some relatively settled understanding of what one's life history has meant, of how it might be characterized within particular normative and representational parameters. In this sense, according to Barthes, "the art of living has no history" (p. 50)—a resounding denial of the Aristotelian tradition of ethics. The deconstructed subject is not subject to, nor interpretable in terms of, mere temporality. Its plots, then, cannot simply be the linear plots of traditional autobiographical narrative. *Roland Barthes by Roland Barthes* proceeds by a "double" movement: the "*straight line*" and the transgressive, atemporal "*zigzag*" (p. 91).

Drifting is another signature Barthesian trope. Drifting is central to "his" life rhythm (he has an "irenic preference for drifting [*le goût irénique de la dérive*]" [p. 102/*p. 106*]). Drifting is also what, in this poststructuralist view, the signifier does: it doesn't lock onto signifieds in any stable way; it floats free, opening out (theoretically at least) interminable possibilities of meaning. It follows for Barthes, as for Derrida, that texts will in some ultimate sense be constitutively interminable; and since both *Doxa* and paradox are for Barthes texts themselves, they too will evince the qualities of shifting interminability. This would suggest that there could be no stable, ascertainable meaning for either of these entities, nor (therefore) any stable or ascertainable relationship between them. In fact, Barthes is not prepared to fully endorse this analysis-annulling implication. While *Doxa* (and so paradox as a kind of reaction formation) will manifest differently in different times and places, particular times and places permit descriptions of at least partially and temporarily determinable relations between *Doxa* and paradox, and between *Doxa* and the "self" that practices paradox's deconstructive critique. Thus, the demarcation of "'private life'"—that central category for the traditional post-Augustinian autobiographer—"changes according to the *Doxa* one addresses" (p. 82).

However, even if a given relation between *Doxa* and, say, a "self" is relatively stable, and even if as part of that relation the "self" in question has internalized certain *Doxic* social prescriptions regarding what a self is or should be like, it does not follow that the resultant "self" is in any sense a "true," or *the* "true," self. Of course Barthes draws precisely the opposite conclusion: the *Doxa* narrative of self is intrinsically false; the "self" that internalizes such narratives is therefore, again intrinsically, an inauthentic "self." If there is such a thing as authentic selfhood (let us leave this question open for the moment), it could only come to one who is prepared to "*let go of the stereotype*" and to use paradox (among other things) to dismantle the *Doxic* narrative. This means that "autobiography," whether written down or as an intrinsic movement of consciousness, must function according to a deconstructive logic in which "self" at once represents and decomposes itself.[67] Writing has to be a kind of suicide that annuls earlier stories of the self. Thus under the heading "The book of the Self," Barthes writes:

> His "ideas" have some relation to modernity, i.e., with what is called the avant-garde (the subject, history, sex, language); but he resists his ideas: his "self" or ego, a rational concretion, ceaselessly resists them. Though consisting apparently of a series of "ideas," this book is not the book of his ideas; it is the book of the Self, the book of my resistances to my own ideas; it is a *recessive* book [*livre récessif*] (which falls back, but which may also gain perspective thereby). (p. 119/*p. 123*)

Here again, there is the suggestion of some kind of provisional relation between self and its milieu; but even as it intimates the existence of such a relation, the passage neutralizes this characterization by depicting the "self" as constantly emergent from and subject to its own self-deconstructions. Of all the intellectual autobiographers I consider in this book, Barthes's relation to his own "ideas" is—if we are to believe his rhetoric—the most suspicious. *Roland Barthes by Roland Barthes* wants to recast the old confessional trope of the disclaimer such that it obtains for all aspects of the self and its awarenesses of the world, be they past, current, or prospective. As John D. Barbour shows in his study of autobiography and "deconversion," this is a highly implausible view of personal transformation.[68] What then *is* this "self" whose susceptibility to *Doxa* requires that autobiography be above all else an act of self-resistance?

II. *Echo Chambers and Mirrors*

To the (limited) extent that one can characterize this self in terms of origins, it seems to have three modes of origination. One is *Doxa* itself: the "self" becomes a "self" by internalizing cultural narratives and modes of emplotment that prescribe the nature of selfhood. A second, which is inextricably connected with the first, is language. Though "Theory" itself is subjected to deconstructive critique in *Roland Barthes by Roland Barthes* (see, for instance, page 54), the book nevertheless presents an account of certain features of selfhood. Like Derrida's account quoted in chapter 2, this one ascribes a central role to language. "Barthes" asks:

In relation to the systems which surround him, what is he? Say an echo chamber: he reproduces the thoughts badly, he follows the words; he pays his visits, i.e., his respects to vocabularies, he *invokes* notions, he rehearses them
under a name; he makes use of [*il se sert de*] this name as of an emblem
(thereby practicing a kind of philosophical ideography) and this emblem dis-
penses him from following to its conclusion the system of which it is the signifier (which simply makes him a sign). (p. 74/*p. 78*)

The echo chamber is one of several metaphors of self-constitution that appear
in this text. It figures the "self" as a space in which *Doxic* materials, couched as
they are in language, reverberate. To some (but what?) degree, these linguistic
materials actually constitute the "self." Without them it is silent, undifferentiated, void of all being. So conceived, the echo chamber would seem to be a shell-
self; a radically contingent mode of being. Yet this isn't ultimately what the passage is saying. It actually gestures at (*describes* would be too strong) a relation
between language and consciousness that is at least partially agential in character. Consciousness seems to be able to intervene in the sign system: it "makes
use" of the "emblem," for instance; and in so doing it subverts, at least to some
extent, the determinative power of the "system." The "self" is not merely a
"sign"; like the signifier, it drifts, and *drifting*—a problematic verb in this instance—is here taken to be a kind of freedom, as in Mallarmé's "*divigations.*" So
there is an intimation of authenticity about this "self."

But reverberation is an unconvincing—no doubt a tactically unconvincing—
way of figuring authenticity. Reverberations start somewhere, somehow; but
they then take on a life of their own, rebounding in an intentionless space, echoing echoes, progressively replacing intended meanings with accidental accretions
of unintended meaning, distorted, overlaid, randomized. An echo is inauthentic. Something similar holds for a visual image that accompanies this auditory
one in *Roland Barthes*: the image of the mirror. *Roland Barthes by Roland Barthes*
means "Roland Barthes" as he appears to himself in the mirror of (linguisticized)
self-consciousness; however, self-consciousness is echo chamber–like in that representations don't just emerge from one surface: they are reflected and refracted
off an infinite set of mirrors, ad infinitum. Barthes avails himself of the fact that
the French *réverbérer* applies to both auditory and visual phenomena:

> The title of this series of books (*X by himself*) has an analytic bearing: *myself
> by myself?* But that is the very program of the image-system! How is it that the
> rays of the mirror reverberate [*réverbèrent*] on me? Beyond that zone of dif-
> fraction—the only one upon which I can cast a glance, though without ever
> being able to exclude from it the very one who will speak about it—there is
> reality, and there is also the symbolic. (p. 153/*p. 155*)

As this passage makes clear, the Barthesian mirror is a version of the Lacanian
mirror: that diffracting "zone" in which the "self" endlessly promulgates and re-

produces the identity-conferring stories it tells itself. The "program of the image-system" is the later, symbolic, articulation of that set of identity-sustaining stories that the child, having first glimpsed what it unconsciously knows to be a spuriously complete image of self in the mirror, produces to deflect recognition of its "fragmented body."[69] Lacan's "mirror stage" is, then, the autobiographical paradigm par excellence for Barthes. Autobiography is in this view a radically specular mode. This is what Barthes means when he says that "the vital effort of this book is to stage an image-system [*mettre en scène un imaginaire*]" (p. 105/*p. 109*). This form of staging does to the image-system what Brechtian theater seeks to do to bourgeois ideology: it makes it strange so that the dishabituated reader/viewer can subject image-system/ideology to rigorous analysis. Barthes has already asserted that "*in the field of the subject, there is no referent*"; that "the pronoun of the imaginary, '*I*,' is im-pertinent"; and that "I myself am my own symbol, I am the story which happens to me" (p. 56). Elsewhere he identifies the subject of his own mirror story as the "deconstructed" (p. 168) subject. Like *A Lover's Discourse*, *Roland Barthes by Roland Barthes* is composed of what purport to be fragments (an indication of how aspects of Romanticism lurk at the heart of the postmodern), many of which have intertextual resonances. In order to underline their subversive distance from conventional autobiographical protocols of self-disclosure, both books arrange their fragments according to one of the most primitive and "ordinary" codes of all: alphabetical order. One might add: according to one of the most innocuous codes of all, since both books are motivated (at least in part) by a horror of the "specter of Totality" (p. 60). Like Koestler, Spender, Beauvoir, and Diana Trilling, Barthes uses autobiography as a means of resisting and responding to what he takes to be the culture of totalitarianism.

His most pressing motivation, however, is to use autobiography to enact a textual "dispersing [of] the enticements of the imaginary" (p. 86); in other words, to strip back the layers of the "self's" psychogenetic myths of consolation. Precisely what this is to achieve is arguably not clear, since in this conception the "self" has no core that might be reached by ridding it of its layers of auto-deception. He concedes that "it is an illusion to suppose that by breaking up my discourse I cease to discourse in terms of the imaginary about myself"; and that "by supposing I disperse myself I merely return, quite docilely, to the bed of the imaginary" (p. 95). The assumption seems to be that the open-ended processes are a good in and of themselves; that they should be embraced even in the absence of any teleological "real" that they might arrive at; perhaps that open-endedness, play, are the activities of consciousness par excellence; and that in pursuing these ideals, consciousness is creating its own freedoms.

But Barthes offers a further, if rather occluded, justification for his use of "autobiography" as an occasion for the deconstructive "staging of image-systems." This justification takes us back to the (provisional) relation between *Doxa* and consciousness. The mirror phase apparently inaugurates both a set of consoling images and a rapacious, unconscious need for more such images. That need is met, albeit incompletely and destructively, by the *Doxa*: it provides spurious accounts of self that arm the ego in its efforts to fend off intimations of psychic and ontological discontinuity. Some of these images perform the further role of misrepresenting to the subject its relation to the structures of power and ideology in which it is embedded. In this sense, Barthes's notion of the imaginary also draws on Althusser's conception of the "imaginary." Indeed the Barthesian imaginary can be read as fusing Lacanian and Althusserian conceptions, while at the same time incorporating some of Barthes's own elaboration of the concept.[70] The psyche is, as it were, primed to internalize the myths of culture. The act of internalization takes place at various levels, most dangerously at the level of the unconscious—a level that on this account is constitutively linguistic. The "*decomposition* of bourgeois consciousness" amounts, then, to a version of the return of the repressed: by staging ideology's saturation of consciousness in a deconstructive narrative, "autobiography" avowedly reverses that saturation, rids the unconscious of the inauthentic narratives of self that lead, in this Lacanian view, to neurosis and, in the Althusserian view, to ideological subjection. This leaves many questions unanswered: What is left of the unconscious if the stories that constitute it are decomposed? Why, if no story is any truer than any other, should a set of replacement images be more conducive to psychic health or political emancipation than the ones they have replaced? What kind of psychic health or political agency can arise from the deconstructive mode of consciousness here envisaged? And so on. Such questions are for more general assessments of the Lacanian position. I turn now to Barthes on the will.

III. *The Willfulness of the Other*

Barthes is with Rousseau, Hegel, Marx, Sartre, Blanchot, and Ricoeur in believing that one cannot "begin to write without taking oneself for another" (p. 99). The autobiographical consciousness is divided into the speaker and subject of the narrative; consciousness appears to itself in the guise of the Other. In this account of negativity, it might be said that a crisis ensues that calls upon—or perhaps even produces—the will. Some power of consciousness is needed to undertake the autobiographer's characteristic imperative of trying to reunite speaker and subject, the self that writes and the self that is written. *A Lover's Discourse* is a marvelous inquiry into, and evocation of, the anguish of Self in its alienation from the Other. Barthes writes brilliantly of the inordinate and desperate ends that the Self will go to in order to reverse—or even just survive—that alienation. Among many intertexts he uses for the fear of abandonment that the Self suffers in the absence of the Other are the *chansons de toile*—later courtly versions of popular songs that appear to have been sung by spinners, sometimes lamenting the absence of their husbands:[71]

It is Woman who gives shape to absence, elaborates its fiction, for she has time to do so; she weaves and she sings; the Spinning Songs express both immobility (by the hum of the Wheel) and absence (far away, rhythms of travel, sea surges, cavalcades).[72]

As the reference to "Myth" following this confirms, the Barthesian intertext extends to the archetypal resonances of the spinner: like Beauvoir in *The Second Sex,* Barthes identifies the spinner as a figure with a gendered history in patriarchy. The spinner may lament the absence of the Other, but it is she who fashions the narrative that lures the Other into the illusory belief that he is free, that his life is the product of his own unconditioned will. Just so, in the Barthesian view, the autobiographical subject-as-Other lives in blissful innocence of its utter dependence on the determinative writerly will of the author. In this intertextual hall of mirrors, chamber of echoes, the writer (for which read *consciousness* itself) is in turn dependent upon the texts of Others: "one copies a role," and Barthes's copy is above all else of Gide's *Journals* (p. 99).

So stated, Barthes's "autobiographical" world might seem to be a substanceless realm of mere simulacra. Mirrors and chambers refracting, texts quoting texts, and so on, ad infinitum. Yet, as I have suggested, the world of *Roland Barthes by Roland Barthes* is not wholly devoid of agency. Self can achieve a degree of resistant distance from—discursive penetration of—the code, and John Eakin is surely right to discern in the text an insatiable "elemental hunger for presence."[73] Here Barthes's repeated emphasis on writing *"through the body"* (p. 80) is important: the body's unique experiential susceptibilities resist the omnipotence of the cultural sign.[74] In Barthes's case, of course, the body has this additional transgressive signification: it is a homosexual body. His classification of this sexuality as a "perversion" (p. 63) captures that word's dual favorable implication (while implicitly repudiating its condemnatory one): it suggests something that is both transgressive and willful. The emphasis on the body is also part of the anti-Cartesian stance of the book, as in the passage I quoted above where Cartesian dualisms are rejected in favor of a dispersion model of the self in which its various features undergo "diffraction" (p. 143), endlessly reconfigured in open-ended forms and combinations.

Here Barthes adduces a problem he would see as a paradox, but that I am inclined to see as an unproductive contradiction. A model of the self as pure dispersion does not appear compatible with any cogent notion of agency. As one would expect of a writer as vastly sophisticated and self-conscious as Barthes, he is aware of the contradiction: "Lavish use of the paradox risks implying (or quite simply: implies) an individualist position" (p. 106). Why? Presumably because paradox in the form it takes here is something that someone *practices*. It does not arise from some merely passive submission to a metaphysical condition. Or does it? Sometimes Barthes would have us see it in just this way:

The book does not choose [*Le livre ne choisit pas*], it functions by alternation, it proceeds by impulses of the image-system pure and simple and by critical approaches, but these very approaches are never anything but effects of resonance: nothing is more a matter of the image-system, of the imaginary, than (self-)criticism. (p. 120/*p. 123*)

In effect, this jettisons the will from autobiography. All is reverberation, mirror, intertext. But it cannot be so. Where there is a text, there is what Barthes calls a "will to work [*envie de travailler*]" (p. 82/*p. 85*), and where there is a will—or a wish—there is an agent who is driven by a "will-to-intelligence [*vouloir-être-intelligent*]" (p. [30]/*p. 34*).[75] This too he will disclaim at times; he quotes one of his earlier works, *The Empire of Signs.*[76] "*No will-to-seize [vouloir-saisir] and yet no oblation*" (p. 59/*p. 64*). The "will-to-seize" is a version of Nietzsche's will to power. A book that ranges, as *Roland Barthes by Roland Barthes* does, from Nietzsche to Eastern mysticism, has room for a whole spectrum of states of the will, and perhaps too for certain notions of will-lessness. But this quotation, and the book in general, does not endorse a posture of mere passivity. Its notion of the self's "contract" (p. 59) with the world is more active, and I would say more Nietzschean, than this. The choice of the alphabet as a narrative schema is an act of will, as is the willing that is required to let go of the stereotype. There is a will to power behind the Barthesian fragments; a will to extend the influence of this way of being, this way of seeing. Barthes wants his deconstructed, dispersed, reverberating conception of self to prevail. His autobiography is willful in the sense both that it is transgressive and that it is infused by a quite steely, if enormously cultured, will, a will that constitutes a mode of existential authenticity. He will present himself as a "dandy" (p. 106), a "hedonist" (p. 43), and this indeed is part of the persona he so brilliantly projects in his "autobiographical" writings. But dandies and hedonists too are creatures of the will. They don't merely drift. The hedonist's will takes its counsel from a rational appraisal of the possibilities of pleasure. The Nietzsche who acknowledged the power of the will wrote eloquently about its Dionysian dimension.

CHAPTER FOUR

Moral Luck in Paris
Luck and Ethical Will in Hemingway's A Moveable Feast

where there is most of mind and reason, there is least chance, and where there is most
chance, there is there least mind.
—Aristotle, *Magna Moralia* (1207a4–6)

In the previous chapter I argued that the will is not so easily denied as its deniers
might have us think. It is one thing for a structuralist Marxist like Louis Althusser to produce a theory that repudiates the will, but another for him to write
an autobiography that sustains that repudiation. Similarly, B. F. Skinner can formulate a behaviorist account of the self that denies the will or its freedom, but
his autobiography clearly writes freedom of the will back into the picture. So too
does Roland Barthes's autobiography, though qua poststructuralist theorist he
seeks to deconstruct will and many of the conceptions of self that go with it. It
seems, then, that will, both as phenomenon and category, is deeply embedded
in the stories we tell; and if, as I believe, the stories we tell have deep structural
roots in the nature of our experiences, such narrative evidence for the will's presence—and indeed its power—cannot be lightly dismissed. But we should not be
surprised to find a degree of contradiction in much of what people write and say
about the will. After all, will, if it exists, is deeply implicated in how we see our
place in the world: in how far we think we can script our lives; in our sense of
human limitation; in various complex psychic structures that involve anticipation, wishing, fear, exertion of power, and so on; and in various aspects of the
lives we have as social beings. These are all complex areas of human experience.

The last of them involves, among other things, the perennially fraught issue
of morality. The drinker described in the preface to this book is inclined to say
that he has a will but that he lacks the power to control it in ways that might be
regarded as morally appropriate. He continues to drink in excess and does all
manner of human damage as a result. We might be inclined to say that he's
morally at fault for this, but he denies it: he believes himself to have inherited an
addictive personality. He believes that his will is powerless to do anything about
this. It's bad luck for those who share his disintegrating life. He wants to say that
in some sense it's a matter of bad *moral* luck that he can't do better. In this area
he just can't do the right thing. But what could this mean?

In the present chapter I discuss an autobiographical text that deals centrally
with the relationship between will, luck, and morality: Ernest Hemingway's *A
Moveable Feast*. I use the somewhat vague phrase "deals with" advisedly, because

this too is a work in which contradictory attitudes to the will run deep. Nevertheless, it is a work that helps to shed light on the kind of excuses that our drinker is inclined to offer.

Ernest Hemingway's Nobel Prize acceptance speech of December 1954 was typical Hemingway—brief, pithy, studiedly unsophisticated. Among his comments was this:

> For a true writer each book should be a new beginning where he tries again for something that is beyond attainment. He should always try for something that has never been done or that others have tried and failed. Then sometimes, with great luck, he will succeed.[1]

The linking of willing—or trying—and luck is also typical of Hemingway. At one level the Hemingway legend is very much about willing: about striving to be a great writer; about pitting the self against dangers that only willpower and courage can ostensibly overcome; about willing various heroic manifestations of the self—writer, big game hunter, drinker, lover, fighter—into being. There is about this writer, who so appealed to Simone de Beauvoir and Jean-Paul Sartre during their early existentialist phase,[2] something of the self-scripting, Nietzschean existential titan of the will. And yet, as any reader of Hemingway's fiction knows, this is not the whole story, because the world within which the Hemingway will is embedded, indeed the world that in a sense calls that will up, is one over which human beings have relatively little control. Frederic Henry's recollection of the plight of ants on a burning log in *A Farewell to Arms* is emblematic of a universe in which human trying seems to be of little avail:

> Once in camp I put a log on top of the fire and it was full of ants. As it commenced to burn, the ants swarmed out and went first towards the centre where the fire was; then turned back and ran towards the end. When there were enough on the end they fell off into the fire. Some got out, their bodies burnt and flattened, and went off not knowing where they were going. But most of them went towards the fire and then back towards the end and swarmed on the cool end and finally fell off into the fire. I remember thinking at the time that it was the end of the world and a splendid chance to be a messiah and lift the log off the fire and throw it out where the ants could get off onto the ground. But I did not do anything but throw a tin cup of water on the log, so that I would have the cup empty to put whisky in before I added water to it. I think the cup of water on the burning log only steamed the ants.[3]

If the ants are like us, Henry is like the Nietzschean god of late modernity who has died, withdrawn, or takes no interest in our fates. We are abandoned in a world that, though perhaps structured by remorseless laws that we can only guess at, strikes our uncomprehending consciousnesses as if it were a realm of pure chance. If you happen to be on that log, it's literally bad luck; your number is up. In this respect, however, Hemingway is not existential in temper: there is no assumption here, as there is in, say, *Being and Nothingness*, that our freedom, our chance to create our own meanings and modes of being in the world, resides in this realm of chance. The ants are figures from naturalistic, not from existentialist, fiction.

Perhaps worlds without messiahs do indeed make the greatest call on human heroism; but if such are beyond our control, and if the heroic will is therefore often unavailing, the nature of the will—its powers, limitations, and ethical bearings—must inevitably come into question. I want to suggest that such questioning goes on in Hemingway's autobiographical volume *A Moveable Feast*; that he is another writer who uses self-life-writing to explore the nature of the will.

A Moveable Feast begins (after preliminary scene-setting) with an image of adulterous desire and draws to a close with a lament to his betrayed wife and son. The first description is of a young woman whom Hemingway sees in a café:

> I've seen you, beauty, and you belong to me now, whoever you are waiting for and if I never see you again, I thought. You belong to me and all Paris belongs to me and I belong to this notebook and this pencil.[4]

At the end Hemingway is temporarily reunited with his wife and child in the mountains:

> When I saw my wife again standing by the tracks as the train came in by the piled logs at the station, I wished I had died before I ever loved anyone but her. She was smiling, the sun on her lovely face tanned by the snow and sun, beautifully built, her hair red gold in the sun, grown out all winter awkwardly and beautifully, and Mr Bumby standing with her, blond and chunky and with winter cheeks looking like a good Vorarlberg boy. (p. 210)

I want to consider Hemingway's account of the will as it infuses and even shapes the narrative's passage from the inaugurating moment to its concluding statement of regret. This involves looking at relations between three factors: will, luck, and ethics.

I. Autobiography, Ethics, and Luck

John D. Barbour rightly pointed out in 1992 that "although recent literary theory and criticism of autobiography raise crucial moral issues, no study has focused specifically on ethical dimensions of autobiography."[5] Most reflective autobiographers are ethicists in the sense that they ask the Aristotelian question: How ought a human life to be lived? One aspect of that question concerns the will: if one thinks the will's power negligible, the sense of what can and should be done with a life must be very different from expectations based on the assumption that the will is powerful and, to some extent at least, free. And, as I have argued, questions about the will must in turn involve questions about other issues. One of these pertains to the condition that dooms the ants on Henry's log—the phenomenon of luck.

For the autobiographer, as for anyone, luck is a strange and disturbing phenomenon. Because it confronts us with our vulnerability to the unpredictable and uncontrollable realm of the contingent, it can seem terrifying and inimical to the rational conduct of a life; yet, as Martha Nussbaum has noted,[6] its very connection with the world of chance, risk, and protean variability can render luck exhilarating and make it seem constitutive of any life we can imagine living, or wishing to live. My interest here is not principally in luck as a general phenomenon, but in the particular conjuncture between luck and ethics about which Nussbaum, Bernard Williams, Thomas Nagel, and others have written: in what has been termed *moral luck.*[7]

The concept of moral luck is complex and much debated, but in essence it contests the Kantian claim that dutiful rational moral agents and their intentions are not subject to the vicissitudes of external contingency, to luck. For Kant, the will so conceived is will as transcendental rationality. As Bernard Williams puts it, the Kantian position is that "both the disposition to correct moral judgment, and the objects of such judgment, are . . . free from external contingency, for both are, in related ways, the product of the unconditioned will."[8] In the *Groundwork of the Metaphysics of Morals,* Kant writes of the good will that

> even if, by some special disfavour of destiny or by the niggardly endowment of step-motherly nature, this will is entirely lacking in its power to carry out its intentions; if by its utmost effort it still accomplishes nothing, and only good will is left (not, admittedly, as a mere wish, but as the straining of every means so far as they are in our control); even then it would still shine like a jewel for its own sake as something which has its full value in itself. Its usefulness or fruitlessness can neither add to, nor subtract from, this value.[9]

The contrasting position, which we might loosely designate as Aristotelian, holds that moral agents, intentions, and outcomes are to some degree subject to contingency, to luck, and that the Kantian image of moral self-sufficiency is untenable, both conceptually and with respect to practical moral conduct.

A Moveable Feast might at first seem too slim a thing to bear the weight of such philosophical implication; and indeed of the autobiographies that I consider in detail in this book, this one is the least "reflective." However, it is not wholly unthinking, and a good deal of implicit philosophizing is buried in its terse and sometimes disingenuous style. Moreover, ethical readings of autobiographical and other forms of literature need not be restricted to morally or aesthetically exemplary texts. The flawed text, too, can tell us much about conceptions of human lives and the ways in which they are narrativized. In this chapter I want to examine the logic and narrativization of Hemingway's conception of luck for what it reveals about a certain popular, if inadequate, conception of the will. Along the way I will have something to say about that resilient cultural myth, the Hemingway legend.

In *The Old Man and the Sea,* the old man muses: "Luck is a thing that comes in many forms and who can recognize her?"[10] In order to help make sense of the various forms of luck that occur in *A Moveable Feast,* it will be useful to make some initial distinctions. For expository purposes I draw upon Thomas Nagel's article "Moral Luck." Nagel identifies kinds as follows. First, there is *constitutive luck:* "the kind of person you are, where this is not just a question of what you deliberately do, but of your inclinations, capacities and temperament." Second, *circumstantial luck:* "the kind of problems and situations one faces." I propose to subdivide this kind into two subsidiary forms: *metaphysical luck,* by which I mean the underlying metaphysical condition that functions as a kind of background to all one's experiences; and *cultural luck:* the kind of cultural environment in which one finds oneself. Third, "luck in how one is determined by antecedent circumstances" (I shall term this *agent-determinative luck*). Fourth, "luck in the way one's actions and projects turn out" (I shall call this *outcome luck*).[11] A further and important qualification is that the notion of luck used here does not carry any implication that the event or influence in question is uncaused. Luck refers merely to the impingement on the agent's life of that which is outside of his or her control.

II. Luck in Art, Racing, and Love

Initial impressions of *A Moveable Feast* tend to focus on its charm, its apparent slightness, and the various cultural myths that converge between its covers: the artistic life in Paris in the thirties; the life of the Lost Generation; the complex fate of American expatriates in Europe; and of course the legend of Hemingway himself, as writer, bon vivant, and will-endowed man of action. The mix is memorable, the writing is generally relaxed and light, as if to suggest that not too much is going on beyond the effort of memorialization itself.

But closer inspection of the kind for which Hemingway had great disdain reveals deceptive complexity. One measure of this is the book's hybrid generic character. It is part memoir and part "autobiography proper"; it veers between fictional invention and quasi-journalistic report; at some levels it is a sad twenties-style story of failed passion, while at others it is a moral fable about the destruction of love from without. It is also an autobiographical *Künstlerroman* in which the artist as young man learns his craft in a complex cultural and social milieu.[12] Then there is a confessional element, complicated by the text's posthumous editorial and publication history,[13] which pertains to the older man looking back on the failings of his younger self—a dimension that might incline us to think of this as a work of quasi-confessional autobiography. And threading its way through much of the above, there is an ethical strand: an exploration of modes and motivations of moral conduct.

The ethical strand yields a kind of code, many aspects of which are familiar in Hemingway's fiction. Despite the suggestion of plenitude in the book's title,[14] the code unfolds within the characteristic Hemingway metaphysic of scarcity: it is a world we cannot really know or possess. The code comprises various values and virtues. I will consider the interrelation between some of these later; for the moment it will be sufficient to note them (in no particular order). First, there is a powerful emphasis upon fidelity, an emphasis that incorporates both truthfulness and sincerity in personal relationships and a fierce emphasis upon authenticity in art, the "true sentence" (p. 12), the fidelity to fact, which is the building block of literary realism. Second, there is a strong emphasis upon friendship—here epitomized by Ezra Pound—and the related virtues of generosity, honor, loyalty (Pound's admiration of his friends' work is "beautiful as loyalty" [p. 107]). Third, a receptiveness to other people, and to experience in general—qualities Hemingway finds in the regulars at one of his favorite cafés, La Closerie des Lilas, people who are "all interested in each other and in their drinks or coffees, or infusions, and in the papers and periodicals which were fastened to rods, and no one was on exhibition" (p. 82). Fourth, the absence of "exhibition" is one of many values that are associated with restraint and discipline: stoicism in the face of the hard facts of existence (this and related virtues are shown to be comically lacking in the profligate and hypochondriacal Scott Fitzgerald), discipline (particularly in respect of art), thrift, durability, courage—especially physical courage—and, importantly, self-sufficiency. Fifth, and in a contrasting vein, there are values that pertain to fullness, satiation, even in some cases to excess: the exercise of one's capacities, immersion in the full, unmediated, sensuous experience of life; the emphasis on action as the mode in which capacities are exercised, in which courage is demonstrated, and, crucially, in which inner conflicts are deferred or dissolved through commitment to particular choices and sensations. Here the emphasis is on risk, submission, daring, and the sating of appetites—what Hemingway calls "the fiesta concept of life" (p. 209). Finally, there is the characteristic emphasis on will. At one point, when he has been complaining to Sylvia Beach about his poor American royalties, he reminds himself with respect to the writer's life in Paris that he has chosen, that "I was doing what I did of my own free will" (p. 72). But the position of will in the code is complex. It resides in each of the two main dimensions of the code: in the dimension characterized by discipline, but also in the "fiesta" one marked by indulgence and risk. Will in Hemingway is apt to seem a monolithic Nietzschean thing, and so to some extent it is; but it has shadings that make it more interesting—if not, finally, more satisfactory—than this.

The shadings help to explain the strangely equivocal power of *A Moveable Feast*'s version of the Hemingway persona: a version that offers the self as at once exemplary in its heroic quest for artistic perfection and as destructively flawed, a fit subject for a kind of gruff and intermittent moral self-scrutiny. Part of the appeal of the legend is apparent in this typical description of Hemingway preparing to work, from the sardonic chapter "Birth of a New School":

> The blue-backed notebooks, the two pencils and the pencil-sharpener (a pocket knife was too wasteful), the marble-topped tables, the smell of early morning, sweeping out and mopping, and luck were all you needed. For luck you carried a horse chestnut and a rabbit's foot in your right pocket. The fur had been worn off the rabbit's foot long ago and the bones and the sinews were polished by wear. The claws scratched in the lining of your pocket and you knew your luck was still there. (p. 91)

What's typical here is the image of Hemingway as the heroically self-sufficient man, the post-Romantic chronicler of the ordinary who needs little more than a café table, a pencil and paper, a coffee, and his own fierce discipline to capture the hard facts of a common condition. Self-sufficiency, of course, is appealing in part because it seems to promise immunity from the unnerving flux of contingency, and the appeal of the Hemingway persona, here, in his fiction and in modern culture generally, derives in large part from this image of a man who is at once sufficiently susceptible to the facts to memorialize them in art, and self-sufficient to a degree that insulates him from the uncontrollable forces that make the shared condition the unnerving thing it is. (It is a significant aspect of the Hemingway legend that he suicided, thereby to some extent dictating the terms of death's otherwise arbitrary impingement.) Yet the passage is not all about control; it's also about flirting and indeed *engaging* with risk, trying your luck, the thrill of pitting the modes of control against the contingent, the sport involved in narrowing the gap between chance and consummate artistry by the exercise of discipline and expertise. The rabbit's foot suggests a link here between Hemingway the writer and Hemingway the hunter: each magnetized by risks they feel compelled to master. As the chapter continues with a report of Hemingway's ferocity toward a pestering aspirant writer in the café, we are reminded that in this case the hunter and the writer share another tendency: the propensity to destroy.

The tension between the ethos of discipline and control, on the one hand, and of risk, submission, and contingency, on the other, runs deep in the narrative. Indeed the contrastive pair contingency/control amounts to a kind of organizing binary in the book that links what might (after Wittgenstein) be termed *families of activity*: activities that are disparate in some ways but that are conceptually and experientially similar in others. One such activity is art, a form of *technē*, of skill that can restrain the powers of *tuchē*, of unordered contingency.[15] Here Hemingway describes writing in a hotel room in Paris:

But sometimes when I was starting a new story and I could not get it going, I would sit in front of the fire and squeeze the peel of the little oranges into the edge of the flame and watch the sputter of the blue that they made. I would stand and look over the roofs of Paris, and think, "Do not worry. You have always written before and you will write now . . ." Up in that room I decided that I would write one story about each thing that I knew about. I was trying to do this all the time I was writing, and it was good and severe discipline.

It was in that room too that I learned not to think about anything that I was writing from the time I stopped writing until I started again the next day. That way my subconscious would be working on it and at the same time I would be listening to other people and noticing everything, I hoped; learning, I hoped; and I would read so that I would not think about my work and make myself impotent to do it. Going down the stairs when I had worked well, and that needed luck as well as discipline, was a wonderful feeling and I was free then to walk anywhere in Paris. (pp. 12–13)

The passage is about art and its relation to the will: how one wills the writing when it is blocked; the will that goes into making the global decisions (one story about each thing) that frame particular subsequent efforts of writing; about knowing when to stop trying so that subconscious energies (or the will in a subconscious modality) can take over and fuel the conscious will for later work. But it's also about the realm of necessity: here, as for Frederic Henry, there is a sense of inevitability about the fire—the fascination of the predictable sputter of peel falling into flame. And it's about the realm of chance, too: the rabbit's foot is to help the will prevail in a world of chance. The need for "luck as well as discipline" encapsulates the tension to which I have referred: it is the play of contingency that renders the discipline of art necessary, just as the disciplines of art are required to organize and memorialize the contingent energies of life.

Another instance of this kind of activity to which the narrative often refers is betting on the races. Here is an example:

You had to watch a jumping race from the top of the stands at Auteuil and it was a fast climb up to see what each horse did and see the horse that might have won and did not, and see why or maybe how he did not do what he could have done. You watched the prices and all the shifts of odds each time a horse you were following would start, and you had to know how he was working and finally get to know when the stable would try with him. He always might be beaten when he tried; but you should know by then what his chances were. It was hard work but at Auteuil it was beautiful to watch each day they raced when you could be there and see the honest races with the great horses, and you got to know the course as well as any place you had ever known. You knew many people finally, jockeys and trainers and owners and too many horses and too many things. (p. 62)

Much of the deceptive charm and interest of *A Moveable Feast* is apparent here. The passage combines two characteristic movements of feeling: a capacity for apparently unreflective and unselfconscious sensuous experience, for submission to that which is "beautiful" but also potentially risky and destructive—a kind of flirtation with a dangerous plenitude ("too many horses and too many things"); and, in contrast, a reassuring sense of familiarity, a particular kind of "work" that yields mastery, expert counsel for the will, an inwardness about the activity that narrows the odds and reduces the risks.

Marital love is the third of a triad of related activities in the text. A passage from the chapter "Shakespeare and Company" shows that for Hemingway luck is deeply implicated in love. Hadley says to Hemingway: "'We'll never love anyone else but each other.'" He replies: "'No. Never.'" They then discuss which books they will borrow from Sylvia Beach's bookshop. Ernest says:

> "And we're going to have all the books in the world to read and when we go on trips we can take them."
> "Would that be honest?"
> "Sure."
> "Does she [Sylvia] have Henry James too?"
> "Sure."
> "My," she said. "We're lucky that you found the place."
> "We're always lucky," I said and like a fool I did not knock on wood. There was wood everywhere in that apartment to knock on too. (p. 38)

The reference to James is significant not only because the couple's fate as innocents abroad in Paris echoes James's international theme, but also because James, who had a powerful influence on Hemingway in the twenties, was responsible for some of the most subtle and elaborate fictional treatments of intimate relationships that were known to him. Knocking on wood in the hope that your marriage holds up—this is the quintessential submission to circumstantial and outcome luck as the arbiter of marital fate. And the motif crops up again in the chapter that prefaces the one about the Fitzgeralds' destructive marriage, "Scott Fitzgerald." Hadley says:

> "We're awfully lucky."
> "We'll have to be good and hold it."
> We both touched wood on the café table and the waiter came to see what it was we wanted. But what we wanted neither he, nor anyone else, nor knocking on wood or on marble, as this café table-top was, could ever bring us. But we did not know it that night and we were very happy. (p. 176)

The verb *hold* implies some sort of effort, a bending of the will toward maintaining that which is fragile and rare in a threatening world; yet this is not what the passage is saying. The implication is that the only thing that might have saved their love is good luck, which his superstition tries to summon: tapping on wood is predicated on occult—or speculative, or wishful—knowledge of the laws that actually drive what seems to be the randomness of chance. It is as good as saying that nothing in their power can resist the contingencies that will destroy their love. All the will can do is enact a thoroughly commonplace kind of occult, irrational hoping. Call this the marble tabletop view of human fate. But consider now a more complex and powerful example from the fine chapter "A False Spring." Here again luck in love is associated, albeit ironically, with luck at the races. After success on the track, Hemingway says:

> "You said we were lucky today. Of course we were. But we had very good advice and information."
> She laughed.
> "I didn't mean about the racing. You're such a literal boy. I meant lucky other ways."
> "I don't think Chink [the friend who had accompanied them] cares for racing," I said, compounding my stupidity. (p. 57)

It's a nice irony that the "stupidity" that in this instance and elsewhere marks the young Hemingway as a man oblivious to certain important truths about love here betrays him into misunderstanding Hadley's meaning and into a resultant defense of the kind of informed gambling that can to some extent counter the play of contingency. It is the hallmark of this "stupidity" that he has no conception of what is needed, or even of the need, to contain the contingencies of love. A similar note of retrospective self-reproach occurs in a striking passage that metaphorically fuses racing and the later state of the Hemingway marriage:

> Racing never came between us, only people could do that; but for a long time it stayed close to us like a demanding friend. That was a generous way to think of it. I, the one who was so righteous about people and their destructiveness, tolerated this friend that was the falsest, most beautiful, most exciting, vicious, and demanding because she could be profitable. (p. 61)

This prefigures the advent of Pauline Pfeiffer and the resultant (or associated?) collapse of the marriage to Hadley. In the published version that results from Mary Hemingway and Harry Brague's editing, this event is later attributed to circumstantial forces beyond Hemingway's control; here he accepts some responsibility, albeit responsibility that is mitigated by his having sought profit to assuage the couple's alleged poverty.[16]

Such inconsistencies in moral appraisal—equivocation between occasional concessions to a measure of responsibility that would imply some freedom of the will, on the one hand, and recourse to the dominant assumption that contingency governs all, on the other—help to explain the oddity of tone and disposition that on closer acquaintance characterize *A Moveable Feast*: its peculiar blend of moral timidity and fearless virility, of nascent self-awareness and crude self-justification. There is a feeling of inevitability about the recurrent lapses from mature recognition to the casuistry of self-mythification: having finally given up on the races, he tells us that "it was enough just to be back in our part of Paris and away from the track and to bet on our own life and work" (p. 64). Like many of the other passages that assimilate love to betting, this one locates marital love in the realm of the contingent.

Such unawareness of the ways of intimacy might seem unlikely in a writer renowned, in some quarters at least, for his fictional treatments of relationships of love. But perhaps not. Hemingway's fictive relationships are after all embedded in a kind of quasi-determinism, a realm of metaphysical luck. Frederic Henry's vision of human life as antlike is soon to be confirmed by his lover Catherine's death after the stillbirth of their child. The Saint Anthony good luck charm that she gives him early in the novel symbolically saves him while she perishes without its powers of protection against the remorseless contingencies that surround their wartime love. Love of this kind has a particular fascination for Hemingway; indeed, despite his schooling in James and other great novelists of character, Hemingway has great difficulty with the subtleties of intimacy that arise in situations not shaped and constrained by immediate external crisis or threat. In *For Whom the Bell Tolls,* Jordan muses: "So if you love this girl as much as you say you do, you had better love her very hard and make up in intensity what the relation will lack in duration and in continuity. Do you hear that? In the old days people devoted a lifetime to it."[17] But what does such a lifetime permit? What is needed to maintain a viable relationship that has "duration" and "continuity"? What part does contingency, luck, in fact play in such relationships?

Martha Nussbaum points out that love of any kind exposes the individuals concerned to the contingency of the Other's being and to the fragility and chanciness of intimacy, its susceptibility to external influence and mutability.[18] But as extreme Hemingway-style assimilations of love and luck show, this view is (as Nussbaum acknowledges) partial at best; indeed it can be quite misleading. Betting comes in various shades, but there is always a moment of choice (or compulsion masquerading as choice) in which one submits to the flux of contingency. Submission to the spin of the roulette wheel is total: a complete forfeiture of control. (In an early letter Hemingway boasts that he can even cut the odds by observing the behavior of the wheel.)[19] Betting on the horses is different, certainly in a case like Hemingway's, where he studied the form, talked to trainers, and so achieved a more favorable configuration of contingency, risk, and mastery. Betting of this kind cannot influence outcomes, but it seeks to predict them through an inwardness with the activity concerned and through a certain kind of preparatory work. Intimate committed relationships are different again. Though such relationships do indeed expose lovers to the contingent, there is also a sense in which engagement with another person works in the opposite way. We could also say of relationships of love that though the unaffiliated Other is a locus of contingency in respect to Self, the consensual bonds of relationship are designed (at least in part) to bring that which is opaque, unpredictable, independent of Self under degrees of control that come with knowability and commitment to shared projects. Indeed it is one of the painful paradoxes of relationships of love that while they ideally delight in the contingent otherness of the Other, control of this kind is an ineluctable feature of them—though the gender ideology and the gendering of control that often come with it are not. As much of the classic fiction Hemingway read will show, the nub here is the configuration of freedom, commitment, and control that arises or, more commonly, is achieved by the lovers. I say "achieved" because if love is more than just passion, more than just submission to contingent and mutable bodily needs and drives, its most viable and substantial form seems to involve a certain kind of work, a moral work that includes negotiating and continually reformulating the balance between commitment, control, and the freedoms of the Other. Hence the title of Gillian Rose's impassioned autobiographical narrative, *Love's Work.*[20]

Hemingway, of course, is renowned for his belief in the moral and therapeutic powers of work. As he says in *A Moveable Feast,* "Work could cure almost anything, I believed then, and I believe now" (p. 21). He dedicated himself to work in Paris (and elsewhere) on writing, to work at Auteuil on the races. *Work* indeed often functions as a synonym for *will* in his writing. Yet he seems to have lacked any developed sense of work as a feature of, a prerequisite for, substantial relationships of love. The thinness of his conception becomes painfully apparent late in *A Moveable Feast* when he owns up to, and tries to explain, his involvement with Pauline. In this moment of what I shall call pseudo-confession, he depicts himself in the mountains at Schruns as "plunged into the fiesta concept of life" (p. 209), as in a state of risky deviation from the exacting demands of his code of discipline. He claims to be led on by "the rich," in particular by a certain "pilot fish" (p. 208: though he is not named, the reference is to John Dos Passos). And then this:

> Before these rich had come we had already been infiltrated by another rich using the oldest trick there is. It is that an unmarried young woman becomes the temporary best friend of another young woman who is married, goes to live with the husband and wife and then unknowingly, innocently and unrelentingly sets out to marry the husband. When the husband is a writer and doing difficult work so that he is occupied much of the time and is not a good companion or partner to his wife for a big part of the day, the arrangement has advantages until you know how it works out. The husband has two attractive girls around when he has finished work. One is new and strange and if he has bad luck he gets to love them both.

Then, instead of the two of them and their child, there are three of them. First it is stimulating and fun and it goes on that way for a while. All things truly wicked start from an innocence. So you live day by day and enjoy what you have and do not worry. You lie and hate it and it destroys you and every day is more dangerous, but you live day to day as in a war. (pp. 209–10)

It seems that Hemingway's final intention was to omit this and to include a more balanced and self-accusative passage about the rich.[21] Nevertheless, this passage constitutes one of several versions he was contemplating and, like much of the material that was reinstated by the editors, it accurately reflects his underlying presuppositions. "Infiltrated" captures nicely Hemingway's assumption that love is not just surrounded but permeated by hostile contingency. One of the problems with the explanation offered here is that even the snatches of marital description that are given of life with Hadley (some snippets were omitted by the editors)[22] lack the depth that is implied in this admission of marital degradation. Though we know Hadley to have been bright and quite sophisticated at the time of their marriage, she is generally given the sort of numpty-brained dialogue that characterizes the intimate relationships in Hemingway's war novels. The sort of exchanges between husband and wife that I have quoted have an evasive banality, a confected "innocence" that is intended as a tragic contrast to the "truly wicked things" that befall the relationship. But what they show is that for Hemingway, living "day to day as in a war" is less a betrayal than a condition of relationships, and that here, as in war, one is a plaything of "luck." Here again, "work" figures, but it is writing work, and the claim is that, in effect, this work leaves the marriage even more open to contingent threats from without than it might otherwise have been.

This pseudo-confession lends credence to Jeffrey Meyers's acerbic claim about Hemingway that "self-justification was always more important to him than friends, wives and children."[23] But it's interesting that here self-justification goes beyond the explanatory invocations of luck as cosmic contingency to luck as a mix of circumstantial and agent-determinative forms. Agent-determination takes the form here of an alleged "innocence," a residuum of his straight-laced Oak Park upbringing; the circumstantial factors have to do with cultural luck—the encounter with a debased code of the kind dramatized in *The Sun Also Rises*: a Dionysian hedonism that reposes in the very play of will as contingent appetite and excess that the code of disciplined work at art seeks to resist. Ernest and Hadley are presented as American innocents abroad and the culture they encounter as destructive of their tender—their fragile—love. The effort at self-exoneration is maudlin and basically absurd: as Michael Reynolds points out, "Ernest was, in fact, ripe for an affair" at this time and would have been a party to one if Duff Twysden had been willing.[24]

Yet earlier, a similar attribution of blame is made with a poetic delicacy and an existential suggestiveness that are typical of Hemingway at his best. In the chapter "A False Spring," the couple stands on a bridge watching the Seine. They have a feeling of "hunger" that for Hadley is later assuaged by a lovely meal and the lovemaking that follows. But for him it is different:

> It was a wonderful meal at Michaud's after we got in; but when we had finished and there was no question of hunger any more the feeling that had been like hunger when we were on the bridge was still there when we caught the bus home. It was there when we came in the room and after we had gone to bed and made love in the dark, it was there. (p. 57)

Hemingway goes on again to reproach himself for "stupidity," this time for his inability to understand his feelings as he lies beside the now-sleeping Hadley in the moonlight: "I had to try to think it out and I was too stupid" (p. 57). But here as virtually everywhere in the book, introspection, and indeed any real reflective penetration of his own code, is beyond him. He simply does not know what drives him, but driven he is, and so the determinative pressure he feels upon his will is constantly imputed to the world beyond self. The chapter concludes with a rumination that is at once haunting and morally problematic:

> But Paris was a very old city and we were young and nothing was simple there, not even poverty, nor sudden money, nor the moonlight, nor right and wrong nor the breathing of someone who lay beside you in the moonlight. (p. 58)

Together these passages intimate the presence of three forms of luck: implicitly, the cosmic kind that lies behind everything; the circumstantial-cultural kind that is the debased culture of Paris and Schruns; and, again implicitly, another kind—a form of constitutive luck, something that has to do with the needs and appetites, the whole psychophysiological disposition of this autobiographical subject. In concert these kinds leave the will stripped of freedom, if not of certain kinds of primitive and compulsive power. Hemingway's conception of will here is profoundly deterministic.

III. Many Sorts of Hunger

Hours before the meal at Michaud's and Hemingway's moonlit rumination about his marriage, the couple are standing on a bridge watching the Seine and become aware that they are hungry. Minutes later they stop outside Michaud's and he ponders:

> Standing there I wondered how much of what we had felt on the bridge was just hunger. I asked my wife and she said, "I don't know, Tatie. There are so many sorts of hunger. In the spring there are more. But that's gone now. Memory is hunger." (pp. 56–57)

This is one of the few intelligent things that Hadley is given to say in the book and it proves to be important. Hunger, of course, is a central feature of the Hemingway world and of the Hemingway legend. His books are preoccupied with gustatory and sexual appetites and their satisfaction. The legend, which seems to me very generous to a man who as person and artist was rather limited, is very much about the scale of Hemingway's needs and appetites: the need for adventure in love and war, in hunting big game, bullfighting, and so on. Charismatic though this may in some respects be, it raises questions about the model of self, and by extension of interaction between selves, that underlies Hemingway's work and reputation, and his conception of will. *A Moveable Feast* brings these questions home with particular point.

The emphasis on hunger, here and elsewhere, needs to be seen in the context of the overall emotional economy of Hemingway's world. I read the generative emotion of this world as a haunting intimation of nullity, of (in Sartre's words) a nothingness that haunts being.[25] "What did he fear?" the older waiter in "A Clean, Well-Lighted Place" asks himself. "It was not fear or dread. It was a nothing that he knew too well. It was all a nothing and a man was nothing too."[26] Characters live on the brink of—and sometimes succumb to—a feeling that is often described as an emptiness. One of the frustrations of Hemingway's writing, however, not least in *A Moveable Feast,* is that the rendering of these feelings seldom gets beyond the sort of primitive emotional notation that Hemingway found in the Mark Twain he so admired: one is lonesome, hollow, empty, or, if things go well, one feels grand or swell. In much of Hemingway's work, these emotional states and possibilities are expressed through existential binaries: emptiness/fullness, hollowness/fullness, loneliness/intimacy, pleasurable will/desolate passivity, hunger/satiation, and so on.

A title like *A Moveable Feast* tends to suggest that all may be well with the self so conceived: so long as your feast goes with you, your needs will be met and your hungers assuaged. But of course neither life nor Hemingway's vision of it offers such reassurances. Martha Nussbaum notes that "the activities associated with the bodily desires not only exemplify mutability and instability in their own internal structure; they also lead us and bind us to the world of perishable objects and, in this way, to the risk of loss and the danger of conflict."[27] In other words, they lay us open to luck. We have seen that Hemingway's fiction locates human hunger in a metaphysic of scarcity where, more often than not, need meets capriciousness and privation. His response to this is not philosophically complex, but it is artistically fraught and powerful, and it has interesting implications.

In fact, I would argue that he has three responses, each finding expression in a particular model of self, will, and self's interactions with other selves. The first is an essentially atomistic model that envisages for the self an incessant quest for satisfaction, a never-ending rhythm of fullness-emptiness-willing-fullness, and so on. Aristotle's emphasis on "replenishment"[28] is helpful here, and we might term this model a *need-replenishment* picture of the self. So conceived, the self is characterized by acquisitive and "taking" relationships with the world in general and with other selves. Its quest for replenishment is compulsive, partly because it is pitted against a reality that at some level it knows to be unpitying, "niggardly"; importantly, it is also fundamentally narcissistic. Little wonder that Hemingway's fiction figures in Christopher Lasch's study of American culture, *The Culture of Narcissism*.[29] The Hemingway persona is deeply narcissistic in Lasch's sense of the term: it is imagined as pitted against an elemental world that it seeks and claims to conquer, yet its real métier is not the wilderness that the rugged individualist confronts, but the mirror to which insecurity drives the self in order to shore up the sense of selfhood.[30] *A Moveable Feast* accords Self absolute supremacy; it gives us Hemingway in the narrative mirror of his own making, at once shameless and desperate in its shoring up of an intensely fragile "heroic" self. George Eliot's references to the "illusion of a concentric arrangement" and to a sense of the world as "an udder to feed our supreme selves"[31] are apt here, not least for their suggestion that many forms of egotistical hunger—including of course gustatory ones—are regressed, repetitions of infantile need. Another passage about writing in Paris captures something of the rhythm of emptiness, willing, and replenishment in which the atomistic Hemingway self is caught:

> It was necessary to get exercise, to be tired in the body, and it was very good to make love with whom you loved. That was better than anything. But afterwards, when you were empty, it was necessary to read in order not to think or worry about your work until you could do it again. I had learned already never to empty the well of my writing, but always to stop where there was still something there in the deep part of the well, and let it refill at night from the springs that fed it. (pp. 25–26)

This deals with two of Hemingway's principal hungers: creative and sexual. Largely unwittingly, it establishes not only an economy of needs, but also a hierarchy among them. Here again, there is a process whereby one disengages the nearly exhausted will, leaving it to replenish itself through the ministrations of the subconscious.

A second model of self, will, and interaction is exemplified in this exchange in *A Farewell to Arms*:

> "You see," [says Catherine to Henry] "I do anything you want."
> "You're so lovely."
> "I'm afraid I'm not very good at it yet."
> "You're lovely."
> "I want what you want. There isn't any me any more. Just what you want."
> "You sweet."[32]

The impulse to fuse with another's being is familiar in Hemingway's fiction and in some of his letters. (The desire to merge or exchange genders with one's partner, explored in the novel *The Garden of Eden,* is a related phenomenon.) It constitutes a reaction to the feelings of emptiness and isolation, of the nullity at the heart of things, and there are times in Hemingway's writing when its powers of consolation and protection seem almost magical. In *A Moveable Feast* this enchanted sense of unison is symbolically associated with the life that Hadley and Ernest have early on in the mountains, away from the debased code of Paris: "In the night we were happy with our own knowledge we already had and other new knowledge we had acquired in the mountains" (p. 21). It also manifests linguistically, as in some of the conversational exchanges I have quoted, where the couple speak an almost childlike idiolect of two, as if from a shared existential core of innocence. We might term this a *fusion* model of self and interaction. Here the self seeks to assuage its emptiness through the absolute solace of an intimacy that abrogates the boundaries upon which isolation depends. Such fusion also abolishes the distance, the difference, that allows contingency, be it circumstantial or the kind associated with linkage to the opaque and contingent qualities of the Other, to "infiltrate" relationships of love. Fusion creates a perfect circuit of desire-and-fulfillment. There need be no wanting, wishing, willing, because the self has incorporated that which embodies its needs and desires—the Other. The fantasized entity that is Ernest-Hadley in the mountains is utterly self-sufficient. Only sinister corruption from without can break the circuit.

Finally, there is a model of self as oriented toward and engaged in *reciprocity* with others. Here the will invests in, and tries to bring about what is best for, the Other. This is where true moral agency enters the picture: Taylor's "strong" moral "evaluators" are agents who can factor the needs of others into their moral decisions. There are not many developed representations of this view of self in *A Moveable Feast* and, not surprisingly given the deeply masculine—indeed masculinist—quality of the Hemingway world, the best examples in fact occur not between Ernest and Hadley but between Ernest and other men, in particular Pound and Fitzgerald. Where it pertains to Ernest and Hadley, it emerges most commonly through expressions of regret: regret that he was not more attentive to her needs; that he put work first; that, in the word that usually expresses his sense of regret, he was "stupid" about their love. Of his strictures on spending, he says: "I knew how severe I had been and how bad things had been. The one who is doing his work and getting satisfaction from it is not the one the poverty bothers . . . I had been stupid when she [Hadley] needed a grey lamb jacket and had loved it once she had bought it. I had been stupid about other things too" (pp. 50–51).

A Moveable Feast is torn between these three models of self, will, and interaction, but ultimately it is narcissism, the need-replenishment view, that prevails. The style of egotism involved is familiar enough. Like the depressive hunger that fuels its various needs, this egotism is in some sense characteristically male. The self is not seen, in the terms used by some feminist theorists of autobiography, as "relational," as being constituted and realized through interaction with others, but as an already-given cite of identity and goal-directed energy; as a compulsive bearer of a Nietzschean will.[33] As Lasch notes, this self is also in some sense characteristically American, a latter-day version of the post-Romantic Imperial Self,[34] isolate, purportedly self-sufficient and self-scripting. For the self so conceived, mutuality is likely to seem not just fragile, but also ancillary, secondary to the project of self-validation through action, creation, and first-person mythification—the mirror. The will here is largely shorn of its ethical dimension. Thus if in Hemingway's world love has little power to resist the encroachments of the contingent, the same is not true of art. The above passage about writing in Paris shows, as does so much else in the book, that Hemingway's deepest need is for, and his deepest commitment is to, art: love and sex have important parts to play in the replenishment of creative energies, but in this emotional hierarchy they are ultimately secondary to such energies and will be sacrificed to them, if need be. To some extent, creativity needs help to renew itself, but, given the right circumstances, it will replenish its almost "empty" "well" in the night. Love, too, needs help; it also needs work. But, as we have seen, the real work here is devoted to art. If at times Hemingway seems aware of these shortcomings and even, almost, to apologize for his "stupidity" in respect to them, the logic of the Hemingway legend, and of the *Künstlerroman* form through which the legend is here given expression, carries the promise of exoneration.

The need for exoneration, justification, is itself a kind of hunger; a kind that is familiar in much autobiographical writing. Hadley is right to say that "'memory is hunger,'" and the comment is particularly apt for *A Moveable Feast*, a work whose desire to memorialize, to contain the play of contingency through writing, is complicated by its imperious need to justify, to shore up the Hemingway legend through appeals to the power of the contingent, of luck, in life.

IV. REGRET, JUSTIFICATION, AND SOMEONE TO BE

In his essay "Moral Luck," Bernard Williams discusses an example, loosely based on the life of Gauguin, in which a morally sentient individual leaves his family in order to pursue a career as a painter. Williams argues that luck plays a big part in moral conduct, and that in this case the moral status of "Gauguin's" decision to leave his family will be subject to various forms of moral luck, including, and perhaps principally, the success or otherwise of the artistic career that follows. If that career is successful, "Gauguin" will from a standpoint that is heavily conditioned by that success deem his decision morally justifiable; if not, he will be subject to "agent-regret": a form of regret that agents can feel toward their past actions, or actions in which they have participated, where regret assumes characteristic forms of expression.

This picture has some relevance to *A Moveable Feast*. Though Hemingway did not leave his wife and son for a career as a writer, we have seen that there is a sense in which his priorities rendered them secondary to that career and in which their secondary status left them highly vulnerable to the contingencies of the appetitive Hemingway soul. Interestingly, his posthumously published novel *Islands in the Stream,* another work that replays his regret about leaving Hadley, features as its central character Thomas Hudson, an artist who likens himself and his life choices to the predicament of Gauguin.[35] The lament with which *A Moveable Feast* draws to a conclusion is a statement of something like agent-regret, and the book's moral fumbling and confusions in general are crude attempts at self-justification. The moral standpoint from which these utterances and attempts are made is complex. It is central to our understanding of the moral sequence described, and to Hemingway's understanding of it, that he writes from the standpoint of a literary legend. To the extent that literary success might in an account like Williams's justify the writer's neglect of wife and son, the justification is, as it were, already in place. Art constitutes its own moral justification. The use of the first-person *Künstlerroman* form reinforces the legend's potential power to expiate because this is a genre often predicated upon the assumption that the artist concerned has achieved a degree of success that renders the reconstruction of the history in which his or her talent developed interesting and worthwhile.

The moral standpoint here is further complicated by the particular nature of Hemingway's regret. To say that this is a form of moral regret is true, but it is not the whole story. Certainly the narrative evinces a sense of guilt and moral failure, and in so doing it summons, or is at least parasitic upon, some of the resources of traditional confessional autobiography in which regret charts a narrative path for a complex autobiographical self in relation to some larger system of value or discourse of self-awareness. Moreover, the element of what Hemingway termed "remorse" in draft passages would have been more pronounced had such passages not been excised by Mary Hemingway and Brague.[36] Yet for a number of reasons, the notion of agent-regret doesn't seem quite right here. One is that the Hemingway persona in the book is not really an agent in the developed sense that, after Taylor, we have imputed to this term. He does not weigh choices in terms of large moral issues and implications; he cannot make sophisticated and dispassionate evaluations, nor give nuanced linguistic accounts of his motivations. He lacks the capacity for reflexive interplay with the moral code in which he is embedded. He is a "weak evaluator" in the sense that his judgments (such as they are) are grounded in self-interest; and in the important sense that, driven as he is by bodily appetite, and incapable of extended rational reflection, his will is not free. Hemingway's regret simply refers to the loss of something that in retrospect he wishes he had not forgone. The processes by which the mistakes were made go largely unscrutinized, and regret has a strong nonmoral dimension in this case. *A Moveable Feast* was written in depressive advancing years in an effort (among other things) to recapture the "innocence" of life with Hadley. Its closing sentence is "But this is how Paris was in the early days when we were very poor and very happy" (p. 211). In fact, the moral and nonmoral concerns tend to merge: grief drives an egotistical review of life priorities, which guilt takes up in its own more empathetic terms.

The attempt to review life priorities in this way amounts to an effort to ask how his life should have been lived and, by extension, how any life ought to be lived. Ethics enters the picture in this general sense, even though the will itself often seems bereft of moral sensitivity. However inadequately and implicitly, *A Moveable Feast* tries to distinguish between the "good life" platitudinously conceived as bohemian indulgence, the fiesta concept of life—cafés, companionship, wine, and writing—and the Good Life that is comprised of optimal human dispositions, activities, and interrelations between these. That it cannot make this distinction with any real success is partly a matter of temperamental and intellectual limitation, partly of contradictions in the code that reflects these limitations, and partly the upshot of contradictions that are inherent in the constellation of values and activities in question—a legacy of conceptual and pragmatic incommensurability.

In fact, the Hemingway code is here riven with contradictions. Four are perhaps particularly noteworthy for a reading of *A Moveable Feast*. The first is the tension between control and submission, where the ethic of discipline, containment of contingency, pulls against the belief in submission to the unmediated play of experience and sensation. Two conceptions of will conflict: will as dedicated to and conditioned by the quest for artistic truth; and Dionysian will-as-excess, unqualified by Apollonian moderation. Second, there is a pull between fidelity as an absolute and overriding commitment to artistic truth and fidelity to those others who, in principle and in practice, cannot but take second place to art. Their betrayal is almost assured. Art is accorded supreme intrinsic value. In part this is because in Hemingway's lexicon of value, "truth" does much of the work that a more fully articulated vision would ascribe to "rationality": for Hemingway, our closest approach to rationality lies in giving the most truthful possible representation of the world; a representation that is structured, given aesthetic-rational form, by the willed and systematically linked intricacies of art. But the quest for truth doubles back on the life that is shaped by that quest: irrationality in the life is justified by the larger end—the pursuit of rationality that is the work. Art is often valued because it treats the Other, which is its subject, as an end-in-itself; but *A Moveable Feast* shows how it may treat others as a means in the quest for artistic perfection. Third, there is a discrepancy between the ethos of self-sufficiency and the belief, both aesthetic and interpersonal, in receptiveness, openness to others. Finally, there is a contradiction between the strong sense of will, of Nietzschean power, which underlies Hemingway's belief in action and self-sufficiency, and the attenuated sense of self-as-plaything of fate that is associated with his appeals to luck, particularly moral luck.

The last of these points picks up on Williams's concern about the actual provenance of the moral self in a world where virtually all aspects of such a self can seem, at least from an external standpoint, the product of luck. This concern is shared by Thomas Nagel, who notes that if we begin the process of attribution of self and acts to "antecedent circumstances," there seems to be no end to the process of regress, and no beginning to the individual agent: "The area of genuine agency, and therefore of legitimate moral judgment, seems to shrink under this scrutiny to an extensionless point."[37] For Nagel and (I think) Williams, there is no conceptual solution to this bind. Both appeal instead to the sense we have by introspection that agency, though more circumscribed than good condition theorists like Kant might wish to think, is real: "We extend to others the refusal to limit ourselves to external evaluation, and we accord to them selves like our own."[38] Nagel's great and memorable concern is that if we hold only to external evaluation—to selves and actions as they appear as parts of networks of cause and consequence—"it leaves us with no one to be."[39] In this view there may be will, but there can be no such thing as free will. It is Hume writ large.

I have argued that one of the great virtues of autobiographical writing is that it takes us beyond external evaluation, the spectator's view of other selves, and gives the sentiment, the logic, the experience of the inner world of first-person agents. Perhaps better than most other forms of discourse, it can express and help to reconcile the puzzling duality of the self; the various senses in which it seems implicated in a threadlike condition: the self as passive, its substance and fate woven from without; or, by contrast, the self as woven, but also a weaver, manipulating the threads of its own being, its own life. But, as Sartre and Beauvoir eventually decided, Hemingway's work generally lacks a productive sense of tension between a developed central self and the world—the "totality" in which it is embedded.[40] This is certainly the case with *A Moveable Feast*. Though its *Künstlerroman* and confessional elements are at times suggestive of such complexity, it continually retreats into a memoir-like modesty about self-revelation. These tendencies are apparent in its implicit and explicit engagements with luck. The thinness of self-description is reflected in the paucity of detail about constitutive or agent-determinative luck. The narrative begins *mediis rebus:* it does not accord the narrated self a past or a moral history; nor does its vignette structure allow for much sense of moral development. There is much about life patterns, drives, needs, and compulsions, but virtually no introspection about possible sources of these patterns, about the psycho-cultural history of the will. The self is in many ways monolithic, a given: the good constitutive luck involved in having talent is taken for granted, and it is assumed that discipline can deliver a destiny of artistic greatness in the face of the contingencies that threaten other aspects of life. Outcome luck seems not to afflict the vocation of art. But for love, and the moral provenance of the self, things are very different. The recurrent references to "stupidity" are suggestive of an element of constitutive luck that contributes to the breakup of the marriage; but the nature and history of such tendencies remain unscrutinized. The major appeals to luck are to its circumstantial forms: the metaphysical kind that surrounds and threatens all human activity, and the cultural form that Ernest and Hadley encounter in Paris and Schruns. It is here that Hemingway ultimately lays the blame for the collapse of his marriage. The world of the book is not just deterministic; it is ultimately fatalistic. Blame and the agent-regret that go with it are not assuaged by artistic success. Hemingway sees the self that arises from its earlier choices largely as a casualty. At some level the book laments that life is not a feast, that one cannot have the good outcomes without the choices and errors that helped to produce them, cannot have the current—legendary—writing self together with all that seems retrospectively desirable about earlier states and experiences of the narrated self. Here Hemingway the tough guy, the man of action, the stoical survivor in a world of scarcity and caprice, gives way to an altogether softer and more sentimental figure, yearning for a plenitude the books that made him famous expressly deny. His earlier caution that "it is only when you can no longer believe in your own exploits that you write your memoirs"[41] is of little avail.

The emphasis on action constitutes an effort of simplification where the complexities that bedevil the self and its code can be deferred or dissolved. The line between action and evasion is fine indeed, and no real demarcation is made between intention and action, between modalities in which the will takes counsel from reflection, on the one hand, and the modality of mere, unthinking assertion, on the other. Fine too is the line between courage and cowardice. The Hemingway who was decorated for bravery in battle and who habitually courted physical risk emerges from the published version of *A Moveable Feast* as something of a moral coward, unable and unwilling to take responsibility for choices that he sheets home to luck. On the last page of *A Moveable Feast,* he looks back nostalgically to the time with Hadley when they thought they were "invulnerable" (p. 211). He now wants us to know that this was an illusion. But the text overcorrects and responds to loss with an odd mix of heroic invulnerability, a monolithic memorialization of self, and despairing moral fatalism suggesting that, ultimately, there is virtually no self left to be. The marble tabletop view of fate supplants the ethos of heroic responsibility. The icon of this world is not Kant's jewel but the rabbit's foot, the Saint Anthony charm.

It is ironic and highly unfortunate that the published version plays up the element of moral cowardice by omitting several expressions of remorse and personal culpability that Hemingway had finally intended for inclusion. However, the editorial history of the text does not in my view substantially affect the reading I offer here. The rationalizations offered in the published version were seriously contemplated by Hemingway among the many drafts he tried, and they are consistent with a conception of luck and agency that dominates not only the earlier parts of the text, but his writing in general—and, I suggest, certain widely occurring narcissistic cultural attitudes to the will that are current today. Moreover, the draft expressions of remorse do not appear to take a high degree of responsibility. Appeals to luck remain prominent, though the appeal features a greater emphasis on constitutive luck ("fault of character")[42] than does the published version. Whatever minor changes the increased emphasis on contrition might have for our sense of Hemingway the man, the published version has made a decisive contribution to the Hemingway legend. The ethical flaws in the published text reflect ethical flaws in the legend.

One such flaw is the failure to see that narcissism constitutes a greater threat to relationships of love than even the unnerving impingements of luck. We know that it was Mary Hemingway and Brague who chose to put the chapter containing the lament to Hadley in *A Moveable Feast* last. Hemingway had apparently decided to drop the last four pages for fear of hurting Hadley and to end the volume with the chapters in which he emerges as a good and empathetic friend to the chaotic Scott Fitzgerald.[43] The impulse to protect Hadley while also securing his own status as a moral being is typical of the moral confusions that pervade the book. Such confusions let in a little moral light, but not a lot and not often. In "A False Spring" he notes that when in their impoverished days a horse (Chèvre d'Or) on which they had bet fell, Hadley "cried for the horse, I remembered, but not for the money" (p. 51). He commends her for her uncomplaining attitude to the poverty to which his quest for artistic greatness had committed them, and he seems aware, but only dimly, of the significance of this episode: his inclination is to curse their bad luck in losing their wager; she cries for the horse. His response is to lament a loss to the self; hers is outward-looking, emotionally cognizant of other beings and their tragic vulnerability to modes of ill luck about which there really is nothing to be done.

CHAPTER FIVE

"Being and Making Oneself Be"

Will and Contingency in Simone de Beauvoir's Autobiography

To talk of luck, as I have done in the previous chapter, is to talk of contingency. For my purposes the two terms can be read as synonyms. However, my discussion of Hemingway focused on a particular form of luck: moral luck. I've argued that *A Moveable Feast* appeals implicitly to a version of the notion of moral luck: Hemingway wants us believe that the breakup of his first marriage occurred because contingency intervened in his life and "caused" him to act, to use his will, in ways that were morally inappropriate.

In the present chapter I look further at the relationship between contingency and the will; but in this instance, I am not concerned first and foremost with the moral dimension of the problem. My principal concern here is with the elemental sense of encounter between a will that wants to control, on the one hand, and a reality that seems, or threatens, to be radically accidental, on the other. This encounter, of course, has profound ethical implications—ethical in the sense that it raises an array of questions about how a life ought to be lived. Simone de Beauvoir is terrified by the thought that reality might be a realm of sheer chance.

I. Necessary and Contingent: This Strange Object, a Life

In Simone de Beauvoir's first published novel, *She Came to Stay,* the central female character, Françoise, has her fortune told by a gypsy. The gypsy rightly surmises facts about the complicated triangular relationship in which Françoise is becoming embroiled with her lover Pierre and a younger woman, Xavière. Françoise returns to the table at which she had been sitting with a companion. Then:

> She was seized by a sudden anguish, so violent that she wanted to scream. It was as if the world had suddenly become a void; there was nothing more to fear, but nothing to love either. There was absolutely nothing. She was going to meet Pierre, they would exchange meaningless phrases, and then they would part. If Pierre's and Xavière's friendship was no more than a mirage, then neither did her love for Pierre and Pierre's love for her exist. There was nothing but an infinite accumulation of meaningless moments, nothing but a chaotic seething of flesh and thought, with death looming at the end.[1]

It is a classic moment in existential fiction: Françoise comes face-to-face with some kind of absolute negation. Her death bears down upon her; the present is a meaningless, whirling, unintelligible flux. She has an intimation of radical contingency. In this instance the experience is all the more terrifying, and in fact is partly precipitated, because the gypsy proves to have occult access to extra-rational orders of experience. Françoise does not. For her the extra-rational is the negation of thought, of understanding, of control. Therein lies its terror. Françoise is closely modeled on Beauvoir herself, and we know from her letters, from accounts of her, and from her autobiographical writings that Beauvoir experienced such moments of appalled intimation of the contingent throughout her life. In *The Prime of Life,* the second volume of her four-volume autobiography, she writes: "The idea of contingency terrifies me; by filling the future with demands and appeals and expectations, I inject an element of determinism into the present [*La contingence m'effraie; en peuplant l'avenir d'attentes, d'appels, d'exigences, je prête au présent une nécessité*]" (*PL,* p. 287/*p. 411*).[2] The opposition of *contingent* and *necessary* (a better translation than "determined" here) is one of several organizing binaries in her writing in various genres. It is powerfully evident in her autobiography and in the associated volumes about the deaths of Sartre and of her mother.[3]

Sartre and Beauvoir generally use the word *contingency* quite conventionally, as a synonym for chance, accident. It comes from the Latin *contingentia* (*con*— with, *tango*—touch), meaning to touch closely or come into contact with. However, it also has a transferential meaning as circumstance, to happen, to befall. Its primary meaning in French is philosophical: *Robert* equates it with "eventuality," but there is a more colloquial French connotation as "things that can change." Beauvoir's and Sartre's customary usage fuses its colloquial and philosophical resonances. Thus, for them, it means that something might or might not happen; that phenomena are not susceptible to prediction; that there is no grand design or inner necessity that determines what will come about, or the way in which phenomena are interrelated. So conceived, *contingency* connotes a metaphysical condition, as in Beauvoir's book on existential ethics, *The Ethics of Ambiguity.* The first paragraph of the *Ethics* contains a characterization of what she calls the "tragic ambivalence" of "man":

> "Rational animal," "thinking reed," he escapes from his natural condition without, however, freeing himself from it. He is still a part of this [natural] world of which he is a consciousness. He asserts himself as a pure internality against which no external power can take hold, and he also experiences himself as a thing crushed by the dark weight of other things. At every moment he can grasp the non-temporal truth of his existence. But between the past which no longer is and the future which is not yet, this moment when he exists is nothing. The privilege, which he alone possesses, of being a sovereign

and unique subject amidst a universe of objects, is what he shares with all his fellow-men. In turn an object for others, he is nothing more than an individual in the collectivity on which he depends.[4]

She goes on to refer to humanity's predicament as "the tragic ambiguity of their condition." There is a fundamental ambiguity in the way in which we experience ourselves and our place in the world: we are of a world of brute facticity, and yet we know ourselves to be part of that world, and that very knowledge seems to set us *apart* from that world; we are purposive beings, drawn on by intimations of freedom, yet we also have powerful intimations of constraint, of inscrutable limits to our freedom; we experience ourselves as inhabiting a present, yet at some level we know this present to be a kind of phantom existence, an extensionless point between past and future; we feel ourselves to be subjects, replete with self-guaranteeing consciousness, but others apprehend us as objects; though we may feel that we are sovereign selves, we in fact depend upon the collectivity for our very being. *Ambiguity* so conceived has deep epistemological and existential links with *contingency.* The passage characterizes a being who has a passion for order and self-determination but who inhabits a world that seems random and is apparently inimical to the exertion of human will and agency.

Even the existence of this being is contingent: we might or might not have existed; our lives occur as if—and apparently by—accident. The for-itself, or consciousness, is consigned to the knowledge of its own chanciness, the freakish absurdity of its having come into being; and it must live, and decide what to make of, this awareness of its own contingent nature. Among other things, it must decide what it might mean to have a life. In several of the great meditative passages scattered through her autobiographical works, Beauvoir asks just this question. One of the finest such passages occurs in the third volume, *Force of Circumstance.* Perhaps few writers have so powerfully and memorably captured the paradoxes that confront the autobiographer:

> Every moment [of her life] reflects my past, my body [*Dans chaque moment se reflètent mon passé, mon corps*], my relations with others, the tasks I have undertaken, the society I live in, the whole of this earth; linked together, and independent, these realities sometimes reinforce each other and descant together, sometimes they interfere with, contradict, or neutralize each other . . .
> A life is such a strange object, at one moment translucent, at another utterly opaque, an object I make with my own hands [*que je fabrique moi-même*], an object imposed on me, an object for which the world provides the raw material and then steals it from me again, pulverized by events, scattered, broken, scored yet retaining its unity; how heavy it is and how inconsistent: this contradiction breeds many misunderstandings. (*FC*, pp. 275–76/*p. 296*)

The verb *fabriquer* is etymologically linked to *fabric* and has deep historical associations with the making of cloth. So the sense of self-as-maker of its own life here partakes, however subliminally, of the metaphor of the self-as-weaver, worker of threads. The passage is rich in tensions that pervade, and to some extent organize, Beauvoir's autobiography. There is a chastening sense, reminiscent of Montaigne, that a life is "a strange object," an "opaque" thing that baffles understanding; yet this feeling competes with the conviction, so important to Beauvoir and Sartre, that to the ideologically unfettered mind, a life could be "translucent," many of its details open to phenomenological inspection and interpretation. There is a tension too between perceptions of present—the present "moment"—and past. On the one hand, the present seems an organic outgrowth of the past: "every moment reflects my past"; seen in another way, however, these temporal "realities" appear "independent." This formulation recalls a contrast that runs deep in existentialism generally and in Beauvoir's writings in particular. The perception of the past as begetter of the present recalls Sartre's famous notion of viscosity in *Being and Nothingness,* where the past is imaged as "sticky," entropic, resistant to change, development, and novelty.[5] The past as an "independent" "reality" recalls the ethos of "transcendence" that animates *Being and Nothingness* and *The Second Sex.* Here what Sartre calls the "absolute heterogeneity" between "past and present"[6] means that we are free to transcend, to remake, ourselves from moment to moment. The past is not sovereign unless we allow it to be so, unless we submit to the cultural dogma of its sovereignty. Once again the double-edged character of the contingent comes into view. Contingency is terrifying, a "meaningless," "seething" "chaos" of "moments"; but just because of this, it is also potentially liberating: contingency means that indeed the present is not the causal upshot of the past, the self not the causal issue of its history. We are free to make and remake ourselves—if we choose to exercise this freedom. The self, then, is a bearer of the contingency that characterizes the world in general. We are not what we are by necessity, and so we can be other than we are by choice, by exertion of the will. Our condition is not just ambiguous but radically *ironic* in that negativity—the Hegelian capacity to imagine and to make ourselves be other than we are—is the constitutive feature of humanity.

What we do with this capacity is an ethical matter. Our condition demands an attitude, and that attitude entails an ethics. In this context, ethics doesn't mean rules and protocols of conduct; nor does it involve meta-ethical theorizing about the nature of moral precepts and agents. Indeed Beauvoir was to become increasingly hostile to such theorizing as her career went on. In *The Ethics of Ambiguity* and in the autobiographical writings, "ethics" retains its Aristotelian signification: it is about how a life should be lived; above all about how the will ought to be exercised—though, as we shall see, the "how" is given little formal content. The book's existentialist prescription is that, in the face of ambiguity and constraint, "man," through whom discourses of value come into the world, must will, and so make, the world in a certain way; in the light of a certain sentiment. This sentiment is the sentiment of freedom: a metaphysical potentiality that follows logically from the contingent nature of things; a potentiality we can and should seize and instantiate in our lives. The attitude involved is one of defiant creativity and "responsibility"; ethics springs into being in the absence of God, and because He is absent: "Far from God's absence authorizing all license, the contrary is the case, because man is abandoned on the earth, because his acts are definitive, absolute engagements. He bears the responsibility for a world which is not the work of a strange power, but of himself, where his defeats are inscribed, and his victories as well."[7] Abandonment, like contingency, is a condition, not an enemy, of action. And action can and should be a political praxis where individual subjectivities share their projects, their visions, and create collective political will: "An ethics of ambiguity" holds that "individual freedoms can forge laws valid for all."[8] In a sense this is a variation on the Will as the Source of Law conception of the will. Beauvoir's version of existentialism is intended to counter charges that Sartrean existentialism cannot yield the ethical dimension that is foreshadowed at the end of *Being and Nothingness*. She argues, not altogether convincingly, that existentialism can meet this requirement, and that ethics entails and informs politics. This is the politics of what in *The Prime of Life* she calls trying to "set freedom free [*à libérer la liberté*]" (p. 434/*p. 627*).

As Richard Rorty notes, contingency needs to be considered in respect not only of world and self, but of language as well.[9] From the standpoint of a Nietzschean version of pragmatism, Rorty argues—much as Davidson, Derrida, and other poststructuralists do—against the realist view that the world has an "intrinsic nature,"[10] that language is a "medium" that enables "expression or representation,"[11] that there is a "Truth" to be "found" (as opposed to made)[12] by the language user. On the contrary, he argues, the "relationship" between language and "the world" is in metaphysical terms a matter of sheer contingency. Humankind *makes* its meanings, *makes* its worlds, in the light of particular needs and agendas, and at the behest of a Nietzschean "will to truth."[13] Such formulations have deep links, both historically and conceptually, with Sartrean existentialism (though Sartre does at times seem to see language as a representational "medium"),[14] and we might therefore expect that Simone de Beauvoir's position would strongly resemble Rorty's, not least in respect of the business of writing life-narratives. At times she does indeed proffer such views, as when she says, echoing a classical figure, that "words are by nature birds of passage" (*FC*, p. 235). Yet some of her most considered statements about autobiographical representation seem to have precisely the contrary implication: she announces, for example, that her intention is to "tell the whole truth [*de raconter [ma vie] en vérité*]" about her life (*FC*, p. v/*p. 7*). Such apparent contradictions reflect Beauvoir's extraordinarily complex relation to autobiography in general, and to existential autobiography in particular. For all this, her autobiography remains one of the great works of its kind.[15] Few autobiographies can rival its capacity to combine intense, intellectually charged introspection with detailed sociohistorical narration. Few can match Beauvoir's rendering of the volatile and unstable interplay between self and its social worlds in times of personal and political upheaval.

That the self, and her sense of life, should be so ambiguous, so conflicted, is entirely consistent with what she tells us about her own history. She associates intellectuality with conflictual accounts of self and world, arguing, with Sartre, that "literature is born when something in life goes slightly adrift" (*PL*, p. 290). In *Memoirs of a Dutiful Daughter*, she recalls how parenting disputes about values and child rearing precipitated her development as an intellectual: "My father's individualism and pagan ethical standards were in complete contrast to the rigidly moral conventionalism of my mother's teaching. This imbalance, which made me the subject of an endless debate, explains to a great extent why I became an intellectual" (p. 45). I read the million or more words of her autobiographical writings as a vast elaboration of this and other debates, and as a vast act of discursive penetration of her social world. In this sense Simone de Beauvoir is the reflective autobiographer par excellence.

II. Beauvoir and Existential Autobiography

Beauvoir is not alone among autobiographers in being preoccupied with contingency. Far from it. Indeed the problem of writing within and about contingency troubles most reflective autobiographers, and certainly those who feature in this study. In one sense, contingency is absolutely central to the autobiographical undertaking: it is the fear of swirling meaninglessness and flux, not least in one's own self, that impels many autobiographers to invest their lives and selves with the kinds of order and intelligibility—with "*nécessité*"—that the formal and epistemological resources of the genre can offer. Yet, as they all know, the very consolations of form can be a source of falsification. Self-life-writing requires order, an avowal of intelligibility, but it must also reproduce some of the disorder that is constitutive of life, that makes a life recognizably human. Beauvoir believes that only an "imaginary object" (*FC*, p. 319), an extended creative artifact, can approach the requisite balance between flux and order, whirl and intelligibility. One vehicle that she sometimes commends above all others is the novel, a form that can render something of the complex weave—she puts it in terms of spinning—of world and meaning: "Only a novel, it seemed to me, could reveal the multiple and intricately spun meanings of that changed world to which I awoke in August 1944 [*Seul un roman pouvait à mes yeux dégager les multiples et tournoyantes significations de ce monde changé dans lequel je m'étais réveillée en août 1944*]" (*FC*, p. 263/*p. 283*); but her highest commendation is generally reserved for autobiography, as in this passage written at the time she was writing *The Mandarins:*

It was a matter of regret for me that a novel always failed to render the contingency of life: the imitations of it a novelist may attempt are soon belied by exigencies [la nécessité] of form. In an autobiography, on the other hand, events retain all the gratuitousness, the unpredictability and the often preposterous complications that marked their original occurrence; this fidelity to real life conveys better than even the most skillful transposition how things really happen to people. (FC, pp. 498–99/p. 523)

Howard's rendering of la nécessité as "exigencies" misses Beauvoir's implication that literary form does indeed encode some of the structures of necessity. However, it is the "gratuitousness," what she elsewhere calls "the surge of backwash, and the contradictions of life itself" (FC, p. 319), that she claims to seek in autobiography. For Beauvoir intellectual life and truth-telling are inextricably related: "I am an intellectual, I take the words and truth to be of value" (FC, p. 365). Yet on even this founding commitment, her views are fraught with contradiction. "Words," after all, "are by nature birds of passage"; moreover, writing the self is bedeviled by "the caprices of memory" (FC, p. vi). The passage quoted above about autobiography and the "contingency of life" continues by acknowledging that even autobiography's "fidelity to real life" has serious limitations:

The danger is that the reader may not be able to discern any clear image amid this welter of caprice, just a hodgepodge. In the same way that it is impossible for a doctor to define both the position of a corpuscle and the length of the wave attached to it, so the writer is unable to depict the facts of a life and its meaning at one and the same time. (FC, p. 499)

Again:

The self has only a probable objectivity, and anyone saying "I" only grasps the outer edge of it; an outsider can get a clearer and more accurate picture. Let me repeat that this personal account is not offered in any sense as an "explanation." Indeed, one of my main reasons for undertaking it is my realization that self-knowledge is impossible, and the best one can hope for is self-revelation. [Le moi n'est qu'un object probable, et celui qui dit je n'en saisit que des profils; autrui peut en avoir une vision plus nette ou plus juste. Encore une fois, cet exposé ne se présente aucunement comme une explication. Et même, si je l'ai entrepris, c'est en grande partie parce que je sais qu'on ne peut jamais se connaître mais seulement se raconter.] (PL, p. 292/p. 419)

Her view, then, appears to be that words can go a long way toward capturing the "facts" in some undifferentiated form, but that where writing the self is concerned, interpretation of the "facts" has to be left to the reader. Self-knowledge is said to be chimerical, a view that should be seen in the context of her claim that she was not introspective;[16] as we shall see, she also regarded certain of its

styles as politically unacceptable. From a person of Beauvoir's philosophical sophistication, so blunt a distinction between fact and meaning is surprising: she
says little about the authorial pre-interpretive selection of "facts" that precedes
the reader's engagement. But the ostensible handing over of meaning-making to
the reader—a familiar claim in Montaigne, Rousseau, and others in the French
memorialist tradition—has profound implications not just for the stories Beauvoir tells about herself, but for the stories she tells about how first-person stories
are constituted. Here we need to consider the metanarrative dimension of her
autobiography in more detail.

Seeking to "tell the whole truth" about the self is, for want of a better term, a
species of realism. In many ways realism is germane to Beauvoir's undertaking:
she wants to offer a full account of the social-ideological determinations of the
self and of the historico-ideological world—features that come under the rubric
of what she calls "situation."[17] She also wants to represent the psychological
processes through which people, exemplified by her own self, internalize and, in
some cases, transcend their social conditioning—what Anthony Giddens terms
reflexive 'monitoring'. However, among the four main volumes of autobiography, there are significant variations of narrative mode. The composing of self
across the four volumes (the books themselves written over a period of fourteen
years) is organized in a manner that seems intended to reinforce certain claims
about her growth and development; in particular, about the attainment of a politically responsible impersonality.[18] The often novelistic *Memoirs of a Dutiful
Daughter* is strongly subjectivist in tone and manner, especially early on. Its form
simulates the egotism that the narrative condemns, and its notion of "duty" suggests (at one of the text's many levels) inauthentic attitudes and acts of the will
that spring from ideological indoctrination. *The Prime of Life* is transitional. It
begins in a similarly personalized register, and its early sections are redolent with
the sense of the self being at the peak of its agential powers—as the phrase "the
prime of life" would suggest. However, as we shall see, its later sections narrate
a turning point wherein Beauvoir supposedly transcends her bourgeois self.
Force of Circumstance is true to its title: the most impersonal of the volumes, it
devotes long tracts to the political and the wider social worlds. Inevitably, the
self is still at the center, and interpersonal relationships remain prominent; but
this book is more devoted than the others to what she had earlier called her determination to "bear witness" to "all experience" (*PL*, p. 26). *Circumstance* here
denotes the constraints that the adult will encounters and must negotiate. In
some respects *All Said and Done* comes full circle. Though not deeply introspective, its tone and focus are personalized, often ruminative. It engages in
open-ended speculation about the relations between self, luck, contingency, and
circumstance. Its title suggests that the quest is at an end, the work done, the
contradictions in life at last conceded. She says: "I have almost always felt happy
and well-adjusted" (*ASD*, p. 462) and, "I accept what I am" (*ASD*, p. 37). She

has come as close as a human being can to that characteristic but ultimately unattainable aspiration of the autobiographer—the desire to "overtake my being, to rejoin and merge with it" (*ASD,* p. 28). The long struggle of introspection and self-definition seems to be over.[19]

These shifts in mode and emphasis are revealing. To some extent they are typical of multivolume autobiographies that are written over long periods. In such narratives, the changes that the writing self undergoes over long periods result in revised forms of expressive mode, so that the reader is confronted with change along several axes: the changes in the self-as-subject that the narrative charts; the alterations in the writing self that charts these changes, alterations that emerge during different phases of composition; revised narrative accounts of the self-as-subject, as later volumes reread aspects of the life that earlier ones had already narrated. And there are other layers of complication as well: for instance, the ways in which later volumes narrate the writing of earlier ones, sometimes seeing those early narrative acts as important life events in and of themselves. Beauvoir's autobiographical volumes exhibit all of these complexities, and her first-person oeuvre is further complicated by the miscellany of modes in which she writes: in addition to autobiography proper, memoir, journals, travel reportage, letters, and hybrid forms like the blend of pathography and interview that she adopts in *Adieux.*[20] But there is a further and crucial set of complexities that arise because of the sort of autobiography she writes. Let us for the moment say that she writes *existential autobiography,* and consider some of the complications this entails.

Depending on how you look at it, the very idea of existential autobiography can seem entirely natural or wildly improbable. It seems natural insofar as existentialism places such emphasis on the self's capacity for change across time—a staple of the traditional autobiographical genre. On the other hand, as Edmund Smyth and Terry Keefe note, there is a sense in which existentialism's account of change constitutes a threat to the very genre of autobiography, because the notion of change in question is so radical.[21] When Sartre talks of a "rupture with determinism," he means that the self undergoes such a radical process of reinvention from moment to moment that it only retains the characteristics of a persisting entity in the most notional and superficial ways; and the same applies to Sartre's slogan that "existence precedes essence." Taken literally, this might seem to suggest there is no ongoing essence that could be represented in autobiography, that the self, being utterly contingent, will elude the representational structures of naming and writing, except—again—in the most notional respects.[22] In chapter 3 I discussed some of the ways in which postmodern "autobiographies" such as *Roland Barthes by Roland Barthes* try to give formal expression to this ontological premise of discontinuity, and I have argued that, strictly speaking, such an attempt is doomed to failure. Autobiography cannot be written without substantial philosophical and formal concessions to the fact that selves do indeed persist, at some fundamental levels, across time.

This applies even to the most intellectually powerful autobiographers, like Simone de Beauvoir. However, her case is even less straightforward than these reflections might suggest. Having "for the moment" characterized her as an existential autobiographer, we now need to qualify this designation, because in fact her autobiographies are, among other things, an unfolding *critique of existentialism*. They show how and why she became an existentialist; but they then go on to show how and why she *ceased* to be one. She narrates a form of what John D. Barbour calls "deconversion." Yet even this doesn't quite capture the full complexity of the case since in some ways Beauvoir always remained indebted to certain aspects, concepts, and attitudes that she learned from existentialism—a pattern that Barbour sees as typical of "deconversion."[23] To take an example: when she explains that in *All Said and Done* she has sought to "overtake my being and merge with it," she is expressing a sentiment that is antithetical to the entire culture of Sartrean existentialism, where the very notion of "nothingness" asserts that consciousness is constitutively Other to itself; that being and consciousness of being can never coincide, can never "merge." In Derridean terms, there is no such thing as "presence." But there are other times when Beauvoir-as-autobiographer sounds every inch the existentialist: "Being means making oneself be" (*ASD,* p. 36) could come straight from the pages of *Being and Nothingness.* So, though not predominantly an existential autobiographer, she is a chronicler of existentialism who remains, to some extent at least, in its debt. In her autobiographical writings, existentialism takes its place alongside various other intellectual discourses: principally feminist, Marxist, Freudian, and humanist.[24] All contribute to what is one of the central activities of these volumes, and one of the principle sources of their greatness: the production of a narrative history of the will.

III. Threads and the History of the Will

The Second Sex explicitly links the mythology of the spinners with woman's subjection under patriarchy. Beauvoir argues that the Moirai exemplify the traditional construction of woman as the occluded, threatening, and essentialized Other, ossified in myth as immanent beings who are responsible for the suffering of the race:

> The cult of germination has always been associated with the cult of the dead. The Earth Mother engulfs the bones of her children. They are women—the Parcae, the Moirai—who weave the destiny of mankind; but it is they, also, who cut the threads. In most popular representations, death is a woman, and it is for women to bewail the dead because death is their work.[25]

The figure of threads and weaving is one of the organizing motifs of Simone de Beauvoir's autobiographical writings. In these volumes she uses the figure, as so many others autobiographers have done, to explore issues of freedom and determinism, fate and volition. The figure is central to her account of how she developed, in particular to the history that she writes of her own will; and because this is in many ways the history of a transgressive female life, threads and weaving play an important part in the feminist dimension of the narrative—in the narrative construction of the female self-as-transcendence. Yet in one respect Beauvoir's use of the figure in the autobiographical writings is conventional: she says nothing about its psychogenesis as historical myth; nor does she reflect on the irony of the fact that in charting her emergence from patriarchal conditioning, she employs a figure that has such deep roots in patriarchal constructions of the feminine. She uses threads and weaving much as male autobiographers like Spender and Koestler do, as a form of gender-neutral philosophical notation. This is consistent with her tendency in the autobiographical works to depict her will as so powerful that the constraints that afflict most women have not obtained for her. Thus in *The Prime of Life* she recalls that as a young woman:

> I attached small importance to the actual conditions of my life: nothing, I believed, could impede my will [*rien n'entravait, croyais-je, ma volonté*]. I did not deny my femininity, any more than I took it for granted: I simply ignored it. I had the same freedoms and responsibilities as men did. I was spared the curse that weighs upon most women, that of dependence . . . To earn one's living is not an end in itself, but it is the only way to achieve securely based inner independence. (*PL*, pp. 291–92/*p. 418*)

The history of the will is encapsulated in the titles of the volumes: *Memoirs of a Dutiful Daughter* suggests the will's subjection to patriarchy and the bourgeoisie; *The Prime of Life* conveys a sense of the self at the peak of its powers, the will as gloriously ascendant; *Force of Circumstance* has the opposite implication: circumstance is that which sets constraints upon the will; while *All Said and Done* seems to imply a cessation of willing, or at least of the colossal investment of will energies that marked the younger Beauvoir's commitment to her life project. This pattern is reflected in the repetition of *force* in the titles of the second and third volumes—*La force de l'âge, La force des choses*—signaling the narrative's displacement of power from the self to the circumstances that surround and constrain it. In *The Prime of Life* she argues that "to divide one's life up into sections is an arbitrary process" (*PL*, p. 285), yet these volumes chart a sequence of relatively distinct phases of the will's development. The first is the daughter of the Catholic bourgeoisie's "submission to divine will [*le recours à la volonté divine*]" (*MDD*, p. 22/*p. 28*), an attitude later given formal articulation in a school curriculum that featured Aquinas as a central figure (*MDD*, p. 160);[26] then there is the velleity she experiences as "the docile reflection of my parents' will" (*MDD*, p. 34); more disturbingly, she senses, as does Maggie in James's *What Maisie Knew*,[27] that she is "the prey of grown-up wills [*les adultes brimaient ma volonté*]" (*MDD*, p. 15/*p. 19*). Later, when she begins to explore versions of the will's emancipation, her first imaginings are narcissistic and conventional: "My life would be a beautiful story come true, a story I would make up as I went along" (*MDD*, p. 178). She figures this fantasy in terms of weaving the threads of her own life: "I took up the threads of my life again [*les fils de ma vie se renouaient*]" (*MDD*, p. 212/*p. 278*); "I took up the threads of my own worried existence [*je repris le fil de mes soucis*]" (*MDD*, p. 218/*p. 286*).

Life as the beautiful story that one spins for oneself is the stuff of fairy tales. The world of the fairy tale is at once contingent and will-governed: while familiar orders of cause and effect—motivation and predictability—do not apply, the will in a Grimms' tale can possess magical and transformative powers that brook no constraint. Yet such narratives scarcely touch subjectivity. They give no real psychological context for the will. As she outgrows such narratives, the young Simone begins to hunger for a vocabulary of inwardness. Feeling betrayed by her parents and the class they represent, she decides:

> I would stand outside myself, watch over and observe myself; in my diary [which she has just begun] I had long conversations with myself. I was entering a world whose newness stunned me. I learned to distinguish between distress and melancholy, lack of emotion and serenity; I learned to recognize the hesitations of the heart, and its ecstasies, the splendor of great renunciations, and the subterranean murmurings of hope. I entered into exalted trances, as on those evenings when I used to gaze upon the sky full of moving clouds behind the distant blue of the hills; I was both the landscape and its beholder: I existed only through myself, and for myself. I was grateful for an exile which had driven me to find such lonely and such lofty joys . . . (*MDD*, p. 202)

The childhood diary is her first venture into first-person writing, and she was to keep a diary intermittently for the rest of her life. This is, as one would expect, a profoundly important moment. The diary signals the opening up of something like adult reflexive consciousness, of the for-itself ("for myself"), and the discovery of a language of inwardness. Wittgenstein would not abide such a phrase, but let us say in phrasing that recalls his that the young Simone is learning a grammar of interiority. The grammar is in part authentic in that it enables distinctions between feelings and conventional social accounts of inner states. But its authenticity is limited, as can be seen from her recourse to pious Romantic sublimities:[28] she now identifies with a deeply individualistic culture of the self; yet this culture too is heavily conventional. Romanticism says "know thyself," but, looking back, she knows that her knowledge was mediated through formulaic Romantic categories. Like George Sand and Mme. de Staël, she uses narrative to explore the history of the individual's struggle to find her bearings in relation to the sublime.

We've seen that Richard Rorty argues that Romantic epistemology tends to construe truth as something that is "made" rather than "found."[29] In this view, the Imagination responds to contingency by doing the weaving. In *Memoirs of a Dutiful Daughter,* Beauvoir uses an array of intertextual allusions in order to bring out a contrast between crude Romantic accounts of world-making and accounts that urge the opposing empiricist and Enlightenment virtues of observation, representation, and constraint upon the will's capacity to fashion its own realities. One of the key texts here is an English work, George Eliot's novel *The Mill on the Floss.* In fact, *Memoirs of a Dutiful Daughter* reads rather like a George Eliot novel, so it is not surprising to find explicit references to Eliot's books therein: "George Eliot's *The Mill on the Floss* made an even deeper impression on me than *Little Women* . . . Maggie Tulliver, like myself, was torn between others and herself: I recognized myself in her. She too was dark, loved nature and books and life, and was too headstrong to be able to observe the conventions of her surroundings, and yet was very sensitive to the criticism of a brother she adored" (*MDD,* p. 148). In Beauvoir's narrative, however, the central character—herself—survives and transcends her surroundings. It is Zaza, the unreconstructed "dutiful daughter," who, like Maggie, is symbolically murdered by her environment.

The young Simone shares with Maggie an imperious need: "I loved being loved," she says (*MDD,* p. 200); Maggie has a "need of being loved."[30] This need is powerfully evident in the way in which, in a key phrase, Simone "composed" her "personality": "Right from the start, I had composed the personality I wished to present to the world; it had brought me so much praise and so many great satisfactions that I had finished by identifying myself with the character I had built up: it was my one reality" (*MDD,* p. 33). In a George Eliot novel this kind of self-invention is seen as a dangerous thing. It reflects alienation from one's true self; the primacy of conventional or fictitious images of self over authentic being. In some respects Beauvoir agrees. At the same time, composing a self, however inauthentic in this instance, is an act of willed self-invention; and self-invention is central to the ethos of existentialism, as well as to Beauvoir's postexistential commitment to transcendence. To quote a key formulation again: "Being means making oneself be." Such self-composition is, then, a precursor of authentic forms that refuse conventional accounts of the self and its narrative possibilities. The ability to "identify" with a self-construct—to live it as an existential reality—is likewise an important and prescient achievement. And of course composing a self is a preparation not only for the experiential construction of alternative self-images; it is also a forerunner of the elaborated and literal (re)composition of self that we call autobiography.

Composing a self exerts a check on event causation. It grasps the freedom implicit in the contingency of life and self, and reinvents the self in the light of some intimation or vision of transcendence. The conception of will at work here is Freedom as the Genus of Volition. The young Simone is drawn to that part of Maggie Tulliver that feels the solicitation of dream, release, sensuousness. In an

odd aside she recalls that in early adulthood, when she was unable to find a publisher for her fiction, she was entranced by an image that in her mind was a composite of Maggie and her creator: "I passionately wanted the public to like my
work; therefore like George Eliot, who had become identified in my mind with
Maggie Tulliver, I would myself become an imaginary character, endowed with
beauty, desirability, and a sort of shimmering transparent loveliness. It was this
metamorphosis [*transfiguration*] that my ambition sought" (*PL*, p. 291/*p. 417*).
Peter Green's rendering of *transfiguration* as "metamorphosis" is problematical,
but to the extent that Beauvoir refers here to a radical transformation of the self,
she is writing counter to George Eliot. In Eliot's fiction, with the exception of
Daniel Deronda, such radical change is seen as the stuff of immature yearning,
of fairy tale. In *The Mill on the Floss* it is said to be downright dangerous because
it disrupts the organic continuity between the self and its past. The world of this
novel is more complicated than Rorty's account of Romantic epistemology
would allow because it is patterned on the Wordsworthian premise that the past
constitutes an immitigable Truth that the present self ignores at its peril. To dis-
rupt the continuities between present and past can only engender division,
alienation, moral incoherence in the self. The anguished Maggie, having dis-
rupted her ties to the past by eloping with Stephen Guest, says to him: "'If the
past is not to bind us, where can duty lie? We should have no law but the inclination of the moment.'"³¹ It is an anxiety that was to be voiced by critics of existentialism. Beauvoir's references to Eliot reflect a complex relationship to Romanticism in both its philosophical and literary manifestations. In terms of
autobiography, her Romantic tendencies betoken a much more strident oppo-
sitional relation between self and social-ideological world than ever appears in
Eliot's work. Beauvoir's is a more hostile, raw, unstable, and narcissistic Romanticism: the kind epitomized by Beauvoir's hero among autobiographers, and a
writer whom George Eliot also revered: Rousseau.³²

Beauvoir's strictures on her early Romanticism are of a piece with her critique of existentialism, and inevitably so since existentialism owes so much to
Romantic epistemology. Her autobiographical history of the will is strong in
its condemnation of existentialism—that "appeal to man's will [*l'existential-
isme . . . en appelait à sa volonté*]" (*FC*, p. 9/*p. 19*), the "antibourgeois anar-
chism" (*PL*, p. 204)—which was to dominate her prewar years with Sartre. It
is one of the great ironies of her autobiography that she effectively turns
Sartre's famous existential diagnostic term—*mauvaise foi*—back upon the life
and thought that characterized their existential phase. She recalls that during
this phase they were hostile to "*la vie intérieure*" (*PL*, p. 24); they sought to cast
off the natural attitude, seeing existence not as the world of bourgeois fabrica-
tion but as "a brutal adventure that was life" (*MDD,* p. 357). This existence
had to be confronted in all its phenomenological immediacy, its teeming contingency, without the consolations of cultural filters. She is drawn to Sartre, in

part at least, because "confronted with an object, he would look it straight on instead of trying to explain it away with a myth, a word, an impression, or a preconceived idea: he wouldn't let it go until he had grasped all its ins and outs and all its multiple significations" (*MDD*, p. 360). This habit of perception and analysis required and expressed a deep hostility to bourgeois norms. But it was riddled with contradiction: "Between the two of us we tore the bourgeoisie to shreds, tooth and nail. In the case of Sartre and myself, such hostility remained individualistic, *ergo* bourgeois" (*PL*, p. 31). This "*ergo* bourgeois" posture, with its "quasi-solipsism and illusory autonomy," was a species of self-indulgent Kantianism. Concluding that, in the early days, she and Sartre "were wrong about almost everything," she continues:

> The mistake we made was in failing to restrict this concept [of freedom] to its proper limits. We clung to the image of Kant's dove, supported rather than hindered in flight by the resistant air. We regarded any existing situation as raw material for our joint efforts, and not as a factor conditioning them: we imagined ourselves to be wholly independent agents. (*PL*, p. 18)

She goes on to talk of their "spiritual pride," "political blindness" (*PL*, p. 18), their "Cartesian rationalism," their belief that they consisted of "pure reason and pure will [*pure conscience et pure volonté*]" (*PL*, p. 19/*p. 23*). Each in a sense "lacked a real family" and they had "elevated this contingency into a principle" (*PL*, p. 19)[33]—the principle of radical, unconditioned freedom—which reflected the fact that, at this stage, "freedom was the very essence of our existence" (*PL*, p. 20). Again: "It was our conditioning as young *petit bourgeois* intellectuals that led us to believe ourselves free of all conditioning whatsoever" (*PL*, p. 22). The Cartesian inheritance of course entailed a sense of the self—whether one's own or others'—as having substance, internality, as being a unique "centre of interiorization [*centre d'intériorisation*]" (*ASD*, p. 2/*p. 12*) of will. Beauvoir's and Sartre's was a "depth" self, a bohemian version of the substantial humanist self. One first-person corollary of this was the habit of detailed, narcissistic introspection: part of Sartre's appeal was also that he would discuss with her "a subject which interested me above all others: myself" (*MDD*, p. 360). A third-person concomitant was an overriding fascination and preoccupation with the lives and selves of other people: "Whether in Paris, Rouen, or Le Havre . . . our main topic of conversation was the various people we knew" (*PL*, p. 103).

One of her most piquant summaries of their outlook at the time suggests that some version of Will as Rational Appetite lurks within their existential commitments. She refers to their "rationalist voluntarist position: in a clear-minded individual, we thought, freedom would win out over complexes, memories, influences, or any traumatic experience" (*PL*, p. 23). At this point she is remarking on their lack of interest in Marxism and psychoanalysis, both of which she now thinks might have challenged some of their illusions. From their "rationalist-voluntarist position," she and Sartre had scorned psychoanalytic theory because of (among other things) "the importance it attached to the unconscious, and the rigidity of its mechanistic theories [that] meant that Freudianism, as we conceived it, was bound to eradicate human free will [*le freudisme . . . écrasait la liberté humaine*]" (*PL*, p. 22/*p. 29*). But if Freudianism in effect dissolved the will into the murky, nondeliberative, contingent depths of the unconscious, Marxism seemed to dissolve it into the realm of material determination. In *The Ethics of Ambiguity* Beauvoir explains that existentialists oppose Marxism because of the degree to which Marxists see consciousness as being externally determined: in this view, "subjectivity is re-absorbed into the objectivity of the given world."[34] Ultimately it is not theory but History that throws out the challenge to their deluded state. Prior to the Second World War she resists the contingent nature of history, its corrosive power to undermine the security of self:

> What I could not accept [in 1939] was that history was being made every day, in all its digressive complexity, and that some unforeseen event might come up over the horizon tomorrow without my knowledge or consent. Such an admission would have spelled danger for me. This concern with my own peace of mind forced me to make time stand still . . . (*PL*, p. 121)

Then, in the spring of 1939, the famous change comes over her:

> Suddenly, History burst over me, and I dissolved into fragments [*l'Histoire fondit sur moi, j'éclatai*]. I woke to find myself scattered over the four quarters of the globe, linked by every nerve in me to each and every other individual. All my ideas and values were turned upside down . . . (*PL*, p. 295/*p. 424*)

This moment, a secular revisioning of the religious confessional conversion in which there is a "paradoxical dying into life,"[35] has many meanings, some of them indeed "contradictory." She contends that at the moment when History bursts over her, rending the self into "fragments," she experiences an absolute break with her prior self, and with the "quasi-solipsism and illusory autonomy" (*PL*, 295) in which she and Sartre had been living. This break, too, is narrated as a metamorphosis: "Later, when I ceased to regard my life as an autonomous and self-sufficient project, I was obliged to rediscover my links with a universe the very face of which I had forgotten. It is this metamorphosis [*transformation*] I now propose to relate" (*PL*, p. 296/*p. 424*).[36] That "face" is the face of the Other, with all its power to rend, threaten, and remake the Self. As she becomes more aware of History, the force of circumstance, culture's complex systems of ideological constraint, she learns not only that she is not free to act in the ways and degrees that existential invocations of the contingent had suggested, but that self-invention, too, is constrained in unsuspected ways. One was not in fact the sole author of one's own script. Threads again: "Not only was I not weaving my life, but its shape, the shape of the time I lived in, the shape of all I loved, depended on the future [*Non seulement ma vie, ce n'était pas moi qui la tissais, mais sa figure, la figure de mon époque et de tout ce que j'aimais, dépendait de l'avenir*]" (*FC,* p. 263/*p. 283*). Now she echoes an emphatically deterministic classical version of the threads and weaving that figures a human life as a thread that unwinds off a spool until it runs out at the moment of death. Writing what she hopes is a truthful autobiography "obliges me to follow obediently the thread the years have unwound" (*FC,* p. 276). The Second World War reveals to her that the threads of one's own life were to a frightening and unsuspected extent in others' hands. When Sartre returns from internment during the war:

> I had been . . . contented—but quite differently from before. Events had changed me; what Sartre used to call my "divided mind" had finally yielded before the unanswerable arguments that reality had brought against it. I was at last prepared to admit that my life was not a story of my own telling, but a compromise between myself and the world at large. (*PL,* p. 385)

In 1961, appalled and alienated by French policy in the Algerian War and reeling from the deaths of Richard Wright and Maurice Merleau-Ponty, she experiences, in more extreme form, this same feeling that one is a witness to, rather than author of, one's own life; that will is unavailing:

> This life I'm living isn't mine any more, I thought. Certainly I no longer imagined I could maneuver it the way I wanted, but I still believed I had some contribution to make toward its construction; in fact, I had no control over it at all. I was merely an impotent onlooker watching the play of alien forces: history, time and death. This inevitability did not even leave me the consolation of tears. I had exhausted all my capacities for revolt, for regret, I was vanquished, I let go. Hostile to the society to which I belonged, banished by my age from the future, stripped fiber by fiber of my past [*dépouillée fibre par fibre du passé*], I was reduced to facing each moment with nothing but my naked existence. (*FC,* p. 587/*p. 615*)

This is the counterpoint to the moment when History, the bearer of contingency, bursts over the self, decimating its protective narcissism, unweaving the fibers that compose it, and reconstituting the individual as an ethical will committed to collective liberation. In 1961 the will undergoes another phase in which its power all but collapses. Contingency no longer delivers the self: it bears down upon it, the menacing "play of alien forces" threatening its viability. Will is for the moment in a pathological state. This is the secular equivalent of the moment of spiritual nadir that occurs in many of the great autobiographies. It is a moment from which Beauvoir qua public intellectual never entirely recovers, though the "private" individual was to find deep reserves of energy and purpose again.

Force of Circumstance ends on a famous note of disillusionment. Looking back on herself as a "young and credulous girl" with life's "gold mine at my feet," she says: "I realize with stupor how much I was gypped" (*FC*, p. 658). In *All Said and Done* she explains that "gypped" refers to the illusions that she inherited from her class: "Bourgeois culture is a promise" (*ASD*, p. 117), and it is this promise—of order, embedded values, good faith, and idealism—that has been broken. "It was," she confesses, "by no means easy to tear myself away from such splendid expectations" (*ASD*, p. 117). The implication, indeed the assertion, of the conclusion of *Force of Circumstance* is that this act of detachment has finally been concluded. *Memoirs of a Dutiful Daughter* ends with the death of a daughter of the bourgeoisie. In a different way *Force of Circumstance* is intended to do something similar. Yet of all the volumes, the last, *All Said and Done*, is the least politically engaged, the most ruminative, the most concerned with the qualitative dimensions of life: aesthetic, interpersonal, recollective. After the long stretches of political-social documentary that occur in *Force of Circumstance*, this volume seems intent on recomposing the self as a substantive, nuanced "centre of interiorization." She now replaces the thread on a spool figure with a more agential conception that sees a life as a "detotalized totality [*totalité-détotalisée*]" in which the past is settled but the future is open to circumscribed shaping by the individual will. In a passage capturing many of the connections that characterize the nexus between autobiography and the figure of the threads of life, Beauvoir argues:

> A life is set within a given space of time; it has a beginning and an end; it evolves in given places, always retaining the same roots and spinning itself an unchangeable past whose opening towards the future is limited. It is impossible to grasp and define a life as one can grasp and define a thing, since a life is "an unsummed whole," as Sartre puts it, a detotalized totality, and therefore it has no *being*. But one can ask certain questions about it. How is a life formed? How much of it is made up by circumstances, how much by necessity, how much by chance [*de la nécessité, du hasard*], and how much by the subject's own options and his personal initiatives? (*ASD*, p. 2/*pp. 12–13*)

She begins the discussion of these issues by querying one of the most puzzling yet taken-for-granted aspects of human existence—the individual's centrality in his or her own life: "What stroke of chance has brought this about?" She itemizes various factors involved in her coming-into-being and concludes with a formulation that includes both contingency and will: "Tossed into the world, I have been subjected to its laws and its contingencies, ruled by wills other than my own, by circumstances and by history: it is therefore reasonable for me to feel that I myself am contingent. What staggers me is that at the same time I am *not* contingent [*Jetée dans le monde, j'ai été soumise à ses lois et à ses accidents, dépendant de volontés étrangères, des circonstances, de l'histoire: je suis donc justifiée de ressentir ma contingence; ce qui me donne le vertige, c'est qu'en même temps je ne le suis pas]" (ASD, p. 1/p. 11).* This seems to mean that though in one sense her coming-into-being is a freak of chance, an entirely contingent event, there is another sense in which "she" constitutes an absolute and "necessary co-incidence of the subject and his history" (ASD, p. 1). If her history had been oth-erwise, she would be someone else. Contingent events can precipitate forms of necessity, presumably because, in this later view, the world is not wholly con-tingent, wholly devoid of "laws." This has implications for the will. The biolog-ical facts of birth—her sex, for instance—are entirely a matter of chance; like-wise, the power that "wills other than my own" has over my life is to some extent a contingent and irresistible thing. But once a life is under way, it seems that the role of chance, of luck, is variable and that my own will comes into play. She ar-gues that given the demographics of her family, much of the course of her child-hood was inevitable and therefore not strictly a matter of chance. Some events, however, are a matter of chance in the sense, first, that they might easily not have occurred and, second, that their impact on her life came to be massively deter-minative. One such event was meeting Zaza, the shadow "dutiful" daughter of *Memoirs of a Dutiful Daughter.* Another was meeting Sartre, the event she con-sistently describes as the most important in her life. Yet even here, she contends, "I find it hard to decide how far our meeting was owing to chance" (ASD, p. 19). On reflection the place of chance seems limited. Given their intellectual pro-clivities and the small circles of the Parisian intelligentsia, it seems likely that if they had not met as and when they did, they would have met at some other time. Moreover, "although to some extent it was chance that brought us into contact, the commitment that has bound our lives together was freely elected [*librement choisi*]: a choice of this kind is not a decree but a long-term under-taking" (ASD, pp. 19–20/p. 34). It was, in other words, an act of will that oc-curred in a setting comprised of contingency, law, and prior volitions. In this set-ting the inaugurating act of will sets certain law-governed causal chains in motion. This appears to be what she means by the strangely theological charac-terization of life as the "fulfilment of a primary design" (ASD, p. 30).

As will now be apparent, Beauvoir's account of contingency is partly framed in terms of an account of luck. Indeed, like Hemingway, Spender, and others, she uses autobiography as a means of exploring various orders of luck and their relations to the will. Near the end of *All Said and Done,* she tells us that "I have trusted in my star" (ASD, p. 462). She frequently reflects on how lucky she has been, and she is fascinated by the luck or ill fortune that befalls people she has been close to. Beauvoir was a risk taker: indeed the ethos of risk—emotional, sexual, physical, political, financial, material—is central to the antibourgeois bo-hemian legend that surrounds her and Sartre as countercultural icons.[37] She characterizes writing as "the feeling of risking and at the same time of tran-scending myself" (FC, p. 127), and the autobiography seems to distinguish, often implicitly, between two kinds of risk in particular. One is a kind of risk-as-submission that we will see in Spender, where one submits to the random play of chance in an undiscriminating and wholly reckless way. This is the realm of pure chance—the roulette wheel rather than the racetrack where Hemingway laid his informed wagers; its ethical correlative is the doctrine of moral luck that I have attributed to Hemingway. In risk-as-transcendence,[38] however, one takes risks that involve an element of rational calculation: various possible outcomes are contemplated; the will takes its counsel from rationality. The individual's choices are predicated, at least in part, on the knowledge that if risks pay off, they will produce significant development and change in the self. Chance might intervene in unproductive, destructive, or unpredictable ways; but the risk is to some extent circumscribed by an initial choice in which certain unpromising fields of possibility are eliminated. When the young Beauvoir refuses to join the public service, as her father had hoped, she runs the risk of not having a financially secure adult life; but the choice to eliminate this option is made, the risk taken, because she senses that she may have an intellectual vocation. This may or may not eventuate; if it does, the dutiful daughter of the bourgeoisie transcends herself and becomes an intellectual. This account of the will is a version of Will as Rational Appetite. While it constitutes a postexistential phase in Beauvoir's thinking, we should not overstate the extent of the philosophical change involved. As Iris Murdoch notes, Sartrean existentialism was strongly rationalist in tendency in the sense that it sees "reflective self-awareness" as humanity's "supreme virtue"[39]—a point borne out by Beauvoir's characterization of her and Sartre's existential position as a species of "rationalist voluntarism."

Beauvoir's later notion of the self as "centre of interiorization" builds on existentialism's respect for rationality—it allows the will still greater access to rational counsel; it predicates a high degree of integration among the self's rational and affective dimensions: "If a theory convinced me, it did not remain an external, alien phenomenon; it altered my relationship with the world, and colored all my experience. In short, I possessed both considerable powers of assimilation and a well-developed critical sense; and philosophy was for me a living reality, which gave me never-failing satisfaction" (*PL,* p. 178). As a consequence, the later view ascribes a reduced presence to contingency, not only in the world but in the self. She now gives unprecedentedly full endorsement to the notion of the self-as-"unity." It is clear that unity so conceived doesn't entail fixity; but it does involve a degree of continuity between the history of the self and its current manifestation, and between choices and consequences. This is the "pattern" to which Beauvoir refers in the preface to *The Prime of Life* (p. 10). References like the following would make no sense in a full-blooded existential autobiography: "my essential self [*la vérité de mon être*]" (*MDD,* p. 115/*p. 151*); "growing up did not necessarily mean denying one's true self [*vieiller n'était pas nécessairement se renier*]" (*MDD,* p. 132/*p. 174*). Such phrases, which are signature terms of the discourses of liberal humanism, suggest a degree of immanence in the self—a conception that pulls against the ethos of transcendence that also figures so powerfully in the autobiography. The pull between self-as-immanence and self-as-transcendence is related to another tension that shadows Beauvoir's entire self-portrait: the disjunction between the self as "glorious singularity" (*MDD*, p. 64), on the one hand, and as Other-directed, fragmented impersonality, on the other; between narcissistic self-assurance and supposed self-abnegation. Whatever her claims to the contrary, the tone of narcissistic self-assurance is seldom absent for long from these volumes.

The autobiography tries to resolve the tension between immanence and transcendence by recourse to a version of the dialectic. In *Force of Circumstance* Beauvoir had argued that "a man's truth includes his objective existence and his past, but it is not inevitably limited to such fossilizations" (*FC*, p. 119). One of the finest meditations on the past, change, and the individual's role in transcending such "fossilizations" comes at the end of the first part of *The Prime of Life* when Beauvoir discusses what she terms the "dialectic of growth" of the individual:

> It is precisely this kind of detailed explanation [the significance of her "feminine status"] which I most mistrust. I have attempted to set out the facts in as frank a way as possible, neither simplifying their ambiguities nor swaddling them in false syntheses, but offering them for the reader's own interpretation. Nevertheless, I reject the crude sort of yardstick against which our more elementary psycho-analysts will in all likelihood attempt to measure them: no doubt it will be asserted that Sartre was a substitute father figure for me, and that Olga took the place of the child I never had. In the eyes of such doctrinaires, adult relationships are non-existent: they take no note of that dialectic process which from childhood to maturity—starting with roots the deep importance of which I am very far from misconceiving—works a slow transformation upon one's emotional ties with other people. It preserves them, but achieves this preservation through a by-passing process which encapsulates the object of one's feelings, and lets one re-examine it afresh. Certainly my attachment to Sartre could, in one sense, be traced back to my childhood; but it also was a result of the sort of person *he* was.(*PL*, p. 292)

"Transformation" here replaces the more radical notion of metamorphosis. She concedes that there is some truth in the psychoanalytic imputation of a transference from father to Sartre: psychoanalysis has it uses. But the relationship with Sartre is not reducible to such formulae. It has to do, also, with the kind of person he was qua Other, and with the fact that, on account of his human particularity, she "freely elected" to be with him. Such freedom is not absolute, and, in contrast to her early existential position, all choices are seen as to some extent conditioned—though not necessarily determined—by one's past. But they are also *enabled* by that past: the "dialectic of growth" means that the past contributes powerfully to the formation of a self that can then reflect and intervene as an agent in shaping its future. The movement is from event to agent causation. This too is a deeply humanistic premise—one that is reinforced in the final volume with its references to "childhood, the key to every life" (*ASD*, p. 35) (though it is in tension with the notion of the "unchangeable past" that appears in the same volume). She is closer here to George Eliot's and John Stuart Mill's conception of volitional intervention in causal sequences[40] than to the existential Sartre on the will. She had argued in *Force of Circumstance* that the "dimension of our existence" that includes "our freedom, our responsibility" cannot be described; that "what can be described is merely our conditioning [*conditionnement*]" (*FC*, p. vii/p. 9). This suggests that, after all, they as existentialists may have been right to think that the will exists in an unconditioned form. Her point now is that in this form it cannot be captured in narrative. Only its forms of instantiation can be described. And yet the autobiographical volumes seem at times to do more than this; they convey the sense of a colossal and deeply rooted power of the will—what she refers to as her own indomitable "will power": "*La volonté qui s'affirmait . . . avait en moi de très anciennes racines*" (*PL*, p. 78/p. 108)—which is something more than the sum of the will's acts and instantiations. It is a power of the self; that which makes transcendence—the surpassing of one's conditioning—possible.

IV. Pacts and Promises: Contingency and the Other

The History that rends Beauvoir into "fragments" in 1939 is but one of the Other's many faces. Consider one of several dream sequences from *Force of Circumstance*. It occurs at a time when she is filled with horror at French atrocities in Algeria. The horror connects with her lifelong terror of aging and death. Of Algeria she says: "And at least my horror had been directed at something outside myself." Now, however, as she grows old, and as her aging is poisoned by the terrors around her, she writes: "I have become an object of horror in my own eyes." Each morning she wakes up saying to herself: "We're going to die." And: "Life is a hell." She has a recurrent dream:

> I am with Sartre in this studio [where she lives]; the phonograph is motionless beneath its cloth cover. Suddenly, music, without my having moved. There is a record on the turntable, it revolves. I twist the control to stop it; impossible to do so, it turns faster and faster, the needle can't keep up, the tone arm gets into the most amazing positions, the inside of the phonograph is roaring like a furnace, there seem to be flames, and the black surface of the record is becoming insanely shiny. At first, the notion that the phonograph is going to collapse under the strain, mild panic which then becomes all-de

vouring: EVERYTHING is going to explode; a supernatural rebellion, incomprehensible, the collapse of all that exists. I am afraid, I am at the end of my rope; I think of calling a specialist. I seem to think he's been here, but then I'm the one who thought of disconnecting the phonograph, and I was afraid when I touched the plug; it stopped. What a mess! The tone arm reduced to a twisted little stick, the needle in shreds, the record shattered, the turntable already ruined, the accessories blasted out of existence, and the disease still lurking inside the machine.

She now offers a gloss on the dream:

> The mysterious and untameable force was that of time and circumstance, it was laying waste my body (that pitiful, blasted twig that had once been an arm), it was hacking away, threatening my past, my life, all that makes me what I am, with total destruction. (*FC,* pp. 584–85)

Passages such as this show how far the process of individuation has come since the days in which the young Simone first discovered her inner world and filtered it through Romantic commonplaces. But the "depth" sense of the self is still there, and some of its concerns are direct continuations from her childhood. One of these is her famous horror of death (she writes memorably of "the joy of being, the horror of being no more" [*PL,* p. 168]); and this in turn connects to her horror of contingency, here imaged as an alien and terrifying force "hacking away" at her past, her life, her self. Few writers have a more highly developed sense than Beauvoir of the body as locus of immitigable contingency, its delights and its inexorable disintegration alike reflections of the "tragic ambiguity" of "the human condition." In part, this has to do with being a woman. She writes in *The Second Sex:* "Women's fate is bound up with that of perishable things; in losing them they lose all."[41] But we have also seen this sense of biological necessity, another "humanist" strand in her conception of the self, in *Roland Barthes by Roland Barthes.*

It is highly significant that the precipitating cause of the dream—atrocities in Algeria—is political as well as personal. As in another discussion of dreams in *Force of Circumstance,* where she speaks of associating her nightmares with "the walking skeletons of Calcutta or those little gourds with human faces—children suffering from malnutrition" (*FC,* p. 654), this one, or more precisely her interpretation of it, suggests a deep link between the contingencies one fears in one's self, in one's constitution as a mortal being, and the appalling contingencies that befall the victims of History. Here self-preoccupation gradates into, almost stands as a metonymy for, that concern for the fate of the Other(s) that the self feels when History rends its unity and casts its fragments "over the four quarters of the globe." It is par excellence an *ethical* response. Like Koestler in his autobiographies, Beauvoir seems here to be intimating the presence of something that resembles what David Parker has termed "the ethical unconscious":[42] in Beauvoir's case, a level at which the unconscious exceeds its centered position in the self and takes on the cares, the "responsibility," of the Other(s). The existential notion of will fails, she argues, because it construes will as unconditioned, and because it is a form of "ethical 'idealism'" (*FC,* p. 290). Will as envisioned in her dream reading is different. It is an emancipated will, driven less by its passion for personal freedom than by a passion for the freedoms of the Other. It pushes against the conditioning—the force of circumstance—that oppresses so many lives. If in "doctrinaire" Freudianism the will seems swamped by the contingencies of the unconscious, this view sees the unconscious as bespeaking ethical concern—concern that, ideally, precipitates a politically efficacious mix of deliberation and commitment to liberation, agency, and subjectivity.

But the dream is not just about the collective Other. It is highly significant that the dream scene occurs in Sartre's studio, and in his presence, because Sartre had an unrivaled position as Other in Beauvoir's life and self-construct. At some absolutely foundational level she needed—or felt that she needed—him in order to exist, and in order to verify her sense of the world. Like so much else, she presents this aspect of her life under the guise of quasi-necessity: as something that, given her early history, was much more likely to happen than not. Long before she meets Sartre, she thinks that "the man destined to be mine would be neither inferior nor different, nor outrageously superior; someone who would guarantee my existence without taking away my powers of self-determination" (*MDD,* p. 154). The expectation was prescient (perhaps suspiciously so). Of Sartre in their early days together, she says: "My trust in him was so complete that he supplied me with the sort of absolute unfailing security I had once had from my parents, or from God" (*PL,* p. 27). Her letters to Sartre, in which she describes in minute—sometimes chilling—detail her day-to-day life, show that the greatest feminist of the century did indeed construct her primary partner as a kind of guarantor: of herself, of the real, of her projects in life, of the power of her will ("my powers of self-determination"). Throughout her life she found it extremely difficult to criticize Sartre, even when he behaved in ways that were deeply wounding to her or contrary to their principles. In one of the letters she writes: "I'm ashamed to say that I never ask myself: 'Have I done well?,' merely, 'will he think badly of me?'"[43] He was Father, superego, libidinal object, and reality principle all in one: a complex, composite projection of her own psyche; the quintessential object of female desire in what Toril Moi calls Beauvoir's "erotico-theoretical relationships."[44] Moreover, as we shall see, the two of them posited the relationship as a "unity" that denied other people "eyes with which to see me." The Other who was Sartre seemed to relieve this woman who as a girl had dreaded "the indifferent glances of the passers-by" in Paris (*MDD,* p. 131) of the frightening burden of the constructive gaze of all Others. However skeptical we may be about the reality of all of this, and however redolent of the patriarchal myths (and indeed Romantic commonplaces) she so brilliantly deconstructs elsewhere, I propose to try to understand, rather than to censure, her near deification of Sartre as "genius," "perfect partner," "the double in whom I found all my burning aspirations raised to the pitch of incandescence" (*MDD,* p. 366).

A passage from *She Came to Stay* gives a particularly illuminating and powerful insight into the relationship. Françoise's dependence on Pierre is described (from her point of view):

> Nothing that happened was completely real until she had told Pierre about it; it remained poised, motionless and uncertain, in a kind of limbo. Formerly, when she still felt shy with Pierre, there were many things she had let fall by the wayside; equivocal thoughts, ill-considered moves. If they were not mentioned, it was almost as if they had not existed at all, and grew instead into a shameful, subterranean vegetation under the surface of her consciousness, where she felt utterly alone and in danger of suffocation. Little by little she had surrendered everything; she no longer knew solitude, but she had rid herself of that swarming chaos. Every moment of her life that she entrusted to him, was given back to her clear, polished, completed, and they became moments of their shared life. She knew that she served the same purpose for him. He had no secret corners, no shame.[45]

The "subterranean vegetation under the surface of her consciousness" is the viscous, chaotic, suffocating stuff of that "swarming chaos" that is the contingent. But when something is shared with and corroborated by him, it is returned to her under the guise of structure, intelligibility, necessity: it is in a state of "completion." Pierre/Sartre can save Françoise/Simone from "the chaotic seething of flesh and thought" that she experiences after her encounter with the gypsy. This identification of Sartre with Pierre and Simone with Françoise might seem too easy, and indeed I don't mean to suggest that the novel is merely a fictional transcription of their two selves. However, we know, not least from Simone's autobiographical testimony, that *She Came to Stay* is modeled on the triangular relationship that occurred between Sartre, Beauvoir, and Olga Kosakievicz (Xavière in the novel); we know, too, again from Beauvoir herself, that as a young woman she found the existence of the Other deeply disturbing. It was the very locus of contingency. She writes in *The Prime of Life*:

> The existence of Otherness remained a danger for me, and one which I could not bring myself to face openly. At the age of eighteen I had fought hard against [class] sorcery that aimed to turn me into a monster, and I was still on the defensive. I had settled the anomaly of Sartre by telling myself that we formed a single entity, placed together at the world's center. Around us other people circled, pleasant, odious, or ridiculous; they had no eyes with which to observe me: I alone could see. (*PL,* p. 105)

The passage is crucial in that it brings together issues that lie at the heart of Beauvoir's autobiographical treatment of Self, Other, contingency, and will: the fear of the Other; the relationship with Sartre as a response to that fear; and the recourse to various forms of contractual agreement as a stay against contingency. The agreement to tell each other everything, to have "no secret corners," is one example of a general fascination in these volumes with promises and pacts.

Before looking more closely at these issues, I want to say more about the philosophical background against which Beauvoir's account of Self and Other unfolds. The key text here is Hegel's *Phenomenology of Mind* in which he writes of the fraught relationship between Self and Other. Self requires the legitimating presence of Other in order to be free; but that very requirement means that Self depends upon Other; that it cannot realize the characteristic desire of conscious being—the desire to be free. In order to break the cycle of dependence and desire "each [consciousness] must aim at the death of the other."[46] Simone de Beauvoir, who read Hegel during the war (before Sartre had done so), used this sentence as the epigraph for *She Came to Stay*. A second source is Sartre's account of being-for-others in *Being and Nothingness*—an account that owes a great deal to Hegel (and, no doubt, to Beauvoir herself).[47] There is no need to dwell at length on this well-known account, and in any case I want to suggest that it throws less light on Beauvoir's autobiographical treatment of other people than is sometimes supposed. But briefly: Sartre pictures the self as harboring a nothingness or "negativity." We crave retreat into the condition of object, of the "thing-in-itself," that we might become substantial, solid. We need other people in order to move from the condition of in-itself to for-itself: a conscious being. We know intuitively that other people exist; and they exist for us as objects, albeit frighteningly elusive, in Beauvoir's word, "mysterious," ones. At the same time, we exist for others as an object; but the relation between self and perceiver is interactive, so that the glance or the "gaze" of the Other in fact contributes to the construction—the constitution—of my Self as a certain kind of object. Like Hegel, Sartre pictures the constitution of Self as interactive, albeit in an oddly provisional sense: it requires the Other, but the role of the Other-as-not-one's-Self expropriates Self even as it seems to help the self into being. For-itself must be a being-for-others. To the extent that I am a construction of the Other, neither my Self nor my world are wholly under my control. I am haunted by a feeling that my Self and my fate are to a significant degree contingent: the Other apparently has the freedom to make and define me. I react by trying to neutralize his freedom by objectifying—making an object of—the Other. But this cannot work: we know the Other to be free; and her or his freedom in some sense penetrates, insinuates its way into, my freedom, taking it over and enslaving me. This is Sartre's version of Hegel's Master-Slave relationship. "Conflict" arises as we—my Self and the Other—battle: each trying to objectify, neutralize, possess, the Other. In the case of lovers, the situation is especially acute:

merely to enslave, possess, the Other is deadly; it kills the relationship. So Self tries to possess Other as a freedom, to link with the Other's freedom without neutralizing it; but, conversely, Self fears that freedom and wants to constitute the limit of that freedom, wants the Other to sacrifice freedom in order to guarantee the security of Self. Love relations, then, have a sadomasochistic quality, veering between the horror of the nihilating impingement of the Other, the terror of the nothingness of solitude, and the need to be loved, to be in control.[48]

We might sum up part of Sartre's picture with a cliché and say that, among other things, his version of being-for-others involves a battle of wills. Will as a means of protecting Self against (real or imagined) subjection by the Other, of coercing the Other into playing the Other-constituting part that is needed for Self to exist, and so on. It seems that will and conflict are constitutive of Self-Other relations. Indeed Sartre says: "Conflict is the original meaning of being-for-others."[49] Beauvoir's fiction and autobiographical writing often seem to endorse this view. In *The Mandarins* Henri tries to find some way of bringing his longtime partner Paula to an acceptance of the fact that he no longer desires an intimate relationship with her. Returning home on a lovely day after an outing with his lover Josette, he muses: "The spring sky was so gay that it seemed possible to live sincerely and without making anyone suffer."[50] It proves not to be possible—Paula almost becomes one of Beauvoir's "women destroyed" by the breakup of the relationship, her "frenzied shamelessness"[51] a response to her feeling that contingency is bearing down where necessity once reigned. In a similar note Beauvoir writes in *Memoirs of a Dutiful Daughter:* "In my own opinion, one cannot love without hating" (*MDD*, p. 350). *She Came to Stay* evokes the sinister impingement of the Other with its associated jealousy and self-alienation. The writing has a murderous intentness that is reminiscent of late James.

The story "The Age of Discretion" reflects through its protagonist on the "dreadful anomaly of the anger that is born of love and that murders love."[52] *The Second Sex* reflects the same outlook, seeing the erotic experience in terms of the familiar "ambiguity of [the human] condition; in it they are aware of themselves as flesh and as spirit, as the other and as subject."[53] One of the great risks of that "condition" is the temptation to refuse the possibility of freedom and subjectivity, to retreat into "immanence, stagnation," which sacrifices "liberty to constraint and contingence." If the subject willingly condemns herself to "contingence," it is a "moral fault" on her part.[54] "The *other* is always a mystery" (but only woman is culturally essentialized as mysterious); the mystery is frightening, and fear, among other things, brings about a destructive ambiguity in all relationships of love: "In all love—sexual or maternal—exist at once selfishness and generosity, desire to possess the other and to give the other all."[55]

Some of the greatest passages in the autobiographies deal with the casualties of the Self-Other struggle. One such is Zaza, the second "dutiful daughter" of the first volume. Zaza is a tragic heroine torn between incommensurable virtues:

duty to her class and duty to herself. She often repeats a line from Ramuz: "'The things I love do not love each other'" (*MDD*, p. 292). Structurally she is the mirror image of Simone in the narrative: Zaza, whose vitality and spontaneity do so much to liberate Simone from the repressive confines of her environment, eventually succumbs to that same environment. In Beauvoir's view she is effectively destroyed by the immanence to which her dutifulness commits her. She does not seem to construe this as a "moral flaw" in Zaza. Simone, by contrast, moves from a kind of immanence—"the docile reflection of my parents' will"—to the transcendence, the "freedom," that she fears she has "paid for" with Zaza's death. The transactional metaphor is ambiguous, but powerful: it suggests that Zaza is not only sacrificed to her class, but in some obscure way by her formerly dutiful friend. This fear appears to have been irrational; but it is the origin of the debt that Beauvoir seeks to "discharge" in *Memoirs of a Dutiful Daughter*. In the narrative it establishes Simone as a person with a moral mission: to avenge her friend's memory and to take on the class that she holds responsible for Zaza's death. Part 1 of *Memoirs* ends with one of those moments of transformation— a moment, we gather, that is precipitated by Zaza, though less by anything she does than by who she is and the feelings this unleashes in Simone. This is the first dramatic moment of rupture from the ethos of the bourgeoisie. After not seeing Zaza for some time, Simone has a "blinding revelation": "All at once, conventions, routines, and the careful categorizing of emotions were swept away and I was overwhelmed by a flood of feeling that had no place in any code" (*MDD*, p. 100). What place Beauvoir's later bisexuality has in this is not clear— not least because she concealed this central fact about herself in the autobiography.[56] But this moment of transformation establishes the primacy of feeling over and above the code, indeed above *any* code that is not of the individual's making. Existentialism is already on the horizon. Zaza's mode of being-for-others is apparently special:[57] she seems to possess a kind of goodness that enables her to confer selfhood on the Other without the accompanying complications of fear, anger, and competitiveness. She doesn't desire the death of the Other. Ultimately she succumbs to the look of the collective Other that is her class: she submits to their construction of her and allows them to crush her will. She thereby avoids "conflict," but also forfeits that which can only be instantiated through conflict: her life. For reasons that are not altogether clear, Beauvoir does not find "moral fault" in Zaza for her submission to immanence. The onus is entirely upon the bourgeoisie. Zaza's fate helps teach Simone that conflict and the freedom of self-construction are mutually entailing. Zaza has taught her to feel; Zaza's death has taught her to fight: the combination of compassion and toughness that marks Beauvoir's self-characterization as a political intellectual springs in large part from this early relationship. Zaza's tragedy lies in her own demise; but her life is liberating for the Other who is Simone.

A very different, but equally tragic, figure is Camille, though her tragedy lacks the redemptive implications for others that marks Zaza's death. Raised by her mother who was a pharmacist, she was a former lover and then a friend of Sartre. She had been a prostitute, a student, and had developed vast intellectual and artistic ambitions. She became the mistress of the director Dullin, staying with him until he died. As a young woman she is strikingly beautiful, apparently highly talented, independent, theatrical. The young Beauvoir is in awe of her. But she also senses a lack: "She had only succeeded in avoiding a condition of dependence by rejecting love . . . The very strength that she derived from her lack of sensibility hinted at a complementary inner weakness" (*PL*, p. 62). Above all, she is the quintessential narcissist, the person in whom Self and Self-as-Other are enclosed in an impenetrable circularity. Beauvoir is highly amusing on Camille's egoistic failures in being-for-others: "The chief object of her cult [of those she worshiped] was her own person" (*PL*, p. 58); she exhibits a "stupendous self-absorption" (*PL*, p. 64); though apparently amorous, "she regarded passionate love as a pre-eminently solitary occupation" (*PL*, p. 59). After some success in the theater, she starts to decline. She drinks heavily. When Dullin becomes terminally ill, she doesn't visit him in the hospital. After his death she develops a sentimental devotion to Dullin but destroys herself with drink. The final scenes of her, in *All Said and Done*, are like something out of Dickens or Balzac: living in filth, amid half-eaten food and rubbish strewn around her room, excrement on the floor and in her hair. She dies an abject human wreck. Beauvoir, who admits to being baffled by the magnitude of this personal catastrophe, remarks: "The emptiness we [she and Sartre] detected in her when we read her pieces had invaded the whole of Camille; and drink and loneliness had completed the destruction—she had sunk into formlessness [*l'inconsistance*]" (*ASD*, p. 75/*p. 108*). Beauvoir's noun *inconsistance* suggests something more specific than "formlessness": it conjures a state that is almost diametrically opposed to that of necessity; a state, that is, very close to contingency. This state is the ultimate descent into contingent servitude—the fate of one who, in the absence of the self-constituting presence of the Other, has no self, no structure of being, to attain. The steely will of the ambitious younger woman, having failed to find the trajectory of transcendence, has circled back upon her, the negativity that should make for growth engulfing her in a state of suicidal fixity. She is a cautionary counterexample in a work that commends transcendence amid and through being-for-others. Similarly, Zaza's liberating impact on Simone shows that the former's fate, though a personal tragedy, is not an absolute tragedy : her mode of being-for-others enables Simone to make herself "be." The chinks of possibility that appear in these cases is consistent with Beauvoir's self-characterization as an essentially optimistic person (*PL*, p. 49). They also suggest something important about her intellectual development: while she ostensibly discarded the naive Kantian optimism of her existential years, her postexistential thought about human relationships is less dark, less tortured and conflict-ridden than the picture that emerges from *Being and Nothingness* would lead one to expect. After all, this mighty figure in the intellectual history of the West counts as her one "undoubted success," not a book, nor a political achievement, but a sustained, close human relationship: her fifty-one-year accord with Sartre.

Interpersonal accords, whether in the form of marriage or other agreements, attempt to protect against contingency by creating pockets of apparent necessity in an otherwise threatening and seemingly random world. Diana Trilling, whose autobiography is the subject of my final chapter, writes that "the miracle of marriage, if it works, is that it makes you the most important person in the world for at least the one other person."[58] This is miraculous because there are so many other people, so many other webs of interconnection, so many other contingent possibilities, in the world. But marriage—if it works—eliminates most of those other possibilities and posits the married person's life as being in large part *for* the Other. Ideally at least, this gives it a kind of purpose, a *telos,* which renders what he or she does meaningful, rational; it invests acts, attitudes, and attachments with a sense of necessity: given the context, there is a logic in things happening this way rather than that. When such an accord breaks down, however, as it does for Paula, necessity gives over to contingency, not only in the sense that the world may seem "seething," unintelligible, "formless" without the Other; but also in the sense that the Self now stands in relation to the Other as a contingent being: as someone who has no particular claim, no particular power to limit the choices that the Other makes, to direct his or her will. Self is now someone whose presence in the life of the Other has become inessential in the sense that the character of the Other's life has ceased to depend in any fundamental way on the presence of (my) Self. Self has now become *contingent on* the Other.

Existentialism's angrily antibourgeois ethos naturally spurned institutions like marriage, and the Sartre-Beauvoir bond remains an icon for many who likewise oppose it. In many respects it made philosophical sense for the existentialists to repudiate marriage and related norms: if the Self's true calling in life is transcendence, then ties that might bind—especially ties that seemed to have deep roots in capitalistic, bourgeois, and Judeo-Christian culture—would be construed as constraints upon the will's project of transcendence. Such a view reflects what might be called the atomistic dimension of existential philosophizing: the view that sees Self as a kind of solipsistic dynamism. However, as I have argued, existentialism has another, and rather different dimension, according to which the Self is not atomistic but rather intersubjective; Self is the product of, and can only subsist within, a relation of mutual constitution with the Other. Depending on how the Other is defined, such a model would seem to be consistent with certain kinds of interpersonal accord—whether state-sanctioned, like marriage, or less orthodox, does not matter. Indeed the Beauvoir-Sartre bond was (we gather) such an accord. Even existentialists, so given to the subjectifying of morality, need some such forms of agreement if they are not to drown in the contingent.

What is required for making such an accord, and for other related forms of agreement? Take one of the forms that figures prominently in Beauvoir's auto-biography: promising. It is the allegedly broken promises of the bourgeoisie that motivate Beauvoir's story of Zaza, the woman destroyed by the treachery of her class; her feeling that she has been "gypped," despite life having kept most of its "promises" (*FC*, p. 658), fuels the anger of the last page of *Force of Circumstance*. There is much, too, about the promises that people make and break with one another.

Promising is a complex thing. In order for a promise to be made and kept, various levels of structure are required. There has to be an embedded convention of promise-making and -keeping that is independent of particular undertakings; as Rawls points out, there must also be associated rules—for instance the rule of fairness[59]—that enable monitoring and enforcement of particular undertakings; there must be particular acts, particular understandings, in which the convention is instantiated, practiced, and learned; and there must be agents who are cognizant of the given socially constitutive conventions and of the rules, and who can exercise morally sentient deliberation and choice in entering into and executing undertakings. Such agents—or "strong evaluators"—enter willingly into agreements: that is, under the guidance of some combination of rationality and feeling, they choose to partake of some binding understanding.

Another, and closely related, form of agreement is the pact. While promising is not necessarily reciprocal—I may promise something to you without expecting anything in return—a pact is reciprocal in structure: at a minimum it has the structure, "I promise *x* on the condition that . . ."; often it entails a joint undertaking: "We promise one another that we will do *x*." The pact, too, requires agential exercise of will in ways that bind. Pacts of course come in many forms, marriage, vows of fidelity, and the like among them. This class of pact exhibits with particular clarity a feature of all pacts and most forms of agreement: not only do they (supposedly) bind participants; they also in a sense quarantine and circumscribe some of their energies. In the case of a vow of fidelity, for instance, the parties become sexually unavailable to all others; and with this comes a certain circumscription of the will, whereby the libidinal dimension of the will is effectively enshrined in the pact and can only be exercised in relation to the Other who is party to the pact. Such a pact is a structure of necessity designed to resist the anarchic temptations of the flesh.

Beauvoir had firsthand experience of a particularly complex form of pact: the triangular affair. Triangulation disrupts the symmetry of the bilateral pact, thereby complicating the patterns of segregation and availability that more conventional pacts are designed to ensure. Triangulation is nevertheless a structure; but it is so complex a structure that many of its emotional effects might well resemble those of contingency. No doubt this structure appealed to the existential Beauvoir and Sartre in part because it was unconventional;[60] also, perhaps, because the sheer complexity of the arrangement put enormous pressure on the authenticity of the individuals concerned, at least on those (Beauvoir and Sartre) for whom the pact was more freely willed than it was for the third person (Olga). Such a pact could not survive without the circulation of a particularly demanding (and no doubt painful) honesty. This nerve-racking configuration must have appealed to the Simone who wrote that she was obsessed by the "relationship between honesty and the will" (*PL,* 271). Philosophizing aside, it is pretty clear from the letters that Beauvoir wrote to Sartre during the war that there was in any case a distinctly voyeuristic dimension to their sexual relationship: their manner of reporting to one another intimate details of their sexual encounters with others was in itself a form of triangulation, since such letters retrospectively invited their recipients in as witnesses of the sexual encounters in question. There is also the possibility that knowing that one would later report such encounters to a third party was part of the thrill of the encounter itself. Just for good measure: that thrill might be heightened by the fact that one's lover in the encounter was unaware that it would be reported to a third party—that some kind of pact was already in place that must compromise the intimacy to which the lover had in good faith surrendered. And then of course there is the French literary tradition of aestheticizing the erotic: Mallarmé, Sade, Anaïs Nin, Genet, and others. Lest the reader think that such suspicious readings pay scant regard to the stature of Beauvoir and Sartre, the letters themselves make interesting, if not always edifying, reading.[61]

Beauvoir gives the same triangular situation that is dramatized in *She Came to Stay* extended treatment in *The Prime of Life,* where Olga appears under her real given name. It is Olga who, more than any other individual, confronts Beauvoir with her horror of the disintegrating power of the Other's contingency. This pact also puts a particular strain on certain of Beauvoir's existential convictions, as in this comment about Olga: "For Olga the present was all-sufficient, and words of definition, limitation, promise, or anticipation—especially the last—seemed wholly irrelevant" (*PL,* p. 192). In a sense this marks Olga as a kind of unwitting existentialist: she lives not in an ethical continuum, but rather in a series of disconnected moments; the past exerts little power to define or predict present or future, or to prescribe conduct therein. So described, Olga is an unusually pure example of the contingency of the Other: she is, so to speak, the cause of her own actions, but there is something radically capricious about the causation in question. For her the very notion of a "promise" is all but unintelligible. Beauvoir admits to the pain that this triangular relation caused her—a pain that barely compares, however, with the anguish recorded in an autobiographical account written by another person who as a young woman became engaged in a triangular relationship with Sartre and Beauvoir, Bianca Lamblin.[62]

To understand Olga's pain we need to consider the famous pact that preceded her encounter with Sartre and Beauvoir; or at least Beauvoir's description of it. She says of meeting Sartre (during her first year at university) that "something *had* happened to me, something that indirectly was to shape the whole of my life to come [*décida de toute ma vie*]" (*MDD*, p. 331/*p. 436*). *Shape* is a powerfully determinative verb: it is the language of necessity. Indeed Beauvoir here uses the *passé simple* to suggest something close to absolute causal power—a power located in a closed past. *Indirectly* modifies it somewhat but leaves the precise force of the description ambiguous. Elsewhere, and for the most part, she seeks to characterize the relationship in terms of a freedom that, remarkably, has the character of necessity, the latter term being conceived not as something that possesses determinative power, but rather as an absolute and unassailable rightness; something that has a natural and unique place in the order of things. In defending the relationship at the end of *Force of Circumstance,* she writes: "It was no matter of chance that I chose Sartre; for after all I did choose him [*Ce n'est pas un hasard si c'est Sartre que j'ai choisi: car enfin je l'ai choisi*]" (*FC*, p. 644/*p. 673*). As we have seen, the account she gives of this "choice" in *All Said and Done* entertains the possibility that "chance" had played a greater role than she had originally thought. But in the end she decides against this possibility and lays the emphasis on choice: however chancy their meeting might or might not have been, the bond was forged and renewed through choice. She repeatedly characterizes the bond in a manner that might seem paradoxical, but that squares with existential accounts of freedom in which commitment to projects enables the liberty of subsequent commitments; she wants us to see this as a bond that is at once totally committed and unconditionally liberating: "That which bound us freed us; and in this freedom we found ourselves bound as closely as possible" (*PL*, p. 26); as an arrangement that honors the contingency (in the best sense) of the Other: "An authentic love should accept the contingence of the other, his idiosyncrasies, his limitations, his basic gratuitousness."[63] Such, she claims, was the relationship, and the style of interrelatedness, they "pioneered," with its "freedom, intimacy, and frankness" (*PL*, p. 287). This was their "morganatic marriage."

According to the autobiography, it was Sartre who set the terms for the "marriage" (a claim questioned by some recent scholarship, in part because of Beauvoir's bisexuality):[64]

> Sartre was not inclined to be monogamous by nature . . . He had no intention, at twenty-three, of renouncing their tempting variety.
>
> He explained the matter to me in his favorite terminology. "What *we* have," he said, "is an *essential* love; but it is a good idea for us also to experience *contingent* love affairs." We were two of a kind, and our relationship would endure as long as we did: but it could not make up entirely for the fleeting riches to be had from encounters with different people. (*PL*, pp. 23–24)

Essential here means something that could not not be; a constitutive part of life itself. It has the connotation of warding off, of lying beyond the contingent: nothing, not even sexual relationships with others, can threaten this bond. Because they are "one," because each requires only the Other in order to "be," other people—those with a lowercase "o"—have no power, be it through their constitutive gaze, the conflict they might seek to engender, the passion they might feel or inspire, to threaten the primary bond. As Pierre tells Françoise:

> "It's impossible to talk about faithfulness and unfaithfulness where we're concerned." He drew Françoise to him. "You and I are simply one. It's true, you know. Neither of us can be defined without the other."[65]

In the autobiography Beauvoir writes: "Love's promises express the passion of a moment only; restrictions and reservations are no more binding; in every case, the truth of the present sweeps all pledges imperiously before it" (*FC,* p. 127); but not in the case of Pierre and Françoise, nor, apparently, in that of Sartre and Simone. Their bond allows for both the "pledge" and the will's liberation. In all of this, telling—the sharing of one's secrets with the Other—plays a central role. The state of mutual transparency to which they are pledged is not just necessary in the sense that it is natural, part of the order of things. Paradoxically, it is also necessary in the sense that they *make* it so: by choosing to tell each other everything,[66] they construct one another as omniscient beings, beings to whom the world of the Other is an open book. Omniscience means that there are no surprises, no occluded regions. Conferring this godlike status is a way of "injecting" necessity into the otherwise unstable, contingent, world of love.

Yet even if all of this were true (and Beauvoir's obsession with jealousy in her fiction and indeed the autobiography suggests that it is not), it would still leave unanswered the question of the other people with a lowercase "o." What if the "fleeting riches" they had to offer didn't seem so fleeting to them? The problem runs deep, not just because of the sensitivities involved, but because it recapitulates the most damaging of challenges to existential ethics: how, if we are all to be radically free, do we avoid the clashes between individual freedoms—clashes that inevitably mean that, in some cases at least, one person's freedom is, and is parasitic upon, another's immanent unfreedom? In *The Ethics of Ambiguity* Beauvoir argues that "individual freedoms can forge laws valid for all," but the process by which this might come about is never explained, and at a level of theory Sartre and Beauvoir never resolved this central problem. Existential ethics never gets beyond a dictum that Beauvoir quotes approvingly: "'I have been true to you after my way'" (*FC,* p. 124). Her autobiography explores it in pained and often frank detail:

> It had been our wish to experience "contingent loves"; but there is one question we have deliberately avoided: How would the third person feel about our

arrangement? It often happened that the third person accommodated himself to it without difficulty; our union left plenty of room for loving friendships and fleeting affairs. But if the protagonist wanted more, then conflicts would break out . . . although my understanding with Sartre has lasted for more than thirty years, it has not done so without some losses and upsets in which the "others" always suffered. (*FC,* p. 125)

She goes on to talk of "this defect in our system" and to discuss the most notable victim of this "defect": the American novelist Nelson Algren, with whom she had an on-off transcontinental relationship between 1941 and 1964. Beauvoir's letters to Algren[67] reinforce what was already known about the suffering her refusal to marry and live with him caused, as well as giving a vivid, if strikingly gender-conventional, testimony to her deep affection for him. The autobiography concedes that in the case of Olga, Algren, and some others, especially Sartre's American lover who is identified as "M" (Dolores Vanetti Ehrenreich), the "conflicts" of intimacy foreshadowed in *Being and Nothingness* did in fact occur. Beauvoir admits to agonies of grief, indecision, and possessiveness periodically throughout the first three volumes. But the claim is that, despite periods of pain, the bond with Sartre remained essentially untainted, above the messy contingencies of feeling associated with intimacy with others with a lowercase "o." There is an obvious contradiction between the admission of suffering, on the one hand, and the claim of exemption, on the other. This tension, and with it the problem of existential freedom—whereby "liberty" is said to be the "foundation stone of all human values" (*PL,* p. 434), yet those "values" cannot be formulated—remains unresolved in the autobiography. Since she cannot resolve it at a level of ethical conceptualization, she tries another strategy: she tries to dissolve it by conferring on Sartre the status of a being to whom the normal canons of ethical expectation do not apply. Having repudiated Sartrean existentialism, she constructs its founder as an existential Overman; a character in whom the will of visionary genius takes precedence over conventional moral mores.

Indeed it is one of the crowning paradoxes of the autobiography of the greatest feminist of the century that her autobiography is also in large part a de facto biography of Sartre. Her story cannot be told without telling his: not just because they shared so much, but because he is in her mind so profoundly responsible for making her "be," making her who she is. Without him, she fears, she might well have lapsed into the "formlessness" she so dreaded. She believes that he gave her life structure in a contingent world; his genius was there to guide the tremendous power of her will. She uses the structures of autobiography, and *Adieux* in which she bids him farewell, to "discharge" her debt to him. She honors their pact in narrative. In this impassioned, narcissistic, yet self-doubting work of hagiography, self-life-writing becomes a strangely moving act of being-for-the-other.

CHAPTER SIX

"Factor x"
Arthur Koestler and the Ghost in the Machine

In chapter 5 I traced some of Simone de Beauvoir's shifting affiliations with various philosophical conceptions of the will—Catholic, Kantian-humanist, existential, quasi-Marxist, liberal humanist, and others. I also drew attention to an emotional pattern that has deep roots in her attitudes toward contingency and that intersects in complex ways with her views about the will. The pattern starts with a fear of contingency that precipitates a rage for control through the will. Later there's a phase in which the self feels overwhelmed by contingency and is convinced that the will is powerless to intervene in a hostile world. Then follows a sentiment of compromise: the will is seen as limited but not utterly powerless, and the world seems forbidding but not entirely unresponsive to the will and its projects. Finally there is a calming of the will as the self, its steely energies now spent, recapitulates and meditates on a past that the will has helped to fashion.

Beauvoir makes her most spectacular claims for the will during her existentialist phase. Here the will is envisaged as a transcendent power—a thing that can surpass, that can remake, the human world. So conceived, the will is the quintessence of freedom. Though Beauvoir's autobiography mounts a sustained repudiation of this conception of will, she is never wholly free of it. In this she is typical of many reflective autobiographers (and of many people): she knows that the world exerts powerful constraints, but this knowledge cannot wholly extinguish her yearning for plenitude, for a place in which the will is author or executor of its own absolute freedom. This same yearning animates much of Arthur Koestler's work, not least his autobiographical writings.

In 1937, during the Spanish civil war, Arthur Koestler was imprisoned in Seville for three months. He spent the first two months in solitary confinement.[1] He was under sentence of death and expected that he might be executed at any moment. What landed him in prison was a desire to witness and to have some influence on historical events: he was there as a journalist, but also as a Communist and a fierce opponent of fascism. What he recalls happening in prison was, however, of a different order: he records a kind of primal encounter with his own selfhood, with the deepest sedimentations of his own being. He promised himself that if he lived he would "write an autobiographical essay where truth would be carried to the point of self-immolation, done with the ruthless sincerity of an X-

175

ray photograph that would make Rousseau's Confessions [*sic*] look like a conventional oil print."[2] After being liberated through a prisoner exchange, he did indeed write about this experience, in a book entitled *Spanish Testament,* and elsewhere.[3] It was to be the first of several works of first-person narrative by one of the great autobiographical writers of the century. *Spanish Testament* is effectively two books in one: the first part is essentially a work of political-historical analysis in which the "I" of the narrator is that of the journalistic witness to events; the second section, *Dialogue with Death,* is very different. It is autobiographical writing of the most intimate and compelling kind—a stunning representation of what it feels like to be on the brink of extinction, to lose all but the use of one's limbs and one's consciousness, and to see how consciousness behaves under such conditions. Thus, he who goes in fear of his life will experience

> that dream-like feeling of having one's consciousness split in two, so that with one half of it one observes oneself with comparative coolness and aloofness, as though observing a stranger. The consciousness sees to it that its complete annihilation is never experienced. It does not divulge the secret of its existence and its decay. No one is allowed to look into the darkness with his eyes open; he is blindfolded beforehand. (*DD,* p. 117)

This is autobiography as a kind of phenomenology: customary conditions and assumptions have been set aside—albeit in this instance, we gather, involuntarily—and consciousness observes its own elemental functionings. It is introspection writ large. This is a register in which Koestler writes with rare power and precision. But to look at *Spanish Testament* in its entirety is to see that Koestler writes with equal authority about the social-historical world. This capacity to move in and out of the theater of consciousness, on the one hand, and the world of external event, on the other, is part of what makes him a major writer of autobiography. It is also what makes him so suited to his central self-appointed task as a writer and intellectual: the analysis and repudiation of totalitarianism.

The passage I have just quoted is typical of Koestler in another way: the reference to consciousness being "split in two" is one of countless such allusions in his massive intellectual and autobiographical oeuvre. Indeed, as we shall see, the figure of the split or the fissure is one of the organizing metaphors of the Koestler world. It applies not only to the self, but also to the baffling reality in which the self is embedded. It is an instance of what I term the *metaphor of self-constitution:* a pivotal metaphor through which the autobiographer constructs and projects an account of self that includes an account of the part that forces external to the self play in its emergence, in constituting it as the self that it is. Why might an intellectual put the figure of the fissure or split to such central use in his work? All manner of influences go into such a choice, and the choice goes on at all manner of levels, some conscious, others less so. In Koestler's case, the figure has deep roots both in his temperament and in his personal history. I will defer speculation about the nature of the figure's appeal for him and simply note at this point the extraordinarily split, fissured, and often contradictory patterns that characterized his life.

Born in 1905 as an only child to middle-class, nonpracticing Jewish parents in Budapest, he had a close but claustral relationship with an emotionally volatile mother and a more distanced one with his quixotic industrialist father. When the father's business went bankrupt in the early twenties, the family moved to Vienna, where Koestler later entered university as an engineering student. Having become involved in Zionism, he discontinued his studies and moved to Palestine, where he lived for three years, at first on a kibbutz, then doing an assortment of work. Here his career as a journalist began. He moved to Paris, became a Communist in 1931, repudiated the faith in 1938, and became a prolific writer in various genres, a sworn opponent of totalitarianism and of all forms of what he saw as intellectual reductionism. An atheist, journalist, and historian of science, he had experienced visionary states since childhood. The New Physics and his explorations of the paranormal converged later in life to confirm him in a position that might be termed *scientistic mysticism*. Here is an atheist who lived as a Zionist in Palestine; a Marxist who became one of the most trenchant and passionate liberal critics of communism; a journalist and historian of science whose writings about the history of scientific discovery assimilate the processes of scientific innovation to those of artistic creativity; a rationalist for whom rational political and social solutions were the only hope of constraining the self-destructiveness of the species, yet a man who believed passionately in the paranormal; a moralist who admits to being pathologically promiscuous;[4] a man of action and of contemplation; a novelist who by his own admission is all too often a propagandist in fictional prose; a spiritualist without a god; a Romantic and yet a hardened pragmatist who advocated mass medication to correct inherent behavioral defects in the species; an ethicist for whom rational moral deliberation is paramount, but who claims that his enlightened life choices were mystically guided in moments of oceanic "grace"; a man magnetized by danger yet prone to pathological levels of anxiety; a proudly self-sufficient individual whose suicide in physically decrepit old age caused a sensation because his third wife, who was well and twenty-two years his junior, took her own life when he did.

One of the great polymaths of the century, Koestler lived on an extraordinary scale. The life, like the conflicts that beset it, has the momentousness of tragedy; and as an autobiographer, he continually maps his life in relation to a tragic dimension.[5] This mapping seeks constantly to understand the place of the will, and of freedom, in human affairs. He recalls that even in solitary confinement there were times in which, having overcome the fear of death, he and his fellow prisoners were "*free*—men without shadows, dismissed from the ranks of the mortal; it was the most complete experience of freedom that can be granted a man"(*DD*, p.196). What is the nature of such freedom? Since it is experienced by those locked away in a cell under threat of death, it cannot be freedom to intervene in one's environment. It must then be a deeply subjective thing, a feature of consciousness itself, or of consciousness's access to an immaterial dimension of being. Koestlerian autobiography is premised on the assumption that consciousness is real, substantial, and multifaceted, and that the relation of consciousness to the world must be thought and reconstructed in multiple dimensions.

I. KOESTLER AND AUTOBIOGRAPHY

To write like Rousseau in the *Confessions* would be to capture some of these dimensions, which is why Rousseau is one of Koestler's "strong"[6] precursors among autobiographers. Nietzsche is another: Koestler writes of the inevitable "*ecce homo* motive" (*IW,* p. 524) in autobiography. Yet notwithstanding his strong Romantic tendencies, the configuration of Koestlerian autobiography is very different from that of either Rousseau or Nietzsche. Despite massive temperamental differences, Koestlerian autobiography is closer to say Mill's *Autobiography,* which he read in his cell in Seville (*DD,* p. 123): like Mill, he chronicles both self and social-historical world; like Mill, too, he weighs mechanistic accounts of reality against more "spiritual" ones; again like Mill, he uses autobiography as a vehicle for philosophical reflection, not least on freedom and the will. Both are reflective autobiographers par excellence. The first work that Koestler identifies as part of his autobiography proper, *Arrow in the Blue,* begins with what he calls his "secular horoscope"—an attempt to chart his own life with reference to two distinct dimensions, the astrological and the material: "Astrology is founded on the belief that man is formed by his cosmic environment; Marx held that he is the product of his social environment. I believe both propositions to be true."[7] Doing autobiography in several dimensions can have its perplexities: what Marxist would concede astrology any validity, and what has Marxist-style causal explanation got to do with astrological accounts of causation? We may well ask, but to this writer, inured as he was to contradiction and to the appearance of synthesis where others could only see contradiction, such apparent impediments to sense-making were an indictment of our sense-making habits, not of the epistemological discourses in question. Doing autobiography in several dimensions also yields rich and historically precious rewards, as in Koestler's notion of autobiography as case history. He concludes the main body of the text of *The Invisible Writing* by saying: "At this point ends this typical case-history of a central-European member of the educated middle classes, born in the first years of our century" (*IW,* p. 515). If there is a degree of disingenuousness about so modest a typicality claim, it is clear that Koestler, an ambivalent and often hostile reader of Freud, has expanded the notion of the case history to take in a great spectrum of forces that shape, engage, and are in turn influenced by the self. Here both astrology and Marxism are misnomers: each is a species of determinism, but, as we shall see, Koestler is no determinist—at least not in any familiar or concerted sense.

The presence of the social-historical dimension in Koestler's autobiographical writings is persistent and powerful. But 'presence' is too weak a word. This dimension—whether in Spain or during travels in Stalinist Russia, or in London or America, or the Indian subcontinent, Southeast Asia, or the many other places in which he lived and traveled—is generally described with a mixture of precision and hard-headed analytic skepticism; yet qua autobiographer he is out to do far more than merely describe: among the authors I discuss in this study, Koestler is the preeminent example of the writer who uses autobiography as what I call a *respondent act*—as a means of morally assessing and of intervening in the world that he experiences and describes.[8] We need some such term for autobiographers like this; we also need one for that large and important group of intellectual autobiographers who, writing in the wake of Hitler and Stalin, use autobiography as a means to explore the meaning and implications of totalitarianism: Koestler himself, André Malraux, Irving Howe, Simone de Beauvoir, Stephen Spender, Primo Levi, and many others. I call this historically crucial subgenre of autobiographical writing *post-totalitarian autobiography.*[9] It is a form that particularly targets three common features of totalitarianism: a conception of the self as infinitely malleable and transformable; the political phenomenon of party or state control over, and *usurpation* of, private morality; and the essentializing of the self in terms of racial and ethnic stereotypes. Early in *Arrow in the Blue,* Koestler sets the scene for such work, tragically and unforgettably:

> At a conservative estimate, three out of every four people whom I knew before I was thirty were subsequently killed in Spain, or hounded to death at Dachau, or gassed at Belsen, or deported to Russia, or liquidated in Russia; some jumped from windows in Vienna or Budapest, others were wrecked by the misery and aimlessness of permanent exile. (*AB,* p. 131)

He hates totalitarianism for many reasons, not least because it constitutes an unprecedented attack on freedom at every level. Autobiography suits his and others' respondent purposes because it permits appropriately emotive accounts by witnesses and victims of totalitarianism; but also because autobiography, certainly in the form that Koestler writes it, is by its very nature an affirmation that consciousness *is* real, substantive, multidimensional—and precious. Post-totalitarian autobiography is consciousness putting its case to the world, where freedom is assumed to be an inalienable constituent of consciousness. Here will enters the picture. In an extraordinary note in the volume *Reflections on Hanging,* Koestler speaks of free will and predestination, having just characterized their competing philosophical claims as "the essence of the human predicament." The note continues (in part):

I think free will is a fantastic notion, but also that man is a fantastic creature. I believe in the unprovable existence of a factor *x*: an order of reality beyond physical causation, about whose nature only a negative statement is possible: namely, that in its domain the present is *not* determined by the past. If it were so determined, 'we would once more revert to the conception of the machine-universe. But a present *not* determined by the past is both a necessary and sufficient condition for the experience of relative freedom—not the freedom of anarchy and arbitrariness, but of an order based on the time-negating concept of the *creatio continua*.[10]

This sort of view is of course by no means particular to Koestler. Such compatibilist accounts of will, which see it as a free power in a determined world but which do not purport to explain the source of this freedom, are familiar in Hume and elsewhere. "Factor *x*" is, then, a constitutive, if elusive, dimension of self. Hard to prove though it may be, we know that we possess it, and the totalitarian dictator knows it too—which is why one of his first moves is to eviscerate the inner self, to try to make inwardness a mere reflection of party ideology, and to annihilate any perceived gap between the will of the individual and some perverted notion of the Will of the People.

Koestler's affirmation of consciousness and the individual will is, then, first and foremost a political thing. But it is not exclusively political, and neither are his polemical and autobiographical targets merely political. His ire could be raised by any deterministic ideology, as by any reductive one;[11] indeed, of course, the two—determinism and reductionism—often go hand in hand. A consistent focus of one such attack was behaviorism. In an encyclopedic work that contains a sustained attack on behaviorist assumptions and methods, Koestler describes behaviorism as a kind of "flat-earth view of the mind,"[12] attacks Skinner and other practitioners,[13] and scorns behaviorist experimental methods as "ratomorphism."[14] Koestler is in no doubt that behaviorism includes among its ranks the philosopher Gilbert Ryle. As we have seen, in his *Concept of Mind* Ryle pours scorn on theories that attribute human intentions and acts to an inner faculty of the will. Such theories seemed to Ryle mere myth—a fanciful positing of a "ghost in the machine" that is the human being.[15] Never one to pass up an opportunity for confrontation, Koestler entitled the volume that contains his most sustained rebuttal of behaviorism *The Ghost in the Machine*. He believed in the ghost as a "ubiquitous presence," a "transparency of phenomena towards a different," immaterial "order of reality." And one of the ghost's names, that which identifies "the god within" the human being,[16] is "factor *x*." Indeed if autobiography can be said to have a de facto subject, an ideal self or dimension of self that the narrative seeks to uncover and render in communicable form, then the ghost as the god within is the de facto protagonist of Koestlerian autobiography.

Koestler tries to figure the relations between cause, effect, the subject and its freedom in terms of threads. In a superb piece about Richard Hillary, the writer and fighter pilot who died in battle in 1943, Koestler tries to understand Hillary's attempts to fathom his own motives for exposing himself to extraordinary levels of risk after being shockingly injured in an earlier battle:

> We find, then, that this last attempt to explain and rationalize his motives is as true as his earlier ones, but not the final truth. The final truth is probably a pattern composed of all the threads we have picked up, and followed for a short while and dropped again. For the pattern is more than the sum total of the threads; it has its own symbolic design of which the threads know nothing. They are ordinary strings, woven of cause and effect; but in the completed design the effect seems to operate the cause. The threads are subject to causality; the pattern to finality.[17]

Here the threads operate in a causal dimension: they converge to form a pattern. But the threads bear traces of a design of which they know nothing, so that as they converge they form an entity—in this case a self—of which they are unaware. The self, which possesses freedom of will, makes choices, and this amounts to reconfiguring some of the strands: now the self-as-agent is doing the weaving. But a scientistic observer who is fixated on Hume-like cause-and-effect will be fixated on the strands and so will miss the "symbolic design," the self; and, having missed this, will miss the most important fact of all—that the self-as-weaver is indeed partially free to orchestrate the threads that in one sense bring it into being. Koestler is acutely aware of the "'crisis of causality'" (*AB,* p. 346) that has beset modern scientific, social, and ethical theory, and he acknowledges the importance of material and other forms of causation. So as autobiographer he wants to reveal the threads; but his ultimate subject is the "symbolic design," the subject that possesses the ghost, the "factor *x,*" the attributes that make it truly and distinctively human, a weaver.

II. Fissured Metaphysics

So conceived, the weaver might seem an enchanted creature in an enchanted world that he or she helps to bring into being. But Koestler's outlook is in fact deeply, though not wholly, tragic: the weaver works in a world riven with contradiction and, being of that world, is him- or herself likewise a riven creature. It is a world in which transcendence is possible, but in which it is often precipitated by pain, and in which it comes in unexpected ways. The autobiographical writings chart a range of life trajectories and inner states, asking which of these have issued in transcendence, which have not, and why. These texts narrate not just one personal quest, but a series, each of which seeks an existential modality that might fuse optimal forms of being, knowing, and willing. These are, inter alia, metaphysical quests, and here the relation of Koestler's autobiographical works to his intellectual position more generally becomes complex. One of the reasons his autobiographical writings are not as widely admired as they deserve to be is that they tend to presuppose an elaborate metaphysics that is at times only sketchily explained in the autobiographical works themselves. (Other reasons include his reputation as a political conservative and reservations about him as a private individual, the latter having gathered force when the details of his death became public.)[18] On the other hand, the autobiographies are also about the life processes that lead to the adoption of some of these metaphysical views. The relation between the life-writing and the other genres is such that the two discourses need constantly to be read with reference to one another.

The metaphysics is worked through in an astonishing range of genres, including psychology, physics (particularly the New Physics), evolutionary theory, anthropology, politics, history, ethics, parapsychology, and sociology. The position that emerges from all of this is at once powerful and paradoxical and, like everything in Koestler's work, operates in various dimensions. I use 'metaphysical' here as an umbrella term for various constituent elements—ontological, epistemological, psychological, and ethical. Each of these in turn needs to be seen in relation to two organizing categories: world and self.

Perhaps the most fundamental feature of Koestler's view of the world is that it is dualistic. This is why, when he wrote a book late in life that was intended to summarize his position, he called it *Janus: A Summing Up*.[19] Much in this world does indeed face in two directions, and survival—and, beyond that, the chance of transcendence—requires that one have the psychological strength to tolerate ambiguity, and the interpretive acuity to read the text of life in its often discrepant and opposing guises. Lest all of this sound rather abstruse, consider an example of the power with which Koestler can render this sense of things in autobiography. Around the age of four or five he endures a tonsillectomy without anesthetic. Looking back he recalls "several indelible minutes of steel instruments being thrust into the back of my mouth, of choking and vomiting blood into the tray beneath my chin; then two more attacks with steel instruments, and more choking blood and vomit":

> Those moments of utter loneliness, abandoned by my parents, in the clutches of a hostile and malign power, filled me with a kind of cosmic terror. It was as if I had fallen through a manhole, into a dark underground world of archaic brutality. Thenceforth I never lost my awareness of the existence of that second universe into which one might be transported, without warning, from one moment to the other. The world had become ambiguous, invested with a double meaning; events moved on two different planes at the same time—a visible and an invisible one—like a ship which

carries its passengers on its sunny decks, while its keel ploughs through the dark phantom world beneath. (*AB,* p. 47)

This is the Romantic child-as-visionary in a moment of ghastly nihilistic inversion: the child's vision is not up in the direction of numinous transcendence, but "down" through a "manhole" to a region of infernal torment. Koestler calls this region "Ahor": "the irrational, archaic horror," and he identifies its discovery as, among other things, the inaugurating moment in his commitment to ethical protest and struggle, in effect the birth of the chronicler of totalitarianism: "Dr. Neubauer [who performed the operation] paved the way for my becoming a chronicler of the more repulsive aspects of our time" (*AB,* p. 48). To this extent the experience proves to be life-enabling.[20] The moment also signals the opening up of his unconscious—the phantasms of the deep—and the inner conflicts that were to characterize his "manic depressive"[21] and anxiety-ridden consciousness. The ambiguity and doubleness of the experience reveal that "reality" has two faces: a demonic one that is entropic, suffocating, annihilating; and a more benign one that, though eerily complicit with the first, makes for life, for insight, for growth, for vision.

What the child sees—or at least the adult's reconstruction of the child's vision—is ontological in the sense that it affirms the existence of a reality that is constituted in a particular (dualistic) way; it is also epistemological in that the vision reveals that modes of human knowing must themselves be dualistic, attuned to the doubleness of the world; and it is psychological as well: he who will henceforth know the world as riven will be riven by that knowledge, a creature whose inner states shift and collide in response to the world that so powerfully affects them. And to know that the world is thus is to know how urgently we need protection from that in ourselves which bears this doubleness: the vision is ethical because it reveals that there is horror in the world, that human beings are its primary instrument, and that curbing our darker propensities requires understandings of value, and social forms that reflect and reinforce those understandings.

Though Koestler theorizes[22] in various places about the ontology of the world, it is the epistemological implications of this ontology that matter most for a reading of his autobiography. In the passage just quoted, the child learns not just that reality exists on two "planes," but that one of these is "visible" and the other "invisible." This, Koestler's version of Romantic epistemology, suggests that our deeper understandings of the world penetrate beyond the veil of appearances to some transcendental level of truth. Of the epiphanic experiences he came to know, he says: "For the first time the veil has fallen and one is in touch with 'real reality,' the hidden order of things, the X-ray texture of the world, normally obscured by layers of irrelevancy" (*IW,* p. 430). The second of his major volumes of autobiography is entitled *The Invisible Writing,* in part to suggest that transcendence is linked to an awareness of the unseen. But there is another organizing binary in Koestler's work that complicates the picture, and this is his distinction between the "tragic" and the "trivial." Though the "tragic" is the dimension of "'real reality'" and the "trivial" that of appearances, it is Koestler's recurrent experience that life's most momentous recognitions come disguised as commonplace, as "trivial": "It is a curious fact that the really important events which alter the whole course of one's destiny usually appear in an insidiously trivial guise. The first symptoms of cancer are much less dramatic than a bruised knee; every psychiatrist knows that the real conflicts of the patient are hidden behind those ideas and dreams which he dismisses as unimportant." Again: "Real tragedy rarely makes good drama. The language of destiny is smooth and full of trivial understatements—like dear old Shubnikov's: 'I wonder now what Hitler did that for?'" (*IW,* p. 183). I will say more about the conception of the "language of destiny" presently; but note here that incongruity and disjunction are the very idiom of this language.

At its best, Koestler's writings have an almost Tolstoyan sensitivity to the bizarreness of this idiom and to the infinite poignancy with which it is associated. On the element of the "grotesque" in "major crises of life": "There is terror and tragedy, but also an absurd incongruity in the ravages of a flood, when saucepans float down the stream next to a hairbrush and a dead hen, and children have the time of their lives being rescued in rowing boats" (*IW,* p. 200). What we get here is an "interlacing of the tragic and the trivial,"[23] and, like Tolstoy, Koestler tracks this idiom all the way from local chance events to the hair-raisingly accidental plane of global history. *Promise and Fulfilment,* a historical study that is marvelously sensitive to chance and its role in history, is rich in examples: "What soldier has not seen that caterpillar crawling along a crack in the bark of the tree behind which he took cover, and pursuing its climb undisturbed by the splattering of the tommy-gun? This intersecting of the tragic and the trivial planes of existence has always obsessed me."[24] The poignancy of this kind of thing, and the extraordinarily chancy way in which the contingent confers historical significance upon the trivial, is captured beautifully in his formulation of what he calls "the Pompeii effect"—that process in which "schoolboys playing with marbles are caught by the lava and petrified into monuments."[25]

The "interlacing" of the tragic and trivial planes produces a kind of threshold that has a particularly important place in Koestler's experiential topography. The most important thing about this threshold is that it is the imaginative habitat of the artist and of other truly creative people. The flood again:

> The tragic plane on which the world moves in times of upheaval has a logic different from the homely reasoning of the trivial plane. For the average citizen it is difficult if not impossible to make the transition; he suffers passively the unreason of floods, wars and revolutions, while apparently crazy

adventurers, artists and other emotionally unbalanced people accustomed to living on the precarious edge where the tragic and trivial planes intersect, jump with alacrity from one to the other. They seem to thrive on catastrophes; their folly is their guardian angel. (*AB*, p. 410)

His own "apocalyptic temperament" of course marks him as one of those "apparently unbalanced people," but on his sort of Romantic view that temperament comes with being an artist. His first major study of creativity, *Insight and Outlook*,[26] expounds a view of creativity that he refines in *The Act of Creation* and elsewhere. On this account, creativity is rooted in what he terms *bisociation*: an ability to think simultaneously on two planes. He proposes a distinction between "the routine skills of thinking on a single 'plane,' as it were, and the creative act which, as I shall try to show, always operates on more than one plane."[27] The central theme of *The Sleepwalkers*, his history of cosmology, is that the artist and the scientist both "think" bisociatively. He writes of "the unitary source of the mystical and scientific modes of experience" and, importantly, of "the disastrous results of their separation."[28] For his or her part, the artist has the gift of "conferring on trivial experiences a new dignity and wonder."[29] Again:

Where the Tragic and Trivial Planes meet, the Absolute becomes humanized, drawn into the orbit of man, while the banal objects of daily experience are transfigured, surrounded by a halo as it were . . . The *locus in quo* of human creativity is always on the line of intersection between two planes; and in the highest forms of creativity between the Tragic or Absolute, and the Trivial Plane . . . This interlacing of the two planes is found in all great works of art, and at the origin of all great discoveries of science.[30]

He might have added "in certain works of autobiography," because his own autobiographical quest narratives are often staged at the threshold where the planes meet.

But the writing self, too, is riven. Figuring it in terms of threads, Koestler sees his earlier self as "a web of contradictions" (*IW*, p. 523), and he cautions the reader that his reconstruction of his period in solitary confinement will be contradictory—inevitably so since any narrative treatment of mind under such duress must move "through strata that are held together by the cement of contradiction" (*IW*, p. 427). Yet he sees such contradiction as being exposed rather than engendered by crisis situations. Human consciousness just *is* internally disjunctive. Hence his endorsement in *The Ghost in the Machine* of neurological researcher Paul McLean's contention that the human brain is comprised of three distinct mutations:

Speaking allegorically of these three brains within a brain, we might imagine that when the psychiatrist bids the patient to lie on the couch, he is asking him to stretch out alongside a horse and a crocodile. The crocodile may be willing and ready to shed a tear and the horse to neigh and whinny, but when they are encouraged to express their troubles in words, it soon becomes evident that their inability is beyond the help of language training. Little wonder that the patient who has personal responsibility for these animals and who must serve as their mouthpiece is sometimes accused of being full of resistances and reluctant to talk.[31]

It is on the basis of such an understanding of the brain that Koestler asserts "the irrationality of the mind's normal functioning" and refers to "split-mind patterns"[32] that arise from the superimposition of evolutionary brain types upon one another:

> The human mind is basically schizophrenic, split into at least two mutually exclusive planes. The main difference between "pathological" and "normal" schizophrenia lies in the isolated character of the irrational component in the former, as opposed to the collectively accepted irrationality of the latter.[33]

So the brain is structurally homologous with reality in general: it too comprises incompatible "planes," and the dismal finding of the passage just quoted is that the rational can never become sovereign over the irrational. What we call rationality is merely the irrational in a form that is socially condoned and regulated. Koestler was often driven to moments of such spectacular biological pessimism by the madness that he saw around him, and it is certainly true that he saw the self as deeply divided and contradictory. But this is not the whole story. This man who believed that what he termed the "Cartesian catastrophe"[34] had undermined the culture of the West yearned for forms of synthesis that might integrate various levels of the self and, by healing the divided creature that humanity had become, save it from itself. His autobiographical writings, while often bemused by the contradictions they reveal in the self as autobiographical "anti-hero,"[35] at the same time narrate a set of quests for psychic integration. Their structure, far from simply replicating alleged structures of psychic contradiction, is in fact teleological: they move, like the arrow in one of their titles, toward higher, if not completely realized, levels of synthesis—though, as we shall see, even this pattern is complicated in various ways.

An aspect of the antibehaviorist stance of the autobiographies is to deny the equation between knowability and external verification. Even the autobiographer who wanted his life-writing to be more revealing than Rousseau's must concede that "the notion of an 'X-ray self-portrait' is obviously a fallacy. Not only because the object is identical with the observer, which fact alone excludes photographic objectivity. But also, because in the realm of psychology no concrete, objective, truth exists, only an almost infinite number of levels of truth" (*IW*, p. 442). In other words, we must learn to live with a degree of mystification—to concede the existence of that which we cannot fully grasp or narrate, and to weave into our autobiographical narratives an awareness that central features of the world transcend conceptual and narrative encapsulation. It also requires that we have a conception of the *subjectively true*: of that which we know to be, without external corroboration. To render this kind of truth is also the business of the autobiographer, as of other artists. One way of putting all of this would be to say that the autobiographer narrates the processes by which she or he learns to be the kind of person who is fit to write autobiography. Because the self that writes can never be "identical" with the self-as-subject (Koestler's phrasing is loose here: his use of "identical" is only intended to suggest that the person who writes and the subject of the narrative are *notionally* the same person; his point is that *ontologically* the two can never in fact completely coincide), and because the truths of the self are multiple and resistant to interpretive closure, the autobiographer will always be pointing her or his narrative at an "elusive receding 'I'" (*AB*, p. 99); but the true autobiographer, like the true thinker or artist, resists the lure of the reductive response to this often threatening situation.[36]

One of the many narrative lines in Koestler's autobiographical writings traces his progress from an alarmed and reductive response to the recessive "I," to a stance that can live with the unencapsulable complexity of the self. The first position is that of a young man (he is in his early teens at the time) whose sense of the world has been shaped by Newtonian mechanics. Indeed, the arrow of *Arrow in the Blue* is a "super-arrow" (*AB*, p. 68) shot out into what is initially assumed to be Newtonian space, which then travels beyond what we know, beyond what we can see or speculate about, into the total unknown. What then? Scandalously, the arrow's flight denies "one's most sacred right—the right to know":

> The idea that infinity would remain an unsolved riddle was unbearable. The more so as I had learned that a finite quantity like the earth—or like myself reclining on it—shrank to zero when divided by an infinite quantity. So, mathematically, if space was infinity, the earth was zero and I was zero and one life-span was zero, and a year and a century were zero. It made no sense, there was a miscalculation somewhere, and the answer to the riddle was obviously to be found by reading more books about gravity, electricity, astronomy, and higher mathematics. (*AB*, p. 68)

At sixteen he comes to think of the arrow not just in terms of an outward journey, but also of an inward one, what he terms the "ego spiral," which curves into the self and which, like its interstellar counterpart, finds no point of arrival but just unanswering infinitude: "The arrow went off at a tangent on its quest for the infinitely remote; the ego spiral curled inward, toward the infinitely close, which was yet as unattainable as the other"(*AB*, p. 99). The correlate of this is a skepticism that insinuates the question "What then?" into the cogito: "A man reads a thriller. He is enjoying himself. He knows that he is enjoying himself.

But does he know that he knows he is enjoying himself? . . . I am thinking of this problem. I know that I am thinking of this problem. I know that I know that I am thinking of this problem. I know that I know that I know . . . and so on" (*AB*, p. 99). True to schematic form—a form that is among other things a defense against the very anxiety it seeks to articulate—he even constructed a diagram of the ego spiral (*AB*, p. 100):

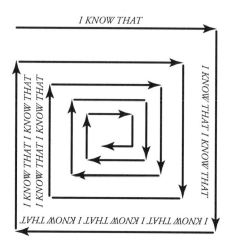

So perceived, the self is an epistemological midget in a world of baffling enormity, terrified by its inability finally to know what is without and what is within. There is an immense temptation to deny complexity, and where this applies to the self it can take the form of the kind of flight from the burdens of consciousness that Sartre calls "bad faith." Koestler believes that much of the horror that humanity begets has its origins here. A crucial moment in the autobiographies comes in his early twenties when he spends a few weeks in a house on Lago di Lugano. The house belongs to a wealthy German widow, one Maria Kloepfer. By this time Koestler is a Communist and still a died-in-the-wool Newtonian metaphysician, and as he says of himself at the time, he is a man crippled by his own system of beliefs. Maria sees the "substance" that lies behind the "ultimate, gaping emptiness" of a personality shaped by

> the void of the nineteenth century's scientific materialism, the world as a clockwork mechanism which, once it had somehow been wound up, would forever follow its course predestined by Newton's laws. But at least in this mechanical universe there were no gaps for poltergeists . . . (*IW*, p. 358)

He has become a sort of clockwork man, an example of the Sartrean figure who aspires to the condition of the thing-in-itself: the status of an object untroubled by the complexities of consciousness. He writes that in a life-changing encounter it is Maria who convinces him that he must assume "the burden of freedom" (*IW*, p. 361) and must question his commitment to a predestinarian view of self and world. The encounter takes the form of an argument about determinism and free will. More of this presently. In essence the admission of "freedom" into consciousness involves opening up to other realms of experience—to a world that might indeed be haunted by poltergeists, and in which one's past might not wholly determine one's present and future self. Maria, a woman haunted by visions, knows that there is indeed a ghost in the machine, and something like a "factor x" that offers freedom, if only we are willing to grasp it.

But what—we must surely ask—*is* this freedom? He says that "factor x" has an "unprovable existence"; yet much of what he writes about the self and the mind is strongly empirical in tendency. Is there no accommodation between the Koestler who renders the mind in terms of evolutionary scenarios and biological metaphors, and the one who locates consciousness beyond the sway of causal law? Consider the most extended of his biological metaphors: the notion of the "holon." According to this hypothetical figure, expounded in most detail in *The Ghost in the Machine,* all sentient life-forms partake of two opposing tendencies: one toward self-assertion, the other toward integration and participation. Each form possesses hierarchically ordered capacities, from simple to increasingly complex. At its metaphoric "base" the entity-as-holon points "downward" toward infinitely more simple and primitive modalities; at the apex it points "up," again infinitely, toward levels of sophistication that extend and even to some extent transform the organism's capacities and nature. Human beings are the most complex holons of all, needless to say, and Koestler argues that several important facts about the race flow from its holon status. One is that we are by nature inclined to transcendence: "Without a transcendental belief, each man is a mean little island. The need for self-transcendence through some form of 'peak experience' (religious or aesthetic) and/or through social integration is inherent in man's condition."[37] Second, it is the integrative tendencies, not the self-assertive ones, that lie behind most human tragedy and destructiveness. Thus he agrees with Hannah Arendt's thesis about Eichmann and the "banality of evil,"[38] and he argues that "the tragedy of man is not his truculence but his proneness to delusions"—the delusions being the compulsion to commit to what are in fact misguided causes in search of belonging and its associated release from the burdens of uncertainty and isolation. Third, true creativity, be it artistic or scientific, is associated with unusually advanced levels of the self-assertive tendency. This is because in its most evolved forms the self-assertive modality becomes a form of self-transcendence. This, in Koestler's view, is what makes a genius.[39] A final point has particular relevance to autobiography. The holon, like so much else, is a Janus-faced entity in which each level of organization points downward toward integrative sameness with other entities, and upward toward differentiation from other entities. Human beings are holons that, like all such entities, are comprised of interlocking sub-holons at all but the highest and lowest levels of organization. Because of this, in Koestler's theory,

> the self or mind is not regarded as a discrete entity, a whole in an absolute sense; but each of its functional holons in the many-levelled hierarchy—from visceral regulations to cognitive habits—is regarded as having a measure of individuality, with the Janus-faced attributes of partness and wholeness; and the degree of their integratedness into a unified personality varies with circumstances, but is never absolute. Total awareness of selfhood, the identity of the knower and the known, though always in sight, is never achieved. It could only be achieved at the peak of the hierarchy which is always one step removed from the climber.[40]

If this has a somewhat homemade quality, it might help to explain something that infuriated Koestler: his lack of acceptance among much of the "mainstream" scientific fraternity. (He was right to think that his mysticism, in particular his belief in the paranormal, was a chief cause of this skepticism.) Be this as it may, as an account of consciousness it is problematical. In part this is because the very metaphorization of self is here performed in such materialist-biological terms that no analytical vocabulary of the nonmaterial, of consciousness construed as ghostlike, is allowed in. The ghost simply enters the description as an agency from another, a "different," metaphoric "order of reality." Koestler offers the holon as an alternative to Cartesian dualistic models. His point is to replace duality with a "serialistic hypothesis, in which 'mental' and 'mechanical' are relative attributes, the dominance of one or the other deriving from a change of levels." However, as he admits, "this still leaves a host of problems unanswered."[41] The idea seems to be that the psyche is a holon within a holon, and that it in its turn is hierarchically constituted, with the "downward" dimension instantiating the unfree—instinctual, determined, passion- and habit-driven—aspects of behavior.[42] Conversely, the "upward" dimension is associated with liberation from these determinative forces: with behavior that is informed by rational self-awareness and choice. There are "degrees of freedom"[43] that correspond with points on the hierarchy, and the further "up" a given action or intention occurs, the greater will be the "responsibility"[44] of the agent who performs it.

Koestler bolsters his case for free will by repeating a claim he makes on the subject in an earlier book, *The Yogi and the Commissar*:

> My disbelief in determinism must be contained in the set of factors which determine my behavior; one of the conditions for fulfilling the prearranged pattern is that I should not believe that it is prearranged. Destiny can only have its way by forcing me to disbelieve in it. Thus the very concept of determinism condemns a man to live in a world where the rules of conduct are based on *As If* and the rules of logic on *Becauses*.[45]

On this view—one that typifies a series of suspiciously slick formulations on Koestler's part—the will at first seems to be free: he argues that even in the case of someone who denies determinism, the will must in a deterministic account be free, since the belief in freedom becomes determinative of the will. Koestler thinks that this proves that the will is free. But does it? Does it not merely prove that even the person who is under the impression of being free is in fact the possessor of a determined will after all, and that the sentiment of freedom, while efficacious in some ways, is ultimately an illusion? Here as elsewhere, his conception of the will comprises a puzzling amalgam of bits of various models: while the existence of "factor *x*" would suggest Freedom as the Genus of Volition, the notion that will is determined by rational belief sounds more like an understanding of Will as Rational Appetite. The claim that belief in freedom structures social arrangements reads like a description of the Will as the Source of Law. Beyond all of this, as we shall see, is the immense complication of certain mystical states that seem to exempt the self from willing in any familiar sense. Perhaps aware that paradox will not quite do, Koestler shores up the position with an empirical claim: "Even psychiatrists of the deterministic school agree that abolition of the experience of having a will of his own leads to collapse of the patient's whole mental structure."[46] He adds that, in effect, the subjective truth that we do in indeed possess freedom of the will cannot be overridden by third-person claims to the contrary: "The subjective experience of freedom is as much a given datum as the sensation of colour, or the feeling of pain."[47]

The holon is a graphic example of a metaphor of self-constitution, and Koestler's autobiographical writings cannot be understood without it. Yet the metaphor highlights a problem that dogs the autobiographical and other writings: Koestler's unsatisfactory account of human psychology. The holon model segments the psyche along various axes; yet it tells us very little about how constituent parts of the entity actually act upon one another. So, for example, we cannot tell how "cognitive" (and presumably self-transcending) components or faculties act upon more primitive, instinctual, "integrative" ones. Koestler talks of feedback "loops"[48] whereby consciousness reflects upon its own reflective capacity to transcend determined inclination, but concedes that such processes lead to an endless process of regression. Ultimately he offers no plausible explanation as to *how* consciousness shakes itself free of instinctual domination; or *how* it becomes the kind of consciousness that can bear the ethical and political responsibilities he asks of it. And these difficulties are consistent with a more fundamental difficulty in Koestler's conception of the self: the role he ascribes to the unconscious.

I have said that Koestler was an ambivalent and often hostile reader of Freud (though he was awed by the experience of meeting the great man).[49] And indeed one of his novels, *Arrival and Departure*,[50] is among other things a sustained attack on the ethical implications of psychoanalysis. Yet it often seems that when he comes to specify the nature of the psyche and its internal dynamics, the unconscious is accorded an unexpectedly powerful determinative role. Consider the following rumination about the ways in which people change:

> I do not believe that anybody, except a very primitive person, can be reborn in one night, as so many tales of sudden conversions will have it. I do believe that one can suddenly "see the light" and undergo a change that will completely alter the course of one's life. But a change of this kind takes place at the spiritual core of the subject, and it will take a long time to seep through to the periphery, until in the end the entire personality, his conscious thoughts and actions, become impregnated with it . . . Nor do I believe that a true spiritual transformation can be the result of a process of conscious reasoning, working its way downward as it were. It begins on the level where the unconscious axioms of faith, the implicit premises of thinking, the innate standards of value, are located. (*IW*, p. 436)

Fine though this is, it ascribes noticeably little capacity for conceptual counseling or modification of the volitional powers of the self. The will (implied though not named here) awaits impulsion from the unconscious. But then the unconscious also contains the murderous crocodile-like tendencies that render the transformation of id energies into ethical ego and superego ones so desperately urgent. There is a gap in the explanation here. Nor does it help that in another explanatory dimension Koestler reads more like a Jungian than a Freudian expositor: his descriptions of epiphanic moments, his belief in the paranormal— these often seem predicated on something like a trans-individual collective unconscious. But there is nothing in principle about such a position that will help to explain individual volition, and arguably nothing sufficiently explicit in Koestler's rendering of such views or experiences to help explain it. Here we see evidence of a "split" in Koestler's worldview that he labored hard to overcome— a kind of paradigm split between mechanistic and mystical conceptions of self and world. He hoped that quantum mechanics might provide a bridge between these two modes of explanation.[51] But we need now to ask why this split is so pronounced; why Koestlerian autobiography is so deeply divided between assertion of the will, on the one hand, and something amounting almost to a denial of it, on the other. Part of the answer lies in Koestler's preoccupation with totalitarianism.

III. The Aquarium

Many of Koestler's titles are binary or paradoxical in form and reflect his split view of things: *The Yogi and the Commissar, Arrival and Departure, Promise and Fulfilment, Insight and Outlook, The Lotus and the Robot, Darkness at Noon, The*

Invisible Writing. The first of these is a good example: the Yogi represents mysticism, the Commissar, of course, totalitarianism. It is this book that contains the early statement of the view that the belief in freedom is determinative of our conduct;[52] the volume also contains fine examples of Koestler's political analyses of the Promethean (*AB*, p. 330) and repressive features of totalitarianism and of alternative forms of political organization.[53] It is here, too, that he speaks of the "split-mind patterns" typical of humankind that take such catastrophic forms under totalitarianism.[54] Koestler's achievement as a journalist and politico-historical analyst is impressive, though the Cold Warrior in some of his postwar writings can betray him into historical simplifications: in particular a tendency to conflate Marxist-Leninist theory with Stalinist social practice, and a failure to explain how, as he asserts, the liberal mind escapes the split and reductive tendencies he discerns in the totalitarian one.[55] However, it is his anatomizations of totalitarianism as a psychological belief-state that are most significant in his autobiographical writings. This former Marxist true-believer has few peers as a chronicler of the particular form of what he sees as addiction (*GTF,* p. 55) that occurs when an individual succumbs to ideological programming. Koestler agrees with Waddington that the human being is a "belief-accepting animal,"[56] and in both *Arrow in the Blue* and his autobiographical essay in Crossman's *The God That Failed,* he describes how he became a Marxist:

> Tired of electrons and wave-mechanics, I began for the first time to read Marx, Engels and Lenin in earnest. By the time I had finished with *Feuerbach* and *State and Revolution,* something had clicked in my brain which shook me like a mental explosion. To say that one had "seen the light" is a poor description of the mental rapture which only the convert knows (regardless of what faith he has been converted to). The new light seems to pour from all directions across the skull; the whole universe falls into pattern like the stray pieces of a jigsaw puzzle assembled by magic at one stroke. There is now an answer to every question, doubts and conflicts are a matter of the tortured past—a past already remote, when one had lived in dismal ignorance in the tasteless, colorless world of those who *don't know.* Nothing henceforth can disturb the convert's inner peace and serenity—except the occasional fear of losing faith again, losing thereby what alone makes life worth living, and falling back into the outer darkness, where there is wailing and gnashing of teeth. (*GTF,* p. 23)

The transition from physics to Marxism is not as great as it might seem: Marx's preface to the first edition of *Capital* appeals to the authority of physics in setting forth its methodological assumptions.[57] But in describing himself as a "convert," Koestler is explicitly invoking the tradition of religious confessional autobiography. Yet this conversion is different: while Augustine recounts his conversion in order to confirm God's existence, Koestler's conversion is narrated in order to *dis*confirm the existence of its putative god; to announce that this god has failed, and to tell us why.[58] This leaves open the question whether Augustine's God might not also have failed. Elsewhere (for instance in *Promise and Fulfilment*) Koestler, the atheistic historian, makes no bones about his belief that Judeo-Christian theism is a human construction and a historically calamitous one at that; but it is Marxism, along with Newtonian determinism and Zionism,[59] that is the subject of what I term *narratives of affiliation* in Koestler's (and others') autobiographical writings. In the case of Marxism, the narrative is deeply ironic because the choice involved is so dreadfully misguided; but it is central to his purposes as an autobiographer that we should understand how such flawed choices come about.

Here again it's important to put Koestler's account into a context that he doesn't always sufficiently provide. His descriptions of how he came to commit to Marxism have a kind of retrospective contempt that borders on self-loathing. Self-loathing is central to the Western autobiographical tradition, from its roots in religious confessional writing, through the anguished mix of self-immolation and compensating self-justification in Rousseau, and into the guilt-ridden self-consciousness of much contemporary autobiography.[60] In a man like Koestler, such hatred of self is a particularly complex thing: while fierce and genuine at one level, it is also complicit in a complex form of narcissistic self-justification— to trounce the earlier self is to affirm later forms of the self, especially the writing self that pens the autobiography. More generally, Koestler's "manic-depressive" tendency to mood swings and splits predisposed him to dramatic oscillations between punitive self-accusation and arrogant self-assertion. The result is that the reader of his self-condemning narratives of Marxist affiliation can be forgiven for having insufficient sense of how justifiable this kind of conversion was *in historical context*. With fascism already on the march, and capitalist democracy appearing to succumb to the internal contradictions that Marx prophesied would destroy it, many Western intellectuals turned to Marxism after due deliberation and in good faith. To put it another way, in many such cases the wills of those concerned did indeed take their counsel, at least in part, from rational appraisal. The failure of the god to which such people turned should not in any simple sense be read as an indictment of the state in which they made their commitments. Post-totalitarian autobiography is important partly because it shows that—and how—reflective individuals can in good faith make commitments that prove with the knowledge of hindsight to be disastrously mistaken.

Koestler's conversion descriptions do not refer to the will directly: the point is rather that ideology drugs the faculty upon which the will relies if it is to function as a free power—a phenomenon close to what Eve Kosofsky Sedgwick calls "epidemics of the will."[61] It is rationality, understood as the capacity to weigh options with a measure of dispassion and to choose appropriately between them, that is slugged as if by a narcotic. In Koestler's terms this means that the higher, self-transcending tendencies in the would-be agent are thwarted, and that the more primitive, integrative, conformist ones take over. Herein lies the danger of the true believer.

If we allow, as we surely must, that *some* conversions of this kind are indeed inauthentic in the sense that they are not associated with processes of rational deliberation, it then becomes important to ask why some individuals have what Koestler calls a particular "proneness to delusion"; why some are liable to bogus conversion. Bogus conversion has its roots in personal history, and Koestler, a man for whom libidinal energy exercised an imperious power,[62] thinks of political and other belief-accepting states as species of libido: "The political libido is basically as irrational as the sexual drive, and patterned, like the latter, by early, partly unconscious, experiences—by traumatic shocks, complexes, identifications, repressions, and the rest. Early emotional conditioning plays a decisive part; the arguments which justify and rationalize the credo come afterwards" (*AB*, p. 122). So conceived, choices of the kind that lead to political commitment are not really choices at all. They are driven by motives rather than conscious intentions. The will plays its part in cathecting a particular ideological option, but in so doing it is determined—indeed (though Koestler does not bring out both of these aspects) *doubly determined*: first by the instinctual drivelike character of libido, and second by the complications of personal history, which in their turn determine that the determinative power of the libidinal drive compels cognition to take irrational forms—forms that must issue in inauthentic choices and so inappropriate and even dangerous emotional investments. And there is a further determinative element to which Koestler rightly imputes enormous power in human affairs: fear—the fear that the epistemological midget feels in a world that he or she cannot fathom; the fear that this, the only creature capable of conceptualizing its mortality, feels at the prospect of death.[63] An immensely anxious man himself, Koestler knew a lot about how fear can precipitate the need to shed "the burdens of consciousness," to have all questions answered in a moment of sheer illumination.

In its turn, inauthentic conversion—and, in some instances, misguided conversion made on reasonable grounds—sets in train processes that have profound human consequences. Koestler likens life in the Communist Party to entering "a strange world, as if he were entering a deep-sea aquarium with its phosphorescent light and fleeting, elusive shapes"; a world that commits the individual to "the gradual transformation of character and of human relationships which a long Party career infallibly produced." The hallmark of this "transformation" is a collapse of trust in others. The motto of the aquarium "might have been: Love your comrade, but don't trust him an inch" (*GTF*, pp. 29-30). Like *Darkness at Noon,* Koestler's autobiographies are brilliant inquiries into the decimation of interpersonal trust and into the processes whereby the will is severed from rational and properly compassionate ethical counseling: "One does not decide at a given moment: 'I am going to be a traitor.' One slides into treason by degrees" (*IW,* p. 125). Again: "To the convert, his conversion appears as a single and indivisible act, a spiritual rebirth in which emotion and reason, the perennial duellists, are for once in complete harmony" (*AB,* p. 318). The convert to Marxism believes that History is "rigidly determined by economic forces" and that "individual responsibility" has no part to play. Where does this leave "ethical values," Koestler asks (*AB,* p. 348). The aquarium, then, is a sort of infernal realm of the ethical, where all faith is bad faith because authenticity no longer has any hold on the self (*SE,* p. 115); where what seems to be courage is in fact something else, since courage requires the sentiment of personal responsibility (*AB,* p. 158); and where a distinctive and sinister phenomenon of totalitarian social-psychological manipulation sets in: the usurpation of the inwardness of self by Party ideology.

Women figure in complex and sometimes objectionable ways in Koestler's autobiographies;[64] indeed one unsuccessful sexual encounter with a particularly strong woman—Simone de Beauvoir—was to reverberate through the autobiographical and other writings of both parties.[65] Perhaps in part because he sensed a deep conflict between his ethical inclinations and his pathological promiscuity, women often figure prominently at moments of particular ethical importance in his autobiographies. On the theme of usurpation he repeats a story—black humor but offered as true—about a colleague of his who picks up a girl wearing a swastika during the carnival season in Berlin in 1932. He takes her back to his flat, whereupon "at the climactic moment" the girl raises herself on one elbow and salutes the führer. She explains to her crushed companion that she and some of her friends had pledged themselves "'to remember the Fuehrer every time at the most sacred moment in a woman's life'" (*IW,* p. 43).[66] But among other stories about women, one is offered in deadly earnest. Indeed it constitutes perhaps the most anguished moment of confession in all of Koestler's autobiographical writings: the story of Nadeshda Smirnova, a young woman with whom he had a relationship during his travels in the Soviet Union in 1932.

He meets her on a train and continues a relationship with her in her hometown of Baku. He is surprised to find that she and the aunt with whom she lives are under suspicion from the Party, and he is persuaded by an official to report on her activities, even as he is having a relationship with her. He writes that his revulsion at his capacity for such betrayal is a turning point: it makes him "a bad Communist, and a bad anti-Communist, and thereby a little more human. I had my first glimpse of the invisible writing" (*IW,* p. 132). But what precisely *is* the "invisible writing," and how does it relate to politics, ethics, the realm of action? In order to get a sense of what this "writing" is, and of its importance, the reader of Koestler needs to consider passages like the following. The "pressure" of life in a totalitarian state seems almost irresistible—slow and steady like soil erosion, or the action of the tides. It results in that gradual thwarting of the mind which I have tried to describe, and is accompanied by an even more fatal corrosion of the spirit. It cuts man off from his metaphysical roots, from religious experience, from the "oceanic feeling" in all its forms. Cosmic awareness is replaced by social vigilance, perception of the absolute by brain-acrobatics. The result is a gradual dehydration of the soul, a spiritual dearth more frightening than the famine. (*IW*, pp. 192–93)

IV. Transcendence

The "dehydration of the soul" involves among other things the death of the will's capacity to take counsel from affective rationality. "Cosmic awareness," the "oceanic feeling," sustains the spirit and connects the will in appropriate ways to the other constituent parts of the psyche. The "invisible writing," or the "language of destiny," is a kind of epiphanic code through which the "cosmic dimension" is revealed to consciousness. This "writing" is no mere rhetorical figure for Koestler. Indeed one of the striking things about Koestler's as-yet-unpublished journals, and those kept by his third wife Cynthia (also unpublished), is that each couches day-to-day experience in terms of the tragic and trivial planes and the language of destiny. This even applies to moments of great crisis. Thus Koestler's anguished journal entries for August-October 1951, after his second wife, Mamaine, has left him, construe what has happened in just these terms:

> The real alternative [to marriage] was, all the time, to shoulder the burden of ultimate loneliness; to settle for good on the tragic plane; to obey the apparent unreason of what I feel to be my destiny.

Again:

> The "langage du destin" [a quotation from Malraux] was this time quite fantastic. The "invisible ink" looked obvious like instructions in brail.[67]

We recall that the child undergoing the tonsillectomy discerns an invisible dimension that is likened to the deeps through which the ship's keel glides. In another passage about the "invisible writing," toward the end of *The Invisible Writing*, Koestler again uses a nautical analogy: a captain of a ship leaves port with sealed directions in his pocket. When he opens them, he finds that they are written in invisible ink. He gets glimpses of the directions written therein, but not enough to decipher them. Yet the awareness of the existence of the illegible text guides his navigation (*IW*, p. 432). Here, as we approach more closely the mystical dimension in Koestler's work, problems—and perhaps also misgivings[68]—

start to multiply. It seems that the "writing" in question enters into volition in an odd way. It is not visionary in the sense that "what has to be done" is laid out in its entirety and merely awaits enactment by a completely compliant individual. The text is in fact fragmentary, and it seems to bypass cognitive processes: the captain does not know in any detail what it is he should do, but he knows intuitively that there is *something* that can be done, and he knows enough to go about doing it—albeit, it seems, in a somewhat dreamlike state. Whether he is free in any significant sense *not* to do what the writing intimates is not clear. Though passages such as this do not have a feeling of compulsion about them, neither do they have a feeling of volition: the suggestion seems to be that the will is coded to pick up and respond to intimations of this kind, and that where they occur the will instinctively, inevitably, and lucently obeys—rather as, according to Plato and Aristotle, the will must inevitably and supinely comply with the bidding of rationality. We need a new term for Koestler's version of things, and if Plato's and Aristotle's view can be described as Will as Intellectual Preference, Koestler's might be termed *Will as Numinous Compliance*—a further complication of his already-puzzling picture of the will.

So conceived, Koestlerian mysticism might seem to be a species of determinism; and so in a sense it is. However, his account of "factor x" and related matters denies this. We recall that when this factor is operating, normal modes of causation are suspended, "the present is not determined by the past," and the agent possesses "relative freedom." So in Koestler's mind at least this is not determinism but rather the reverse—exemption from causation. In another of his ontological figures, he explains that in a moment of transcendence he becomes aware that

a higher order of reality existed, and that it alone invested existence with meaning. I came to call it later on "the reality of the third order." The narrow world of sensory perception constituted the first order; this perceptual world was enveloped by the conceptual world which contained phenomena not directly perceivable, such as gravitation, electromagnetic fields, and curved space. The second order of reality filled in the gaps and gave meaning to the absurd patchiness of the sensory world.

In the same manner, the third order of reality enveloped, interpenetrated, and gave meaning to the second. It contained "occult" phenomena which could not be apprehended or explained either on the sensory or the conceptual level, and yet occasionally invaded them like spiritual meteors piercing the primitive's vaulted sky. Just as the conceptual order showed up the illusions and distortions of the senses, so the "third order" disclosed that time, space and causality, that the isolation, separateness and spatio-temporal limitations of the self were merely optical illusions on the next higher level. (*IW*, pp. 431–32)

So the "invisible writing" appears also to be the language of the "third order"—an order not intelligible to us in "conceptual" terms. By extension we can suppose that when this "order" acts, say, upon the will, it does so with the spectacular, baffling, and irresistible force of a meteor entering the atmosphere above the bewildered Neanderthal's head. This is not an entirely reassuring thought.

While in general I don't find Koestler's mysticism uninteresting, or even necessarily implausible, there is only so much that rational analysis can say about it.[69] However, it is clear that in a schematic way his visionary experiences, in which the will is cut free from normal orders of determination, are intended as an antidote—a respondent act—to species of totalitarian thought that are predicated on versions of material causation, and to forms of totalitarian practice that invoke notions like the Will of the People or the Will of the Leader. The epiphanic self is totalitarianism's visionary Other. What is more interesting about Koestler's autobiographical accounts of his otherworldly revelations is their relation to his psychological history and his temperamental makeup. In particular, there is a complex and intriguing relationship between his pathological levels of anxiety, his political involvements, his ethical commitment to the virtue of courage, and his devotion to the "invisible writing." Here yet again, Koestler seems split in a variety of ways, some of them apparent to him, others not. He expresses his awareness of certain inner contradictions through one of many (too many!) modulations of the arrow metaphor. Two years he spent in Berlin (1930–32) stayed in his memory "under the sign of the split arrow, the dual temperament which drove me in two opposite directions: into the fanatical ranks of the Communist Party and towards detached scientific contemplation" (*AB*, pp. 349–50). The "split" between action and contemplation is as we have seen entirely characteristic of him; but he has more to say about his "temperament" than just this.

Koestlerian autobiography reports a self that is compulsively active but also pathologically fearful, and it acknowledges a link between these things: action is an antidote to anxiety. "Though subject to frequent fits of depression, real disasters usually fill me with a wild elation . . . It is, I suppose, part of the apocalyptic temperament, of the all-or-nothing type of mentality—a temperament that lacks fortitude in minor crises but thrives on catastrophes" (*IW*, p. 200). It is not uncommon for those who are prone to dread to be magnetized by risk, whether because the actuality of danger is less painful and threatening than its anticipation; or because danger's "highs" can blot out the sensation of fear; or because the indignity of "being" a fearful person is more psychologically devastating than the fear that has to be overcome in facing real or imagined dangers—no doubt there are all manner of possibilities and permutations. In Koestler's case being magnetized by risk drew him quite literally to the clashing planes of historical threat and conflict—to Spain during the civil war, for instance. Here the psychological payoffs could be great: he sniggers that Stephen Spender and other thirties writers had a "good historical time" in Spain (*IW,* p. 399), but he is open to similar suspicions—"the invisible writing" was apt to come into view at the scene of crises, for the language of destiny is the language of the threshold. But to be "magnetized" is to be impelled, and on this view of things it is not freedom but compulsion that brings him to the threshold. The will is active, but it is also determined. Having got there, however, it is the "invisible writing" that ostensibly frees his will.

What does this tell us about the ethical implications of Koestler's account of the will? Obviously it suggests that courage is not always what it seems. Koestler objects to the "embarrassingly exhibitionistic, adolescent, dumb hero quality" of courage in Hemingway's fiction (*IW,* p. 400); and he is similarly hard on himself. "There are two kinds of courage: the brave man's and the coward's," he writes. And he continues: "Mine has always been the coward's courage, which is often the more stubborn variety." As a young man, aware of this deficiency in himself, he writes a motto of which Aristotle would have approved and props it against the foot of his bed: "COURAGE IS NEVER TO LET YOUR ACTIONS BE INFLU-ENCED BY YOUR FEARS" (*AB,* p. 158). Courage cannot survive in the aquarium. How then does one learn or recover it? Koestler's autobiographies seem to give two answers: by forfeiture of the entire personality structure that sustains cowardice, and by an act of benediction by the Other.

The first of these is exemplified in cell no. 40 in Seville, and the narrative account is Koestler as visionary autobiographer at his best. The culmination of the transition from anxiety to transcendence is the "oceanic" vision he has in cell no. 40. Using a wire spring from his mattress, he begins to scratch mathematical formulae on the wall. The third formula he tries is Euclid's proof that the number of primes is infinite; that "to whatever astronomic regions we ascend in the scale, we shall find numbers that are not the product of smaller ones, but are generated by immaculate conception, as it were" (*IW,* p. 428). He recaptures the "enchantment" that the formula had given him as a child at school:

> And then, for the first time, I suddenly understood the reason for this enchantment: the scribbled symbols on the wall represented one of the rare cases where a meaningful and comprehensive statement about the infinite is arrived at by precise and finite means. The infinite is a mystical mass shrouded in a haze; and yet it was possible to gain some knowledge of it without losing oneself in treacly ambiguities. The significance of this swept over me like a wave. The wave had originated in an articulate verbal insight; but this evaporated at once, leaving in its wake only a wordless essence, a fragrance of eternity, a quiver of the arrow in the blue. I must have stood there for some minutes, entranced, with a wordless awareness that "this is perfect—perfect"; until I noticed some slight mental discomfort nagging at the back of my mind—some trivial circumstance that marred the perfection of the moment. Then I re-

membered the nature of that irrelevant annoyance: I was, of course, in prison
and might be shot. But this was immediately answered by a feeling whose verbal translation would be: "So what? is that all? have you got nothing more serious to worry about?"—an answer so spontaneous, fresh and amused as if the
intruding annoyance had been the loss of a collar-stud. Then I was floating on
my back in a river of peace, under bridges of silence. It came from nowhere
and flowed nowhere. Then there was no river and no I. The I had ceased to
exist. (*IW*, p. 429)

This is what, elsewhere, he calls "the un-selfing of the self":[70] it is the "oceanic
experience" par excellence. That term of course comes from Freud.[71] But the experience is describable in other ways. Seen in terms of the model of human-as-
holon, it is the ultimate and infinite expression of the organism's capacity for
self-transcendence.[72] As an instance of the individual's life among the metaphysical planes, it is the quintessential moment in which the tragic renders trivial—transcends—the greatest anxiety of all: the fear of death. This is "spiritual
experience" in its purest form: he was later to define "spiritual life" as "the training for the acceptance of death."[73] Seen as a moment of mystical transcendence,
not least transcendence of earlier states of the self, it is the instant in which the
self-deluding and scientist quest for the arrow gives way to an infinite expansion of consciousness that registers as "a quiver of the arrow in the blue": an acceptance that its flight is indeed infinite, that we live now in the relational space
of an Einsteinian universe. And what of the ego spiral? This moment of vision
does not identify a point at which introspection arrives; rather, it sets that diagram and the gestalt it expresses aside. In its moment of infinite expansion, the
agonies of self-consciousness evaporate as self is gathered into some higher
modality, a third order, in which the ego dissolves; and with it—Koestler would
argue—goes the bane of the autobiographer: the distinction between the self-
as-object and the self-as-subject. The overarching rationale of Koestlerian autobiography is the quest for this point of intersection between time and infinity,
tragic and trivial, action and narration. So conceived, autobiography would constitute a fusion of what he identifies as two mystical modes:

> In the "arrow state" consciousness expands towards mystic union with the All-
> One while the ego is felt to dissolve in the infinite. In the opposite "spiral
> state" consciousness contracts, is focused on the self, strives to establish iden-
> tity between subject and object, to permeate the self with awareness of itself.
> (*AB*, p. 101)

Once more, the arrow is the arrow of transcendence; the ego spiral has been replaced by the "spiral state" in which absolute, but noncognitive, self-awareness—as opposed to self-knowledge—has been attained. The un-selfed self, of
course, cannot—need not—possess a will. The will is also rendered superfluous

because this is a life-out-of-time experience, and will, constituted as it is for temporal instantiation, can have—need have—no life out of time. Schopenhauer, the pessimist of the will, holds out the hope that for the person who learns from experience, there might be deliverance from the strife of willing, that will-lessness may be within the human compass. Koestlerian un-selfing, too, delivers the self from the anxiety and the exactions of willing, though the state seems to come less by wisdom than by fiat or grace.

Consider again his encounter with Maria Kloepfer, another of those crucial women in the narratives. When he comes to stay with her in her house on the lake, he is a dissociated, clockwork man. I mentioned earlier that what changes him is a conversation with Maria. Maria, who has been mentally ill and is soon to die of a combination of epilepsy and mental illness, "had the gift of occasionally reading fragments of the writing" (*IW*, p. 359). During a meal she and Koestler have a heated argument about "Determinism versus Free Will" (*IW*, p. 361). Koestler knows that the New Physics is already undermining Newtonian determinism, and he feels "an attraction" (*IW*, 363) to the other order that Maria knows and that he secretly yearns for. As the argument becomes more angry, he reduces her to tears by a threat that is also a piece of logical trickery: he says that if she is right that he possesses free will, he will get so angry that he will smash a treasured piece of her china, since her words will determine his deeds. On the other hand, if she withdraws her claim, the piece will inevitably be saved. Either way, free will is denied. Things between them are strained thereafter, and within days Koestler leaves. They (and one other) walk across the square to the railway station and:

> Suddenly Maria stopped in the middle of the square. It was the second and last time that I saw her crying. But this time she put her long, thin arms round my neck and her face against mine. For a moment she stood like that, trying to control her trembling. Then I felt the cool touch of her metal brace [on her teeth] against my temple, and I had the instant sensation of infinite peace, as if a faith-healer had laid his hand on me. (*IW*, p. 366)

He speaks of it as her "giving me absolution with that single, soothing touch of her lips" (*IW*, p. 367). The kiss is an act of forgiveness, but of a special kind— the kind that by honoring the Other's flawed mode of being confers the power to change—and the will to do so. Koestler does change: he comes to believe in and to live by the presumption of freedom of the will. Maria's kiss of absolution is another survival of religious narrative in this, the autobiography of what I have termed a "scientist mystic".

Living as if one were free, enacting that mysterious inwardness that cannot be silenced by ideology or reductionism—this is what in *Darkness at Noon* Koestler calls the "grammatical fiction"[74] of selfhood. Often he concedes the contradictions implicit in living this way. But to learn to live with contradiction and to maintain the activity of the ethical will in the face of apparent pointlessness is central to what he sees as a new form of humanism:

> "If the pessimism of the philosopher is a valid attitude, the duty of the militant humanist to go on hoping against hope is no less valid. The reproach of morbid despair which is so often levelled against us, seems to me provoked by a mix-up between two parallel planes in our minds which should be kept separate: the plane of detached contemplation in the sign of infinity, and the plane of action in the name of certain ethical imperatives. We have to accept the perpetual contradiction between these two. If we admit that defeatism and despair, even when logically justified, are morally wrong, and that active resistance to evil is a moral necessity even when it seems logically absurd, we may find a new approach to a humanist dialectic . . ." (*AB,* p. 133, quoting from his novel *The Age of Longing*)

There is something heroic about this, as there is about much in Koestler, but also something unsatisfactory that comes from too great a preparedness to repose in contradiction. To separate "contemplation" and "action" in this way is implausible—and indeed dangerous. It means that action, the activity of the will, is informed by a spontaneous, intuitive apprehension of the Good. It is a species of moral intuitionism. Koestler quotes Schopenhauer approvingly: "To preach morality is hard; to give it an intellectual justification is impossible."[75] But the moral agent, the "strong evaluator," is one who exercises the will in the light of a complex deliberative process of which he or she can give a nuanced reflective account. Koestler's moral protagonist cannot be an agent in this sense. Acting by moral intuition means that the will is determined by the affective faculties—a thing he elsewhere fears, and rightly so: such a person could, if sufficiently disturbed, be a Nazi rather than a fighter for democratic freedom.

In the end it is very hard to say whether Koestler's conceptions (plural) of the will amount to a form of free will or not. There are just too many contradictions. Similarly, it is hard to know whether his ultimate position amounts to a politics of transcendence or a transcendence of politics. An epiphany is indeed a dramatic alternative to ideological "addiction"; but epiphanies are a minority— some would say a privileged minority—pursuit. What we need to know is why more readily available alternatives, like various forms of liberalism and humanism, are preferable to totalitarian ones, and how it is that some liberal-humanist options manage to avoid the perils of the closed ideological system. Here we need a distinction that Koestler never seems adequately to make: between thinking that is systematic and "closed," on the one hand, and thinking that is systematic and nonreductive or "open," on the other.

Nevertheless, Koestler is undoubtedly important: a central figure in the life of the twentieth century and a writer who takes autobiography's fascination with the will in startling and challenging directions. He was aware of the plight of the will in his century, and he tried to steer a course among various and often incommensurable options. Having shed his early allegiance to seventeenth-century Newtonian/Humean-style understandings of causation, he encountered and explored new perspectives, only to find in Freud and Marx another set of determinisms that denied the will its freedom. Less worldly intellectuals of the time saw in Nietzsche the ultimate and salving release from determinism, but Koestler's understanding of totalitarianism's abuses of the concept of will, together with his powerful grasp of how destructive Dionysian man could be if stripped of rational regulation, meant that he could not and would not countenance the Nietzschean option. His descriptions of a will-less state can be reminiscent of Schopenhauer and of other Romantic literary and philosophical sources, but his mysticism is hard to place. His "All-One" is perhaps reminiscent of the Buddhist notion of totality[76] but is really the secular god of quantum mechanics. It is certainly not the sort of being to whom Augustine wishes his will to tend. Like Augustine and others, Koestler yearns for some perfect form of absorption where affiliation shades into fusion with something beyond and greater than Self. He tries all manner of conceptions of the will in pursuit of this ideal. His autobiographical writings are a record of the contradictions that ensued, but also of the passionate intensity of his quest and its importance for twentieth-century understandings of metaphysics, ethics, and political choice.

CHAPTER SEVEN

"Strange Identity"
Stephen Spender and Weakness of Will

Hence also it is no easy task to be good. For in everything it is no easy task to find the middle, e.g. to find the middle of a circle is not for every one but for him who knows.
—Aristotle, *Nichomachean Ethics* (2.9)

The essential point in every determination of the will by the moral law, is that being a free will it is determined simply by the moral law, not only without the co-operation of sensible impulses, but even to the rejection of all such, and to the checking of all inclinations so far as they might be opposed to that law.
—Kant, *Critique of Practical Reason* (book 1, chapter 3)

I can also find myself engaged in acts which reveal my possibilities to me at the very instant when they are realized.
—Sartre, *Being and Nothingness* (part 1, chapter 1, V)

Politics without ideology and with a strong tendency towards autobiography equals liberalism.
—Stephen Spender, postscript, *The Thirties and After*

In my reading of Koestler in the previous chapter, I argued that his autobiographical and other writings are deeply, if in some ways laudably, conflicted about the will. At times the will is presented as free—the ghost that inhabits the human machine. But in this ghostly, otherworldly register the will can also look decidedly unfree. Koestler's visionary states are such that the will is not so much owned and counseled by the self, as it is guided, perhaps even determined, by forces and intimations that are quite beyond the self. The ghost—the will—may be "in" the machine, but it's not at all clear that the machine owns the ghost; that a human being can exert free will in response to a rational appraisal of the options that present themselves.

Koestler was passionate about human rights, and he exhibited a quite phenomenal power of the will in pursuit of his ethical and political commitments. This is one of the very impressive things about him; but it does not mean that the theoretical and autobiographical accounts he gives of the will present a picture of will as strong or effective. Indeed, much of what he tells us about himself in the autobiographies is suggestive of what we might think of as weaknesses of will: his binge drinking, his promiscuity, his susceptibility to violent mood swings, his bouts of depressive apathy, his need for otherworldly intimations in order to spark his will into action.

Though Koestler implicitly grapples with the problem of weakness of will—the problem that some would say besets people like the drinker, the gambler, the overeater, and the agoraphobic of my preface—his autobiographies seldom get the issue into focus. For a more pointed treatment of this thematic of the will, I turn now to Koestler's contemporary, Stephen Spender.

Paul laments: "The good which I want to do, I fail to do." Augustine, comparing the willing that moves a limb with his current and infinitely greater longing—the will for God's grace—bemoans: "I was not doing what with an incomparably greater longing I yearned to do."[1] Each is pondering a phenomenon that is as familiar as it is puzzling: the phenomenon of weakness of the will. For those who deny the existence of the will altogether, there can be no such phenomenon, however real it might feel to us. (Though some who deny the will in theory nevertheless ponder its appearance of weakness in certain practical contexts.) But anyone who believes in the existence of the will is likely at some stage to ask questions like: "How is it that I want to do something so badly and yet do not, or cannot, do it?" Or, "How is it that I can recognize the importance of doing something, yet lack the willpower that is commensurate with that recognition, and so lack the ability to do whatever it is?" Among those who frequently pose such questions are the reflective autobiographers, many of whom want to know about the powers, limitations, and nature of the will. One of the most extended modern autobiographical treatments of weakness of will and related issues occurs in Stephen Spender's *World Within World,* which contains this line from one of his poems: "O strange identity of my will and weakness!"[2]

Philosophical discussions of weakness of will have a long, complex, and sometimes forbiddingly technical history. To do this history justice requires book-length studies. There are several such books, some of them excellent and wide-ranging.[3] I don't propose to embark on a detailed historical account here, but merely to indicate some of the main points that are at issue in debates about weakness of the will and to cite a few of the better-known discussions, together with a few qualifications of my own, in order to provide a context for my reading of Spender's autobiography.

I. Can the Will Be Weak?

To the question "Can the will be weak?" common sense says, "Yes, of course"; but as soon as one considers particular philosophical accounts of the will—and indeed of the self in general—matters become more complex. Judeo-Christian accounts, which impute to the individual a free will that can be exercised at her or his discretion, appear to accommodate the notion that one's will might be weak; but as Augustine's puzzlement shows, it is not easy to explain *how* weakness comes about, nor how it can be corrected. His conversion comes after much unavailing trying, but it comes, as it were, in another register. When he reads Paul, something transformative happens: willing gives over to a new state that somehow fuses faith and love. The state is essentially God-given and not, therefore, in any direct sense the consequence of a newly self-generated strength of will. We may see it as in some measure the result of earlier willings, but Augustine does not philosophically explain how the weakness and ineffectuality of those earlier willings give over to efficaciousness—to strength of will.

For the Greeks, the problems are of a different order. Their conception of Will as Intellectual Preference construes will as enactment of rational assessment. Willing and rationality are thought to be both logically and pragmatically indivisible. People are so constituted that it ought to be impossible for someone who has made a rational assessment as to which is the best course of action in a particular situation to act in a way that does not reflect that assessment. And yet it is palpably the case that people can at times act in ways that do not correspond with what appears to be the best option open to them. Plato tries to deal with this, one of the so-called "Socratic paradoxes," in several texts. The best-known early discussion comes in the *Protagoras*. Socrates says:

> It must follow that no one willingly goes to meet evil or what he thinks to be evil. To make for what one believes to be evil, instead of making for the good, is not, it seems, in human nature, and when faced with the choice of two evils no one will choose the greater when he might choose the less.[4]

The discussion, which begins at 351, brings out various issues. For instance: What is the force of the terms *evil* and *good* in this context? Are these ethical categories in a narrow sense—categories pertaining to how one lives the Good Life—or are their entailments other, or more general, than this? In the case of this, Plato's early hedonistic view of the self,[5] these terms are linked closely to pleasure: one's assessment of what is best will turn on what is most likely to yield pleasure. But this in turn raises other questions: To what extent is a human being's pleasure in fact linked to the Good in an ethical sense? Can a person whose soul is rationally constituted take real pleasure (whatever this might mean) in something that is not ethically good? Again: Are there not various degrees and intensities of pleasure, various forms, some of which are "better" than others? Can rational appraisal be "dragged about" by certain passions so that, even when we try to make rational assessments, they are distorted by emotional interferences? Another set of questions has to do with the manner in which we make our appraisals: What processes actually go into the sort of practical reasoning that points us to this choice rather than that? Are they purely "rational," or do the passions also enter in? How do we weigh, for example, pleasures that might come in the form of short-term satisfactions against delayed, and perhaps deeper, ones? And so on. Socrates' conclusion here is that we can only act inappropriately as a result of ignorance; that judgment cannot be dragged about by passion; and that wrong choice results from cognitive interference, whether in the way modes of assessment are applied or in the choice of the modes themselves. In this view, the possibility of weakness of will does not make sense: where cognition is impaired, will is inoperative.

Later, however, Plato's view seems to change. In the *Laws* he introduces a term that was to have a long and complex history: *akrateia*,[6] which here covers intemperate behavior rooted in ignorance, lack of self-control, or both. The notion of "unwisdom,"[7] a judgment originating in disharmony of the soul, enters the picture. The earlier, one-dimensional account of motivation has given way to a more complex model—the model that is elaborated in *The Republic*'s tripartite picture of the soul. Now we have a "plurality"[8] of motivational factors or desires, each with its own object. Because plural, such desires can conflict with one another; moreover, as Justin Gosling notes, desires are now conceived as replenishments of current lacks.[9] Among the motivational factors that now obtain are the passions. So it is possible for judgment to be skewed not just by ignorance, but by the interference of passions as well: "The impulses which draw and drag come through affections and diseases."[10] Further, passions can be conceived not just in terms of particular motivational states, but in terms of more general dispositions of character. When impulses, whether they be momentary or expressive of character disposition, cause the individual to act in a way that is not consistent with the best rational assessment of available options, the behavior is *akratic*. Now further questions arise: How do we differentiate between rationality and passion? Is a virtue like, say, loyalty a rational value commitment, a passion, or both? Might various "passions" not impinge equally and in the same way upon judgment: for instance, do loyalty and anger impinge in the same ways, and to the same degrees? And so on.

Aristotle takes up many of these issues in the *Nichomachean Ethics,* the majority of his remarkably rich and suggestive, but also often cryptic, discussion coming in 1145b21–47b19. These passages have generated a massive secondary literature in which questions as fundamental as "does Aristotle believe in the possibility of 'clear eyed' *akrasia?"*—that is, weak behavior that accompanies a just rational assessment of options—are still in dispute.[11] Aristotle contests the Socratic view in the *Protagoras* that "there is no such thing as incontinence"; that people act weakly "only by reason of ignorance."[12] Aristotle claims that incontinence does occur; that the passions can interfere with rational appraisal; and that while the virtuous person will be rational and continent (just as the properly ordered state will be rational), so persons with flawed character dispositions can be incontinent. The incontinent man is one "whom passion masters so that he does not act according to right reason"; however, this man has the saving quality that he maintains some grasp of right principles, even though he may not always enact them.[13] Whatever the scholarly disagreements about Aristotle's views and their relation to Plato's positions, it is sufficient for our purposes to say that the two thinkers work within the same basic paradigm of Will as Intellectual Preference. Thus Aristotle says: "No one *wishes* for what he does not think to be good, but the incontinent man does *do* things that he does not think he ought to do."[14] Two further elements of Aristotle's discussion are particularly relevant for my purposes: first, his brief allusion to behaviors that result in harm to the self[15] and, second, his earlier equation of bodily desire with replenishment of deficiency.[16]

As would be expected, another famous and influential account—Aquinas's—follows Aristotle's quite closely, though it also resembles Augustine's in having to explain—or try to explain—how and why weakness of will in the form of sin enters the world. Aquinas's writings about weakness of will are characteristically intricate; they are also often hard to interpret.[17] His Will as Rational Appetite view entails that it must be very difficult to conceive of situations in which a person could knowingly act against the counsel of reason. In the case of natural modalities of the will, where there is a necessary connection between human acts and happiness, there can be no question of weak-willed behavior, since here the will is not free; however, where deliberative processes obtain—where there is no necessary connection between a particular good and happiness—the will is at least in part free and *akratic* behavior becomes conceivable, albeit within a limited scope. Aquinas likens weakness of will to impairment of the body and allows for passional interference with cognitive functions:

> Accordingly, when the concupiscible or irascible power is affected by any passion contrary to the order of reason, with the result that an impediment arises in the aforesaid manner to the due action of man, it is said to be a sin of weakness. Hence the Philosopher [Aristotle] compares the incontinent man to a paralytic whose members move in a manner contrary to his intention.[18]

Hume's Judeo-Christian treatment of these matters breaks the nexus between rationality and the will—as one would expect of the philosopher who writes that "reason is, and ought only to be, the slave of the passions." However, his comments on weakness of will tend to grant parity to reason and passion, while also productively complicating that very distinction. Indeed he insists that the distinction is itself misleading:

> The common error of metaphysicians has lain in ascribing the direction of the will entirely to one of these principles [calm desires and tendencies or real passions], and supposing the other to have no influence. Men often act knowingly against their interest: For which reason the view of the greatest possible good does not always influence them. Men often counter-act a violent passion in prosecution of their interests and designs: 'Tis not therefore the pres-

ent uneasiness alone, which determines them. In general we may observe, that both these principles operate on the will; and where they are contrary, that either of them prevails, according to the *general* character or *present* disposition of the person. What we call strength of mind, implies the prevalence of calm passions above the violent . . .[19]

It is a flexible and nuanced view. It extends the notion of a "passion," as Aristotle tries in places to do, so that some motivational elements that might prima facie look like reason are actually reclassified as "calm" passions: states in which complexity is processed in an orderly but affective way. And the view is very case-specific: if at times violent passion dominates the present disposition of the character, then rational assessment will give way; and the contrary is also true. Either way, however, it is the will that is determined in a given direction. Unlike Plato and Aristotle, Hume does not conclude that the will is only active when rational counsel prevails.

Hume's empiricist account contrasts strikingly with Nietzsche's comments on weakness of will. Here again, the ambivalence of prophetic late modernity's sense of the will is evident. At a raw, rhetorical level, Nietzsche of course enjoins his reader to will change and transformation in the world; to shed the will-dulling nullity of conventional German life. But his theoretical conviction that the will does not exist commits him to a denial of relative terms: if there is no will, there cannot be strong or weak will.

> *Weakness of the will:* that is a metaphor that can prove misleading. For there is no will, and consequently neither a strong nor a weak will. The multitude and disgregation of impulses and the lack of any systematic order among them result in a "weak will"; their coordination under a single predominant impulse results in a "strong will": in the first case it is the oscillation and the lack of gravity; in the latter, the precision and clarity of the direction.[20]

The most efficiently integrated and directed organism will have the appearance of strength of will, but will does not function here as an explanatory term. It is not will that makes for strength, but integration and direction that make for a condition for which the term *will* is a metaphoric label.

I have argued that the other two great prophets of late modernity—Freud and Marx—deny the freedom, though not the actuality, of the will; and in their work, as in Nietzsche's, the sense that the will can be weak is everywhere implicit, but seldom if ever given proper theoretical articulation. Freud's aspiration to put ego where id used to be is a way of saying that the will is weak when we are dominated by instinctual forces. As a rationalist, he associates domination of the psyche by irrational id forces, and the repressed materials that drive neurosis, with enfeebling of the ego and of the self's capacity to negotiate reality. Psychoanalysis is a means of fortifying the Will as Rational Appetite mode of engagement with the world. Similarly, Marx's account of ideology can be taken to imply that when the self's capacity for rational appraisal and response is drugged by false understandings, an ideologically ensnared person's will is in effect weak. It is enfeebled by a failure of understanding and, of course, by material constraints. Constraints are external; ideology begins in externality but infiltrates the mind, enfeebling faculties like the "will" that take their counsel from rationality, and from the passions that flow freely and creatively in an emancipated being.

I want to mention one further modern variant that has particular relevance for Spender.[21] Sartre's *Being and Nothingness* gives grounds for regarding bad faith as a form of weakness of the will. This rather elusive concept, which Sartre pointedly pits against the Freudian notion of the unconscious,[22] involves a flight from the recognition and seizure of freedom. Sartre does not give a compact definition of the term (its most memorable encapsulations come by way of examples), but this typically knotty passage from *Being and Nothingness* gives some indication of his position:

> Bad faith flees being by taking refuge in "not-believing-what-one-believes." It has disarmed all beliefs in advance—those which it would like to take hold of and, by the same stroke, the others, those which it wishes to flee. In *willing* this self-destruction of belief . . . it ruins the beliefs which are opposed to it, which reveal themselves as *being only* belief.[23]

The idea seems to be that bad faith retreats into a kind of soft skepticism: not the hard kind that, by acknowledging the possibility that I am not what I am, opens the self out to new self-scripting incarnations; but rather a kind that, by a self-protective act of the will, leaches all possibilities of such conviction as could empower the will to seek its freedom. The self remains captive to conventional attitudes. The will has participated in its own debilitation. This is indeed, in Spender's words, a case of "strange identity" of "will and weakness."

With Spender in mind, I want to suggest some further qualifications and possibilities in thinking about weakness of will. For instance, one might want hypothetically to posit a condition of apparent "will-lessness," not in the sense proposed by those like Skinner and the Saussurean Barthes, where freedom of the will is denied altogether, but perhaps in a more mystical sense such as one finds (in their different ways) in Augustine and Schopenhauer, where the will gives over to a higher state that resembles passivity. Will-lessness might also be associated with much less luminous states like severe depression, where even basic instinctual drives like hunger and the will to communicate can be immobilized. Let's for the moment speculate that there are human states in which the will is almost wholly passivized (a very different matter, of course, from metaphysical denials of the will), and refer to this, the first of what I shall term *modalities of the will*, as *radical passivity*. The example of depression suggests further possible variations, some of which raise interesting questions about whose interests the will might actually be serving—or compromising—in particular instances. For example, depression can skew the will so that it is exerted in ways that are contrary to what seem to be the best interests of the agent. We've seen that Aristotle allows for the possibility that people can at times knowingly and deliberately act in ways that cause harm to themselves. Robert Dunn is interesting on such apparently self-destructive exertions of will.[24] Let's simply call this complex phenomenon (is suicide in or against the best interests of someone who is in catastrophic psychological pain?) a *self-destructive* modality of the will. In addition to this phenomenon of acting against one's best interests, there are cases in which will takes rational counsel as to how the individual's interests would be best served, but in which the counsel itself is flawed. The least profound form of this is the kind of cognitive interference that Plato and Aristotle allow for: defects in practical reasoning. However, there is a deeper form of the phenomenon that we have seen in Sartre. This is the phenomenon of *inauthenticity* in which will is guided not by courageously free-seeking intimations of "self"-hood, but rather by conventional expectations and understandings as to what a self is and ought to be. Here will enacts the natural attitude; or, in Sartre's terms, the will has taken flight into, and hides behind, the natural attitude. It is in bad faith—a psychologically, morally, and sometimes politically deeper affliction than mere cognitive interference.

I now want to suggest a modality that doesn't fit neatly into any of the categories we have seen so far, and that might, depending upon your point of view, be seen as an instance either of weak or strong will. What I have in mind is a modality in which the will is exerted in a way that precipitates the agent into a situation involving contingencies that she or he makes no real effort to anticipate or to control. This submission to the pure play of contingency is a kind of indiscriminate, content-free choice that is familiar in Nietzsche and in existentialist literature. I'll call it *Will as Submission,* to get the sense that will hands the self over to sheer contingency. I also want to identify what might be called the *Heuristic Exercise of the Will,* where actions or moral inclinations occur in order not so much to affect an outcome for the Self (or Other), but rather to discover more about the Self (or Other). Like *Will as Submission,* this conception bears some resemblance to existential ones that see will as a kind of synthesis of cause, motive, and end, a synthesis that transforms a proto- or potential self into one that assumes transitive self-definition through action. As Sartre puts it in *Being and Nothingness:* "The cause, the motive, and the end are the three indissoluble terms of the thrust of a free and living consciousness which projects itself toward its possibilities and makes itself defined by these possibilities." And again: "I can also find myself engaged in acts which reveal my possibilities to me at the very instant when they are realized."[25] Though it would be possible to see them as instances of the Freedom as the Genus of Volition view, I shall characterize *Will as*

Submission and *Heuristic Exercise of the Will* as instances of weakness of will, but in a definitional, not a moral, sense. In my graduated conception of will, both occupy a position toward the end of the spectrum in which rational counsel has little bearing upon will-acts.

Finally, and again with Spender in mind, it is worth distinguishing between different *spheres* of the will's activity, in particular, private and public spheres; and between different, though overlapping, guises of the self-as-agent: citizen, artist, autobiographer, and lover.

II. Eccentricity and Confessional Autobiography

In *The Thirties and After* Spender comments: "I myself am, it is only too clear, an autobiographer. Autobiography provides the line of continuity in my work."[26] Certainly Spender's work in many genres—poetry, criticism, journalism, drama, short fiction, novels, travel diaries, journals, political commentary, and theory, as well as autobiography—evinces a powerful integrating concern with the authorial self. Published in 1951 when he was forty-two, *World Within World* is a fine example of the kind of Dantean autobiography written in the middle of the journey, or as Spender puts it, "the centre of life" (p. 335). Often quoted for its accounts of the "Auden generation" and of the cultural politics of the thirties and forties, *World Within World* is also well-known for the frankness of its self-representation. As Brian Finney notes, the work is especially valuable for the "double perspective" through which Spender narrates a reality that is both historical and intensely personal.[27] This perspective is profoundly heuristic. Spender seeks not simply to report, but also to explore and even to reformulate the relationship between the self and the social-historical world. The historical impulse for such an endeavor is clear enough. Writing in the wake of Hitler and in the shadow of Stalin, Spender, like Koestler, writes post-totalitarian autobiography as a means of trying to understand totalitarianism and of warning against its remaining dangers.

In autobiography no less than in any other form, historical context constitutes a field of symbolic possibility and political significance for choices among narrative genres. Spender notes that "a pastoral poem in 1936 was not just a pastoral poem. It was also a non-political poem" (pp. 249–50). In a related way, the mere act of writing a personalized autobiography in 1951, through what Spender calls "this frame of European ruins" (p. 151) and at what appeared to be "the end of an individualistic epoch" (p. 263), was to make a political statement, to affirm the humanistic culture of the self against the encroachments of the totalitarian.

Louis MacNiece writes of Spender's efforts toward "redeeming the world by introspection."[28] The description is barbed but incisive: it hints at what many readers view as an excessive self-preoccupation in Spender's writing; but it also acknowledges the sincerity of Spender's endeavor to pit self-consciousness against the forces that threaten the freedom and integrity of the self. For Spender introspection is a respondent act and autobiography is an elaborated form of such an act. *World Within World* works principally within two overlapping traditions: Romantic autobiography in which the self-as-agent aspires to transcend the cultural ideology that has shaped it, and the tradition of modern secular confessional autobiography, where intimate self-revelation affirms the sacred particularity of the self—its exemplary difference. Spender adumbrates these forms of life-writing in his critical study *The Struggle of the Modern*. He distinguishes between the "Voltairean I," which participates in the changing social forces it seeks to satirize and redirect, and the "modern 'I,'" which through "receptiveness, suffering, passivity, transforms the world to which it is exposed."[29] Each of these reflects a condition of the will: in the first the will is active, transformative; in the second, it is paradoxically active by inaction, using its passivity as a power to precipitate change. His own autobiographical persona comprises elements of both of these postures, but his "strong" precursors are Wordsworth and Rousseau.

For Spender the relationship between the writer, not least the autobiographer, and the cultural code is an anguished one—an anguish memorably expressed in an important essay, "Confessions and Autobiography." The following could easily be a description of Rousseau:

> All confessions are from subject to object, from the individual to the community or creed. Even the most shamelessly revealed inner life pleads its cause before the moral system of an outer, objective life. One of the things that the most abysmal confessions prove is the incapacity of even the most outcast creature to be alone. Indeed, the essence of the confession is that the one who feels outcast pleads with humanity to relate his isolation to its wholeness. He pleads to be forgiven, condoned, even condemned, so long as he is brought back into the wholeness of people and things.[30]

John Sturrock describes the conflicted relationship between "inner" and "outer" in autobiography in somewhat different terms—but in a way that highlights the presence of the will: "The tension in autobiography derives from the conflict in it between the will to apartness and the will to association; and if the evidence of the will to apartness pervades all autobiographical narrative, then the evidence of the will to association lies in the existence of autobiography itself, as the most sociable of literary acts."[31] *World Within World* both advocates and practices intimate confessional introspection. It is at once a private and a "sociable" book. Spender claims that "most lives are like dishonest works of art in which the values are faked, certain passages blurred and confused, difficulties evaded, and refuge taken by those bad artists who are human beings, in conventions which shirk unique experiences" (p. 316). Confessional autobiography reconstitutes the human self as a good, an exemplary, artist: one who faces and finds appropriate forms of expression for the frightening complexity she or he finds within. In *World Within World* he says in connection with his discussions of his bisexuality:

> The things I am now writing of are difficult to explain. Very few people dare to have a clear view of their own complexity. They would prefer to simplify themselves even at the expense of condemning their way of life rather than maintain complex and perhaps contradictory attitudes towards it, from which a harmony might finally be achieved. (p. 185)

Spender is strongly influenced by the nineteenth-century conception of the individual life as a quasi-artifact, a thing shaped in partial conformity with genre-like specifications. In this view—familiar in Keats, Wilde, and others—individual life choices are in part guided by the desire to give one's existence a certain aesthetically consequent shape and pitch, and, as in religious confessional autobiography, to invest it with particular structural constellations of meaning.[32] The autobiographer is a life-crafter twice over: first, crafting the life as it is lived, and then writing that life. What makes both aspects of this enterprise so difficult, according to Spender, is the fact that the autobiographer, like the artist in general, confronts two ineluctable conditions of being human: our solitude and our immersion in a contingent reality that we can neither fully control nor understand. In "Confessions and Autobiography" he characterizes the artist thus:

> To feel strange, to retain throughout life the sense of being a voyager on the earth come from another sphere to whom everything remains wonderful, horrifying, and new, is, I suppose, to be an artist. Artists—whether they are writers or painters—are people who continue throughout life to realize that every experience is a unique event in time and space, occurring for the first and last time.[33]

World Within World is an autobiographical *Künstlerroman* that recalls the writer's development as an artist and young man. This is the self-as-voyager; but the book is also a map, or a topography of the self and its manifold relations with the world.

Spender believes that the autobiographer must seek and undergo an encounter with the "real self" (p. 311), his or her radical *eccentricity.* He takes Rembrandt's quest for his "ultimate self" in self-portraiture[34] as a model for the autobiographer, and indeed for each individual's confrontation with his or her own separation, even isolation: "'I am alone in the universe.'"[35] But just as Rembrandt's occluded self-image shadows forth through a public painterly language, so the autobiographer as writer must memorialize self through public signs that threaten the very eccentricity he or she wants to preserve. This is a version of Spender's central theme: the relation between "private" and "public."

For Spender, as for Hemingway, the will to art and memorialization is set against the forces that threaten the will's efficacy, even its existence. The first poem in his sequence "Spiritual Explorations" contemplates the ego's inexorable loss of control as the self voyages toward "the multitudinous loneliness of death" and the enforced desuetude of the will:

> Beneath our nakedness, we are naked still.
> Within the mind, history and stars expose
> Our bodies' frailty and a new day blows
> Away huts and papyri of the will.[36]

The cosmological imagery suggests the depths of the self's immersion in the contingent. Mortality ties us to a body that in turn links us to the fate of perishable and contingent things; the mind, aware of the cosmic enormity that surrounds it, internalizes that enormity in the act of registering it, takes the uncontrollable vastness into the self, which then knows not only the inevitability of death but the powerlessness and perilousness of which death is the consummation and the ultimate symbol. The self cannot finally withstand the colossal forces that surround it, nor the knowledge of the will's fragility.

So stated, Spender's account of the self and the contingent might seem bleak, almost deterministic. But this is not the case. His work is centrally about education; about learning what it means to have a will, and about how to exert the will in ways that reduce the disintegrating impact of the contingent and dilute the determinative power of the past. Learning about the will includes confronting the will's limitations. In this autobiography, error is accorded unusual prominence: "I have learned largely from mistakes, so that this book seems to me, among other things, a catalogue of errors" (p. xxii). This is consistent with his position in "Confessions and Autobiography," where he defines confessional autobiography as "the record of a transformation of errors by values."[37]

Like Sartre, Spender thinks that the self will generally choose flight over recognition of its aloneness; in particular, it will tend to recoil from the moral implications of its isolation, its "real moral solitude."[38] Real though Spender believes this possibility to be—he was raised with the fear of being "a moral outcast" (p. 9)—the temptation is always to deny one's unbearable isolation by a gesture of self-inclusion in some wider moral totality.[39] Whether in Augustine's confessions to God or Rousseau's to "the spirit of democracy,"[40] the principle is the same; indeed Spender exemplifies modern autobiography's transition from a confessional mode that, as in Augustine, reposes in the confident belief that there is a divine auditor for personal apologia, to a confessional register that disbelieves in God and is haunted by doubts about the nature—even the existence—of Self and human Other. I shall suggest that one of the ways in which Spender tries to counter such doubts, and to reaffirm the self's social dimension without lapsing into Sartrean bad faith, is to imagine the will as a constitutively social—or at least intersubjective—phenomenon.

But this too has its dangers. "Intimacy," Spender concedes, "has terrors for me" (p. 20). It may be that "true goodness is based on abnegation" (p. 280), but what he calls the "fantasy of utterly generous love" (p. 88) is actually inimical to intimacy because the lover becomes absolutely subsumed in the beloved. Intimacy threatens the distinctness of lover and beloved. For Spender, anything that endangers the self constitutes a danger to the wider totality. "Utterly generous love" can defuse the self-definition required for action and so the power of agency. We must maintain the intentionality that is intrinsic to what he calls "integrity of purpose" (p. 32).[41] In a brilliant formulation in *Love-Hate Relations,* Spender says that for Hemingway "courage was not just action: it was a kind of transcendent self-consciousness."[42] The linkage of the courage to know the self, to "aim beyond" it and to act, is highly characteristic of Spender as an autobiographical and political ethicist.

The will learns outer-directed purposiveness in a variety of interrelated spheres, "private" and "public," including the very important sphere of friendship. We shall see that the boundaries between various forms of friendship—intimate and platonic, same-sex and heterosexual—are heuristically blurred in *World Within World;* but in all cases creative relationship is conceived as combining independence and interdependence, such that love is an act, rather than an exercise in quiescence, the sort of "prolonged and deceptive docility" (p. 175) that characterized Spender's relationship with Christopher Isherwood in the late twenties and early thirties.

Sanford Sternlicht understates the speculative, quasi-mystical, and metaphysical dimensions of Spender's work when he characterizes Spender's position as consistently "empirical, totally nonmetaphysical, programmatic, and immediate,"[43] but certainly Spender's emphasis tends to be empirical, especially when it comes to human relations. He rejects the sociopolitical abstractions of Marxist-Leninism just as he had repudiated his father's invocations of Victorian precepts like "Discipline, Purity, Duty" (p. 9). "Individuation," he says in *The Struggle of the Modern,* "is the basic pattern of all experiencing."[44] Individuation can only come from experience. This is particularly so for moral knowledge, which he, like Aristotle, believes must principally be gained in situ, with a proper understanding of the specificities of a given set of circumstances.[45] What Spender calls his "thirst for moral knowledge" (p. 210) is perhaps the generative emotion of a narrative that, though open and even indulgent about the appetitive dimensions of the soul, ultimately repudiates hedonism in favor of love (p. 120) and sees life as a process undergone but also shaped by an aesthetically sentient moral subject.

In his essay in *The God That Failed,* Spender writes that "the artist is simply the most highly developed consciousness in a society," and continues: "Literature and art are therefore a *témoignage,* a witnessing of the human condition within the particular circumstances of time and place."[46] But there is a danger that the artist will not fulfill his or her communicative function, that the modern condition will eviscerate the most important kinds of creativity. This is a central concern of *The Creative Element,* a work published two years after *World Within World.* Here Spender argues that the artist must transcend the

> distinction between an external world which is "real" and an inwardness supposedly "unreal." One has to ask what, in a world which is "spiritually barren," can the real attitude of the inner life to external things be? Significant reality is, surely, a balanced relationship between outer and inner worlds. The inner world of a writer may become incommunicable, but in a time when the external world has become "spiritually barren" outer reality is only real in the sense of being factual. The result of that excessive outwardness of a "spiritually barren external world" is the excessive inwardness of poets who prefer losing themselves within themselves to losing themselves outside themselves in external reality.[47]

In *The Struggle of the Modern* he embraces the aesthetics of modernism insofar as it involves "the reinstating of imagination as primary, central, the verb."[48] In this Romantic view (in Rilke, Lawrence, Joyce), imagination is an exercise of the will in its most creative register: "The idea that the life and works of the imagination somehow provide an incandescent centre in which human personality and even social forms can become molten and transformed";[49] herein lies the "hope" in the possibility that "art might re-connect the life, which has been driven inwards into the isolated being of the artist, with the external world, by accomplishing a revolution in the lives of people converted to share the visions of modern creation."[50] So conceived, imagination itself is centripetal: "The poetic imagination is centripetal, a bringing together of experiences from a circumference which could theoretically be enlarged to include all pasts and presents, all things known and experienced into the centre of the artist's individual sensibility where they are the projected patterns which can also be the consciousness of readers."[51] A related formulation, which describes the "imagistic poetic method" that Spender associates with the "moderns" (as opposed to the "contemporaries") also speaks of the

> action of the external world upon inner sensibility. Individual consciousness is the centre which is acted upon by the environment. Contemporary economic conditions, politics, etc., affect it as discords in music, screaming colours, distorted form or lack of form. These conditions, that affect sensibility, form a "climate" or "atmosphere"—moral, intellectual or aesthetic— which is the complex result of material and social circumstances, seen by the mind's eye . . .[52]

Then follows a more detailed, if somewhat—and typically—loose, characterization of the innerness of creative consciousness:

While, from the outside, the centre of consciousness is acted upon by impressions attacking it from the circumference of the environment, reaching
into the whole world, it also contains within itself another universality, that
of subconscious life, childhood, personal history, sleep, dream, the subjective
ego which moves into pasts and depths beyond individuality, where it is pure
existence and no longer knows its name.[53]

To characterize the "subjective ego" as "universal" may seem contradictory, but
Spender is trying to balance two commitments here. He wants to retain an important presence for the Marxist emphasis upon "material and social conditions," but also to insist that the innermost circles of self transcend social determination.

The sense of movement, of process, is fundamental to *World Within World.*
It is associated with one of the book's most characteristic effects—the impression that the self is unfolding according to subtle and irregular rhythms and that
these rhythms help to orchestrate the self's subjective and social energies.[54] The
narrative is directional but not teleological; the voyage of the self is about the
journey, not the destination. To write in the middle of the journey is by definition not to arrive. There is a part of Spender that would agree with Sartre that
"transcendence" is the "constitutive structure of consciousness."[55] But his agreement would be qualified: while he does not think it possible wholly to capture
some synthetic "current" self in narrative, neither does he believe that we can
make sense of what we "are" now without reference to the past. On the contrary,
the best narrative account we can give of what we currently "are" must emerge
from a recapitulation of that past, and of the forms the self has taken hitherto.
Spender has a good deal of faith in the authenticity of the resultant life-narrative,
in its ability to represent what has occurred, and to intimate—even to help bring
about—a state of "harmony" in the future. Late in the book Spender says: "I
have written of many presences, ghosts from the past, which surround me, and
my aim has been to describe what I am, by making a large sum of a great many
ever-present pictures of experience. I want to depict these omnipresent selves
rather than a new and emergent self of today" (p. 322). This narrational "aim"
translates into a complex interplay of directional and circular structures, and
into an equally complex topography of the self and its interrelations. It is here
that Spender tries to characterize the central but elusive feature of his self-world
conceptualization: the will.

III. Concentricity and the Will

The central theme in all of Spender's work is the relationship between the
"inner" world of the self—be it artist or citizen—and the "outer" world of history, society, brute facticity. The dual perspective of *World Within World* is in

part a sustained narrative device for exploration, negotiation, and reformulation of this relationship. The title of the autobiography may derive from Lawrence's poem "Red Moon-Rise," which contains the lines

> for now I know
> The world within worlds is a womb, whence issues all
> The shapeliness that decks us here-below . . . [56]

The poem figures the whole of creation as sustained within and energized by some womblike fecundity. Spender's estimation of Lawrence is ambivalent but generally admiring.[57] One of several references to Lawrence in *World Within World* indicates just how important the novelist was in the poet-autobiographer's quest for an adequate self-world conceptualization: "He had a sense that distinctions between outer and inner are sacred: that whilst the inner life should meet the outer world, the outer should not become the inner world of the writer" (p. 97). The imputation of sacredness to this relation can be understood in at least three ways. It derives from Spender's sense that rationalism and scientistic modernity have occasioned a "shrunken inner world of individuated experience."[58] More personally, it goes deep to the roots of his psychological history. This is the history of a highly sensitive child who, even before the loss of both parents early in life (his mother when he was twelve, his father when he was seventeen), learned the need, the habit, of protective emotional withdrawal. Like Koestler, he withdrew from the emotional extremity of his mother's swings in health and mood, from her "sense of catastrophe" (p. 4), and from the alienating emotional barrenness, the "unreality" (p. 7), of a father who seemed unable to connect with his children and who was driven by a need for success. He withdrew, too, from the "atmosphere of moral compulsiveness" (p. 27) that his grandmother provided after his father's death and, later, from the bruising male ethos that he encountered in school, the "hearty" impudence that he met at Oxford. His being "at least a quarter Jewish" was also a factor: it seemed to symbolize and to help account for the pervasive sense of difference, of disconnection from his environment, that he experienced as a child. Of the Hampstead Jews he met at school, he writes: "I began to realize that I had more in common with the sensitive, rather soft, inquisitive, interior Jewish boys, than with the aloof, hard, external English" (p. 13). His ambiguous ethnic status, like his sexual ambivalence, was later to play a major part in the dynamics of his emotional and intellectual life; and in all that he did and wrote the contrast between the "soft" interiority of the self and the "hard" externality of the world was to be a recurrent preoccupation.

The sense of a sacred relation was also a response to historical events; indeed, we shall see that the central motif in Spender's personal life and work attempts to figure relations between the personal and the historical. This figure was in essence a response to totalitarianism. I have argued that a defining feature of post-totalitarian autobiography is the attempt to use life-writing as a way of resisting the totalitarian culture of the self, and that three common aspects of totalitarianism are particularly pertinent here: a conception of the self as infinitely malleable and transformable; the political phenomenon of party or state control over, and *usurpation* of, private morality; and the essentializing of the self in terms of racial and ethnic stereotypes. *World Within World* resists these tendencies in various ways. One example is its "thirst for moral knowledge," the insistent ethical emphases that reflect a search for a private morality that will create an acceptable habitation for this mercurial and ambivalent self in a wider moral totality, a totality it also seeks to transform. Another, to which I shall return, is its exploration of the relationship between love and social stereotyping. Still another is its cautioning against ways in which the world of external events can, as it were, hollow the self out until it seems little more than a cluster of responses to external conditions. Spender would abhor a condition that Alfred Kazin attributes to Henry Adams: that of the "self living history as its own fate."[59] Of his preoccupation with the rise of Nazism, Spender writes: "External things over which I had no control had usurped my own deepest personal life, so that my inner world became dependent on an outer one, and if that outer one failed to provide me with its daily stimulus of crime and indignation, I felt often a kind of emptiness" (pp. 190–91).

Another strategy that, as we have seen, is common to autobiographies of this kind is the construction of politically charged metaphors of self-constitution. The organizing metaphor of this kind in *World Within World* is that of *concentricity*, according to which the self is figured as possessing an innerness that is likened to a central core or circle. The core comprises ego, subjectivity, identity; but it also contains deeper spheres in which the intellectualizing, self-reflexive subject disappears from view and in which consciousness gradates into archetypal unconscious, individuality into primordial impersonality. Around this center, and moving outward from it, are farther and larger circles, their distance from the center corresponding to progressively more "public" spheres of being: the progression is from "inner" to more public aspects of the self, thence to increasingly "external" aspects of the public, politico-historical world. Hence the title *World Within World*, which captures the interplay between the two dominant and cognate figural motifs of the narrative: eccentricity and concentricity. These motifs are part of a larger and quite complex system of ontological imagery that figures relations between aspects or "regions" of reality and the forces that generate, link, or articulate them.

The concentric metaphor can seem cumbersome and too insistent. It reminds us, at times at least, that this is a young man's book. Nevertheless, the metaphor echoes several of the subnarratives in *World Within World*. One of these is the narrative of affiliation, which recalls the individual's history of religious and/or political affiliation and disaffiliation. Here Spender the recanted Marxist (albeit one who was only briefly and adventitiously a member of the

Party)[60] uses the concentric metaphor as a rejoinder to Marx's dictum that "it is not the consciousness of men that determines their being, but on the contrary, their social being that determines their consciousness." Spender, "who revolts against the concept of himself as 'social man'" (p. 310), counters with what he takes to be "the only true hope for civilization—the conviction of the individual that his inner life can affect outward events and that, whether or not he does so, he is responsible for them" (p. 285). The passage in which he alludes to his feeling of revolt is worth quoting at greater length:

> I am I: hero of a potential autobiographic novel in which I give the hero and the other characters their real names and their attributes: curve on a psychiatrist's chart which I paste on my wall: and in spite of this, in fact because of it, I insist that I am a citizen, that I have views and take sides and accept responsibilities, and even hold opinions about public affairs. I am a citizen who revolts against the concept of himself as "social man," with a respectable, official outside life, and two secret selves—a fictitious hero and a clinical case history. It is in the individual who accepts the responsibility of his own complexity, that the diversity of society attains a unity of consciousness where opposites are reconciled. (pp. 310–11)

This is a circumspect revision of an earlier bald claim in *Forward from Liberalism* that "the future of individualism lies in the classless society."[61] He is defending himself against the (anticipated) charge that he should have written with greater discretion—either in the form of an autobiographical novel or a psychoanalytic case history. But the "hero" of post-totalitarian autobiography is an agent, and introspection is an act with a social-political trajectory. Fiction is more evasive, and psychoanalysis more impersonal, than he wishes to be in having his say. (He did in fact write, and much later publish, a heavily revised form of an autobiographical novel, *The Temple,* about some of the events covered in the Cambridge and prewar German sections of the autobiography.)[62] He hopes that autobiographical introspection might help to redeem the outer circles of the world that surround the self. The reference to psychoanalysis is important. One's own case history can have various effects. As an account of the shaping of the self by circumstance, it might neutralize agency by casting the self as preordained, the powerless product of external determination. On the other hand, and ideally, the case history might release the capacity to act by neutralizing impeding conflict, trauma, and neurosis. In this intellectual autobiography Marx, Freud, and (as we shall see) Darwin are towering and influential, but also flawed, figures whose own self-world conceptualizations threaten the self's "integrity of purpose," its capacity to exert enlightened will.

Releasing the capacity to act is at best a limited possibility; but to the extent that it can be done, the chief faculty involved is the will. Yet as "Darkness and Light," the poem originally published in 1935 and that prefaces

World Within World, shows, Spender is haunted by the fear that life—his life and so the life of the world he wished to influence—may be blighted by a certain weakness of the will:

> To break out of the chaos of my darkness
> Into a lucid day, is all my will.
> My words like eyes in night, stare to reach
> A centre for their light: and my acts thrown
> To distant places by impatient violence
> Yet lock together to mould a path
> Out of my darkness, into a lucid day.
>
> Yet, equally, to avoid that lucid day
> And to preserve my darkness, is all my will.
> My words like eyes that flinch from light, refuse
> And shut upon obscurity; my acts
> Cast to their opposites by impatient violence
> Break up the sequent path; they fly
> On a circumference to avoid the centre.
>
> To break out of my darkness towards the centre
> Illumines my own weakness, when I fail;
> The iron arc of the avoiding journey
> Curves back upon my weakness at the end;
> Whether the faint light spark against my face
> Or in the dark my sight hide from my sight,
> Centre and circumference are both my weakness.
>
> O strange identity of my will and weakness!
> Terrible wave white with the seething word!
> Terrible flight through the revolving darkness!
> Dreaded light that hunts my profile!
> Dreaded night covering me in fears!
> My will behind my weakness silhouettes
> My territories of fear, with a great sun.
>
> I grow towards the acceptance of that sun
> Which hews the day from night. The light
> Runs from the dark, the dark from light
> Towards a black and white total emptiness.
> The world, my life, binds the dark and light
> Together, reconciles and separates
> In lucid day the chaos of my darkness.

It is no great poem; indeed it exemplifies some of the limitations in Spender's poetry. (The poem was included, with minor revision of the title and some lines, in Spender's *Collected Poems 1928–1953* of 1955, but omitted from *Collected Poems 1928–1985.*)[63] The sense of anguished uncertainty is studied, ponderous, the product of an uneasy alliance between Spender's subjectivist confessional voice and the more detached, intellectual virtuosity of Audenesque wit. If some of the details are obscure, the general import of the poem seems in the first instance to be to dramatize existential binaries that correspond to modalities of the will. One modality involves asserting the will in a way that can deliver the self from the "dark" "chaos" of paralyzing confusion—an exercise of the will in which intimations of freedom embolden the will to seek more profound forms of emancipation. This is perhaps will in its heuristic dimension. An opposing modality, which is fundamentally inauthentic, entails not quite the suppression, but the turning away of the will such that it thwarts its own drive toward enlightened deliverance, deliberately consigning the self to the very darkness that at another level it seeks to transcend. Here will uses what freedom it has to repudiate that freedom, to render itself a determined thing. In Sartrean terms, it is in bad faith. The imagery of darkness and light intersects in sometimes opaque ways with Spender's customary notation of center and circumference. In the first modality, the self is figured as on a circumference, seeking through path-forging "acts" a light at the center that will in turn center, existentially ground, the self. In the second modality, the self is again on the circumference, but now its energies, its acts, chart an "avoiding journey" away from the "light." In each case the will functions, but in the second the will might be said to be weak, albeit in a highly specific way. Whether through failing in its quest for the light at the center, or through refusing the light and embracing the darkness of the periphery, the self's benighted exertions forge a paradoxical link between weakness, center, and circumference: "Centre and circumference are both my weakness." The powerful line that follows—"O strange identity of my will and weakness!"—sets the emotional and indeed conceptual terms for much of the moral action and reflection in *World Within World*.[64] But what of the last stanza? "I grow towards the acceptance of that sun" suggests a process of maturation in which the will gravitates toward the light. The "black and white total emptiness" then referred to seems obscure (and quite possibly poetically inept). But the concluding three lines seem again to suggest a process of at least partial resolution in which consciousness—"the world, my life"—at once affects and constitutes the only possible situation in which a productive relationship between opposing tendencies—light/dark, chaos/lucidity—can occur. The nature of this relationship is far from clear, but it seems to involve a rhythm of synthesis and separation out of which comes an empowering differentiation, or capacity to differentiate, between darkness and light, lucidity and confusion; in other words, some degree of emancipation for the will whereby its intimations of greater freedom constitute its primary precipitating influence. This rhythm is echoed in the larger structure of the autobiography.

How does this conflicted and impaired condition of the will come about? In part through general cultural factors that bear upon the will; but also through influences that, while deriving in part from general cultural conditions, have deep roots in Spender's personal history. Consider a fine poem on the death of his father, "The Public Son of a Public Man":

> When I left your funeral, my face was hard
> With my contempt for your failure still.
> But, father, the hardness was a scabbard
> For your resurrected will.[65]

World Within World is about social redemption, but it is also about the taking up of an incomplete paternal task: the redemption of the father's will in a massively ambivalent son. This is a deeply transferential book in which the worlds of the son—public and private—intersect with but seek to separate from the disablingly public world of the father, and in which will seeks to take other than paternal forms. Spender's strong feelings of affinity with John Stuart Mill are obvious in the long discussion of Mill's "unhappy passivity" in relation to his father in *Forward from Liberalism*.[66] The desire to achieve a feminized male subjectivity or private sphere from which one can participate in a patriarchal public sphere, and transform the public sphere in the self's own nuanced interior image, makes Spender one of the quintessential male British writers of the thirties.[67] The father embodies an enormous Nietzschean power of the will: steely, phallic, directed at the public world in which it seeks influence and acclaim. The son, who cannot sustain the weight of this unrelenting patrimony, fears that his life will be blighted by radical passivity. The father's attitude to his son is highly ambivalent, and he represents (and urges) an inauthentic path for the son's self-realization. Stephen, torn between the "sequent path" of authentic self-realization and the "avoiding journey" of conformity to the paternal example, has to find a modality of the will that enables him to balance rational and passional inclinations, and that traverses private and public, central and circumferential spheres.

His class background further complicates the private-public relation. As a child he rebels against the compulsive and elitist Spender family ethos:

> My revolt against the attitude of my family led me to rebel altogether against morality, work and discipline. Secretly I was fascinated by the worthless outcasts, the depraved, the lazy, the lost, and wanted to give them that love which they were denied by respectable people. This reaction was doubtless due to the fact that I wanted to love what I judged to be the inadmissible worst qualities in myself. (p. 9)

This pattern was to repeat itself well into his adult life. It seems to combine a rejection of conventional accounts of his "best interests" with a strong inclination to self-destructiveness, but also with an instinct for heuristic exercise of the will in directions that might reveal as well as reflect aspects of the self. There is also a feeling of wanting to effect an existential disconnection between present and past, rather like what Sartre calls a relationship of "absolute heterogeneity" between the two.[68] The passage shows how deeply authenticity in this work is implicated in a relation with the code that is at once anguished and, at least in intention, transformative: in seeking to love those who mirror the aspects of self spurned by bourgeois respectability, he also seeks to extend the margins of respectability, to personalize the code. The movement of feeling involved is at once paralyzingly self-centered and nascently outward-turned. It sets a pattern for later development and for his neo-humanist vision of postwar reconstruction. He imagines a new Venice:

> For our individualistic civilization to be reborn within the order of a new world, people must be complex as individuals, simple as social forces. They must recognize their public duties, accept sacrifices, recognize necessity: but at the same time they must insist on their individuality, their difficulties, their privacy, their irrationality. The simplifying struggle to achieve social justice and pacification of the world preoccupies men today. But yesterday there was that complexity which made the Renaissance prolific, wonderful, rich, mysterious: and tomorrow there must be the miracle of a just civilization which is also capable of the complex folly of building a Venice. (pp. 191–92)

Building a new Venice is really a matter of learning how to live in one. *World Within World* charts a learning process in which autobiography becomes the imaginative extension of a revived liberalism. In *The Thirties and After* Spender writes that "politics without ideology and with a strong tendency towards autobiography equals liberalism."[69] According to Spender, the deepest lessons we learn are about how to exercise the will, and we most deeply learn those lessons in relationships of love.

IV. The *Akrates* as Lover

One of the journal entries that Spender includes in *World Within World* reads in part as follows:

> My own work is to write poetry and novels. I have no character or will power outside my work. In the life of action, I do everything that my friends tell me to do, and have no opinions of my own. This is shameful, I know, but it is so. Therefore I must develop that side of me which is independent of other people. I must live and mature in my writing.
>
> My aim is to achieve maturity of soul . . . After my work, all I live for is my friends. (pp. 104–5)

Written at the age of twenty in Hamburg during the midyear Oxford vacation, this is one of Spender's earliest formulations about the self as *akrates* (a use of the term that in this instance presupposes that clear-eyed *akrasia* is possible). Already, however, it is qualified: the will is inactive, the self, he fears, even radically passive, in most areas; but in one, the "private" sphere of writing, it seems to function effectively—so much so that it may ultimately yield the Spenderian ideal of "maturity of soul." The place of "friends" in this personal economy is complex. His present predicament is such that friendship renders him passive, almost selfless; yet there is a sense in which friends do actually elicit will of some kind: after writing, it is they he lives for. He can live *for* others but not live—be properly alive—*with* them. His hope is that the authenticity of self that comes from writing may radiate out to other areas of life and enable him eventually to enter into friendship as an "independent" being.

Friendship is an elastic term in *World Within World,* and it is one of a number of related, overlapping, and shifting designations in the book for various forms of interpersonal relation. Indeed this autobiography canvasses some of the West's most abiding categories of human connection: libido, *eros, philia, caritas.* In this world where men often had sexual associations with male (and in some instances female) friends, the line between friendship and romantic love is blurred. It is also blurred in a moral sense: Spender's reconstructive critique of the code of bourgeois propriety involves a reassessment of what friendship and love mean, and of the appropriate terms for their moral appraisal. If he seeks in some respects to be liberated, he is no libertine: he rejects the practice of putting "sex before love";[70] he believes that "love is the essential thing in life" and that, again in concentric terms, "no one should want anything except to find his place in life, the centre of his potentiality to love and be loved."[71] When he reproaches himself for the will-lessness, the "prolonged and deceptive docility" of his part in the relationship with Isherwood, the comment has a powerful ambiguity: "deceptive" suggests that Stephen was not in fact irredeemably passive, that he would and could develop a will in love; it also has an ethical import: to live as an inchoate self for one's beloved is to deceive the Other into a relation with a misleading construction of Self. The "fantasy of an utterly generous love" is just that—a fantasy. Love can be neither humanly profound nor ethically sound if it does not express the will of the lover.

The place of will in loving is extraordinarily complex, and there has been a persistent historical tendency to dissociate the two. For Aristotle and Plato, if the lover's power of rationality is "dragged about" by passion, the will is thought to be inoperative. Kant thinks that romantic love is an inherently appetitive, will-less phenomenon; and since for Kant moral appraisal only obtains where conduct is deliberative and will-governed, romantic love cannot on his account be subject to moral assessment. In *The Metaphysics of Morals* and elsewhere, Kant in fact draws a distinction between will-less and will-governed love: *pathological love* is romantic, non-will-governed love; the contrasting form, *practical love,* is an attitude of concern for the Other that one can will one's self to have. The former sort lies outside the realm of morality; the latter falls within its domain:

> For love, as an affection, cannot be commanded, but beneficence for duty's sake may; even though we are not impelled to it by any inclination—nay, are even repelled by a natural and unconquerable aversion. This is *practical love,* and not *pathological*—a love which is seated in the will, and not in the propensions of sense—in principles of action and not of tender sympathy; and it is this love alone which can be commanded.[72]

Spender, we might say, does believe in the possibility of weakness of will, but he does not conceive of the weakness of will as intrinsic to romantic love. Just as importantly, he does not see such weakness as beyond moral appraisal or as beyond retrieval through educative moral development. On the contrary, the moral action of *World Within World* centers on a process whereby what I shall call the *affective will* is emancipated and educated in relationships of love. The narrative deals with a series of romantic relationships in which this development takes place: principally his early homosexual relationships with the undergraduate "Marston," whom he meets at Oxford (this was a case of unrequited attraction on Stephen's part); "Walter," an unemployed youth whom he meets while living in Germany; Christopher Isherwood; and Jimmy Younger (Tony Hyndman), a Welshman he employed while living in London. The later relationships with which he deals here are heterosexual: with the American divorcee "Elizabeth" (Muriel Gardiner),[73] whom he meets in Vienna in 1934 while he is still involved with Jimmy; Inez Pearn, his first wife, whom he marries after a brief acquaintance; and his second wife, and partner from then on, the pianist Natasha Litvin. In all but the last case much is made of the nature of the *choice* involved in entry into relationships of this kind. As Martha Nussbaum notes, this is indeed a profound issue. Kant and others who consider romantic love to lie beyond the purview of moral discourse have a point insofar as the movement of feeling involved in falling in love seems less volitional than does the feeling involved in some other forms of interpersonal behavior.[74]

Here is the description of Spender's first encounter with Marston:

> I first noticed him—I remember—in the train to Oxford, at the beginning of my second term. He was with a crowd of the other "hearties," but there was something watchful, withdrawn, in his attitude which made him seem separate from them. Sometimes he smiled to himself with the secret jauntiness of a very modest person who does not realize that his modesty makes him different from the others.
>
> At that moment I made a decision to get to know him, when I quite well might not have done so. There was a moment of pure arbitrariness when I

thought: "I need not do this, but I will do it." This decision remained like a core of emptiness at the very centre of everything I felt afterwards, however strong the feeling might be. (p. 64)

The designation of this movement of feeling as "arbitrary" is interesting and typical. Paul Ricoeur refers to the misleading sense in which "an *arbitrary act* can appear as a healthy reaction at the end of hypercritical reflection"; but he also cautions, in phrasing reminiscent of Spender, that the attempt to "crystallize a definite intention out of the chaos of unformed possibility" can result in a despair born of "freedom without values."[75] In *The Temple* the Spender surrogate, Paul, says to his friend Joachim of Joachim's latest infatuation: "'I don't really understand that you can fall in love with someone because you have said that you were going to fall in love.'"[76] In the Marston passage the motivational state is offered as an instance of weakness of will, yet it is a complex thing. Clearly, will of a kind is exerted; a choice is made.[77] What is missing is not volition but certain forms of deliberation and passional engagement that might ideally condition volition (though there is a hint of desire in the sense that Stephen may identify with and be attracted to Marston's apparent insularity). The choice in question precipitates the chooser into a situation that he seeks neither to know, to predict, nor to control. He chooses to submit to sheer contingency. This is the will as submission; a sort of existential projection of and beyond self that is to have painful but mixed consequences. Existential though it might in some ways be, the choice proves destructive in the sense that the lack of deliberative, and in particular of affective, motivation results in a "core of emptiness" at the center of the friendship. The choice lacks personal investment; the will operates in a mode of pure assertion. The "core" metaphor is of course highly significant: this is a relationship in which the self-as-innermost-center is absent from the concentric configuration of commitment and action. It proceeds from an empty choice. Nevertheless, the relationship has important developmental implications: it "influenced my life. Immediately after the walking tour [with Marston] I began to write poems different from any others I had done. A concrete situation had suddenly crystallized feelings which until then had been diffused and found no object. A relationship which had thus acquired a significant place in my development continues to exist in my mind now that I have developed beyond it" (pp. 66–67). Does this episode demonstrate weakness of will? It depends upon one's conception of will. In mine, which associates strength of will with rationally informed choice, it is weakness of a kind—though not moral weakness. But there is clearly a sense in which Stephen's will at this point could be deemed active, even strong.

The next important "phase of a search for the identification of my own aims with those of another man" (p. 67) is with Walter. Here again, the initial moment of interested engagement is characterized as arbitrary: "At one *Lokal* [in

Hamburg] I met an unemployed young man called Walter, in whom I rather arbitrarily decided to take an interest" (p. 117). Walter exploits Stephen for money, but exploitation is to some extent mutual: Stephen repeats the pattern of identification with the outsider that had earlier been a feature of his rebellion against his family. Yet there is more to the relationship than mutual convenience:

> I cannot just dismiss Walter as part of my very gullible past when I allowed myself to be victimized by a tramp. For in this relationship there was a grain of real affection of a kind which I had not had before. It is as though I was in need of some precious ore and had been driven to seek it in the smallest quantities and the roughest places. What my friends—and even I myself, at moments, saw—was that I returned with clothes tattered, and having been robbed and degraded. But as a matter of fact I did have a little of the precious ore: there were moments when in the middle of cheating me Walter trusted me, and when I gave him more than money. With him I escaped to some extent from the over-spiritualized, puritan, competitive atmosphere in which I had been brought up, to something denser, less pure, but out of which I could extract and refine little granules of affection. From such experiences I gradually learned a feeling which I could later bring to the highest relationships.
>
> Through Walter, I imagined the helplessness, the moral weakness, the drift, of unemployment. I imagined, I suppose, that something which I was now beginning to call in my mind "the revolution" would alter his lot, and I felt that as a member of a more fortunate social class I owed him a debt. (pp. 117–18)

Once again, there is a moment of choice, and though it is to some degree and in some respects arbitrary, there are clear psychological and sociological factors conditioning this choice. The situation here is morally complex. To the extent that the decision to get involved with Walter is exploitative and lacks developed emotional investment, it is morally suspect. It involves a kind of categorial love where one loves the other in part as Other, but also in part as the embodiment of a social stereotype. Insofar as it exposes him to dangerous risk, the act of will involved is also in a sense self-destructive. But there are also senses in which the choice seems authentic: it is part of the repudiation of the "best interest" account of self he receives in childhood and of a heuristic search for his own true best interests—interests that include release from puritanic attitudes toward the body, and the capacity to give and receive affection. It also has some positive moral-political content because it contains an element of genuine political sympathy. While Marston was roughly of Stephen's class, Walter is not. The will to love Walter is in part motivated by the desire to bring about a fairer world. In love the *akrates* is beginning to learn more authentic—affective—private forms of the will, but also the possibility of deep interconnections between will of this kind and the political will. If the will is weak here, it is again weakness of a particular kind; it is also less pronounced than in the case of Marston. Here growth presages not only greater strength of will, but a greater range of the will's applications.

Prior to joining Isherwood in Berlin in 1930, Spender lives a somewhat paradoxical life of reclusive Weimar Republic hedonism. Looking back, he sees in his combination of "sympathy with weakness" at the time something like Yeatsian "passive suffering." He has

> strength, to the extent to which I was master of my own kingdom of the creative imagination, my own work wherein I might create as I chose. Within this inner world even weakness could become a kind of strength. It isolated me and disqualified me from other kinds of work than poetic writing. I needed only the strength of my own weakness to say that I had no other responsibilities than simply to exist in order to write. It [his social attitude of "pity"] enlarged my sympathies by leading me down paths where people were insulted, oppressed, or vicious. It saved me from having to judge them by conventional rules of conduct, since I did not observe these myself. (p. 119)

His own conduct at the time, in the red light districts of Hamburg, again involves various modalities of the will. The seeker after pleasure "has in his hands this magic key of entrance into a perpetual stream of fulfillment which he can use whenever he wills. When he even no longer feels desire, he can in an idle, abstract and unwishing kind of way prove to himself, almost for no reason except a mysterious and remote compulsion to reaffirm that it is so, that the hidden life of forbidden wishes exists in extravagant nakedness behind the mazes of walls" (p. 120). This suggests a distinction between will as mere sensual inclination and will as submission, the latter taking such a pure form as to be almost wholly severed from felt inclination ("almost unwishing"). But passional inclination—desire—also projects the self into an under-, or alternative, world that becomes crucial to his reconstitutive critique of the code and his later political engagements. Through it all he retains an authentic will in his work.

The relationship with Isherwood begins with Christopher's suggestion that Stephen live near him in Berlin. Spender's account of the friendship focuses repeatedly on his own "docility": "About three years of my life, I realize now, were lived precariously off the excitement of being with Isherwood. I told him everything, I showed him every letter of any interest I received, I looked to his judgement of my friends and activities" (p. 127); "I had lived vicariously on his life in Berlin" (p. 174). Here again, however, it would be misleading to construe Spender's role merely in terms of "passivity." In one of the most important observations he makes about anyone in *World Within World,* he says of Isherwood that "he also recognized that nearly everyone wanted something out of life which he or she had been taught to conceal" (p. 128). The choice to enter a relationship with someone who was "on the side of the struggle towards self-realization" (p. 128) is, potentially at least, self-transformative: paradoxically, his docile devotion is to another, and to a bond, that holds out the promise of an effective linkage between personal wanting and willing, being and becoming. Such a friendship can be emancipatory. At the same time the political world is starting to impinge. They witness the rise of Nazism and think seriously, but hesitatingly, about communism as perhaps the only viable alternative to fascism. Stephen becomes preoccupied with two issues: the freedom of the individual, and guilt. The two are connected through the sort of class guilt that he feels, and he comes to see the necessity of distinguishing between different kinds of guilt in order to shed the useless form that inhibits action and to respond to the productive kind that promotes it. It was useless to feel class regret that forbids any criticism of Walter's dishonesty; but useful, necessary, to feel such class responsibility as would motivate one to seek a fairer society. In the imagistic logic of the narrative, guilt becomes associated with both the will-negating darkness at the center and the "sequent path" that links center and circumference in the light of action: "Thus although guilt may create for us a kind of stumbling darkness in which we cannot act, it is also the thread leading us out of a labyrinth into places where we accept, instead of being overwhelmed by, the responsibility of action" (pp. 137–38). Guilt is here a thread of life, a prompt to the will.

Guilt nevertheless figures strongly in the relationship with Jimmy that Stephen establishes when he returns from Germany to London in January 1933. This relationship, which is accorded more detailed description and analysis than any other in the book, begins characteristically: Spender describes his decision to invite Jimmy to be a live-in secretary as "this very arbitrary decision of mine to take him as a companion" (p. 177). Companionship develops into an intense and tortured bond that the narrative anatomizes in emotional, moral, political, and gender terms. The central moral problem is one to which Spender refers in his *Journals*: the threat of a loss of self, or "absorption," in a relationship. Unhealthily dependent relationships are

> a way of entering into a kind of dual subjectivity, a redoubled and reciprocal egotism; it is an alliance of two people who form a united front to deal with the problems of the objective world. The problem of married people is not to become absorbed in each other, but how not to become absorbed in each other; how, in a word, to trust one another in order to enter into a strong and satisfactory relationship with the outside world.[78]

Hitherto it has been Stephen who feels absorbed, selfless, with others; but the situation with the unemployed, working-class former soldier Jimmy is reversed: away from the army Jimmy "seemed lacking in will and purpose" (p. 176); he develops what Stephen sees as a "hopeless dependence on me" (p. 183). Spender concludes: "My character undermined his belief in himself; his dependence and lack of anything to do threatened my creativeness" (p. 183). Here again, however, the submission mode in which he initiates the relationship returns to haunt it. As with Walter, "there was real affection, real happiness, real interest in our life together: but also a sterility which sometimes affected me so much that I would lie down on my bed with a sensation I have never known before or since, as though my mouth were full of ashes" (p. 176). The asymmetry of the two wills involved—Stephen dominant, Jimmy subordinated—leads to passionate struggles and conflicts during which Jimmy "broke through the barrier of self-protection" that had for so long been "surrounding" (p. 182)—encircling—Stephen. This is crucial to Stephen's development, but this relationship can only develop so far. In part this is because of the way in which the externality of its political entailments shadow, in a sense usurp, its emotional center. Again, on the initial decision: "This very arbitrary decision of mine to take him as a companion, having once been made, became a social phenomenon, as though in him I had taken into my home the purposelessness of the life of the Depression outside" (p. 177). Jimmy is body and soul, but also social embodiment. This, too, is a categorial love: "I was in love, as it were, with his background, his soldiering, his working-class home" (p. 184). *World Within World*'s preoccupation with this kind of loving is partly a matter of the inauthenticity of will that is involved, where the will, proceeding from the inaugurating moment of submission and "abstraction," draws too much of its subsequent emotional impetus and inspiration from the circumference, too little from the "centre" that is the self's "potentiality to love and be loved." But this has still wider implications, because the book's critique of the affective will so conceived is an aspect of the post-totalitarian autobiographical attack on the essentializing of self through social and ethnic stereotypes. Spender's "dual perspective" combines an intellectual attack on the totalitarian culture of the self as a political phenomenon with a confessional exposé of the self's early propensity for related and destructive attitudes to the Other.

The gender dimension of Spender's account of the relationship introduces further, and controversial, considerations. The "sterility" Stephen feels is more than a matter of abstract and disarticulated will; it also arises from the fact that this is a same-sex relationship:

> We had come against the difficulty which confronts two men who endeavor to set up house together. Because they are of the same sex, they arrive at a point where they know everything about each other and it therefore seems impossible for the relationship to develop beyond this. Further development being impossible, all they can do is to keep their friendship static and not revert to a stage of ignorance or indifference . . . Thus a kind of sterility was the result of the loyalty of each to the other; or rather of his loyalty to the relationship itself which he did not wish to grow beyond. (pp. 183–84)

What is missing is "some element of mystery" for which the "differences of class and interest," Jimmy's categorial appeal, can compensate only to a limited degree. Whatever the general validity or otherwise of these comments, their importance for this discussion lies in the way in which *World Within World* identifies the contingency of the Other, his or her "element of mystery," with heterosexual polarity. Spender's debt to Lawrence is again apparent. This identification in turn says much about the place of the body in Spender's narrative, and about the interplay of the "Puritan" conditioning of will and desire with which he has had to contend:

> My brothers and sister and I were brought up in an atmosphere which I would describe as "Puritan decadence." Puritanism names the behaviour which is condemned; Puritan decadence regards the name itself as indecent, and pretends that the object behind the name does not exist until it is named. The Puritans have stern faces; but their eyes have looked on life. The Puritan decadents have unseeing, rhetorical faces, faces of immature boys who are prematurely aged, faces of those upon whose minds some operation has been performed removing those centres which were conscious of the body.
>
> To the son of the Puritan decadent, his body is a nameless horror of nameless desires which isolate him within a world of his own. He is divided between a longing to become like the others who walk about in their clothes without desires and as though they had no bodies, and a sense that nevertheless for him his guilt gives him back his body. But if guilt is knowledge of what is real, nevertheless this knowledge is locked within himself, and as he grows older his relationships with others appear unreal unless he can involve them in a guilt as deep as his own. (pp. 314–15)

Denied the "centre" that integrates body and soul, he is locked into his own "world" and into destructive forms of "guilt": the intricacy of the narrative's conceptual-imagistic organization in this instance is striking. Here too one must learn to differentiate between productive and unproductive guilt in order to emerge from solipsistic inwardness, to "develop beyond" forms of relatedness that are grounded in a damaged subjectivity. The self, we might say, is ideologically marked by social, gender, and sexual attitudes; the will is inclined to enact this conditioning through inauthentic and submissive choices in respect to the Other. But the body is not wholly captive to cultural ideology because, according to Spender, will has the capacity to forge reconstitutive relations between center and circumference, body and soul, Self and Other. It does so through authentic, "centred," balanced, and heuristic modes of choosing.

Spender's next substantial relationship is heterosexual, with "Elizabeth" (Muriel Gardiner), a medical student and divorced single mother from Chicago, in the spring of 1934. In one of the most resonant comments in the book, he says of Elizabeth that she was "in possession of all of the threads of her life" (p. 200). By contrast, he remains emotionally disorganized. His attraction is again partly categorial: the fact that she was American "mystified and attracted me"

(p. 194). She also represents one of a sequence of powerful women—mother, grandmother, his aunts, his governess Caroline—who elicit highly ambivalent responses from him. In this instance his ambivalence is directly sexual. The relationship assumes what he sees as a distinctly modern "texture of catastrophe" (p. 196) as he finds himself torn between the ill Jimmy (with whom he is still involved) and Elizabeth. There is "a real inability on my part to choose . . . Something which we called my 'ambivalence' forever kept unsleeping watch between us, like a sword" (p. 197). Eventually he returns to London, and Elizabeth, who like most of his lovers was to remain a lifelong friend (his *Journals* are dedicated to her), becomes engaged to an Austrian socialist. His parting comments about Elizabeth are revealing: ultimately he was too undecided to satisfy her; for her part, she was too much committed to a "rationalist" conception of the world, and she lacked his understanding of "religious experience." In sum, she was (to give the full formulation) "too much in possession of all the threads of her life" (p. 200). Here, as in the poem "The Double Shame," the *akrates* regrets the frailties of his will:

> At first you did not love enough
> And afterwards you loved too much
> And you lacked the confidence to choose
> And you have only yourself to blame.[79]

Yet blame does not extend to wanting to be quite so concerted, decided, unmystified as Elizabeth. His will is to disambiguate and escape much of the darkness, but he is unsuited to the absolute lucidity of day. This is the Spender who hopes that Auden will say in his obituary that "my life was in some way ambiguous."[80]

Marriage to Inez, a politically engaged student and would-be novelist, begins with another moment of sudden decision. He meets her at a function at which he speaks in Oxford in 1936; asks her to his housewarming party a few days later; thence, the next day, to lunch, when he proposes to her. They marry three weeks later. Of his impulse to propose, he says:

> It is difficult at this distance of time to understand why I did this. I certainly felt strongly attracted and this made me suspect that if I did not marry her quickly someone else would . . . My lack, of previous impulse [to marry] could be used as evidence that now I was not acting on impulse. But, of course, beneath this fallacious and superficial ratiocination was my despairing knowledge that if I did not act on impulse I decided nothing. So that action for me consisted of seizing on to impulses without considering the results, and letting them carry me whither they would. (p. 205)

It is, then, another assertion of will as submission, at best vaguely conditioned by initial attraction. This time, however, a less turbulent relationship results, though the two differ fundamentally. Importantly, their "imaginations were in-compatible," not least because she does not share his "thirst for moral knowl-edge" (pp. 209, 210). Precisely why the relationship fails is not clear, but his pre-occupation with other concerns—Jimmy's well-being, the Spanish civil war, fascism—was a contributing factor, and at some level they did not manage to create a viable adult relationship (p. 257). He is consumed with jealousy when she leaves him for another man, but later counts the marriage "a constructive phase in her development, as well as mine" (p. 209). In 1941 he marries Natasha Litvin. Nothing is said of the prior stages of the relationship and very little of the relationship itself. The sequence of the *akrates* in love essentially concludes with this paragraph:

> When we were first married, I suffered from an exacerbated sense of guilt aris-ing from the break-down of the relationships I have described in these pages. I was for ever attaching blame either to others or myself for what I regarded as failures. One day, Natasha said to me: "From now on there is no question of blame. There is only us," and this was the faith, the research for a unity which was ourselves belonging to one another, on which our marriage was founded. (pp. 279–80)

No longer immobilized in his own "blame," he has found the "faith" that the humanist seeks in "the highest relationships." He can now live with, not merely through, another. They have a unity with independence; subjectivity that is re-ciprocal rather than "dual"; belonging without "absorption" of one in the other. The progression of feeling involved in this transition is not otherwise described; but the affective will, it seems, has found the place from which it can attain a balanced, a properly articulated, relatedness with inner and outer worlds—a mode of what Richard Eldridge calls "reason-shaped inclination."[81] Spender says in his *Journals*: "I've always felt some saving angel does guard me from the worst."[82] Though the *Journals* also suggest that Spender's sexual "ambivalence" persists in other relationships later in life, *World Within World* has something of a benignly comic outcome: having bucked conventional morality and willed a series of dangerously contingent intimacies, he arrives at a relationship in which tensions are reconciled, harmony established.

V. The Self at the Center

Spender's conception of a properly articulated relationship between inner and outer, private and public in a sense fuses the Kantian binaries of pathological and practical love. The lover learns an appropriate—affective—exercise of will in relationships that is both passional and practical: passional, in that desire pro-ceeds from an existential "centre"; practical, in that the object of that desire is also the focus of moral discrimination and solicitude. The lover, who is now an intentional agent, then supposedly takes this knowledge out into the political world, where it infuses his or her practical commitment to the general well-being of others. For Kant the question as to "how a free will is possible" is "for human reason, an insoluble problem." If the question seems ultimately intractable, an autobiographer like Spender seeks perhaps not to explain precisely how freedom of the will is possible, but at least to show something of how will so conceived looks, feels, and even originates. In order to follow him further here, we need to look in more detail at the conception of self at the "centre" of *World Within World.*

In fact, the narrative entertains at least four competing, in places overlapping, conceptions of self. According to the first, the self is wholly socially determined, ideologically constructed. Even subjectivity is here conceived as a cultural construct, such that the circumferential social world entirely shapes the innerness of the person at the center. This is the determinist Marxism that *World Within World, Forward from Liberalism,* and other works repudiate. A second model is (roughly) social Darwinian: the self so conceived is a product of an amoral, competitive natural order whose logical extension is the wars—the two world wars, the Spanish civil war—with which the narrative deals. A third model might be termed a version of rationalist humanism. This position, which is exemplified by Elizabeth, focuses in a highly practical and nontranscendental way on the human individual: this individual is at once the locus of moral value, the precipitating cause of moral-political struggle, and the agent of moral-political change. No attempt is made to provide a wider metaphysical context for this entity, nor to account for the wellsprings of its capacity and inclination for ethical action. This conception of the human being is profoundly secular; it is a version of the agent as strong evaluator. A fourth and related projection might be termed a species of post-Romantic humanism. Here too the self is preeminent as locus, cause, and agent; but in this case two dimensions are added: a wider metaphysical context that informs the narrative's predominantly Christian sense of ethics and the quest to realize value through action, and some depth psychological account of unconscious processes—an account more archetypal Jungian than Freudian. This model can also include an apostolic dimension of a particular, naturalistic, kind, where the self that has borne witness to its own complexities and to those of the natural and political worlds espouses a secularized redemptive personal and social doctrine. Spender, who as subject of his autobiography best embodies this view, writes elsewhere that "individual conscience is the repository of witnessed truth."[83] These models are, so to speak, subjected to various forms of conceptual and figural inquiry, always with a view to seeing whether they are compatible with the concentric conception of self.

The self in *World Within World* is at the center in a number of ways. It is topographically at the center of its concentric universe; it is temporally at the center of its own life, at the middle of the journey; it is ontologically at the center of its own being, a being that shades almost imperceptibly into that which surrounds and helps to shape it; but it is also at the center in the sense that, at the deepest levels, the self is an atemporal emanation from the child we once were and continue to be. In *World Within World* the structural correlate of the self-at-the-center is a design whereby the narrative begins and ends in childhood: in a variant concentric formulation, "childhood is like wheels within wheels of this book, which begins, and revolves around, and ends with it" (p. xxii).[84] This recursive structure is one of the main instances of the interplay of directional and circular energies that so characterize the narrative. In its majestic final paragraph the story, having circled back to childhood, concludes with a vision of the child at the center:

> Now that I am old I am encumbered by many childish things. Yet the fact remains that I am and was the same person: when I was a child there were moments when I stood up within my whole life, as though it were a burning room, or as though I were rowing alone on a sea whose waves were filled with many small tongues of fire: and where I thought of my son, and my daughter, and my ancestors, and when I remembered how my mother, the night before she died, said to Ella, who was lighting the little gas fire in her bedroom, "Tell them I have had a very happy life." (p. 336)

The visionary child is omniscient, seeing not only his own past and future, but beyond into the ancestral history of the family, even the race. For the reader this moment of vision embraces and reconfigures what has gone before it: we see that the child had in some sense foreseen the tumult and the grandeur of his subsequent development. The fact that this could be so in turn retrospectively conditions our sense of the particular self at the center of this narrative, and of the potentialities of the self—*any* self—in general. Together with the book's intricate—if sometimes opaque and confusing—weave of concept, formulation, and figuration, what we might term this re-visionary moment is part of an attempt to find, and ultimately to *will and choose,* an appropriate mode of selfhood.

Few of the modes, and their associated models, survive the searching inquiry the book undertakes. The first—the ideological determinist—model is rejected as an unconscionable and dangerous totalitarian fantasy. The self is not infinitely malleable and transformable, and much of the action of the narrative charts the emergence of, in some sense, an already-established self from the constraints of its early conditioning, and a pattern of self-realization through choice among options that personal and social conditions make available. Here the narrative targets both Marx and Freud. It also targets Darwin, or rather social Darwinian elaborations of *The Origin of Species.* The return to childhood at the end of the narrative focuses on the child's early encounters with nature. These encounters assume subtly different characters as they are described. This one, about a pond in the home garden at Sheringham, Norfolk, is Darwinian in quality:

I soon observed that activity which as little disturbed the gelatinous stillness of the pond as a fly or a leaf fossilized thousands of years ago disturbs the amber in which it is enclosed. Newts moved along the pond-floor, and little water boatmen with their tiny jerking oars cut their courses up and down and across, through the water, as sharp as needles, and straight as ruled lines. Slow beetles stirred, and the snails clinging to the water plants with their mouths, moved a few centimetres up a stalk like a sheep nibbling its way to another pasturage.

The life of the pond was like a theatre whose surface was the front of the stage; and peering down upon this stage I saw naked dramas, glutinous loves, voracious murders, incredibly fertile births, taking place in the utter stillness of unnatural light.

My ambition was to be a naturalist, an old man with a long white beard, like a photograph I had seen of Charles Darwin. (p. 325)

"All this was during the First World War" (p. 325): the pond is a microcosm of the murderousness that is going on beyond the deceptive innocence of the childhood garden. The self so conceived is, like Darwin in *The Origin of Species,* at once a detached observer and a minuscule point of life in a vast, impersonal cosmic drama in which human beings have no privileged place and little capacity for moral intervention. The tone and import of this passage are subtly but significantly different:

In autumn and winter the prevailing winds which caused the branches of the stunted hedges to bend all in one direction, blew across the cliff-edge fields between Sheringham and East Runton. One day the wind was so strong that I could lean against it; like an invisible door in a wall of air, it would yield slightly if I pushed it, and then spring back against me. Then I started singing into the wind. Then I stopped singing and I heard a very pure sound of choral voices answering me out of the blowing sky. It was the angels. (p. 324)

This is closer to Wordsworth than Darwin and typifies the post-Romantic humanist self. As in the book's final paragraph, the child here has some sort of visionary capacity. As in *The Prelude,* the capacity is instantiated and activated through encounters with the natural world. Again, as in Wordsworth's poem, the sublimity of nature takes morally educative forms: leaning against the wind is one of Stephen's first introductions to the imperious but limited power of the will that dwells within him. The power is, so to speak, there; but it can only emerge through primal encounters with the noumenal. Later, again as in Wordsworth, it takes on social and political forms and force. A key late passage indicates that such early moments of encounter function like Wordsworthian "spots of time": they infuse and help to articulate later forms of the self; the self returns to these moments, as it does in the act of writing this autobiography, for inspiration, direction, consolation: "My early childhood was marked by a quite exceptional harmony, and it is perhaps this which has enabled me to retain throughout life a central calm and happiness, amid violent divisions of my own nature" (p. 311). In some mysterious way, the angels of the wind and the guardian angel who brings him his good luck are one. The center of the self at the center contains a special and salving "calm" that generates "harmony" and makes it seem achievable, despite the various ambiguities that trouble his adult life. As the image of the child in the sea of tongues of fire shows, this self possesses not only the nuanced interiority of the liberal humanist, social self; it also possesses a *depth* that is primordial, archetypal, protean, in its inclusiveness. As another poem in "Spiritual Explorations" has it:

> Yet all the past, the race,
> Knowledge and memory remain unfurled
> Within the individual, lonely
> With time, winning, losing, his world.[85]

Life is a process of "winning," finding one's "world," one's worlds, which death then takes away. But not entirely. In the sense that time lives, and only lives, in the mind, the self not only suffers, but contains and transcends its own death. There is cosmic enormity within. Again, it is the child who sees and continues to remind the adult of this:

> In the night of my childhood, I saw that the smallness and brevity of a human life, compared with the infinitude of time and the immensity of the universe, dwarf each separate person, and the most the cleverest can know is that he knows nothing. Within each there is a world of his own soul as immense as the external universe, and equally with that, dwarfing the little stretch of coherent waking which calls itself "I." (p. 334)

Like many of the best passages in *World Within World,* this powerfully captures the surpassing strangeness of that which the narrative contemplates. This is both a statement of strength (the self in a sense contains all) and an admission of smallness, of weakness. Such admissions are emotionally complex in this book: its call to action, to exertion of the ethical-political will, is a call to the sort of actions that are performed by those who, unlike the "special race of monsters"[86] (totalitarian and other) who rule the world, have a just spiritual sense of human limitation, of the limits of the will. Weakness is not always what it seems. It can be, and indeed is intrinsic to, the best kinds of strength. Thus in "Variations on My Life":

> Having accepted then
> This weakness beyond dispute
> Which is the strength I reject

Blessed weakness reaching back with dark root
Where earth and womb connect[87]

The deepest, transpersonal, sources of the self yield a weakness that is strength, and a strength fashioned out of weakness.

It is for this reason that the rationalist humanist model of self—a model that corresponds roughly with the Will as Intellectual Preference—is ultimately rejected. A still fuller quotation from the passage about Elizabeth and "the threads of life" indicates what is at issue here:

> I did not satisfy her; and from my point of view, she was too clear, too decided, too much in possession of all the threads of her life, too confident in what she knew, too little mystified by what she did not know. For instance, to her religious belief was simply an encumbrance to clear thinking. I had a kind of piety of not judging what I did not understand, a reverence for the beliefs of others, and even a certain understanding of religious experience. I could not accept such a rationalist view. (p. 200)

World Within World seeks a balance between the human need and right to control a mysterious, contingent world, and the ethical, emotional, even religious, requirement that we respect much of that mystery; that will does not seek entirely to master the strangeness, the chanciness, the tragic as well as the sublime possibilities of the human estate. Weakness of the will is a danger; but so too is the excessive strength that would gather all of the "threads of one's life," write out so much of the contingency that constitutes that life as human.

At this historical distance it may seem that Spender's account of will is at once too ambivalent and too naive. Yet seen in historical context, the ambivalence about will makes eminent sense: in 1951 a too-Nietzschean account of the will would have seemed reminiscent of the excesses of totalitarianism; on the other hand, a too-nebulous conception would leave the world without the resources—ethical and political—to power reconstruction. Nevertheless, certain tensions remain in Spender's account. One of these concerns the relationship between weakness of will and ideology. On the face of it, he pays too little heed to the power that ideology has not only to constrain, but also to condition the will. Part of the problem here is that his conception of ideology names rather than investigates a condition. In his *Journals* he says with reference to the Holocaust: "Ideology, that bridge between the old religion of superstition and the new religions of pseudo-science—whether Marxist or fascist—is what connected this atavistic hatred of nation for nation, class for class, to the scientific means of murder and torture."[88] This again must be seen in the context of a time when Hitler and Stalin seem to have created something like a new metaphysical condition, a hell on earth. For Spender as for many reflective autobiographers and other intellectuals of his generation writing at this time, "ideology" names the psychotic thought and attitude systems that rationalized and helped to produce incommunicable levels of catastrophe. This is understandable. But from the point of view of analysis, it robs the concept of ideology of its diagnostic and descriptive power.

The difficult work of understanding how and to what extent ideology actually functions, how it impinges upon the will, and in whose interests, does not sufficiently occur here, powerful though the text's evocations of various forms of ideological pressure are. Instead it resorts to the configurative metaphor of an inner circle relationally linked to and impacting upon a circumferential world through the medium of the will that traverses private and public spheres. Perhaps because some of this analysis does not happen, the all-important point of conjuncture at which pre-ideological properties of the self encounter ideology is not adequately explored. It would be massively reassuring to think that the self at the center were inviolable; but *World Within World* leaves the reader more in hope than with conviction on this point. Perhaps will would be stronger, which is to say more efficacious, if it knew more precisely what in ideology it was up against.

I note two further sources of tension in Spender's account. One concerns the extent to which he does in fact urge or achieve some degree of reconstitution in the narrative. His denial that he writes about an "emergent self," together with his organicist Wordsworthian premise about identity over time, would seem to suggest that his conception of self is incremental rather than transformative: "If I have changed, I have done so not so much in having shed some of these presences [earlier states of the self], as in having re-arranged them in their relation with one another, shifting the emphasis slightly, changing a pattern, rather than outgrowing the old, or making an entirely new pattern out of new elements" (p. 322). This is consistent with the child self at the center; and no one seriously imagines that an entirely new self can arise. Yet there is a tension between this organicist conception, and the associated concentric metaphor of self-constitution, on the one hand, and the book's emphasis on will and transformation, on the other. The tension is reflected in the structural pull between directional and circular energies. It is artistically powerful, but conceptually unresolved.

This in turn connects with a tension between an acknowledgment of ideology (as Spender conceives of it) that would draw the alarmed self out of itself, out of its protective center, and a horror of ideology that tempts it to withdraw into the implausibly transformative region of the centripetal poetic and autobiographical imagination. Here *World Within World* seems to recant the attack on the unworldliness of Romanticism that appears in *Forward from Liberalism*.[89] This tension, too, is unresolved but artistically powerful: the dual impulses of engagement and withdrawal are defining characteristics of this fascinatingly ambivalent autobiographical self. The "tongues of flame" and the wind that the child at the center envisions recall the apostolic calling of the feast of the Pentecost in Acts 2:

While the day of Pentecost was running its course they were all together in one place, when suddenly there came from the sky a noise like that of a strong divining wind, which filled the whole house where they were sitting. And there appeared to them tongues like flames of fire, dispersed among them and resting on each one. And they were all filled with the Holy Spirit and began to talk in other tongues, as the Spirit gave them power of utterance. (New English Bible)

What the child envisions is a summons to a new mode of belief, and a summons to surmount the mere interiority, the hidden will, of personal vision—to carry the vision, and the doctrine it reveals, out into the world. The moment of visionary plenitude is the inaugurating moment of the will's education. The enlightened will can diminish the corrosive moral impact of contingency upon this life, and life in general. The wind and the tongues of fire are a summons to surmount the insularity of personal vision—to promulgate that vision in the sociopolitical world in the form of a nuanced intersubjective conception of conduct. The conception is flawed and incomplete, and the world may not want to listen. But whatever its shortcomings as philosophy, theory, social prescription, *World Within World* makes a fine and courageous contribution to the post-totalitarian effort to imagine new forms of self-world conceptualization at a time when, for many, the hope of truly civilized polity seemed literally almost unimaginable.

CHAPTER EIGHT

"Custodians of Their Own Fates"?

Diana (and Lionel) Trilling in The Beginning of the Journey

> . . . our bodies are gardens, to the which our wills are gardeners.
> —*Othello*, I.iii

My discussion of Stephen Spender focused on his fear that his will might be—or might have been—weak, and on the autobiographical account he gives of how his will became stronger, more effective, more deeply grounded in the cognitive and emotional energies of the self. The education of the will in *World Within World* occurs principally in the "private" sphere of personal relationships, but Spender believes education of this kind empowers the will to intervene in the public sphere—in post-totalitarian Europe. Spender's concentric metaphor of self-constitution is a calculated repudiation of totalitarian attempts to expropriate and usurp the inwardness of the individual agent. The metaphor puts self at the center of its world, and will at the center of the self. In effect, Spender says that we cannot fulfill our capacities and our obligations as human beings unless we reappropriate and retrain the will. In order to operate as complex, reflective, and socially oriented agents, we must in a sense own our own wills.

As we approach the end of this study of autobiography and the will, I want to circle back to where it all began, to Augustine. Augustine is preoccupied with the question: Who owns the will? Thus at the beginning of book 5 of the *Confessions* he says:

> He who is making confession to you is not instructing you of that which is happening within him. The closed heart does not shut out your eye, and your hand is not kept away by the hardness of humanity, but you melt that when you wish, either in mercy or in punishment, and there is "none who can hide from your heat."[1]

Human beings possess a will. But the will is a gift from God—in many Judeo-Christian versions a kind of power that is ours to exert as and when we wish. The will, it would seem, is "ours." Yet God has the power—and indeed the right—to compel that will to submission to His Will. So what actually happens when Augustine's conversion allegedly brings these two wills into a state of complete congruence? Does Augustine somehow "get his will going" in that direction? Yes, perhaps; yet it is God's grace that makes such an initiative possible, that in a sense precipitates it. But if grace is the precipitating factor, how can Augustine be said to have willed his own submission? Perhaps grace can be thought of as an option that God makes available, and will as a means of choosing or refusing that option. But then the self itself has been made available, brought into being, by God, and though the will is in a sense part of the gift that is the individual's life, it is not an unconditional gift: it comes with the expectation that it will be exercised in a manner that connects the self and God in a particular way; indeed, the will cannot be whole, itself, cannot be what God intends it to be, *unless* it is exerted in this way. In a sense it is a gift that is not fully given until it is given back.

Throughout the course of this book I have drawn attention to several thematics of the will that crop up repeatedly in Western autobiography, even in narratives written in widely discrepant cultures and cultural epochs. The issue of ownership of the will is one of these. In the present chapter I read a contemporary American Jewish autobiography, Diana Trilling's *The Beginning of the Journey,* in light of this issue. Trilling doesn't quite put it in terms of owning the will. Her formulation refers not to ownership but to the idea that one might be the "custodian" of certain powers, capacities, and life trajectories. I now want to ask what this means and precisely how it relates to the will.

Early in her "autobiography," *The Beginning of the Journey,* Diana Trilling offers one of her many assessments of her husband, the renowned New York Jewish literary intellectual Lionel Trilling. Having commented on his modesty about his appearance, she continues:

> He was similarly modest on the score of his intellectual and literary abilities. He felt of colleagues whom he plainly outdistanced that all of them knew more than he knew, reasoned better, wrote more boldly and cogently. Yet behind this inaccurate self-assessment lay a secure sense of his own worth—he was a good custodian of his strengths. He liked to quote the admonition of Joyce's Stephen Daedalus: "Silence, exile and cunning." He was not at all a calculating person but there was a considerable natural cunning in his subversion of his upbringing and in his quiet handling of his professional career.[2]

The passage is typically fine-grained. Though a combative and often opinionated woman—she spoke of intellectual life as "the life of significant contention" (p. 420)—her psychological accounts of herself and others are often nuanced, even delicately equivocal. The New York Jewish intellectual milieu in which she spent her adult life produced many highly self-conscious autobiographical works,[3] but few if any are as subtle about the complexities of the soul as this one. Moreover, Diana Trilling's is one of only a small number of women's autobiographies to emerge from what was an intensely male milieu.[4]

Most of the New York Jewish intellectuals, not least Lionel himself, were heavily influenced by Freud,[5] but in Diana Trilling's writing the influence is more pervasive than in most. Even when she is not consciously invoking Freud, her accounts of herself and her world are characteristically suffused with a

Freudian way of seeing. Thus the assessment of Lionel I have quoted modulates from a level at which he exhibits a sort of punitive conscious and preconscious sense of self that is characterized by insecurity and low self-esteem, to a deeper, more unconscious level at which he has a "secure" sense of his own worth. Here, as in so many other places, affinities between their intellectual outlooks are clear: Lionel himself often referred to Rousseau's notion of the "sentiment of being,"[6] the noble savage's primal intuitive grasp of his or her own existence and value; and his work repeatedly grapples with the nature of the self's relation to, and modes of appraisal of, itself.

This passage reveals another feature of Diana's outlook that is every bit as pervasive as—and indeed complexly entwined with—her Freudianism, and this is her unswerving belief in the agential capacities of the self. It's there in the arresting notion that one might achieve an effective "subversion" of one's upbringing; that one is both a product and an author of one's own history. It's there, too, in the formulation that comes two sentences earlier: "He was a good custodian of his own strengths." The notion of the self as a "custodian" of the elements (like the will) that go into its making is familiar in the history of conceptualizations of the will; yet her way of putting it is both striking and suggestive. It suggests that one of the elements that comes into the world with us as a kind of given is the capacity to shape ourselves, to emancipate ourselves *from* the realm of the given. This is the will's great calling, and already it is clear that she thinks of the will in much more than simply instrumental terms: though will sometimes works merely to impose the needs and desires of a relatively settled self upon the world, it is often, and more interestingly, a force that lives in subtle and variable relations with the self that "possesses" it, that is its "custodian." One of these relations is self-transformative: the will can change that which is its custodian. This idea commands assent among a strikingly miscellaneous range of authors, including Mill, Nietzsche, and Sartre. Another of her formulations extends the idea further: she speaks of women who in the twenties were "custodians of their own fates" (p. 107): if we have the power to choose, and to transform the self that does the choosing, then in an important sense our "fates" are in our own hands. We are their "custodians." And with fates—a modern understanding of *the* Fates—we are back again where this study of autobiography and the will began.

But Diana Trilling knows better than most that the will also has its life in intersubjective relations, and *The Beginning of the Journey* is a fascinating study of intersubjectivity—Self and Other—in autobiography.

I. WHOSE STORY?

The book's title says a lot. In 1947 Lionel published an anti-Stalinist novel that was to become a minor classic. He called it *The Middle of the Journey.* Diana's autobiographical title echoes his, thereby signaling a role for Lionel that is even more central to her life narrative than is Sartre's role in Simone de Beauvoir's autobiographical writings. Diana further underlines Lionel's place in her life-story with her subtitle: *The Marriage of Diana and Lionel Trilling.* Though Lionel died in 1975, some twenty years before Diana's death in October 1996, her autobiography is often focused on and through their life together. In her preface she writes: "This book is in part an autobiography, in part a biography of my husband, Lionel Trilling, and in largest part a memoir of our marriage. It is not a literary study but a personal story" (p. ix). And she admits that one of her motives for writing is to set the record straight for books that might later be written about them, either singly or as a couple (p. x). The will to power is on view from the outset.

In a remarkable unpublished letter, she alludes to what is in effect her will to power and its psychological roots. Writing to Lionel on May 26, 1962, while he is away in Europe, she reports a conversation with their friend and colleague Steven Marcus. She is "bowled over by the accuracy of his insight" that "I use my sense of reality in everyday life as a defense against my analytical reality." She continues:

And I caught a new glimpse of what reality must be for me—the phallic truth. Or, rather, my power to perceive reality must represent my phallicism, which power I guard against losing in analysis. Maybe I don't make myself clear, I haven't really the sense of having got hold of the insight as I should, but I feel it is supremely important esp. when I recognize the aggressiveness with which I thrust (sic) my reality-insistence upon any one I deal with— my belief that there is only a single reality, that which I happen to perceive, and that the best help I can be to anyone I love, the most creative thing I can do, is enforce my reality upon the other person. It's like a rape. (By the way, perhaps you might keep this letter so that if I forget all of this promptly, I can refresh my memory.)[7]

The "(sic)" is hers; the sense of how apparently blind and abrasive she could be with respect to others' views of the world seems to have been widely held by many who met her; but the letter shows her to have been less insensitive than she often seemed. She knew that her need to prevail was rooted in insecurity, that her will in this area was a product of weakness, and that her psyche harbored some kind of conflict between male didacticism and her training in the arts of female self-subordination.

She assures the reader of *The Beginning of the Journey* that no serious falsification follows from the way the book is structured because after 1950 "there were now no significant changes in the basic pattern of our lives" (p. ix). They had married in 1929, when they were both twenty-four years of age; so the "pattern" is set during the first twenty-one years of their marriage. The book's design adds weight to the proposition that women's autobiography tends to be "relational" in conception and structure. There is fragmentary evidence that Lionel could have been an accomplished autobiographer.[8] Had he lived to write the autobiography he had begun when he succumbed to pancreatic cancer, there is no doubt that Diana would have figured prominently. But it seems doubtful, not least because of his personal diffidence, that she would have figured as decisively in his as he does in hers.

However, the situation is somewhat more complex than her preface would suggest. A relative and close friend of Diana's believes that her original intention was to write two books—one about the marriage, the other about herself—but that she decided to conflate the two as her health, and in particular her eyesight, declined.[9] (*The Beginning of the Journey* was composed by dictation when she was almost blind.) Secondly, the book that actually unfolds is more concertedly autobiographical than the subtitle's emphasis on a portrait of a marriage would give us to expect. Certainly Lionel is always strongly present; but the preeminent focus is Diana's pained and paradoxical sense of self: her long struggle for individuation, her need to find and to fashion a viable self out of the extraordinary mix of arrogance and insecurity that formed a kind of bedrock of her personality. Here is a further, though familiar, sense in which *The Beginning of the Journey* is a book about the will: the struggle for individuation and self-definition that gives it its poignant power is itself an intricate and extended act of will. I use the bedrock analogy advisedly because Trilling at times figures her struggle as a process of chipping away at deeply embedded sedimentations of the self. Writing of the way in which her parents trained her to avoid surpassing the achievements of her siblings (she had a brother who was three years older than she and a handicapped sister five years her senior), she laments that psychoanalysis only enabled her to see the limiting later impact of this training—her tendency to "people the world with brothers and sisters whom I must not excel" (p. 247)—relatively late in life: "This corner of my emotional history was opened to me too late for me to do more than chisel away at the loose fragments of so solid an obstacle to my free course in life" (p. 248). The sense of tension between deeply embedded internal constraints and the will to a "free course" is the hallmark of the book.

The narrative's account of how this struggle is played out within the marital context is subtle and is notable for the ways in which it refuses formulaic gender understandings. Here something needs to be said about Diana Trilling's relation to feminism. She considers "women's liberation" the "most successful revolution of our century" (p. 155), but she has her own perspective on it. In an essay entitled "Women's Liberation," written in 1970 and published in her collection *We Must March My Darlings,* she argues for a more complex differentiation between the sexes: "Free of the cultural shards of our sexual differences, perhaps we can now come to a more satisfactory knowledge of our distinctive maleness and femaleness, and from this knowledge bring biology and culture into sounder relation with each other."[10] She is, then, for difference, but for difference understood in the light of a general reconceptualization of the relationship between culture and biology. In *The Beginning of the Journey* she says:

> I have never supposed that I have any special wisdom to impart on the subject of women. I separate from the feminists of our present day in thinking of men, not as the opponents of women, but as their companions in the same hard business of being human. If, as is surely the case, they have had advantages in this difficult enterprise which have been denied to women, it has not made them any happier. I am not convinced that it is harder to be a woman than it is to be a man. I have also had far too many pleasures and privileges in being a woman to think of myself as a victim in the way in which feminist doctrine now seems to dictate. (pp. 352–53)

The passage is somewhat misleading in that some of her work, especially *Mrs. Harris*,[11] her account of the trial of the woman accused of murdering the Scarsdale Diet doctor, is notable for its gender analyses, particularly its discussions of female masochism. The passage just quoted does, however, reveal much about her own generational conditioning: elsewhere she says that "to live by deference to the needs of those one loves is among the pleasanter modes of existence; also, I might add, among the most taxing";[12] it is also consistent with much of what she reveals about her personal history. So powerful are these generational and personal factors that this most combative of women harbors no particular resentment toward men. But there is another and still more individual reason why this should be so: Lionel himself was far from "typical" of even the intellectual men of his time; indeed he was not even temperamentally typical of his often feisty and strategic New York Jewish intellectual colleagues. As she says, his personality was to a considerable degree the result of the "subversion" of his own conditioning, and while he had "natural cunning," he was not "calculating." His work returns again and again to the possibility that one might choose a style for the self that will be more than style in the honorific sense: his hope is that style can reach down and deeply condition the person. I will say more about this when I discuss the Trillings on the will presently. What I want to suggest here is that the self Diana imputes to Lionel is an amalgam of temperament and, to a very significant degree, *choice,* and that the act of choice that so profoundly shapes this self also sets it apart from conventional masculine conditioning.

Lionel's attitude to her career is one example of his unusual disposition toward gender expectations. Like many women, she found her profession "by accident" (p. 325): Margaret Marshall, the literary editor of the *Nation,* rang Lionel to ask if he could suggest someone to do unsigned reviews for the journal. After he hung up Diana suggested, rather to her own surprise, that she do it. Lionel, who had a high estimation of her intellectual and stylistic abilities, encouraged and recommended her. She was thirty-six at the time and was to go on to make a substantial—if controversial—reputation as a reviewer and critic. She says of his attitude throughout: "He placed no barriers in my literary path. Far from putting any restraints on me, Lionel constantly encouraged my career and delighted in its every advance. He was much quicker to my literary defense than to his own" (p. 349). Earlier she comments that though she learned to be an intellectual from him, the process was informal, never one of "conscious pedagogy" (p. 19). Like Simone de Beauvoir, she concedes pride of place to her intellectual partner: "Lionel was a writer of broader vision than mine and of more complex purpose and in the course of time he developed a prose which I could only envy" (p. 20). While Beauvoir's intellectual deference to Sartre is open to debate, Diana Trilling's deference to Lionel is not. Indeed, what's impressive about this estimate is its frankness, accuracy, and lack of rancor. There seems to have been remarkably little professional competitiveness in the marriage. In part because of this, she was later able to write an autobiography that set out to be both "her" story and "his."

But her account of the marriage is much more clear-eyed than, say, Beauvoir's version of her relationship with Sartre. She is open about the tumult that characterized the middle years of the marriage and painfully frank about the "annihilating verbal assaults" that (according to her) Lionel launched upon her "perhaps at most five or six" times a year (p. 254). Here the darker side of Lionel that she conjures so powerfully into view is strikingly apparent—a darker side that is, in her account, much more captive to gender conditioning than his customary self, and that is in this instance a legacy of his conflicted relationship with his mother. It is this assessment, among others, that the Trillings' son, James, has contested in a recent article about his father.[13] It's clear, then, that when Diana Trilling speaks of the "miracle" (p. 419) of marriage, she doesn't mean something that is made in heaven, but rather something that is remarkable given the profoundly flawed and conditioned nature of human life in the here and now. In such a place a "successful marriage" constitutes a "remarkable" "accident." I want to quote the passage from which this last comment comes for what it says about the will as a lived and shared challenge in the Trilling marriage:

> To live one's life without a sense of time is to squander it. For more than a decade Lionel and I squandered life not in pleasure but in fearfulness. We were afraid to be fully grown up and to be in command of ourselves and others, even children. Ours was a successful marriage on the score of this shared impediment as well as on the score of more attractive features. It was one of those unconscious conspiracies between a man and a woman which make a successful marriage so remarkable an accident. (p. 191)

Her account of this "shared impediment" is frank and fascinating. Elsewhere she refers to it as a sort of "diffidence": "We were both of us crippled by a curious diffidence in our dealings with other people" (p. 113). Even sending back a substandard meal in a restaurant was too much for a couple thus afflicted. They seemed to share, at least in the earlier years, a kind of affliction of the will—a sharing that made the marriage at once secure and weak: "It met the requirements of our weaknesses no less than of our strengths" (p. 152). Now and then in his literary essays, Lionel lets slip an observation about relations between the sexes that has a strongly autobiographical feel about it. In *The Liberal Imagination* he writes that "marriages are often unsatisfactory for the very reasons that make it impossible to dissolve them"[14]—an assessment that could easily have come from Diana's pen.

The question "Whose story?" is, then, not easy to answer. Like Beauvoir's autobiographical writings, *The Beginning of the Journey* is in part a de facto biography of the Great Man who was the woman's partner. This Other-directed focus of autobiographical energy in Trilling's and Beauvoir's books complicates the already-complicated interweaving of the two lives and selves. Carolyn Steedman's comment that "children are always episodes in someone else's narrative"[15] applies equally to adult selves: our stories are so deeply enmeshed in the stories of others that autobiography must always be, to varying degrees, an amalgam of self-writing and biography. But when laudation—in Beauvoir's case hagiography—is a principal motive for self-writing, the focus of the story must be equivocal. It remains so in *The Beginning of the Journey,* despite Diana Trilling's determined, courageous, and sometimes deeply ambivalent effort to restore for posterity a Lionel Trilling whose darker side seems only to have been known to her.

II. THE FORCE OF THE PAST; OR, TWO MEANINGS OF *Determined*

Like many avowed Freudians, not least, as I have argued, Freud himself, Diana Trilling's attitude to the past is contradictory. At times she can sound like an all-out determinist: "There would seem, however, to be no aspect of my mind and no activity of my mature life whose source cannot be traced to one or the other of my parents. Only the mix is mine" (p. 100); or "unfortunately, the mistakes in our upbringings are never really compensated for" (p. 38). Yet, her position on the past is much more complex, and ultimately more sanguine, than this. In a review of *Arrival and Departure,* a novel that explores the relations between neurosis, political commitment, and psychoanalysis, she criticizes what she sees as Koestler's failure to make "any value distinction between determined conduct and volitional conduct."[16] Similarly, the comment just quoted about our inability to compensate for our "upbringings" actually comes in the section in which she speaks of Lionel as a "good custodian," and the phrase that's appended to the previous quotes—"Only the mix is mine"—has major possible implications. I've argued that such implications are on the side of will, choice, and a margin of freedom: the past may determine those antecedent factors that converge upon "me"; but in "me" they assume unprecedented forms of combination, "mix." In the sense that I am unprecedented I am radically individual; and if, as Trilling believes, the "mix" includes an innate capacity to formulate and enact desires, resolutions, and so on, then "I" am an individual possessed of an individual will—and a will, moreover, that is to some extent free. So conceived, "I" am at once a product of a past and a producer of a present and a future. But I can only be effective in this way if the particular contingent circumstances in which I operate permit effective response (some situations are more constraining than others), and if I am prepared to will the will into activity. On this view, the will looks very much like the Freudian ego: it is, in her words, "the organizing principle of the personal life,"[17] which coordinates both intrapsychic activity and the self's relations with "reality." For Diana Trilling, *determined,* then, means two things: it refers to the conditioning power of the past and also to that which opposes that conditioning power—the will to shape one's own life, to "subvert" that past. She knows, too, that the shaping power of the past need not be paralyzing: it is as apt to equip us for choice as to impose paralysis. Of her mother she says: "My mother left me a substantial legacy of determination" (p. 99). A self-proclaimed legatee of the past, she was as critic and social commentator a fierce opponent of the victim culture. She always requires of literature that it give us "stories about people and not about victims."[18]

This is essentially how she tries to tell the stories of Lionel and herself, even if her hypersensitivity toward the power of the past at times pulls *The Beginning of the Journey* in the direction of plaintive lament: "I sometimes think that my heart has never stopped aching, whether with my masked and injured love for my father or my injured and buried love for my mother" (p. 100). Her parents were immigrant eastern European Jews. After working as a braid salesman, her father established a successful braid manufacturing business. Unlike many of the New York Jewish intellectuals, Lionel and Diana came from families that were already middle class. They did not have to struggle for this status. Nor did they have to contend with a powerful pull between the old eastern European Jewish ways and the allure of assimilation that beset so many of their friends and colleagues: "Like Lionel but unlike most of the Jewish intellectuals of our generation, I had the childhood of an American who happened to be a Jew, not that of a Jew who happened to be an American" (p. 43). The book's structure reflects and expresses its defining concern: the will as a response to the determinative threat that is posed by the past. The first chapter gives something of an overview, but is predominantly about Diana. The second deals principally with Lionel's childhood, the third largely with her own. The fourth chapter takes her to her undergraduate days at Radcliffe, then switches to Lionel and brings him to his undergraduate career at Columbia. The next is about both, and brings them to the point of marriage. Thereafter it is largely a joint narrative. The structure encourages the reader to see the adult self as pitted against a constraining past, and also to see that each has carried internalized versions of the past's constraints into the marriage, so that their bond is at once regressive, protective, and requiring of joint and individual response: a power of determination in response to the past's determinative power.

The overall effect is to conjure the two personalities and their stories in a way that gives graphic access to what Lionel (after Freud) calls "the 'night side' of life."[19] The past, which includes one's biological inheritance, really does menace and threaten the self, and Diana Trilling is surely one of the greatest autobiographical chroniclers of a characteristic—though not exclusively—Jewish cultural legacy: the use of anxiety as a means of processing and dealing with the world. I put it in this way because we're not talking here about anxiety as a kind of background to life; nor as a reactive symptom that wells up at times of particular stress and fatigue. What's at issue here is anxiety as life's generative emotion—as an existential orientation that structures, orchestrates, and infuses the individual's transactions with the world, day in and day out. Anxiety in this sense is not an epiphenomenon of the psyche—it is the psyche's constitutive structure. In another of those autobiographical glimpses in his academic writings, Lionel gives as an example of a client visiting a physician, someone who wishes to be cured "let us say, of a fear of walking in the street."[20] For readers of *The Beginning of the Journey,* the example is poignant indeed because in the autobiography Diana reveals that she suffered for many years from agoraphobia. Indeed, friends say that right to the last she was prone to phobias and that on account of her fear of heights she would not visit apartments that were higher than about the second floor.[21] The scale of Diana Trilling's internal conflicts is startling: this woman who as a tough and uncompromising reviewer struck fear into the hearts of the authors who came her way (she loved the story of a novelist and refugee from Nazi Vienna who was reputed to have said that he had lost his country, his home, and his language but at least had had the good fortune not to have been reviewed by her [p. 330]) was the same woman who for over a decade (from about 1931 to the early 1940s) suffered such severe panic attacks that she was afraid to leave her apartment in uptown Manhattan without Lionel or some other companion, hired a companion to keep her company during the day, was at times only able to travel if doing so with her analyst, and took up radical politics in part as a way of getting herself out of the house and into some collective environment. To get the measure of the conflict involved, we have to imagine her a virtual prisoner of dread in that apartment, yet fearlessly pronouncing upon the literary and broader cultural life of her time. The irony is not lost upon her. She speaks of an intellectual "arrogance" (p. 20) that comes as part of her conflicted childhood endowment, and of her early work for the *Nation* she says: "It astonishes me that with so little ground for authority I claimed so much right to be heard. Apparently, whatever my private timidities, my public voice was firm and courageous" (pp. 336–37). Yet the reader is perhaps even more astonished than she is at the sheer scale of these contradictions (she, after all, knew them as a routine aspect of the world). Perhaps the letter to Lionel about her "phallicism" holds a key: if phobias are in part a fear of the contingent, uncontrolled dimensions of life, then one can see why a phobic person might in certain aspects of her own life be controlling, even domineering and judgmental.[22] In Beauvoir's terms, such a person might be "injecting determinism" where only contingency seems to reign.

How many autobiographers have been so possessed by fear that they draw up a list of their dreads? Here is Diana's account of what she and her family used to fear:

> lightening, thunder, wind, heavy snow, driving cars, driving in cars, horses, snakes, worms, germs, poisonous plants and berries, electrical appliances, gas and gas fixtures, fire, cows, bulls, all boats including rowboats, swamps, quicksand, flies, mosquitos, bees, Greek ice-cream parlours, bats, mold, rust, gangrene, spiders, caterpillars, strange cats and dogs, mice, rats of course, canned goods, bad fish, damp, drafts, whooping cough, blood poisoning, influenza, infantile paralysis, ruptured appendices, syphilis, other people's towels or tubs or toilet seats (much the same as syphilis), subways, bananas, tomatoes, oranges, oysters, fruit pits, any medicine taken even once in excess of a prescription, any two medicines taken in conjunction, foods in unusual combination with other foods, deep water, undertow, waves, leeches, toads, eels, dyes, hospitals, insanity, imbecility, brain fever, pinkeye, ghosts and ghosts stories, cemeteries, Saint Vitus' dance, the poorhouse, lockjaw, rabies, heredity, sunstroke, trains, gypsies, beggars, intermarriage, leprosy, lice, nits, pimples (related to syphilis), anything swallowed without sufficient chewing, ice water, the dark, burglars. (pp. 3–4)

True, she claims that such fears were common to many adults of the time (Michael Woolf writes of the "Haunted House" of American Jewish autobiography),[23] but to suffer intense emotional investment across the whole range of them—this was surely an experience reserved for the pathologically fearful few, many of whom had been schooled in the ways of Jewish apprehension. Little wonder that she tells us—and it's worth noting the prominence these passages about dread assume by virtue of their appearance right at the start of the narrative—that "fear is the emotion I remember best from childhood" (p. 3) and that "I regarded myself as preternaturally fearful" (p. 217). And the list gets extended as the narrative unfolds: fear of self-display (p. 52), fear of freedom (p. 176), fear of prominence as a writer (p. 247)—and so on. Characteristically, though, the second most important emotion she recollects from her childhood is "longing": "I would always long for someone or something which could not be named, a transcendence, I suppose" (p. 3). Here then is the tension between anxiety and transcendence that we have seen in Arthur Koestler's autobiographical writings. Like Koestler (another Jew, of course) she sees herself as afflicted by "a classical anxiety neurosis" (p. 229); again like him, she sees transcendence as both a pre-condition and a property of the will. *The Beginning of the Journey* is about both fear and its overcoming.

It would, however, be misleading to press the comparison between Trilling and Koestler too hard: while Trilling was a virtual prisoner in her apartment and rarely ventured beyond Manhattan until her panic attacks ceased, Koestler, as we have seen, positively courted danger and lived by an ethos of risk. These strikingly different responses to anxiety reflect a vast divide between the genders: anxious men are conditioned to act, anxious women to visit the anxiety upon themselves, thwarting and disabling the will. But there is also a deep psychological disparity between the two individuals concerned. Koestlerian anxiety and the psychic structures with which it is associated are counterbalanced by states of mystical exemption from apprehensiveness—the "oceanic states" in which his customary psychic structures melt away. Nothing remotely like this occurs in Diana Trilling's account of herself. Always, there is a sense of steely will and strategizing to survive; never any real sense of exemption or internal repose, such as Schopenhauer thinks we might find on the other side of struggle. Characteristically, she both comments on and tries to explain her incapacity to transcend the past and its menacing accumulation of conditioning and fear. She recalls a deranged woman called Bobolinka who lived next door and was brutally murdered when Diana was a child. To Bobolinka (in part at least) she traces her life-long "fear of insanity"—a fear that has "blocked the free play of my imagination and made me too intent upon reasonableness" (p. 8). Wondering why she lacked the wherewithal to fulfill her intellectual gifts, she says: "My literary life was just one more territory through which I dragged the heavy anchor of my childhood instruction" (p. 352). And she goes on to track this to various specific family attitudes and even specific incidents. One of these involves an activity that she pursued later in life and even contemplated as a career: singing. Her penchant for singing around the family used to attract derision, and on one occasion her father says sarcastically that he will build her a stage in the toilet. Here is part of her gloss on this incident:

> The remark was critical in my life. In consigning me to the place of excrement he could not more vividly have put his ban on self-display. I permanently incorporated the prohibition into the system of law by which my life is governed. Without psychoanalysis, I would not have been enough free of it even to make a start as a published writer. (p. 52)

There is no sense that the effects of this incident might just be cast aside by or during some gestalt shift in the orientation of consciousness. *The Beginning of the Journey* does not report—or even really contemplate the possibility of—a fundamental shift whereby the psychic orientation and structure that are constituted by anxiety might give way to some other structure or orientation.

Trilling is to a considerable degree stuck for life with the toilet-as-a-stage incident and its effects, and the best she can do to get "free of it" is to "chisel away"
at the memory, and at other particular fears, with the aid of psychoanalysis. The
past so conceived carries an enormous determinative charge; and in the economy of her life, the thing that is imputed the power to counter, or at least ame-
liorate, that charge is psychoanalysis. In effect, psychoanalysis is called upon to
act as a kind of circuit breaker for the determined will. Freud says that unconscious motives determine the will; but analysis, by bringing such determinative
forces to consciousness, switches the source of determination from the id to the
ego, thereby supposedly lessening the hold of the original impulsions and letting rationality take firmer roots in conduct. Analysis is a kind of assisted and
partial liberation of the will, the analyst a figure who, if her or his presence is
truly willed by the analysand, can in effect help to intervene in the causal sequences that have shaped the individual's behavior hitherto.

Few autobiographies give so prominent a place to psychoanalysis as *The Beginning of the Journey*. Not only does Freudianism infuse Trilling's way of seeing the world; she repeatedly draws upon her experiences in analysis in offering explanations of her self. Beyond this, she actually narrates her experiences
with her seven therapists, naming each and reporting on what she thinks they
did to help or hinder her struggle for confidence and individuation. (There is
a strange resemblance between Diana's account of her intense and disturbing
experiences with these therapists and Saint Teresa's autobiographical account
of the eight persons to whom she turned for spiritual guidance and mentor-
ship.)[24] This is Freudian autobiography par excellence. The contest between
the extremity of Trilling's symptoms and the salving aspirations of psychoanalysis is gripping indeed—as are her biographical sketches of the analysts
themselves. The account of her agoraphobia is the most graphic example. The
following, a description of the terror of contingency, is reminiscent of Beauvoir
and indicates what Diana and her therapists were up against. Lionel has grown
a mustache during a brief absence and so confronts her with the need to adapt
to a minor change:

> Emotionally I was unable to handle the change in his appearance. I trembled
> with anxiety before the unknown; in the next months and years any change
> in my familiar circumstances, even a sudden shadow across a window or an
> unanticipated sound, filled me with terror. I was like a child whose world
> must be not be altered lest she be left without protection against all the un-
> named dangers of a hostile universe. (p. 187)

The most alarming symptom, however, was her fear of being away from Lionel—a factor that presumably needs to be borne in mind when weighing his
verbal assaults upon her. There could be few internal constraints more binding
and debilitating than this—a dependence upon one's partner that amounts

both to a loss of freedom for oneself and a profound impingement on the freedom of the Other. What does this mean?

She makes and reports various attempts to answer this question. The first person she sees about the problem—a neurologist called Wechsler—poses it quite openly, and his question "hangs in my mind like a balloon in a comic strip" (p. 175). The image is oddly discordant, coming from such a champion of high culture and psychological acuity; but the question makes an impact, not least because it "implied an element of choice in my symptom" (p. 175). Passages like these reflect the depth of Trilling's Freudianism: the unconscious is functioning here as an agent-surrogate, willing a certain kind of sickness at the behest of determinative elements of her personal history. There was a "hidden motive" in her "burgeoning neurosis" (p. 175). In such willing the will is not free. It is determined. She now goes on to gloss the rather confused answer that she gave to Dr. Wechsler—that she depends more on Lionel than he does on her—as follows:

> What I was trying to say was that I wanted Lionel to be more commanding, more in charge of me. I wanted him to be more like my father even if this would involve a curtailment of my freedom—perhaps especially if it curtailed my freedom. I wanted him to be the chaperon my father had been. The fact that he did not exercise parental authority over me exposed me to all the illicitness and temptation I had been taught to fear. (p. 176)

In existential terms it is a willing of bondage that is rooted in a fear of freedom. The Freudian dimension casts Lionel as a displaced version of the Father—both the biological parent and the father as the Law by which the superego aspires to thwart the libido, the id more generally. Again, "fear" is the constitutive, the generative emotion in all of this. The figure of the chaperone sits interestingly with that of the custodian: the chaperone (generally an older woman) protects her charge from the threat of the "illicit"; the custodian (of whom more anon) is a guardian in a more general sense. The chaperone-custodian figure in Trilling's passage is one who protects the young woman from a full engagement in experience. But women who are truly "custodians of their fates" function in just the opposite way: it is, as we have seen, their fate to have a will, and to have adult custody of the will is to exercise, to engage fully—however riskily—with the world.

This explanation of her agoraphobia seems to be important but not definitive. A later therapist, Dr. Schidler, tries to apply counterphobic principles—to get her over her fears through "willpower" (p. 233). This doesn't work: the will that wills its own paralysis can't be acted upon by a direct countervailing act of will. More subtle means are needed—or so she thought. In the event, another analyst, Dr. Brunswick, makes the breakthrough. This person's position in the narrative is complex indeed. Fifty years later Trilling still fumes at the fact that she had been referred to and treated by a woman who was a morphine addict.

She describes her five years under Dr. Brunswick's "vagrant care" (p. 242) as "the hardest of my life" (p. 240). She is intensely critical of the doctor's habit of lecturing her about her condition. And yet, it is in the course of such inappropriately didactic sessions that Dr. Brunswick provides the insight that breaks the spell. Diana's panic attacks—though not her general propensity to fear—cease. It is the great frustration of *The Beginning of the Journey* that we don't learn what the insight was. But it is significant that it came in the form it did: as an insight, the outcome of an analysis in the more familiar discursive sense, not of the transference that Freud saw as so central to the practice of psychoanalysis. And yet Diana's anger fifty years later suggests that some very powerful transferential processes were in fact at work.

III. The Trillings on the Will

At the age of twenty-three Lionel Trilling contracted scarlet fever. For a time his life was in danger, and the experience of the illness and convalescence was to have a profoundly formative effect for him. Eight years later, when his friend and Columbia colleague Alan Brown was on sick leave, Trilling wrote to him, saying:

> It seems to me that the best members of the intellectual middle-classes should all have a course (not as dramatic as yours is being) in the Abandonment of Responsibility . . . I myself have only once had forced on me that relaxation of which you speak and it was impressively effective—when eight years ago I had scarlet fever and was they tell me like [*sic*] to die and I let everything slip—and did I find out what I was really about! with no effort but just a gradual unfolding, so that I was entirely a different person when I got up a couple of months later, which, by the way, I didn't want to do, the process, apparently, being still incomplete.[25]

Eleven years after this, in *The Middle of the Journey,* Trilling recreated the illness experience in fictional form. Laskell, the protagonist, recalls the period he spent in bed with scarlet fever as a kind of golden time:

> During the latter part of his time in bed he had been able, for quarter-hours at a time, to stare at a rose that had survived the death of eleven other roses that had been sent to him. For as many days as the rose lasted, Laskell had kept it on a little table near his bed, handy for contemplation. He could become lost in its perfection, watching the strange energy which the rose seemed to have, for it was not static in its beauty, it seemed to be always at work organizing its petals into their perfect relation with each other. Laskell, gazing at it, had known something like desire; but it was a strange desire which *wanted* nothing, which was its own satisfaction.

Just prior to this he reflects: "Some remarkable thing had happened to his mind and will."[26] Herein lies the deepest significance of the "real life" episode: Lionel had a lifelong fascination with the will—it is, as Diana says, "a signal word throughout Lionel Trilling's writing"[27]—and the illness seems greatly to have extended his sense of what the will, or the cessation of the will's "normal" activities, might be like. He was no mystic, yet these descriptions bespeak a kind of mystical deliverance from the quotidian that claimed so much of his intellectual and personal attention. He was also no philosopher, but he was a historian of ideas and his writings grapple repeatedly with different conceptions and gradations of the will; indeed one of his great intellectual achievements lies in his ability to capture in discursive (and, early in his career, creative) prose manifestations of the will that often go unnoticed, or that are often not even recognized as forms of the will at all. When Trilling uses phrases like "letting everything slip" and "desire which *wanted* nothing," he doesn't mean that the will is in abeyance; he means that it is active, but in subtle and special ways that require subtle and special forms of perception and representation in order to see what is occurring.

When former friends and colleagues published a volume of essays in his honor after his death, they called it *Art, Politics, and Will*[28]—a title that reflects the fact that Trilling speaks of the will across the entire human spectrum from public life to private, from art to subjective experience, from existential orientation to interpersonal relations. These explorations inevitably and manifestly affected Diana Trilling's view of the world and her way of doing literary and cultural criticism. And there is this further and fascinating twist: when she came to write Lionel's de facto biography in *The Beginning of the Journey*, she framed her portrait of him very much in terms of the condition of his will. I discuss this portrait in the next section. Here I want to give a more detailed account of Lionel's, and then of Diana's, work on the will, and to trace some of the patterns of affinity and difference between them. I then relate these matters to autobiography.

Lionel Trilling wrote within a composite European humanist tradition that accords centrality to the individual self. He was an extraordinarily wide-ranging critic, and he traced the cultural articulation of the will all the way from Greek drama to his own day. In an admirable account of Trilling's work, Mark Krupnick argues that Trilling was a "reactive critic."[29] What he means by this is that Trilling needed a polemical target to work against in order to produce his best criticism. This is true in the sense that much of his best work—and, importantly, Diana's best work too—was written in opposition to cultural Stalinism and indeed against all vestiges of totalitarianism. In this they were quintessential postwar liberal intellectuals. But, as Krupnick acknowledges, Trilling was "reactive" in the further sense that his literary and cultural criticism was geared to what he perceived to be the pressing social needs of the time. His diagnosis of the ills of late modernity, for instance, centers on what he terms "the hypertrophy of the will"[30]—a condition in which the will is distended and dangerously distorted by a disturbance in the economy of the faculties that share its psychic domain. He made this kind of diagnosis as early as his Ph.D. dissertation, which was written in the mid-thirties and was to appear as a major work of scholarship on Matthew Arnold in 1939;[31] but awareness of Hitler and Stalin quickened his sense of urgency about the will and moved him to argue in *The Liberal Imagination* (1950) that "surely the great work of our time is the restoration and reconstitution of the will,"[32] "the great former will of humanism."[33] What was this will? There is no simple answer to this question, but one thing is certain: the Trillings saw in both totalitarian ideology and in avant-garde cultural modernism what Lionel termed "an affirmation of the unconditioned nature of the self."[34] *Sincerity and Authenticity,* the source of this last quotation, tracks this "affirmation" to many sources: to Hegel's vision of the emancipated spirit, to Nietzsche's hypostasization of the will, to modernist literature's fascination with the disintegrated consciousness. Trilling, whose natural temperamental habitat was what he called "the temperate zone,"[35] feared such excesses and was on the side of the Nietzsche who affirmed the Apollonian check on Dionysian excess; the English moderation of Arnold, Mill, or E. M. Forster; and, perhaps above all, Freud's affirmation of the ego's role in taming and integrating the forces of the id. But Freud and others—Keats, even Nietzsche in places—offered a corrective in another crucial direction. Trilling objected to what he termed "the negative transcendence of the human,"[36] a denial-by-disgust of the human condition that he found in much major modernist, or protomodernist, writing: Dostoyevsky's *Notes from the Underground,* Kafka. This kind of denial sought to go "beyond culture" through refusal of the actual and, importantly, a refusal of pleasure. Trilling affirms the pleasure principle, not as Dionysian excess but as an inalienable aspect of the integrated psyche's reaching toward its fullest self-realization. When he entitled one of his volumes of essays *The Opposing Self,*[37] he did not mean to affirm Romantic refusals of the actual; on the contrary, he insisted (in terms reminiscent of Koestler) that "the spirit of man is always at the mercy of the actual and trivial," and that, notwithstanding modernism's fascination with the unconditioned, the challenge, which only the greatest literature can meet, is to represent the conditioned. This reads more like Mill than Hegel or Kant: "To comprehend unconditioned spirit is not so very hard, but there is no knowledge rarer than the understanding of spirit as it exists in the inescapable conditions which the actual and the trivial make for it."[38] Here, in capsule, is Trilling's sense of literature's great calling in modern culture.

It's clear from this that he is a "reactive" critic not only in the sense that he often gears his critical commentary to perceived current cultural need, but also because such needs will always in his view reflect or articulate in their terms requirements that spring from something like a universal human condition—the condition of being conditioned. As a critic Trilling self-consciously writes within and seeks to endorse the great Western tragic tradition, which addresses itself to the fate of human need in a conditioned universe. His encapsulations of this view often have a Schopenhauerian ring: "The world is a complex and unexpected and terrible place,"[39] a place that baffles and constrains the will—"such is the nature of the human will, so perplexed is it by the disparity between what it desires and what it is allowed to have."[40] One of the great dangers is that human beings, whether through totalitarian assertion or various modes of intellectual reduction, will seek to shatter or to eschew the "complexity" of things. Hence his critique of what he saw as the reductive postwar condition of the "liberal imagination" in the book that bears that title. Hence too his attack on Skinnerian behaviorism. He sees in *Beyond Freedom and Dignity* and Skinner's entire program of "reinforcement" "a new and clandestine mode of aggression" under the guise of a utopian attempt to bring about a peaceable form of human society.[41] Trilling's line of critical defense against such attitudes is the notion of "moral realism" in literature (and other arts). He finds it in many of his favorite writers, among them E. M. Forster. In his study of Forster, he writes: "All novelists deal with morality, but not all novelists, or even all good novelists, are concerned with moral realism, which is not the awareness of morality itself but of the contradictions, paradoxes and dangers of living the moral life."[42] This emphasis, which displaces American New Criticism's preoccupation with local stylistic paradox and irony into the realm of ethics, links Trilling's humanism with his tragic outlook: it is the self as understood and prioritized by humanism that registers and must learn to live within the tragically constraining complexities of the moral life. Trilling's conception of the self is of a moral being, a moral agent, in Taylor's terms a "strong evaluator," possessed of capacities for reflection, deliberation, and discerning conduct. At least this is his ideal picture of self. Many selves, he believes, are not like this—hence, in part, the need for literary and cultural criticism.

In *A Gathering of Fugitives* Trilling argues that "in complex lives, morality does in some part determine destiny; in most lives it does not."[43] The suggestion that straightforward (by which I suppose he means nonreflective) lives are not shaped by moral factors is surely just wrong. Further, the notion of morality as a determinant of destiny clearly needs elaboration. More of this in a moment. But if we accept—as we surely must—that moral discernment is to some degree assisted by moral reflectiveness and intentionality, then Trilling's commitment to what might rather vaguely be termed the *culture of the self* makes sense. His affirmation of this culture takes both general and specific forms. He complains that modernity has "lost the *mystique* of the self,"[44] and his account of Romanticism and the Enlightenment cherishes those in whose writing this mystique is profoundly apparent: principally Wordsworth, Rousseau, and Keats. Of the former he says, wonderfully I think, that he was "haunted by the mysterious fact that he existed";[45] he is, as I have said, fascinated by Rousseau's notion of a "sentiment of being" that infuses the self with an effortless, prereflective grasp of its own existence, and his great essay on Keats's letters in *The Opposing Self* construes the young poet as a man whose sense of "attachment," both to himself and to "reality" in general,[46] is unusually, perhaps uniquely, strong.

Great literature, then, can convey the salving mystique of the self. However, mystique is less a particular set of qualities than an inducement imaginatively to invest the mysterious self with particular qualities, and each writer will fashion the self after his or her own passions, fears, and predilections. Moreover, their visions of self can vary from text to text. Wordsworth's sense of the self's mystique impels him to invest the Leech Gatherer with a kind of elemental, prereflective selfhood; yet the self of *The Prelude* is supremely inquiring and self-conscious. So too of course is the self of Rousseau's *Confessions*—its agonized self-awareness a far cry from the untroubled immediacy of "the sentiment of being." The Keatsean self is a quicksilver thing, and his notion of "soul-making" is more an activity, or a capacity for an activity, than a set of settled properties. Even these three figures show that what the great literature of the self's mystique conjures is a vast *array* of accounts of the self and, however majestic and fascinating these may be, the reader who takes the issue of her or his own selfhood seriously is confronted with that distinctively modern dilemma of having to *choose* among this vast and often incommensurable array of existential possibilities. Literature can revitalize the sense of the self's mysteriousness, but our choices must ultimately be our own; and such choices involve an exertion of the will.

To put the matter this way is to see why Keats held such particular fascination for Trilling. As Trilling sees it, Keats combines a profound and secure sentiment of his own being with the heroic will to shape a self against a hostile world:

> Negative Capability, the faculty of not having to make up one's mind about everything, depends upon the sense of one's personal identity and is the sign of personal identity. Only the self that is certain of its existence, of its identity, can do without the armor of systematic certainties.

And again:

> The faculty of Negative Capability has yielded doctrine—for the idea of "soul-making," of souls creating themselves in their confrontation of circumstance, is available to Keats's conception only because he has remained with half-knowledge, with the double knowledge of the self and of the world's evil.[47]

Perhaps, as Trilling thinks, the genius can defy the contradictions that beset ordinary mortals; but be this as it may, there is an apparent circularity at work here: soul-making is about choosing a self, and yet Trilling tells us that one can only choose a self if one's self is already securely in place. But if this were the case, why would one bother—or need to bother—to make the choice in the first place? I want to underline two points here. The first is that this conundrum represents a tension that runs deep in Trilling's work: the tension between a notion of a substantial self that chooses, on the one hand, and, on the other, the conception of choices that are made in search of such a self. Second, these two versions of selfhood entail different, and to some extent competing, accounts of the will. On the first, the will is a property or—to recall one of the themes of this study—a possession of, something that belongs to, a relatively settled self; and because the self is settled to this degree, it might seem that the will's capacity for self-transformation is limited. Nevertheless, the choices it makes, the acts of will it performs, are authentic not in the existential sense, but in the way Spender represents centered choices—ones that are made from a being that has a metaphoric "core" of selfhood.[48] On the second version, however, the will is more like the faculty envisaged by Nietzsche and later existentialism: the "I" to which it "belongs" is so notional and thin an entity that "belonging" is a misnomer. The will so conceived is more like a floating, almost unattached, faculty or power that conjures temporary "selves" into "being."

Mark Krupnick, who is rightly troubled by an "ambivalence" in Trilling's work that goes beyond the self-assured play of irony and complexity (Trilling writes in a letter of his own "special indecisiveness"),[49] tracks this ambivalence to a variety of factors, and principally to the problems involved in choosing styles of selfhood. Noting the vast differences between the primordial selfhood of the Leech Gatherer and the drive to self-invention in an American figure like Jay Gatsby, Krupnick suggests that "Trilling never decisively chooses between" such models and that "the result is a pervasive ambivalence about a host of related issues."[50] Again rightly, Krupnick sees this "ambivalence" as an aspect of Trilling's unfolding response to the political and social realities of his day. Like so much else in Trilling's work, it needs to be seen in the context of his flirtation with leftist politics and the later recantation that resulted in his entrenched anti-Communist position; from the 1950s onward it relates also to his misgivings about mass culture.[51] In *The Beginning of the Journey*, Diana Trilling describes how the couple was instructed in the ways of Marxist dialectic by Sidney Hook while at Yaddo, an artists' and writers' retreat in Saratoga, in 1931 (pp. 176-86). At the time nothing was known about the realities of Stalinism, and their commitment to something like historical materialism lasted until the show trials of the late thirties. As Krupnick notes, by the time Lionel published his study of Arnold in 1939, the dialectic in his work had undergone a mutation into something more like a form of immensely sophisticated intellectual equivocation—a holding of competing forces and options in a state of unresolved tension. The old Marxist model of struggle-synthesis-struggle-synthesis had disappeared from his writing for good; so too, as I have argued, had the precursor Hegelian model in which contradiction and synthesis eventually issue in the unconditioned. Much of what Trilling now commends to his readers—Arnoldian "free play," Forster's fuguelike orchestration of countervailing themes and tendencies, the unresolved tensions of moral realism, the anti-Stalinist open-endedness of the "Liberal Imagination"—reflects a commitment (in Krupnick's words) to "stasis," "equilibrium," and "willing suspended,"[52] and a withdrawal from direct political engagement. Here Trilling parts company with many of the other New York Jewish intellectuals with whom his name is often associated. Their styles remained more dialectical, more blunt—as indeed did Diana's own style. Krupnick believes that the results of this eschewal of the dialectic for Trilling's practice as a "cultural critic" were ultimately deleterious.[53] He may well be right. But I am less concerned with this dimension of Trilling's work than with his account of the will; and here I want to argue that his post-thirties fascination with states of apparent disengagement is central to the distinctive intellectual contribution he made.

This brings us back to the complex issue of choosing a self. Krupnick says that Trilling's "voluntarism has a strongly aesthetic coloration. He envisions the self defining itself not by its choice of actions but by its choice in styles of selfhood."[54] It's certainly true that Trilling sets a good deal of store by the style of the self in this sense. In the famous essay "Manners, Morals and the Novel," he argues that in the great and normative tradition of the European novel, "manners make men";[55] the late *Sincerity and Authenticity* betrays (*expresses* would be too strong a word) a preference for "sincerity," which aligns self with culturally given styles or accounts of identity, over the search for unconditioned "authenticity"[56]—for who we "really" are when cultural modes of definition are removed; and in an early essay (quoted by Krupnick) he poses this rhetorical question: "Is not the political choice fundamentally a choice of personal quality?"[57] The two statements aren't identical: the first suggests that "manners"—the external trappings of the self that we present to the world—are expressive of a "true" inner self; the second that the inner self, which reflects our broad philosophical disposition toward the world, is the product of a choice, the choice of "personal quality." Combined, the statements suggest that, at least to some considerable extent, we choose to be who we are, and that who we thus become can be discerned from the way we present ourselves to the world. Krupnick's gloss on the position suggests a strong distinction between "actions" and choosing a self. Such a distinction is essentially foreign to Trilling's work; it is also, I want to suggest, an unhelpfully blunt distinction. The choice of a self, if (or to the extent that) it can be effected, is no mean feat. Given the array of forces that threaten to shape and determine us, it is an astonishing thing to be able to script one's own being. To do so effectively requires a special kind of exertion of the will: a kind that calls on the greatest powers that the will possesses, and on a high degree of discernment and deliberation in choosing among options that culture makes available. Such an activity surely deserves to be termed an (*intentional*) *action,* even if its trajectory is inward, toward the beingness of the self, rather than outward in the form of interventions in the world. To withhold the term "action" in such cases is to repeat the behaviorist mistake of reducing action to external behavioral manifestation. This is not to say, as Trilling wants at times to do, that choosing a self necessarily warrants the appellation *political;* but then neither should "politics" be seen, as Krupnick tends to see it, as a synonym for "action."

At any rate, Trilling sees the choosing of the self as an act of will, and as one that is to some extent achievable. It can only be achievable "to some extent" because like all other acts of will it is constrained; it goes on in an ineluctably conditioned world. The constraints are partly cultural—he never denies that cultural ideology will set some limits to "soul-making"; they are also personal in the sense that one's psychological history will set some parameters for and limits to self-fashioning; and very importantly, there are biological constraints as well. Here Trilling's account of Freud is revealing and important. He sees Freud (as he sees himself) as writing within the great Western tragic tradition that posits "some meaningful relation between free will and necessity."[58] Like others in that tradition, Freud takes as one of his "tasks" the challenge "to define the borders of necessity in order to establish the realm of freedom."[59] Trilling defends Freud against the charge of determinism, though he makes the common defense by inference from the practice of psychoanalysis rather than mounting a philosophical case: "The whole intention of psychoanalysis . . . is to free the soul from bondage to necessities that do not actually exist so that it may effectually confront those that do exist."[60] In such passages Freud emerges as a proponent of the (conditioned) will. Elsewhere, however, in his later writings, Trilling lays heavy emphasis on the biological. In the great essay "Freud: Within and Beyond Culture," he argues that "culture is not all-powerful"; that "beyond the reach of cultural control . . . this residue of human quality, elemental as it may be, serves to bring culture itself under self-criticism and keeps it from being absolute."[61] Given his general position, this affirmation of biology may seem an odd—and indeed a high-risk—move, but his motives are clear: in setting limits to culture's construction of the self, he affirms the self's powers to reflect on its cultural conditioning and if necessary to refuse and to change that conditioning; indeed to change culture itself. This, a version of what Anthony Giddens calls *recursive self-monitoring,* is after all one of the main missions of criticism. Trilling's position implies a relationship of mutual entailment between culture-resisting margins of selfhood and the capacity for critical reflection, but he does not justify this implication. There is no obvious reason to assume that biological determination of aspects of the self will produce, or be associated with, the capacity for critical reflection. But, like so many of his tactical shifts, this one is a "reactive" response—in this instance, a response to totalitarian fantasies about the cultural usurpation of the self, and to behaviorist and constructivist determinisms that allow the self no margin of self-determination, of free will. Trilling wants to say that the biological "human quality" is associated with the existence of the will. We can't be more precise than this because he isn't: the implied structural account of the self here doesn't say whether the will is *of* that "human quality," or merely able to function because that "quality" leaves a space that culture can't invade.

In the same essay Trilling, speaking of the conviction that the self possesses "a hard, irreducible, stubborn core of biological urgency," proclaims it a "liberating idea."[62] The word "urgency" is clearly carefully chosen, yet it provides one of many instances in which Trilling's alluringly subtle style can seem evasive, or at least insufficiently precise. The notion of a biologically encoded "urgency" or energy sounds reminiscent of Schopenhauer and Nietzsche, but so far as one can generalize about Trilling's position, it does not really accord with such views. He is a rationalist who affirms the existence of the critical faculties and—what is equally important—the capacity of such faculties to guide the enlightened will. He is no proponent of Schopenhauerian blind striving. At times he comes close to a Will as Intellectual Preference position on the will: he regrets that modernity isn't more sympathetic to Aristotle's belief that the will is directed by reason;[63] he says that Blake, Whitman, and Lawrence knew that "what begins as an act of will grows to be an act of intelligence";[64] and the last paragraph of *The Liberal Imagination* argues that we must learn to "think of ideas as living things, inescapably connected with our wills and desires, and susceptible of growth and development by their very nature."[65] For rationality to operate in this way, there must indeed be a "space" that culture cannot invade; but this is a very sketchy metaphor. What he really wants to say, and what is much more informative, is that "the inner life is real"[66] and that this dimension contains, or perhaps *is,* an "internal, meditative, slowly-precipitating part of" the self.[67] It is significant that this marvelous phrase appears in his first published book, the study of Matthew Arnold, because, as I have argued, Trilling's greatest and most lasting contribution is to have affirmed the existence of this "part" of the self, to have rendered it in a critical and fictional prose that can at times attain the suggestiveness of meditative poetry, to have affirmed complex literature's important cultural role in representing this dimension of the self, and to have insisted that the will has its home and proceeds from this inner sanctum of the individual. Trilling's "will," then, unlike Skinner's or Ryle's, has a concealed but still partially knowable inner dimension; unlike Nietzsche's conception, Trilling sees the will as part of a continuum that begins in meditation, reflection, deliberation, and issues—but only in some cases—in outwardly visible "actions." Like Kant's, this conception allows rationality an important part to play for the will and sees the will as essentially an ethical phenomenon (more of this in a moment), though Trilling allows more room for affective dimensions like "desires" than does Kant.

How and in what ways one "owns" this will is, as I have suggested, not clear in Trilling's account, but the existence of the will he never doubts.

We need to think of will in Trilling not only as a faculty that resides within the self, but also as a certain kind of process that *connects* the self with that faculty in a certain way. His admiration for Forster springs partly from that writer's notion and representation of "the relaxed will"[68]—in other words, a kind of willing that, like Laskell's in the presence of the rose, is receptive rather than active, subtle rather than steely (though he does also find in Forster a "whim of iron"),[69] meditative rather than instrumental. His disinclination to drive a firm distinction between slow precipitation and action is clear in his comment that Wordsworth's notion of "'wise passiveness' is of course an activity."[70] Some of his greatest readings of novels also focus on places in which the will emerges as a gentle, internal, even recessive thing. He is fascinated by Dickens's Clennam in *Little Dorrit* whose first words include the claim: "'I have no will.'" Like Laskell, Clennam is a man "in middle life," the middle of the journey, who finds himself puzzled by the condition—and the social expectations—of the will. He is in some ways the quintessential fictional representation of Trilling's sense of self. After announcing that he no longer has a will, however, Clennam continues: "'That is to say,'—he coloured a little,—'next to none that I can put in action now'";[71] in other words, the will is active even if instrumentally constrained. Trilling's gloss on the character is consistent with these qualifications:

> Some grace—it is, of course, the secret of his birth, of his being really a child of love and art—has kept Arthur Clennam from responding to the will of his mother with a bitter, clenched will of his own. The alternative he has chosen has not, contrary to his declaration, left him no will at all. He has by no means been robbed of his ethical will, he can exert energy to help others . . .[72]

Unlike Melville's Bartleby, this is not a case of "the will in its ultimate fatigue."[73] In Trilling's account, Clennam in a sense makes two choices: one, the choice not to respond to his mother's diseased will with a "clenched will" of his own; the other, to exert the more gentle, less instrumental, will that he has chosen to have in the interests of others. One choice is of a modality of the will that thenceforth infuses whatever he does; the other is a particular exercise, or series of exercises, of the will so chosen and constituted. Through this process Clennam forges a connection between will and self, and between self and the acts it wills. Clennam (the argument implicitly runs) cannot not have a will; he must make that choice of mode, and the mode he chooses is intrinsically ethical: it is directed toward the well-being of others, it subordinates self to the needs of those others, and it has that "slowly precipitating" internality that Trilling sees as a necessary condition of the moral agent. This is a notion of will as moved by and expressive of love—the notion I have termed Heart, Affection, and Will. There is a by now familiar unanswered question in all of this: in virtue of what "personal quality" does Clennam make that inaugurating choice of mode? As I have argued, there can be no simple answer to this question save to say that human beings possess propensities to both good and evil and, within certain constraints, the freedom to choose (at least in part) rationally between these propensities. This kind of choosing goes on within the shifting and often scarcely discernible space that neither culture nor biology can subjugate. Clennam chooses the good—indeed the Good Life as Aristotle understands it. In so doing he does with respect to his mother what, in a passage admired by Freud and quoted by Trilling, Goethe enjoins his readers to do with respect to their fathers (here meaning one's inheritance in general): "'What you have inherited from your fathers, truly possess it so as to make it your very own.'"[74] Understood in this way (and I find Trilling's reading entirely persuasive), Clennam exemplifies the "complex" life in which "morality determines destiny." Indeed we are now better placed to see what Trilling means by this intriguing formulation. It is clear that, not withstanding the almost provocative use of the word "determines," his is not a deterministic statement. In "complex lives" morality can to some extent determine what happens in a person's life, but "morality" in the sense that the term is used here, is a property of a *moral agent,* and this entails that such a person's moral orientation is a consequence of articulable *choice,* of rationally electing among available cultural models to be a certain kind of (ethical) self. It also entails that having exercised the freedom to be such a person, freedom (albeit freedom in a constraining context) persists as an abiding condition for subsequent moral choices. To the extent that the moral agent so conceived shapes her or his life-plot through a choice of moral orientation, and through subsequent moral choices, she or he *transforms "destiny" into a story of her or his own making.* That is, "destiny" ceases to be a fate imposed from without and becomes a co-creation of self and circumstance.

Goethe's notion of possession is clearly not, then, a kind of grasping or coveting; it is more like an act of assimilation in which the receptive self concedes the reality of the past (both psychological and biological), lets it in, then allows the "relaxed will" to bring its combined subtleties of feeling, intellection, and understanding to bear upon it. When, and only when, that past has been possessed in this way, the will, informed by a deep intuitive sense of the genesis and nature of this self, may confer upon it the grace of novelty—the status of the self that is both product of a past and producer of an identity in which the materials of the past converge and are transformed in an unprecedented way. The will is author of the self's particularity, but it works with the already-given. It is a dimension of "sincerity" rather than of "authenticity." It is this kind of process that gives birth to a self for which morality is determinative of the will. Such a picture hovers somewhere between philosophical psychology and mysticism. It tries to capture in language and metaphor what Trilling calls "awareness of the will in its beautiful circuit of thought and desire."[75] He would be the first to claim—

along with Hume, Locke, and so many others—that, finally, this cannot be done. At least not in discursive prose. However, it is done best, and done with remarkable subtlety, in fine literature. He says that the rendering of this "beautiful circuit" of the will has been "the peculiar property of the novel";[76] and in another passage he uses the metaphor of the "emotional space in the human mind" and goes on to refer to "the interplay between free will and circumstance upon which all literature depends."[77] Little wonder that the will is a "signal term" in Lionel Trilling's criticism.

But he doesn't think of literary art as merely a mode of representation, as something that can describe the inner worlds of moral life in superior ways. He also sees it, as his critical apprenticeship in Arnold would incline him to do, as a mode of deliverance—something that has the capacity to remove us from the coercive claims of the world and to take us to a place where the will can be at ease. Such a view has a long and honorable history, a history that verges in places on mysticism. It's no accident that early in *Matthew Arnold* Trilling quotes Schopenhauer at length. The passage contrasts "subjective" states that are directed "to the will" with "objective" ones that are self-transcending. Here is a part of what Trilling quotes:

> "Thus genius is the faculty of continuing in the state of pure perception, of losing oneself in perception, and of enlisting in this service the knowledge which originally existed only for the service of the will; that is to say, genius is the power of leaving one's own interests, wishes, and aims entirely out of sight, thus of entirely renouncing one's own personality for a time, so as to remain *pure knowing subject,* clear vision of the world . . ."[78]

So conceived, genius finds expression in the work of art and so creates something that not only represents modalities of the will, but also schools the reader's will in the modes of relaxed contemplation. Trilling asks of art that it do both of these things—render the conditions and modalities of the will in the finest possible ways, and refine the condition of the reader's will through the transcendence that great literature can bring.

In general Diana Trilling's views about the will closely resemble those of her husband. However, to turn from his comments about it to hers is to register a sharp difference in tone. While his affirmations of the "Liberal Imagination" emerge from delicate shadings of suggestion, qualification, and equivocation, her style is altogether more blunt. It is virtually inconceivable that the following assertion from *We Must March My Darlings* could have come from his pen: "No one can call himself a liberal who is not an anti-Communist."[79] It may indeed be that Lionel would have concurred with such a sentiment; the point is that his less pressing endowment of the will to power would not have compelled him to put it on the public record. Qua public intellectual, her world is more black-and-white than his. As she concedes in that letter about her "phallicism," people tend to be saints or sinners in her eyes. One such saint was President Kennedy, whom the Trillings both met during a visit to the White House. Diana was to describe the occasion in near-ecstatic terms in a report that was only published after her death.[80] But the following comment about Kennedy—made in reference to the president's habit of vacationing in the traditional family compound at Hyannis Port rather than in some newly chosen, self-scripting location—shows how deeply she shares Lionel's view about the unconditioned: the president's behavior suggests that "a man is truly free only when he is released from the search for an unconditioned selfhood."[81] Like Lionel's, her notion of freedom is one that can only exist within—and against—a constraining context: "Far from believing that the self is best comprehended or realized apart from society, I am of the older opinion that it is society which provides the self with its best possibilities of ascendancy, even of transcendence."[82] I have argued that transcendence seems to have been largely beyond her, but "ascendancy," by which I take her to mean taking the dominant hand in one's own destiny, was what she sought through all those years of struggle and analysis; and "ascendancy," she insists, requires that we make choices: "It is *the* progressive fallacy of our time to suppose that we can rationalize all of life's anomalies. The notion that life demands choice and that choice inevitably implies sacrifice is something which only the religious intelligence seems, at the moment, willing to entertain."[83]

I want to track this sentiment into her literary criticism in a moment, but consider, first, this reflection upon her marriage from the autobiography:

> In the actual conduct of our lives, the two of us, in fact, silently accepted the premise that my first responsibility was to my home and family. Had this been put in words, I daresay that even as far back as the thirties and forties I would have protested it. But so long as it was not formulated, I was able to deceive myself that it was as a matter of free will and competence that I took on the tasks of the home—they were easier for me to do than they would have been for Lionel and I was better at them. (p. 21)

What are we to make of this avowal of self-deception? It's not said as a criticism of Lionel, who, according to her, was more attentive to household chores than most men of his day; nor, though it is offered as a reflection on her gender conditioning ("the way that nice girls were raised" [p. 21]), is it said in anger against conventional gender expectations. No doubt there is a hint of regret and resentment, but the passage is primarily drawing attention to something that is for her positive, necessary, an inevitable feature of social life. That something is the capacity to make accommodations as part of a certain trade-off between self and the code. The trade-off is roughly this: In return for society's provision of the structures that offer the self "its best possibilities of ascendancy, even of transcendence," I will use my intellectual faculties, including even my capacity for

dissimulation, to trick my will into thinking that the way I live is the consequence of a freely chosen mode of existence. In so doing I don't surrender the belief that the will is free, nor the principle that insists on my right to exercise that
freedom. I simply misrepresent to my will the extent of the constraints under
which, in this instance, I am actually operating. Sartre and Beauvoir would call
this bad faith—self-deception motivated by the fear of freedom. Postmodern
theories like Althusser's would see in it the insidious capacity of ideology to enlist the imagination in stories about the self's relation to the world that misrepresent that relation and that conceal the thwarting of "desire" (often their de
facto word for *will*), which is associated with ideologically saturated subjectivity. But this isn't what Diana Trilling means; it isn't what her brand of liberalism
says. What her brand says is that just as we have no freedom without constraint,
so we have no freedom without the facilitating structures of a cultural order. I've
argued that in fetishizing constraint, power, and ideology, postmodern theory
has all but eclipsed the notion of facilitation and the necessarily dialectical relation between constraint and freedom. Though they don't put it this way, the
Trillings are on the side of those like Anthony Giddens and Charles Taylor who
posit a reflexive relationship between agency and social structure. For the passage
above, and indeed for the totality of the Trillings' work, we need to expand the
notion of structure to include a repertoire of structurally interrelated models of
self that both help to shape this particular self and enable it to make choices that
shape its own being.

As an essayist and reviewer, Diana Trilling urges that the condition of the will
be seen not in terms of a stark opposition between free will and determinism,
but in terms of a spectrum that allows for the shades of reciprocal relation that
actually characterize most agents' lives within cultural systems. Here is a typical
passage from a review of 1948:

> The problem [of free will and determinism] is of course a very complex one.
> Obviously, in standing against an absolute of determinism, I do not mean to
> close out all social or personal causality. I do ask, however, for some degree of
> mediation between the extremes of causality and freedom.[84]

Again: "No matter how bad the dominant social tendencies of our time, the creative will of the individual is not always at their mercy."[85] Like Lionel, she reacts
against what she sees as late modernity's condition of being "paralyzed in will,"[86]
and she is critical of literature that seems to her to replicate this condition: Roth's
Portnoy's Complaint, where determinism seems to offer anger as the only choice
open to the victim of his conditioning;[87] by contrast she prefers the "non-de-
terministic view of life," which she identifies as more British in tendency. She
finds this in J. R. Ackerley's poignant but understated autobiography, *My Father
and Myself,* because unlike Roth's book it "proposes . . . the not inconsiderable
virtues of courage, kindliness, responsibility"[88]—in other words, it is infused

with a belief in the ethical efficacy of the will; a belief that is both a necessary and a sufficient condition for the exercise of the will as an ethical faculty.

This criticism of Roth is interesting in another and related respect. Her impatience with fatalism and its neglect of the will is reminiscent of William James, and it applies not only to individuals but to social groups as well. In another comment that erodes the distinction between notions of destiny and self-determination, she says that even minority groups have "responsibility for their own destinies,"[89] and this includes Jews and Jewish writers. Her criticism of Roth is consistent with, for instance, her reservations about Saul Bellow's *Dangling Man*, where pessimism is unaccompanied by the "grandeur" that she requires of art.[90] Her markedly unsentimental attitude toward Judaism is I think fundamental to her disposition as a cultural critic: her impatience with modernist pessimism seems to spring in significant degree from her ambivalent reaction to what she saw as the rather bruising and self-pitying nature of the New York Jewish literary milieu she moved in. Lionel's like-minded reservations about modernism do not seem to be so obviously influenced in this way. His attitude to Judaism was typically ambivalent, but he began his publication career in the *Menorah Journal*, and there is a kind of apologetic curiosity about Judaism in some of his essays—most notably "Wordsworth and the Rabbis" in *The Opposing Self*—that finds no parallel in Diana's work. *The Beginning of the Journey* ends with a moving but still highly ambivalent tribute to the "strange difficult ungenerous unreliable unkind and not always honest people who created the world in which Lionel and I shared, and to which we tried to contribute" (p. 420). And she goes on to name many of the prominent Jews among them (the group of course included many distinguished non-Jewish intellectuals): Elliot Cohen, Philip Rahv, Irving Howe, and others.

Most of those on the list are men. Earlier in the book she complains of Elliot Cohen's "suffocating" editorial "will" (p. 92) at the *Menorah Journal,* and throughout she gives the impression of having been bruised by the tough and disingenuous environment that such men created. Her focus on the gendering of this world, and of the styles of masculinity that characterized and shaped it, is one of the great fascinations of *The Beginning of the Journey,* it also provides the primary context within which we receive and assess her account of Lionel. That context in turn reflects one of her major, if often implicit, themes as a literary and cultural critic: the relationship between masculinity and the will. Her views about this are particularly apparent in her commentary on three authors: Hemingway, D. H. Lawrence (she edited an anthology of his writing and a selection of his letters),[91] and her friend and sometime combatant Norman Mailer. Of course, each of these is associated, at least in the popular mind, not just with masculinity but also virility; and Diana Trilling's interest in the masculine will often focuses on the libidinal dimension.

I will suggest in the next section that she had a particular reason for being preoccupied with Hemingway. In an essay on Mailer, she characterizes Hemingway as a good and sometimes great writer who developed a style that at its best could evoke the "areas of retirement and indecision and even discordance"[92] of feeling that characterize complex sensibility. All too often, however, he gives the impression that it is through violent activities that "man confirms his virility"—an "unhealthy confusion of manliness with brutality."[93] Lawrence, the author to whom she devoted more words than any other, is a different story. Like Henry Miller and Mailer, he is "concerned with the body as the gateway to heaven,"[94] but this doesn't mean that he is a proselytizer of pleasure. On the contrary, "Lawrence's erotic manifesto had little or nothing to do with the investigation of pleasure, everything to do with the deep connections of body and spirit and the subtle resonances of love."[95] Lawrentian sexuality, then, is of the realm of the conditioned: it isn't about the pursuit of unlimited narcissistic pleasure: "The sexuality for which Lawrence spoke was nothing if not conditioned, and not merely by the full-scale emotions which he insisted upon both as its source and justification but also by the larger social purpose to which he thought sexuality must minister."[96] She is more ambivalent about Mailer than about Hemingway, though she can be quick to Mailer's defense, even likening his attitude to sexuality to Lawrence's: "For Mailer, as for Lawrence, sexual activity is never its own justification; its good is measured by the quality of the emotions it produces or expresses."[97] And she further links the two writers by alluding to Lawrence's famous remark about freedom being a mere rattling of chains in this endorsement of Mailer's depiction of Hollywood sexuality in *The Deer Park*:

> The inhabitants of Mailer's Hollywood are wracked by a fever without cure; in their freedom from conventional sexual restraint there sounds the rattling of the chains of a bondage as awful as that of the Army [in *The Naked and the Dead*]. Only love and tenderness, only the terrible self-denying imperatives of feeling can release these victims from the tyranny of their unimpeded sexual compulsions . . .[98]

Mailer, she thinks, poses with particular urgency the "ultimate pressing question of our time," namely: "Where do we, where shall we, where can we derive our moral sanctions—from a failing tradition or from the wild free impulses of our racial infancy, from the Ego or the Id?"[99] Yet in the same essay she rejects Mailer's hipsterism as a homegrown species of existentialism hell-bent on the pursuit of the unconditioned.[100]

If these three writers highlight the problem of modernity's "moral sanctions," they also raise a related issue that exercised Lionel Trilling: the relationship between body and culture in general and the consequences of this relation for the will. In a remarkable essay on Marilyn Monroe, Diana Trilling sees the recently deceased actress as "a biological victim"[101]—as someone who, with the aid of her sex-obsessed culture, was essentially destroyed by the great bio-

logical endowment of her apparent sexuality. The notion that one can be a victim of one's own libidinal energies recurs in Diana's writing—as in the illusory
freedom of Mailer's imprisoned Hollywood characters of lust. As I have argued, the intellectual rationale for this view is that mere lust is unconditioned,
a drive that lacks the constraining entailments that are needed for true human
fulfillment. No doubt there are more personal factors at work in the sexual attitudes of this woman who carried a childhood fear of the "hidden intimacies
of the body" into adult life, and who was so appalled to learn of Frieda
Lawrence's marital infidelities that she complained that in everything he wrote
Lawrence sought to "deceive us that he wrote from within the boundaries of a
monogamous marriage."[102]

IV. Lacking the Will to Be Hemingway: Diana Trilling on Lionel Trilling

How is it, then, that she can say of Lionel: "I could have wished him to have a
thousand mistresses were this to have released him from the constraints upon
him as a writer of fiction. I would willingly have been his female Leporello and
sung his conquests" (p. 373). Part of the answer lies in that word "constraints"
because for Lionel Trilling, as for most of us, constraints were easier to commend
in principle than to tolerate in practice. Great and internationally renowned
critic that he was, Lionel wanted above all else to be a novelist, with all the promise this held—at least in his mind—for a life in the realm of the unconditioned.
One of the most arresting things about *The Beginning of the Journey* is Diana's
determination to lay bare the part of Lionel that longed for the unconditioned
and that silently raged against the terms on which the world had permitted him
success. Painfully she asks:

> Did his friends and colleagues have no hint of how deeply he scorned the very
> qualities of character—his quiet, his moderation, his gentle reasonableness—
> for which he was most admired in his lifetime and which have been most cel-
> ebrated since his death? (pp. 372–73)

At this distance it is hard to know the answer to her question, but my impression is that, no, his friends and colleagues had very little hint of such things, little sense that in "the dark recesses of his heart where unhappiness was so often
his companion, he was contemptuous of everything in his life which was dedicated to seriousness and responsibility" (p. 372). Quentin Anderson, Trilling's
former student, colleague, and friend, says that these passages came as something of a surprise to him, but agrees that "Lionel didn't want to be known for
his amenity alone."[103] In conversation, James Trilling also evinces surprise, saying that such deep resentments and frustrations were not apparent to him
(though his article about his father presents Lionel as a repressed man who re-

sented the constraints that were associated with this repression).[104] Clearly, if Diana is right about this, it shows Lionel's work—not least his writing about the will—in a different, though by no means a diminished, light. His work would now need to be seen, at least in part, as an act of compensation for the unease that arose from the stultification of his own will. But one wants corroborating evidence before jumping to such conclusions.

The evidence Diana presents is striking indeed. She quotes two published excerpts from Lionel's notebooks, both of them about Hemingway. The first, written in 1933, describes a letter he has seen from Hemingway to Clifton Fadiman:

> "A crazy letter, written when he was drunk—self-revealing, arrogant, scared, trivial, absurd: yet felt from reading it how right such a man is compared to the 'good minds' of my university life—how he will produce and mean something to the world ... how his life which he could expose without dignity and which is anarchic and 'childish' is a better life than anyone I know could live, and right for his job. And how far-far-far I am going from being a writer—and how less and less I have the material and the mind and the will." (pp. 369–70)

Lionel was twenty-eight at the time and had published several short stories. Fourteen years later he was to publish *The Middle of the Journey* to considerable critical acclaim. But this was to be his only novel and eventually he became a critic but not a writer, just as he had feared. And he feared this would happen not primarily because he lacked talent (though this was part of it), but because he lacked the "will" to be a Hemingway.[105] Diana then quotes a passage from Lionel's notebooks written twenty-eight years later, in 1961. It is about Hemingway's death:

> "Death of Ernest Hemingway. Except Lawrence's 32 years ago, no writer's death has moved me as much—who would suppose how much he haunted me? How much he existed in my mind—as a reproach? He was the only writer of our time I envied. I respected him in his most foolish postures and in his worst work (except *The Old Man and the Sea*)." (p. 371)

Diana notes that the reference to Lawrence is unsurprising given his stature as a writer, but that it is harder to understand why Lionel should have been so "haunted" by Hemingway. Her explanation is that "Hemingway pre-eminently stood for what he [Lionel] had himself sacrificed in his life and work. In Freudian terms, Hemingway represented the triumph of id over superego, with the resultant release of his creative powers" (p. 371). It's of course typical of Diana that her understanding of Lionel should be mediated by Freud, and interesting that in order to legitimate her own interpretation of Lionel's attitude toward Hemingway, she invokes an article by Louis P. Simpson that appeared in an issue of *Partisan Review* containing the notebook excerpts.[106] Simpson's view is that Lionel desired but could not seize the bohemian life.

At this point we need to remind ourselves that autobiographers, too, write under various "constraints," and that intellectual autobiographers like Diana Trilling often encounter a particular species of constraint in which ethical beliefs about how a life should be lived come into conflict with their feelings about particular individuals with whom they have shared their lives. Qua intellectual and cultural commentator, Diana is clear about her answer to the question I quoted in the last section: "Where do we, where shall we, where can we derive our moral sanctions—from a failing tradition or from the wild free impulses of our racial infancy, from the Ego or the Id?" Her answer is: from the ego, and in answering thus, the ego represents not only the principle of psychic organization, but also of historico-cultural organization whereby the individual self attains appropriate and functional relations with the world beyond it, including the world of "tradition." Diana (like Lionel) wants criticism to reaffirm and, where necessary, to reconstruct that tradition so that it is availing, rather than "failing," for modern life. But when Diana, confirmed in her Freudian way of seeing, looks back at Lionel and says that, contra Hemingway, Lionel is a victim of the superego's conquest of the id, she cannot blithely repose in her answer to the larger cultural question. It is simply (one supposes) too painful to do so—to look back and say that one's partner's suffering was acceptable because it conformed to one's prescription for general cultural well-being. Certainly Diana's generational (and Jewish) conditioning as a woman who enjoyed "living by deference to the needs of those one loves" doesn't allow her to do this. She'd rather have been his "female Leporello and sung his conquests"—or so she thinks.

Her account of the condition of Lionel's will can't be disinterested, and it is the source of various tensions and inconsistencies. One of these has major implications. Lionel, we recall, commends the "relaxed will" that takes its counsel from a "slowly precipitating part" of the self. This "part" is characterized by a form of intelligence in which rationality is infused with emotional subtlety. In her literary and cultural criticism, Diana too embraces this view. However, her deeply Freudian account of Lionel and his will is very different in emphasis. This reading construes Lionel's commitment to the ethos of the "relaxed will" as the product of repression. On this view, the commitment loses much of its status as ethical vision and is reconfigured as a symptom. Moreover, the Diana who says that she'd "willingly" have been Lionel's Leporello if it would have enabled him to write more novels is essentially giving permission to the Hemingwayesque will that Lionel has repressed, and thereby to the Nietzschean notion of will—the will to power, Will as Dynamic Power—that, qua intellectuals, both she and Lionel rejected. It is one of the great ironies of *The Beginning of the Journey* that in this sense it switches allegiance away from the very conception of will and its relation to culture that it sets out to reaffirm.

Another tension concerns the condition that Lionel's will was in fact in, because although Diana is prone to see it as a thwarted will, she also believes that he was "a good custodian of his strengths"—that, as an intellectual and a professional man, he in fact put his will to good use in developing such powers as he possessed. Among the powers he did *not* possess, she believes, was high-order literary creativity: "Lionel lacked the genius of a Joyce to bring the traditional novel into alignment with the demands of our atomizing and sterilizing century" (p. 395). Here he was always going to have to compromise. Nevertheless, she thinks that he applied his will to very good effect in achieving a "subversion of his upbringing." Good Freudian that she is, she provides a lot of information about this background. She presents the young Lionel as a kind of victim of love—or at least a kind of Jewish American parental mollycoddling: his father fusses over imagined physical threats to the boy, his mother explains that Lionel was such a beautiful baby that a sign had to be posted on his baby carriage: "PLEASE DON'T KISS THE BABY" (p. 36), and in general he was denied normal childhood engagement with the world. The parental marriage was never close and became distressingly distant as time went on. The mother was quite forceful, the father underconfident. In the draft pages of the autobiography that Lionel had commenced shortly before his death, there are multiple attempts to get started, each beginning with the observation that his father gave up his business as a tailor when Lionel was born because he did not want him to be the son of a tailor.[107] He then started a business making men's fur-lined coats, but the venture failed through lack of business acumen and the ravages of the Depression. Thereafter he became increasingly depressed, prone to violent outbursts of temper, hypochondriacal, and paranoid. Like Stephen Spender and Arthur Koestler, Lionel was "maddened by his father's unreality" (p. 32); like them he was a reactive son whose choice of life task was powerfully but ambivalently shaped by the untenable paternal model. Lionel becomes an intellectual; more than this, his intellectuality was to be markedly anglicized in character, less influenced by his eastern European Jewish heritage than that of most of his New York intellectual colleagues. Diana says that "Lionel's life was dangerously dedicated to being as unlike his father as possible" (p. 34). When David Trilling died in 1943, Lionel was left at the age of thirty-seven to support his mother and sister, as well as Diana and himself. He did so uncomplainingly for many years. According to Diana, his mother, Fanny, was more forceful and cultured than his father; yet throughout his life Lionel harbored what Diana saw as a "hard primitive core of hostility" (p. 253) toward her. This was a matter of great moment for Diana, in part because she thought this hostility to a woman she came to like and admire unwarranted; but more particularly because she saw in this rage the genesis of the Lionel's "annihilating verbal assaults" upon her.

Insofar as one can generalize about the complex play of insight, speculation, and emotion that make up Diana's portrait of Lionel, it is probably fair to say that she puts the emphasis upon his emancipation from, rather than on his victimization by, his childhood. But even here the account is often ambiguous:

"His essential character was undamaged by the extravagances of his upbringing. He was apparently able to take from his family the best of its intention for him and to discard the absurdities" (p. 38). To what extent can his transcendence of what was wrong in his childhood be imputed to an act of will? To say that "his essential character was undamaged" might suggest that he survived by good grace or good genetic luck; but the verb "discard" implies a more active response—a conscious and or instinctively wise sifting of the past and a willed process of selection whereby what can be used is retained and the rest dispensed with. So perceived, Lionel was adept at finding what David Reisman, a sociologist he much admired, calls "the useable past."[108] This is consistent with being "a good custodian of one's strengths"—it is also, of course, what the literary critic, at least as the Trillings conceived this person, does: she or he too is a custodian of those texts of value that have been passed on by the tradition; but she or he also actively engages in reconstituting that tradition by arguing for the retention of what is still relevant and fine, and the rejection of that which seems no longer of use or value.

"His essential character was undamaged" has a further set of possible implications, but they are implications of a kind that Diana does not take up. In order to put the usable past to use, it may be that one's will needs to be essentially undamaged by the unusable, destructive aspects of that past. And by will in this context I mean more than striving; I mean the prudent, discerning activity of a volition informed by a combination of rational deliberation and feeling. I think this is basically what Diana means to say about Lionel's powers of growth and survival, and her account of him is compelling in this respect. In this she has his own testimony, written at the time when he had to overturn a decision not to grant him tenure at Columbia. She speaks of his experiencing "a sudden access of self-esteem" (p. 267) at the time and quotes the following lines (among others) from one of his notebooks (June 1936):

> "Going through change of life and acquiring a new dimension . . . A new emotional response to all things. New response to people, a new tolerance, a new interest. A sense of invulnerability. The result of my successful explosion at Columbia?" (p. 267)

Yet important questions remain. One is conceptual: our understanding of what such survival means will depend in part on what relation we think the will has to the self, to one's "essential character." If we think that it occupies some kind of inviolate psychic space that early trauma or distress cannot readily reach, then we will say that (within reason) victims should be able to overcome, to "subvert," their pasts. But if on the contrary we see the will as woven threadlike through the whole emotional-psychological fabric of one's character, then it is hard to see how that "thread" can remain "undamaged" while the rest is ravaged by circumstance. Then again, we might think in terms of different endowments of will, such that regardless of whether it inhabits an inviolate space or threads its way through all regions of the psyche, some individuals "have" it in greater, more resilient and effective, quantities than others. While it is hard to reconstruct Diana's underlying views about such things, I suspect that, if asked, she would have subscribed to the last of these possibilities and have said that the thread of will in Lionel's psyche was strong by virtue of its natural endowment. He owned a will that was naturally resilient. Like him, she sets great store by biology, and this is roughly what she means by "essential character." But she still insists that each person has a choice about whether to exercise the endowment he or she possesses, and her ethical commendation of Lionel rests on the way, and the extent to which, he took up this challenge.

What then of the Lionel who wanted but lacked the will to be a Hemingway; or of the man whose past took such hold that he launched excoriating "verbal assaults" upon his wife several times a year? The question is never really adequately answered in *The Beginning of the Journey.* As I have said, such uncertainties are hardly surprising; but certainly Diana provides clues along with her Freudian sense of how clues ought to be pressed into interpretive service. It would seem that, to invoke again the metaphor of will as dwelling in a psychic space, culture did indeed "invade" this space in Lionel, wise though he was in so many ways, and that the invasion was effected through the medium of what we might call the "Hemingway principle." So that Lionel Trilling, who seemed to most people so superlatively adapted to the conditioned life, in fact harbored a dimension of will that had been emboldened to despise and want to transcend such a life. He wanted to possess and exercise an artistic genius that he did not have. This emboldening happened (the argument might run) because of the complications that beset the process of choosing a self. In Lionel's terms, the "sincere" person, who is adapted to the conditioned nature of the world, settles for choices among available cultural models of selfhood; but what if he chooses a model that *is itself a model of the unconditioned?* He then craves the "authenticity" of the cultural outrider; he craves to be "authentic" in the manner of a Hemingway, a Mailer, or a Henry Miller (or a Nietzsche). There is a kind of catch-22 at work here, and, given the internal conflicts we all carry into our professional lives, it is hard to see how a literary critic, for instance, can entirely avoid it. As a rational man Lionel Trilling can affirm the conditioned and can see through the swashbuckling nonsense in Hemingway's version of the will, but at other, more subliminal levels this version has such dramatic appeal for Trilling that he can't rid it from his mind or from his criticism. We might even say that his "choice" of Hemingway is unconsciously determined, less than, say, his admiration for *Anna Karenina.* To return to a question that has come up throughout this study: Is a choice that is unconsciously determined really a choice? I have argued that it is not; that choices require some exertion of the freedom of the will, some capacity to articulate reasons for choosing, and that where this does not happen we have not a choice but a reflex reaction to a motive. Clearly, there is some degree of reflection and so choice in Trilling's attachment to Hemingway, but much of it, I suspect, is unconscious in origin.

If we ask why it was Hemingway, and not one of the other and greater novelists that Lionel admired—the great nineteenth-century chroniclers of the ethical will in a conditioned world—we would have to say, I suppose, that the will's space is not inviolate, either with respect to cultural influences or with respect to other dimensions of the psyche. As Diana argues, Hemingway "haunts" precisely because Lionel's superego has had such a comprehensive victory over the id. So we need something resembling the threadlike conception of will here— something that sees it as partaking of psychic regions, as well as being in some hard-to-represent way a discernible psychic presence of its own. What I have termed a *graduated conception of will,* where will is a power that is instantiated through engagement with other faculties, is intended to accommodate these conceptual needs. We need a further proposition to the effect that Lionel was unable to moderate the superego's decimation of the id because he knew too little in the analytic sense of what went on in his own psyche. In the course of revealing that Lionel too spent periods under analysis, Diana says: "He was absorbed with the literature of human motivation and much gifted in its comprehension, but in the living of his life he was not drawn to the probing of motive. The disinclination probably carried over into his [psychoanalytic] treatment and hindered its progress" (p. 226).

In writing about Lionel, then, Diana is urging understandings that he (in her account) did not, and could not, have; and one of these understandings is precisely the extent to which his capacity for self-understanding had been impaired by the cataclysmic act of repression that resulted from the id's capitulation to the superego. Here she writes about her beloved exactly as a Freudian biographer might write about her or his subject. But in other respects, of course, she cannot approach even the distanced biographer's levels of compromised objectivity. She would have us believe otherwise. She insists (ironically enough, in deterministic terms) not only on her ability to tell it like it was, but on her inability to do otherwise: "The lust for honesty in my family was ravaging and incurable: I am its product." And again on the same page: "The need not to deviate from truth drags like an anchor on this book" (p. 50). Yet it is virtually inconceivable that the resentment that surfaces intermittently in *The Beginning of the Journey* will not distort the portrait of Lionel to some extent; that, for instance, her recollection of his "annihilating verbal assaults" upon her, assaults that left her shaken and racked with feelings of inadequacy, wouldn't have produced at least a vestigial need to have the last word, to exercise her will to power in shaping posterity's perception of their life together.

It is in the foreword to one of the volumes of Lionel's essays and reviews that Diana compiled and edited after his death that she defines the will as "the or-

ganizing principle of the personal life." And she continues: "The will that kept
Lionel at his desk day after day confronting his blank sheet of paper was not the
will of imposition. It was the will of freedom and individual affirmation, the will
that mobilizes itself against all despotisms, even those of our own temperaments."[109] There is a now-familiar circularity in the notion of a will that "mobilizes itself." I have nothing further to say on this. But the idea that one's own
temperament can be a kind of "despotism," and that one's will can, at least to
some significant degree, overcome it, is typically arresting. Diana Trilling affirms
such power in the will, but without claiming anything like complete sovereignty
for it. Because conditioned, the will can have only partial victories; and even
these victories are likely to be assisted triumphs in which psychoanalysis plays a
necessary part. According to friends, Diana found the inner resources to "blossom" after Lionel's death.[110] But how typical of her strange blend of feisty pride
and painful dependency that as Lionel is dying she derives desperately needed
reassurance about his love for her not from him, not from her own stock of
memories or certainties, not from letters, but from his then psychoanalyst, Dr.
Abbate, who comes to visit. The doctor and Lionel talk privately in his hospital
room, and then she leaves.

> I had never before met Dr. Abbate, but at the door she leaned over and kissed
> me. She said that she wanted me to know how much Lionel had always loved
> me. It was not something which she had to say, nor was it much to say, but it
> was enough. (p. 256)

CONCLUSION

In this study I have argued that the will is intrinsic and fundamental to human beings, and that our descriptions of human life must therefore take account of it. Autobiography is one among many narrative forms in which we try to produce such descriptions, and I have suggested that it is particularly well suited to explorations of the will. From Augustine onward, autobiographers have tried to fathom the will and its operations. This is not surprising: it is virtually impossible for an even minimally reflective person to ponder his or her life without asking what part the will has played in making that life the thing it is. I have proposed the term *reflective autobiographer* to describe the kind of first-person writer who achieves a reflective distance from conventional ideological attitudes, and who uses autobiography to explore, critique, and sometimes reformulate cultural understandings of the world. Such writers operate as—and should be understood as—agents; albeit ones who, like all agents, are constrained in various ways.

I've acknowledged, and indeed shown, that the will is a very difficult thing to conceptualize. The history of attempts to locate, define, and characterize the will is itself a complex and shifting narrative. I have suggested, however, that throughout this history certain problems and positions keep coming up, and not just in theological, philosophical, and psychological writings, but also in autobiography. One of the many things that make Augustine so remarkable is the fact that the *Confessions* raises and gives detailed attention to many of the will-related issues that preoccupy later writers in various genres. My main focus, however, has been on modern autobiography, and on what it can tell us about the condition of the will in late modernity. I have argued that late modern culture is deeply confused, conflicted, and often wantonly incurious about the will, and that some of the roots of these difficulties can be discerned in the major shapers of late modernist thought: Nietzsche, Marx, and Freud. They can also be seen in lesser but still representative figures like Skinner, Ryle, Barthes, and Derrida. Further back, these difficulties also have roots in the rise of that radical, threatening, and intoxicating sentiment of freedom that increasingly characterizes the modern period.

My own conception of the will sees it as an inalienable power of the self (though one that is in varying degrees constrained by specific practical, and in particular ideological, contexts). This power is instantiated though engagement with particular psychic faculties. My "graduated conception" of the will proposes that we conceptualize it in terms of a spectrum: at one end, where will is instantiated through engagement with id, the unconscious, unreflective affect, it is least "free." It is most "free" at the other end of the spectrum where it is instantiated through engagement with rationality—though on my account the term "rationality" is expanded to include emotional components in reflective deliberation. In terms of my central metaphor for self and will—the metaphor of threads—I see the self as a weaver who is possessed of certain innate powers to shape and create. These powers enable the weaver to shape the pattern that is his or her life—but only to some degree. The threads out of which that pattern must be shaped bring with them certain built-in possibilities and limitations. The weaver can't just make anything out of those threads. And it's not just the threads themselves that constrain what the weaver can do; it's also the weaver's culture—a culture that enables him or her to conceive of certain life-plots and possibilities, but not of others. So the self-as-weaver is a constrained agent who possesses the will and the wherewithal to shape his or her life, but only within certain limitations. Something like this conception occurs in that first-person fictional epic *Moby-Dick*. In chapter 47, "The Mat-Maker," Ishmael, who is working at a loom, muses on weaving, threads, freedom, and destiny:

> Chance, free will, and necessity—no wise incompatible—all interweavingly worked together. The straight warp of necessity, not to be swerved from its ultimate course—its every alternating vibration, indeed, only tending to that; free will still free to ply her shuttle between given threads; and chance, though restrained in its play within the right lines of necessity, and sideways in its motions modified by free will, though thus prescribed to by both, chance by turns rules either, and has the last featuring blow at events.[1]

What of the autobiographer? I see this figure as a weaver at a second remove, shaping an account of the life that he or she has played a significant part in shaping. The autobiographer's weave will represent many things, including a representation of the part will has played in the life that is being represented. It is not necessary to my view of autobiography that such representations be regarded as objectively "true" in some ultimate sense. I simply argue that we must concede certain substantial kinds and degrees of authority to the autobiographer's accounts of his or her life, precisely because it is *his or her life,* and that however desirable absolute "truth" might be, we can—and often have to—make do with the more humble criterion of "probability."

Chapter 3's discussion of autobiographies by will-denying intellectuals reflects the views I have just outlined. It argues that the will is real and at least partially free; that it must have a place in descriptions of human life; and that it emphatically *does* have a place in the autobiographies of Althusser, Skinner, and Barthes. Chapter 4 focuses on the relationship between will and morality. I argue that though the Hemingway persona is associated in the popular imagination with willpower and resilience, the conception of will that dominates *A Moveable Feast* is actually thin—too thin to bear any real moral weight. In this book, and indeed elsewhere, Hemingway appeals to a version of moral luck according to which one's moral conduct is almost wholly determined by luck. If one's conduct is morally "bad," circumstances have caused it to be so. This view of the will sees it as essentially passive, as determined by fate. Chapter 5, which traces the relationship between will and contingency in Simone de Beauvoir's autobiographical writings, discusses the various emotional phases that, in her autobiographical account, she goes through in negotiating her fear of the contingent; and it charts these phases in terms of the various philosophical understandings of the will that she endorses at various times of her life. I read Beauvoir as a recanted existentialist whose autobiographical thought charts a movement from understandings of will as solipsistic and radically free, to one in which will is profoundly linked to collective interests and is only partially free. Beauvoir's final position is a version of constrained voluntarism.

Koestler's case, the subject of chapter 6, is especially complex. Perhaps the most divided of the major autobiographers I discuss, he dichotomizes the will into two dimensions: one, a realm of natural causality where the will is law-governed and (in this sense) not ultimately free; the other, a noumenal realm in which the will is exempt from natural causation and absolutely free. The will is the noumenal "ghost" in the natural machine. But in what sense is the ghost "in" the machine, and what are the implications of its alleged presence there? There is no clear answer to the first question (Koestler's theory of the holon is brave but unavailing here), but Koestler believes that the ghost's presence means that human beings carry a spark of the transcendental will, and that this spark can and should drive what they do as ethical—in particular as *political*—agents. This is the essence of his work as a post-totalitarian autobiographer. The ambiguities in Koestler's position are clear in the mix of metaphors he uses (for instance, jostling metaphors of dimensionality and habitation), and in his conception of the noumenal itself, where the will actually seems to be mystically guided, rather than free.

Stephen Spender, too, is deeply interested in the possible freedoms of the will, but he approaches the issue from another direction: in *World Within World* he explores the ancient topic of weakness of will. Like Koestler, Spender is desperate to reconstitute the will as ethical and political agency. He too is a post-totalitarian autobiographer. Spender thinks, however, that this can only be done through the education that the will receives in the private sphere of personal relationships. Spender's metaphor of self-constitution, according to which the self is at the center of concentric circles that radiate "out" toward the social world, entails that the will's education, too, will radiate "out" into the public sphere of politics and culture. Education here involves a transition from arbitrary and decentered acts of will, to acts that result from existentially centered choices—

choices rooted in forms of deliberation that fuse emotion and rationality. This is Spender's version of liberalism—a version that conceives of the will as a constrained power that can enact and bring significant degrees of freedom into the world. Chapter 8 returns to one of the inaugurating questions that I raise in this book: In what sense can we be said to "own" our wills? Diana Trilling, too, is a liberal autobiographer who is deeply antitotalitarian, deeply committed to the will as a partially free power of the self. Her literary and cultural criticism, like that of her husband, Lionel, sees the will as fundamentally ethical and as rooted in affective and rational deliberation. Though she thinks that much of our fate is "given" to us, she also thinks that we are "given"—that we possess, or more precisely, have a "custodial" relation to—our wills. In this view, will can be exercised for better or for ill, not least in the shaping of our own life patterns. But *The Beginning of the Journey* is conflicted on the matter of the will because when Diana writes about the condition of Lionel's will, she switches her affiliation from the will as a deliberative aspect of the ego to the will as enactment of the id; from the liberal culture of the conditioned self that she and Lionel admired in Arnold, Forster, Mill, and others to a more unconditioned Nietzschean view—a view that both Diana and Lionel associate with Hemingway.

It should not come as a surprise that these readings of autobiography evince a good deal of textual complication and even confusion. I have argued that reflective autobiography is a heuristic mode. If, as I contend, we are to learn from this mode, we will learn from the range of possibilities it opens out, quite as much as from the matters it seems to settle or to get "right." When it comes to the will as a lived reality, we must go to the testimony of particular individuals. Without such testimony, our understanding of the will cannot get far, however powerful the more abstract philosophical, theological, psychological, and other accounts of it we have might be.

My own discussion has drawn chiefly on autobiography, philosophy, and the history of ideas. I have attempted to give a philosophically framed account of autobiography and its engagements with the will. Where I have used philosophical terms and perspectives pertaining to the will, they have been intended to function, in part at least, as aspects of a humanistic theory of autobiography. I have argued that the will needs much more searching and respectful exploration than it generally receives at the moment. My particular lines of inquiry can make a contribution here, but they are by no means exhaustive. The history of autobiography's engagements with the perplexities of the will cannot be comprehensively reconstructed without attention to material circumstantial factors that bear upon the will's activity in a conditioned world. Those who write what are now termed "material histories" of various aspects of human life and mythologization (feminists, postcolonialists, Marxists, and others) will continue to make an important contribution to our understanding of autobiography in this respect. And since the central metaphor of this book—weaving—refers to an activity that has traditionally been heavily gendered, I want again to acknowledge the part that feminist scholarship has played, and will continue to play, in our understanding of autobiography and the will. Accounts of autobiography must attend closely to what Ricoeur calls "collective representations."[2] I have tried to do some of this work here, but there is a great deal more still to be done.

In closing, however, I want to repeat two qualifications I have made throughout this study concerning the will and its embeddedness in material histories. One is that some postmodern approaches cannot adequately deal with the will (whether historically or otherwise) because they are predicated on a denial of the will, or at least of its freedom. The other is that when considering the place of will in human life, attention to mere materiality is not enough. The will is one of those deeply puzzling issues that pervade our often puzzling experience as human beings. We should not in my view try to eliminate what Ricoeur calls "the mystery of incarnation"[3] from our personal and social descriptions. This is why, for instance, I find Koestler's autobiographical accounts of mystical experience and the will interesting. The complexities of the will can lead those who are interested into several dimensions: philosophical (the history and analysis of various accounts of the concept), material (its life and conceptualization in particular social-historical settings), narratological (the ways it is figured in narrative, not least in autobiography), and spiritual—its haunting presence at the heart of our experience in a world we cannot fully fathom; a world from which we want so much, but in which we often find that our efforts are compromised, imperfectly rewarded, or even unavailing. How strange the shifts and fluctuations in our own volitional histories: how we can so ferociously will at twenty-five what looks unimportant or worthless at forty-five; how, having got what we willed, we sometimes find that it is other than we imagined, or insufficient in ways that we did not envisage; how some of what has most abiding value in our lives comes to us apparently unwilled, as if by grace. Will enters into our sense that life—for instance, an individual life that is set down in an autobiography— is at once of colossal import and, in the vast sweep of which we are a minuscule part, a matter of precious little moment, where "precious" has an ineffable ambiguity. Emily Dickinson:

> So large my Will
> The little that I may
> Embarrasses
> Like gentle infamy—
>
> Affront to Him
> For whom the Whole were small
> Affront to me
> Who know His Meed of all.

Earth at the best
Is but a scanty Toy—
Bought, carried Home
To Immortality.

It looks so small
We chiefly wonder then
At our Conceit
In purchasing.[4]

APPENDIX A
SOME EARLIER CONCEPTIONS OF THE
WILL: MAIMONIDES TO MILL

I. Medieval Accounts

1. *Maimonides*

Maimonides, the leading philosophical figure of the Jewish Middle Ages, was as much influenced by Aristotle as was Aquinas (see below). Indeed one of Maimonides' great achievements was to effect a synthesis between certain aspects of Judaism and certain elements of Aristotelianism. Like Aquinas, he fashioned a form of theistic Aristotelianism; again like Aquinas, Maimonides wrote extensively about the human will—though not as extensively or as intricately as his Christian counterpart. The two men's views on the will are strikingly different. But before comparing this dimension of their thought, some more general points of comparison are needed.

While Maimonides shares with Aquinas the view that God cannot be known directly, in His "essence," Maimonides' version of this doctrine contains suppositions and emphases that clearly differentiate it from Aquinas's. We shall see that Aquinas in effect qualifies this doctrine by positing two levels at which humankind may know—or know of—God: one, a level of transcendence that eludes the grasp of human rationality but can be known through revelation and embraced through faith; two, a level of immanence in which God is present to humankind through Being and can be known indirectly, through various forms of deductive and extrapolative human intellection.[1] In Maimonides' thought the second of these two levels is largely absent—at least ostensibly. While God's wishes for human beings can be grasped through the Torah and the 613 *mitzvot* (or precepts) therein, the study of these is seen as an aspect of revelation, not (at least in the first instance) of cognition.[2] Only a believer will be moved to study the Torah—so the theory goes—and the believer is one for whom revelation has already occurred. This means that the study of Torah, while often intricately analytical, does not aim to penetrate to a divine essence by analytical means: analysis is conceptualized not as a mode of syllogistic progression toward the truth, but as an activity that facilitates and internalizes revelation. On this view, to study the Torah gives the individual a special kind inwardness with God's will; and the greater this inwardness, the more expertly appropriate the carrying out of God's commands, the closer the individual draws to human perfection. Yet we cannot know *how* or *why* God exists, except through negative postulations (He is not like us) and through what the Torah reveals of His attributes, such as mercifulness, though even these are not revelations of His essence, but manifestations in modes that are apprehensible to human understanding. We can know merely that He *does exist,* that He has attributes in this sense, and that His will should be obeyed.[3] According to Maimonides, then, God's existence is radically ulterior: it is not immanent in, nor is it linked to, nor dependent upon, creation: "We do not comprehend His knowledge, nor do we fathom its extent at all, for He is His knowledge and His knowledge is Him."[4]

God's radically transcendent status with respect to creation has complex implications for human conduct, and in particular for the role of human will. Maimonides accepts as an unarguable first premise the doctrine that God has bestowed free will on humankind. He represents the mainstream of Jewish theology in believing that the Torah and the *mitzvot* presuppose humankind's freedom to choose: "Free will is granted to all men. If one desires to turn himself to the path of good and be righteous, the choice is his. Should he desire to turn to the path of evil and be wicked, the choice is his."[5] In other words, humankind possesses a will, and will is understood as being constitutively free. In Vernon J. Bourke's terms, Maimonides sees Freedom as the Genus of Volition. So profound is this freedom of the will that "there is no one who can prevent" a human being "from doing good or bad"[6]—not even God, for He has given freedom of choice as an absolute gift (though only in the sense that choice is free: not in the sense that sin is exempt from punishment). Here one of the important distinctions between Aquinas and Maimonides on the will comes to light. For Aquinas, the will is, as it were, already encoded to incline toward the Good, if it is engaged. But for Maimonides the will does not have a constitutive appetitive inclination to the Good. It is for the owner of that will to so direct it. God wishes that he or she do so—"It is fitting for a person to control all the powers of his soul by his thought"[7]—and punishment awaits those who do not. But the will itself is a power awaiting direction. It is not, as in Aquinas (and Augustine), a power that can only move in a certain direction. All that can be said about the nature of the will is that it is by nature free and that it is God's will that it be so:

> Just as the Creator desired that [the elements of] fire and wind rise upward and [those of] water and earth descend downward, that the heavenly spheres revolve in a circular orbit, and all the other creations of the world follow the nature which He desired for them, so too, He desired that man have free choice and be responsible for his deeds, without being pulled or forced. Rather, he, on his own initiative, with the knowledge which God has granted him, will do anything that man is able to do.[8]

The apparent contradiction between this account of the will and the doctrine that God is all-knowing cannot be resolved: it is beyond human comprehension.[9] What can be said, however, is that, allowing for minor variations, people are all born with a capacity to be good or otherwise: "Each person is fit to be righteous like Moses, our teacher, or wicked, like Jeroboam."[10] The person who chooses the path of the Good will reveal a kind of godliness that is in the self; but some never make this revelation. Either way, an element of spiritual travail accompanies earthly life, and mystical union with God is not a possibility. For Maimonides, as for Aquinas, "the highest bliss is the contemplation of God."[11]

Maimonides' account of the will is typically Judaic in that it has a strong ethical emphasis. The godliness that is present in creation is conceived of as an intrinsically moral thing, and a human being who chooses in the direction of self-perfection must do so through a commitment to the morally Good Life.[12] Though the will is not inherently moral, it will be so if it is exercised as God would wish. Maimonides contends that the soul comprises five elements and that these govern nutrition, sensation, imagination, stimulation, and conceptualization, respectively.[13] There is no special place or faculty for the will, though the element of sensation has certain will-like characteristics.[14] On Maimonides' account, the will is a sort of first principle of psycho-spiritual organization: a power that suffuses all aspects of the person, whether he or she uses it to pursue or to eschew activities that are conducive to the Good Life and to an inwardness with the will of God.

II. *Aquinas*

Aquinas's account of the will is one of the most intricate ever given. Its historical importance lies not only in its later influence, but in the way in which it synthesizes aspects of both the Greek (specifically, Aristotelian) and the Augustinian conceptions. Aquinas, of course, was massively influenced by Aristotle, who had been widely translated into Latin in the twelfth century. But many of his analyses of the will also refer to Augustine. This is hardly surprising given the changes in metaphysical orientation that mark the transition from Greek to (some versions of) Judeo-Christian culture. The Greeks' account of the will is embedded in a metaphysic that takes it for granted that the world is rationally structured and that the will enacts rational knowledge of the world so conceived. The task of philosophy is to describe the structures in question and the will's operation within them. But in Judeo-Christian, and especially medieval, accounts some of this confidence is missing. As Frederick Copleston says, *faith* has become an issue: confidence in the structured nature of the world, and of the will's role in that world, must be sought and won, and this is done, at least in part, through activities of intellectual understanding.[15] Moreover, philosophy now has to contend with the Fall and with the will's part in it. As a result of original sin, God is now not known, but believed in. Nevertheless, Aquinas's account of the will owes more to Aristotle than to Augustine—at least to that strand in Aristotle that sees choice as (possibly) springing from "appetitive intellect." In the *Summa Theologica* Aquinas writes:

> Aristotle leaves it in doubt whether election belongs principally to the appetitive or the cognitive power: since he says that election is either *an appetitive intellect or an intellectual appetite*. But he inclines to its being an intellectual appetite when he describes election as *a desire proceeding from counsel.*[16]

As this indicates, Aquinas's conception is of the Will as Rational Appetite: a desire for human goods, though this does not entail that it is always a reasonable or moral desire. It is a potentiality or power in the self that may be activated by the understanding so that it inclines toward those objects deemed worthy by the "counsel" that understanding provides. However, even this basic tenet needs to be seen in the broader context of Aquinas's outlook in general.

Much of what he says about the will occurs in the *Summa Theologica*—a work that has important generic implications for our purposes. Aquinas distinguishes between works of theology and works of philosophy. The first of these are written from the point of view of one who knows God's revealed truth; who has faith and can contemplate humankind's ultimate destiny, which is salvation. The second seeks a rational grasp of the phenomenal, created world in its own terms.[17] In these terms the *Summa* is both theology and philosophy: it is theology insofar as it is written by a man who has faith; but it is philosophy in the sense that it engages, reconstructs, and philosophizes about the processes by which fallenness proceeds to faith. In this sense it is a conceptually elaborate form of theodicy: a thought journey back to the divine origin from which the Fall has separated humanity, thence through the history of salvation, to the ultimate end of earthly life—"happiness," albeit such flawed forms of happiness as are available to humankind in this life. These forms of happiness come through philosophic knowledge of God and through the exercise of humankind's natural (or God-given) virtues.[18]

However, God cannot be known directly in His essence, His modes of His transcendent Otherness. For instance, we cannot comprehend the inaugurating act of free will through which He created the universe.[19] What we can know, according to Aquinas, is the realm of Being, where substance and accident combine in the form of objects we perceive and, in some cases, understand. It is about Being that mind formulates rational propositions, and such propositions can yield knowledge of God. We possess a cognitive ability to derive understanding of universal truths from sensory data, and Aquinas's empiricism proposes that it is from the level of sense experience that human knowledge first comes. It is upon such data that the intellect—or cognition—goes to work. However, as is so often the case in Aquinas, this level of human engagement—the intellectual level—subdivides, in this case into two modalities of knowing. First, there is "understanding": a process whereby the intellect grasps some aspect of the world in an immediate and synthesizing act of consciousness. It sees what something means. Experiences of this kind pertain to first principles and certain universal forms of truth such as justice. Second, there is "reason," here construed as a discursive moving from one proposition to the next until understanding is achieved.[20] But, either way, the general trajectory of the agent's movement is from sensory to rational apprehensions of the world.

We can come to faith either by revelation or by reason; but nothing can be known that has not been grasped through some form of understanding, and faith is a form of knowledge. Thus faith cannot simply be "willed" without understanding. Where, then, does the will lie in the configuration of human-and-divine that I have so far sketched? The will's potentiality is, as it were, encoded such that if it is activated it must necessarily behave in certain ways, and not in others. In particular, when activated the will must incline to what has been apprehended as "happiness": that is, the life infused and animated by the Good. And the will is, as it were, precipitated toward the Good by the counseling of the intellect.[21] Thus, if a person inclines toward evil, for instance, the will cannot be responsible: other forces must be at work, and the will must be inoperative. So the will takes its counsel from rationality; it is an "appetitive" faculty in the sense that when activated it will incline in certain directions; it is a mode of intellectual appetition because it requires intellectual apprehension to activate it. Aquinas distinguishes between intellect and will in terms of a kind of experiential trajectory: while the object of intellect is internal to it, the object of the will is external to it; in other words, will is the part of us that is oriented toward external goods.[22]

Aquinas holds that human beings are in some senses, and some situations, "free" to exercise the will; and he denies any contradiction between this tenet about the will and the doctrine of predestination. According to this doctrine, God already knows all that will happen, yet he does not intervene in such freedom as he has given human beings to shape their own destinies.[23] They can choose (within certain parameters) their fates, and it is because the world is populated by flawed but will-endowed entities called human beings that error enters the picture. The "freedom" of the will is, however, a very complex matter. In fact, Aquinas scarcely uses the phrase "free will" at all, and in practice the margin of freedom he ascribes to the will is very restricted. To the extent that will is free, it is so because of its relation to intellect, whose judgments are free; indeed a judgment is not a judgment if it is not free.[24] Another of the distinctions he makes is between "natural" and "deliberative" modalities of the will:

> There are certain particular goods which have not a necessary connection with happiness, because without them a man can be happy; and to such the will does not adhere of necessity. But there are some things which have a necessary connection with happiness, namely, those by means of which man adheres to God, in Whom alone true happiness consists.[25]

The natural modality, which adheres to goods that are necessary for happiness, is the volitional correlate of the epistemological notion of understanding. Just as there are certain things that we can immediately "know," so there are certain (natural) volitions that we will inevitably perform, if certain conditions are met. These conditions are as described by Aristotle: that the agent knows an action to be in his or her power; that he or she knows something of the nature, means, ends, and circumstances of the action; that external forces do not intervene; and that the action will either be a means to, or a means of, securing the end that is the Good.[26] Again, it is the intellect that identifies and formulates this end. Aquinas's doctrine of the will lays greater emphasis on the notion of volition than on that of freedom. The will that acts by necessity is nevertheless operating as the will; but it is not free to do other than what rational apprehension advises. In the case of deliberative volition, however, there is a dimension of freedom, because here the options open to the agent are not intrinsically or self-evidently desirable; that is, it is not immediately apparent that they are necessary to the attainment of happiness or the Good. Volition here operates in the epistemological register of reason: it takes advice on pros and cons that arise from a process of discursive consideration, and then it decides how it will act. The decision in this case is free in the sense that the will might have directed the agent to act otherwise. There is a further, albeit complicated, sense in which deliberation can enter into the life of the volitional agent, and this is that the mind can elect not to focus on certain things, thereby obviating the need to make choices about them.

Aquinas's account of these matters is typically medieval in that it conceives of phenomena hierarchically. His philosophy of the will does not seek, as Augustine's does, to identify the will as a separate faculty; rather, it sees the whole soul as indivisible and tries to understand how will relates, both procedurally and hierarchically, to the other components of the soul. On his account, the cognitive dimension of the soul is higher than the will.[27] It is the cognitive dimension that distinguishes humans from animals, and it is in this dimension that the peculiarly human drive to self-perfection is located. The fulfillment of that drive to perfection is the state of true happiness in which humankind knows God without having to exert the will. At this point she or he has apprehended reality in its universal aspect—not God, as such, but God in the terms in which we can know Him.

How do we know what we know of human will, according to Aquinas? It cannot be through some direct, extra-empirical encounter between one part of the soul (say, the rational faculties) and another (the will). The soul and therefore its constituent parts are said to be immaterial, but the human mind can only have direct knowledge of material substances.[28] Therefore, mind cannot directly know the will—cannot grasp it, as it were, in its essence. But it can know the will through its acts, and in this context acts include both external actions consequent upon movements of the will, and mental will-acts themselves:

> And just as through the soul itself we know *that* the soul is, inasmuch as we perceive its acts, and seek by a study of its acts and their objects to know *what* it is, through the principles of speculative sciences, so, too, concerning those things that are in our soul, namely its powers and habits, we know indeed *that* they are, inasmuch as we perceive their acts, but *what* they are we gather from the nature of these same acts.[29]

Aquinas often quotes both Aristotle and Augustine when discussing the kinds of knowledge that the mind can have of itself, and of the will in particular. His account of how and to what extent the mind can know the will combines introspection by which we know *that* we will, and intellection, which helps us to understand *what* the will is: how it fits into the general scheme of things and what powers it has.

> Now whatever is intelligibly in an intelligent subject is understood by that subject. Therefore the act of the will is understood by the intellect, both inasmuch as one perceives that one wills, and inasmuch as one knows the nature of this act, and consequently, the nature of the principle which is the habit or power.[30]

It follows from Aquinas's general position that any such knowledge we may have of the human will must be imperfect. But it is knowledge nevertheless, and knowing about the will is an indispensable aspect of knowing Being—and so drawing closer to God.

II. The Naturalization of Mind: The Seventeenth and Early Eighteenth Centuries

In the theistic accounts offered by Augustine, Aquinas, and Maimonides, the human will is explained and described, in the first instance, with reference to God. It is only after deity's role in the creation and activity of the human will has been elucidated that the human experience of possessing and exercising such a faculty is examined. This dimension is and remains logically secondary to speculation about God's role in the life of the will. In the next major period of philosophical speculation about the will—the seventeenth century—this general orientation changes. A process that might be termed the *naturalization of the mind* occurs. Now God is conceived of as being present as a presiding First Cause, but the phenomena of mind—including the will—have been emancipated from transcendental causal explication and are now charted in terms of natural laws, causes, and psychological states. Before turning to the seventeenth-century empiricists, however, we should note two important and dissenting accounts: one from the seventeenth century itself; the other from the sixteenth century.

I. *Martin Luther, Spinoza*

Martin Luther is of massive historical importance with respect to the will. In *The Bondage of the Will*, Martin Luther expounds a form of predestinarian doctrine. Humankind may have a measure of freedom in matters that do not pertain to salvation, but in matters that do so pertain, the will cannot dictate its own condition, nor the condition of the soul. Only God can do that, and His decisions hold, irrespective of our deeds:

> This, therefore, is essentially necessary and wholesome for Christians to know: *that God foreknows nothing by contingency, but that He foresees, purposes, and does all things according to His immutable, eternal, and infallible will.* By this thunderbolt, "Free-will" is thrown prostrate, and utterly dashed to pieces. Those, therefore, who would assert "Free-will," must either deny this thunderbolt, or pretend not to see it, or push it from them.[31]

Luther's "thunderbolt" does not, however, signal a kind of resignation, and certainly not fatalism. A Christian does indeed experience freedom; a special sort of freedom through his spiritual and social life: "A Christian lives not in himself, but in Christ and in his neighbor. Otherwise he is not a Christian. He lives in Christ through faith, in his neighbor through love. By faith he is caught up beyond himself into God. By love he descends beneath himself into his neighbor."[32] The Christian's freedom, then, lies in a kind of self-transcendence; but he is also free in the sense that he escapes the bondage entailed in living as though God were not sovereign. To deny the sovereignty of God is to commit oneself to a life lived by human precept and regulation, and to cut oneself off from the one true source of freedom—the Holy Spirit. To the extent that he counsels a form of giving over whereby the will gradates into a love that receives grace, Luther is closer to Augustine than is often supposed.

Spinoza's account of the will looks back to the intellectualism of the Greeks, and forward to some eighteenth-century attempts wholly to identify the will with rationality:

> *Corollary.*—Will and understanding are one and the same.
>
> *Proof.*—Will and understanding are nothing beyond the individual volitions and ideas . . . But a particular volition and a particular idea are one and the same (by the foregoing Prop.); therefore, will and understanding are one and the same. *Q.E.D.*[33]

II. *Descartes*

It is in the work of Descartes that seventeenth-century understandings of the will take a turn that is especially momentous for a history of the will and its relations with autobiography. Much of Descartes's philosophical prose is of course couched in a heuristic first-person mode, and his method of trying to resolve doubt through recourse to introspective analysis was to have a major influence on modern autobiographical writing. The second *Meditation* makes clear that the cogito incorporates more than just thought in its narrowly cognitive sense. The cogito includes a range of aspects and activities of consciousness. No less than Augustine, Descartes links introspection and (among other things) the will: "But what then am I? A thing which thinks. What is a thing which thinks? It is a thing which doubts, understands, [conceives], affirms, denies, wills . . ."[34] Though an individual is a creation of God, and in that sense a determined being, the individual will is in some hard-to-define sense an autonomous faculty of the soul. So much so, indeed, that the individual can withhold assent to the proposition that God exists. In *The Passions of the Soul*, article XLI, Descartes writes:

> But the will is so free in its nature, that it can never be constrained; and of the two sorts of thoughts which I have distinguished in the soul (of which the first are its actions, i.e. its desires, the others its passions, taking this word in its most general significance, which comprises all kinds of perceptions), the former are absolutely in its power, and can only be indirectly changed by the body, while on the other hand the latter depend absolutely on the actions which govern and direct them, and they can only indirectly be altered by the soul, excepting when it is itself their cause. And the whole action of the soul consists in this, that solely because it desires something, it causes the little gland [the pineal gland] to which it is closely united to move in the way requisite to produce the effect that relates to this desire.[35]

Here, then, is the protomodern theater of the mind, what John Sturrock refers to as Descartes's "intimate transparency,"[36] replete with a faculty that is the seat of volition and instigates acts of consciousness and physical acts alike through an organic intermediary: the pineal gland. On this account the will is fundamentally free: it "can never be constrained."

III. *Locke, Hobbes, and Hume*

Like Augustine and Descartes, Locke wants to know how it is that we know we possess wills, and how we can best understand what the will is. And like them, he believes that we can best know the will through introspection. This in the *Essay Concerning Human Understanding*:

> The act of *volition* . . . being a very simple act, whosoever desires to understand what it is will better find it by reflecting on his own mind and observing what it does when it *wills*, than by any variety of articulate sounds whatsoever.[37]

Having so reflected, Locke concludes that the precipitating cause of willing is a certain "uneasiness"—a kind of discomfort, or urge or feeling of lack—that demands resolution. Introspection tells us that there are "a great many *uneasinesses* always soliciting and ready to determine the *will*,"[38] and on Locke's rationalist account human freedom resides in the fact that we can generally (not always) suspend responses to these solicitations until reason has arbitrated among them. Since reason is intrinsically geared to the greatest Good, we shall will the Good where reason is in the ascendancy. The "great privilege of finite intellectual beings" is that

> they can *suspend* their desires and stop them from determining their *wills* to any action, till they have duly and fairly *examined* the good and evil of it, as far forth as the weight of the thing requires. This we are able to do; and when we have done it, we have done our duty, and all that is in our power, and indeed all that needs. For, since the *will* supposes knowledge to guide its choice, all that we can do is to hold our *wills* undetermined, till we have *examined* the good and evil of what we desire. What follows after that follows in a chain of consequences, linked one to another, all depending on the last determination of the judgment . . .[39]

On Locke's empiricist-rationalist account, it is reason that orders and interprets the "ideas" that are furnished by experience,[40] and reason that, by determining the will, precipitates mechanistic causal sequences of action and judgment. Locke's position is complex: while reason's role is suggestive of a Will as Intellectual Preference view, there is also an appetitive dimension (he says much about "desires") and a sense that "liberty" is the true genus of the will.[41]

Hobbes's description of volition is quite explicit in construing deliberation as a composite thing comprising cognitive and affective dimensions. He ponders the term *deliberation* itself, noting that it means "putting an end to the *liberty* we had of doing,"[42] and he defines will as "*the last appetite in deliberating*."[43] It is a crucial insight about the psychology of willing, not just for what it says about the psychological mechanisms involved, but because it helps explain why the whole topic of the will and willing can be emotionally threatening: if to will is, as Hobbes argues, to act, and to do so in a way that closes off other possibilities, then will can seem the enemy of liberty, of freedom. In this respect Hobbes's position is antithetical to that of, say, Kant, who equates rational choice and freedom. Readers who have concluded or been told that they have a "commitment problem" will perhaps recognize what is at issue here. Hobbes's description of deliberation is as follows:

> When in the mind of man, appetites, and aversions, hopes and fears, concerning one and the same thing, arise alternately; and divers good and evil consequences of the doing, or omitting the thing propounded, come successively into our thoughts; so that sometimes we have an appetite to it; some-

times an aversion from it; sometimes hope to be able to do it; sometimes despair, or fear to attempt it; the whole sum of desires, aversions, hopes and fears, continued till the thing be either done, or thought impossible, is that we call DELIBERATION.[44]

Hobbes expressly opposes the medieval conception of Will as Rational Appetite,[45] arguing that there is only will where there is genuine temptation to act against the counsel of rationality. Hobbes's account, which sees the will as a kind of power or faculty of the self, graphically illustrates that now familiar paradox in some conceptualizations of the will: for him, the will itself is determined, and therefore not "free"; but that which determines it—deliberation—is substantially under our control. To this extent, the will is (substantially) free in effect, but not in essence. Hobbes's account is also notable for the extent to which it relates volition not just to mental states, but to bodily ones as well.

Hume's contribution to empiricist accounts of the will is revealing in a number of ways, not least for the kinds of historically significant tensions it exhibits. One of these is a tension between a confident determination to produce a comprehensive Newtonian science of humankind, on the one hand, and, on the other, an awareness of how extraordinarily complex a phenomenon the self—in particular personal identity—is. In the appendix to *A Treatise of Human Nature*, he says of his treatment of personal identity in the main body of the text: "I find myself involv'd in such a labyrinth, that, I must confess, I neither know how to correct my former opinions, nor how to render them consistent."[46] In *An Enquiry Concerning Human Understanding*, he had figured this complexity as threadlike: his account of human nature seeks to "unravel all its intricacies."[47] A second source of tension, and one that recurs often in the history of thinking about the will, is between the desire to anatomize the will and its relation to other psychophysiological constituents of the self, and the conviction that the will itself is beyond human understanding: even the "power or energy" whereby the will precipitates such apparently simple actions as the movement of limbs is, "like that in other natural events . . . unknown and inconceivable."[48] Hume agrees with Hobbes that some kind of "uneasiness" is an inaugurating condition of volitional activity,[49] but unlike Hobbes, he does not think that we can know the will by introspection; indeed he disclaims the tradition that tries to understand "liberty and necessity . . . by examining the faculties of the soul."[50] What we can know of it can only be known through experience: "We learn the influence of our will from experience alone. And experience only teaches us, how one event constantly follows another; without instructing us in the secret connexion, which binds them together, and renders them inseparable."[51] Experience, then, reveals to us the will's place in those causal sequences that lie at the heart of his essentially deterministic conception of the world. However, even "experience" is a fraught term: it refers not so much to what is objectively "out there" to be observed, as to the forms the world assumes when processed or rendered by the mind. Hume argues that even the relational configuration of necessity we perceive "exists in the mind, not in objects."[52] Among the impressions (that is, strong perceptions) we have is the sense that the will is radically free, that it is characterized by "liberty" in the sense that we can do whatever we want: "By the *will*, I mean nothing but *the internal impression we feel and are conscious of, when we knowingly give rise to any new motion of our body, or new perception of our mind.*"[53] Hume's general position commits him to seeing any such impression as a "false sensation" that will not survive intelligent reflection on the structures of experience itself.[54] Thus he argues that "the conjunction between motives and voluntary actions is as regular and uniform as that between the cause and effect in any part of nature."[55] However, he is no crude determinist. In the first place, he draws a distinction that is crucial and too seldom made in discussions of these matters: a distinction between how volitional behavior might look to an observer, and how it *feels* to the person performing the volition.[56] The feeling of free choice, while strictly speaking a "false sensation," is not entirely that: there is a difference between the doctrine of the "liberty of indifference," according to which the world is contingent and acausal and the will therefore radically free, and that of the "liberty of spontaneity," which imputes to agents a limited but genuine margin of *perceived* freedom within a causally determined world. Precisely what that margin consists in is not altogether clear, but it seems to involve the at times defensible feeling that one sometimes acts without powerful external constraint;[57] that one is free to exercise will at the behest of what one wants to do—at the behest of one's "motives."[58] Motives, which are themselves the causal products of one's inherited temperament and personal history, are determinative of the will. And so Hume arrives at the following famous but puzzling formulation:

> By liberty, then, we can only mean *a power of acting or not acting, according to the determinations of the will;* that is, if we choose to remain at rest, we may; if we choose to move, we also may.[59]

As Godfrey Vesey points out, this could mean one of two things: "according to how *the will determines*" or "according to how *the will is determined,*"[60] but the latter interpretation seems the most plausible. In a paradoxical sense that we have already seen and will see again (for instance in Schopenhauer), the will is both determined and (to some extent at least) free. This particular form of qualified psychological determinism is very apparent in the short autobiographical document Hume wrote a few months before his death, *My Own Life,*[61] where his sanguinity of temperament is presented as the key determinant in his life.

A brief description such as I am giving here can only hint at the remarkable complexity of Hume's account of the will, but two other points are especially important, not least for later developments. One concerns his speculations about the relationship between will and other behavioral phenomena, and the "identity" of the agent. His "bundle" theory of the self essentially sees identity as a fictitious imposition on an entity—the "self"—which is a constantly changing summation of myriad "impressions." He speaks of the self as "but a bundle or collection of different perceptions, which succeed each other with an inconceivable rapidity, and are in a perpetual flux and movement."[62] Second, he departs from Locke, Spinoza, and the intellectualists in seeing the passions, and not the reason, as the primary determinant in the moral "decisions" we make. As the famous formulation in *A Treatise of Human Nature* would have it, "Reason is, and ought only to be, the slave of the passions, and can never pretend to any other office than to serve and obey them."[63] Though "passions" is here an inclusive word for a great array of motivational factors and states, it is clear that Hume is not a rationalist in any narrow sense. Yet he does not see "passions" alone as a basis for the moral life: rather it is a predominantly affective mixture of reason and passion, such as one finds in the wise and temperate individual, that is fundamental to moral life.[64] Hume, it seems, was one such individual; yet, as his autobiography makes clear, the temperaments of such people are a genetic given, which then determines the will. So on this view even moral sagacity is the product of causal antecedence.

III. Toward the Unconditioned Will: Later Eighteenth and the Early Nineteenth Centuries

1. *Rousseau*

Rousseau's place in the history of thought about the will is complex. Though profoundly democratic in intent, *The Social Contract* has been read by some as a forerunner of totalitarianism; and the *Confessions,* which figures in the popular imagination as one of the great resistant acts of the solitary will, is in its own way a pained admission of the determined nature of human life. *The Social Contract* proclaims early on that "to renounce our freedom is to renounce our character as men,"[65] yet true freedom is something that only comes into being when humankind has made the transition from "brute" to the early stages of civilized social being. Thus in *Discourse on the Origin and Foundations of Inequality,* Rousseau writes: "Nature alone does everything in the operations of a beast, whereas man contributes to his operations by being a free agent."[66] Once the state of (early) civilized social being obtains, three forms of the will come into being as possible modes of human presence in the world. One is the "personal will":[67] an essentially egoistic expression of personal want and aspiration. Second there is "the will of all," which is a mere agglomeration of the imperfect individual wills of all. Finally, there is the "general will," a descendent of Pascal's "will of the majority":[68] that quasi-mystical form of social relatedness that is the "contract" itself. Here the individual, motivated by a mix of rationality and passion, enters voluntarily into a "pact" with fellow citizens whereby the imperfections of egoistic need give way to the freedoms of true social life. The "pact" both expresses and actualizes the true, virtuous social being of the species. Each individual is now part of an "indivisible" whole and is free to enact his or her powers of rationality and virtue therein.[69] While certain practical safeguards are required to ensure the reliability of the common will,[70] it is held to be potentially sagacious in a way that the isolated individual cannot be.

Like Augustine's *Confessions,* the *Confessions* of Rousseau bring will and autobiography into close, albeit less systematic, relationship. Rousseau is yet another autobiographer who figures the complexities of the self in terms of threads or strands. Of an unjust childhood punishment and its psychological consequences, he writes: "I do not feel capable of unravelling the strands or even remotely following all that happened at that time within me."[71] Just prior to this he has made one of his most scandalous confessions: that he has a masochistic sexuality stemming from, he believes, his experience of corporal punishment at the hands of his foster mother, Mlle. Lambercier. He recalls the "admixture of sensuality"[72] he feels when she beats him, and he continues in a tone of bemused lament:

> Who could have supposed that this childish punishment, received at the age of eight at the hands of a woman of thirty, would determine my tastes and desires, my passions, my very self for the rest of my life, and that in a sense diametrically opposed to the one in which they should normally have developed.[73]

This is Rousseau the "arch catastrophist" in deterministic mode. He believes that in the condition that results from the inaugurating moment of emotional distortion, the passions are deflected from their natural course and the rational counsel of the will is powerless to intervene. He hypothesizes that the condition arises from, and perpetuates itself as, a dysfunction in the relation between Self and Other: Self cannot give and receive love except in a state of masochistic subjection to the Other. At the close of *Discourse on the Origin and Foundations of Inequality,* Rousseau offers one of his great formulations about such dysfunctions in the Self-Other relation. He again contrasts the "savage" and the "sociable man": "The savage lives within himself; the sociable man, always outside of himself, knows how to live only in the opinion of others; and it is, so to speak, from their judgment alone that he draws the sentiment of his own existence."[74] This fear of the Other's power to construct Self was to reverberate through many later texts—Hegel, Marx, the existentialists—and to reemerge in post-totalitarian liberal discourses in writers such as Diana and Lionel Trilling.

II. *Kant: Reason and Transcendental Agency*

Kant's account of the will, like that of Aquinas, has to be read in several dimensions. On one of these many levels, Kant can be read as seeking to emancipate the will from what he saw as its excessive subordination to naturalistic mental processes in empiricist accounts. He wants to retain their scientistic sense of the natural world, and a phenomenal domain within which we perceive through the senses; but he also wants to exempt some aspects of humankind from this domain. In particular, he wants to posit intellectual concepts—here associated with the faculty of Understanding—which are necessary conditions for the possibility of experience. These concepts are the Categories. Kant's critical idealism seeks to understand the powers of reason; it concludes that reason is the faculty of the principles we may know—those principles being the rules by which the natural and moral worlds operate. But reason can also take us beyond the phenomenal world to the noumenal one. Kant equivocates as to how far we can know the noumenal—or unconditioned—world, and it can be argued that the distinction between phenomena and noumena is merely methodological; however, I believe that one strain of his thought presupposes a "transcendental" human capacity to apprehend the unconditional. In this admittedly contentious respect, he is proto-Romantic, even though his positing of reason as the route to the unconditioned marks him as a speculative rationalist.

It is useful to read Kant in relation to Hume. Kant argues that unless we possessed the categorial concept of causality, we would not be able to make causal sense of reality in the way that Hume says we do. Kant's critique of the Hume-style view extends to—and indeed entails—a repudiation of Hume's "bundle" theory of the self. Kant insists that there must be a prior subjectivity, a unitary activity of consciousness, already in place in order so to register experience. This prior activity of consciousness is "transcendental apperception":

> There can be in us no modes of knowledge, no connection or unity of one mode of knowledge with another, without that unity of consciousness which precedes all data of intuitions, and by relation to which representation of objects is alone possible. This pure original unchangeable consciousness I shall name *transcendental apperception.*[75]

This self, however, is not the simple substance, the complex self-validating and defining theater of the mind, predicated by Descartes. It is, rather, a foundational, nonreflective awareness, an "I am," that cannot be identified with a complex, individual account of "*what*" or "*who*" "*I am*": "I have no *knowledge* of myself as I am but merely as I appear to myself. The consciousness of self is thus very far from being a knowledge of the self."[76] This self is a dual entity: it has a higher part, which is of the intelligible (that is, reason-bearing) world, and a lower part (the animal or "sensible" self).[77] The lower part will obey the edicts of the higher. Here the will enters the picture. The will is a faculty of the higher self. It acts in accordance with the understandings of reason:

> Only a rational being has the power to act *in accordance with his idea* of laws—that is, in accordance with principles—and only so has he a *will.* Since *reason*

is required in order to derive actions from laws, the will is nothing but practical reason. If reason infallibly determines the will, then in a being of this kind the actions which are recognized to be objectively necessary are also subjectively necessary—that is to say, the will is then a power to choose *only that* which reason independently of inclination recognizes to be practically necessary, that is, to be good.[78]

Kant is one of those thinkers whose conception of the will seems to fall within several of the categories that Vernon J. Bourke and others have proposed. The passage just quoted sounds like the Will as Rational Appetite: when operative, the will inclines toward the Good, as conceived of in practical terms and as ascertained by rationality. Kant sometimes refers to the will so conceived as the "Rational Will" and distinguishes between this and the so-called "Elective Will." The latter of these is "affected, but not *determined,* by impulses"; the former is "the appetitive faculty . . . which determines the elective will to action." If one acts at the behest of the Elective Will only, one is exercising a form of freedom that is impure, illusory—however "free" one might feel in so doing. If, on the other hand, the Elective Will is determined in its actions by the Rational Will, true freedom is attained.[79] Herein lies one of the many puzzling complications of Kant's conception: if in places he seems to restrict the notion of will to that which is rationally governed, passages such as the one I have just alluded to sunder the will into two modalities, one of which is rationally determined while the other is, at least in some registers, not so determined.[80]

Because it is not driven by the (animal) passions, the will is "autonomous."[81] The categorical imperative—"Act only on that maxim through which you can at the same time will that it should become a universal law"[82]—is uttered by a moral agent who is cognizant of a universal moral order and whose awareness of that order includes the cognizance that, as an intelligible being, she or he is free. This Rousseauian sentiment is a practical, not a metaphysical, proposition: "A will which can be determined . . . through motives which are represented only by reason, is entitled *freewill* (*arbitrium liberum*), and everything which is bound up with this will, whether as ground or as consequence, is entitled *practical.*"[83] The agent who espouses the categorical imperative is an individual legislator, and to this extent Kant's view partakes of the theory of Will as the Source of Law; but insofar as the will is conditional upon freedom, Kant's account also reflects the assumption of Freedom as the Genus of Volition. The ethical will, then, is (in the sense just described) unconditioned, part of—or a path to—the world of the noumena. Critical philosophy cannot, and does not seek to, explain how this can be so. Like Hume, Kant believes that such explanations are beyond human understanding. Defining free will as "the power of spontaneously beginning a series in time," he adds parenthetically that it cannot be "understood."[84] Similarly, there are limits to what we can know of ourselves through introspection, because to introspect is to approach the self as a thing-in-itself; that is, without mediating categorial understanding "we can never, even by the most strenuous self-examination, get to the bottom of our secret impulsions."[85] And again: "Consciousness of self according to the determinations of our state in inner perception is merely empirical, and always changing. No fixed and abiding self can present itself in this flux of inner appearances."[86] This fluxlike interiority Kant calls "*empirical apperception.*"[87] What we can know through introspection is not a private Cartesian sphere, but rather a supra-personal one that is structured by universal laws: "The original and necessary consciousness of the identity of the self is thus at the same time a consciousness of an equally necessary unity of the synthesis of all appearances according to concepts, that is, according to rules, which not only make them necessarily reproducible but also in so doing determine an object for their intuition."[88]

Kant, then, is both important and paradoxical for a discussion of autobiography and the will. His importance lies in the centrality he accords the will, the intrinsically moral conception he has of it, and in the will's part in transcendental apprehension—the orientation toward the unconditioned. His conception of the self is paradoxical in this: on the one hand, he posits a self-as-agent that seems substantive, the bearer of complex cognitive and affective states, a being that acts in the light of complex processes of deliberation and self-reflection and that ascribes to other beings morally entitled agent status (this is the *kingdom of ends* referred to in the *Groundwork*);[89] on the other hand, this self lacks the individual specificity that we might associate with such an agential conception. The inward gaze of the Kantian agent reveals its participation in trans-individual processes; but the rich reflective self-consciousness that we associate with the substantial romantic and modern self is missing. As we have seen, the tension between personalized and impersonal conceptions of self, and of the will's place in selfhood, was to haunt autobiography from the eighteenth century onward, most notably in antihumanist modernism and postmodernism.

III. *Hegel: Romantic Rationalist Optimism*

Hegel provides what is perhaps the greatest—and certainly the most complex—Romantic philosophical account of the will. As M. H. Abrams argues in *Natural Supernaturalism,* Hegel, particularly in *The Phenomenology of Mind,* has a place of particular importance in the history of autobiographical narrative. The *Phenomenology* is par excellence a philosophical version of the journey as theodicy: the hero (in this case, at least in its ultimate manifestation, the Spirit) undertakes a journey from a fallen and divided condition, through the perils of self-contradiction and alienation; a journey that is in fact a spiraling up to a condition of transcendence in which contradiction is resolved and the lost unity restored. Since this is a narrative of restitution, its end is in its beginning. Hence the circular architectonic of Hegel's system. Abrams's encapsulation of the *Phenomenology* is, I believe, definitive for present purposes. For him, the work is

> the representative autobiography of a spiritual education, told explicitly in the mode of two consciousnesses (the enlightened spirit's present recollection of things past); it justifies evil and suffering as necessary conditions to the achievement of maturity and the recognition of one's identity and aim, is climaxed by the discovery of the implicit principles governing its own organization, evolves both into its own genesis and into the masterwork to which it serves as prelude, and reaches at its end the very stage in time at which the *Phenomenology* in fact begins . . .⁹⁰

Abrams's allusion to a "prelude" alerts us to the momentousness of the date of the *Phenomenology*'s publication: 1807, a year after the publication of the first text of Wordsworth's *The Prelude*. No less than Wordsworth, Hegel epitomizes one of Romanticism's great cultural shifts: the deification of mind (or of some faculties thereof); the attribution to the human intellect, imagination, or whatever of powers hitherto imputed only to God.

But if the *Phenomenology* and *The Prelude* share elements of one of the master plots of Romanticism, they differ in ways that are fundamental for a consideration of autobiography and the will. The *Phenomenology* is not in any conventional sense autobiographical. In saying this I don't mean what is self-evidently the case: that it is speculative philosophy and not personal narrative, that it is written in the third and not the first person. (Though it purports to arrive at a transcendent form of consciousness that perfectly fuses Self and Other, first and third person, the narrative has the structural properties of the third person.) I mean, rather, that the constitution of the central consciousness of Hegel's narrative is structurally dissimilar to the "I" of, say, *The Prelude*. Though singular in nomenclature, Hegel's Spirit is in fact a collective noun— the highest realization of the consciousness of the race. In Abrams's words: "The collective human consciousness figured as a single agent."⁹¹ In this sense Hegel is closer to Kant than to Wordsworth: his conception of the Spirit is indebted to the impersonal conception of Kant's transcendental self.

But while Kant divides the self into higher and lower elements, Hegel's Spirit journeys from a fallen to a transcendental state. The Spirit is an agent-in-process; Hegel's dizzying array of conditions, subdivisions, contradictions, syntheses, and so on map what is at once a conceptual and a historical journey: this is the conceptual path that is required for the envisioning of transcendence, but it is also the path that history, which is preeminently the history of thought (or philosophy), is taking. Herein lies Hegel's optimism.

The Spirit, then, is in a sense the race-as-collective-philosopher-agent, reflecting philosophically on a journey that it was always destined to take. (Here again, Hegel resembles Kant in believing that reason, which for Hegel is inherently dialectical, is the only avenue to transcendence.) But in what sense was it so destined? To answer this question is to consider Hegel's at times baffling account of the will. In order to do this, all aspects of his account need to be seen in terms of the process within which they are embedded. The following example from the famous chapter "The Unhappy Consciousness" describes a transcendence of the individual will that seems to be, and in one sense is, exemplary:

> For giving up one's own will is only in one aspect negative; in principle, or in itself, it is at the same time positive, positing and affirming the will as an *other*, and, specifically, affirming the will as *not* a particular, but universal.[92]

The antithesis between the will as "particular" (reflecting only the inclinations of the individual self) and "universal" (subsumed into the collective will of the Spirit) is fundamental to Hegel's system. So too is the process, depicted above, whereby the protagonist of the narrative passes from one condition to the other: from particular to universal will. In this instance, however, the protagonist is not (yet) the Spirit; it is an earlier manifestation that Hegel calls "self-consciousness," a phase of development in which the consciousness of the protagonist is divided against itself. The "unhappy consciousness" is "the consciousness of self as a divided nature, a doubled and merely contradictory being."[93] This dividedness is not bad in itself: it is a necessary stage of development; but it is flawed in that the protagonist's cardinal and potentially salving capacity to imagine being other than it is—its "negativity"[94]—is here a source of conflict and unease. Thus the protagonist neither acknowledges the full import of, nor welcomes, the process of transition that it has undergone in moving from one modality of the will to another: "The giving up of its own will as particular is not taken by it to be in principle the positive element of universal will."[95] This incomplete othering of the self, the sense of being alienated both from a formerly unified self bearing an individual will, and from collective forms of consciousness, takes us into the world of *Rameau's Nephew* and of course Rousseau's *Confessions*. The notion of the Unhappy Consciousness depicts and presages much of the inner drama of modern autobiography. In an earlier section of the *Phenomenology*, Hegel anatomizes some of the processes that occur when consciousness posits itself as Other:

> Consciousness is for-itself and on its own account, it is a distinguishing of what is undistinguished, it is Self-consciousness. I distinguish myself from myself . . . I, the selfsame being, thrust myself away from myself . . . Consciousness of an other, of an object in general, is indeed itself necessarily self-consciousness, reflectedness into self, consciousness of self in its otherness.[96]

The autobiographer, of course, makes a biographical subject of him- or herself, posits the self as Other; and, like Hegel's protagonist, the modern autobiographer must deal with the gap that thereby opens up—either by trying to close it (Wordsworth) or by embracing radical otherness as the only authentic mode of being (existential autobiography). In either case, as I have argued, acts of will are involved. In Hegel's case, however, the gap is already destined to be closed: the will is a kind of inherent force, moving through consciousness and moving consciousness toward, a state of unconditioned plenitude. It is, in Abrams's words, "immanent energy."[97] In Bourke's terms it seems at times to be an instance of Will as Dynamic Power. If we return to one of the questions that I posed in relation to the Augustine passage in the first chapter of this study, we might ask of Hegel's conception: Who owns the will? The answer seems to be that it can have a kind of contingent and transitory existence as the property of particular individuals who may exert it in various limited and incidental ways, but that such individuals are actually more custodians or conduits than owners. The will moves in and through them, thence upward toward forms that are transpersonal, collective, purified of the dross of individual caprice. Thus in the *Encyclopedia* Hegel says of (individual) "inclinations" and "feelings" that "although they are self-determinations of the free will in itself, in terms of content they are not free for themselves, nor have they reached generality and objectivity."[98] Here there are hints of Rousseau's General Will. Again, in the *Phenomenology* Hegel speaks of the "vanished immediacy" of the individual will as it is subsumed into the universal one.[99]

As his architectonic dictates, Hegel withholds detailed characterizations of the fully emancipated will until the final section of the *Phenomenology*, the one entitled "Spirit." Here, in a series of portentous and highly abstracted formulations, he tries to picture the ascension (the figure of rising up often occurs) of the individual will to the realm in which all wills are harmonized in an impersonal, interpersonal, one. I quote another passage that was to have massive philosophical and political ramifications for the twentieth century:

> Each individual consciousness rises out of the sphere assigned to it, finds no longer its inmost nature and function in this isolated area, but grasps itself as the notion of will, grasps all the various spheres as the essential expression of this will, and is in consequence only able to realize itself in a work which is a work of the whole. In this absolute freedom all social ranks or classes, which are the component spiritual factors into which the whole is differentiated, are effaced and annulled; the individual consciousness that belonged to any such group and exercised its will and found its fulfilment there, has removed the barriers confining it; its purpose is the universal purpose, its language universal law, its work universal achievement.[100]

Vernon J. Bourke sees in passages such as these evidence of a conception of Will as Reality:[101] insofar as the historical dialectic works through the will and brings about the state that fuses all wills into an ideal entity, the will is, potentially at least, the very stuff of reality. Marx was to reply that no blessed necessity of contemplative release from constraint was at work in history. Class divides had to be leveled through struggle; revolutions in the social order had to be made through a very different kind of will—through *praxis*. But for Hegel the ascent of the Spirit through reason would culminate in "laws and functions of the state"[102] as consciousness contemplates and fuses with its true object—"consciousness itself."[103] Freedom is for Hegel a fundamental and inalienable feature of the mind, and as that freedom is realized the mind's distinctive medium—reason— will reshape the world.

IV. *Schopenhauer: Romantic Pessimism*

In his account of the will, Schopenhauer is almost eerily prescient of late modernity. Here is a typical passage:

> Thus everywhere in nature we see contest, struggle, and the fluctuation of victory, and later on we shall recognize in this more distinctly that variance with itself essential to the will. Every grade of the will's objectification fights for the matter, the space, and the time of another.[104]

The foreshadowings of Darwin are unmistakable, as are, in other places, the anticipations of Freud (who much admired Schopenhauer). Schopenhauer's tragic sense, so apparent in the passage just quoted, is principally expressed through his conception of the will. He follows (while also critiquing aspects of) Kant in conceptualizing the world in two principal dimensions: phenomena, that which is of the causal world of nature; and noumena, or, the "thing-in-itself"—the true being of things. There is also a transcendental dimension, associated with Platonic Ideas, that reveals itself to certain individuals in states of mystical cessation. More of this in a moment.

Schopenhauer aligns particular modes of knowing with these various dimensions. He follows Kant in claiming that the phenomenal world is known through a process in which mind actively participates in the perception of "reality," such that "reality" is a product of mind and world, and of the mind's relationship to "reality." The world so perceived is the world as Idea (or "Representation"). But the world known in this dimension is "not the only side of the world, but merely its external side, so to speak, and that the world has an entirely different side which is its innermost being, its kernel, the thing-in-itself."[105] The will is "the *thing-in-itself* proper."[106] Hence the title of Schopenhauer's great work: *The World as Will and Representation* (or *Idea*).

But what manner of thing is this "will"? It is not in any substantive sense "my will," a faculty that I exert in a conventional mode of free choosing. Rather, it is a transpersonal force that is in all of creation: "The inner being itself . . . is present whole and undivided in everything in nature, and in every living being."[107] This is Will as Dynamic Power. Will for Schopenhauer is the Almighty; creation is the instantiation of the will. Humankind is a "microcosm"[108] of the whole: each of us is the bearer of a force—the primal, constitutive force—that is the very stuff of life. If this sounds sanguine, Schopenhauer's characterization of will in its most primordial aspect again makes clear that—and why—his thought is essentially pessimistic: "Here we see at the very lowest grade the will manifesting itself as a blind impulse . . . it appears as such a blind urge and as a striving devoid of knowledge in the whole of inorganic nature."[109] We embody and are driven by this "blind" "striving"; the will is not the rational thing envisaged by Kant or Hegel, nor is it separate from its manifestations in action: in contrast to dualistic theories like that of Descartes, action for Schopenhauer is merely the externalization of the will. However, the gloom of this view is alleviated somewhat by the fact that natural phenomena exist in a hierarchy, with organisms that possess no power of intellection, and so no capacity to reflect upon the will that is within, at the bottom, and humankind, which has the ability so to reflect, at the top. In human beings "the light of knowledge penetrates into the workshop of the blindly operating will, and illuminates the vegetative functions of the human organism";[110] in us will becomes "the object of the knowing subject."[111] Here, then, is one version of the conjuncture of introspection and the will that, as I have been arguing, is so fundamental to autobiography.

As might be expected given the atavistic view he has of the world, Schopenhauer's account of introspection allows for little edifying interiority. There are a number of reasons for this. One is that he holds the will to be constitutively resistant to explanation: like a natural phenomenon such as a mote in a sunbeam, "the human will . . . is in its inner nature not subject to explanation."[112] So that which is the primary focus of introspection—the will—is in fact unyielding to human understanding. Moreover, the powers of understanding, or rationality, are on this view very limited: the light of knowledge does not penetrate very far. Unlike Descartes and other rationalists, Schopenhauer speaks (puzzlingly) of "the complete difference between the will and the intellect . . . the former's primacy and the latter's subordinate position."[113] Further, one of the many respects in which Schopenhauer anticipates Freud is his insistence that the will is buried in, or is perhaps the very being of, the unconscious: "The will, as the thing-in-itself, constitutes the inner, true, and indestructible nature of man; yet in itself it is without consciousness."[114] Again:

> In fact, the intellect remains so much excluded from the real resolutions and secret decisions of its own will that sometimes it can only get to know them, like those of a stranger, by spying out and taking unawares; and it must surprise the will in the act of expressing itself, in order merely to discover its real intentions.[115]

Moreover, the main focus of the will is the libido.[116] Elsewhere he likens consciousness to a plant, where the root is the will; the corona, the intellect; and the stem, the "I" or (in our terms) the egolike intermediary between the two.[117] Thus, "man's real inner nature" is "not in consciousness, but in the will."[118] It follows that introspection will not reveal our own motives for action prior to action taking place. We can only know of such things *a postiori,* and then "knowledge is merely added to"[119] the action in question. However, the *a postiori* view can under certain conducive circumstances reveal much that is true about the person and his or her acts. One example of this is letter writing; another is autobiography:

> The man who records his life surveys it as a whole; the individual thing becomes small, the near becomes distant, the distant again becomes near, motives shrink and contract. He is sitting at the confessional, and is doing so of his own free will. Here the spirit of lying does not seize him so readily [as in, say, a conversation], for there is to be found in every man an inclination to truth which has first to be overcome in the case of every lie . . .[120]

Here is another of those redemptive moments that intermittently relieve the gloom of Schopenhauer's worldview. But this passage is about retrospection—a kind of inference drawn on the basis of what one has done—rather than introspection, a looking inward in the present tense. And we still need to ask: Given his views about the will in general, what can be the force of the phrase "of his own free will" here?

This brings us to one of the least plausible aspects of Schopenhauer's account of will. And since it is also one of the most important, its flaws must weigh heavily against his outlook in general. The following passage sets out his position on freedom of will in *The World as Will and Representation.* (The position was restated, with some elaboration, in the essay *On the Freedom of the Will*):[121]

> This man is never free, although he is the phenomenon of a free will, for he is the already determined phenomenon of this will's free willing; and since he enters into the form of all objects, the principle of sufficient reason, he develops the unity of that will into a plurality of actions. But since the unity of that will in itself lies outside time, this plurality exhibits itself with the conformity to law of a force of Nature. Since, however, it is that free willing which becomes visible in the man and in his whole conduct . . . every particular deed of the man is to be ascribed to the free will, and directly proclaims itself as such to consciousness.[122]

In other words: an individual comes into being through the (inscrutable) action of a free power or will; but the person him- or herself is determined by the "free volition" of that will, and being of the order of Nature is subject to Nature's causal laws. The individual experiences a sensation of freedom in making choices because what he or she senses within is a localization of the power that is free; but so localized in the self, that power is in fact not free but determined. To this extent the sentiment of freedom of choice is an illusion. Schopenhauer further anatomizes the processes in question as follows: We have an "empirical character"—"the unalterable nature of the empirical character"[123]—which is fixed and unchanging; this character provides "motives" to the will (in fact he distinguishes between cause, stimulus, and motivation);[124] the will is so configured that it must act in accordance with these motives. Because in a sense we provide our will with our own motives, we feel that we choose freely; but in fact our given characters have the force of necessity in all we do.[125] However, all is not lost, because through what he terms the "*acquired character,*" the individual can attain a consummate form of self-knowledge, "the most complete possible knowledge of our own individuality."[126] One of the apparent oddities of Schopenhauer's position is that the empirical self through which the blind, impersonal will moves is an irreducibly particular self and that there exists "great difference of individual characters."[127] The person who can gain profound knowledge of the (empirical) self also gains profound knowledge of the world-that-is-will and, with that, a kind of philosophical detachment from the strife-torn human condition.

And so to what might be termed the mystical side of Schopenhauer's thinking. On this version of the unconditioned, the reflective individual, through "the sanctifying force" of "resignation,"[128] through aesthetic experience,[129] and through altruistic moral activity,[130] may, like the philosopher-autobiographer George Santayana, achieve a state in which "the will now turns away from life."[131] It is now that mind apprehends the Platonic Ideas; the old determining character can be "eliminated"[132] and the will, now released from the impairments of its conditioned state, can now perhaps be said to be free. Schopenhauer cites Christian dogma and Eastern mysticism in asserting, with due qualification, that seen in these terms the "old philosophical argument of the freedom of the will . . . is not without ground."[133] "*Necessity,*" he tells us in italics, "*is the kingdom of nature; freedom is the kingdom of grace.*"[134] Whether this vision of "salvation"[135] is compelling in the light of Schopenhauer's general position is in my view doubtful. Certainly he does not ultimately share Kant's faith in reason nor Hegel's faith in rational process, though in a phrase that resonates for this study he says that History, in charting the ways of the will, "follows the thread of events."[136] Yet the will-less sage that is History seems to have achieved a miraculous exemption from a condition to which the great majority of the species seem perpetually doomed. For them the threads are the threads of determination.

IV. NINETEENTH-CENTURY AFFIRMATIONS

After Schopenhauer, nineteenth-century Continental philosophy was to produce further and massively influential accounts of the will (see chapter 2). However, it is essential to acknowledge the prevalence and importance of what might in very general terms be called empiricist-liberal writings about the will by

British and American philosophers, psychologists, and social theorists. While generally not as audacious or ambitiously systematic as their Continental counterparts, many of these writers matter not only because they affirm the existence and the (partial) freedom of the will, but because they also affirm the existence of a substantial self—a notion that was to persist into twentieth-century liberal accounts. One of the strands of the story I have to tell in this book is that such liberal understandings of the will become very important once the nature and dangers of totalitarianism dawn upon Western intellectuals, and that intellectual autobiographers were prominent among those who took up the challenge of trying to imagine a complex, discerning, and volitionally endowed self after Hitler and Stalin.

1. *William James*

In *The Principles of Psychology* William James gives one of the most fine-grained of all accounts of the will. Indeed there are few better places to go for an introduction to the subject. James's discussion ranges over neurophysiological, experimental, psychological, philosophical, and everyday experiential ground and offers a compelling synthesis of information from these areas. Not for nothing was James the brother of one of the great novelistic explorers of the intricacies of the will. Some of William's phrases might well have appeared in a Henry James novel: "*the dread of the irrevocable*"; "the slow dead heave of the will"; and, with reference to the temptation of doing "bad acts," he speaks of a "vertiginous fascination."[137] The chapter that James devotes to the will concludes its penultimate section with an impassioned invocation of the centrality of the will in human life—"'*will you or won't you have it so?*' is the most probing question we are ever asked"[138]—and a plea that we should trust the intuitive sense we have that the will is real, that it is free, that it is fundamental. James is yet another commentator on the will who figures it in threadlike terms, writing of "the web of motivation."[139]

James construes the will entirely in mentalistic terms: "Volition is primarily a relation, not between our Self and extra-mental matter (as many philosophers still maintain), but between our Self and our own states of mind."[140] The essence of this "relation" is an act of "attention" whereby the mind holds a certain idea about what the agent ought to do for long enough to enable the idea to have "a quiet hearing."[141] James agrees with many of the commentators we have so far considered, that if a "quiet hearing" occurs, it is highly likely that the agent will make the rational and reasonable decision.[142] James sums up as follows:

> *The essential achievement of the will, in short, when it is most "voluntary," is to* ATTEND *to a difficult object and hold it fast before the mind. The so-doing is* the *fiat;* and it is a mere physiological incident that when the object is thus attended to, immediate motor consequences should ensue.[143]

The strong-willed person is one who can maintain attention on objects for longer than others.[144] We can know certain things about volition—for instance, feelings of uneasiness rather like those posited by Locke, certain experiences of deliberation, and above all the "ideas" that precipitate action. James is thoroughly empiricist in his insistence that such ideas can only be derived from experience.[145] However, he denies that through introspection we can capture the microprocesses of willing itself.[146]

James's discussion is impressive for the range of modalities and experiences of the will it considers. He is one of the first theoretical commentators to write perceptively about what might be thought of as pathological states of the will.[147] For this reason (among others) he is important for relations between autobiography and the will, since reflective autobiographies so often explore states of the will that seem to them aberrant, dysfunctional, or pathological. Stephen Spender's fear of masochistic, passive, and reckless modalities of the will—the subject of chapter 7 of this study—is a case in point.

On the question of free will, James is refreshingly modest and chary of monolithic accounts. He believes that "the question of free-will is insoluble on strictly psychologic grounds,"[148] and so proceeds—as one surely must—to consider it from several points of view. One is to question the foundational physicalist assumptions on which versions of determinism often rest. In true pragmatist form, James suggests that we see what happens if we proceed instead from "a *moral* postulate about the Universe, the postulate that *what ought to be can be, and that bad acts cannot be fated, but that good ones must be possible in their place,* which would lead one to espouse the contrary view."[149] In a classic phrase he argues that "freedom's first deed should be to affirm itself,"[150] and that it is only by assuming freedom of the will that we can undertake a proper investigation of any topic, this one included. Even then, conclusions must necessarily be provisional, but he urges an important distinction between "determinism," which admits of the subjective experience of effort, and "fatalism" understood as a surrender of effort;[151] and he enjoins the kind of effort that is expressed in a brave facing of life's complexities, and a refusal of simple—for instance, scientistic deterministic—formulations about "the huge world that girdles us."[152] James employs a figure that is very close to one Nietzsche uses for the will: James uses the figure of the tide; Nietzsche, the wave. Determinism "admits something phenomenal *called* free effort, which *seems* to breast the tide, but it claims this as a *portion of the tide.*"[153] His belief is that we do indeed "breast" the tide; that, at least to some extent, we chart our course amid the coercive currents. At the center of this picture is the substantial individual self that cannot be reduced to mere experiential and ideational clusters[154] and that possesses a heroic capacity to refuse simple myths of defeat and consolation, and to confront the contingent and strange thereness of the world. This, too, sounds like Nietzsche; but, as I have argued, James's German contemporary was in essence a denier, not a defender, of the will.

II. *John Stuart Mill*

John Stuart Mill occupies a special place in the history of autobiography and its relations with the will. His *Autobiography* is one of the best known and most influential examples of the use of autobiography to chronicle the emotional impact, and the eventual transcending, of a deterministic view of the world. In Mill's footsteps follow many modern intellectual autobiographers, not least those like Stephen Spender and Arthur Koestler, who use autobiography to narrate their experience of living with, and outliving, the deterministic premises of Marxism.

Mill's account of the will is not particularly detailed philosophically; but his conception of how will should operate in an open society is of great moment. *A System of Logic* sets out his position on the nature and the powers of the will. His underlying assumptions are essentially empiricist: we learn from experience what forms of action are available to us,[155] and it is on the basis of such knowledge that we can initiate volitions. Introspection can reveal certain physical sensations that are attendant upon the state of mind in which we intend, and the action that executes that intention; however, consciousness cannot register causal connections between intentions and actions:

> A volition is not an efficient, but simply a physical cause. Our will causes our bodily actions in the same sense, and in no other, in which cold causes ice, or a spark causes an explosion of gun-powder. The volition, a state of our mind, is the antecedent; the motion of our limbs in conformity to the volition is the consequent. This sequence I conceive to be not a subject of direct consciousness . . .[156]

The physical analogies suggest the presence of a strong Hume-style causal theory, and this is indeed the case. However, Mill's proposed discipline of "ethology"—the "science of the formation of human character"[157]—suggests that human beings are both embedded in a world of necessity *and* that they are to a significant degree potentially free. His argument turns on a particular construal of the term "necessity." He rejects the common understanding of the term as a simple synonym for the strictly inevitable. "Philosophical Necessity" rightly claims that if we know someone well enough we can predict how they will act in a given situation, but this is not inconsistent with our being free; nor does it invalidate the subjective sense of freedom that sometimes accompanies our actions.[158] The fact is, he believes, that human motivation is almost always multiple, and it follows from this that no single determinant will inevitably hold sway. Of human actions he says:

They are never (except in some cases of mania) ruled by any one motive with such absolute sway that there is no room for the influence of any other. The causes, therefore, on which action depends are never uncontrollable, and any given effect is only necessary provided that the causes tending to produce it are not controlled. That whatever happens could not have happened otherwise unless something had taken place which was capable of preventing it, no one surely needs hesitate to admit.[159]

The multiplicity of possible determinants allows for the possibility of some kind of intervention in causal sequences, and that possibility is greatly augmented by the fact that one of the key determinants in our conduct is an entity we have the capacity to change: "our characters." Of character Mill writes:

> Its being, in the ultimate resort, formed for him [any human being], is not inconsistent with its being, in part, formed *by* him as one of the intermediate agents. His character is formed by his circumstances, (including among these his particular organisation,) but his own desire to mould it in a particular way is one of those circumstances, and by no means one of the least influential.

And again: "We are exactly as capable of making our own character, *if we will,* as others are of making it for us."[160]

It is this position that, at least in part, rescues Mill from the depression that he describes in the *Autobiography,* a work Olney likens to "a syllogism on private human experience":[161]

> During the later returns of my dejection, the doctrine of what is called Philosophical Necessity weighed on my existence like an incubus. I felt as if I was scientifically proved to be the helpless slave of antecedent circumstances; as if my character and that of all others had been formed for us by agencies beyond our control, and was wholly out of our own power. I often said to myself, what a relief it would be if I could disbelieve the doctrine of the formation of character by circumstances . . .[162]

He ponders the problem and eventually perceives that the term "necessity" carries a misleading implication with respect to human action. And then:

> I saw that though our character is formed by circumstances, our own desires can do much to shape those circumstances; and that what is really inspiriting and ennobling in the doctrine of freewill, is the conviction that we have real power over the formation of our own character; that our will, by influencing some of our circumstances, can modify our future habits or capabilities of willing.[163]

The emphasis on "desires" is crucial: this is an autobiography that famously chronicles the discovery of an affective dimension in life, and it is this dimension that instigates the will's reflexive action upon character and its circumstances. Here yet again the question "Who owns the will?" arises. Mill's answer seems to be that while the affective dimensions of the psyche are inactive, the will too is inactive, at least in the sense that it can do no more than reflect the power that external determinants have over the self. In this sense the self does not have real "ownership" of it. But when the affective powers are activated, the will becomes a power at our disposal. We can exercise it as a thing that is ours to use. Elsewhere, Mill insists that the will is an aspect of an "enduring I"[164] and that we can modify and otherwise influence it.

The notion that the will can be modified and educated is of course central to Mill's political and social philosophy. *On Liberty*'s espousal of Humboldt's principle of "the absolute and essential importance of human development in its richest variety"[165] is in part a call for the education of the will such that it will be brought to bear upon personal and social development. The book's vision of "a greater fullness of life"[166] requires, first, that social beings are social agents in a full sense: "He who chooses his [life] plan for himself employs all his faculties." Such a person succeeds in proportion as he exercises "decision," "discrimination," "firmness," "self-control," and a combination of "judgement and feelings."[167] Second—and importantly—*On Liberty* acknowledges that the will necessarily has its life in the realm of the socially conditioned. It must be as free as it can reasonably be, but this version of liberalism is in no doubt that the will must acquiesce in certain constraints: "The sole end for which mankind are warranted, individually or collectively, in interfering with the liberty of action of any of their number is self-protection."[168] Whether this formulation makes sufficient allowance for constraint, and whether liberalism could adequately grasp other and more insidious kinds of social constraint, was to become a matter of major dispute for late modernity.

APPENDIX B
SOME OTHER LATE MODERN INSTANCES

I. Voluntary and Involuntary: Paul Ricoeur

In *Freedom and Nature*, the first volume of his massive study of the will, Paul Ricoeur alludes to "the grandeur of choice."[1] The phrase sounds Sartrean, and indeed Ricoeur shares some of Sartre's fascination with the drama of the human will's life in the world. Yet Ricoeur's account of the will is in part intended as a corrective to what he sees as the reductive excesses of Sartrean ontology. Ricoeur believes that the Sartrean binary of being/nothingness is at once too insubstantial and too voluntaristic in its account of the self: insubstantial in that, on this view, the self "exists" in a mode of pure negativity; voluntaristic in the sense that so conceived the unfettered will encounters no limits to its projects of transcendence.[2] Ricoeur's inquiry, which seeks to combine a hermeneutic investigation of human meaning-making with a phenomenological description of the will in its various modalities, replaces the being/nothingness pairing with that of voluntary/involuntary; but while the existential being/nothingness is binary in structure, Ricoeur's voluntary/involuntary is dialectical:[3] each of these terms entails, requires, and interacts with the other. Ricoeur insists on the "*reciprocity of the involuntary and the voluntary*"[4]—a reciprocity that is both empirical in the sense that we only know freedom in a context of constraint, and theoretical in that, conceptually, the two terms are mutually entailing. This way of conceptualizing the issue moves the axis of discussion from constraint and transcendence, as in Sartre, to constraint as a necessary condition of a qualified freedom. Thus Ricoeur: "We shall say that freedom is immersed in necessity, that necessity is the locus of freedom."[5] Here is a typically counter-Sartrean formulation:

> Self-imputation and motivation indicate the liaison of a specific activity and receptivity at the heart of deciding. It would be a total misconception of man—and we shall progressively discover that man's condition has the being of Transcendence as its limiting index—if we considered willing a pure act. Activity has not only a contrary, but also a complement: a contrary in the passivity whose prototype is the bondage of passions, a complement in the passivity of which motives are a prime example and which is illustrated in still another way by the organs of voluntary motion and the necessity of a given

condition. I do my acts to the extent to which I *accept* reasons for them. I provide the basis for the physical being of my actions even while I base myself on their value, that is, their moral being.[6]

This gives Ricoeur's characteristic emphasis on the inevitability of some degree of limitation; it also reflects his habit of careful and intricate attention to the actual phenomenological structures and experiences of the life of the will. While his conceptualization of these matters is less dramatic than Sartre's, and his exposition less arresting in stylistic and literary terms, the nuanced and inclusive nature of Ricoeur's descriptions is of real value for literary textual readings, not least readings of autobiography. His treatment of "motives" in the passage just quoted typifies one of the great virtues of his account: his understanding of the importance of such intangible and shifting internal phenomena as hesitation, changes of mind, shades of inclination, and the like, in the life of the agent. He argues that "the deciding will cannot be reduced to a terminal act, to a final *fiat* bursting suddenly into the warp and woof of an internal situation which makes no allowances for it."[7] Volitional events have a history, and it is a history that needs to be traced through a "succession" that is the "progress of decision through detours, stagnation, leaps and returns."[8] He acknowledges the importance of "intellectualism"[9] and its positing of the will's inherent dependence on rational assessment; however, he cautions that "it is false that determination by reasons rather than by impulses or desires is enough to make us free,"[10] and he accords a central place to "attention"[11]—a kind of meditative focus on possibilities—in the life of the "free" agent. His conception of will is also fundamentally ethical, at least in some dimensions. This is the "moral value" in the life of the agent: "On the one hand, will seeks its justification in values and turns to them to receive a blessing of the good; on the other hand, valuation is only a moment in the initiative of the will which enlists in its service."[12] He emphasizes the inalienably social dimension of values: the cogito always occurs within a social setting ("the act of myself is at the same time participation"),[13] and "collective representations are a source of motives distinct from organic needs."[14]

As the reference to a "moment" indicates, Ricoeur's picture of the will is spread across various dimensions—a feature of the theory that is only loosely captured by a temporal term like "moment." Some of these dimensions pertain to will-acts themselves, others to stages in his descriptive methodology. Indeed *Freedom and Nature* is a difficult book to summarize, in part because the line between will-dimensions and description-dimensions is often hard to draw. In his desire to honor the "mystery of incarnation"[15] that we know through the lived experience of the will, Ricoeur constructs an intricate but flexible analytic grid. It all "begins" with the cogito: "I understand myself in the first place as he who says 'I will.'"[16] (Ricoeur insists on the inclusiveness of the cogito as an experience comprising "'I desire,' 'I can,' 'I intend,' and, in a general way, my existence as a body.")[17] In one dimension, that inaugurating "'I will'" can be understood in terms of three noetic (or intentional) "acts" of the will: "deciding," "moving," and "consenting." In phenomenological terms, each of these can be understood as having intentional objects that can be analyzed in noematic terms: deciding— the decision made; moving—bodily movement undertaken; consent—acquiescence in a set of conditions/limitations. At another level, and in keeping with the doctrine of the reciprocity of voluntary and involuntary, each component can be understood in terms of its manifestation in the mode of the involuntary. Here deciding is construed in terms of needs, motives, values; moving with respect to skills, emotions, habits; and consenting is grounded in character, the unconscious, life.[18] In this series of "moments," the involuntary is increasingly primary with respect to the voluntary. It is also important to note that one of the main aspirations of the account is to deconstruct traditional binaries of mind and body.

The picture of the self that emerges from this phase of the analysis is highly particular at some levels, and universalist at others. The particularist tendency is obvious in a statement such as: "All motivation is in the first place irremediably particular: every consciousness has its own style which distinguishes it from all others."[19] Particularity is also implied in the notion (Ricoeur is closer to Sartre on this point) of the self as an "open totality."[20] When he writes about "character," the self emerges as a universal particular that is both determined and free: "My character in its changeless aspects is only *my freedom's mode of being*"; and, "I have a way of choosing and of choosing myself which I do not choose."[21] In other words, the universal structures of selfhood impose upon each individual a kind of power of freedom that permits each to choose the particular form he or she, and his or her life-narrative, will take. Of course, the "eidetic method" employed in the phenomenological analysis is intended to uncover universal structures, and the further the "successive deepenings of the descriptive method"[22] proceed toward the "involuntary" end of the spectrum, the more universalist (for want of a better term) the account becomes.

A central feature of Ricoeur's general description of the human condition and the will's place therein is the notion of the "fault," which he thinks of as "an alien body in the essential structure of man."[23] The "fault," here understood as human frailty and fallibility—those aspects of the human constitution that allow evil into the world and that impede the satisfactory operations of the will—is the subject of the second part of Ricoeur's study of the will, *Finitude and Guilt*. This work is in turn divided into two parts, *Fallible Man* and *The Symbolism of Evil*.[24] In pursuit of the "global disposition" that is the fault, this "certain non-coincidence of man with himself,"[25] Ricoeur now moves into a different set of analytic and descriptive registers. In *Fallible Man*, eidetic description gives over to a form of reflection in which the "internal aberration" that is the "fault" is approached "regressively through reflection on unstable syntheses."[26] This description has three dimensions: transcendental, practical, and affective. The next volume, *The Symbolism of Evil,* abandons the phenomenological method altogether for what is in effect a textual quest for evidences of human frailty. Here Ricoeur's project has striking potential applications for autobiography in that his main source of textual evidence is religious confessions. This investigation, which focuses on three protean myths—the myths of chaos, divine binding, and exile—is hermeneutic in character. What it tries ultimately to characterize is the phenomenon of the "servile will," which at some fundamental but rather inarticulable level has to do with "the unavailability of freedom to itself"[27]—a kind of thwarting of the freedom of the will. The phases of hermeneutic analysis of this condition are intricate and do not need to be rehearsed for our purposes;[28] but we can say in general terms that Ricoeur sees in the whole practice of religious confession a source of, in principle, reliable insight into humanity's fallen condition. The complexity of his hermeneutic method acknowledges the difficulty of rendering that condition intelligible, but it does not deny the possibility of (significant) intelligibility itself. Ricoeur's own modest venture into autobiography, his "Intellectual Autobiography,"[29] does not dwell on the condition of his own will, but it records a life marked by a capacity for initiative, change, and growth, both intellectual and personal. It is an unassuming but by no means a "servile" document.

II. Wittgenstein and Anglo-American Analytic Philosophy

I have noted that it is hard to generalize about modern analytic philosophy because it comprises so many styles and themes of philosophizing. The will has certainly had its defenders, like Brian O'Shaughnessy in his monumental *The Will: A Dual Aspect Theory.* O'Shaughnessy says of the will: "I actually believe in the phenomenon it [the word] purports to designate."[30] But the more general tendency has been to deny the existence of a psychic faculty that might be construed as the will, or free will. An important but complex case is that of Wittgenstein. As Charles Altieri says: "Wittgenstein's approach to the will is difficult to state in general terms."[31] In part this is because of the intense aphoristic difficulty of his work in general; also because of the difficulties involved in tracking his views as between the early *Tractatus* and the later *Philosophical Investigations.*[32] (His *Notebooks* help to chart some of the patterns in question.)[33] A study of autobiography and the will must take account not just of Wittgenstein on the will, but also of the implications that some of his views in general have for autobiography. It should also be noted that, as in the case of Descartes, Nietzsche, and others, Wittgenstein's very manner of doing philosophy has a strong autobiographical flavor.

Perhaps the most important of these implications concerns Wittgenstein's account of the self, in particular his attack on the mainstream Western philosophical assumption—an assumption that is dramatically evident in Augustine—that there exists an inner world that can be understood on the model of a metaphysically objective world:[34]

> *Where in* the world is a metaphysical subject to be noted?
>
> You say that this case is altogether like that of the eye and the field of sight. But you do *not* really see the eye.
>
> And from nothing *in the field of sight* can it be concluded that it is seen from an eye.[35]

While he does not deny that we have inner lives, Wittgenstein denies that any such inner world—a kind of self-guaranteeing theater of the mind that is ontologically independent from the world—exists: "An 'inner process' stands in need of outward criteria."[36] We don't, for example, have thoughts that then "go into" or "get expressed in" language; we don't formulate intentions that then cause actions. To put it another way, Wittgenstein rejects the notion of mental contents and intermediaries: thoughts are already linguisticized, intentions spring up in the context of the subject's embeddedness in a social setting. This embeddedness constitutes the link between "subject" and "world": subjects are agents who internalize social grammars and engage with the world accordingly, while also having the capacity to react back upon those grammars in ways that change them and the linguistic community itself.

The description I have just given pertains largely to Wittgenstein's later thinking, however, and in turning more specifically to his account of the will, we need to backtrack for a moment to the early position of the *Tractatus*. Here Wittgenstein distinguishes between the phenomenal will (the alleged empirical psychological faculty we habitually think of as the will) and the transcendental will—that which we assume to exist when we characterize the subject as, say, Kant does; a will that takes its counsel from sources that are in some sense extrasocial or absolute. We can say that that the will as pictured in the *Tractatus* is essentially the transcendental will. When Wittgenstein says that "the world is independent of my will,"[37] he seems to mean that (a) since there are no causal laws that I can master, my will can only determine my attitude to the way things are, though its shape may change the things themselves; (b) the will is in some sense severed from the world of events and actual states of affairs, and so from the forms and evaluations associated with these; (c) the will so conceived lacks—or might arguably lack—the ability to grasp the subject's position in the world as a whole. (There is scope here for some notion of weakness of will.) Peter Winch argues that there is a connection of some sort between the two forms of the will, phenomenal and transcendental.[38] Be this as it may, the account of the will in the *Tractatus* seems to reflect that work's general tendency to see the relation between subject and world on the model of a proposition: something that can describe, but cannot change, a given state of affairs. To this extent, it is a kind of otherworldly will; something that cannot intervene in the social settings it transcends.

The *Philosophical Investigations* crystallizes the notion of a social setting (as I have called it) into what Wittgenstein calls "forms of life,"[39] by which he means particular social practices that constitute agents who enact and modify these forms. Since philosophizing itself takes place within particular forms of life, it cannot make meaningful sense of the transcendental; and so the distinction between the transcendental and phenomenal remains problematical. The will operates in a given setting. To say it "operates" is in fact apt, because Wittgenstein wants to avoid what he sees as the old mistake of duplication wherein some sort of mental act is posited in order to get the will going; in other words, the will wills itself into activity: "It makes no sense to speak of willing willing."[40] As Charles Altieri suggests, Wittgenstein's later view is best characterized in terms of words like *disposition* and *orientation*.[41] "The will is an attitude of the subject to the world."[42] What we construe as the "will" is not in fact a faculty of mind, replete with its own shadow theater of energies and prior willings, but rather the particular mode of belonging that a given subject has to its social world; a mode of belonging that entails a certain disposition or orientation toward (among other things) one's acts. It is within that social world and its forms of life, and within the context of that agent's mode of belonging, that "willing" takes place—the kind of willing that seems immediate in the sense that there is no Augustinian or Cartesian intermediary dimension behind it. Such willing is socially constructed in the specific sense that the circumstances in which the will has its life, and the meanings we assign to that life, are social in origin.

What this view entails for the practice of autobiography is (like so much else about Wittgenstein) open to debate. It might suggest that an autobiographer's account of her or his motives for doing something must be unreliable in the sense that the writer is directing her or his attention to the wrong place: to an imagined "inner" world rather than to a nexus between subject and social setting. Indeed Wittgenstein does distinguish between "reasons" and "causes" in a way that generally limits the former to first-person accounts, while the latter are seen as third-person observational statements.[43] The *Investigations* also distinguishes between willing and wishing: while willing cannot be a cause, wishing, which has that capacity, requires the disposition of commitment entailed in willing, in order to find expression: "Willing, if it is not to be a sort of wishing, must be the action itself."[44] What would the status of an autobiographer's account of her or his reasons be? The answer here seems to be mixed. To the extent that Wittgenstein thinks that mental life is already linguisticized, he might say that first-person reports on reasons can have considerable legitimacy, since language here reports on what is already linguistic; but in the sense that he does not think that self-reflection can capture that which is reflected upon, he might see such reports as little more than a kind of post facto fictionalizing. But this seems unlikely. Wittgenstein's philosophical method depends so heavily upon scrutinizing language usage as a key to understanding of forms of life that it would make no sense to deny in principle the authority of first-person reports. Rather, the point might be that such reports illuminate in ways and places that are not necessarily intended or envisaged by the reporters. There might even be a sense in which an autobiographical account of the will is a kind of double reflection: a reflection on what was itself a way of talking about an inclination that was not of the agent's making.

There can be few more preposterous experiences in life than trying to summarize Wittgenstein in a few paragraphs; but, as Altieri argues, there is no reason to think that Wittgenstein's account of will is inimical to a deep conception of agency. Nor is there reason to feel that Wittgenstein's views are essentially inimical to the exploration of the will. What his views do suggest, however, is that exploration is always a form or an offshoot of conversation. There is no "private language"[45] in which we can commune with our "inner" selves; but there are public languages—autobiography among them—in which we can and do explore the experience of having an inner life, of having, for instance, a will. Though Wittgenstein's accounts of the will, and of the self in general, are more attenuated than the conceptions I propose in this study, his outlook on the will is congenial to the extent that he sees the will as discussable because the medium of discussion—language—has such a powerful role in making it the sort of thing that it is. Will springs from language games,[46] games that induct agents into complex reciprocal engagements with the world, and autobiography is a language game that we might expect to shed light on the will.

Another complex and nuanced analytic philosophical denial of the will and its supposed freedoms has come from Donald Davidson. For Davidson, "cause is the cement of the universe";[47] but does this entail that the intentional states— for instance, the willings—of human beings are causally determined? One of the many layers of complication in Davidson's account arises from his contention that laws relate to events—say internal events and "actions"—only insofar as these things are described in a certain way. His "*anomalous monism*" argues that "psychological events are physical events" but that "events do not fall under strict laws when described in psychological terms."[48] Psychological—or mental— events can only then be described under physical laws, and this for Davidson amounts to saying that mental events *are* physical events.[49] While some of his remarkably detailed and incisive comments about agency might seem to suggest otherwise,[50] the general import of his position seems to be that, ultimately, the inner world of the agent is externally caused, and that—by implication—freedom of will is logically impossible. More precisely, Davidson sees these causal relations as extensional and objective, and causal explanation (and description) as the opposite.

GLOSSARY OF TERMS

AGENT: The capacity of an individual to act in the light of complex forms and combinations of reflection, deliberation, and appraisal. Agents can be "strong" or "weak" "evaluators"; the former are individuals who weigh options in terms that pertain to larger implications and conceptions of what is good in life. The "stronger" the evaluator, the more developed are the agential powers of the self. Agents have "reflexive" relations to the social structures in which they are embedded (*see reflexive monitoring of conduct*), and their evaluations generally include a developed ethical dimension—a dimension upon which they are able to report through the use of sophisticated linguistic capacities. The agent possesses a substantial margin of freedom, be it freedom to act or to reflect. The writing of a substantive, *reflective autobiography* (*see below*) is an example of the exertion of agential powers so conceived.

AGENT CAUSATION: Similar to Aristotle's notion of an *efficient cause,* agent causation describes an occurrence that is caused by the freely willed activity of an agent.

APPETITION: Roughly equivalent to "inclination," appetition can be inflected in many ways—rational, passional, and so on.

CAUSE: A term with an array of not always compatible connotations. The most fundamental feature that is common to the greatest range of usages is that a cause is clearly prior to and independent of that which it brings about. Aristotle's fourfold typology of causes is foundational. He distinguishes between *efficient cause* (that by which a change is wrought), *final cause* (the end or purpose for which a change is pursued), *material cause* (that in which a change is wrought), and *formal cause* (that into which something is changed). Three often used senses for the word *cause* are as follows: one, the Humean view (taken up by Mill) that one event is the cause of another if and only if the first kind of event can universally be seen to result in the second kind, and vice versa. Here the occurrence of the first event is both a necessary and sufficient condition for the occurrence of the second. Two, the view that a cause is a necessary but not a necessarily sufficient condition for bringing something about. Three, the idea of "cause" as a "lever," a means of setting in train something that brings something else about.

CONFIGURATIVE METAPHORS: Metaphors that figure relations between aspects or "regions" of reality, and the forces that generate, link, or articulate them.

CULTURAL SPECIFICITY OF THE WILL: The view that both conceptions and lived manifestations of the will have a high degree of specificity to particular forms of

325

culture, or, as Wittgenstein has it, particular *forms of life*.

EVENT CAUSATION: Where events are caused by other events (rather than by the freely willed activity of agents).

EXISTENTIAL POSITING: A foundational "act" of consciousness in which the self tries to establish the nature of its relationship to the world. Speculation about and exploration of the will is central to such acts, since the nature of one's relation to the world must in large part depend on whether the self is seen as causative of—as efficiently willing—its own being and life events, or whether the self and its life events are seen as being causally determined (in which case free will has little role). I read reflective autobiography as an elaborated and culturally central form of existential positing.

EXPLANATORY POSTULATES: Hypothetical features of self and/or world that are dramatized and articulated in narrative in an effort to understand the nature of experience as it is lived. So conceived, narrative is a *heuristic* (*see below*) activity. But of course narrative has other modalities as well: representational, fictional, and so on. The will is one of the most widely occurring explanatory postulates in reflective autobiography.

HEURISTIC: Activities undertaken in a spirit of open-minded inquiry. Complex narrative—for instance, reflective autobiography—often embodies this spirit.

INTROSPECTION: Looking "inward" to examine the contents and nature of consciousness. But on the issue of temporality, *see retrospection* (*below*). Introspection can occur in a mode of direct phenomenological encounter, as well as in ways that are mediated (in various degrees) by culturally provided modes of analysis and understanding. At some level, even the products of direct phenomenological encounter require culturally provided means for recognition and articulation.

LUCK: *constitutive luck:* the kind of person you are, where this is not just a question of what you deliberately do, but of your inclinations, capacities, and temperament; *circumstantial luck:* the kinds of problems and situations one faces; *metaphysical luck* (a subcategory of circumstantial luck): the underlying metaphysical condition that functions as a kind of background to all of one's experiences; *cultural luck* (another subcategory of circumstantial luck): the kind of cultural environment in which one finds oneself; *agent-determinative luck:* luck in how one is determined by antecedent circumstances; *outcome luck:* luck in the way one's actions and projects turn out.

METAPHORS OF SELF-CONSTITUTION: A pivotal or controlling metaphor in an autobiography that expresses an understanding both of what the—or a—self is like, and of the forces that bring it into being, which constitute it as the thing it is. I use *constitution* rather than, say, *construction,* because the latter term is now widely read as a synonym for fictive invention—an implication I do not want. *Constitution* can refer both to the constitution of the "actual" historical self and to the self that is the subject of autobiographical narrative. A related and valuable term is James Olney's "metaphors of self."

MODES OF EMPLOTMENT: Culturally provided, sanctioned, and in some cases imposed plot structures for the narrative representation of individual human lives. The reflective autobiographer's relationship to such modes (like that to other cultural materials) is *reflexive*.

MOTIVE: An impulsion to act that is often associated with illicit behavior and disguises its status as the precipitating factor of the behavior in question.

NARRATIVES OF AFFILIATION: Autobiographical narrative treatment of patterns of affiliation to and repudiation of intellectual, political, and other movements/causes/belief systems. I use the term largely with reference to narratives about subscription to and repudiation of Marxism ("the God that failed"); but such narrative patterns have deep roots in religious confessional autobiography.

NUMINOUS COMPLIANCE: My term for a state, described by Koestler and some other autobiographers, in which the will complies with—is in a sense rendered passive by—direction revealed or intuited in a "visionary" state.

POST-TOTALITARIAN AUTOBIOGRAPHY: Autobiography written by postwar intellectuals in an attempt (among other things) to explore the nature and implications of totalitarianism.

PRECONSCIOUS INTENTIONS: Intentions of which the agent is not aware, but that are not in principle unavailable to him or her.

PROTOCOLS OF SELF-DISCLOSURE: Culturally provided, sanctioned, and, in some cases, imposed parameters and practices for autobiographical self-revelation. Such protocols, like Foucault's "discursive regimes," can apply to a range of narrative dimensions, from style and taste to the presumed structural properties of the self, rhetorical relations with the reader, and so on. They can, then, have a powerful political-ideological dimension.

REASON: The description under which an agent formulates (and often justifies) his or her reason(s) for doing something.

RECEDING CAUSAL EFFICACY: The sense in which causal forces can "thin out" over time (or in other dimensions), so that something that has a powerful determinative force in a certain time and place may have a reduced causal force twenty years later or in another setting. The principle applies to individual psychological life in some instances, though Freud and others have taught us that certain events can maintain their (destructive) causal efficacy over a lifetime; that is, that almost no thinning takes place. Some of the Romantics held that certain positive experiences could be similarly powerful across time. Here, the failure of "thinning" is a positive thing.

RECOLLECTION: Obviously, "looking back"; but the term is more complex than it might seem. For instance, to what can it be contrasted? Is there any kind of "looking" that is not a form of "looking back"? To recollect is not necessarily to reassemble something (say, memories) in their original form, though it might be taken to have this implication. It might equally imply that elements are reassembled in novel ways, as when we talk about someone "putting himself back together" after a breakdown, but in a way that involves fashioning a revised configuration of self.

REFLECTIVE AUTOBIOGRAPHY: Autobiography in which there is a significant and sophisticated component of reflection on the meaning and larger implications of the life being written, and of life in general; and in which there is a significant sense of reflective, critical distance between the attitudes and assumptions of the autobiographer, and the attitudes and assumptions that were/are prevalent in her or his cultural-ideological milieu.

REFLEXIVE MONITORING OF CONDUCT: A continuous reciprocal activity whereby agents, who are knowledgeable participants in a cultural system, enact but also react back upon the values that inform the system, thereby changing those values, that system. The agent's ability to "react back" upon the system is a consequence of the fact that she or he possesses knowledge of the system and an ability to reflect upon its values and the enactments these prompt. The more developed an agent, the more pronounced the reflexive dimension of conduct. Reflective autobiographers are reflexive actors in this sense. The systems upon which they react are both social (their social worlds) and genre-specific (the structures, protocols, and so on, of autobiography itself).

RESPONDENT ACT: The use of autobiography as a means of responding to and intervening in external political and social events.

SCIENTISTIC MYSTICISM: The kind of mysticism without a god that occurs in, for example, Koestler. It is scientistic in the sense that it aligns itself with the New Physics and related developments.

SELF: A global term that denotes the existence of a human individual. The term can incorporate the notion of a subject, where, for example, this is understood to indicate a certain mode of being through rational self-conceptualization. However, *self* is a broader term than this and can be applied to an individual who does not possess self-reflexive consciousness in, say, a Cartesian sense. Yet the term is not infinitely elastic. A human organism that possessed, for instance, no language, or no engagement in/familiarity with patterns of identity-confirmation, could not be a self.

STRONG EVALUATORS: Agents whose assessments of possible actions are based on criteria that transcend mere personal pleasure or advantage, and that take in broader concerns about the nature and implications of the Good Life. Such agents have a strongly reflexive relationship to social structures and values and possess the ability to give complex linguistic articulations of their reasons for acting as they do. Their evaluations generally have a strong ethical dimension. Strong evaluators also possess a substantial degree of freedom. A reflective autobiographer is a strong evaluator.

SUBJECT: A term that I generally do not use, because efforts to specify it, and to differentiate it from the self, have thus far been inconclusive. The two meanings most commonly associated with it are (a) the notion of the individual as *subject to* certain social forces and systems of ideological power; and (b) the individual as understood by, say, Descartes, Kant, and Husserl: a self-guaranteeing consciousness that is to a high degree independent of the world in which it resides.

SUBJECTIVITY: One of the most widely used and abused terms in current literary theory, where it has come to be associated, inter alia, with Althusserian and other notions of subjection. The consequence of this has been to assume or claim that subjectivity is, as it were, wholly ideologically constructed from without. I reject this construal of the term and use *subjectivity* to mean something like "what it feels like to be me"; the "texture" of my consciousness, how it feels to have *my* experience of the world rather than someone else's. This construal of the term does not preclude explanatory accounts of factors that cause my subjectivity to be the way it is; but such accounts are not "built into" the term. The term itself should not in my view be taken as implying any particular kind or degree of causal determination of consciousness. Issues of kind and degree need to be specified on a case-by-case basis. The contents of subjectivity cannot be "read off" some grid comprising assumptions about, for example, particular ideological systems and their impact on selves. Such a methodology relies on third-person points of view. But information about subjectivity must principally come from first-person sources—such as autobiography.

TYPICALITY CLAIMS: Implicit or explicit dimensions in an autobiography in which the autobiographer claims that aspects of his or her life are typical of, and have evidential value as a source of information about his or her time, place, milieu. Such claims can relate either to the writer's "inner" or public life, or a combination of the two.

UNCONSCIOUS INTENTIONS: Intentions that impel action but of which the actor cannot be aware without assistance (for instance, psychoanalysis).

USURPATION: Processes whereby totalitarian and other regimes try to commandeer the contents of individual consciousness and to replace these with party ideology.

WEAK EVALUATORS: People whose procedures of appraisal are based on criteria of pleasure and/or other forms of self-interest, and whose assessments lack awareness of larger—and in particular ethical—implications. Weak evaluators cannot give complex linguistic accounts of their reasons for acting as they do. It would be hard for a weak evaluator to be a strong reflective autobiographer (though the autobiographies of weak evaluators can be of great evidential value for sociologists and others).

WILL, CONCEPTUAL DENIAL OF: The denial that there is any such thing as the human will.

WILL, DETERMINISTIC ACCOUNTS OF: Accounts that concede the existence of the will but that see the will as wholly determined and therefore unfree.

WILL, AS DYNAMIC POWER: This conception sees the will as a kind of raw power or energy that the individual possesses and can exert.

WILL, FREEDOM AS THE GENUS OF VOLITION: On this view the will is by definition free. To speak of the will as constrained or blocked, whether by internal or external factors, is a contradiction in terms. Many people actually take this view for granted: they assume (erroneously) that will and free will are synonymous.

WILL, GENERAL WILL: Rousseau's term for the quasi-mystical notion of a form of collective will that gives objective embodiment to humankind's essential—and essentially rational and moral—nature. The General Will is not imposed from "outside"; rather, individuals willingly subscribe to it and find their freedom through participation in it. The General (as opposed to the Individual or the Collective) Will is held to be morally infallible, and it underpins Rousseau's notion of the Social Contract. Variations of the concept appear in Pascal, Hegel, Marx, and others.

WILL, GRADUATED CONCEPTION OF: The will conceived in terms of a spectrum. The will is seen as a power to precipitate that is inherent in the self but is instantiated though engagement with other faculties. At one end of the spectrum, where engagement is with affective faculties only, the will lacks freedom; at the other end, where engagement is with rationality (or some mix of rational and affective in which rationality is sovereign), the will is relatively free. Rationality and so freedom can be impeded by a variety of factors, including inherited temperament, various forms of ideological conditioning; and the "I" of the will-endowed self is inevitably linked to a cultural grammar, a "form of life," that provides it with such things as models of selfhood, recognizable and desirable life patterns, desirable life projects, and so on. *Graduation* also refers to *receding causal efficacy* (*see above*): the thinning of determinative power through time (and other dimensions).

WILL, AS INTELLECTUAL PREFERENCE: Here the exercise of will is thought to be indistinguishable from cognition, both logically and in practical terms. Will can only enact what is rationally deemed to be the best course of action. Where such courses of action are not pursued, it is because the will has been rendered inoperative and some other influence (passion, for instance) has taken over.

WILL, OF THE PEOPLE: The notion that a collection of individuals can possess a single will, either by virtue of some binding force that makes each will identical or because the various things they will coalesce to form one supra-will.

WILL TO POWER: Nietzsche's notion whereby any entity seeks to expand its sphere of influence; to makes its views, its sense of entitlement, prevail. The will to power is a major precipitating factor in the writing of autobiography.

WILL, AS RATIONAL APPETITE: On this view willing is an entirely different kind of activity from cognition. Will is seen as a psychic power that enables its possessor to incline toward objects intellectually apprehended as good (and away from those apprehended as "bad" objects). Understanding is not the initial cause of volitions; rather, understanding, or the objects it makes known, provides the sense of purpose, and the understanding of the mode in which a purpose might be achieved, which attracts the appetitive (inclining) thing that is the will to operate in certain ways.

WILL, AS REALITY: On this view will is the very stuff of life—a kind of life force that is in, and is constitutive of, everything.

WILL, AS THE SOURCE OF LAW: This view sees laws as being promulgated by some fiat of a legislator and as binding upon those for whom the laws were brought down.

WILL, IN TERMS OF HEART AND AFFECTION: This view sees love as the central and definitive aspect of volition.

NOTES

NOTE ON TEXTS AND TRANSLATIONS

1. Eva Hoffman, *Lost in Translation* (London: Vintage, 1998).
2. Paul Ricoeur, *Oneself as Another* (Chicago: University of Chicago Press, 1992), pp. 1-4.

INTRODUCTION

1. Apart from philosophical discussions of the will in Augustine and others, one of the remarkably few direct treatments of the will and the genre of autobiography I have been able to find is Roger J. Porter, "'In *Me* the Solitary Sublimity': Posturing and the Collapse of the Romantic Will in Benjamin Robert Haydon," in *The Culture of Autobiography: Constructions of Self-Representation,* ed. Robert Folkenflik (Stanford: Stanford University Press, 1993), pp. 168-87.
2. Alain Touraine, *Critique of Modernity,* trans. David Macey (Oxford: Basil Blackwell, 1995), p. 5.
3. Nelson Mandela, *Long Walk to Freedom* (London: Little, Brown & Co., 1994), p. 377.
4. For a subtle discussion that offers characterizations of various states of the will in relation to "addictive behavior," see Harry G. Frankfurt, "Freedom of the Will," in *The Importance of What We Care About: Philosophical Essays* (Cambridge: Cambridge University Press, 1988), pp. 11-25. On the vexed issue of "addiction attribution" and characterizations of the will, see Eve Kosofsky Sedgwick's powerful essay "Epidemics of the Will," in *Tendencies* (Durham, N.C.: Duke University Press, 1993), pp. 130-42.
5. Barry Humphries, *More Please: An Autobiography* (London: Viking, 1992), p. 288.
6. Vernon J. Bourke, *Will in Western Thought: An Historico-Critical Survey* (New York: Sheed and Ward, 1964).
7. Hannah Arendt, *Willing,* in *The Life of the Mind* (New York: Harcourt Brace & Co., 1978).
8. Lionel Trilling, *The Liberal Imagination: Essays on Literature and Society* (1950; reprint, New York: Harcourt Brace Jovanovich, 1976), p. 58.

CHAPTER ONE

1. Homer, *Iliad,* trans. Richmond Lattimore (Chicago: University of Chicago Press, 1956), 24.523-30, p. 489.
2. Robert Dessaix, *A Mother's Disgrace* (Sydney: Angus & Robertson, 1994), p. 186.
3. Stephen Spender, *World Within World: The Autobiography of Stephen Spender* (1951; reprint, New York: St. Martin's Press, 1994), p. 200.
4. Arthur Koestler, *The Yogi and the Commissar* (1945; reprint, London: Jonathan Cape, 1964), p. 58.
5. Simone de Beauvoir, *Force of Circumstance*, trans. Richard Howard (1963; reprint, New York: G. P. Putnam's Sons, 1964), p. 263.
6. Diana Trilling, *Mrs. Harris: The Death of the Scarsdale Diet Doctor* (New York: Harcourt Brace Jovanovich, 1981), pp. 4, 288.

7. My thanks to John Gillies for stimulating me to think further about some of these implications and for his astute comments on an early draft of this chapter.

8. For a deconstructive reading of the Ariadne myth and its hermeneutic implications, see J. Hillis Miller, "Ariadne's Thread: Repetition and the Narrative Line," *Critical Inquiry* (autumn 1976): pp. 57-77. The theme is developed further in Hillis Miller's *Ariadne's Thread: Story Lines* (New Haven: Yale University Press, 1992).

9. *Iliad,* 15.185-93, p. 314.

10. On the ambiguities in question, see D. J. Conacher, *Aeschylus' Prometheus Bound: A Literary Commentary* (Toronto: University of Toronto Press, 1980), pp. 51-54.

11. *Iliad,* 24.208-13, p. 480.

12. Hesiod, *Theogony,* trans. Dorothea Wender (Harmondsworth: Penguin, 1973), 218-21, p. 30; 903-5, p. 52.

13. *Iliad,* 3.182, p. 105.

14. There has been much scholarly debate about the details and import of this description. For a meticulous account, complete with diagrams, see *The Republic of Plato,* ed. James Adam (Cambridge: Cambridge University Press, 1969), vol. 2, pp. 440-63.

15. All quotations are from *Plato: The Collected Dialogues,* eds. Edith Hamilton and Huntington Cairns (Princeton: Princeton University Press, 1963), 616b-621b, pp. 840-44.

16. Simone de Beauvoir, *The Second Sex,* trans. and ed. H. M. Parshley (1949; reprint, London: Picador 1988), p. 179.

17. For a feminist autobiographical and social historical perspective on weaving, see Carolyn Steedman, *Landscape for a Good Woman: A Story of Two Lives* (London: Virago, 1986). See especially, part 2, "The Weaver's Daughter." Another historical source is Jill Liddington and Jill Norris, *One Hand Tied Behind Us: The Rise of the Woman's Suffrage Movement* (London: Virago, 1978).

18. For implications that fall outside my area of particular interest, see Hillis Miller, "Ariadne's Thread," pp. 70-72.

19. Henry James, *Autobiography: Including A Small Boy and Others, Notes of a Son and Brother, and The Middle Years,* ed. Frederick W. Dupee (Princeton: Princeton University Press, 1983), p. 410.

20. Nicholas Mosley, *Efforts at Truth: An Autobiography* (London: Minerva, 1996), p. 157.

21. James Olney, *Memory and Narrative: The Weave of Life-Writing* (Chicago: University of Chicago Press, 1998), p. xiv.

22. Michel Leiris, *La règle du jeu, III, Fibrilles* (Paris: Gallimard, 1967), p. 287. The translation is mine. The other three volumes of *La règle du jeu* are *Biffures* (Paris: Gallimard, 1948), trans. Lydia Davis, as *Scratches* (Baltimore: Johns Hopkins University Press, 1997); *Fourbis* (Paris: Gallimard, 1955), trans. Lydia Davis, as *Scraps* (Baltimore: Johns Hopkins University Press, 1997); and *Frêle bruit* (Paris: Gallimard, 1976). His earlier volume of autobiography is *L'âge d'homme* (Paris: Gallimard, 1939), trans. Richard Howard, as *Manhood* (Chicago: University of Chicago Press, 1992).

23. As in Martha Nussbaum's fine study, *The Fragility of Goodness: Luck and Ethics in Greek Tragedy and Philosophy* (Cambridge: Cambridge University Press, 1986).

24. Richard Wollheim, *The Thread of Life* (Cambridge: Harvard University Press, 1984). Wollheim has little to say about free will, noting that "it would have required a change of philosophical persuasion" (p. xiv) for him to dwell on this topic.

25. James Olney, *Metaphors of Self: The Meaning of Autobiography* (Princeton: Princeton University Press, 1981), p. 27.

26. George Eliot, *Middlemarch,* Cheap edition (1874; reprint, Oxford: Clarendon Press, 1986), book 1, chap. 15, p. 139.

27. Frank's powerful account of the experience of illness (heart disease and cancer) is deeply concerned with the relation between what he conceptualizes as "the will of the body," on the one hand, and the will that we want to exercise over our own bodies, on the other. See Arthur W. Frank, *At the Will of the Body: Reflections on Illness* (Boston: Houghton Mifflin, 1991).

28. Richard Eldridge, *Philosophy, Literature, Criticism, and Self-Understanding* (Chicago: University of Chicago Press, 1989), p. 32.

29. Benjamin Franklin, *An Autobiography and Other Writings,* ed. Ormond Seavey (Oxford: Oxford University Press, 1993), p. 84. Another, more recent, and disturbing, American autobiographical account of alleged strength of will is G. Gordon Liddy, *Will: The Autobiography of G. Gordon Liddy* (New York: St. Martin's Press, 1980).

30. Karl Joachim Weintraub's more elegant, but also more general, term is *self-orientation.* See his important study, *The Value of the Individual: Self and Circumstance in Autobiography* (Chicago: University of Chicago Press, 1978).

31. Paul Ricoeur, *Freedom and Nature: The Voluntary and the Involuntary,* trans. Erazim Kohák (Chicago: Northwestern University Press, 1966), p. 5.

32. Saint Augustine, *The Confessions,* trans. Henry Chadwick (Oxford: Oxford University Press, 1991), VIII.vi (15), p. 143.

33. Ibid., VIII.vi (15), p. 144.

34. Ibid., VIII.vii (16), p. 144.

35. Ibid., VIII.vii (18), p. 146.

36. Ibid., VIII.viii (19), p. 147.

37. Ibid., VIII.viii (20), p. 147.

38. Ibid., VIII.ix (21), p. 147.

39. Ibid.

40. Ibid., VIII.ix (21), p. 148.

41. Ibid., VIII.viii (19), p. 146. The reference is from Matthew 11:12.

42. Ibid., XIII.xi (12), p. 279. On the semantic history of *voluntas,* see John M. Rist, *Augustine: Ancient Thought Baptized* (Cambridge: Cambridge University Press, 1994), pp. 187–88.

43. Saint Augustine, *The Trinity,* trans. Stephen McKenna (Washington, D.C.: Catholic University of America Press, 1963), XV (20), p. 506.

44. Augustine, *Confessions,* X.xi (18), p. 189.

45. Augustine, *Trinity,* XI, 2, 5, p. 321.

46. Augustine, *Confessions,* XIII.ix (10), p. 278.

47. Ibid., VIII.xii (28), p. 152.

48. Ibid., VIII.xii (29), p. 153.

49. On the relationship between grace and freedom in Augustine, see Eric Osborn, *Ethical Patterns in Early Christian Thought* (Cambridge: Cambridge University Press, 1976), pp. 167–70.

50. This is not of course to deny that many of the narrative-theological elements of the *Confessions* are conventional in origin—a point made by Georg Misch, *A History of Autobiography in Antiquity,* trans. E. W. Dickes, 2 vols. (Cambridge: Harvard University Press, 1951),

vol. 1, p. 17; and Avrom Fleishman, *Figures of Autobiography: The Language of Self-Writing in Victorian and Modern England* (Berkeley: University of California Press, 1983), pp. 53–69.

51. Albrecht Dihle, *The Theory of the Will in Classical Antiquity* (Berkeley: University of California Press, 1982), p. 144. Hannah Arendt concurs, calling Augustine the "first philosopher of the will" in *Willing*, in *The Life of the Mind*, pp. 84ff.

52. See, for example, Robert Edward Brennan, *Thomistic Psychology: A Philosophic Analysis of the Nature of Man* (Toronto: Macmillan, 1941), pp. 28–29.

53. I use the term as it is employed by Bourke, *Will in Western Thought*, p. 29.

54. Plato, *Republic*, IV.439d–439e, in *Collected Dialogues*, pp. 681–82.

55. Ibid., IV.439d, p. 681.

56. Aristotle, *Nichomachean Ethics*, III.1111b11–15, in *The Complete Works of Aristotle*, ed. Jonathan Barnes, 2 vols. (Princeton: Princeton University Press, 1984), vol. 2, p. 1755.

57. Ibid., VI.1139b4–5, p. 1799.

58. Olney, *Memory and Narrative*, p. 98. William C. Spengemann makes a similar point. He proposes a subgenre of "philosophical autobiography," and discusses its presence in Augustine's *Confessions*. In general, however, he identifies "philosophical autobiography" with the eighteenth century—a more limited application of the term than I would wish to make. See William C. Spengemann, *The Forms of Autobiography: Episodes in the History of a Literary Genre* (New Haven: Yale University Press, 1980), p. xiv. See also Stanley Cavell's autobiography, *A Pitch of Philosophy: Autobiographical Exercises* (Cambridge: Harvard University Press, 1994), p. vii: "There is an internal connection between philosophy and autobiography . . . each is a dimension of the other."

59. *The Philosophical Works of Descartes*, trans. Elizabeth S. Haldane and G. R. T. Ross, 2 vols. (Cambridge: Cambridge University Press, 1974), vol. 1, p. 153.

60. Reprinted in David Hume, *On Human Nature and the Understanding*, ed. Antony Flew (New York: Macmillan, 1962), pp. 304–10.

61. Jean-Jacques Rousseau, *The Confessions*, trans. J. M. Cohen (Harmondsworth: Penguin, 1953), p. 29.

62. Ibid., p. 25.

63. Ibid., p. 26.

64. The nice epithet is from John Sturrock, *The Language of Autobiography* (Cambridge: Cambridge University Press, 1993), p. 142.

65. Olney, *Metaphors of Self*, p. 259.

66. John Stuart Mill, *Autobiography*, ed. Jack Stillinger (London: Oxford University Press, 1971), p. 101.

67. Ibid., p. 102. See James Olney's finely weighted discussion of this aspect of Mill's *Autobiography* in *Metaphors of Self*, pp. 254–59. Olney underlines an important distinction: between determinism and fatalism.

68. The term is from Richard Freadman and Seumas Miller, *Re-thinking Theory: A Critique of Contemporary Literary Theory and an Alternative Account* (Cambridge: Cambridge University Press, 1992).

69. Eduardo Cadava, Peter Connor, and Jean-Luc Nancy, eds., *Who Comes After the Subject?* (London: Routledge, 1991), pp. 104–5.

70. Ibid., p. 103.

71. On humanism, see Vincent Descombes, "Apropos of the 'Critique of the Subject' and of the Critique of this Critique," in ibid., p. 132; on capitalism, see Gérard Granel's contribution, "Who Comes After the Subject?," ibid., p. 151.

72. On Aristotle see, for example, the essay by Mikkel Borch-Jacobsen, "The Freudian Subject," ibid., p. 63.

73. Ibid., pp. 129, 103.

74. Ibid., pp. 120–34.

75. Charles Taylor, *Sources of the Self: The Making of the Modern Identity* (Cambridge: Harvard University Press, 1989).

76. Anthony Cascardi, *The Subject of Modernity* (Cambridge: Cambridge University Press, 1992). For a subject-as-subjection view of the autobiographical subject, see Felicity Nussbaum, *The Autobiographical Subject: Gender and Ideology in Eighteenth-Century England* (Baltimore: Johns Hopkins University Press, 1989).

77. A typical example is Catherine Belsey, *Critical Practice* (London: Methuen, 1980). See, for instance, the summation of the "subject" on p. 67.

78. William Lyons, *The Disappearance of Introspection* (Cambridge, Mass: Bradford Books, 1986).

79. Gilbert Ryle's preferred term, see his *Concept of Mind* (1949; reprint, Harmondsworth: Penguin, 1963).

80. Lyons, *The Disappearance of Introspection,* p. 96.

81. Ibid., p. 126.

82. Augustine, *Trinity,* book X, 14, p. 308.

83. The best-known exposition of this elusive concept, which is Heideggerian in origin, appears in Jacques Derrida, *Of Grammatology,* trans. Gayatri Spivak (Baltimore: Johns Hopkins University Press, 1974).

84. See Dihle, *The Theory of the Will in Classical Antiquity,* on this background.

85. Ibid., p. 144.

86. Lyons argues in *The Disappearance of Introspection* that we do not introspect as such. Rather, we engage in a process of modeling whereby we "replay" abstracted versions of particular "cognitive and appetitive episodes" by "means of perceptual memory and imagination" (p. 152).

87. See for example Robert Smith, *Derrida and Autobiography* (Cambridge: Cambridge University Press, 1995).

88. See for example, Richard Freadman and Seumas Miller, *Re-thinking Theory.*

89. Two important books that argue such a position are Charles Altieri, *Act and Quality: A Theory of Literary Meaning and Humanistic Understanding* (Amherst: University of Massachusetts Press, 1991); and C. A. J. Coady, *Testimony: A Philosophical Study* (Oxford: Clarendon Press, 1992). The latter book gives an important philosophical defense of testimonial authority—a defense that has clear implications for autobiography.

90. Several connected issues converge here. One concerns whether or not there is such a thing as a kind of inner Cartesian "theater" of the self; that is, whether we possess an inner "space" that is somehow "private" and "unique." Or is "subjectivity" (to use that much-abused term) merely an internal manifestation of conventional social materials, constructed and determined from without? If we affirm the presence of a "private" interior "space," how, if at all, can we prove its existence? And if we believe in its existence (whether we can prove it or not), how—if at all—can it be reported or represented in a public medium like language? My position is that there are such things as inner "states" and other internal phenomena; that we know these in part through introspection; that some aspects of this innerness are, as it were, already verbal and therefore readily susceptible to linguistic communication; that others, however, are pre- or subverbal and are only therefore susceptible to verbal approximation and

various kinds of creative reconstruction (for instance, in autobiography); and that because innerness is (in varying degrees) communicable, we are able to share our experiences of it and to confirm that my innerness is generically like yours, though each person's "subjectivity" will comprise a unique configuration of elements (we could think of them as threads), some of them widely occurring, others more particular to my own history.

91. I use *constitution* rather than, say, *construction* because the latter term is now widely read as a synonym for fictive invention—an implication I do not want. *Constitution* can refer both to the constitution of the "actual" historical self and to the self that is the subject of autobiographical narrative. A related and valuable term is James Olney's *metaphors of self* (See his *Metaphors of Self*, pp. 30–35). For discussion of Olney's notion, see Robert Sayre, "Revolutionary Concepts of Self," in *Interface: Essays on History, Myth and Art in American Literature,* ed. Daniel Royot (Montpellier: Publications de la Recheche, 1985), pp. 3–12; and John Pilling, *Autobiography and Imagination: Studies in Self-Scrutiny* (London: Routledge & Kegan Paul, 1981). Sayre argues that concepts of the self are more general than metaphors (p. 4); Pilling contends that the metaphoricity of self-constructs threatens their "substantiality" and coherence (p. 119).

92. A related and useful term occurs in Regenia Gagnier's valuable study *Subjectivities: A History of Self-Representation in Britain, 1832–1920* (New York: Oxford University Press, 1991). Gagnier refers to an "axiology of the self," defining it as "the systems of values, expectations, and constraints that come into play when one represents oneself to others in the concrete circumstances of daily life" (p. 3). See also her helpfully variegated definition of subjectivity (pp. 8–9).

93. I take the term from the British sociologist Anthony Giddens. See, for example, his *Central Problems in Social Theory: Action, Structure and Contradiction in Social Analysis* (London: Macmillan, 1979), p. 80.

94. Charles Taylor, *Human Agency and Language: Philosophical Papers* (Cambridge: Cambridge University Press, 1985), vol. 1, p. 15. See also Amélie Oksenberg Rorty, ed., *The Identities of Persons* (Berkeley: University of California Press, 1976): "Humans are just the sorts of organisms that interpret and modify their agency through their conceptions of themselves" (p. 323). In a recent volume on autobiography and postmodernism, Leigh Gilmore seems to want to have it both ways—to have agents whose characteristic agential activity is to show how fragmented they in fact are: "The lamentably decentered human agent of so many postmodernisms does not emerge here [in these essays] as *the* subject of autobiography; rather, we see human agents as producers of discourse who tend to heighten the contradictions in the discourses of self-representation and let those form the explanation for disruption or discontinuity." The comment appears in her essay "The Mark of Autobiography: Postmodernism, Autobiography, and Genre," in *Autobiography and Postmodernism,* eds. Kathleen Ashley, Leigh Gilmore, and Gerald Peters (Amherst: University of Massachusetts Press, 1994), p. 8. Writing of the possible "creation of self through process and relationship," Nicole Ward Jouve argues that "it is because subjecthood has become so difficult, has been so deconstructed, that there is need to work towards it," in *White Woman Speaks with Forked Tongue: Criticism as Autobiography* (London: Routledge, 1991), pp. 10–11.

95. Taylor, *Human Agency and Language*, p. 16.

96. Ibid., p. 23.

97. See the discussion of Skinnerian behaviorism in chapter 3.

98. Taylor, *Human Agency and Language*, p. 28.

99. Ibid., p. 29. See the discussion of Sartre on will in chapter 2.

100. Ibid., p. 31.

101. Ibid., p. 43.

102. Ibid., p. 39.

103. Giddens, *Central Problems in Social Theory*, p. 5.

104. Ibid., p. 5. For a more detailed exposition of his theory of "structuration," see Anthony Giddens, *The Constitution of Society* (Oxford: Polity Press, 1984).

105. Giddens, *Central Problems in Social Theory*, p. 26.

106. Ibid., pp. 38, 44.

107. See Giddens, *The Constitution of Society*, chap. 2.

108. Harry G. Frankfurt, "Freedom of the Will," in *The Importance of What We Care About: Philosophical Essays* (Cambridge: Cambridge University Press, 1988), p. 17.

109. Ibid., p. 16.

110. Hayden White, *Tropics of Discourse: Essays in Cultural Criticism* (Baltimore: Johns Hopkins University Press, 1978), p. 66.

111. See Charles Altieri's searching and persuasive elaboration of this Wittgensteinian concept with respect to agency in *Subjective Agency*.

112. See Bourke's discussion of some of these in *Will in Western Thought*, chap. 10.

113. A less comprehensive, but penetrating and valuable account is Hannah Arendt, *Willing*, in *The Life of the Mind*. For a phenomenological/hermeneutic account, see Paul Ricoeur's three volumes *Freedom and Nature: The Voluntary and the Involuntary, Fallible Man*, and *The Symbolism of Evil*. (Publication details are given in appendix B, "Some Other Late Modern Instances," p. 375.) For psycho-cultural perspectives, see Rollo May, *Love and Will* (London: Fontana, 1972); Leslie Farber, *The Ways of the Will* (London: Constable, 1966); Francis Aveling, *Personality and Will* (New York: D. Appleton Press, 1931); Otto Rank, *Will Therapy and Truth and Reality*, trans. Jessie Taft (New York: Alfred A. Knopf, 1947); Viktor E. Frankl, *The Will to Meaning* (New York: World Publishing Co., 1969); Silvano Arieti, *The Will To Be Human* (New York: Quadrangle Books, 1972); Roberto Assagioli, *The Act of Will* (New York: Penguin Books, 1973); Gerald May, *Will and Spirit* (San Francisco: Harper & Row, 1987); and Joanne H. Stroud, *The Bonding of Will and Desire* (New York: Continuum, 1994).

114. It should be noted that many accounts of the will contain elements of more than one of these positions, and that Bourke's list is by no means exhaustive. However, it provides invaluable signposting and helps to capture the essence of some of the best-known positions. In summarizing Bourke's categories, I have simplified the language in some cases, especially where he refers to various notions of causation: a matter I want to defer until the end of this chapter.

115. *The Complete Works of Aristotle*, vol. 1, *Physics*, bk. 2, pp. 329ff.

116. Alisdair MacIntyre, *Against the Self-Images of the Age* (New York: Schocken Books, 1971), pp. 195–96.

117. Ibid., p. 200.

CHAPTER TWO

1. I am indebted to John Deigh for discussion of this point. This sort of compatibilist argument is well known in Hume (see appendix A, "Some Earlier Conceptions of the Will: Maimonides to Mill"). A subtle and influential version of it appears in Harry G. Frankfurt, *The Importance of What We Care About: Philosophical Essays* (Cambridge: Cambridge University Press, 1988). See especially essays 2 and 3. For an overview of compatibilist, incompati-

bilist, and other philosophical positions on the will, see Galen Strawson, "Luck Swallows Everything: Can Our Sense of Free Will Be True?" *Times Literary Supplement* (June 26, 1998), pp. 8–9.

2. Questions: Is there such a thing as the will? If so, is it determined or free? Can the will be conceived on the model of a single faculty? What part, if any, do acts of attention pay in willing? To what extent, and in what ways, is the will culturally mediated? Who owns the will? What roles do rational appraisal and the emotions respectively play in willing? Is it necessary to presuppose the existence of a substantial self in order to presuppose the existence of the will? Is the will susceptible of knowledge through introspection? What might it mean to speak of pathological states of the will? What is the relationship between determinism and fatalism, and between freedom and volition? Should the will be conceived of as separate from/prior to "acts," or are willing and acting the same thing? What is, or might be, the relationship between writing autobiography and the "will to power"? What becomes of the will if the individual is in a state of alienation? What is the relationship between will and the unconscious? How does the notion of ethical responsibility relate to various conceptions of the will? Does the concept of will require a contrastive term such as *constraint?* Can there be such a thing as weakness of will? In what ways might the will be oriented in a world that is seen as contingent? How are causes, reasons, and motives related to willing? What connections—and disconnections—might there be between will and love? What conditions of the will seem to be typical of our time?

3. Charles Taylor, *Sources of the Self: The Making of the Modern Identity* (Cambridge: Harvard University Press, 1989).

4. I don't want or need to enter complex debates about periodization. I make the fairly standard assumption that the modern period stretches from about the Renaissance to the French Revolution and the Industrial Revolution in England. I use the term *late modernity* to designate the cultural epoch that follows, and is to some extent shaped by, Nietzsche, Marx, and Freud; in other words—albeit only in certain cultural dimensions—from the second half of the nineteenth century to the present day.

5. Taylor, *Sources of the Self,* p. 395.

6. See appendix A, "Some Earlier Conceptions of the Will: Maimonides to Mill," pp. 289–317.

7. See the discussion of Sartre later in this chapter.

8. Leslie Farber, *The Ways of the Will* (London: Constable, 1966), p. 48.

9. Rollo May, *Love and Will* (London: Fontana, 1972), p. 9.

10. Lionel Trilling, *The Liberal Imagination: Essays on Literature and Society* (1950; reprint, New York: Harcourt Brace Jovanovich, 1976), p. 58.

11. Alain Touraine, *Critique of Modernity,* trans. David Macey (Oxford: Basil Blackwell, 1995), p. 2.

12. Michael Domeyko Rowland, *Absolute Happiness: The Whole Untold Story: The Way to a Life of Complete Fulfilment* (Bellingan, NSW: Self Communications, 1993), pp. 25, 21. Thanks to Anne Marie Sawyer for drawing my attention to this text.

13. I note with admiration that analytic philosophy has maintained a continuous, though perhaps a minority, commitment to explorations of the will. Three recent books further confirm this trend: Richard Double, *Metaphilosophy and Free Will* (New York: Oxford, 1996), which argues that our position on free will must largely be determined by our metaphilosophical commitments; Thomas Pink, *The Psychology of Freedom* (Cambridge: Cambridge University Press, 1996), which construes the will as an executive capacity that allows us, in

given situations, to apply our earlier deliberations about how to act; and Robert Kane, *The Significance of Free Will* (New York: Oxford University Press, 1996), a wide-ranging account of various positions on the will whose own position draws heavily upon the language of quantum mechanics.

14. Eve Kosofsky Sedgwick argues that there is a deep structural (historical and psychological) link between alleged addictive "epidemics" that are said to afflict and master the will, and the process of "addiction attribution" itself: attributions of addiction are part of a process whereby idealized proffered freedoms of the will are rhetorically purged of all traces of unfreedom. She argues that this phenomenon is rampant in contemporary Western society. See "Epidemics of the Will" in Sedgwick's *Tendencies* (Durham, N.C.: Duke University Press, 1993), pp. 131–34.

15. See, for example, Charles Altieri, *Subjective Agency: A Theory of First-Person Expressivity and Its Social Implications* (Oxford: Basil Blackwell, 1994); Anthony Giddens, *The Constitution of Society* (Oxford: Polity Press, 1984); Jürgen Habermas, *The Structural Transformation of the Public Sphere: An Inquiry into a Category of Bourgeois Society*, trans. Thomas Burger (Cambridge: M.I.T. Press, 1989); Seyla Benhabib, *Situating the Self: Gender, Community and Postmodernism in Contemporary Ethics* (New York: Routledge, 1992); Alisdair MacIntyre, *After Virtue: A Study in Moral Theory* (London: Duckworth, 1981); C. B. Macpherson, *Democratic Theory: Essays in Retrieval* (Oxford: Oxford University Press, 1973); John Rawls, *A Theory of Justice* (Oxford: Oxford University Press, 1972); and Charles Taylor, *Human Agency and Language: Philosophical Papers* (Cambridge: Cambridge University Press, 1985).

16. Donald Davidson, *Essays on Actions and Events* (Oxford: Oxford University Press, 1980), p. 179.

17. Friedrich Nietzsche, *Thus Spoke Zarathustra*, trans. Walter Kaufmann (New York: Viking Press, 1954), pp. 138–39.

18. Friedrich Nietzsche, *The Will to Power*, trans. Walter Kaufmann and R. J. Hollingdale (New York: Vintage, 1968), no. 993, p. 517.

19. Nietzsche, *Thus Spoke Zarathustra*, p. 13.

20. Friedrich Nietzsche, *Beyond Good and Evil*, trans. R. J. Hollingdale (Harmondsworth: Penguin, 1990), no. 208, p. 137.

21. Ibid., no. 203, p. 126.

22. Friedrich Nietzsche, *The Genealogy of Morals*, in *The Birth of Tragedy and The Genealogy of Morals*, trans. Francis Golffing (New York: Doubleday, 1956), p. 191.

23. Friedrich Nietzsche, *Ecce Homo*, trans. R. J. Hollingdale (London: Penguin, 1979), p. 18.

24. Ibid., p. 67. On *Ecce Homo* and the "ideology of genius," see Carl Pletsch, "On the Autobiographical Life of Nietzsche," in *Psychoanalytic Studies of Biography*, eds. George Moraitis and George H. Pollock (Madison: International Universities Press, 1987), pp. 405–34.

25. On Schopenhauer, see appendix A, "Some Earlier Conceptions of the Will: Maimonides to Mill," pp. 309–12.

26. Hannah Arendt, *Willing*, in *The Life of the Mind* (New York: Harcourt Brace & Co., 1978). p. 163.

27. Nietzsche, *Thus Spoke Zarathustra*, p. 12.

28. Nietzsche, *The Will to Power*, no. 692, p. 369; no. 671, p. 354.

29. Nietzsche, *The Genealogy of Morals*, in *The Birth of Tragedy and The Genealogy of Morals*, pp. 178–79.

30. Alexander Nehamas, *Nietzsche: Life as Literature* (Cambridge: Harvard University Press, 1985), pp. 44–45.

31. On Kant, see appendix A, "Some Earlier Conceptions of the Will: Maimonides to Mill," pp. 302–5.

32. Nehamas, *Nietzsche*, p. 82.

33. Ibid., p. 78.

34. Nietzsche, *The Will to Power*, no. 632, p. 336.

35. Ibid., no. 633, p. 337.

36. Nietzsche, *Beyond Good and Evil*, no. 259, p. 194.

37. Nietzsche, *The Will to Power*, no. 1067, p. 550.

38. Nietzsche, *Ecce Homo*, p. 45.

39. Nietzsche, *The Will to Power*, no. 479, pp. 265–66.

40. Friedrich Nietzsche, *The Gay Science*, trans. Walter Kaufmann (New York: Random House, 1974), no. 310, p. 247.

41. For Mill, see appendix A, "Some Earlier Conceptions of the Will: Maimonides to Mill," pp. 315–17.

42. Nietzsche, *The Will to Power*, no. 689, p. 367.

43. For Hegel, see appendix A, "Some Earlier Conceptions of the Will: Maimonides to Mill," pp. 305–9.

44. Arendt, *Willing*, in *The Life of the Mind*, p. 171.

45. Nietzsche, *The Will to Power*, no. 636, p. 340.

46. Ibid., no. 625, p. 334.

47. Ibid., no. 616, p. 330.

48. Nehamas, *Nietzsche*, p. 80.

49. Ibid., p. 68.

50. Friedrich Nietzsche, *Twilight of the Idols*, trans. R. J. Hollingdale (Harmondsworth: Penguin, 1968), p. 102.

51. Nietzsche, *The Will to Power*, no. 617, p. 331.

52. Ibid., no. 966, p. 507.

53. Ibid., no. 967, p. 507.

54. Nietzsche, *The Gay Science*, no. 290, p. 232.

55. Ibid., no. 347, pp. 289–90.

56. Nietzsche, *Beyond Good and Evil*, no. 19, pp. 48–49.

57. D. H. Lawrence, letter to Edward Garnett, June 5, 1914, in *Selected Literary Criticism*, by D. H. Lawrence, ed. Anthony Beal (London: Heinemann, 1956), p. 18. Of course Lawrence himself had a lot to say about the will and particularly abhorred what he saw as the dehumanized, egotistical will of mechanized man and woman. *Women in Love* (1920; reprint, New York: Viking, 1960) is a powerful source here, as when Hermione tells Gerald, another character of unreconstructed will, about how she has changed herself by sheer determination: "'And by learning to use my will, simply using my will, I *made* myself right'" (p. 131).

58. Nietzsche, *The Will to Power*, no. 488, p. 270.

59. Nietzsche, *Beyond Good and Evil*, no. 6, p. 37.

60. Nietzsche, *The Gay Science*, no. 354, p. 297.

61. Nietzsche, *The Will to Power*, no. 689, p. 367.

62. Karl Marx, *Capital: A Critique of Political Economy*, ed. Frederick Engels, trans.

Samuel Moore and Edward Aveling, rev. by Ernest Untermann (New York: Random House, 1906), vol. 1, p. 195.

63. Karl Marx, "Concerning Feuerbach," in *Early Writings*, trans. Rodney Livingstone and Gregor Benton (Harmondsworth: Penguin, 1975) p. 423.

64. Ibid., p. 98.

65. Karl Marx and Frederick Engels, *Manifesto of the Communist Party*, in *The Revolutions of 1848*, ed. Frederick Engels, trans. Samuel Moore (Harmondsworth: Penguin, 1973), p. 70.

66. For Rousseau, see appendix A, "Some Earlier Conceptions of the Will: Maimonides to Mill," pp. 301–2.

67. Karl Marx, *Grundrisse: Foundations of the Critique of Political Economy (Rough Draft)*, trans. Martin Nicholaus (Harmondsworth: Penguin, 1973), p. 84.

68. Karl Marx, *Economic and Philosophical Manuscripts*, in *Early Writings*, p. 379.

69. Ibid., p. 328.

70. Karl Marx, "Excerpts from James Mill's *Elements of Political Economy*," in *Early Writings*, p. 260.

71. Karl Marx and Frederick Engels, *The German Ideology*, trans. anonymous (Moscow: Progress Publishers, 1976), p. 348.

72. Marx, *Economic and Philosophical Manuscripts*, in *Early Writings*, p. 366.

73. Marx, *Capital*, vol. 1, p. 708.

74. For instance, Marx, *Capital*, vol. 1, p. 248.

75. Ibid., p. 687.

76 Marx, "A Contribution to the Critique of Hegel's Philosophy of Right. Introduction," in *Early Writings*, p. 251.

77. Ibid., p. 256.

78. Karl Marx, *The Holy Family*, in *Selected Writings*, ed. David McLellan (Oxford: Oxford University Press, 1977), p. 135.

79. See chapter 3 for Althusser's claims about an "epistemological break" between early and late Marx.

80. Marx, *Economic and Philosophical Manuscripts*, in *Early Writings*, p. 348.

81. Ibid., p. 353.

82. Ibid., p. 357.

83. Marx and Engels, *The German Ideology*, p. 67.

84. Marx and Engels, *Manifesto of the Communist Party*, in *The Revolutions of 1848*, p. 81.

85. Marx and Engels, *The German Ideology*, p. 67.

86. Marx, preface to *A Critique of Political Economy*, in *Early Writings*, p. 425.

87. See for example Marx's discussion of the arts in the introduction to *Grundrisse*, pp. 110–11.

88. Marx and Engels, *The German Ideology*, p. 49.

89. This passage occurs in volume 3, which does not appear in the Moore and Aveling translation. I have quoted it from *Capital: An Abridged Edition*, trans. anonymous, ed. David McLellan (Oxford: Oxford University Press, 1995), vol. 3, p. 470.

90. Sigmund Freud, "A Difficulty in the Path of Psycho-Analysis," in *The Standard Edition of the Complete Psychological Works of Sigmund Freud*, ed. James Strachey, trans. Joan Rivière (London: The Hogarth Press, 1955), vol. 17, pp. 143–44.

91. In Freud's essay "The 'Uncanny,'" in ibid., p. 236.

92. Frank J. Sulloway, *Freud: Biologist of the Mind* (London: Burnett, 1979), p. 94.

93. Sigmund Freud, *The Ego and the Id*, trans. Joan Rivière (New York: W. W. Norton, 1962), p. 46.

94. Ibid., p. 15.

95. Freud, *The Psychopathology of Everyday Life*, in *The Standard Edition*, vol. 6, pp. 253–54.

96. Sigmund Freud, *General Introduction to Psychoanalysis*, trans. Joan Rivière (New York: Garden City Publishing, 1938), p. 95.

97. Here a comparison of Freud and Hume (see appendix A, "Some Earlier Conceptions of the Will: Maimonides to Mill," pp. 299–301) is instructive and shows how slippery these matters can be. Hume's notion of a cause is problematical, but in essence it commits him to the view that (a) causes are external to that which they effect; (b) that there is a fairly clear demarcation between a cause, an effect, and a reason; and (c) causes only qualify as such if they can be seen so to operate in all instances. Freud seems to agree on the third point, but on the other two things look very different. There are times when he writes as if causes are extensional (for instance, sexual traumas during early infancy), but not all of the things he adduces as causes are external in this sense. For instance, the unconscious functions as a cause, yet many of its contents are archaic and therefore not an environmental imposition on the individual; further, as I've suggested, there's a sense in which the unconscious is a part of that which is said to be subject to causation. So we have the odd notion of (a part of) a thing having a causal impact on itself. The complications multiply when we consider what becomes of reasons and motives in Freud's view. We tend to think of a reason as something that is, or at least can be, consciously formulated: I have a known reason for doing something, and I do that something in consequence of having and knowing that reason. But Freud says that reasons aren't what they seem to be. The reasons we think we have for doing things are not the real reasons. The real ones are lodged in the unconscious, where we can't have access to them. "Down" there they function not as reasons in the ordinary sense but as—what? Perhaps as causes in the sense that they dispose or compel us to certain activities and states without our *necessarily* being aware that they are doing this. So now we have "reasons" that are a kind of smoke screen, and we have causes. But the plot thickens further because there are also things that might be termed *motives*. This is because Freud often writes as if the psyche, and/or parts thereof, has the status of an agent. Thus the ego-as-chief-executive of the psyche sees to it that whatever is intolerable to conscious awareness is repressed "down" into the unconscious. It does this because avoidance of pain is a priority for the self-protection of the organism. To this extent, the ego (or whatever) has a motive for bringing repression about. Having executed this motive, the repressed material can function as a cause under the guise of reasons that the unwitting individual trots out to him- or herself. And there are further twists that occur if the person undergoes (successful) analysis: now the reasons are revealed to be false; the causes are known and can be replaced by reasons in the ordinary sense—behavior is now more often driven by rational and conscious appraisal—and the analysand now at least knows something of the motives that impel his or her mind. Hume's terms, then, have in several instances been transformed, even turned on their heads.

98. Sulloway, *Freud*, p. 95.

99. Freud, *The Psychopathology of Everyday Life*, in *The Standard Edition*, vol. 6, p. 275.

100. In *A Structural Study of Autobiography: Proust, Leiris, Sartre, Lévi-Strauss* (Ithaca: Cornell University Press, 1974), Jeffrey Mehlman argues that Freud's "self-analysis," which included his letters and his theoretical texts, distinguishes him as "the practitioner of the most radical form of autobiography we know" (p. 14).

101. Sigmund Freud, *An Autobiographical Study*, trans. and ed. James Strachey (New York: W. W. Norton, 1952), p. 6.

102. Freud, *The Ego and the Id*, p. 40, n. 1.

103. Ibid., p. 25.

104. Ibid., pp. 18, 26.

105. I am thinking here of the impersonalist doctrines of T. S. Eliot, James Joyce, Virginia Woolf, Gertrude Stein, and of later writers like Alain Robbe-Grillet. In terms of autobiography, Stein's *The Autobiography of Alice B. Toklas* is a classic example of a modernist text that, though intensely willful in its way, scrambles the categories such as "inner" and "outer" upon which a concept of will is likely to depend.

106. Jean-Paul Sartre, *Nausea*, trans. Lloyd Alexander (New York: New Directions, 1964), p. 131.

107. I do not deal here with other existential accounts. On Heidegger's transition from an essentially Nietzschean position to one in which will seeks its own dissolution, see Hannah Arendt, *Willing*, in *The Life of the Mind*, pp. 172–94. As Heidegger's former student, Arendt is ideally qualified to comment; as his former lover, she has a strong investment in deflecting ideological blame from Heidegger. Here, as elsewhere in her writings about him, the discussion is colored by an attempt to exempt him from criticism for his support of Nazism.

108. Jean-Paul Sartre, *Being and Nothingness: An Essay on Phenomenological Ontology*, trans. Hazel E. Barnes (New York: Philosophical Library, n.d.), p. 440.

109. Ibid., p. 119.

110. Jean-Paul Sartre, *The Words*, trans. Bernard Frechtman (New York: George Braziller, 1964), p. 164. On Sartre's "deconversion" from the values of his childhood upbringing, see John D. Barbour, *Versions of Deconversion: Autobiography and the Loss of Faith* (Charlottesville: University Press of Virginia, 1994), chap. 7.

111. Sartre, *The Words*, p. 200.

112. Sartre, *Being and Nothingness*, p. 137.

113. Ibid., p. 529. See an excellent Ph.D. dissertation whose title bears this phrase: Graham Storey, "Condemned to Freedom: The Othering of Self in Existentialism, Deconstruction and the Literature of Self-Consciousness" (La Trobe University, 1997).

114. Sartre, *Being and Nothingness*, p. 90.

115. Jean-Paul Sartre, *Existentialism and Humanism*, trans. Philip Mairet (London: Methuen, 1948), p. 32.

116. Sartre, *Being and Nothingness*, p. 25.

117. Ibid., p. 452.

118. Ibid., p. 495.

119. Ibid.

120. Ibid., p. 444.

121. Ibid., p. 452.

122. Ibid., p. 449.

123. Ibid.

124. Ibid., p. 136.

125. Ibid., p. 444.

126. Ibid., p. 627. Sartre offers a famous and more detailed formulation about ethics in *Saint Genet*, trans. Bernard Frechtman (New York: Mentor, 1963), p. 207.

127. Sartre, *Being and Nothingness*, p. 155.

344 NOTES TO PAGES 76-81

128. William Wordsworth, *The Prelude* (text of 1805–6), ed. J. C. Maxwell (Harmondsworth: Penguin, 1971), 2.31–33, p. 74.

129. For other important figures of this kind—Wittgenstein in particular, but also Davidson and O'Shaughnessy—see appendix B, "Some Other Late Modern Instances," pp. 318–24.

130. Gilbert Ryle, *The Concept of Mind* (Harmondsworth: Penguin, 1963), pp. 61, 63.

131. For Skinner on the will, see chapter 3, pp. 96–100.

132. Ryle, *The Concept of Mind,* p. 66.

133. Ibid., p. 71.

134. Ibid.

135. Ibid., p. 72.

136. Ibid., p. 63.

137. Ibid., pp. 66–67.

138. Ibid., p. 65.

139. Ibid., p. 67.

140. Ibid., p. 63.

141. Stephen Spender, *World Within World: The Autobiography of Stephen Spender* (1951; reprint, New York: St. Martin's Press, 1994), p. 64.

142. Gilbert Ryle, "Autobiographical," in *Ryle: Modern Studies in Philosophy,* eds. Oscar P. Wood and George Pitcher (London: Macmillan, 1971), p. 11.

143. Charles Taylor, *Sources of the Self: The Making of the Modern Identity* (Cambridge: Harvard University Press, 1989), p. 57.

144. Ryle, *The Concept of Mind,* p. 78.

145. Harold Bloom, *The Anxiety of Influence: A Theory of Poetry* (New York: Oxford University Press, 1973), p. 30.

146. For evidence of a trend back toward agential conceptions of the self in literary studies, see Jane Adamson, Richard Freadman, and David Parker, eds., *Renegotiating Ethics in Literature, Philosophy, and Theory* (Cambridge: Cambridge University Press, 1998); and Meili Steele, *Theorising Textual Subjects: Agency and Oppression* (Cambridge: Cambridge University Press, 1997).

147. Jonathan Culler, *Structuralist Poetics: Structuralism, Linguistics and the Study of Literature* (London: Routledge & Kegan Paul, 1975), pp. 29, 30.

148. Jacques Derrida, *Writing and Difference,* trans. Alan Bass (London: Routledge & Kegan Paul, 1978), p. 289.

149. Jacques Derrida, *Of Grammatology,* trans. Gayatri Chakravorty Spivak (Baltimore: Johns Hopkins University Press, 1974), p. 166.

150. Derrida, *Writing and Difference,* pp. 12–13.

151. In my attempts to grasp the passage, I have discussed it with two colleagues, both of them distinguished Derridean scholars: Kevin Hart and Alex Segal. While these discussions have not resolved all of the interpretive uncertainties, they have helped to show how and why an admirer of Derrida would value the account of the will given here, and how and why someone like myself finds it unsatisfactory. Derrida's views on autobiography receive further elaboration in Jacques Derrida, *Demeure: Maurice Blanchot* (Paris: Galilée, 1998). Robert Smith's *Derrida and Autobiography* (Cambridge: Cambridge University Press, 1995) is particularly interesting on comparisons/relations between Derrida, on the one hand, and Nietzsche and Levinas, on the other. Another influential deconstructive study is Paul de Man, *The Rhetoric of Romanticism* (New York: Columbia University Press, 1984), not least for his denial that any

such genre as autobiography exists. See his "Autobiography as De-Facement," pp. 67–82. For an extended rejoinder to Derrida, especially with respect to the implications of his views for the practice of autobiography, see Stanley Cavell, *A Pitch of Philosophy: Autobiographical Exercises* (Cambridge: Harvard University Press, 1994)—the autobiography of a philosopher who is particularly well credentialed to assess Derrida's thought and its implications for autobiography.

152. Derrida, *Of Grammatology*, p. 167.

153. Benito Mussolini, *My Autobiography*, trans. anonymous (Westport: Greenwood Press, 1970), pp. 203, 241.

154. Adolf Hitler, *Mein Kampf*, trans. Ralph Manheim (London: Pimlico, 1992), pp. 273–74, 108.

CHAPTER THREE

1. Louis Althusser, *Essays in Self-Criticism*, trans. Grahame Lock (London: Verso, 1976), pp. 126–31.

2. Louis Althusser, *For Marx*, trans. Ben Brewster (London: New Left Books, 1969), pp. 233–34.

3. Ibid., p. 233.

4. Louis Althusser, "Ideology and Ideological State Apparatuses," in *Essays on Ideology*, trans. anonymous (London: Verso, 1984), p. 45.

5. Althusser, "A Letter on Art," ibid., p. 174.

6. Louis Althusser and Étienne Balibar, *Reading Capital*, trans. Ben Brewster (London: New Left Books, 1970), p. 133.

7. Althusser, *For Marx*, p. 227.

8. Althusser and Balibar, *Reading Capital*, p. 106.

9. Althusser, *For Marx*, p. 113.

10. Althusser and Balibar, *Reading Capital*, p. 58.

11. Ibid., pp. 188–89.

12. Althusser, *For Marx*, p. 143.

13. Ibid., p. 217.

14. Althusser and Balibar, *Reading Capital*, p. 250.

15. Ibid., p. 180.

16. Anthony Giddens, *Central Problems in Social Theory: Action, Structure and Contradiction in Social Analysis* (London: Macmillan, 1979), p. 52.

17. Ibid., p. 66.

18. Ibid., p. 180.

19. Ted Benton, *The Rise and Fall of Structural Marxism: Althusser and His Influence* (London: Macmillan, 1984), p. 21.

20. Louis Althusser, *The Future Lasts a Long Time*, eds. Olivier Corpet and Yann Moulier Boutang, trans. Richard Veasey (London: Chatto & Windus, 1993). This edition also contains *The Facts*. The French edition is *L'avenir dure longtemps; suivi de, Les faits: Autobiographies* (Paris: Éditions Stock/Imec, 1992). Where I quote from the French, page numbers in the text will be given in italics.

21. John Sturrock, "The Paris Strangler" [a hostile review of Althusser's autobiographical writings], *London Review of Books*, 14:24 (December 17, 1992), p. 6.

22. The scholar's temptation! Althusser writes of the normal criminal who has paid his debt to society: "*Il peut en toute conséquence rentrer normalement dans la vie*" (p. 17). Veasey

translates this as "he is free to pick up the threads of his life" (p. 21), but, alas, I don't see it in the French.

23. Althusser and Balibar, *Reading Capital*, p. 180.

24. Althusser, *For Marx*, p. 234.

25. On what seems in fact to have been quite a reasonable childhood, see Yann Moulier Boutang, *Louis Althusser: Une biographie*, vol. 1, *La Formation du mythe (1918–1955)* (Paris: Grasset, 1992).

26. I believe that Paul John Eakin understates the impact of Freudian theory on autobiography when he argues: "Beyond a general acceptance that frankness is a desideratum, however, and that sexuality ought to be included in the story of a life, the impact of the Freudian concept of the unconscious on autobiography has not been very substantial." The comment appears in his *Touching the World: Reference in Autobiography* (Princeton: Princeton University Press, 1992), p. 84.

27. Warren Montag, "A Process without a Subject or Goal(s): How to Read Althusser's Autobiography," in *Marxism in the Postmodern Age: Confronting the New World Order*, eds. Antonio Callari, Stephen Cullenberg, and Carole Biewener (New York: Guilford Press, 1995), p. 58.

28. See Sturrock, "The Paris Strangler," p. 6.

29. Benton, *The Rise and Fall of Structural Marxism*, p. 16.

30. B. F. Skinner, *About Behaviorism* (1974; reprint, London: Penguin, 1993), p. 59.

31. B. F. Skinner, *Science and Human Behavior* (New York: The Free Press, 1953), p. 18.

32. B. F. Skinner, *The Behavior of Organisms: An Experimental Analysis* (New York: Appleton-Century-Crofts, 1938), p. 6.

33. B. F. Skinner, *Contingencies of Reinforcement: A Theoretical Analysis* (New York: Appleton-Century-Crofts, 1969), p. 266.

34. B. F. Skinner, *Beyond Freedom and Dignity* (New York: Bantam, 1972), p. 12.

35. This position is set out in various of Skinner's books, including *Contingencies of Reinforcement*.

36. Skinner, *The Behavior of Organisms*, p. 47.

37. Skinner, *Beyond Freedom and Dignity*, p. 19.

38. B. F. Skinner, *Walden Two* (New York: Macmillan, 1948), p. 262.

39. Skinner, *About Behaviorism*, p. 4.

40. Skinner, *Science and Human Behavior*, p. 17.

41. Ibid., p. 20.

42. Skinner, *Beyond Freedom and Dignity*, p. 46.

43. Skinner, *Contingencies of Reinforcement*, p. 46.

44. Skinner, *Science and Human Behavior*, p. 286.

45. Ibid., p. 228.

46. Skinner, *Beyond Freedom and Dignity*, p. 179.

47. Skinner, *Science and Human Behavior*, p. 228.

48. Skinner, *Contingencies of Reinforcement*, p. 98. On Hitler, see pp. 257–58.

49. Skinner, *About Behaviorism*, p. 188.

50. B. F. Skinner, *A Matter of Consequences: Part Three of an Autobiography* (1983; reprint, New York: New York University Press, 1984), p. 412. The earlier volumes are *Particulars of My Life: Part One of an Autobiography* (1976; reprint, New York: New York University Press, 1984), and *The Shaping of a Behaviorist: Part Two of an Autobiography* (1979; reprint, New York: New York University Press, 1984). Hereafter I will give quotations under abbreviations

in the body of the text: *Particulars of My Life: PML; The Shaping of a Behaviorist: SB; A Matter of Consequences: MC.* A further autobiographical piece is "B. F. Skinner," in *A History of Psychology in Autobiography,* eds. E. G. Boring and G. Lindzey (New York: Appleton-Century-Crofts, 1967), vol. 5, pp. 387–413.

51. In a letter quoted in Fred Kaplan, *Thomas Carlyle: A Biography* (Berkeley: University of California Press, 1993), p. 534.

52. I *Henry IV,* act 2, scene iv, lines 371–72.

53. Quoted in Daniel W. Bjork, *B. F. Skinner: A Life* (New York: Basic Books, 1993), p. 38. The quotation is from an interview with Bjork, March 7, 1990.

54. Skinner, *Beyond Freedom and Dignity,* pp. 11–12.

55. Skinner was named "Humanist of the Year" by the American Humanist Association in 1972—an honor that those who read him as I do will ponder with puzzlement.

56. The poem, "Science and Human Behavior," was originally published in the *Partisan Review* in 1957. It was reprinted in John Hollander, *A Crackling of Thorns* (New Haven: Yale University Press, 1958), pp. 52–53.

57. Roland Barthes, "The Death of the Author," in *Image-Music-Text,* trans. Stephen Heath (London: Fontana, 1977), p. 148.

58. Roland Barthes, *S/Z: An Essay,* trans. Richard Miller (New York: Hill & Wang, 1974), p. 10.

59. Roland Barthes, *Roland Barthes by Roland Barthes,* trans. Richard Howard (New York: Hill & Wang, 1977), p. 143.

60. Ibid., p. 144.

61. Roland Barthes, *Mythologies,* trans. Annette Lavers (1957; reprint, New York: Hill & Wang, 1973).

62. Roland Barthes, *A Lover's Discourse: Fragments,* trans. Richard Howard (1977; reprint, New York: Hill & Wang, 1978).

63. Roland Barthes, *Camera Lucida,* trans. Richard Howard (1980; reprint, London: Vintage, 1993), p. 67.

64. Ibid., p. 98.

65. The English text from which I quote is *Roland Barthes by Roland Barthes,* trans. Richard Howard (New York: Hill & Wang, 1977); the French edition is *Roland Barthes par Roland Barthes* (Paris: Seuil, 1975). Where I quote from the French, the page numbers will be in italics after the English page numbers. For a discussion of the book's various possible titles, see Andrew Brown, *Roland Barthes: The Figures of Writing* (Oxford: Oxford University Press, 1992), pp. 119–27. Where translation issues require consideration, I cite Barthes's French in square brackets.

66. Patricia Meyer Spacks, *Imagining a Self: Autobiography and Novel in Eighteenth-Century England* (Cambridge: Harvard University Press, 1976), finds just the contrary tendency in classic eighteenth-century English autobiography (and fiction) where the "obsession and final achievement" of these works is "selfhood and consistent identity" (p. 315).

67. Johnnie Gratton identifies three positions with respect to the relationship between subject and language in *Roland Barthes by Roland Barthes*: "(a) a pre-critical subject, for whom expressivity remains a natural function of language; (b) a critical subject, who calls into question both the efficiency of the expressive process and the credibility of a self predating it, dispensing ready-made contents into it; and (c) a post-critical subject . . . who prizes the act of writing for its salutary dispersal of the ego-ideal and who experiences that dispersal as an ecstatic undoing of limits." The comment appears in his essay "*Roland Barthes par Roland*

Barthes: Autobiography and the Notion of Expression," *Romance Studies* 8 (1986): 57–65. Quoted by Eakin, *Touching the World,* pp. 16–17.

68. Barbour argues that personal transformation can never be a process of total disconnection from the past. He writes of "the autobiographer's double consciousness of the self's continuing identity and its transformation." See John D. Barbour, *Versions of Deconversion: Autobiography and the Loss of Faith* (Charlottesville: University Press of Virginia, 1994), p. 111. Barbour also insists that apostasy must always call on already-embedded values and conceptualizations.

69. Jacques Lacan, *Écrits: A Selection,* trans. Alan Sheridan (London: Tavistock, 1977), p. 4.

70. In an illuminating discussion of the imaginary in Barthes, Michael Moriarty argues that Barthes extended the conception to include the construction of the Other in the eyes of the subject. See his *Roland Barthes* (London: Polity, 1991), p. 172.

71. I owe my knowledge of these songs to Patricia Harris Stablein.

72. Barthes, *A Lover's Discourse,* p. 14.

73. Eakin, *Touching the World,* p. 19. Paul Jay also senses a nostalgia at the heart of the "disappropriated" Barthesian textual subject. See his *Being in the Text: Self-Representation from Wordsworth to Roland Barthes* (Ithaca: Cornell University Press, 1984), p. 181.

74. Eakin notes that in *Roland Barthes by Roland Barthes,* the body goes "far toward filling the absent center of the subject" (*Touching the World,* p. 12).

75. The English translation does not begin pagination until page 44. The page number in square brackets corresponds to the number the page would have if paginated. The quote is from a caption beside a photograph of Barthes as a young man.

76. Roland Barthes, *The Empire of Signs,* trans. Richard Howard (1970; reprint, Hill & Wang, 1982).

CHAPTER FOUR

1. Quoted in Matthew J. Brucolli, ed., *Conversations with Hemingway* (Jackson: University Press of Mississippi, 1986), p. 196.

2. Simone de Beauvoir, *The Prime of Life,* trans. Peter Green (1960; reprint, Cleveland: World Publishing Co., 1962), p. 114.

3. Ernest Hemingway, *A Farewell to Arms* (1929; reprint, London: Triad, 1977), pp. 232–33.

4. Ernest Hemingway, *A Moveable Feast* (New York: Charles Scribner's Sons, 1964), p. 6. Subsequent references to this work will be given in parentheses after quotations in my text.

5. Barbour's book, an original and deeply considered study, is *The Conscience of the Autobiographer: Ethical and Religious Dimensions of Autobiography* (London: Macmillan, 1992). The quotation is from page 3.

6. See her fine study, Martha C. Nussbaum, *The Fragility of Goodness: Luck and Ethics in Greek Tragedy and Philosophy* (Cambridge: Cambridge University Press, 1986).

7. Bernard Williams, "Moral Luck," in *Moral Luck: Philosophical Papers 1973–1980* (Cambridge: Cambridge University Press, 1981), pp. 20–39; Thomas Nagel, "Moral Luck," in *Mortal Questions* (Cambridge: Cambridge University Press, 1979), pp. 24–38. I would like to thank Dr. Alex Segal for drawing my attention to some of the philosophical connections noted here and for his helpful early comments on some of the ideas I develop in this chapter.

8. Williams, *Moral Luck,* p. 20.

9. Immanuel Kant, *Groundwork of the Metaphysics of Morals,* trans. H. J. Paton (New York: Harper & Row, 1964), p. 62.

10. Ernest Hemingway, *The Old Man and the Sea* (London: Jonathan Cape, 1952), p. 117.

11. Nagel's definitions are given in *Mortal Questions,* p. 28.

12. Though strictly a term for the "novel of the education" of the writer, *Künstlerroman* will suffice for a case like *A Moveable Feast.*

13. The text was edited by Mary Hemingway and Harry Brague. Scholarship on the various manuscript drafts seems conclusively to show that the published text departs significantly from the one intended in Hemingway's final drafts. In particular, the published version omits some formulations in which he sought to take more responsibility for the breakup of his marriage with Hadley and includes a key passage, which he had apparently decided to excise, in which he blames the "rich" for the advent of Pauline Pfeiffer in his life. I discuss these matters later in the chapter. For scholarship on the manuscript and the publishing history of *A Moveable Feast,* see Gerry Brenner, "Are We Going to Hemingway's Feast?" *American Literature* 54, no. 4 (December 1982) 528–44; Ronald Weber, *Hemingway's Art of Non-Fiction* (London: Macmillan, 1990), chap. 6; and, by far the most detailed treatment, including tabulation of the various manuscript emendations and drafts, Jacqueline Tavernier-Courbin, *Ernest Hemingway's* A Moveable Feast: *The Making of a Myth* (Boston: Northeastern University Press, 1991). For a rich and intricate reading of Hemingway's manuscript revisions and the light they throw on both the inner tensions of *A Moveable Feast* and on modern autobiography more generally, see Susanna Egan, *Mirror Talk: Genres of Crisis in Contemporary Autobiography* (Chapel Hill: University of North Carolina Press, 1999), pp. 29–47.

14. The title was selected by Mary Hemingway and Harry Brague from a list that Hemingway had left. See Ronald Weber, *Hemingway's Art of Non-Fiction,* chap. 6.

15. Nussbaum discusses these terms and their implications in Greek philosophy at length in *The Fragility of Goodness.* See especially chapter 4.

16. Tavernier-Courbin conclusively demonstrates that this poverty was an invention of Hemingway's. See *Ernest Hemingway's* A Moveable Feast, pp. 90–94.

17. Ernest Hemingway, *For Whom the Bell Tolls* (1941; reprint, London: Granada, 1976), p. 153.

18. Nussbaum, *The Fragility of Goodness,* p. 221.

19. Ernest Hemingway, *Selected Letters, 1917–1961,* ed. Carlos Baker (New York: Charles Scribner's Sons, 1981), p. 33.

20. Gillian Rose, *Love's Work* (London: Vintage, 1997). I am indebted to Margaretta Jolly for drawing this extraordinarily powerful work to my attention.

21. See Tavernier-Courbin, *Ernest Hemingway's* A Moveable Feast, pp. 177–80, 201–3.

22. Ibid., p. 180.

23. Jeffrey Meyers, *Hemingway: A Biography* (London: Macmillan, 1985), p. 482.

24. Michael Reynolds, *Hemingway: The Paris Years* (Oxford: Basil Blackwell, 1989), p. 319.

25. Jean-Paul Sartre, *Being and Nothingness: An Essay on Phenomenological Ontology,* trans. Hazel E. Barnes (New York: Philosophical Library, n.d.), p. 11.

26. *The Complete Short Stories of Ernest Hemingway,* Finca Vigia edition (New York: Charles Scribner's Sons, 1987), p. 291.

27. Nussbaum, *The Fragility of Goodness,* p. 7.

28. Aristotle, *Nichomachean Ethics*, 1118b17, in *The Complete Works of Aristotle*, ed. Jonathan Barnes, 2 vols. (Princeton: Princeton University Press, 1984).

29. Christopher Lasch, *The Culture of Narcissism: American Life in an Age of Diminishing Expectations* (London: Abacus, 1980), p. 204.

30. See Lasch, *The Culture of Narcissism*, p. 10.

31. George Eliot, *Middlemarch* (1871; reprint, Harmondsworth: Penguin, 1965), pp. 297, 243.

32. Hemingway, *A Farewell to Arms*, p. 96.

33. For a feminist reading of Hemingway, see Nancy R. Cromley and Robert Scholes, *Hemingway's Genders: Rereading the Hemingway Text* (New Haven: Yale University Press, 1994). On relational and associated tendencies in women's autobiography and proposed contrasts with male models, see Sidonie Smith's critique of the "androcentric paradigm" in *A Poetics of Women's Autobiography: Marginality and the Fictions of Self-Representation* (Bloomington: Indiana University Press, 1987), p. 10; Regenia Gagnier, "The Literary Standard, Working-Class Autobiography and Gender," in *Revealing Lives: Autobiography, Biography and Gender*, eds. Susan Groag Bell and Marilyn Yalom (Albany: State University of New York Press, 1990). Gagnier argues that "the organic, self-regarding, typically male and middle-class self of literary autobiography was always only one 'self' among others, even before it was dispersed under the conditions of postmodernism" (p. 101). Susan Friedman writes of the "fundamental inapplicability of individualistic models of the self to women and minorities" in "Women's Autobiographical Selves: Theory and Practice," in *The Private Self: Theory and Practice of Women's Autobiographical Writings*, ed. Shari Benstock (Chapel Hill: University of North Carolina Press, 1988), p. 34. Mary Mason argues for a wide diversity of models of female identity-in-writing and identity-in-community; see "The Other Voice: Autobiographies of Women Writers," in *Life/Lines: Theorizing Women's Autobiography*, eds. Bella Brodzki and Celeste Schenck (Ithaca: Cornell University Press, 1988), pp. 19–44. One of the first scholars to draw attention to the relational properties of women's life-writing was Estelle C. Jelinek, ed., *Women's Autobiography: Essays in Criticism* (Bloomington: Indiana University Press, 1980). Jelinek writes of the "multidimensionality of women's socially conditioned roles" (p. 17). Other influential formulations have come from Mary C. Mason, "The Other Voice: Autobiographies of Women Writers," in *Autobiography: Essays Theoretical and Critical*, ed. James Olney (Princeton: Princeton University Press, 1980), where Mason talks of the senses in which the female autobiographical self is "linked to the identification of some 'other'" (p. 210); and Julia Watson in her essay "Shadowed Presence: Modern Women Writers' Autobiographies and the Other," in *Studies in Autobiography*, ed. James Olney (Oxford: Oxford University Press, 1988), pp. 180–89. See also Julia Swindells, ed., *The Uses of Autobiography* (London: Taylor Francis, 1995), especially the introduction; and Norine Voss, "'Saying the Unsayable': An Introduction to Women's Autobiography," in *Gender Studies: New Directions in Feminist Criticism*, ed. Judith Spector (Bowling Green, Ohio: Bowling Green State University Popular Press, 1986), pp. 218–33.

34. Lasch, *The Culture of Narcissism*, p. 8. For the Imperial Self, see Quentin Anderson, *The Imperial Self* (New York: Knopf, 1971).

35. Ernest Hemingway, *Islands in the Stream* (New York: Charles Scribner's Sons, 1970), p. 7.

36. Tavernier-Courbin, *Ernest Hemingway's* A Moveable Feast, pp. 178–79.

37. Nagel, *Mortal Questions*, p. 35.

38. Ibid., p. 37.

39. Ibid., p. 38.

40. Beauvoir, *The Prime of Life*, p. 114.

41. Ernest Hemingway, "Pamplona Letter," *The Transatlantic Review* 2 (September 1924): 301. Quoted in Weber, *Hemingway's Art of Non-Fiction*, p. 136.

42. Tavernier-Courbin, *Ernest Hemingway's* A Moveable Feast, p. 180.

43. Ibid., chap. 8.

CHAPTER FIVE

1. Simone de Beauvoir, *She Came to Stay*, trans. anonymous (1943; reprint, New York: Dell, 1963), p. 132.

2. The four volumes of Beauvoir's autobiography proper are *Mémoires d'une jeune fille rangée* (Paris: Gallimard, 1958): *Memoirs of a Dutiful Daughter*, trans. James Kirkup (Cleveland: World Publishing Co., 1959); *La force de l'âge* (Paris: Gallimard, 1960): *The Prime of Life*, trans. Peter Green (Cleveland: World Publishing, 1962); *La force des choses* (Paris: Gallimard, 1963): *Force of Circumstance*, trans. Richard Howard (New York: G. P. Putnam's Sons, 1965); *Tout compte fait* (Paris: Gallimard, 1972): *All Said and Done*, trans. Patrick O'Brian (New York: G. P. Putnam's Sons, 1974). When quoting from these texts I use the following abbreviations: *Memoirs of a Dutiful Daughter* (*MDD*), *The Prime of Life* (*PL*), *Force of Circumstance* (*FC*), *All Said and Done* (*ASD*). Where I also quote from the French, page references will appear in italics after the page references to the English volumes. Another important first-person source is *Journal de guerre: Septembre 1939-Janvier 1941* (Paris: Gallimard, 1990).

3. Simone de Beauvoir, *La cérémonie des adieux; suivi de Entretiens avec Jean-Paul Sartre* (Paris: Gallimard, 1981): *Adieux: A Farewell to Sartre*, trans. Patrick O'Brian (Harmondsworth: Penguin, 1985); *Une mort très douce* (Paris: Gallimard, 1964): *A Very Easy Death*, trans. Patrick O'Brian (Harmondsworth: Penguin, 1969).

4. Simone de Beauvoir, *The Ethics of Ambiguity*, trans. Bernard Frechtman (1945; reprint, New York: Citadel Press, 1994), p. 7.

5. Jean-Paul Sartre, *Being and Nothingness: An Essay on Phenomenological Ontology*, trans. Hazel E. Barnes (New York: Philosophical Library, n.d.), pp. 604–15.

6. Ibid., p. 119.

7. Beauvoir, *The Ethics of Ambiguity*, pp. 15–16.

8. Ibid., p. 18.

9. Richard Rorty, *Contingency, Irony, and Solidarity* (Cambridge: Cambridge University Press, 1989). See especially chapter 2.

10. Ibid., p. 4.

11. Ibid. p. 11.

12. Ibid., p. 9.

13. Ibid., p. 13.

14. For instance, when Sartre says that "each man finds himself in the presence of *meanings* which do not come into the world through him" (*Being and Nothingness*, p. 520).

15. A view not shared by the doyen of French autobiographical scholarship, Philippe Lejeune. On Lejeune's surprisingly critical assessment, see Marylea MacDonald, "'For Example': Simone de Beauvoir's Parenthetical Presence in Philippe Lejeune's Theory of Autobiography," *Simone de Beauvoir Studies* 10 (1993): 237–40.

16. "I don't apply my analyses to myself all that often. It is not in my nature." From an interview with Beauvoir, quoted in Judith Okely, *Simone de Beauvoir: A Re-reading* (London: Vi-

rago, 1986), p. 122. Kathleen Woodward suggests, unconvincingly in my view, that "Beauvoir's memoirs disappoint us because they are too connected with the outside world and do not seem motivated by a need to discover her own past," in her essay "Simone de Beauvoir: Aging and Its Discontents," in *The Private Self: Theory and Practice of Women's Autobiographical Writings,* ed. Shari Benstock (Chapel Hill: University of North Carolina Press, 1988), p. 101.

17. See for example Simone de Beauvoir, *The Second Sex,* trans. and ed. H. M. Parshley (1949; reprint, London: Picador 1988), pp. 65–69.

18. Tilde Sankovitch argues that the articulation of the authorial persona across the volumes is partly handled through the association of Beauvoir with a "hidden mythic structure" of elemental character types. See her essay "Simone de Beauvoir's Autobiographical Legacy," *Simone de Beauvoir Studies* 8 (1991): 93–101.

19. Eleanore Holveck summarizes Beauvoir's position in *All Said and Done* as follows: one's "own reflection unifies the disconnected and fragmentary into the single project of one complete and successful life." See her "Simone de Beauvoir: Autobiography as Philosophy," *Simone de Beauvoir Studies* 8 (1991): 109. On Beauvoir's perspective in *All Said and Done,* see also Terry Keefe, "Simone de Beauvoir's Second Look at Her Life," *Romance Studies* no. 8, "French Autobiography: Texts, Contexts, Poetics" (summer 1986): 41–55.

20. For a more detailed discussion of the shifts and inconsistencies that occur from volume to volume of Beauvoir's autobiography, see Terry Keefe, *Simone de Beauvoir: A Study of Her Writings* (Totowa, N.J.: Barnes & Noble, 1983), chap. 2.

21. In an excellent and wide-ranging collection of essays on existentialism, autobiography, and related matters: see Terry Keefe and Edmund Smyth, eds., *Autobiography and the Existential Self: Studies in Modern French Writing* (New York: St. Martin's Press, 1995). See especially Smyth's essay "Autobiography, Contingency, Selfhood: A Reading of *Les Mots,*" pp. 25–38; and Keefe's judicious conclusion to the volume, pp. 183–94.

22. Terry Keefe shrewdly observes that Sartre's slogan does not *deny* essence, but merely places it in a secondary position (ibid., p. 187). One might add that the "anguish" about which Sartre writes at such length describes a deeply *troubled* relationship between the self and its essence (see, for example, *Being and Nothingness,* p. 35). I thank Graham Storey for highlighting this dimension of Sartre's position.

23. John D. Barbour, *Versions of Deconversion: Autobiography and the Loss of Faith* (Charlottesville: University Press of Virginia, 1994), p. 111.

24. For a comparison of Beauvoir and Sartre as autobiographers in relation to existential and other traditions, see Beth Yalom, "Sartre, Beauvoir and the Autobiographical Tradition," *Simone de Beauvoir Studies* 8 (1991): 75–82.

25. Beauvoir, *The Second Sex,* p. 179.

26. For Aquinas on the will, see appendix A, "Some Earlier Conceptions of the Will: Maimonides to Mill," pp. 291–95.

27. Beauvoir would not have agreed: she thought James's novel "a bore." See Simone de Beauvoir, *Beloved Chicago Man: Letters to Nelson Algren 1947–64* (London: Victor Gollancz, 1998), p. 115.

28. On the sublime in the nineteenth-century French tradition and its relations to the twentieth century, see Suzanne Guerlac, *The Impersonal Sublime: Hugo, Baudelaire, Lautréamont* (Stanford: Stanford University Press, 1990).

29. Rorty, *Contingency, Irony, and Solidarity,* pp. 3–7.

30. George Eliot, *The Mill on the Floss,* ed. Gordon S. Haight (Oxford: Clarendon Press, 1980), p. 33.

31. Ibid., p. 417.

32. Beauvoir cites Rousseau as an exemplar of autobiographical writing in the preface to *The Prime of Life* (p. 10) and the introduction to *Force of Circumstance* (p. vi); however, references to Rousseau in *The Second Sex* are, for obvious reasons, much more critical. In an early letter, George Eliot describes Rousseau as one "of the writers who have most influenced me" and says that "Rousseau's genius has sent that electric thrill through my intellectual and moral frame which has awakened me to new perceptions, which has made man and nature a fresh world of thought and feeling." She stresses that she does not, however, necessarily agree with all of Rousseau's views. Letter to Sara Sophia Hennell, February 9, 1849, *The George Eliot Letters,* ed. Gordon S. Haight, 9 vols. (New Haven: Yale University Press, 1954–78), vol. 1, p. 277.

33. Nancy K. Miller considers the question of Beauvoir's "freedom" in relation to her decision not to have children. See her "Writing Fictions: Women's Autobiography in France," in *Life/Lines: Theorizing Women's Autobiography,* eds. Bella Brodzki and Celeste Schenck (Ithaca: Cornell University Press, 1988), p. 53.

34. Beauvoir, *The Ethics of Ambiguity,* p. 19.

35. Jerome Hamilton Buckley, *The Turning Key: Autobiography and the Subjective Impulse Since 1800* (Cambridge: Harvard University Press, 1984), p. 52. See also Barbour, *Versions of Deconversion.*

36. For a careful assessment of Beauvoir's tendencies to egotism, on the one hand, and solidarity, on the other, see Sylvie Rockmore, "Simone de Beauvoir: Égoïsme ou Solidarité?" *Simone de Beauvoir Studies* 12 (1995): 73–79.

37. On Beauvoir and risk, see Debra B. Bergoffen, *The Philosophy of Simone de Beauvoir: Gendered Phenomenologies, Erotic Generosities* (Albany: State University of New York Press, 1997), chap. 5.

38. I discuss this notion in chapter 7 with reference to Stephen Spender.

39. Iris Murdoch, *Sartre: Romantic Rationalist* (1953; reprint, London: Fontana, 1967), p. 77. Judith Okely argues that "Beauvoir's 'I' of the adult autobiographies is the rational actor and intellectual who seeks to repress and control any underlying contradictions in the self" (*Simone de Beauvoir: A Re-reading,* p. 122).

40. See appendix A, "Some Earlier Conceptions of the Will: Maimonides to Mill," pp. 315–17. In a letter George Eliot argues that "one cannot flourish until one has 'conciliated necessitarianism'—I hate the ugly word—with the practice of willing strongly, of willing to will strongly, and so on" (*The George Eliot Letters,* vol. 6, p. 166). For a comparative discussion of Eliot and Mill on determinism and the will, see George Levine, "Determinism and Responsibility," *PMLA* 77 (June 1962): 268–79.

41. Beauvoir, *The Second Sex,* p. 613.

42. See David Parker, *Ethics, Theory and the Novel* (Cambridge: Cambridge University Press, 1994). See especially chapters 1–5. Parker's excellent discussion of these matters tends to construe the ethical unconscious in a more negative manner than I do here. For him, this unconscious tends, as one might expect, to contain repressed materials that are implicated in the individual's having a restricted mode of being in the world. I am using the term in a more positive sense, to suggest that the unconscious may contain certain constructive and fructifying ethical inclinations.

43. Simone de Beauvoir, *Letters to Sartre,* trans. Quintin Hoare (1990; reprint, London: Vintage, 1992), p. 17.

44. Toril Moi, *Simone de Beauvoir: The Making of an Intellectual Woman* (Oxford: Basil Blackwell, 1994), p. 18. On Beauvoir's "paradoxical impulse of attachment and individuation,"

see Catherine Portuges, "Attachment and Separation in *The Memoirs of a Dutiful Daughter*," "Simone de Beauvoir: Witness to a Century," *Yale French Studies*, no. 72 (1986): 107–18.

45. Beauvoir, *She Came to Stay*, p. 23.

46. Ibid., p. 233.

47. It seems clear that Beauvoir was deeply involved in working out many of the ideas in *Being and Nothingness* and in the editorial processes of the book's production. I do not, however, accept Kate and Edward Fullbrook's contention that she was in fact the principal author of *Being and Nothingness*. See Kate Fullbrook and Edward Fullbrook, *Simone de Beauvoir and Jean-Paul Sartre: The Remaking of a Twentieth-Century Legend* (New York: Basic Books, 1994).

48. Sartre, *Being and Nothingness*, part 3.

49. Ibid., p. 364.

50. Simone de Beauvoir, *The Mandarins*, trans. Leonard Friedman (1954; reprint, London, Fontana, 1960), p. 376.

51. Ibid., p. 329.

52. Simone de Beauvoir, "The Age of Discretion," in *The Woman Destroyed*, trans. Patrick O'Brian (1967; reprint, New York: Pantheon, 1969), p. 44.

53. Beauvoir, *The Second Sex*, p. 423.

54. Ibid., p. 29.

55. Ibid., p. 437.

56. A fact perhaps more surprising in a French autobiography of the time than it would be in an English or American one, given attitudes to bisexuality in the respective cultures. For a balanced assessment of Beauvoir's autobiographical suppression of her bisexuality, see Hazel Barnes, *The Story I Tell Myself: A Venture in Existentialist Autobiography* (Chicago: University of Chicago Press, 1997), p. 186. Barnes is especially well qualified to comment: a renowned scholar and translator of existentialist texts, her autobiography is structured along existential lines; it is also the autobiography of a lesbian.

57. In *Simone de Beauvoir: Feminist Mandarin* (London: Tavistock, 1985), p. 19, Mary Evans contrasts Beauvoir and Sartre with respect to their ability to endow individuals of the opposite sex with psychological specificity when writing about them. Zaza is an interesting variation on this issue, the question being whether Beauvoir's agenda of class critique in *Memoirs of a Dutiful Daughter* brings Zaza to the edge of a kind of characterization by category.

58. Diana Trilling, *The Beginning of the Journey: The Marriage of Diana and Lionel Trilling* (New York: Harcourt Brace, 1993), p. 419.

59. John Rawls, *A Theory of Justice* (Oxford: Oxford University Press, 1973), pp. 342–50.

60. Though less so in France than in Britain or the United States. On French women novelists and their use of narrative to rethink the conventions governing sexual relationships, see Joan DeJean, *Tender Geographies: Women and the Origins of the Novel in France* (New York: Columbia University Press, 1991).

61. Beauvoir, *Letters to Sartre*. For a judicious view of these letters, see Barnes, *The Story I Tell Myself*, pp. 186–87.

62. Bianca Lamblin, *Mémoires d'une jeune fille dérangée* (Paris: Bolland, 1993).

63. Beauvoir, *The Second Sex*, p. 664.

64. Fullbrook and Fullbrook, *Simone de Beauvoir and Jean-Paul Sartre*.

65. Beauvoir, *She Came to Stay*, p. 23.

66. There is a good deal of evidence that Beauvoir was more open in volunteering information to Sartre than he was in volunteering it to her.

67. Beauvoir, *Beloved Chicago Man*.

CHAPTER SIX

1. Koestler's recollections of these events are notoriously variable. Some of his autobiographical accounts put the period of imprisonment at five months. On such matters of factual detail I generally follow Koestler's most recent biographer, David Cesarani, *Arthur Koestler: The Homeless Mind* (London: William Heinemann, 1998). Cesarani's most concerted treatment of Koestler's Spanish civil war experience occurs on pp. 118–35.

2. Arthur Koestler, *The Invisible Writing: The Second Volume of an Autobiography: 1932–40* (1954; reprint, New York: Stein and Day, 1984), p. 441. Hereafter *IW.*

3. Arthur Koestler, *Spanish Testament* (London: Gollancz, 1937). The Danube edition, *Dialogue with Death,* trans. Trevor and Phyllis Blewitt (London: Hutchinson, 1966), begins with some sections that in *Spanish Testament* appear in the final chapter of section 1, "The Last Days of Malaga." There are numerous other structural and textual differences between the two editions. Hereafter *DD.*

4. Cesarani's biography has caused a stir by claiming that Koestler raped two women, and probably several more (pp. 399–401). It also gives graphic accounts of his promiscuity and his intermittent emotional cruelty to women. Highly disturbing though these charges are, they don't—even if confirmed—materially affect what I have to say about Koestler. Having studied Koestler's published work and some of his personal papers before the publication of Cesarani's study, I had concluded that his attitude toward women was highly conflicted and at times very destructive. Further, I have always seen him as a monumentally divided man: one capable of great goodness, generosity, and courage; but also a man with a dark—indeed demonic—side. His heavy drinking, cyclical depressions, and self-confessed neuroses played their parts in his mercurial personal patterns.

5. Derick Marsh, to whom I am indebted for discussions of Koestler and other matters, points out the aptness for Koestler of Yeats's claim that "we begin to live when we conceive life as tragedy."

6. I use the term as Harold Bloom uses it in *The Anxiety of Influence: A Theory of Poetry* (New York: Oxford University Press, 1973). Bloom's term entails both the precursor's provision of necessary expressive forms and possibilities, and the disciple's inevitable oedipal rebellion against the father, and the resultant distortion of the exemplar's voice.

7. Arthur Koestler, *Arrow in the Blue: The First Volume of an Autobiography: 1905–31* (1952; reprint, New York: Stein and Day, 1984), p. 15. Hereafter, *AB.* The other autobiographical volumes, in addition to *Dialogue with Death,* are *Scum of the Earth,* trans. Daphne Hardy (London: Victor Gollancz, 1941), hereafter *SE;* and Arthur Koestler and Cynthia Koestler, *Stranger on the Square* (London: Abacus, 1985)—a volume that was coauthored by the Koestlers and was found in manuscript form among Arthur's papers after the joint suicide. Hereafter *SS.* See also his important essay about repudiating communism in Richard Crossman, ed., *The God That Failed* (1949; reprint, New York: Books for Libraries Press, 1972), pp. 15–75. Hereafter *GTF.*

8. An important study of autobiography that construes the genre as a form of "act" is Elizabeth W. Bruss, *Autobiographical Acts: The Changing Situation of a Literary Genre* (Baltimore: Johns Hopkins University Press, 1976). Bruss's "acts" are illocutionary acts (p. 6).

9. Susan G. Figge draws attention to an autobiographical subgenre that could also be regarded as an instance of post-totalitarian autobiography: books by children of Fascist fathers. See "'Father Books': Memoirs of the Children of Fascist Fathers," in *Revealing Lives: Autobiography, Biography, and Gender,* eds. Susan Groag Bell and Lillian S. Yalom (Albany: State University of New York Press, 1990), pp. 193–201. Paul John Eakin quotes a striking passage

from Mary McCarthy's *Cast a Cold Eye* (1950; reprint, New York: New American Library, 1972), in which McCarthy uses a totalitarian metaphor for the psyche: "discarded selves languish in the Lubianka of the unconscious." See Paul John Eakin, *Fictions in Autobiography: Studies in the Art of Self-Invention* (Princeton: Princeton University Press, 1985), p. 28.

10. Arthur Koestler, *The Trail of the Dinosaur/Reflections on Hanging*, Danube edition (London: Hutchinson, 1970), p. 244.

11. See Arthur Koestler and J. R. Smythies, eds., *Beyond Reductionism: The Alpbach Symposium* (London: Hutchinson, 1969).

12. Arthur Koestler, *The Ghost in the Machine* (1967; reprint, London: Hutchinson, 1976), p. 17.

13. On Skinner, see ibid., pp. 7–15. For an assessment of Koestler on behaviorism, see Kathleen Nott, "The Trojan Horses: Koestler and the Behaviorists," in *Astride Two Cultures: Arthur Koestler at 70,* ed. Harold Harris (London: Hutchinson, 1975), pp. 162–74.

14. Koestler, *The Ghost in the Machine,* p. 15. David Cesarani's treatment of these matters seems to me too perfunctory and dismissive. To say that Koestler was a "quasi-determinist" is too vague and that his attack on behaviorism lacks penetration because he too was "quite capable of reducing human behaviour to the product of electronic impulses," (p. 469) does little justice to the complexity of Koestler's position.

15. Gilbert Ryle, *The Concept of Mind* (Harmondsworth: Penguin, 1963), p. 62.

16. Koestler, *The Ghost in the Machine,* p. 220.

17. Arthur Koestler, *The Yogi and the Commissar* (1945; reprint, London: Jonathan Cape, 1964), p. 58.

18. See Cesarani's reading of the suicide "pact" in *The Homeless Mind,* pp. 548ff.

19. Arthur Koestler, *Janus: A Summing Up* (Richmond South, Vic.: Hutchinson Group, Australia, 1978).

20. Cesarani—who is convinced that Koestler greatly overstates the unhappiness of his childhood and that he characteristically reads grand meanings back into events that were not in fact of determinative importance—thinks that the tonsillectomy description is a put-up job (pp. 11–12). I suggest that neither Cesarani nor anyone else can ultimately know this. What we can say is that, however authentic or laced with fantasy, Koestler's narrative account of this event takes us deep into his sense of self and world.

21. He describes himself as "manic depressive" in *The Invisible Writing,* p. 307. The assessment is disputed by Celia Goodman, the sister of Koestler's second wife, Mamaine, in a volume of Mamaine's letters. Celia Goodman, ed., *Living with Koestler: Mamaine Koestler's Letters 1945–51* (London: Weidenfeld & Nicolson, 1985), p. 21.

22. Stephen Spender, who reviewed both *Arrow in the Blue* and *The Invisible Writing,* complains of the first volume that it is "theory-ridden." See Stephen Spender, "In Search of Penitence," in *Arthur Koestler: A Collection of Critical Essays,* ed. Murray A. Sperber (Englewood Cliffs, N.J.: Prentice-Hall, 1977), p. 103.

23. Koestler, *The Yogi and the Commissar,* p. 63.

24. Arthur Koestler, *Promise and Fulfilment: Palestine 1917–1949* (London: Macmillan, 1949), p. 190.

25. Koestler, *The Yogi and the Commissar,* p. 61.

26. Arthur Koestler, *Insight and Outlook: An Inquiry into the Common Foundations of Science, Art, and Social Ethics* (London: Macmillan, 1949).

27. Arthur Koestler, *The Act of Creation* (1964; reprint, London: Hutchinson, 1969), pp. 35–36.

28. Arthur Koestler, *The Sleepwalkers: A History of Man's Changing Visions of the Universe* (1959; reprint, London: Hutchinson, 1968), p. 426.

29. Koestler, *The Act of Creation*, p. 69.

30. Ibid., pp. 364–65.

31. Koestler, *The Ghost in the Machine*, p. 277.

32. Koestler, *The Yogi and the Commissar*, pp. 110, 109.

33. Ibid., p. 109.

34. Koestler, *The Act of Creation*, p. 148.

35. Koestler, preface to the Danube edition of *Arrow in the Blue*.

36. Stephen Spender feels that in response to this situation, Koestler resorts to a mode of mechanical self-analysis that lacks "the element of love" with the result that "his own personality seems a blank in the story of his life." See Spender, "In Search of Penitence," p. 105.

37. Koestler, *The Ghost in the Machine*, p. 297.

38. Ibid., p. 269.

39. Koestler, *The Act of Creation*, p. 259.

40. Koestler, *The Ghost in the Machine*, p. 213.

41. Ibid., p. 219.

42. Ibid., p. 217.

43. Ibid., p. 216.

44. Ibid., p. 217.

45. Ibid., p. 215.

46. Ibid., p. 248.

47. Ibid., p. 249.

48. Ibid., p. 217.

49. The meeting is described in *The Invisible Writing*, p. 497.

50. Arthur Koestler, *Arrival and Departure* (1943; reprint, London: Hutchinson, 1966).

51. Koestler's most sustained effort to argue this position is *The Roots of Coincidence* (London: Hutchinson, 1972).

52. Koestler, *The Yogi and the Commissar*, p. 205.

53. See especially the analysis of Stalinist Russia in part 3 of *The Yogi and the Commissar*.

54. Ibid., p. 109.

55. A point that John Gatt-Rutter has highlighted in various conversations. I take this opportunity to express again my thanks to John for his wise commentary on this and related matters. Maurice Merleau-Ponty has a different view again, declaring Koestler a "*mediocre Marxist.*" See "Koestler's Dilemmas," in *Arthur Koestler: A Collection of Critical Essays*, ed. Sperber, p. 84. In Koestler's (partial) defense, it is worth pointing out that he does at times acknowledge the analytical value of certain Marxist concepts and perspectives (see, for example, *Arrow in the Blue*, p. 337), and that he sees liberal democracy as offering "cold comfort"—a comfort that is however preferable to the "totalitarian blizzard" (*Promise and Fulfilment*, p. 184).

56. Arthur Koestler, *The Heel of Achilles: Essays 1968–1973* (London: Hutchinson, 1974), p. 20.

57. Karl Marx, *Capital: A Critique of Political Economy*, ed. Frederick Engels, trans. Samuel Moore and Edward Aveling (New York: The Modern Library, 1906), vol. 1, p. 12. I am grateful to Dr. Thomas Hoy for pointing out this connection. These and other matters are explored in his admirable Ph.D. dissertation, "Fiction, Science and the Cultural Moment: Paradigms in Science and Fiction" (La Trobe University, 1998). Marx's reference, however, is by implication to Newtonian physics. The "wave-mechanics" to which Koestler refers above

are Einsteinian physics, and Koestler's intellectual development can in part be traced in terms of his transition from the Newtonian to the Einsteinian paradigm.

58. John D. Barbour makes this connection in *Versions of Deconversion: Autobiography and the Loss of Faith* (Charlottesville: University Press of Virginia, 1994), p. 48.

59. One of Cesarani's strongest claims is that Koestler's autobiographies give a "de-Ju-daised" (p. 62) account of various aspects of his life, including his experiences of deconversion. I find him quite persuasive on this point.

60. For a discussion of the closely related topic of shame in autobiography, see John D. Barbour, *The Conscience of the Autobiographer: Ethical Dimensions of Autobiography* (London: Macmillan, 1992), chap. 7.

61. Koestler, one might argue, tries to use autobiography to break the cycle of "addiction attribution" proposed by Sedgwick, whereby anyone might be said to be condemning the addictions of others from the standpoint of their own consciousness-numbing thralldom: by narrating his own experience of ideological addiction, while also demolishing its logic and its emotional appeal, he claims a place for himself "beyond" the reach of addiction's coercive powers. His detractors have in effect said that he merely switched substances: from the dependencies of the totalitarian ideologue to those of the impassioned Cold Warrior. On my reading of Koestler, this view is substantially, though not wholly, inaccurate. Either way, Mark Levene is right to say that "for a generation of writers, Koestler was the embodiment of 'the god that failed.'" See Mark Levene, *Arthur Koestler* (New York: Frederick Ungar, 1984), p. 151. On "addiction attribution" see "Epidemics of the Will," in Eve Kosofsky Sedgwick, *Tendencies* (Durham, N.C.: Duke University Press, 1993), p. 131.

62. One of Cesarani's most compelling findings is that Koestler feared a bisexual "streak" in himself. He quotes a notebook entry of May 1944 in which Koestler actually uses the phrase "Bi-sexual streak" (p. 227). Given Koestler's strong homophobic tendencies, it would not be surprising if his aggression, his promiscuity, and his destructive behavior toward women were in part compensation responses to a fear of the feminine in himself.

63. Koestler, *The Ghost in the Machine,* p. 311. In his brief and composed suicide note, Koestler says that he is leaving this life with "some timid hopes for a de-personalised after-life beyond due confines of space, time and matter, and beyond the limits of our comprehension." Quoted in George Mikes, *Arthur Koestler: The Story of a Friendship* (London: André Deutsch, 1983), p. 79.

64. In *Stranger on the Square,* p. 199, the adoringly—perhaps (as Michael Scammel has suggested in conversation) masochistically—uncritical Cynthia repeats with amusement Arthur's story of how he seduced a young woman whom he saw with her fiancé in a restaurant. The incident suggests a kind of predatory ruthlessness toward women on his part that is corroborated by a good many other incidents, but this has to be set against the obvious, if damaged, kind of fondness he had for Cynthia and others.

65. Deirdre Bair gives evidence for the sexual encounter in *Simone de Beauvoir: A Biography* (London: Jonathan Cape, 1990), p. 316. Koestler fell out with Beauvoir and Sartre and satirized the latter in his novel *The Age of Longing* (1951; reprint, London: Hutchinson, 1970). Beauvoir then satirized Koestler in *The Mandarins,* and he returned the favor in *Stranger on the Square.* See also Beauvoir's descriptions of Koestler in Simone de Beauvoir, *Beloved Chicago Man: Letters to Nelson Algren 1947–64* (London: Victor Gollancz, 1998).

66. Quaintly, the Danube edition transposes "sacred" as "scared."

67. Both quotations from a journal entry dated Sunday, August 19, 1951. The Koestler Archive, Rare Books section, Edinburgh University Library.

68. Iain Hamilton, author of the regrettably limited *Koestler: A Biography* (New York: Macmillan, 1982), confesses to impatience with Koestler's mystical explorations (p. xvi).

69. I may be in a minority here. Cesarani dismisses these beliefs as "odd" (p. 81), much as Iain Hamilton does in the earlier biography. Cesarani even sees Koestler's account of his visionary experience in prison as "mumbo-jumbo" (p. 142). This is strong stuff. Though a stranger to visionary experience, I like to read autobiography as a possible opening-out onto new modes of experience. Indeed this is a very good reason for reading visionary autobiography in a scientistic age.

70. Koestler, *The Ghost in the Machine*, p. 218.

71. Sigmund Freud, *Civilization and Its Discontents*, trans. James Strachey (New York: W. W. Norton, 1962), pp. 11ff.

72. Koestler, *The Ghost in the Machine*, p. 218.

73. Koestler, *The Yogi and the Commissar*, p. 10.

74. Arthur Koestler, *Darkness at Noon*, trans. Daphne Hardy (1940; reprint, London: Hutchinson, 1973), pp. 109–12.

75. Koestler, *The Heel of Achilles*, p. 109.

76. As John Gatt-Rutter has pointed out in conversation with the author.

CHAPTER SEVEN

1. For discussions of the Paul and Augustine passages, see chapter 1.

2. Stephen Spender, *World Within World: The Autobiography of Stephen Spender* (1951; reprint, New York: St. Martin's Press, 1994). The line appears in the poem that prefaces the early editions of the volume, "Darkness and Light." St. Martin's Press, New York, reissued the book with a new introduction by Spender in 1994. Spender died in 1995.

3. See, for example, Robert Dunn, *The Possibility of Weakness of Will* (Indianapolis: Hacket Publishing, 1987); William Carlton, *Weakness of Will* (Oxford: Basil Blackwell, 1988); Justin Gosling, *Weakness of the Will* (London: Routledge, 1990); and G. Mortimore, ed., *Weakness of Will* (London: Macmillan, 1971).

4. Plato, *Protagoras*, 358c–d, in *The Collected Dialogues of Plato, Including the Letters*, eds. Edith Hamilton and Huntington Cairnes (Princeton: Princeton University Press, 1961), p. 349.

5. See Gosling, *Weakness of the Will*, p. 9.

6. Plato, *Laws*, 734b, in *The Collected Dialogues*, p. 1320.

7. Ibid., 689b, p. 1284.

8. Plato, *Republic*, 436e, in *The Collected Dialogues*, p. 678.

9. Gosling, *Weakness of the Will*, p. 21.

10. Plato, *Republic*, 439d, in *The Collected Dialogues*, p. 681.

11. In *Practical Reason, Aristotle, and Weakness of the Will* (Minneapolis: University of Minnesota Press, 1984), Norman O. Dahl asserts that Aristotle believes genuine cases of weakness of will can occur (p. 6). Amélie Oksenberg Rorty argues that the *akrates* "is precisely the sort of person who is conflicted because his moral development is uneven." See her "*Akrasia* and Pleasure: *Nichomachean Ethics* Book 7," in *Essays on Aristotle's Ethics* (Berkeley: University of California Press, 1980), p. 283.

12. Aristotle, *Nichomachean Ethics*, 1145b8-27, in *The Complete Works of Aristotle*, ed. Jonathan Barnes, 2 vols. (Princeton: Princeton University Press, 1984) vol. 2, pp. 1809–10.

13. Ibid., 1151a21–25, p. 1819.

14. Ibid., 1136b7–9, p. 1794.

15. Ibid., 1136b20, p. 1794.

16. Ibid., 1118b17–18, p. 1766.

17. See Gosling, *Weakness of the Will*, for a discussion that identifies and discusses some of the salient complexities. See also my discussion of Aquinas on the will in appendix A, "Some Earlier Conceptions of the Will: Maimonides to Mill," pp. 291–95.

18. Thomas Aquinas, *Summa Theologica*, I–II, 77, 3, in *Basic Writings of Saint Thomas Aquinas*, ed. Anton C. Pegis, trans. Laurence Shapcote, 2 vols. (New York: Random House, 1945), vol. 2, p. 635.

19. David Hume, *A Treatise of Human Nature*, ed. L. A. Selby-Bigge, 2nd ed. (Oxford: Oxford University Press, 1978), p. 418.

20. Friedrich Nietzsche, *The Will to Power*, trans. Walter Kaufmann and R. J. Hollingdale (New York: Vintage, 1968), no. 46, pp. 28–29.

21. I have omitted several prominent discussions, including Donald Davidson's much-debated attempt to revive a Will as Intellectual Preference view that allows for the possibility of clear-eyed *akrasia*. Though brilliantly ingenious, I find little textual correlation for Davidson's argument in *World Within World*. See Donald Davidson, *Essays on Actions and Events* (Oxford: Oxford University Press, 1980), essay 2.

22. Jean-Paul Sartre, *Being and Nothingness: An Essay on Phenomenological Ontology*, trans. Hazel E. Barnes (New York: Philosophical Library, n.d.), pp. 50–53.

23. Ibid., p. 70.

24. Dunn, *The Possibility of Weakness of Will*, chap. 5.

25. Sartre, *Being and Nothingness*, pp. 449, 36.

26. Stephen Spender, *The Thirties and After: Poetry, Politics, People, 1933–1970* (New York: Vintage, 1979), p. 235.

27. In *The Inner I: British Literary Autobiography of the Twentieth Century* (London: Faber & Faber, 1985), Brian Finney uses the term *double perspective* in his discussion in chapter 10 of the relation between "self and history." The chapter includes an interesting discussion of *World Within World*.

28. Louis MacNiece, *The Strings Are False* (London: Faber & Faber, 1965), p. 114.

29. Stephen Spender, *The Struggle of the Modern* (1963; reprint, London: Methuen, 1965), p. 72.

30. Stephen Spender, "Confessions and Autobiography," reprinted from *The Making of a Poem* (New York: W. W. Norton, 1962), in *Autobiography: Essays Theoretical and Critical*, ed. James Olney (Princeton: Princeton University Press, 1980), p. 120.

31. John Sturrock, *The Language of Autobiography: Studies in the First Person Singular* (Cambridge: Cambridge University Press, 1993), pp. 18–19.

32. On nineteenth-century autobiography and the shape of a life, see Avrom Fleishman, *Figures of Autobiography: The Language of Self-Writing in Victorian and Modern England* (Berkeley: University of California Press, 1983).

33. Spender, "Confessions and Autobiography," p. 116.

34. Stephen Spender, *Journals 1939–1983*, ed. John Goldsmith (New York: Oxford University Press, 1983), p. 179.

35. Spender, "Confessions and Autobiography," p. 117.

36. Stephen Spender, *Collected Poems 1928–1985* (London: Faber & Faber, 1985), p. 113.

37. Spender, "Confessions and Autobiography," p. 121.

38. Ibid.

39. Ibid.

40. Ibid.

41. Spender would regard with skepticism the asymmetrical relation between Self and Other proposed by Levinas. See Emmanuel Levinas, *Totality and Infinity: An Essay on Exteriority,* trans. Alphonso Lingis (The Hague: Martinus, 1979).

42. Stephen Spender, *Love-Hate Relations: English and American Sensibilities* (New York: Vintage Books, 1975), p. 22.

43. Sanford Sternlicht, *Stephen Spender* (New York: Twayne, 1992), p. 99.

44. Spender, *The Struggle of the Modern,* p. 54.

45. See Aristotle, *Nichomachean Ethics,* II.1104a4–9, in *The Complete Works of Aristotle,* vol. 2, p. 1744: "Matters concerned with conduct and questions of what is good for us have no fixity, any more than matters of health. The general account being of this nature, the account of particular cases is yet more lacking in exactness; for they do not fall under any art or set of precepts, but the agents themselves must in each case consider what is appropriate to the occasion, as happens also in the art of medicine or of navigation."

46. Stephen Spender, in *The God That Failed,* ed. Richard Crossman (1949; reprint, New York: Books for Libraries Press, 1972), p. 270.

47. Stephen Spender, *The Creative Element* (London: Hamish Hamilton, 1953), p. 21.

48. Spender, *The Struggle of the Modern,* p. 17.

49. Ibid., p. 4.

50. Ibid., p. 86.

51. Ibid., p. 55.

52. Ibid., p. 117.

53. Ibid.

54. John Sturrock does less than full justice to *World Within World*'s technical inventiveness when he writes of "Spender's conformism" as autobiographer. See *The Language of Autobiography,* p. 261.

55. Sartre, *Being and Nothingness,* p. lxi.

56. D. H. Lawrence, "Red Moon-Rise," in *The Works of D. H. Lawrence* (London: Wordsworth, 1994), pp. 53–55.

57. See Spender's study of Lawrence, *D. H. Lawrence: Novelist, Poet, Prophet* (London: Weidenfeld & Nicolson, 1973).

58. Spender, *The Struggle of the Modern,* p. 7.

59. Alfred Kazin, "The Self as History: Reflections on Autobiography," in *The American Autobiography: A Collection of Critical Essays,* ed. Albert E. Stone (Englewood Cliffs, N.J.: Prentice-Hall, 1981), p. 32.

60. For the history of Spender's identification with Marxism, see his autobiographical piece in *The God That Failed,* pp. 229–73.

61. Stephen Spender, *Forward from Liberalism* (London: Victor Gollancz, 1937), p. 71.

62. Stephen Spender, *The Temple* (London: Faber & Faber, 1988).

63. The earlier collection is Stephen Spender, *Collected Poems 1928–1953* (London: Faber & Faber, 1955).

64. In his recent biography of Spender, David Leeming quotes a letter from W. H. Auden to Spender (May 12, 1942) in which Auden questions Stephen's insistence that his will is weak. Auden suggests that the so-called "weakness" is a disguise for what is in fact an "excess of will." See David Leeming, *Stephen Spender: A Life in Modernism* (London: Duckworth, 1999), p. 140. Whilst too brief and lacking in interpretive aspiration to do Spender full jus-

tice, Leeming's book is the first attempt at a full-scale biography of Spender. It is a useful introduction to Spender's life, work, and relation to modernism.

65. Spender, *Collected Poems 1928–1985*, p. 100.

66. Spender, *Forward from Liberalism*, p. 97.

67. For a more mixed assessment of homosexuality and its impact on British writers of the thirties, and for a detailed literary account of the period, see Valentine Cunningham, *British Writers of the Thirties* (Oxford: Oxford University Press, 1988), especially pp. 148–53.

68. Sartre, *Being and Nothingness*, p. 119.

69. Spender, *The Thirties and After*, p. 236.

70. Spender, *Journals*, p. 33. The account Spender gives of his changing sexual orientation in *World Within World* has drawn sharp criticism from some queer theorists and historians of homosexual autobiography. For a particularly hostile reading that alleges serious autobiographical bad faith on Spender's part, see Paul Robinson, *Gay Lives: Homosexual Autobiography from John Addington Symonds to Paul Monette* (Chicago: University of Chicago Press, 1999), pp. 65–90. Robinson sides with David Leavitt, author of *While England Sleeps*, a novel that imagines certain explicit homoerotic details that do not appear in Spender's sexually inexplicit narrative, and that led to litigation by Spender. For Spender's outraged response to Leavitt, see Stephen Spender, "My Life Is Mine; It Is Not David Leavitt's," *New York Times Book Review*, September 4, 1994, p. 11. It will be clear from the present chapter that I consider *World Within World* a much more substantial and worthy book than does Paul Robinson. Indeed some aspects of *World Within World* that Robinson reads as deplorably inauthentic appear in my reading as probing explorations of various modalities of the will. Having said this, I can see why Robinson's political commitments might lead him to read the book as he does. For a more sympathetic account of identity and sexual orientation in *World Within World*, one that reads Spender's history in terms of bisexuality, see Marjorie Garber, *Vice Versa: Bisexuality and the Eroticism of Everyday Life* (New York: Simon & Schuster, 1995), pp. 355–64.

71. Ibid., p. 43.

72. Immanuel Kant, *Selections*, ed. Theodore M. Greene (New York: Charles Scribner's Sons, 1957), p. 278, this passage trans. T. K. Abbot. See Kant's "The Doctrine of Virtue," in *The Metaphysics of Morals*, trans. Mary Gregor (Cambridge: Cambridge University Press, 1991), pp. 418ff., for further elaboration of this kind of distinction.

73. See her autobiography, *Code Name "Mary": Memoirs of an American Woman in the Austrian Underground* (New Haven: Yale University Press, 1983), which contains her account of her relationship with Spender.

74. Martha C. Nussbaum, *Love's Knowledge: Essays on Philosophy and Literature* (New York: Oxford University Press, 1990), p. 338.

75. Paul Ricoeur, *Freedom and Nature: The Voluntary and the Involuntary*, trans. Erazim V. Kohák (1950; reprint, Chicago: Northwestern University Press, 1966), p. 83.

76. Spender, *The Temple*, p. 122.

77. Rollo May argues that the contrary of will is not indecision but apathy. See his *Love and Will* (London: Fontana, 1972), p. 29.

78. Spender, *Journals*, p. 33.

79. Spender, *Collected Poems 1928–1985*, p. 85.

80. Spender, *Journals*, p. 244.

81. Richard Eldridge, *On Moral Personhood: Philosophy, Literature, Criticism, and Self-Understanding* (Chicago: University of Chicago Press, 1989), p. 45.

82. Spender, *Journals*, p. 481.

83. Spender, *The Thirties and After,* p. 17.

84. Carolyn Steedman observes that "the particular legacy of romanticism within Western society . . . has been the establishment of childhood as an emblem of the self lying deep within each individual." The comment appears in her essay "Woman's Biography and Autobiography: Forms of History, Histories of Form," in *From My Guy to Sci-Fi: Genre and Women's Writing in the Postmodern World,* ed. Helen Carr (London: Pandora, 1989), pp. 108–9. For some related discussion of narrative and identity structures in autobiographies of childhood, see Richard N. Coe, *When the Grass Was Taller: Autobiography and the Experience of Childhood* (New Haven: Yale University Press, 1984), p. 79.

85. Spender, *Collected Poems 1928–1985,* p. 115.

86. Spender, *Journals,* p. 415.

87. Stephen Spender, "Variations on My Life," in *The Still Centre* (London: Faber & Faber, 1939), p. 92.

88. Spender, *Journals,* p. 286.

89. Spender, *Forward from Liberalism,* p. 34.

CHAPTER EIGHT

1. Saint Augustine, *Confessions,* trans. Henry Chadwick (Oxford: Oxford University Press, 1991), V.i (I), p. 72. The reference is to Ps. 18:7.

2. Diana Trilling, *The Beginning of the Journey: The Marriage of Diana and Lionel Trilling* (New York: Harcourt Brace, 1993), p. 39. All subsequent page references will be given in the body of my text.

3. For instance, Alfred Kazin's three-volume autobiography: *A Walker in the City* (San Diego: Harcourt Brace Jovanovich, 1951), *Starting Out in the Thirties* (Boston: Little, Brown, 1962), and *New York Jew* (New York: Alfred A. Knopf, 1978); Philip Roth, *The Facts: A Novelist's Autobiography* (London: Jonathan Cape, 1989) and *Patrimony: A True Story* (London: Vintage, 1992); Norman Mailer, *Advertisements for Myself* (1959; reprint, New York: Perigee Books, 1981); Norman Podhoretz, *Making It* (London: Jonathan Cape, 1968), *Breaking Banks: A Political Memoir* (New York: Harper & Row, 1979), and *Ex-Friends: Falling Out with Allen Ginsberg, Lionel and Diana Trilling, Lillian Hellman, Hannah Arendt, and Norman Mailer* (New York: The Free Press, 1999); Lillian Hellman's four autobiographical volumes, three of which were later collected under the title *Three: An Unfinished Woman* (1969), *Pentimento* (1973), and *Scoundrel Time* (1976) (Boston: Little, Brown, 1979), and *Maybe* (Boston: Little, Brown, 1980). An interesting and admirable variation on a theme is Irving Howe's pointedly subtitled *A Margin of Hope: An Intellectual Autobiography* (London: Secker & Warburg, 1983), which largely eschews the inner life. The most detailed study of this milieu is Alexander Bloom, *Prodigal Sons: The New York Intellectuals and Their World* (New York: Oxford University Press, 1986).

4. Apart from Lillian Hellman's works (cited in the previous note) and Diana Trilling herself, there is not a great deal more. Of the two most eminent female intellectuals in the group, Hannah Arendt and Mary McCarthy, the former did not write an autobiography; the latter did but was not Jewish. (To be precise, she was technically one-third Jewish.) See McCarthy's *Memories of a Catholic Girlhood* (New York: Harcourt Brace Jovanovich, 1957) and *How I Grew* (San Diego: Harcourt Brace Jovanovich, 1987). For related listings see Patricia K. Addis, *Through a Woman's I: An Annotated Bibliography of American Women's Autobiographical Writings, 1946–1976* (Metuchen, N.J.: The Scarecrow Press, 1983).

5. On suggested links between Freudianism and Jewish culture, see Jerry Victor Diller,

Freud's Jewish Identity: A Case Study in the Impact of Ethnicity (London: Associated University Press, 1991).

6. Lionel Trilling, *Sincerity and Authenticity* (London: Oxford, 1974). Though he cites the Masters and Masters translation, Trilling does not in fact follow their translation exactly: he substitutes "being" for their word, "existence" (p. 179).

7. The Lionel Trilling Papers, Columbia University.

8. Two pieces that show an autobiographical gift are his lovely essay on Edmund Wilson, "Edmund Wilson: A Background Glance," in his *A Gathering of Fugitives* (1956; reprint, Oxford: Oxford University Press, 1980), pp. 53–60; and his unfinished tribute to his great friend and colleague Jacques Barzun, "A Personal Memoir," in *From Parnassus: Essays in Honor of Jacques Barzun*, eds. Debora B. Weiner and William R. Keylor (New York: Harper & Row, 1976), pp. xv–xxii.

9. Dr. Stephen Koch, conversation with author, November 1, 1997.

10. Diana Trilling, *We Must March My Darlings: A Critical Decade* (New York: Harcourt Brace Jovanovich, 1977), p. 198.

11. Diana Trilling, *Mrs. Harris: The Death of the Scarsdale Diet Doctor* (New York: Harcourt Brace Jovanovich, 1981).

12. Diana Trilling, *We Must March My Darlings*, p. 194.

13. In essence James Trilling argues that Lionel suffered from attention deficit disorder and that it is this disorder, and not the influences that Diana's Freudian reading of Lionel adduces, that explains Lionel's fits of temper and some of the other problematical aspects of his personality to which she refers. Thus James's account is essentially medicalist while Diana's is psychoanalytic; yet they do agree on some important points: each sees Lionel as a victim of some form of repression, and each reading is essentially deterministic in character. To put it another way: both see Lionel as a man substantially bereft of effective will. See James Trilling, "My Father and the Weak-Eyed Devils," *American Scholar* (spring 1999): 17–41.

14. Lionel Trilling, *The Liberal Imagination: Essays on Literature and Society* (1950; reprint, New York: Harcourt Brace Jovanovich, 1978), p. 28.

15. Carolyn Steedman, *Landscape for a Good Woman: A Story of Two Lives* (London: Virago, 1986), p. 122.

16. Diana Trilling, *Reviewing the Forties* (New York: Harcourt Brace Jovanovich, 1978), p. 71.

17. Diana Trilling, foreword to *Speaking of Literature and Society*, by Lionel Trilling (Oxford: Oxford University Press, 1982), p. vii.

18. Diana Trilling, *Reviewing the Forties*, p. 5.

19. Lionel Trilling, *The Liberal Imagination*, p. 39.

20. Ibid., p. 41.

21. Dr. Stephen Koch, conversation with author, November 1, 1997.

22. I am grateful to Dr. Stephen Koch for his part in a conversation we had about this aspect of Diana Trilling's emotional life.

23. Michael Woolf, "The Haunted House: Jewish-American Autobiography," in *First Person Singular: Studies in American Autobiography*, ed. A. Robert Lee (New York: St. Martin's Press, 1988), pp. 198–216.

24. Teresa's mentor figures were Francisco de Salcedo, Gasper Daza, Diego de Cetina, Juan de Pradanos, Baltasar Alvarez, García de Toledo, Pedro Ibaañez, and Domingo Bañez. See *The Collected Works of Saint Teresa of Avila*, trans. Kieran Kavanaugh and Otilio Rodriguez, 3 vols. (Washington, D.C.: ICS Publications, 1976).

25. Letter to Alan Brown, August 26, 1936. The Lionel Trilling Papers, Columbia University.

26. Lionel Trilling, *The Middle of the Journey* (1947; reprint, New York: Harcourt Brace Jovanovich, 1975), pp. 16–17.

27. Diana Trilling, foreword to *Speaking of Literature and Society,* by Lionel Trilling, p. vi.

28. Quentin Anderson, Stephen Donadio, and Steven Marcus, eds., *Art, Politics, and Will: Essays in Honor of Lionel Trilling* (New York: Basic Books, 1977).

29. Mark Krupnick, *Lionel Trilling and the Fate of Cultural Criticism* (Evanston, Ill.: Northwestern University Press, 1986), p. 100.

30. Lionel Trilling, *The Liberal Imagination,* p. 58.

31. Lionel Trilling, *Matthew Arnold* (1939; reprint, London: Unwin University Books, 1949).

32. Lionel Trilling, *The Liberal Imagination,* pp. 250–51.

33. Ibid., p. 251.

34. Lionel Trilling, *Sincerity and Authenticity,* p. 56.

35. Lionel Trilling, *A Gathering of Fugitives,* p. 32.

36. Lionel Trilling, *Beyond Culture: Essays in Literature and Learning* (1965; reprint, New York: Harcourt, Brace Jovanovich, 1980), p. 71.

37. Lionel Trilling, *The Opposing Self: Nine Essays in Criticism* (1955; reprint, Oxford: Oxford University Press, 1980).

38. Ibid., p. 66.

39. Lionel Trilling, *The Liberal Imagination,* preface.

40. Lionel Trilling, *The Opposing Self,* p. 52.

41. Lionel Trilling, *The Last Decade: Essays and Reviews, 1965–75,* ed. Diana Trilling (Harcourt Brace Jovanovich, 1979), p. 159.

42. Lionel Trilling, *E. M. Forster* (1969; reprint, New York: Harcourt Brace Jovanovich, 1980), p. 6.

43. Lionel Trilling, *A Gathering of Fugitives,* p. 43.

44. Lionel Trilling, *The Opposing Self,* p. 40.

45. Ibid., p. 120.

46. Ibid., p. 36.

47. Ibid., pp. 33, 40.

48. In a letter to Lionel Trilling dated December 1945, Stephen Spender, while congratulating him on *The Middle of the Journey,* contends that the novel is too soft on Marxism and pseudo-Marxist individuals. The Lionel Trilling Papers, Columbia University.

49. Letter to David Riesman, July 22, 1962. The Lionel Trilling Papers, Columbia University.

50. Krupnick, *Lionel Trilling and the Fate of Cultural Criticism,* p. 15.

51. On conservative American intellectuals and mass culture after the war, see Richard H. Pells, *The Liberal Mind in a Conservative Age: American Intellectuals in the 1940s and 1950s* (New York: Harper & Row, 1985).

52. Krupnick, *Lionel Trilling and the Fate of Cultural Criticism,* p. 54.

53. See for instance Krupnick's discussion of historical agency, ibid., p. 131.

54. Ibid., p. 15.

55. Lionel Trilling, *The Liberal Imagination,* p. 204.

56. Lionel Trilling, *Sincerity and Authenticity,* p. 47.

57. Lionel Trilling, *Speaking of Literature and Society,* p. 112.

58. Lionel Trilling, *A Gathering of Fugitives*, p. 63. Alexander Bloom argues that "for Trilling, Freudian psychology offered not only a guide to the contemporary human predicament but also illumination about its possible resolution" (*Prodigal Sons*, p. 192).

59. Lionel Trilling, *A Gathering of Fugitives*, p. 63.

60. Ibid.

61. Lionel Trilling, *Beyond Culture*, p. 98.

62. Ibid., p. 99.

63. Lionel Trilling, *A Gathering of Fugitives*, p. 39.

64. Lionel Trilling, *The Liberal Imagination*, p. 25.

65. Ibid., p. 284.

66. Lionel Trilling, *E. M. Forster*, p. 58.

67. Lionel Trilling, *Matthew Arnold*, p. 28.

68. Lionel Trilling, *E. M. Forster*, p. 5. Forster uses the term in *A Room With a View* (1908; reprint, Harmondsworth: Penguin, 1976), p. 141.

69. Ibid.

70. Lionel Trilling, *The Opposing Self*, p. 112.

71. Charles Dickens, *Little Dorrit*, ed. John Holloway (1857; reprint, Harmondsworth: Penguin, 1967), p. 59.

72. Lionel Trilling, *The Opposing Self*, p. 53.

73. Ibid.

74. Quoted in Lionel Trilling, *A Gathering of Fugitives*, p. 64.

75. Lionel Trilling, *The Liberal Imagination*, p. 252.

76. Ibid.

77. Ibid., p. 92.

78. Quoted in Lionel Trilling, *Matthew Arnold*, p. 25.

79. Diana Trilling, *We Must March My Darlings*, p. 49.

80. Diana Trilling, "Washington Memoir: A Visit to Camelot," *The New Yorker* (June 2, 1997), pp. 54–65.

81. Diana Trilling, *We Must March My Darlings*, p. 11.

82. Diana Trilling, *Claremont Essays* (New York: Harcourt, Brace & World, 1964), p. viii.

83. Ibid., p. 63.

84. Diana Trilling, *Reviewing the Forties*, p. 232.

85. Ibid., p. 151.

86. Ibid., p. 25.

87. Diana Trilling, *We Must March My Darlings*, p. 160.

88. Ibid., p. 171.

89. Diana Trilling, *Reviewing the Forties*, p. 229. On William James, see appendix A, "Some Earlier Conceptions of the Will: Maimonides to Mill," pp. 313–15.

90. Ibid., p. 91.

91. Diana Trilling, ed., *The Viking Portable D. H. Lawrence* (New York: Viking, 1947); Diana Trilling, ed., *Selected Letters of D. H. Lawrence* (New York: Viking, 1958).

92. Diana Trilling, *Claremont Essays*, p. 201.

93. Diana Trilling, *Reviewing the Forties*, p. 18.

94. Diana Trilling, *We Must March My Darlings*, p. 205.

95. Ibid., p. 297.

96. Ibid., p. 298.

97. Diana Trilling, *Claremont Essays*, p. 191.

98. Ibid., pp. 191–92.

99. Ibid., p. 195.

100. Ibid., p. 189.

101. Ibid., p. 243.

102. Diana Trilling, "Lawrence in Love," review of *Mr. Noon,* by D. H. Lawrence, *New York Times Book Review* (December 16, 1984): 24–25.

103. Quentin Anderson, conversation with author, October 23, 1997. Anderson adds as an instance of Trilling's less urbane side his liking for Henry Miller's work. Mark Krupnick is one of several reviewers who take exception to Diana's autobiographical portrait of Lionel. In "The Trillings: A Marriage of True Minds?" he complains of her "unsparingly deflationary portrait of Lionel" (*Salmagundi,* no. 103 [summer 1994]: 214). Krupnick also suggests that, notwithstanding her psychoanalytic self-explorations, Diana is in fact "a very unself-conscious autobiographer" (p. 216).

104. James Trilling, conversation with author, October 21, 1997. On repression, see James Trilling, "My Father and the Weak-Eyed Devils," pp. 38–41.

105. Edward Joseph Shoben, a trained therapist who knew Lionel Trilling through academic contact, speculates interestingly on the impact that unfavorable reviews of *The Middle of the Journey* might have had on him. See Shoben's study of Trilling, *Lionel Trilling: Mind and Character* (New York: Frederick Ungar, 1981), especially pp. 49–52.

106. Louis P. Simpson, "Lionel Trilling and the Agency of Terror," *Partisan Review* (winter 1987): 18–35.

107. The Lionel Trilling Papers, Columbia University.

108. See Lionel Trilling's two admiring reviews of Riesman in *A Gathering of Fugitives,* pp. 91–107.

109. Lionel Trilling, *Speaking of Literature and Society,* editor's foreword, p. vii.

110. Quentin Anderson, conversation with author, October 23, 1997.

CONCLUSION

1. Herman Melville, *Moby-Dick,* eds. Harrison Hayford and Hershal Parker (1851; reprint, New York: W. W. Norton, 1967), p. 185.

2. Paul Ricoeur, *Freedom and Nature: The Voluntary and the Involuntary,* trans. Erazim V. Kohák (1950; reprint, Chicago: Northwestern University Press, 1966), p. 123.

3. Ibid., p. 15.

4. *The Complete Poems of Emily Dickinson,* ed. Thomas H. Johnson (London: Faber & Faber, 1975), no. 1024, p. 471.

APPENDIX A

1. On the extrapolative dimension in Maimonides, see Rabbi Dr. S. D. Cowen, *Jewish Thought in Context: Studies in the Relationship between Jewish and General Thought* (Melbourne: Institute for Judaism and Civilization, 1998), chap. 2. I am indebted to Rabbi Cowen's account of Maimonides and have profited greatly from our discussions of Jewish theology. For an arresting reading of Maimonides and his relation to modernity, see Aryeh Botwinick, *Skepticism, Belief, and the Modern: Maimonides to Nietzsche* (Ithaca: Cornell University Press, 1997). Botwinick argues for deep continuities between Maimonides and modern thought, all the way through to postmodernism.

2. See Moses Maimonides (Rambam), *The Mishneh Torah: Hishot Teshuvah,* trans. Rabbi Eliyahu Touger (New York: Moznaim Publishing, 1990), chap. 8, 2–3, pp. 182–83.

3. Moses Maimonides, *The Guide for the Perplexed,* trans. M. Friedländer (New York: Dover Publications, 1956), I, LVIII, p. 83.

4. Moses Maimonides, *Pirkei Avot,* trans. Rabbi Eliyahu Tonger (New York: Moznaim Publishing, 1994), chap. 8, p. 60. See also *The Guide for the Perplexed,* I, XXXV, p. 49.

5. Maimonides, *The Mishneh Torah: Hishot Teshuvah,* chap. 5, 1, p. 114.

6. Ibid., chap. 5, I, pp. 114–16.

7. Maimonides, *Pirkei Avot,* chap. 5, p. 34.

8. Maimonides, *The Mishneh Torah: Hilchot Teshuvah,* chap. 5, 4, p. 126.

9. Ibid., chap. 5, 4, p. 130.

10. Ibid., chap. 5, 4, p. 116.

11. Julius Guttmann, *Philosophies of Judaism: A History of Jewish Philosophy from Biblical Times to Franz Rosenzweig,* trans. David W. Silverman (New York: Schocken Books, 1973), p. 199.

12. Maimonides, *Guide for the Perplexed,* II, XXXVI, p. 226.

13. Maimonides, *Pirkei Avot,* chap. 1, p. 15.

14. Ibid., p. 17.

15. Frederick Copleston, *A History of Philosophy,* vol. 3, part 2 (London: Burns & Oates, 1963), pp. 412–13.

16. All quotations from Aquinas are from *Basic Writings of Saint Thomas Aquinas,* trans. Laurence Shapcote, ed. Anton C. Pegis, 2 vols. (New York: Random House, 1945). I will cite quotations from the *Summa Theologica* giving part number, question number, and article number, followed, in parentheses, by the volume and page numbers from the Pegis edition. The first quotation is from I, 83, 3 (I, p. 790).

17. Ibid., I, 1, 8 (I, pp. 13–14).

18. Aquinas, *Summa Contra Gentiles,* XXXVII (II, p. 60).

19. Aquinas, *Summa Theologica,* I, 19, 4 (I, p. 201).

20. Ibid., I, 79, 8 (I, p. 759).

21. Ibid., I, 83, 3 (I, p. 790).

22. Ibid., I, 27, 4 (I, pp. 279–80).

23. Ibid., I, 23, 3 (I, p. 242).

24. Ibid., I, 83, 1 (I & III, p. 787).

25. Ibid., I, 82, 2 (I, p. 779).

26. Ibid., I–II, 6, 1 (II, p. 227); See Aristotle, *Nichomachean Ethics,* III.1111b10–17 in *The Complete Works of Aristotle,* ed. Jonathan Barnes, 2 vols. (Princeton: Princeton University Press, 1984), vol. 2, p. 1755.

27. Aquinas, *Summa Theologica,* I, 82, 3 (I, p. 780).

28. Ibid., I, 75, 5 (I, p. 689).

29. Aquinas, *Summa Contra Gentiles,* XLVI (II, p. 81).

30. Aquinas, *Summa Theologica,* I, 87, 4 (I, p. 842).

31. Martin Luther, *The Bondage of the Will,* trans. Henry Cole (Grand Rapids, Mich.: Baker Book House, 1976), sec. IX, pp. 38–39.

32. Martin Luther, "The Freedom of a Christian," in *Luther's Works,* ed. Helmut T. Lehmann, vol. 31, *The Career of the Reformer: I,* ed. Harold J. Grimm (Philadelphia: Fortress Press, 1957), p. 371.

33. *The Chief Works of Benedict de Spinoza,* trans. R. H. M. Elwes, 2 vols. (New York: Dover Publications, 1951), vol. II, p. 121.

34. *The Philosophical Works of Descartes,* trans. Elizabeth S. Haldane and G. R. T. Ross, 2 vols. (1911; reprint, Cambridge: Cambridge University Press, 1973), vol. I, p. 153.

35. Ibid., I, p. 350.

36. John Sturrock, *The Language of Autobiography: Studies in the First Person Singular* (Cambridge: Cambridge University Press, 1993), p. 102.

37. John Locke, *An Essay Concerning Human Understanding,* ed. John W. Yolton, 2 vols. (London: Dent, 1965), vol. I, p. 206.

38. Ibid., I, p. 217.

39. Ibid., I, pp. 220–21.

40. Ibid., I, chap. I.

41. Ibid., I, chap. XXI, p. 220.

42. Thomas Hobbes, *Leviathan,* ed. J. C. A. Gaskin (Oxford: Oxford University Press, 1996), I, 6, 50 (p. 40).

43. Ibid., I, 6, 53 (p. 40).

44. Ibid., I, 6, 49 (p. 39).

45. Ibid., I, 6, 53 (p. 40).

46. David Hume, *A Treatise of Human Nature,* ed. L. A. Selby-Bigge, 2nd ed. (Oxford: Oxford University Press, 1978), p. 633.

47. David Hume, *An Enquiry Concerning Human Understanding,* ed. Antony Flew (La Salle, Ill.: Open Court, 1988), p. 123.

48. Ibid., p. 107.

49. Hume, *A Treatise of Human Nature,* p. 414.

50. Hume, *An Enquiry Concerning Human Understanding,* p. 129.

51. Ibid., p. 106.

52. Hume, *A Treatise of Human Nature,* p. 165.

53. Ibid., p. 399.

54. Hume, *An Enquiry Concerning Human Understanding,* p. 130.

55. Ibid., p. 125.

56. Ibid., p. 130.

57. Hume, *A Treatise of Human Nature,* p. 407.

58. Ibid., p. 401.

59. Hume, *An Enquiry Concerning Human Understanding,* p. 131.

60. Antony Flew and Godfrey Vesey, *Agency and Necessity* (Oxford: Basil Blackwell, 1987), p. 102.

61. Reprinted in David Hume, *On Human Nature and the Understanding,* ed. Antony Flew (New York: Collier Books, 1962), pp. 304–10.

62. Hume, *A Treatise of Human Nature,* p. 252.

63. Ibid., p. 415.

64. See Alisdair MacIntyre, ed., *Hume's Ethical Writings: Selections from David Hume* (Notre Dame: University of Notre Dame Press, 1965), p. 11.

65. Jean-Jacques Rousseau, *The Social Contract,* trans. Christopher Betts (Oxford: Oxford University Press, 1994), p. 50.

66. Jean-Jacques Rousseau, *Discourse on the Origin and Foundations of Inequality,* in *The First and Second Discourses,* ed. Roger D. Masters, trans. Roger D. Masters and Judith R. Masters (New York: St. Martin's, 1964), p. 113.

67. Rousseau, *The Social Contract,* p. 58.

68. Blaise Pascal, *Pensées,* trans. A. J. Krailsheimer (Harmondsworth: Penguin, 1966), p.

51. For a detailed history of the concept of the General Will prior to Rousseau, see Patrick Riley, *The General Will Before Rousseau: The Transformation of the Divine into the Civic* (Princeton: Princeton University Press, 1986).

69. On the General Will, see especially book I, chap. VI, of *The Social Contract*.

70. See *The Social Contract*, book II, chap. III.

71. Jean-Jacques Rousseau, *The Confessions*, trans. J. M. Cohen (London: Penguin, 1953), p. 29.

72. Ibid., p. 25.

73. Ibid., p. 26.

74. Rousseau, *First and Second Discourses*, p. 179. Rousseau's phrase is "*le sentiment de sa propre existence.*"

75. Immanuel Kant, *Critique of Pure Reason*, trans. Norman Kemp Smith (London: Macmillan, 1929), I, II, 2A107, p. 136.

76. Ibid., I, II, B158, p. 169.

77. Immanuel Kant, *Groundwork of the Metaphysic of Morals*, trans. H. J. Paton (New York: Harper & Row, 1964), p. 119.

78. Ibid., p. 80.

79. The bemusing intricacies of this position are most concisely stated in *Kant's Critique of Practical Reason and Other Works*, trans. T. K. Abbott (London: Longmans, 1954), pp. 281–83.

80. Graeme Marshall, to whom I am much indebted for counsel on Kantian and other accounts of the will, reads Kant as saying that the will is always determined by reason, whether it is influenced by inclination or not.

81. *Kant's Critique of Practical Reason and Other Works*, p. 100.

82. Ibid., p. 89.

83. Kant, *Critique of Pure Reason*, II, II, A802, p. 633.

84. Ibid., B478, p. 413.

85. Kant, *Groundwork of the Metaphysic of Morals*, p. 75.

86. Kant, *Critique of Pure Reason*, I, II, 2A107, p. 136.

87. Ibid.

88. Ibid., I, II, 2A108, pp. 136–37.

89. Kant, *Groundwork of the Metaphysic of Morals*, p. 100.

90. M. H. Abrams, *Natural Supernaturalism: Tradition and Revolution in Romantic Literature* (New York: W. W. Norton, 1973), pp. 236–37.

91. Ibid., p. 228.

92. G. W. F. Hegel, *The Phenomenology of Mind*, trans. J. B. Baillie (New York: Harper & Row, 1967), p. 266.

93. Ibid., p. 251.

94. Ibid., p. 96.

95. Ibid., p. 267.

96. Ibid., p. 211.

97. Abrams, *Natural Supernaturalism*, p. 175.

98. G. W. F. Hegel, *Encyclopedia of the Philosophical Sciences in Outline and Critical Writings*, ed. Ernst Behler, trans. Steven A. Taubeneck (New York: Continuum, 1990), pp. 237–38.

99. Hegel, *The Phenomenology of Mind*, p. 609.

100. Ibid., pp. 601–2.

101. Vernon J. Bourke, *Will in Western Thought: An Historico-Critical Survey* (New York: Sheed and Ward, 1964), pp. 204–5.

102. Hegel, *The Phenomenology of Mind*, p. 602.

103. Ibid.

104. Arthur Schopenhauer, *The World as Will and Representation*, trans. E. F. J. Payne, 2 vols. (New York: Dover, 1969), vol. I, pp. 146–47.

105. Ibid., I, pp. 30–31.

106. Ibid., I, p. 162.

107. Ibid., I, p. 129.

108. Ibid., I, p. 162.

109. Ibid., I, p. 149.

110. Ibid., I, p. 151.

111. Ibid., I, p. 150.

112. Ibid., I, p. 124.

113. Ibid., II, p. 211.

114. Ibid., II, p. 201. The earlier translation, by R. B. Haldane and J. Kemp (London: Routledge & Kegan Paul, 1883), actually uses the term unconscious (II, p. 411).

115. Schopenhauer, *The World as Will and Representation*, II, p. 209.

116. Ibid., I, p. 329.

117. Ibid., II, p. 203.

118. Ibid., II, p. 199.

119. Ibid., I, p. 292.

120. Ibid., I, p. 248.

121. Arthur Schopenhauer, *On the Freedom of the Will*, trans. Konstantin Kolenda, 2nd ed. (Oxford: Basil Blackwell, 1985).

122. Schopenhauer, *The World as Will and Representation*, I, pp. 288–89.

123. Ibid., I, p. 301.

124. Schopenhauer, *On the Freedom of the Will*, pp. 30–32.

125. Ibid., p. 95.

126. Schopenhauer, *The World as Will and Representation*, I, p. 305.

127. Ibid., I, p. 131.

128. Ibid., I, p. 395.

129. Ibid., I, p. 184.

130. Ibid., I, p. 370.

131. Ibid., I, p. 379. George Sanatayana, *Persons and Places,* eds. William G. Holzberger and Herman J. Saatkamp, Jr. (Cambridge: MIT Press, 1986). Late in his narrative, Santayana, who gives a summary of each paragraph in the margin, summarizes the section about to begin as follows: "The solution is to renounce the world as Will while retaining it as Idea" (III/XXV, p. 427).

132. Ibid., I, p. 521.

133. Ibid., I, p. 403.

134. Ibid., I, p. 404.

135. Ibid., I, p. 233.

136. Ibid., I, p. 184.

137. William James, *The Principles of Psychology* (1891; reprint, Chicago: William Benton, 1952), pp. 795, 798, 811.

138. Ibid., p. 827.

139. Ibid., p. 795.

140. Ibid., p. 819.

141. Ibid., p. 817.

142. Ibid.

143. Ibid., pp. 815–16.

144. Ibid., p. 817.

145. Ibid., p. 768.

146. Ibid., pp. 776–77.

147. Ibid., pp. 799–806.

148. Ibid., p. 822.

149. Ibid., p. 823.

150. Ibid.

151. Ibid., p. 824.

152. Ibid., p. 826.

153. Ibid., p. 824.

154. Ibid.

155. John Stuart Mill, *A System of Logic Ratiocinative and Inductive* (1843; reprint, London: Longmans, Green & Co., 1967), p. 233.

156. Ibid., p. 232.

157. Ibid., p. 562.

158. Ibid., pp. 547–48.

159. Ibid., p. 549.

160. Ibid., p. 550.

161. James Olney, *Metaphors of Self: The Meaning of Autobiography* (1972; reprint, Princeton: Princeton University Press, 1981), p. 259.

162. John Stuart Mill, *Autobiography,* ed. Jack Stillinger (London: Oxford University Press, 1971), p. 101.

163. Ibid., p. 102. See James Olney's finely weighted discussion of this aspect of Mill's *Autobiography* in *Metaphors of Self,* pp. 254–59. Olney underlines an important distinction between determinism and fatalism.

164. In "On the Freedom of the Will," in *An Examination of Sir William Hamilton's Philosophy* (1867); quoted in *Willing,* in *The Life of the Mind,* by Hannah Arendt (San Diego: Harcourt Brace & Co., 1978), p. 97.

165. John Stuart Mill, *On Liberty,* ed. Gertude Himmelfarb (Harmondsworth: Penguin, 1974). Mill's quotation, from Wilhelm Von Humboldt's *Sphere and Duties of Government* (1852), appears as the epigraph to *On Liberty.*

166. Ibid., p. 127.

167. Ibid., p. 123.

168. Ibid., p. 68.

APPENDIX B

1. Paul Ricoeur, *Freedom and Nature: The Voluntary and the Involuntary,* trans. Erazim V. Kohák (1950; reprint, Chicago: Northwestern University Press, 1966), p. 170. A valuable American phenomenological inquiry into autobiographical consciousness that bears some resemblances to Ricoeur's project is William Earle, *The Autobiographical Consciousness* (Chicago: Quadrangle Books, 1972).

2. On this aspect of the Ricoeur-Sartre comparison, see David Stewart, "Existential Humanism," in *Studies in the Philosophy of Paul Ricoeur,* ed. Charles E. Reagan (Athens: Ohio University Press, 1979), pp. 24–25.

3. A point well made in Charles E. Reagan, *Paul Ricoeur: His Life and His Work* (Chicago: University of Chicago Press, 1996), p. 18.

4. Ricoeur, *Freedom and Nature,* p. 4.

5. Ibid., p. 352.

6. Ibid., p. 78.

7. Ibid., p. 137.

8. Ibid., p. 150.

9. Ibid., p. 170.

10. Ibid., p. 158.

11. Ibid.

12. Ibid., p. 76.

13. Ibid., p. 18.

14. Ibid., p. 123.

15. Ibid., p. 15.

16. Ibid., p. 5.

17. Ibid., p. 9.

18. Ricoeur seldom expresses these networks of interrelation in clear summary fashion. Part of the picture I have just sketched is given in *Freedom and Nature,* p. 341. I have relied heavily in this paragraph on an admirably clear schematic summary given by John B. Thompson, *Critical Hermeneutics: A Study in the Thought of Paul Ricoeur and Jürgen Habermas* (Cambridge: Cambridge University Press, 1981), p. 42.

19. Ricoeur, *Freedom and Nature,* p. 341.

20. Ibid., p. 144.

21. Ibid., p. 368.

22. Ibid., p. 17.

23. Ibid., p. 24.

24. Paul Ricoeur, *Fallible Man,* trans. Charles A. Kelbley (1965; reprint, New York: Fordham University Press, 1986); *The Symbolism of Evil,* trans. Emerson Buchanan (1967; reprint, Boston: Beacon Press, 1969).

25. Ricoeur, *Fallible Man,* p. 1.

26. Thompson, *Critical Hermeneutics,* p. 43.

27. Ricoeur, *The Symbolism of Evil,* p. 151.

28. Ibid., pp. 155–57.

29. Paul Ricoeur, "Intellectual Autobiography," trans. Kathleen Blamey, in *The Philosophy of Paul Ricoeur,* vol. XXII, The Library of Living Philosophers, ed. Lewis Edwin Hahn (Chicago: Open Court, 1995), pp. 4–53.

30. Brian O'Shaughnessy, *The Will: A Dual Aspect Theory,* 2 vols. (Cambridge: Cam-

bridge University Press, 1980), vol. 1, p. 1xi. O'Shaughnessy offers a dualistic account that sees will as a psychic force that comes between deliberation and action.

31. Charles Altieri, *A Theory of First-Person Expressivity and Its Social Implications* (Oxford: Basil Blackwell, 1994), p. 30. Altieri characterizes his methodology in this important book as a "proleptic quasi-Wittgensteinian phenomenology" (p. 13).

32. Ludwig Wittgenstein, *Tractatus Logico-Philosophicus* (1921; reprint, London: Routledge & Kegan Paul, 1962); *Philosophical Investigations*, trans. G. E. M. Anscombe (1953; reprint, Oxford: Basil Blackwell, 1956).

33. Ludwig Wittgenstein, *Notebooks 1914–1916*, eds. G. H. von Wright and G. E. M. Anscombe, trans. G. E. M. Anscombe, 2nd ed. (Chicago: University of Chicago Press, 1984). The entry dated November 4, 1916 (pp. 86e–88e) is especially pertinent for the issues I discuss here.

34. See H. L. Finch, *Wittgenstein* (Rockport, Mass.: Element, 1995), pp. 75–79.

35. Wittgenstein, *Tractatus*, 5.633, p. 151.

36. Wittgenstein, *Investigations*, 580, p. 153e.

37. Wittgenstein, *Tractatus*, 6.373, p. 181.

38. Peter Winch, *Ethics and Action* (London: Routledge & Kegan Paul, 1972), p. 119. Winch's chapter 6, "Wittgenstein's Treatment of the Will," is an excellent—though itself advanced—introduction to the topic.

39. Wittgenstein, *Investigations*, p. 11e.

40. Ibid., p. 159e.

41. Altieri, *Subjective Agency*, p. 50.

42. Wittgenstein, *Notebooks*, p. 87e.

43. Wittgenstein, *Investigations*, 477–81, pp. 135e–36e.

44. Ibid., 615, p. 160e.

45. Ibid., 269–75, p. 94e.

46. Ibid., 7, p. 5e.

47. Donald Davidson, "Agency," in *Essays on Actions and Events* (Oxford: Oxford University Press, 1980), essay 3, p. xi.

48. Ibid., p. 231.

49. Ibid.

50. Ibid., pp. 43–62.

INDEX